Managing Quality

Third edition

Barrie G. Dale

Copyright © Blackwell publishers Ltd 1999
Editorial apparatus and arrangement copyright © Barrie G. Dale 1999

First edition published by Prentice Hall Europe in 1990
Second edition published by Blackwell Publishers in 1994

Third edition published by Blackwell Publishers in 1999
Reprinted 2000 (twice)

Blackwell Publishers Ltd
108 Cowley Road
Oxford OX4 1JF
UK

Blackwell Publishers Inc.
350 Main Street
Malden, Massachusetts 02148
USA

British Library Cataloguing in Publication Data

A CIP catalogue record for this book is available from the British Library.

Library of Congress Cataloging-in-Publication Data
Managing quality / [edited by] Barrie G. Dale. - - 3rd ed.
cm.
  Includes bibliographical references and index.
  ISBN 0–631–21409–7 (alk. paper). — ISBN 0–631–21410–0 (pbk : alk. paper)
    1. Engineering management. 2. Total quality management.
  I. Dale, B. G.
  TA190.M38   1999
  658.5'62—cd21   99–16395
                                                      CIP
Typeset in 10/11½pt Galliard
By Graphicraft Limited, Hong Kong
Printed in Great Britain by TJ International, Padstow, Cornwall

This book is printed on acid-free paper

Contents

Figures

Tables

Contributors

John Aldrige is Quality Manager with Siemens Standard Drives, Congleton.

Bernard Burnes is a Lecturer in Operations Management at the Manchester School of Management, UMIST.

Ian Ferguson is the Managing Director of Ferguson Associates, Birmingham.

David Lascelles is the Managing Director of David Lascelles Associates, Carrington Business Park, Manchester.

Roy Lee is a Squadron Leader, Support Management Group at Royal Air Force Wyton.

Rory Love is a Quality Engineer at Alexanders Ltd., Falkirk.

Barbara Lewis is a Senior Lecturer in Marketing at the Manchester School of Management, UMIST.

John Macdonald is the Managing Director of John Macdonald Associates, Surrey.

Peter Shaw is a TQM Project Officer at the Manchester School of Management, UMIST.

Adrian Wilkinson is Professor in Human Resource Management at the University of Loughborough.

Preface

The first edition of *Managing Quality* sold well, and the second edition sold even more copies which, according to the publisher, is unusual for a book of this type. The third edition builds on the success of these two editions.

In the spirit of continuous improvement, a complete revision of the book has been undertaken with some chapters having undergone extensive revision, sometimes by new contributors, and additional chapters introduced to reflect developments in the field. For example, new material is introduced on: the Role of Management in Total Quality Management (TQM), Policy Deployment, Sustaining TQM, Business Process Re-engineering (BPR), and Self-Assessment, Models and Quality Awards. I have also contributed, sometimes in association with colleagues, more material to this third edition. In addition, there has been some re-ordering of material, changes made to terminology, and some chapters have been dropped.

The book is a very comprehensive TQM text and has developed a track record and following among students, academics and practitioners. Its purpose is to provide the reader with an appreciation of the concepts and principles of TQM. It has proved to be a wide-ranging source of reference for the many tools, techniques and systems associated with the concept. The feedback indicates that the book has been useful to industrialists, management consultants, academics, and undergraduate and postgraduate students from a variety of disciplines; TQM is not the special province of one group of people or one discipline. People studying for professional examinations which involve considerations of quality have also benefited from use of the book.

In a book of this size and format, it is not easy to decide the depth and detail of the text, what is to be put in and what is to be left out, and who should contribute. The comments from reviews and users of the first and second editions and the views of colleagues have assisted in this task. I have tried to achieve a balance between the number of contributions from practitioners and those from the academic community; the views and ideas expressed by both parties are supportive of each other. I believe this mixture of approaches, under one cover, adds to the value of the book.

I hope readers will read the whole book to gain an understanding of the breadth and depth of TQM. However, most of the chapters do stand alone and readers may choose to dip in to the book to learn more about a particular subject.

The subject of TQM is vast. There are many issues and interfaces to consider, and there are a considerable number of tools, techniques and systems which can assist an organization in the introduction and development of the concept. An attempt has been made in the text to cover the main aspects and functions of TQM, from identifying customer needs and requirements through to design, quality planning, supply and subcontract, human resources, and production/operations. While there is nothing particularly radical in the text, the book does cover the main concepts and issues currently being debated and considered by business leaders throughout the world. The academic contributors have also outlined some of their recent research findings. I do hope that readers will find some new ideas and angles on subjects which have been brought to their attention.

The brief given to the contributors was to keep the level of technical detail to a minimum and to write in non-specialist language. This is much easier in some topics than others, but I believe that this objective has been achieved, and I hope the reader will find that the structure of the book is logical, and that the content is clear and free from confusing jargon.

For the purposes of presentation, the text is conveniently arranged into five parts:

1 The development of TQM
2 The business context of quality management
3 The introduction of TQM
4 Quality management systems, tools and techniques
5 TQM through continuous improvement

The initiative for editing and contributing to the first edition of this book arose from the UMIST TQM research and education and training activities which, at that time, had been carried out for some seven years. These activities have remained at a very high level during the intervening period with the award of a number of major research contracts and continuation of the TQM-based TCS programmes. Supported by the responses and comments with respect to the second edition, I believe the need for the book has become even stronger. It is to be hoped that readers, through study of the text, will be encouraged to take up the challenge of strengthening their commitment and dedication to TQM and continuous improvement.

In my role as editor, I have attempted to ensure that each topic is adequately covered in breadth and depth, and that it is presented simply and clearly. Subject to these constraints, I have tried not to interfere with contributors' styles because I believe an author's style is an integral part of getting his or her message across to the reader. I should add too that, apart from the chapters bearing my name, the views and opinions expressed in individual contributions are those of the authors and not myself.

Finally, I wish to thank all the contributors for making this book possible. I have learned much from them. I hope the readers will too.

Barrie Dale
United Utilities Professor of Quality Management
Head of the Operations Management Group
Manchester School of Management
UMIST
Manchester

Standards

The standards listed here are referred to within this book. Copies of the standards can be obtained from BSI, London or ISO, Geneva.

British Standards

BS600 (1935) *The Application of Statistical Methods to Industrial Standardisation and Quality Control*
BS600R (1942) *Quality Control Charts*
BS4778 *Quality Vocabulary*
    Part 2 (1991) *Quality Concepts and Related Definitions*
BS4891 (1972) *A Guide to Quality Assurance* (withdrawn in 1994)
BS5179 (1974) *A Guide to the Operation and Evaluation of Quality Assurance Systems* (withdrawn in 1981; superseded by BS5750)
BS5750 *Quality Systems* (this standard has been superseded by the ISO9000 series)
    Part 0 (1987) *Principle Concepts and Applications*
       Section 0.1 *Guide to Selection and Use*
       Section 0.2 *Guide to Quality Management and Quality System Element*
    Part 1 (1987) *Specification for Design/Development, Production, Installation and Servicing*
    Part 2 (1987) *Specification for Production and Installation*
    Part 3 (1987) *Specification for Final Inspection and Test*
    Part 8 (1991) *Guide to Quality Management and Quality Systems Elements for Servicing*
    Part 13 (1991) *Guide to the Application of BS5750 Part 1 to the Development, Supply and Maintenance of Software*
BS5760 *Reliability of Systems, Equipment and Components*
    Part 1 (1996) *Dependability Programme Elements and Tasks*
    Part 2 (1994) *Guide to the Assessment of Reliability*
    Part 3 (1993) *Guide to the Reliability Practices: Examples*
    Part 5 (1991) *Guide to the Failure Modes, Effects and Criticality Analysis (FMEA) and FMECA*
    Part 7 (1991) *Guide to Fault Tree Analysis*
    Part 14 (1994) *Guide to Formal Design Review*

BS6143 *Guide to the Economics of Quality*
  Part 1 (1992) *Process Cost Models*
  Part 2 (1990) *Prevention Appraisal and Failure Model*
BS6548 *Maintainability of Equipment*
  Part 2 (1992) *Guide to Maintainability Studies During the Design Phase*
BS7000 *Design Management Systems*
  Part 1 (1993) *Guide to Managing Product Design*
BS7511 (1989) *General Criteria for Certification Bodies Operating Product Certification*
BS7512 (1989) *General Criteria for Certification Bodies Operating Quality System*
BS7513 (1989) *General Criteria for Certification Bodies Operating Certification for Personnel*
BS7782 (1994) *Control Charts – General Guide and Introduction*
BS7785 (1994) *Shewart Control Charts*
BS8800 (1996) *Guide to Occupational Health and Safety Management Systems*
PD3542 (1988) *The Operation of a Company Standards Department*
PD6470 (1981) *The Management of Design for Economic Production*
PD6489 (1987) *Guide to the Preparation of a Company Standards Manual*
PD6538 (1993) *Vision 2000: A Strategy for International Standards, Implementation in the Quality Arena
      during the 1990s*

International Standards

Note that the ISO series are designated BS EN ISO in the UK and Europe.
ISO8402 *Quality Management and Quality Assurance*
  Part 1 (1994) *Vocabulary*
ISO9000 *Quality Management and Quality Assurance Standards* (this standard superseded BS5750)
  Part 1 (1994) *Guidelines for the Selection and Use*
  Part 2 (1997) *Generic Guidelines for the Application of ISO9001, ISO9002 and ISO9003*
  Part 3 (1997) *Guidelines for the Applications of ISO9001 to the Development, Supply and Maintenance
      of Computer Software*
  Part 4 (1993) *Guide to the Dependability Programme Management*
ISO9001 (1994) *Quality Systems – Model for Quality Assurance in Design, Development, Production,
      Installation and Servicing*
ISO9002 (1994) *Quality Systems – Model for Quality Assurance in Production, Installation and Servicing*
ISO9003 (1994) *Quality Systems – Model for Quality Assurance in Final Inspection and Test*
ISO9004 *Quality Management and Quality System Elements*
  Part 1 (1994) *Guidelines*
  Part 2 (1991) *Guidelines for Services*
  Part 3 (1993) *Guidelines for Processed Materials*
  Part 4 (1993) *Guidelines for Quality Improvement*
ISO10011 *Guidelines for Auditing Quality Systems*
  Part 1 (1990) *Auditing*
  Part 2 (1991) *Qualification Criteria for Quality Systems Auditors*
  Part 3 (1991) *Management of Audit Programmes*
ISO10013 (1995) *Guidelines for Developing Quality Manuals*
ISO14001 (1996) *Environmental Management Systems – Specification with Guidance for Use*

Abbreviations

ABC	Activity-based costing	CWQC	Company-wide quality control
APQP	Advanced product quality planning	DHU	Defects per hunded units
AQ+	Aeroquip Quality Plus	DOE	Design of experiments
AQAP	Allied Quality Assurance Publications	DPA	Departmental purpose analysis
AQL	Acceptable quality level	DPU	Defects per unit
ASI	American Supplier Institute	DTI	Department of Trade and Industry
ASQC	American Society for Quality Control (now the American Society for Quality)	EDI	Electronic Data Interchange
		EFQM	European Foundation for Quality Management
ATM	Automated teller machine		
BACS	Bankers automated clearing system	EOQ	European Organisation for Quality
BPM	Business Process Management	EPSRC	Engineering and Physical Sciences Research Council
BPR	Business process re-engineering		
BSI	British Standards Institution	EQA	European quality award
BU	Business unit	FMEA	Failure mode and effects analysis
CAD	Computer-aided design	FTA	Fault tree analysis
CAM	Computer-aided manufacture	GM	General Manager
CANDO	Cleanliness, arrangement, neatness, discipline and orderliness	HR	Human resources
		HRM	Human resources management
CAPD	Check Act Plan Do	IQA	Institute of Quality Assurance
CAPEX	Capital expenditure	ISO	International Organization for Standardization
CEDAC	Cause and effect diagrams with addition of cards		
		IT	Information technology
CEN	European Committee for Standardisation	JIT	Just-in-time
CENELEC	European Committee for Electrotechnical Standardization	JUSE	Japanese Union of Scientists and Engineers
CEO	Chief executive officer	KJ	Kawakita Jiro
CPA	Critical path analysis	KPI	Key performance indicator
C_{pk}	Process capability index	LSL	Lower specification limit
CQAD	Corporate QA Department	MBNQA	Malcolm Baldrige National Quality Award
CRIP	Check, Reflect, Improve, Pass	MBO	Management by objectives
CRISP	Check-reflect-improve-scrutinize-pass	MIS	Management information systems

MITI	Ministry of International Trade and Industry	QCT	The seven quality control tools
MOD	Ministry of Defence	QCs	Quality circles
MRP II	Manufacturing Resources Planning	QCD	Quality, cost, delivery
NACCB	National Accreditation Council for Certification Bodies	QFD	Quality function deployment
		Q-map	Quality management activity planning
NAMAS	National Measurement Accreditation Service	QSATs	Quality Service Action Teams
		QSG	Quality Steering Group
NATLAS	National Testing Laboratory Accreditation Service	R&D	Research and development
		RPN	Risk priority number
NATO	North Atlantic Treaty Organization	SDT	Supplier Development Team
NIST	National Institute of Standards and Technology	SMED	Single Minute Exchange of Die
		SMMT	Society of Motor Manufacturers and Traders
np	Number defective charts		
NWW	North West Water	S/N	Signal-to-Noise
OEE	Operating equipment effectiveness	S and P	Standard and Poor
OEM	Original equipment manufacturer	SPC	Statistical process control
O&M	Organization and Methods	SQA	Supplier Quality Assurance
p charts	Proportion/percentage charts	STA	Success tree analysis
PAF	Prevention-appraisal-failure	SWOT	Strength, Weakness, Opportunities and Threats
PAL	Pooling, Allying and Linking Across Organizations		
		TARP	Technical Assistance Research Programs
PAT	Project Action Team	TMC	Total management control
PCB	Printed circuit board	TOR	Terms of reference
PDCA	Plan-do-check-act	TPM	Total productive maintenance
PDPC	Process decision program chart	TQ	Total Quality
PDSA	Plan-do-study-act	TQC	Total quality control
PERA	Production Engineering Research Association	TQM	Total quality management
		TQMSAT	Total quality management sustaining audit tool
PERT	Programme evaluation and review technique		
		TQSG	Total quality steering group
POC	Price Of Conformance	UKAS	UK Accreditation Service
PONC	Price Of Non-Conformance	UMIST	University of Manchester Institute of Science and Technology
P_{pk}	Preliminary process capability index		
PPM	Parts per million	USL	Upper specification limits
PR	Public Relations	VFO	Vital few objective
QA	Quality assurance	YIT	Yield improvement teams

The Development of Total Quality Management (TQM)

The purpose of this part of the book is to introduce the reader to some of the fundamentals of TQM.

Chapter 1 examines the evolution of quality management 'all activities of the overall management function that determine the quality policy, objectives and responsibilities, and implements them by means such as quality planning, quality control, quality assurance and quality improvement within the quality system' from inspection 'activity such as measuring, examining, testing or gauging one or more characteristics of an entity and comparing the results with specified requirements in order to establish whether conformity is achieved for each characteristic' to quality control 'operational techniques and activities that are used to fulfil requirements for quality' to *quality assurance* 'all the planned and systematic activities implemented within the quality system, and demonstrated as needed to provide adequate confidence that an entity will fulfil requirements for quality' and, finally, to TQM 'management approach of an organisation centred on quality based on the participation of all its members and aiming at long-term success through customer satisfaction, and benefits to all members of the organisation and to society.' (ISO8402). In describing this evolution, a comparative analysis is made of the essential difference between detection and prevention-based approaches. The key elements of TQM are also discussed.

Quality management experts such as Crosby, Deming, Feigenbaum and Juran have had a considerable influence on the development of TQM throughout the world, and their views and teachings are summarized in this chapter.

The chapter examines why companies decide to embark on TQM and the various ways they can get started and develop the concept in conjunction with a process of quality improvement 'actions taken throughout the organization to increase the effectiveness and efficiency of activities and processes in order to provide added benefits to both the organization and its customers' (ISO8402). TQM is a vision, and a process of continuous and company-wide improvement is the means for progressing towards the vision. The chapter also summarizes a list of points which organizations should keep in mind when developing TQM.

Chapter 2 outlines the main reasons why senior management should become personally involved in TQM. It examines what they need to know about TQM, and what they need to do in terms of actions. The role of middle and first-line management is also key to putting in to place the principles of TQM and the activities with which they need to become involved are outlined and examined.

No book on TQM would be complete without some discussion of the way in which Japanese companies develop and manage the concept. Some of the Japanese wisdom is touched upon in chapter 1 but chapter 3, based on the findings of four Missions of European executives led by the editor to Japan to study TQM, and supported by work carried out in conjunction with Japanese companies with manufacturing facilities in the UK, examines the key essentials of their approach. Among the issues explored are customer satisfaction, long-term planning, R&D, organizing and planning for quality, management of improvement, visible management systems, people involvement, education and training, Total Productive Maintenance and just-in-time (JIT).

Companies adopt and commit themselves to TQM in a variety of ways. Chapter 4 examines six different characteristics and behaviour which have been found to be typically demonstrated by organizations across the world. These six levels of TQM adoption can be used as an internal measure by which organizations can compare their standing, and assist them in the review of their performance.

chapter one

TQM: An Overview

B. G. Dale

Introduction

In today's global competitive market-place, the demands of customers are forever increasing as they require improved quality of products and services but are prepared to pay less for their requirements. Continuous improvement in total business activities, with a focus on the customer throughout the entire organization, is one of the main means by which companies meet these demands. This is why quality and its management and continuous improvement, the focus of this chapter, is looked upon by many organizations as the means by which they can maintain a competitive edge over their rivals. However, it should be pointed out that, in many markets today, quality is not the competitive weapon it once was. It is now expected as a given requirement and is considered an entry level characteristic to the market. As a result of all this effort, it is very clear that, during the last decade, the quality of products, services and processes have increased considerably.

This opening chapter provides an overview of TQM and introduces the reader to the subject. Many of the themes outlined here are explored in greater detail later in the book.

These days, the most progressive organizations are embarking on a journey of transformation towards TQM, and this is coupled with its spread, from the manufacturing to the service sector and on to public services. What is TQM? According to ISO8402, it is the:

> Management approach of an organisation, centred on quality, based on the participation of all its members and aiming at long-term success through customer satisfaction, and benefits to all members of the organisation and to society.

This chapter opens by examining the evolution of quality management – 'All aspects of the overall management function that determines the quality policy, objectives and responsibilities, and implement them by means such as quality planning, quality control, quality assurance and quality improvement within the quality system', ISO8402 – through the stages of inspection, quality control, quality assurance (QA) and onwards to TQM. In presenting the details of this evolution, the drawbacks of a detection-based approach to quality are compared with the recommended approach of prevention. Having described these stages, this chapter examines the key elements of TQM: commitment and leadership of the CEO; planning and organization; using tools and techniques; education and training; employee involvement; teamwork; measurement and feedback and culture change.

A number of quality management experts have had a major influence in organizations throughout the world in shaping the development of TQM as it is known today. In the Western world, the four best known are Crosby, Deming, Feigenbaum and Juran. No book on quality management would be complete without some discussion of the teachings of these experts. Taguchi has popularized design of experiments and his contribution is reviewed in the section on the 'received wisdom' as are some of the familiar concepts associated with the Japanese approach to quality management.

This chapter then goes on to examine why organizations decide to embark on TQM. Five factors – the CEO, competition, demanding customers, a greenfield venture and restart situation – are reviewed. The chapter also looks at how companies can get started on TQM and reviews the main approaches. It is closed by presenting a summary of the points which organizations need to keep in mind when developing and advancing TQM. This is done under the broad groupings of organizing, systems and techniques, measurement and feedback and changing the culture.

The Evolution of Quality Management

Systems for improving and managing quality have evolved rapidly in recent years. During the last two decades or so, simple inspection activities have been replaced or supplemented by quality control, QA has been developed and refined, and now many companies, using a process of continuous and company-wide improvement, are working towards TQM. In this progression, four fairly discrete stages can be identified: inspection, quality control, QA and TQM; it should be noted that the terms are used here to indicate levels in a hierarchical progression of quality management (figure 1.1). British and International standards definitions of these terms are given to provide the reader with some understanding but the discussion and examination is not restricted by these definitions.

Inspection

> Activity such as measuring, examining, testing or gauging one or more characteristic of an entity and comparing the results with specified requirements in order to establish whether conformity is achieved for each characteristic.
>
> ISO8402

At one time, inspection was thought to be the *only* way of ensuring quality. 'Totality of characteristics of an entity that bear on its ability to satisfy stated and implied needs', (ISO8402). Under a simple inspection-based system, one or more characteristics of a product, service or activity are examined, measured, tested, or assessed and compared with specified requirements to assess conformity against a specification or performance standard. In a manufacturing environment, the system is applied to

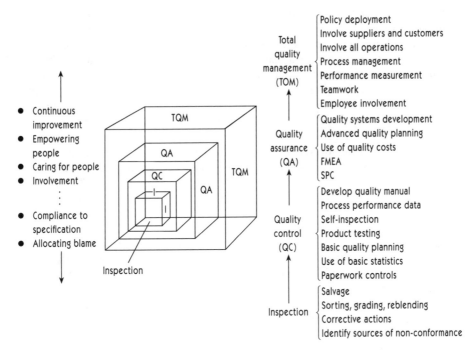

Figure 1.1 The four levels in the evolution of TQM

incoming goods and materials, manufactured components and assemblies at appropriate points in the process, and before passing finished goods into the warehouse. In service, commercial and public services type situations, the system is also applied at key points, sometimes called appraisal points, in the producing and delivery processes. The inspection activity is, in the main, carried out by dedicated staff employed specifically for the purpose, or by self-inspection of those responsible for a process. Materials, components, paperwork, forms, products and goods which do not conform to specification may be scrapped, reworked, modified or passed on concession. In some cases, inspection is used to grade the finished product as, for example, in the production of cultured pearls. The system is an after-the-event screening process with no prevention content other than, perhaps, identification of suppliers, operations, or workers, who are producing non-conforming products/ services. There is an emphasis on reactive quick-fix corrective actions, and the thinking is departmental based. Simple inspection-based systems are usually wholly in-house, and do not directly involve suppliers or customers in any integrated way.

Quality control

Operational techniques and activities that are used to fulfil requirements for quality.

ISO8402

Under a system of quality control one might expect, for example, to find in place detailed product and performance specifications, a paperwork and procedures control system, raw material and intermediate stage product testing and reporting activities, logging of elementary process performance data, and feedback of process information to appropriate personnel and suppliers. With quality control, there will have been some development from the basic inspection activity in terms of sophistication of methods and systems, self-inspection by approved operators, use of information and the tools and techniques which are employed. While the main mechanism for preventing off-specification products and services from being delivered to customers is screening inspection, quality control measures lead to greater process control and fewer incidence of non-conformances.

Organizations whose approach to the management of quality is based on inspection and quality control are operating in a detection type mode, i.e. finding and fixing mistakes.

What is detection?

In a detection or 'firefighting' environment, the emphasis is on the product, procedures and/or service deliverables, and the downstream producing and delivery processes. Considerable effort is expended on after-the-event inspecting, troubleshooting, checking, and testing of the product and/or service and providing reactive 'quick fixes' in a bid to ensure that only conforming product and services are delivered to the customer. In this approach, there is a lack of creative and systematic work activities, with planning and improvements being neglected, and with defects being identified late in the process with all the financial implications in terms of the working capital employed. Detection will not improve quality but only highlight when it is not present, and sometimes it does not even manage to do this. Problems in the process are not removed, but contained. Inspection is the primary means of control in a 'policeman' or 'goalkeeper' type role and thereby a 'producing' versus 'checking' situation is encouraged, leading to confusion over people's responsibilities for quality: 'Can I, the producer, get my deliverables past the checker?' It also leads to the belief that non-conformances are due to the product/service not being inspected enough and also that operators are the sole cause of the problem, not the system.

A question which organizations operating in this mode must answer is: Does the checking of work by inspectors affect an operator's pride in the job? The production–inspection relationship is vividly described by McKenzie (1989).

With a detection approach to quality, non-conforming 'products' (products are considered in their widest sense) are culled, sorted and graded, and decisions made on concessions, rework, reblending, repair, downgrading, scrap, and disposal. It is not unusual to find products going through this cycle more than once. While a detection type system may prevent non-conforming product, services and paperwork being delivered to the customer (internal or external), it does not prevent them being made. Indeed, it is questionable whether such a system does, in fact, find and remove all non-conforming products and services. Physical and mental fatigue decreases the efficiency of inspection and it is commonly claimed that, at best, 100 per cent inspection is only 80 per cent effective. It is often found that, with a detection approach, the customer also inspects the incoming product/service, thus the customer becomes a part of the organization's quality control system.

In this type of approach, a non-conforming product must be made and a service delivered before the process can be adjusted, and this is inherently inefficient in that it creates waste in all its various forms; all the action is 'after-the-event' and

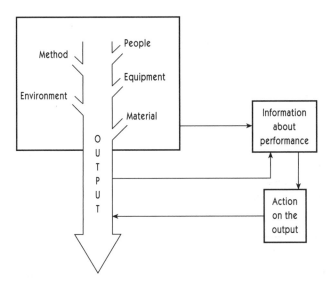

Figure 1.2 A detection-based quality system
Source: Ford Motor Company (1985)

backward looking. The emphasis is on 'today's events', with little attempt to learn from the lessons of the current problem or crisis. It should not be forgotten that the scrap, rework, retesting, reblending, etc. are extra efforts, and represent costs over and above what has been budgeted and which, ultimately, will result in a reduction of bottom line profit. Figure 1.2 taken from the Ford Motor Company (1985) three-day SPC course notes is a schematic illustration of a detection type system.

An environment in which the emphasis is on making good the non-conformance, rather than preventing it arising in the first place, is not ideal for engendering team spirit, co-operation and a good climate for work. The focus tends to be on switching the blame to others, people making themselves 'fireproof', not being prepared to accept responsibility and ownership, and taking disciplinary action against people who make mistakes. In general, this behaviour and attitude emanates from middle management, and quickly spreads downwards through all levels of the organizational hierarchy.

Organizations operating in a detection manner are often preoccupied with the survival of their business and little concerned with making improvements.

Quality assurance (QA)

Finding and solving a problem after a non-conformance has been created is not an effective route towards eliminating the root cause of a problem. A lasting and continuous improvement in quality can only be achieved by directing organizational efforts towards planning and preventing problems occurring at source. This concept leads to the third stage of quality management development: QA.

All the planned and systematic activities implemented within the quality system and demonstrated as needed to provide adequate confidence that an entity will fulfil requirements for quality.

ISO8402

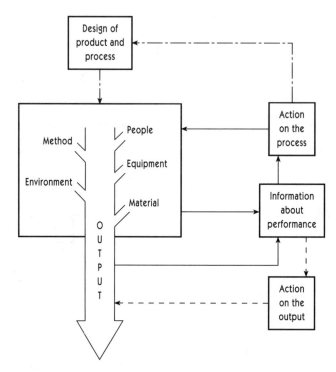

Figure 1.3 A prevention-based quality system
Source: Ford Motor Company (1985)

Examples of additional features acquired when progressing from quality control to QA are, for example, a comprehensive quality management system to increase uniformity and conformity, use of the seven quality control tools (histograms, check sheets, Pareto analysis, cause and effect diagrams, graphs, control charts and scatter diagrams), SPC, FMEA, and the gathering and use of quality costs. The quality systems and practices are likely to have met, as a minimum, the requirements of the ISO9000 series of quality management system standards. Above all, one would expect to see a shift in emphasis from mere detection towards prevention of non-conformances. In short, more emphasis is placed on advanced quality planning, training, improving the design of the product, process and services, improving control over the process and involving and motivating people.

What is prevention?

QA is a prevention-based system which improves product and service quality, and increases productivity by placing the emphasis on product, service and process design. By concentrating on source activities, it stops non-conforming products being produced or non-conforming services being delivered in the first place and, even when defects occur, they are identified early in the process. This is a proactive approach compared with detection, which is reactive. There is a clear change of emphasis from downstream to the upstream processes and from product to process, see figure 1.3 (Ford Motor Company, 1985). This change of emphasis can also be considered in terms of the PDCA cycle. In the detection approach, the act part of the cycle is limited, resulting in an incomplete cycle. Whereas, with prevention, act is an essential part of individuals and teams striving for continuous improvement, as part of their everyday work activities.

Quality is created in the design stage and *not* at the later control stage; the majority of quality-related problems are caused by poor or unsuitable designs of products and processes. In the prevention approach, there is a recognition of the process as defined by its input of people, machines, materials, method, management and environment. It also brings a clearer and deeper sense of responsibility for quality, and to eliminate the root cause of waste and non-value adding activity to those actually producing and delivering the product and/or service.

Changing from detection to prevention requires not just the use of a set of tools and techniques, but the development of a new operating philosophy and approach. This requires a change in management style and way of thinking; it requires the various departments and functions to work and act together in cross-functional teams to discover the root cause of problems, and to pursue their elimination. Quality planning and continuous improvement truly begins when top management includes prevention, as opposed to detection, in their organizational policy and objectives, and they start to integrate the improvement efforts of various departments together. This leads to the next level, that of TQM.

Total quality management (TQM)

The fourth and highest level, that of TQM, involves the application of quality management principles to *all* aspects of the organization, including customers and suppliers, and their integration with the key business processes.

TQM requires that the principles of quality management should be applied in every branch, and at every level, in the organization with an emphasis on integration into business practices, and a balance between technical, managerial and people issues. It is a company-wide approach to quality, with improvements undertaken on a continuous basis by everyone in the organization. Individual systems, procedures and requirements may be no higher than for a QA level of quality management, but they will pervade every person, activity and function of the organization. It will, however, require a broadening of outlook and skills, and an increase in creative activities from that required at the QA level. The spread of the TQM philosophy would also be expected to be accompanied by greater sophistication in the application of tools and techniques, increased emphasis on people (the so-called soft aspects of TQM), process management, improved training and personal development and greater efforts to eliminate wastage and non-value adding activities. The process will also extend beyond the organization to include partnerships with suppliers and customers, and all stakeholders of the business. Activities will be reoriented to focus on the customer, internal and external with the aim of building partnerships, and going beyond satisfying the customer to delighting them. The need to self-assess progress towards business excellence is also a key issue.

There are many interpretations and definitions of TQM, but, put simply, TQM is the mutual co-operation of everyone in an organization and associated business processes to produce products and services which meet and, hopefully, exceed the needs and expectations of customers. TQM is both a philosophy, and a set of guiding principles for managing an organization.

The Key Elements of TQM

Despite the divergence of views on what constitutes TQM, there are a number of key elements in the various definitions which are now summarized. (Other chapters provide more detail of these elements.)

Commitment and leadership of the CEO

Without the total demonstrated commitment of the CEO and his/her immediate executives and other senior managers, nothing much will happen, and anything that does will not be permanent. They have to take charge personally, lead the process, provide direction, exercise forceful leadership, including dealing with those employees who block improvement and maintain the impetus. However, while some specific actions are required to give TQM a focus, as quickly as possible, it must be seen as the style of management and the natural way of operating a business.

Planning and organization

This features in a number of facets of the improvement process:

- Developing a clear long-term strategy for TQM which is integrated with other strategies such as IT, production/operations and HR and, also, with the business plans of the organization
- Deployment of the policies through all stages of the organizational hierarchy with objectives, targets, projects and resources agreed with those responsible for ensuring that the policies are turned from words into actions; see chapter 5
- Building product and service quality into designs and processes
- Developing prevention-based activities, e.g. mistake-proofing devices
- Putting QA procedures into place which facilitate closed-loop corrective action
- Planning the approach to be taken to the effective use of quality systems, procedures and tools and techniques, in the context of the overall strategy
- Developing the organization and infrastructure to support the improvement activities, including allocating the necessary resources to support them – while it is recommended to set up some form of steering type activity to provide direction and support and to make people responsible for co-ordinating and facilitating improvement, the infrastructure should *not* be seen as separate from the management structure
- Pursuing standardization, systematization and simplification of work instructions, procedures and systems

Using tools and techniques

To support and develop a process of continuous improvement, an organization will need to use a selection of tools and techniques within a problem-solving approach. Without the effective employment and mix of tools and techniques, it will be difficult to solve problems. The tools and techniques should be used to facilitate improvement, and should be integrated into the routine operation of the business. The organization should develop a route map for the tools and techniques which it intends to apply. The use of tools and techniques as a means, helps to start the process of improvement, employees using them feel involved and that they are making a contribution, quality awareness is enhanced, and behaviour and attitude change starts to happen, and projects are brought to a satisfactory conclusion.

Education and training

Employees, from the top to bottom of an organization, should be provided with the right level and standard of education and training to ensure that their general awareness and understanding of quality management concepts, skills and attitudes are appropriate and suited to the continuous improvement philosophy; it also provides a common language throughout the business. A formal programme of education and training needs to be planned and provided on a timely and regular basis to enable people to cope with increasing complex problems. It should suit the operational conditions of the business; is training done in a cascade mode (everyone is given the same basic training within a set time frame) or is an infusion mode (training is provided on a gradual progression basis to functions and departments on a need-to-know basis) more suitable? This programme should be viewed as an investment in developing the ability and knowledge of people and helping them to realize their potential. Without training, it is difficult to solve problems and, without education, behaviour and attitude change will not take place. The training programme must also focus on helping managers to think through what improvements are achievable in their areas of responsibility. It also has to be recognized that not all employees will have received and acquired adequate levels of education. The structure of the training programme may incorporate some updating of basic educational skills in numeracy and literacy, but it must promote continuing education and self-development. In this way, the latent potential of many employees will be released, and the best use of every person's ability achieved.

Involvement

There must be a commitment and structure to the development of employees, with recognition that they are assets which appreciate over time. All available means, from suggestion schemes to various forms of teamwork, must be considered for achieving broad employee interest, participation and contribution in the improvement process; management must be prepared to share some of their powers and responsibilities and loosen their reins. This also involves seeking, and listening carefully to, the views of employees and acting upon their suggestions. Part of the approach to TQM is to ensure that everyone has a clear understanding of what is required of them, how their processes relate to the business as a whole and how their internal customers are dependent upon them. The more people who understand the business, and what is going on around them, the greater the role they can play in the improvement process. People need to be encouraged to control, manage and improve the processes which are within their sphere of responsibility.

Teamwork

Teamwork needs to be practised in a number of forms. Consideration needs to be given to the operating characteristics of the teams employed, how they fit into the organizational structure and the roles of member, team leader, sponsor and facilitator.

Teamwork is one of the key features of involvement and, without it, difficulty will be found in gaining the commitment and participation of people throughout the organization. It is also a means of maximizing the output and value of individuals.

There is also a need to recognize positive performance and achievement, and to celebrate and reward success. People must see the results of their activities, and that the improvements they have made really do count. This needs to be constantly encouraged through active and open communication. If TQM is to be successful, it is essential that communication must be effective and widespread. Sometimes, managers are good talkers but poor communicators.

Measurement and feedback

Measurement, from a baseline, needs to be made continually against a series of key results indicators – internal and external – to provide encouragement that things are improving, i.e. fact rather than opinion. The latter indicators are the most important as they relate to customer perceptions of product and/or service improvement. The indicators should be developed from existing business measures, external, competitive and functional generic and internal benchmarking, as well as customer surveys and other means of external input. This enables progress and feedback to be assessed against a roadmap or checkpoints. From these measurements, action plans must be developed to meet objectives and bridge gaps.

Ensuring that the culture is conducive to continuous improvement activity

It is necessary to create an organizational culture which is conducive to continuous improvement, and in which everyone can participate. QA also needs to be integrated into all an organization's processes and functions. This requires changing peoples' behaviour, attitudes and working practices in a number of ways:

- Everyone in the organization must be involved in 'improving' the processes under their control on a continuous basis, and take personal responsibility for their own QA.
- Employees must be encouraged to identify wastage in all its various forms.
- Employees can stop a process, without reference to management, if they consider it to be not functioning correctly.
- Employees must be inspecting their own work.
- Defects must not be passed, in whatever form, to the next process. The internal customer–supplier relationship (everyone for whom you perform a task, service or provide information is a customer) must be recognized.
- Each person must be committed to satisfying their customers, both internal and external.
- External suppliers and customers must be integrated into the improvement process.
- Mistakes must be viewed as an improvement opportunity. In the words of the Japanese, every mistake is a pearl to be cherished.
- Honesty, sincerity and care must be an integral part of daily business life.

Changing people's behaviour and attitudes is one of the most difficult tasks facing management, requiring considerable powers and skills of motivation and persuasion;

considerable thought needs to be given to facilitating and managing culture change. In the words of a Government Chief Engineer in the Hong Kong Civil Engineering Department:

> Getting the quality system registered to ISO9001 is the easy bit, it is changing people's attitudes and getting them committed to continuous improvement what is presenting the greatest challenge.

What is the 'Received Wisdom'?

In a booklet, *How to Take Part in the Quality Revolution: A Management Guide,* Smith (1986) argues that the CEO will draw little comfort from the writings of the quality gurus in the task of leading a process of improvement in his/her organization:

> Just deciding where to begin is so difficult that many never get off the starting block. The condition is so common it even has a name – 'Total Quality Paralysis'.

The experience of the UMIST Quality Management Centre supports Smith's argument in that there is little doubt that managers are confused by the amount, and variety, of advice that is available, and this can hamper the spread and development of quality improvement. This condition is not as evident in Japan where there is less conflicting advice – the criteria of the Deming Application Prize and the influence of JUSE have seen to that; see chapter 3. Perhaps the MBNQA (US Department of Commerce, 1998) and the EQA (EFQM, 1998) will do the same for America and Europe, respectively (see chapter 22); only time will tell.

In the Western world, the four best known quality management experts, and arguably the most influential, are all Americans: Crosby (1979), Deming (1982), Feigenbaum (1991) and Juran (1988). Because of the considerable influence which these four men have had in the development of TQM in organizations throughout the world, their writings are explored, albeit in brief.

Crosby

Crosby's audience is primarily top management. He sells his programme to top management, and stresses increasing profitability through quality improvement. His argument is that higher quality reduces costs, and raises profits. He defines quality as conformance to requirements. Crosby's (1979) programme has 14 steps that focus on how to change the organization and tend to be a specific action plan for implementation; see table 1.1.

Crosby's approach is based on four absolutes of quality management:

- Quality means conformance, not elegance.
- It is always cheaper to do the job right the first time.
- The only performance indicator is the cost of quality.
- The only performance standard is zero defects.

Crosby also has produced a 'quality vaccine' comprising 21 areas, divided into five categories – integrity, systems, communications, operations and policies – which he treats as preventive medicine for poor quality.

Table 1.1 Crosby's 14-step quality improvement programme

1	Management commitment
2	Quality improvement team
3	Quality measurement
4	Cost of quality evaluation
5	Quality awareness
6	Corrective action
7	Establish an ad hoc committee for the zero defects programme
8	Supervisor training
9	Zero defects day
10	Goal setting
11	Error cause removal
12	Recognition
13	Quality councils
14	Do it over again

He does not accept the optimal quality level concept, because he believes that higher quality always reduces costs and raises profit. Cost of quality is used as a tool to help to achieve that goal. With respect to cost of quality, he produced the first serious alternative to the prevention–appraisal–failure categorization with the price of conformance and price of non-conformance model. In terms of employee roles, Crosby allocates a moderate amount of responsibility to the quality professional. Top management has an important role, and the hourly workforce has a role limited to reporting problems to management. One way that Crosby measures quality achievement is with a matrix, the quality management maturity grid, that charts the stages which management goes through from ignorance to enlightenment.

In summary, Crosby is acknowledged as a great motivator of senior management in helping to start the improvement process. His approach is generally regarded as simple and easy to follow. His critics often claim that he lacks substance in giving detailed guidance on how to apply quality management principles, tools, techniques and systems; however, on the other hand, it can be argued that he simply wishes to avoid being prescriptive.

Deming

Deming's thesis is that quality, through a reduction in statistical variation, improves productivity and competitive position. His early thinking was influenced by Shewhart, who is considered as the father of statistical quality control. He defines quality in terms of quality of design, quality of conformance, and quality of the sales and service function. Deming aims to improve quality and productivity, jobs, ensure the long-term survival of the firm, and improve competitive position. He does not accept the trade-off shown in economic cost of quality models, and says there is no way to calculate the cost of selling defective products to customers, which he believes is the major quality cost.

Deming advocates measurement of quality by direct statistical measures of manufacturing performance against specification. While all production processes exhibit variation, the goal of quality improvement is to reduce variation. Deming's approach is highly statistical and he believes that every employee should be trained in statistical

Table 1.2 Deming's 14 points for management

1	Create constancy of purpose towards improvement of product and service, with the aim to become competitive, stay in business, and to provide jobs.
2	Adopt the new philosophy – we are in a new economic age. Western management must awaken to the challenge, learn their responsibilities and take on leadership for future change.
3	Cease dependence on inspection to achieve quality. Eliminate the need for inspection on a mass basis by building quality into the product in the first place.
4	End the practice of awarding business on the basis of price tag. Instead, minimize total cost. Move toward a single supplier for any one item on a long-term relationship of loyalty and trust.
5	Improve constantly and forever the system of production and service, to improve quality and productivity, and thus constantly decrease costs.
6	Institute training on the job.
7	Institute leadership (see point 12): the aim of supervision should be to help people, machines and gadgets to do a better job. Supervision of management, as well as supervision of production workers, is in need of overhaul.
8	Drive out fear, so that everyone may work effectively for the company.
9	Break down barriers between departments. People in research, design, sales and production must work as a team, to foresee problems of production and problems in use that may be encountered with the product or service.
10	Eliminate slogans, exhortations and targets for the workforce that ask for zero defects and new levels of productivity. Such exhortations only create adversarial relationships, as the bulk of the causes of low quality and low productivity belong to the system and thus lie beyond the power of the workforce.
11a	Eliminate work standards (quotas) on the factory floor; substitute leadership instead.
11b	Eliminate management by objectives, by numbers and by numerical goals; substitute leadership instead.
12a	Remove barriers that rob the hourly worker of his or her right to pride of workmanship. The responsibility of supervisors must be changed from sheer numbers to quality.
12b	Remove barriers that rob people in management and in engineering of their right to pride of workmanship. This means, inter alia, abolishment of the annual or merit rating, and of management by objectives.
13	Institute a vigorous programme of education and self-improvement.
14	Put everybody in the company to work to accomplish the transformation. The transformation is everybody's job.

quality techniques. A 14-point approach (Deming 1986) summarizes his management philosophy for improving quality; see table 1.2.

Deming's view is that quality management and improvement is the responsibility of all the firm's employees: top management must adopt the 'new religion' of quality, lead the drive for improvement and be involved in all stages of the process. Hourly workers should be trained and encouraged to prevent defects and to improve quality, and be given challenging, rewarding jobs. Quality professionals should educate other managers in statistical techniques and concentrate on improving the methods of defect prevention. Finally, statisticians should consult with all areas of the company.

Other contributions of Deming include the PDCA or the PDSA cycle of continuous improvement, which Deming himself termed the Shewhart cycle and the pinpointing of the seven 'deadly diseases' which he used to criticize Western management and organizational practices:

1. Lack of constancy of purpose
2. Emphasis on short-term profits
3. Evaluation of performance, merit rating or annual review
4. Mobility of management
5. Running a company on visible figures alone
6. Excessive medical costs
7. Excessive cost of liability

A number of Deming user groups and associations have been formed which are dedicated to facilitating awareness and understanding of his work and to helping companies introduce his ideas. Also, a considerable number of authors – Aguayo (1990), Kilian (1992), Scherkenbach (1991) and Yoshida (1995) – have written books and papers explaining Deming's ideas.

In summary, Deming expects the managers to change – to develop a partnership with those at the operating level of the business, and to manage quality with direct statistical measures without cost-of-quality measures. Deming's approach, particularly his insistence on the need of management to change the organizational culture, is closely aligned with Japanese practice. This is not surprising in view of the assistance he gave to the Japanese after World War II.

Feigenbaum

Feigenbaum was General Electric's world-wide chief of manufacturing operations for a decade until the late 1960s. He is now president of an engineering consultancy firm, General Systems Co., that designs and installs operational systems in corporations around the world. Feigenbaum was the originator of the term 'total quality control', defined in 1961 in his first edition of *Total Quality Control* (1991) as:

> Total Quality Control is an effective system for integrating the quality-development, quality-maintenance, and quality-improvement efforts of the various groups in an organization so as to enable marketing, engineering, production, and service at the most economical levels which allow for full customer satisfaction.

Feigenbaum does not try so much to create managerial awareness of quality as to help a plant or company to design its own system. To him, quality is a way of managing a business organization. Significant quality improvement can only be achieved in a company through the participation of everyone in the workforce who must, therefore, have a good understanding of what management is trying to do. Fire-fighting quality problems has to be replaced with a very clear, customer-oriented quality management process that people can understand and to which they can commit themselves.

Senior management's understanding of the issues surrounding quality improvement and commitment to incorporating quality into their management practice is crucial to the successful installation of Feigenbaum's total quality system. They must abandon short-term motivational programmes that yield no long-lasting improvement. Management must also realize that quality does not mean only that customer problems have to be fixed faster. Quality leadership is essential to a company's success in the market-place.

Feigenbaum takes a very serious financial approach to the management of quality. He believes that the effective installation and management of a quality improvement process represent the best return-on-investment opportunity for many companies in today's competitive environment.

Feigenbaum's major contribution to the subject of cost of quality was the recognition that quality costs must be categorized if they are to be managed. He identified three major categories: appraisal costs, prevention costs and failure costs (Feigenbaum, 1956). Total quality cost is the sum of these costs. He was also the first of the international experts to identify the folly of regarding quality professionals as being solely responsible for an organization's quality activities.

Table 1.3 Feigenbaum's ten benchmarks for total quality success

1	Quality is a company-wide process.
2	Quality is what the customer says it is.
3	Quality and cost are a sum, not a difference.
4	Quality requires both individual and team zealotry.
5	Quality is a way of managing.
6	Quality and innovation are mutually dependent.
7	Quality is an ethic.
8	Quality requires continuous improvement.
9	Quality is the most cost-effective, least capital-intensive route to productivity.
10	Quality is implemented with a total system connected with customers and suppliers.

Source: Feigenbaum (1991)

According to Feigenbaum, the goal of quality improvement is to reduce the total cost of quality from the often quoted 25–30 per cent of sales or cost of operations to as low a percentage as possible. Therefore, developing cost of quality data and tracking it on an ongoing basis is an integral part of the process.

Feigenbaum says that management must commit themselves:

- To strengthening the quality improvement process itself
- To making sure that quality improvement becomes a habit
- To managing quality and cost as complementary objectives

In summary, though he does not espouse fourteen points or steps like Deming or Crosby, it is obvious his approach is not significantly different; it simply boils down to managerial know-how. He does however identify ten benchmarks for success with TQM; see table 1.3.

Juran

Joseph Juran has made, perhaps, a greater contribution to the quality management literature than any other quality professional. Like Deming, he has had an influence in the development of quality management in Japanese companies. While Deming provided advice on SPC methods from the late 1940s onward, Juran in the mid-1950s focused on the role of senior people in quality management. The focus of his series of lectures was that quality control must be an integral part of the management function, and practised throughout the organization. It can be argued that the teachings of Juran provided the catalyst which resulted in the involvement in first-line supervisors and operators in the improvement process.

Part of his argument is that companies must reduce the cost of quality. This is dramatically different from Deming. Deming ignores the cost of quality while Juran, like Crosby and Feigenbaum, claim that reducing it is a key objective. A ten point plan summarizes his approach; see table 1.4.

Juran defines quality as 'fitness for use', which he breaks into quality of design, quality of conformance, availability, and field service. The goals of Juran's approach to quality improvement are increased conformance and decreased cost of quality, and yearly goals are set in the objective-setting phase of the programme. He developed a quality trilogy comprising of quality planning, quality control and quality improvement.

Table 1.4 The Juran method

---

1 Build awareness of the need and opportunity for improvement.
2 Set goals for improvement.
3 Organize to reach the goals.
4 Provide training.
5 Carry out projects to solve problems.
6 Report progress.
7 Give recognition.
8 Communicate results.
9 Keep the score.
10 Maintain momentum by making annual improvement part of the regular system and processes of the company.

Source: Juran (1988)

Basically, his programmes work in three segments: a programme to attack sporadic problems, one to attack chronic problems, and an annual quality programme, in which top management participates, to develop or refine policies. Juran defines two major kinds of quality management – breakthrough (encouraging the occurrence of good things) that attacks chronic problems, and control (preventing the occurrence of bad things), that attack sporadic problems. He views the improvement process as taking two journeys – from symptom to cause (diagnosis) and cause to remedy (diagnosis to solution).

Juran also allocates responsibility among the workforce differently from Deming. He puts the primary responsibility to quality professionals (who serve as consultants to top management and employees). The quality professionals design and develop the programme, and do most of the work. While granting the importance of top management support, Juran places more of the quality leadership responsibility on middle management and quality professionals. The role of the workforce is mainly to be involved in quality improvement teams.

In summary, Juran emphasizes the cost of quality, because the language of top management is money, and he recommends cost of quality for identifying quality improvement projects and opportunities and developing a quality cost scoreboard to measure quality costs. Juran's approach is more consistent with American management practices – he takes the existing management culture as a starting point and builds a quality improvement process from that baseline. In contrast to Deming, he considers that, if the energy from fear is harnessed and focused in a positive direction, it can be a positive rather than a negative factor.

Are the approaches of these gurus different?

Advocates of each guru are apt to claim that 'their man's approach' is the only one likely to work. This is an arrogant and myopic stance to adopt; each approach has its strengths and weaknesses, and they are all proven packages. None of the experts has all the answers to the problems facing an organization, despite each guru and, in particular, their supporters stressing the exclusivity of their approaches/methods. It is also worth remembering that all four of these experts are consultants (not forgetting that Deming is now dead), and it is in their own business interests and that of their supporters to distinguish their approach from that of their peers and to appear to have all the answers.

It is suggested that any person interested in learning about the approaches and methods of any of these four men goes to the source of the original work rather than that of their disciples.

The ways of approaching quality management as suggested by Crosby, Deming, Feigenbaum and Juran are variations on a theme, the essential difference is the focus of their approach. A number of writers, such as Bendell (1989), Fine (1985), Gerald (1984) and Main (1986), have compared and contrasted the approaches of the four gurus, and these commentaries are helpful in assessing the value of each approach. Broadly speaking, the teachings of these four gurus can be characterized by the main focus of their approach:

- Crosby – company-wide motivation
- Deming – statistical process control (SPC)
- Feigenbaum – systems management
- Juran – project management

McBryde (1986) says that the 'golden thread' running through the philosophies of all four (and other, unnamed) gurus is the concept of adopting quality as a fundamental business strategy permeating the culture of the entire organization. Fine (1985) concludes that the teachings of Crosby, Deming and Juran (Feigenbaum is not included in his comparison) have four points in common:

- The importance of top management support and participation
- The need for workforce training and education
- Quality management requires careful planning and a philosophy of company-wide involvement
- Quality improvement programmes must represent permanent, ongoing activities

The approach of the Japanese to the management of quality

In addition to the approaches and philosophies of these four experts, the Japanese approach to quality management is also widely publicized. In recent times, the work and ideas of a number of Japanese quality experts have been published in English, including Imai (1986), Ishikawa (1985), Mizuno (1988), Nemoto (1987), Ozeki and Askaka (1990), Shingo (1986) and Taguchi (1986).

The Japanese define quality as uniformity around the target, and their goal is continual improvement towards perfection. They allocate responsibility for quality management among all employees. The workers are primarily responsible for maintaining the system, although they have some responsibility for improving it. Higher up, managers do less maintaining and more improving. At the highest levels, the emphasis is on breakthrough and on teamwork throughout the organization.

There are a number of now-familiar concepts associated with Japanese style TQM or TQC or CWQC as they sometimes term it. Earlier work tried to make a distinction between TQC and CWQC but, in Japanese companies today, they appear to be one and the same. This is recognized by recent publications from JUSE (1997); today, Japanese companies tend to use the term TQM rather than TQC. These concepts are listed here.

- Total commitment to improvement
- Perfection and defect analysis
- Continuous change
- Taking personal responsibility for the QA of one's own processes
- Insistence on compliance
- Correcting one's own errors
- Adherence to disciplines
- Orderliness and cleanliness

The ideas of Imai, Ishikawa and Shingo are all being applied in the West but, perhaps, it is the work of Taguchi which is the best known. For this reason, his work is reviewed before going on to describe some of the general concepts of Japanese style TQM; more details of Taguchi and the Japanese approach to TQM are provided in chapters 16 and 3 respectively.

Genichi Taguchi is a statistician and electrical engineer who was involved in rebuilding the Japanese telephone system. He was contracted to provide statistical assistance and design of experiment support. Taguchi rejected the classical approach to design of experiments as being too impractical for industrial situations and revised these methods to develop his own approach to design of experiments. He has been applying design of experiments in the Japanese electronics industry for over 25 years.

His ideas fall into two principal and related areas known as 'the loss function' and 'off-line quality control'. In his ideas about the loss function, Taguchi (1986) defines quality as: 'The quality of a product is the loss imparted to society from the time the product is shipped.' Among the losses, he includes consumers' dissatisfaction, warranty costs, loss of reputation and, ultimately, loss of market share.

Taguchi maintains that a product does not start causing losses only when it is out of specification, but when there is any deviation from the target value. Further, in most cases, the loss to society can be represented by a quadratic function, i.e. the loss increases as the square of the deviation from the target value; see figure 1.4. This leads to the important conclusion that quality (as defined by Taguchi) is most economically achieved by minimizing variance, rather than by strict conformance to specification.

This conclusion provides the basis for Taguchi's ideas for off-line quality control. Off-line quality control means optimizing production process and product parameters in such a way as to minimize item to item variations in the product and its performance. Clearly, this focuses attention on the design process. Taguchi promotes three distinct stages of designing-in quality:

1. *System design* – the basic configuration of the system is developed.
2. *Parameter design* – the numerical values for the system variables (product/process parameters which are called factors) are chosen so that the system performs well, no matter what disturbances or noises are encountered by the system. There are three types of design factors – control, signal and null. The emphasis is on using low-cost materials and processes in the production of the system.
3. *Tolerance design* – if the system is not satisfactory, tolerance design is then used to improve performance by tightening the tolerances.

Taguchi's emphasis is on parameter design. Underlying the parameter design process is the concept that process and product performance is defined by two different kinds of factor – control factors (which can be controlled easily) and noise factors

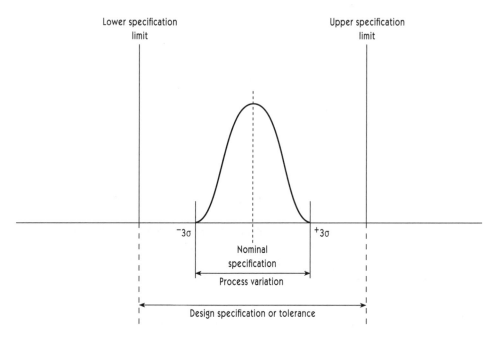

Figure 1.4 Design tolerance and process variation relationship
Source: Dale and Cooper (1992)

(which are virtually impossible or prohibitively expensive to control). Taguchi's methods look for a set of control factors which will produce a process or product insensitive to the effects of noise factors.

When seeking to optimize production process and product or service parameters, it is frequently necessary to determine, experimentally, the effects of varying the parameter values. This can be a very expensive and time-consuming process which may produce a lot of redundant information. By using fractional factorial experiments, which Taguchi calls orthogonal arrays, the number of experiments required can be reduced drastically, though it must be said that there are eminent statisticians who do not wholly agree with the claims made about the efficacy of orthogonal designs.

The attention given to what are commonly termed 'Taguchi methods' has been largely responsible for organizations examining the usefulness of experimental design in making improvements. Quite apart from the successes derived from using his methods, the level of awareness he has promoted in design of experiments is an achievement in itself. On a more negative note, he provided little advice on the management of the experiments themselves.

Various practices underpin the TQM approach in Japanese companies:

- Policy deployment of targets for improvement
- Use of statistical methods
- Housekeeping
- Daily machine and equipment checking
- Successive and self-check systems
- Visual management

- Mistake-proofing
- Detailed QA procedures
- Visual standards
- The concept that the next person or process is the customer
- Improvement followed by standardization
- The JIT philosophy
- Total productive maintenance
- Quality circles (QCs)
- Suggestion schemes
- Treating suppliers as part of the family

Change and Continuous Improvement*

Changing the life-long behaviour, customs, practices and prejudices of an organization is not easy. Organizations committed to quality will strive continually to improve the quality of their goods or services, and are committed to change but, in many cases, they were intended to be stable and unchanging. Good reasons must exist inside and/or outside the organization to precipitate the process of change and make managers recognize that they need to improve their business.

Lascelles and Dale (1989) report that the continuous improvement process is often triggered by one or more of these forces for change:

- The CEO
- Competition
- Demanding customers
- A fresh-start situation, e.g. a greenfield venture

Figure 1.5, from Lascelles and Dale (1993), shows that demanding customers are the most effective force or agent for change, closely followed by a need to reduce costs/improve profitability. The forces can be viewed as links in a chain, with competition acting as a catalyst setting off a chain reaction which enhances quality awareness in the market, resulting in demanding customers and CEOs behaving as change agents; see figure 1.6 from Lascelles and Dale (1993).

Forces for change: The CEO

Many writers on the subject of quality management are agreed that unless the CEO takes the lead to improve quality within an organization, attempts and gains made by individuals and departments will be short-lived; this is explored in more detail in chapter 2. However, most CEOs want tangible proof of the need for continuous improvement and for their own involvement, because they usually have a number of urgent matters which need their attention. Thus, other forms of factors must be present also, of which market pressure, e.g. intense competition, demanding customers, has by far the greatest impact. A restart situation or greenfield opportunity may also aid the process by eliminating some of the barriers to change or reducing their effects.

* The contribution of Dr David Lascelles contained in the section 'Change and Continuous Improvement' is acknowledged.

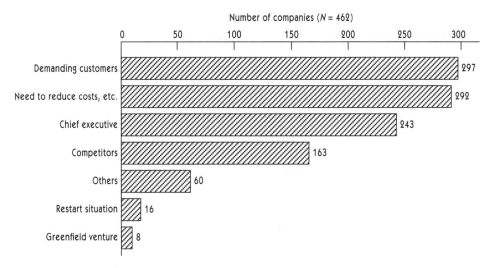

Number of companies (N = 462)

Figure 1.5 Factors motivating quality improvement
Source: Lascelles and Dale (1993)

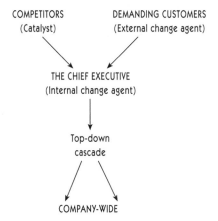

COMPETITORS
(Catalyst)

DEMANDING CUSTOMERS
(External change agent)

THE CHIEF EXECUTIVE
(Internal change agent)

Top-down
cascade

COMPANY-WIDE

Figure 1.6 Market-led paradigm of TQI
Source: Lascelles and Dale (1993)

Forces for change: Competition

Competition is fierce in today's business environment and quality is becoming increasingly recognized as a key consideration in many purchasing decisions. There is little doubt that quality is an essential part of the marketing mix as companies seek ways to differentiate effectively their products and/or services from those of their competitors. Many successful companies (in market share terms) now advertise their products and/or services on the basis of quality and reliability rather than price. (Consider, for example, the number of advertisements in which the word quality is featured.) There are numerous well-publicized cases (e.g. DTI, 1990) in which intense competition has been the change agent compelling companies to develop their quality systems to meet the requirements of the ISO9000 series of quality system standards and/or to introduce a TQM strategy to improve quality. The options may be to go out of business, to lose market share, or to have to withdraw from a particular market. The motivation for improvement is provided here by the need to stay competitive, and the change agent is the customer whose awareness of quality has been enhanced. As a result of such pressures, suppliers of goods and services have, in turn, themselves become demanding customers and seek improved levels of quality conformance from their own suppliers.

Forces for change: Demanding customers

Demanding customers with high product and service quality expectations and an established reputation for quality can be very effective change agents. In addition to providing tangible evidence of the value of reputation and standing, they have the potential for bringing about radical and permanent changes in attitudes towards continuous improvement among their suppliers through the requirements they place on them. Many major purchasers have policies which outline what is required of suppliers in terms of their approach to quality management, e.g. the QS9000 quality system standard. Documents such as these describe fundamentals that must be incorporated into a supplier's quality planning methods and quality system to control and improve quality. Each supplier is responsible for building on these fundamentals to develop an effective quality system and products and services which are defect free. Many quality conscious purchasers assess and evaluate supplier performance. Some also provide resources to help suppliers to implement tools and techniques, improve workplace layout, and give guidance on problem solving. For example, Nissan Motor Manufacturing (UK) Ltd among others have a supplier development team who are working with suppliers on a continuous basis to teach them how to make incremental improvements; see Lloyd et al. (1994) for details. Companies that take an active interest in their suppliers are likely to provoke a far-reaching effect on the way in which they manage continuous improvement.

Forces for change: 'Fresh-start' situations

The degree of entrenchment of attitudes, and hence the difficulty of changing them, is related to the length of time an organization has been established, its size, staff turnover rate, managerial mobility, markets, competitors, and many other factors which influence the 'performance' of an organization. A fresh-start situation therefore provides excellent opportunities to make rapid, fundamental, changes to attitudes and relationships.

A 'greenfield' venture may be the setting up of a new company, a new operational direction for an existing company – e.g. creation of a new strategic business unit as part of a diversification programme – an established company relocating to a new factory, or a company establishing a new operation in existing premises after rationalizing plant, product lines, manpower, etc. It may be argued that most greenfield ventures are in areas where growth expectations are high and where demanding customers are at their most influential. Furthermore, most greenfield companies tend to be small at the outset so that the purchasing power of individual customers is considerable. A greenfield venture provides an opportunity for the introduction of a process of continuous improvement in a situation where there is no prior history of lame excuses, acceptance of non-conformance, shipping non-conforming products just to meet production targets, providing and accepting a poor level of service, poor delivery performance, and where 'we have always done it this way', 'it will not work here' and other unhelpful attitudes are absent. In a greenfield venture, there is an opportunity to start from scratch without any vested interest or inhibiting procedures to overcome. It is an opportunity for senior management to try to do all the things that should be done to engender a culture of continuous improvement.

A hiatus, no matter how brief, brought about by an interruption of a company's operations may present the same kind of opportunity. Intentional temporary dislocation or cessation of normal activities may be another way of breaking with tradition, deflating the pressures of expediency, and removing the barriers to improvement. Moving to a new site, a takeover, management buy-out, large-scale refurbishing of premises or equipment, bankruptcy, or a major catastrophe, might also be the catalyst for change.

How do Companies get Started?

Once change has been triggered, organizations need to translate enhanced quality awareness and organizational need for improvement into effective action. At this stage, an organization's senior management team ask many questions:

- What should we do? What are the priorities?
- What advice do we need? From whom should we be taking advice? Can we get unbiased advice?
- Should the approach be top-down or bottom-up?
- Do we need an umbrella term? Do we have to use the term TQM? What are the alternatives – quality improvement, continuous improvement, business improvement, customer care, customer focus, customer first?
- How quickly should we proceed?
- Which tools and techniques should we apply? How do we apply these tools and techniques?
- What training do we need? What courses and conferences should we attend? What packages and programmes should we buy?
- Can we make use of one of the recognized Models for Business Excellence?
- Which companies should we visit? Which network of companies should we attempt to join?
- Should we call in a management consultant, and which one?
- Should we develop the quality system to meet the requirements of the ISO9000 quality management system series?
- How important is quality management system registration?
- How do we embrace our current improvement initiatives under the TQM banner?

Their dilemma is often compounded not just by a lack of knowledge of TQM and the process of continuous improvement, but also by a lack of experience in managing organizational change. The overwhelming quantity and variety of available advice, which is often conflicting, sometimes biased and sometimes incorrect and misdirected, simply adds to the confusion and chaos. It is not surprising then that there is sometimes inertia on the part of senior management teams who are faced with the task of introducing a formal process of continuous improvement in their organizations.

Each writer on the subject of TQM develops and outlines an approach which reflects their own background, values and experience:

- Methods outlining the wisdom, philosophies and recommendations of the internationally respected experts on the subject
- Prescriptive step-by-step approaches
- A listing of TQM principles which are presented in the form of a TQM implementation plan and a set of guidelines
- Non-prescriptive methods in the form of a framework or model
- Self-assessment methods based on the business excellence models on which the MBNQA and the EQA are based

Thus it can be seen that there are a number of ways to get started, and it is up to each organization to identify the approach which best suits their needs and business operation. Indeed, it is not unusual for an organization to find that its TQM approach is not working out as planned and switch to another approach. Some of the main ways of starting TQM are now examined.

Applying the wisdom of the TQM experts

The writings and teachings of Crosby (1979), Deming (1986), Feigenbaum (1991) and Juran (1988) discussed earlier in the chapter, is a sensible starting point for any organization introducing TQM. These four men have had a considerable influence in the development of TQM in organizations throughout the world. The usual approach is for an organization to adopt the teachings of one of these quality management experts and to attempt to follow their programme. The argument for this approach is that each expert has a package which works, the package gives some form of security, it provides a coherent framework, gives a discipline to the process and provides a common language, understanding and method of communication. To facilitate this, some companies have purposely opted for the simplest package. The approach of Crosby is generally recognized as being the easiest to follow. Dale (1991) found that Crosby followed by Juran, and then Deming, were the most frequently used experts. Observations of organizations setting out on this road is that, sooner or later, they will start to pull into their improvement process the ideas of other quality management experts. This is understandable because none of these experts has all the answers to the problems facing an organization, despite the claims made about the exclusivity of approach.

Whichever man's programme or approach is being followed, it should be used as a quality management tool to focus on the improvement process and not treated as an end in itself.

Applying a consultancy package

Some companies (usually large concerns) decide to adopt the programme of one of the major management consultancies on the grounds that it is a self-contained package which can be suitably customized for application throughout their organization. Some companies are very comfortable with consultants, others not so. It should also be noted that most of the 'gurus' have their own consultancy activities to help organizations to implement the ideas and principles of the expert in question.

It is important for a company to understand that the use of a consultant organization does not relieve the senior management team of their own responsibilities for TQM; it is their responsibility to own the improvement process and to exercise leadership. Executives should never allow the consultant to become the 'TQM champion' or the company expert on TQM. A key part of consultancy is transfer of skills and knowledge, and when the project is complete the training and guidance, provided by the consultant must remain within the organization in order that the process of improvement can progress and develop. The consultant should be perceived by the organization as an 'implementation' tool, and not as an initiator of TQM and the improvement process. It may be that the consultant is also learning on the job and that the organization is acting, unknowingly, in the role of guinea pig and any ideas, proposals and decisions should always be scrutinized carefully by the TQM steering committee for their applicability to the company's operations.

Quality management consultancies bring their expertise to the company and provide the resources, experience, disciplines, objectivity and catalyst for getting the process started. The consultants are usually involved in a wide range of activities from planning through to training and project work and implementation of specific improvement initiatives. There are a myriad of consultancies offering a variety of TQM products and packages, and not all of them will suit every organization. It is likely that organizations, in particular large ones, will use more than one consultancy as they make progress along the TQM journey.

A company intending to use a consultancy must carefully consider its selection so as to ensure that the one chosen is suited to their needs; this also applies to the individual consultant(s) who will actually carry out the work. The selection issue generally involves a presentation of the TQM approach used by the consultancy to senior management and other interested parties. There are a number of factors to be taken into consideration:

- The personality of the consultant(s) and the perceived interaction with the people with whom they will work
- The presentation and proposal made
- Previously published material
- The availability and adequacy of educational material and supporting systems, programmes and tools, including delivery style of the material
- The consultant's willingness to carry out ongoing reassessment and to fine-tune the training programme
- The reputation, experience and track record of the consultancy and individual consultant(s), with existing clients
- The consultant's knowledge of TQM and its application in practice in similar or related companies – not just in consulting, research and/or teaching
- The consultant's rapport and ability to communicate with staff at all levels in the organization
- The consultant's ability to develop a bond with the organization
- The consultant's training skills and ability
- The consultant's grasp of the client organization's culture and management style

- The extent to which the consultancy is prepared to assist in carrying out a quality management diagnosis, and to tailor and adopt the package and delivery methods to suit the needs of the client

The decision to use a consultant organization is usually made by the CEO with support from the Quality Director. It is dangerous for the consultant to assume that other Board members will contribute more than vocal support to the process of improvement.

The company needs to understand clearly what is being bought from a consultancy. It is often difficult to define in precise detail what is required in a TQM assignment with the consequence that the terms of reference are vague. This sometimes results in a difference between what was ordered and what was delivered; wrangling over the deliverables from a TQM contract is a major detractor in a process of continuous improvement. The company should also take care that a TQM assignment is not used to open the door for other consultancy work in problem areas such as manufacturing management, business process re-engineering (BPR), logistics, HR, organization development, accountancy and business management. The easiest way of selling consultancy is on the back of a short-term successful assignment; this might have a negative influence on the long-term success of TQM.

A major complaint about consultancies is the use of 'off-the-shelf' packages and prescriptive solutions that fail to maximize client involvement, do not reflect the client's business process, and business constraints, and the use of prescriptive words and terms which do not suit the culture of the client organization.

For those considering the utilization of an external consultant, the main issues to be addressed and agreed on can be summarized:

- Clear terms of reference specifying the expected benefits to the organization of the consultancy project, with tangible objectives, milestones and time-scales
- The precise nature of the relationship between the client management team and the consultant – the management team will need to consider the precise form of consultancy input required, and to identify success criteria for the project
- The mechanism for implementing the improvement strategy and managing the change process, together with the resources required – the issues involved include the role of the senior management team, the amount of time and energy individual senior managers are able or prepared to commit, and who might assume the day-to-day role of project co-ordinator

A booklet, *Choosing and Using a Consultant*, produced by the Employment Department (1991) and which is aimed at directors and managers, contains a number of useful pointers to identify, select and work with consultants.

Frameworks and models

A framework or model is usually introduced to present a picture of what is required in introducing TQM. They are the means of presenting ideas, concepts, pointers and plans in a non-prescriptive manner, and are usually not considered to be a 'how-to' guide to TQM introduction and subsequent development. They are guides to action and not things to be followed in a slavish manner. Step-by-step approaches have a set starting point, and usually follow one route, and are rigid in general. They are more concerned with the destination than the route to get there. A framework allows the users to choose their own starting point, course of action and to build gradually on the individual features and parts at a pace which suits their business situation and available resources. Aalbregtse et al. (1991) provide an excellent description of what a framework should consist and its objectives. A number of writers, such as Burt (1993), Chu (1988), Dale and Boaden (1993), Flero (1992) and Johnson (1992), have proposed a range of TQM improvement frameworks. A typical framework for managing continuous improvement is the UMIST improvement framework as described by Dale in chapter 8. It provides on indication of how the various aspects of TQM fit together, and is particularly useful for many organizations:

- Those who are taking their first steps on the continuous improvement journey
- Those with ISO9000 quality management series registration, who require some guidance and advice on what to do next
- Those attempting to develop improvement plans and controls across a number of sites
- Those with less than three years' operating experience of TQM

Developing a tailor-made organizational route map

A variation on these approaches is to absorb the 'received wisdom' and the experiences of other companies and to extract the ideas, methods, systems and tactics which are appropriate to the particular circumstances, business situation and environment of the organization. Organizations starting with any of the more popular approaches to TQM will eventually use this method.

In this approach, management have to think through the issues and to develop for themselves a vision, quality objectives, policy, approach, a route map for quality improvement and the means of deploying the philosophy to all levels of the organization. A feature of organizations following this approach is that senior management will have visited other companies with a reputation for being 'centres of excellence' to see, at first hand, the lessons learned from TQM; they will have become involved in meetings relating to TQM with executives of like minds from different companies. They are also frequent attendees at conferences and are generally well read on the subject.

When starting on the improvement process, it is always beneficial for organizations to establish contacts with others that have a reputation for excellence in systems and products. There is much to be said for learning by association, and sharing information through networks. Companies working with, or competing directly against, companies with advanced management processes, develop their knowledge of TQM and continuous improvement at a fast rate. A case in point is the influence which the Japanese automotive and electronic companies have had on the UK supply base.

From the outset, organizations must accept that TQM is a long and arduous journey, which has no end. Unfortunately, there are no short cuts and no one has a monopoly of the best ideas. Furthermore, once started, the momentum needs to be maintained, otherwise even the gains may be lost. Even the most successful improvement process has periods when little headway is made.

The method of starting on TQM is less important than management commitment to continuous improvement and the leadership they are prepared to demonstrate; this is the key determinant of long-term success.

Self-assessment

If a process of continuous improvement is to be sustained and its pace increased, it is essential that organizations monitor, on a regular basis, what activities are going well, which have stagnated and what needs to be improved. Self-assessment (discussed in detail in chapter 22) against a recognized Model for Business Excellence provides such a framework and it is defined by the EFQM (1998) as:

> Self-assessment is a comprehensive, systematic and regular review of an organization's activities and results referenced against a model of business excellence. The self-assessment process allows the organization to discern clearly its strengths and areas in which improvements can be made and culminates in planned improvement actions which are monitored for progress.

Summary: Developing TQM

In concluding this chapter, a list of points is offered which organizations should keep in mind when developing TQM. Many of them are expanded upon in the chapters which follow.

Organizing

- There is no ideal way of assuring the quality or an organization's products of services. What matters is that improvement does occur, that it is cost-effective, and that it is never-ending.
- There is no one best way of starting a process of continuous improvement which suits all organizations and cultures.
- Senior management's commitment is vital to gain credibility, assure continuity and establish longevity of the process. They need to think deeply about the subject and commit to it the necessary resources. Managers must also place more emphasis on leadership and create an environment in which people can develop and apply, to full potential, all their skills.
- Planning should have a ten-year horizon to ensure that the principles of TQM are firmly rooted in the culture of the organization. Patience and tenacity are key virtues.
- Quality objectives and strategies must be developed and deployed down through the organizational hierarchy, along with agreeing goals for improvement.
- The improvement process needs to be integrated with other organizational improvement initiatives and business strategies.
- A multi-disciplinary TQM steering committee, chaired by the CEO, must be established and appropriate infrastructure established to support the improvement process. It is important that this infrastructure is integrated into the existing structure.
- At the outset, the main quality problems must be identified and tackled by the senior management team – 'lead by example'.

Systems and techniques

- The quality management system must be well documented, provide direction and feedback and be audited internally on a regular and effective basis.

- The day-to-day control and assurance activity must be separated from the improvement process.
- There must be a dedication to removing basic causes of errors and wastage.
- At the design stage, all potential non-conformances must be identified and eliminated.
- A system by which all staff can raise those problems which prevent them turning in an error-free performance should be in place.
- It should be recognized that tools, techniques, systems, and packages are used at different stages in different organizations in their development of TQM.
- The timing of the introduction of a particular tool, technique, system or package is crucial to its success.
- Mistake-proofing of operations should be investigated.
- Statistical methods should be used.

Measurement and feedback

- It should be recognized that customer satisfaction is a business issue.
- All available means must be used to determine customer requirements and to develop systems and procedures to assess conformance.
- It should be easy for the internal and external customer to complain. Ensure that all customer complaints are picked up and analysed, and that there is appropriate feedback.
- The attitude that 'the next process/person is the customer' must be encouraged.
- Measures of customer satisfaction and quality indicators for all internal departments must be developed.
- Regular self-assessment of the progress being made with continuous improvement against the criteria of the MBNQA for performance excellence and the EFQM model for business excellence, or a similar model should be carried out. This will assist in making the improvement efforts more efficient and cost effective.

Changing the culture

- All aspects of customer and supplier relationships should be developed, improved and assessed on a regular basis.
- Teamwork must be practised at all levels.
- People must be involved at all stages of the improvement process, and not simply in those aspects which directly affect their role.
- Education and training should be continuous and widespread, to foster changes in attitudes and behaviour, and to improve the skills base of the organization.

References

Aalbregtse, R. J., Heck, J. A. and McNeley, P. K. 1991: TQM: how do you do it? *Automation*, 38(8), 30–2.

Aguayo, R. 1990: *Dr. Deming: The American Who Taught the Japanese About Quality*. New York: Simon and Schuster.

Bendell, T. 1989: *The Quality Gurus: What Can They Do for Your Company?* London: Department of Trade and Industry.

Burt, J. F. 1993: A new for a not-so-new concept. *Quality Progress*, 26(3), 87–8.

Chu, C. H. 1988: The pervasive elements of total quality control. *Industrial Management*, 30(5), 30–2.

Crosby, P. B. 1979: *Quality is Free*. New York: McGraw Hill.

Dale, B. G. 1991: Starting on the road to success. *TQM Magazine*, 3(2), 125–8.

Dale, B. G. and Boaden, R. J. 1993: Improvement framework. *The TQM Magazine*, 5(1), 23–6.

Dale, B. G. and Cooper, R. 1992: *Total Quality and Human Resources: An Executive Guide*. Oxford: BPI.

Deming, W. E. 1982: *Quality, Productivity and Competitive Position*. Cambridge, Mass.: Massachusetts Institute of Technology, Centre of Advanced Engineering Study.

Deming, W. E. 1986: *Out of the Crisis*. Cambridge, Massachusetts: Massachusetts Institute of Technology, Centre of Advanced Engineering Study.

DTI. 1990: *The Case for Quality*. London: Department of Trade and Industry.

EFQM (European Foundation for Quality Management). 1998: *Self-Assessment 1998: Guidelines for Companies*, Brussels: EFQM.

Employment Department. 1991: *Choosing and Using a Consultant*. London: HMSO.

Feigenbaum, A. V. 1956: Total quality control. *Harvard Business Review*, 34(6), 93–101.

Feigenbaum, A. V. 1991: *Total Quality Control*. New York: McGraw Hill.

Fine, C. H. 1985: *Managing Quality: a Comparative Assessment*, Manufacturing Issues, Booz Allen and Hamilton Inc.

Flero, J. 1992: The Crawford slip method. *Quality Progress*, 25(5), 40–3.

Ford Motor Company. 1985: *Three-day Statistical Process Control Course Notes*, Ford Motor Company, Brentwood, Essex.

Gerald, V. 1984: *Three of a Kind: A Reflection on the Approach to Quality*, Corporate Quality Bureau, Philips Group N. V., Eindhoven.

Imai, M. 1986: *Kaizen the Key to Japan's Competitive Success*. New York: Random House Business Division.

Ishikawa, K. (translated by D. J. Lu) 1985: *What is Total Quality Control? The Japanese Way*, Englewood Cliffs, NJ: Prentice Hall.

Johnson, J. W. 1992: A point of view: life in a fishbowl: a senior manager's perspective on TQM. *National Productivity Review*, 11(2), 143–6.

Juran, J. M. (Editor-in-Chief) 1988: *Quality Control Handbook*. New York: McGraw Hill.

JUSE, The Deming Prize Committee. 1997: *The Deming Prize Guide for Overseas Companies*, Tokyo: Union of Japanese Scientists and Engineers.

Kilian, C. S. (1992): *The World of W. Edwards Deming*. New York: SPC Press Inc.

Lascelles, D. M. and Dale, B. G. 1989: Quality improvement: what is the motivation? *Proceedings of the Institution of Mechanical Engineers*, 203(B1), 43–50.

Lascelles, D. M. and Dale, B. G. 1993: *The Road to Quality*. Bedford: IFS Publications.

Lloyd, A., Dale, B. G. and Burnes, B. 1994: Supplier development: a study of Nissan Motor Manufacturing (UK) and her suppliers. *Proceedings of the I.Mech.E.*, 208(D1), 63–8.

Main, J. 1986: Under the spell of the quality gurus. *Fortune*, August 18, 24–7.

McBryde, V. E. 1986: In today's market: quality is best focal point for upper management. *Industrial Engineering*, 18(7), 51–5.

McKenzie, R. M. 1989: *The Production-Inspection Relationship*. Edinburgh and London: Scottish Academic Press.

Mizuno, S. 1988: *Company-Wide Total Quality Control*. Tokyo: Asian Productivity Organisation.

Nemoto, M. 1987: *Total Quality Control for Management*. Englewood Cliffs, N.J.: Prentice Hall.

Ozeki, K. and Asaka, T. 1990: *Handbook of Quality Tools*. Bucks: Productivity Europe.

Scherkenbach, W. W. 1991: *The Deming Route to Quality and Productivity: Road Maps and Roadblocks*. Milwaukee: ASQC Quality Press.

Shingo, S. 1986: *Zero Quality Control: Source Inspection and the Poka-Yoke System*. Cambridge, Mass.: Productivity Press.

Smith, S. 1986: *How to Take Part in the Quality Revolution: A Management Guide.* London: PA Management Consultants.

Taguchi, G. 1986: *Introduction to Quality Engineering.* New York: Asian Productivity Organisation.

US Department of Commerce. 1998: *Malcolm Baldrige National Quality Award 1998 Criteria for Performance Excellence,* Gaithersburg: National Institute of Standards and Technology.

Yoshida, K. 1995: Revisiting Deming's 14 points in light of Japanese business practice. *Quality Management Journal,* 3(1), 14–30.

chapter two

The Role of Management in TQM

B. G. Dale

Introduction

It is the responsibility of the senior management team to create the organizational environment, atmosphere, values and behaviour in which TQM can achieve its potential. This has been well articulated by the international authorities on quality management (e.g. Crosby, Deming, Feigenbaum and Juran) who typically point out that the leadership provided in these matters is the key to the success, or failure, of the initiatives. This requires changing – through a deliberate, structured and systematic process – the behaviour and attitudes of people at all levels in the organization hierarchy. People who, because of the respective cultures of the organizations in which they have worked – lack of TQM education and training, lack of opportunity, neglect, mistreatment, etc. – have, in manufacturing industry, regarded quality as a means of sorting conforming from non-conforming product, and reworking product to prevent non-conforming goods being passed to customers and, in service situations and public services, have sometimes adopted a 'take it or leave it' attitude to the consumer and the public.

It is not an easy task to create an organizational culture in which each person in every department is fully committed to improving their own performance and is dedicated to satisfying their internal customers' needs and future expectations. This takes many years and requires senior managers to take a long-term view. Along the TQM journey, it is easy for people, especially when under pressure, to slip back into the old traditional firefighting way of doing things. It should be expected that a number of employees will tend to be cynical and expect TQM to go the way of all new initiatives and eventually fizzle out. So it is not surprising that organizations do encounter a wide range of obstacles in pursuing a process of continuous and company-wide improvement.

This chapter outlines the main reasons why it is important that senior managers should become personally involved in TQM. TQM is the prime responsibility of senior management and they need to become immersed in it; without this commitment nothing of significance will happen. It examines what they need to know about TQM, and what they should do in terms of actions. Middle management and first line management also have a key role to play in putting the principles of TQM in place at the sharp end of the business, and the activities in which they need to get involved are also outlined.

The Need for Senior Managers to get Involved in TQM

The decision to introduce TQM can only be taken by the CEO in conjunction with the senior management team. Senior management have to devote time to learn about the subject, including attending suitable training courses and conferences. Developing and deploying organizational vision, mission, philosophy, values, strategies, objectives and plans, and communicating the reasons behind them together with the underlying logic is the province of senior management. This is why senior management have to become personally involved in the introduction and development of TQM, and to demonstrate visible commitment and confidence to it by leading this way of thinking and managing the business. This not only requires their personal commitment but a significant investment of time. To ensure that senior management focus their attention on issues of continuous improvement, there is emerging evidence that a proportion of their remuneration (such as bonus or performance-related pay) is related to metrics such as customer satisfaction and employee satisfaction figures and scores achieved against the EFQM Model for Business Excellence.

TQM requires the commitment, confidence and conviction of the senior management team; if this is achieved it avoids false starts and helps to ensure longevity. They have to encourage a total corporate commitment to improve, continually, every aspect of the business. Everyone in the organization has a role to play in continuous improvement but this effort is likely to be disjointed and spasmodic if senior managers have not made the organizational requirements clear. If they fail to become involved, it is likely that the improvement process will stagnate and disillusionment will set in among employees. Quality is an integral part of the management of an organization, and its business processes, and is too important an issue to delegate to technical and quality specialists.

The ultimate aim is to have people taking ownership for the QA of their processes, and to have a mindset of continuous improvement. This state of affairs is not a natural phenomenon and does not happen overnight, and senior managers must be prepared to spend time coaching people along this path and providing the necessary influences. Once people have seen senior managers leading the TQM initiative and respect has been earned, then this will start to happen and will encourage the emergence of followers in the form of quality leaders and champions from various parts and levels of the business.

Senior managers should be sensitive to the fact that some employees will resist the change to TQM. The usual reasons for this are that they are uncertain of the nature and impact of TQM and their ability to cope, the change will lessen their authority over decisions and allocation of resources, and it threatens their prestige and reputation. If senior managers are personally involved in the change process, it can help to breakdown these barriers.

There is a very strong relationship between the business achievements of an organization and senior managers understanding and commitment to TQM. The cost of non-conformance or mismanaging quality, is likely to be 5 to 25 per cent of an organization's annual sales turnover or operating costs in not-for-profit organization;

see chapter 7. If these figures are compared to profit as a percentage of sales turnover or expenditure in not-for-profit organizations, the key questions are – 'Can the CEO afford *not* to get involved in TQM?', 'How much will it cost the organization *not* to put in place a process of continuous improvement?', and 'Is investment in TQM and continuous improvement worthwhile?'

In a survey of the CEOs of the top 500 European Corporations in relation to the key requirements for success in TQM, McKinsey and Company (1989) identified six key points:

1 Top management attention – 95% agreement
2 People development – 85% agreement
3 Corporate team spirit – 82% agreement
4 Quality performance information – 73% agreement
5 Top management capability building – 70% agreement
6 Sense of urgency – 60% agreement

These findings support the point made earlier that the role of senior management is critical to success. Lascelles and Dale (1990) reporting on their research also say: 'The CEO is the primary internal change agent for quality improvement.' They point out that, in this capacity, he/she has two key roles: 'shaping organizational values, and establishing a managerial infrastructure to actually bring about change'.

The CEO must have faith in the long-term plans for TQM, and not expect immediate financial benefits. However, there will be achievable benefits in the short-term, providing that the introduction of TQM is soundly based. Senior managers need to create and promote the right environment for TQM to work:

- People can work together as a team and teamwork becomes an integral part of business activities.
- People co-operate with their peers and teams work with teams.
- Mistakes are freely admitted without recriminations, and these mistakes are perceived as an opportunity for improvement, i.e. a 'blame free' culture.
- People are involved in the business through decision making.
- People genuinely own process.
- People improve, on a continuous basis, the processes under their control, i.e. they have the continuous improvement mindset.
- People direct their attention to identifying, satisfying and delighting and winning over customers, whether they be internal or external.
- Ideas are actively sought from everyone.
- Development of people is a priority.
- Employee involvement in the business is worked at continually.
- Permanent solutions are found to problems.
- Departmental boundaries between functions are non-existent.
- Effective two-way communication is in place.
- Recognition is given for improvement activities.
- Status symbols are removed.

Change is not something that any department or individual takes to easily, and administering changes in organizational practices has to be considered with care. In the majority of Western organizations, people have witnessed the latest fads, fashions and 'flavours of the month' which have come and gone. They have become accustomed to senior managers talking a lot about a topic or issue, but failing to demonstrate visible commitment to what they are saying. Here are some of the typical comments made by employees:

- 'He is at it again, let's humour him/her.'
- 'TQM will go the way of all other fads and fancies.'
- 'Let's keep our heads down and things will revert to normal.'
- 'They are all talk and don't really believe what they say.'

It is only senior managers who can break down this cynicism, influence the indifference and persuade people that the organization is serious about TQM. It is they who have to communicate in person to their people why the organization needs continuous improvement and to demonstrate that they really care about quality. This can be done by becoming involved in activities:

- Setting-up and chairing a TQM steering committee or quality council
- Identifying the major quality issues facing the organization and becoming personally involved in investigating the issues, ideally as a leader, member, sponsor or foster parent to an improvement team, problem elimination team or the like
- Getting involved in quality planning, audit, improvement meetings and organizational housekeeping
- Leading and/or attending quality training courses
- Chairing individual sessions with operatives about the importance of following, and adhering to, procedures and working instructions
- Organizing and chairing defect review and customer return committees
- Instigating and carrying out regular audits, self-assessment and diagnosis of the state-of-the-art of TQM
- Dealing with customer complaints, and visiting customers and suppliers
- Leading customer workshops, panels and focus groups
- Visiting, on a regular basis, all areas and functions of the business, and discussing improvement issues
- Developing, communicating and, then, following a personal improvement action plan
- Communicating as never before on TQM, e.g., carrying out team briefs, preparing personal thank you notes to both teams and individuals and writing articles for the company newsletter
- Practising the internal customer-supplier concept, see figure 2.1.

With the internal customer – supplier approach, a supplier identifies his/her customers and determines their requirements. In some cases, the supplying process may have to be developed to meet the stated requirements. The supplier then undertakes the task and carries out self-inspection and control before the work is passed to the internal customer. Taking responsibility for following processes is part of this approach.

In these ways, senior managers lead and teach by example, and employees can develop a sense of purpose to continuous improvement. Once commitment and leadership has been demonstrated then ideas, innovations and improvements will start to feed through from the lower levels of the organizational hierarchy. At this stage in the development of TQM, senior managers must also be aware that some

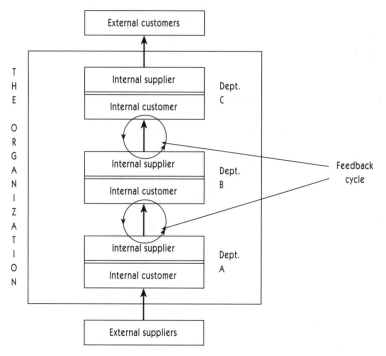

Figure 2.1 The customer – supplier network
Source: Dale and Cooper (1992)

employees will be complying through fear and have no real commitment or belief in the concept; it takes time to change attitudes and culture.

The improvement process is a roller-coaster of troughs and peaks; see figure 2.2. At certain points in the process, the situation will arise that while a considerable amount of organizational resources is being devoted to improvement activities, little progress appears to be being made. In the first three or so years of launching a process of continuous improvement and, when the process is in one of these low points, it is not uncommon for some middle and first line managers and functional specialists to claim that TQM is not working and to start asking questions:

- 'Why are we doing this?'
- 'Are we seeing real improvements?'
- 'What are the benefits?'
- 'Have we the time to spend on these 'outside our function' activities?'
- 'Improvement teams are a waste of time'
- 'Such and such a concept would be a better bet.'

Consequently, they will perhaps wish to switch their attention on what they claim are other more pressing matters. If the CEO is personally involved in TQM and visibly perceived to be so, people are much less likely to express this type of view. The CEO and senior managers have a key role to play in helping people through this crisis of confidence in TQM. There are a number of mechanisms which can

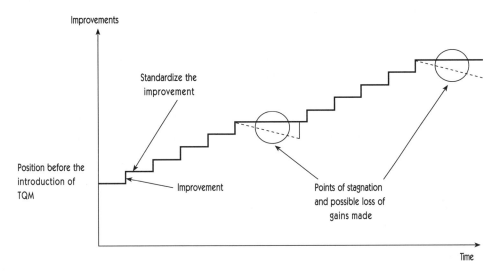

Figure 2.2 The quality improvement process
Source: Dale and Cooper (1992)

assist with this. For example, the MD of a speciality chemicals company introduced the concept of 'quality action days' to give all employees the opportunity to meet him and to express their views and concerns on the company's progress with TQM and what could be done to speed up the process of employee involvement.

In most Western organizations, a few key people are vital to the advancement of the improvement process and, if such a person leaves, it can result in a major gap in the management team. In the case of leadership and organizational changes, the CEO plays a major role in developing the understanding and diffusing beliefs with respect to TQM to new managers and technical and business specialists. In this way, the effects of any organizational changes are minimized. When key people leave and the improvement process continues without interruption and improvement teams continue to meet and make a contribution, this is an indication that an environment which is conducive to TQM is firmly in place. These type of issues are explored in detail by Bunney and Dale (1996) as part of a longitudinal study in a speciality chemical manufacturer.

Organizations are not usually experienced in holding the gains made in TQM. In addition to leadership and organizational changes, factors such as take-overs, HR and industrial relations problems, short-time working, redundancies, cost cutting, streamlining, no salary increases, growth of the business, and pursuit of policies which conflict with TQM in terms of resources, etc., can all have an adverse effect on the gains made, and damage the perception of TQM. People will be looking to senior managers to provide continuity and leadership in such circumstances.

What Senior Managers Need to Know about TQM

The first thing senior managers must realize, from the outset, is that TQM is a long-term and *not* a short-term intervention, and that it is an arduous process. They must also realize that TQM is *not* the responsibility of the quality function.

- There are no quick fixes.
- There are no easy solutions.
- There are no universal panacea.
- No tool, technique and/or system will provide all the answers.
- There are no ready-made packages which can be plugged in to guarantee success.

What is being talked about here is a long-term culture change. The planning horizon to put the basic TQM principles into place is between eight and ten years. The Japanese manufacturing companies typically work on 16 years, made up of four 4-year cycles – introduction, promotion into non-manufacturing areas, development/expansion, and fostering advancement and maintenance; see chapter 3 for details. Consequently, senior managers have to practise and communicate the message of patience, tolerance and tenacity. It is highly likely that there will be some middle management resistance to TQM, in particular, from those managers with long service, who are concerned with the new style of managing, more so than from staff and operatives.

In spite of the claims made by some writers, consultants and 'experts', senior managers must recognize that there is no single or best way of introducing and developing TQM. There are, however, common strands and principles which apply in all organizations. Organizations are different in terms of their people, culture, history, customs, prejudices, structure, products, services, technology, processes and operating environment.

What works successfully in one organization and/or situation will not necessarily work in another. A good example of this is TQM awareness training. As mentioned in chapter 1, there are two main approaches:

1 Cascade ('sheep dipping'), in which training is given to everyone over a relatively short time frame
2 Infusion, where people are trained on a need to know basis

In some organizations 'sheep dipping' has been successful and, in others, it has been a dismal failure. The same two-way argument is true for the infusion approach. With respect to training, it is important that senior managers have a clear idea of the strategic direction of the improvement activities after the training has been given.

In the long run, what really matters is that senior managers demonstrate long-term commitment and leadership to the process of continuous improvement. They must be prepared to think through the issues for themselves and to test out ideas and thoughts, to modify them and to adapt, as appropriate, to the operating environment of the business. The key point is to learn from experience. Employees are usually forgiving of management, if mistakes are openly admitted and explanations given, rather than covered up.

Senior managers need to commit time to develop their own personal and group understanding of the subject; cohesion in the senior management team, which comes from understanding, is important in making the changes which are necessary with TQM. They need to read books, attend conferences and course, visit the best practices in terms of TQM and talk to as many people as possible. The self-assessment criteria of the MBNQA and EFQM performance and business excellence models (as outlined in chapter 22) can assist in developing this overall understanding. It is also important that improvement ideas are forever circulating in the minds of senior managers along the lines of the PDCA cycle. In this way, they will avoid the false trails laid down by their own staff, consultants and 'experts'.

This understanding of TQM will also assist the CEO in deciding, together with other senior managers and key staff, how the organization is going to introduce TQM:

- What method and format of training is required?
- How many and what type of teams will be introduced?
- How many teams can be effectively supported?
- Is a TQM steering committee necessary and, if so, what form should it take?
- Which tools and techniques should be used?
- What is the role of a quality management system?
- How will TQM contribute to reducing warranty claims? etc.

To start, and then develop, a process of continuous improvement, an infrastructure is required to support the associated tasks and departments, and people need to be able to devote time to quality planning, prevention and improvement activities. Cook and Dale (1995) point out that management do not give sufficient care in reviewing the effectiveness of their organizational improvement infrastructure to ensure that the momentum of the improvement process is being maintained. Their research evidence indicates that the initial infrastructure is sometimes removed too quickly before the process has become embedded.

People have to be encouraged to take part in improvement activities and, to do this, they need to be released from their day-to-day work routines. The employment of a full-time quality co-ordinator and/or facilitator(s) relieved of day-to-day work pressures, can help to integrate individual improvement activities under a common umbrella, in addition to providing advice and guidance on matters of improvement. The issue of getting started is not an easy one. Prior to embarking on TQM, most organizations will already have undertaken a number of improvement initiatives, and a key issue is how to bring together those initiatives and build on them. A number of elements of TQM, such as empowerment, are nebulous and senior managers sometimes have difficulty in seeing how they might operate in their organization. It is important that the more nebulous elements are combined with the readily understood aspects, such as quality systems, procedures and practices, teamwork, and tools and techniques. As part of getting started, senior managers must diagnose the organization's strengths and opportunities for improvement in relation to the management of quality. This typically takes the form of an internal assessment of employees' views and perceptions (internal and group assessments, and question-naire surveys), a systems audit, a cost of quality analysis, and obtaining the views of suppliers and customers (including those accounts which have been lost) about the organization's performance in terms of product, service, people, administrative, innovation, strengths and weaknesses, etc. This type of internal and external assess-ment of perspectives should be carried out on a regular basis to gauge the progress being made towards TQM and to help decide the next steps. This is the benefit of self-assessment against a recognized model for business excellence. Once senior management have realized the need for TQM, they need to translate this awareness into effective action.

Their dilemma is often compounded, not just by a lack of knowledge of TQM and the process of continuous improvement but also, by a lack of experience in managing organizational change. The overwhelming quantity and variety of available advice, which is often conflicting, sometimes biased and sometimes incorrect, simply adds to the confusion and chaos.

In terms of the quality management structure, it should be understood that day-to-day control and assurance of quality should be separated from improvement and TQM promotion activities. If this is not done, QA staff quite naturally will focus their efforts on the daily short-term type activities and activities related to the quality management system, and commit little time to long-term planning and improvements. It is a fact of business life that people will give more priority to the day-to-day activities for which they are responsible. These tasks are more easily recognized, assessed and rewarded than are those related to improvement, especially those involving some form of teamwork. In particular, this applies when assessment and appraisal of individual performance takes no account of improvement achievements.

The CEO and senior managers may need to develop a company vision and mission statement; this should include developing an organizational definition of quality. However, the vision and mission has to be supported by organized changes rather than by stand-alone statements of objectives.

As a final point, senior managers should be sufficiently knowledgeable about TQM to know what type of questions to ask their people in relation to the improvement mechanisms. They should also be able to query results and the process by which they were obtained, and have some indication of what non-conforming products and/or service is costing their organization.

What Senior Managers Need to Do about TQM

This section first reviews the leadership criteria of the EFQM model (EFQM, 1998); see also chapter 22. The criteria detail the behaviour of all managers in driving the company towards business excellence. It concerns how the executives, and all other managers, inspire and drive excellence as an organization's fundamental process for continuous improvement. The leadership criterion is divided into four parts:

1 How leaders visibly demonstrate their commitment to a culture of TQM
2 How leaders support improvement and involvement by providing appropriate resources and assistance
3 How leaders are involved with customers, suppliers and other external organizations
4 How leaders recognize and appreciate people's efforts and achievements.

Senior managers need to decide the actions they are going to take to ensure that quality becomes the number one priority for the organization. They need to allocate time and commitment:

- To communicate their views on TQM – executives should take every opportunity to talk and act in a manner consistent with the principles of TQM
- To decide how the company will approach the introduction and advancement of TQM
- To lead education and training sessions, including the review of courses
- To assess the improvements made

- To become personally involved in improvement activities
- To determine if the main principles of TQM are being absorbed into the day-to-day operations of the business
- To understand how key competitors are using TQM
- To become involved in benchmarking – this will enable them to see, for example, what the superior performing organizations have achieved, and the discrepancies or gap with their organization's performance
- To lead and encourage the use of self-assessment methods and principles

Senior managers should consider how they are going to demonstrate to people from *all* levels of the organization their commitment to TQM. They need to visit every area to see what is happening in relation to TQM, ask about results and problems, give advice, and create good practice through leadership. In relation to this latter point, senior managers should take the lead in organizational housekeeping with the objective of seeing that the operating and office areas are a model of cleanliness and tidiness.

Senior managers should work as a team to develop improvement objectives and plans, and identify the means by which they can measure organizational improvement, i.e. self-assessment. They are responsible for pinpointing opportunities, prioritizing projects and steering the improvement efforts.

Teamwork is an essential element of TQM, providing an opportunity for co-operative action in pursuit of continuous improvement. The CEO and senior managers need to give more thought to the means by which teamwork may be facilitated, and how the achievement of effective team members can be recognized. The use of teams is a way of involving everyone in a continuous improvement initiative; see also chapter 21.

- Teams aid the commitment of people to the principles of TQM.
- Teams provide an additional means of communicating between individuals, management and their direct reports, across functions, and with customers and suppliers.
- Teams provide the means and opportunities for people to participate in decision making about how the business operates.
- Teams improve relationships, develop trust and facilitate co-operative activities.
- Teams help to develop people and encourage leadership traits.
- Teams build collective responsibility.
- Teams aid personal development and build confidence.
- Teams develop problem-solving skills.
- Teams facilitate awareness of improvement potential, leading to behaviour and attitude change.
- Teams help to facilitate a change in management style.
- Teams solve problems.
- Teams improve morale.
- Teams improve operating effectiveness as people work in a common direction.

There are considerable demands on senior managers' time, and a vast number of projects and matters seeking his or her attention. A CEO of a complex high-technology printed circuit board manufacturer uses the term 'spinning like a top' to describe this situation. However, if TQM is to be successfully introduced it has to take precedence over all other activities. The CEO should plan their diary to ensure that they devote some time each week to TQM activities.

It is the responsibility of senior managers to ensure that everyone in the organization knows why the organization is adopting TQM, and that people are aware of its potential in their area, department, function and/or process. Their commitment must filter down through all levels of the organization. It is important that all employees feel they can demonstrate initiative, and have the responsibility to put into place changes in their own area of work. This involves the establishment of owners for each business process. Consideration needs to be given to how this should be addressed.

A company-wide education and training programme needs to be planned, and undertaken, to facilitate the right type and degree of changes. The aim of this programme should be to promote a common TQM language, awareness and understanding of concepts and principles, to ensure that there are no knowledge gaps at any level in the organization and to provide the skills to assist people with improvement activities; this should include team leadership, counselling and coaching skills. A planned programme of training is required to provide employees with tools and techniques on a timely basis. In most organizations, it is frequently found that there is a good deal of variation in relation to understanding what the process of continuous improvement actually involves. Executives also need to consider the best ways of making an input to leading some of the quality-related training.

The senior management team needs to commit resources to TQM. For example, people need to be released for improvement activities and key decision makers must be made available to spend time on TQM issues. The CEO needs to delegate responsibility for continuous improvement to people within the organization. Some organizations appoint a facilitator/manager/co-ordinator to act as a catalyst or change agent. However, if this is to be effective, the CEO must have a good understanding of TQM and the continuous improvement process. The CEO needs to develop an infrastructure to support the improvement activities:

- Monitoring and reporting the results – there is nothing like success to convert cynics and counter indifference
- Providing a focus and the people to make it happen
- Developing and deploying improvement objectives and targets
- Involving people from all areas of the business

It is helpful to establish a TQM steering committee or quality council type of activity to oversee and management the improvement process. These are the typical roles of such a group:

- To agree plans, goals, provide and manage resources
- To monitor progress
- To determine actions
- To create an environment which is conductive to continuous improvement
- To concur on issues of continuous improvement
- To facilitate teamwork
- To ensure that firm foundations are laid down
- To identify impediments to progress

From the vision and mission statements, a long-term plan needs to be drawn up which sets out the direction of the company, in terms of its development and management targets. This plan should be based on the corporate philosophy, sales forecast, current status, previous achievements against plan and improvement object-ives. From this long-term plan, an annual policy should be compiled, and plans, policies, actions, and improvement objectives established for each factory, division, department and section. These plans and objectives typically focus on areas affecting quality, cost, delivery, safety and the environment. Middle managers and first-line supervisors should, at the appropriate point, participate in the formulation of these plans, targets and improvement objectives. This ensures that the policies and object-ives initiated by the CEO and senior management team are cascaded down through the organizational hierarchy so that all employees in each function of the business can carry out their activities within their own area of influence with the aim of achieving common goals and improvement targets. A typical framework for policy deployment is shown in figure 2.3 and details of policy deployment are given by Dale (1990) and Akao (1991), and also in chapters 3 and 5.

The process of policy deployment ensures that the quality policies, targets and improvement objectives are aligned with the organization's business goals. The ideal situation in policy deployment is for the senior person at each level of the organ-izational hierarchy to make a presentation to their staff on the plan, targets and improvements. This ensures the penetration and communication of policies, objectives and continuous improvements throughout the organization, with general objectives being converted into specific objectives and improvement targets. In some organ-izations, as part of this policy deployment they formulate, every year, a plan which focuses on a different improvement theme. One of the key aspects of policy deploy-ment is its high visibility, with company and departmental policies, targets, themes and projects being displayed in each section of the organization.

There must also be some form of audit at each level, to check whether targets and improvement objectives are being achieved, and the progress being made with specific improvement projects. This commitment to quality, and the targets and improvements made, should be communicated to customers and suppliers. Some organizations use seminars to explain these policies and strategies. The respective reporting and control systems must be designed and operated in a manner which will ensure that all managers co-operate in continuous improvement activities. They also need to ensure that the tasks delegated to staff with respect to TQM are being carried out in the manner ascribed.

The CEO must ensure that his or her organization really listens to what their customers are saying, and what they truly need, and their concerns. This is more easily said than done; none of us like criticism and we have a tendency to think we know best. This customer information is the starting point of the improvement planning process. In many organizations, information is collected directly by com-puter links to and from customer's processes, particularly in process industries.

Executives must ensure that they do not disguise things from the customer; honesty is the byword in TQM. Senior managers should ensure their organization takes every opportunity to join the customers' and suppliers' improvement pro-cesses; mutual improvement activities can strengthen existing partnerships and build good working relationships. For example, in a major blue chip packaging manu-facturer, they work with their customers to ensure that the packaging they produce is suited to the packaging equipment of their customers. Senior managers must

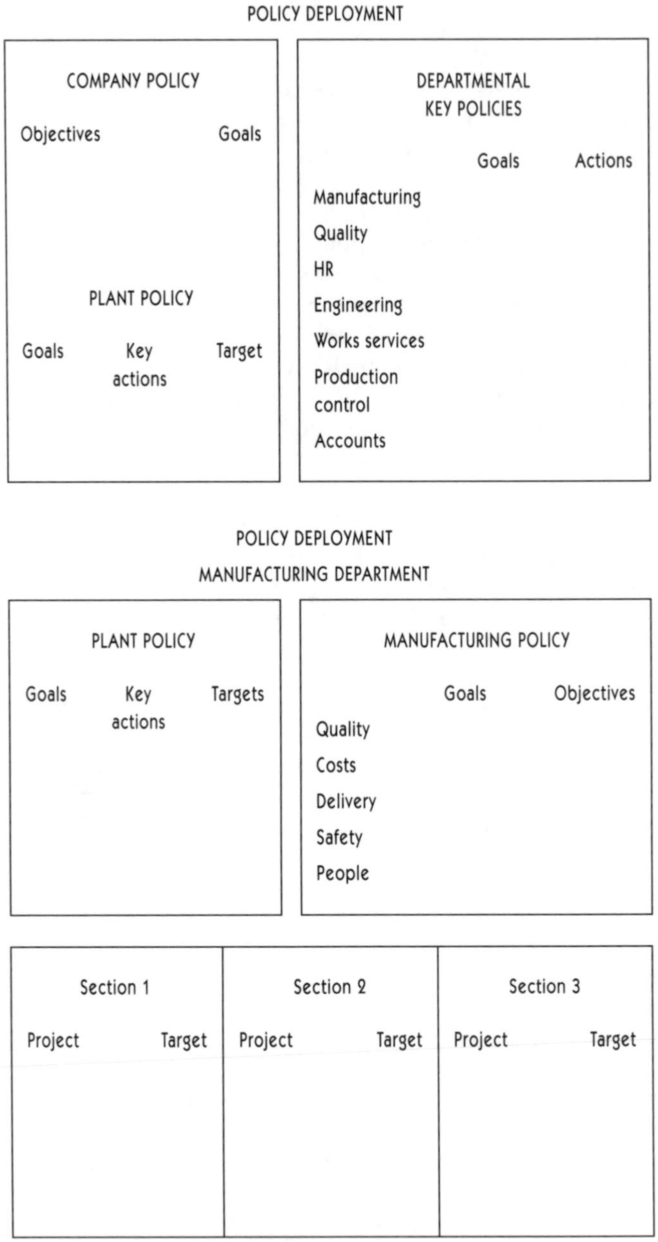

POLICY DEPLOYMENT

COMPANY POLICY		DEPARTMENTAL KEY POLICIES

COMPANY POLICY

Objectives   Goals

PLANT POLICY

Goals   Key   Target
           actions

DEPARTMENTAL
KEY POLICIES

                    Goals   Actions
Manufacturing
Quality
HR
Engineering
Works services
Production
control
Accounts

POLICY DEPLOYMENT

MANUFACTURING DEPARTMENT

PLANT POLICY

Goals   Key   Targets
           actions

MANUFACTURING POLICY

                    Goals   Objectives
Quality
Costs
Delivery
Safety
People

Section 1	Section 2	Section 3
Project Target	Project Target	Project Target

Figure 2.3 A typical framework for policy deployment

ensure that corrective action procedures and defect analysis are pursued vigorously and a closed-loop system operated to prevent repetition of mistakes.

It is important that the CEO ensures that the organization has positive quantifiable measures of quality as seen by their customers. This enables an outward focus to be kept on the market in terms of customer needs and future expectations. These are some typical performance measures:

- Field failure statistics
- Reliability performance statistics
- Customer returns
- Customer complaints
- 'Things gone wrong' data
- Adverse customer quality communications
- Customer surveys
- Lost business
- Non-accepted tenders
- Prospect to customer conversion rate

They also need to develop internal performance measures on metrics:

- Non-conformance levels
- Quality audit results
- Yield results
- Quality costs
- Employee satisfaction
- Employee involvement
- Service level agreements
- Score achieved against the EFQM or MBNQA models
- Percentage of employees satisfied that the organization is customer focused and that it is a quality company

It is usually necessary to evaluate the current internal and external performance measure to assess their value to the business.

A measurement system to monitor the progress of continuous improvement process is a key necessity; without it improvement will be more difficult. In the words of Scharp, former President and CEO of A. B. Electrolux (1989): 'What gets measured gets done'. Consequently, people will focus on those actions necessary to achieve the targeted improvements. All the evidence from the Japanese companies (Dale, 1993) indicates that improvement targets and objectives act as key motivators. However, these need to be carefully set and monitored. It is possible to improve indicators without improving real performance, especially if targets are unrealistic or not seen as controlled by individuals responsible for them. These individuals may fear they will be blamed and, consequently, they may focus on indicators not performance.

Senior managers should never overlook the fact that people will want to be informed on how the improvement process is progressing. They need to put into place a two-way process of communication for ongoing feedback and dialogue; this helps to close the loop. Communications, up, down and across the organization are one of the most important features of the relationships between directors, managers and staff. Regular feedback needs to be made about any concerns raised by employees; this will help to stimulate further involvement and improve communication. This also pinpoints any impediments to the process of continuous improvement.

Senior managers should be prepared to learn about statistical methods, to use them in their decision-making processes, and to demonstrate an active interest and involvement in techniques such as SPC and DOE. This ensures that knowledge and decisions are based on fact, not opinion. For example, when passing through manufacturing and office areas, they should adopt the habit of looking at the control charts which are on display and direct questions to the people responsible for charting and analysing the data. They can also learn, from the data portrayed on the charts, of any problem which the 'operator' is experiencing with the process. The control chart is a communication to senior management on the condition of the process – it is a 'window' on the operating world of processes. Ignoring the message will only cause frustration among those involved with SPC and will hinder the process of continuous improvement. It should also not be forgotten that SPC teaches people to ask questions about the process.

Continuous improvement can be facilitated by the rapid diffusion of information to all parts of the organization. A visible management system and a storyboard style presentation in which a variety of information is collected and displayed is a very useful means of aiding this diffusion. The CEO needs to consider seriously this form of transparent system.

The CEO and senior managers must never become satisfied and complacent with the progress the organization has made in TQM; they must strive continually to achieve improvements in the product, service and associated processes. They need to adopt the philosophy and mindset that there is no ideal situation and the current state can always by improved upon. Areas of organizational waste and uselessness need to be identified, and attacked in a ruthless manner.

The Role of Middle Managers

Middle managers have a vital part to play in the introduction and development of TQM. They will only be effective, however, if they are committed to it as a concept. Senior managers should not lose sight of the fact that middle and first-line management have been victims of previous 'flavour of the month' management. There is also a fear from middle management that they will be bypassed as a result of improvement activities. A number of middle managers shine as troubleshooters (this is how they achieved promotion) and do not know anything else. They commonly express the concern that if there is no firefighting what else can they do and naturally fear for their jobs, especially in the current climate of developing flatter organizational structures.

The middle manager's role typically involves these activities:

- Developing specific improvement plans for the departments and processes for which they are responsible
- Ensuring that the objectives, values, policies and improvement initiatives of their departments are aligned with the company's business goals, TQM strategy, and quality management system
- Communicating the company's approach to TQM in common sense and jargon-free language to first-line managers and other employees
- Acting as TQM coach and counsellor to the employees for whom they are responsible
- Ensuring that first-line managers are individually trained in the use of tools and techniques, and that these are used effectively

- Acting as a 'guardian, or sponsor or mentor' to improvement teams, and securing the means to reward employees
- Providing top management with considered views on how to manage the continuing implementation and development of TQM, taking into account feedback from first-line managers and employees on potential difficulties or obstacles

The Role of First-Line Managers

First-line managers and supervisors are at the forefront of TQM. They have the key role of encouraging its implementation in the workplace, and are especially important because of the numbers of people they influence and lead. If first-line managers lack commitment, training, appropriate resources and a supportive management system and culture then the TQM cascade will fail at its most critical level. First-line managers are directly responsible for these activities:

- Analysing the individual procedures and processes for which they are responsible so as to identify areas where improvements might be initiated and made
- Encouraging individual employees and operators to contribute improvement ideas, and ensuring that good ideas and efforts are acknowledged and rewarded by middle and top management
- Ensuring that any quality concerns reported by employees are analysed and resolved through permanent long-term corrective action
- Participating in improvement teams in their own and related work areas
- Providing workplace training in the use of specific techniques and tools to capture improvement data
- Communicating the results of improvement activities and initiatives effectively to middle managers
- Providing the data and responses required by the company's formal quality management system, including where applicable the requirements of the appropriate part of the ISO9000 series
- Providing the data for the self-assessment process
- Representing the people and processes they supervise in management discussions about TQM resources and strategies

Summary

This chapter has examined the role which senior managers need to take, and the leadership they need to display, if TQM is to be successful. They will often ask what they need to do to demonstrate their commitment to TQM. The chapter has outlined some of the things they need to become involved with, including chairing the TQM steering committee, organizing and chairing defect review boards, leading self-assessment of progress against a model for business excellence, developing and then following a personal improvement action plan and sponsoring improvement teams. The chapter has summarized in brief what senior management need to know about TQM, and what they need to do to ensure TQM is successful and treated as part of normal business activities.

It is also pointed out that middle managers and first-line managers have a vital role in putting the principles of TQM in place, and that they must have unified thinking with senior management. Typical activities with which they should become involved have been outlined.

References

Akao, Y. (ed.) 1991: *Hoshin Kanri: Policy Deployment for Successful TQM*. Massachusetts: Productivity Press.

Bunney, H. S. and Dale, B. G. 1996: The effect of organisational change on sustaining a process of continuous improvement. *Quality Engineering*, 8(4), 649–57.

Cook, E. and Dale, B. G. 1995: Organising for continuous improvement: an examination. *The TQM Magazine*, 7(1), 7–13.

Dale, B. G. 1990: Policy deployment. *The TQM Magazine*, 2(6), 125–8.

Dale, B. G. 1993: The key features of Japanese total quality control, *Quality and Reliability Engineering International*, 9(3), 169–78.

Dale, B. G. and Cooper, C. L. 1992: *Total Quality and Human Resources: An Executive Guide*. Oxford: Blackwell Publishers.

EFQM (European Foundation for Quality Management). 1998, *Self-Assessment 1998 Guidelines for Companies*. Brussels: EFQM.

Lascelles, D. M. and Dale, B. G. 1990: Quality management: the Chief Executive's perception and role. *European Management Journal*, 8(1), 67–75.

McKinsey and Company, 1989: *Management of Quality: The Single Major Important Challenge for Europe*, European Quality Management Forum, October 19th, Montreux, Switzerland.

Scharp, A. 1989: *What Gets Measured Gets Done: The Electrolux Way to Improve Quality*, European Quality Management Forum, October 19th, Montreux, Switzerland.

chapter three

The Japanese Approach to TQM

B. G. Dale

Introduction

Most experts are agreed that quality, in its widest sense, is the dominant factor in the success of Japanese companies in world markets, and much has been written on this during the last decade or so.

In describing the development of quality control in Japan (JUSE, 1996) the point is made:

> It is well known both inside and outside Japan that Company-Wide Quality Control (CWQC) on Total Quality Management (TQM), through the use of statistical methods has been widely practised in Japanese industry and has produced remarkable results, such as improved product and service quality, enhanced productivity and reduced costs.

In any text dealing with the subject of TQM, it would be a serious omission not to discuss the ways in which Japanese companies manage continuous and company-wide improvement. There is also considerable benefit in learning from best practice and, in this way, it is possible to discover pointers to the future strategic directions along which Western organizations should move if they are to gain competitive advantage.

TQC or CWQC are usually the terms used in Japan to refer to TQM. It is the integrative strategic framework of the Japanese company, and it is the qualifying criterion in their home market-place. In the view of the author, there is no difference between TQC, CWQC and TQM and the reader should treat them as the same.

CWQC is defined by the Union of Japanese Scientists and Engineers (JUSE, 1996) company-wide as:

> CWQC is a set of systematic activities carried out by the entire organisation to effectively and efficiently achieve company objectives and provide products and services with a level of quality that satisfies customers, at the appropriate time and price.

TQM is not perceived as desirable; it is considered as essential by Japanese companies for their continued survival. A number of Japanese companies, through their considerable efforts over the last 25 to 30 years, have put the principles of TQM firmly in place and are totally committed to sustaining and advancing a process of continuous and company-wide improvement. Freeman (1996) provides an extremely interesting insight on how this is achieved using some of the principles of scientific management.

This chapter is structured under a number of broad headings: customer satisfaction, long-term planning, R&D, the motivation for starting TQM, organizing and planning for quality, management of improvement, visible management systems, involvement of people, education and training, TPM, and JIT.

The data on which this chapter is based has been collected by the author from leading four Study Missions of European manufacturing executives to Japan to examine their approach to TQM in a selection of major manufacturing companies. At relevant points in the text, comparisons are made between Japanese and European approaches to managing continuous improvement, based on the author's empirical research work in both Japanese and European companies.

Customer Satisfaction

In Japan, the internal market-place is dominant and competition is fierce. This means that organizations need to be totally dedicated to satisfying customers. This effort must be long-term and continuous; otherwise, they will be overtaken by the competition. Their internal market is saturated and demands ever-increasing product diversification and attractiveness, speedy response to market needs, rigorous reliability and quality of conformance. The Japanese companies believe that bringing new products to the market-place quickly is the means by which they can sustain their competitive edge. 'The customer always comes first' and 'the customer is king' are terms used by organizations to describe their market-orientated spirit. Organizations are forever looking at the needs of the market. Japanese managers also comment that their customer quality requirements are becoming increasingly rigorous, and these requirements are a moving target. The Japanese companies concentrate on increasing market share and net sales, and not the rate of return on investment.

There is a total belief that business operations and efficiency can always be improved by reflecting the customer needs and requirements. Japanese organizations have a variety of systems, procedures or mechanisms by which they can properly identify these needs and keep focused on the market. They go to considerable lengths to collect information (through talking and listening) on the wants and needs of customers, to obtain their opinions, better understand their expectations, and assess their satisfaction with products and services. For example, a manufacturer of ceramic products has 4,500 fixed points of observation from which data is collected.

Japanese companies believe it is important for the engineers who are involved in the development of new products to go to the customer and the location where the equipment is being used and to ask the user (including field operators) questions:

- What they feel about the product?
- What bothers them?
- What features new products should have?
- What is required to satisfy customer needs, expectations, thinking and ideas?

This knowledge, together with that accumulated through various means at the company and other means of listening to 'customer voices', is used in new product development to pinpoint the technical gaps of the competition. It also helps to identify product features and characteristics which the customer finds attractive and charming, and which differentiate the product from those of competitors.

In Japan, there is an implied expectation that customer expectations will be beaten. It is also common practice for Japanese organizations to use QFD in conjunction with the seven management tools, M7* (see Mizuno (1988) and chapter 14 for details) as the mechanisms for co-ordinating this type of data. They are also employed to clarify the required quality (objective and subjective) from the customer, and to translate customer wants into design requirements and hence build in quality at source. Detailed information is also developed on customer profiles, their current needs and future expectations. The databanks which Japanese organizations have built-up on this are far in advance of anything encountered in European companies.

Long-term Planning

Quality (including service), cost, and delivery (accuracy and lead time) – QCD – are the main organizational objectives as they strive to become the best in class in relation to QCD. This is a prime consideration in company vision, mission and policy statements. The evidence collected indicates that this has been the case in most Japanese companies for the last 30 years or so. Extensive use is made of mottos expressing some appropriate message on QCD. This assists in keeping the theme in the forefront of employees minds.

Japanese companies believe that their corporate strength is built up through TQM, and customer oriented quality is foremost in every aspect of organizational corporate policy. This view is encapsulated in the point made by one organization that even if only one out of 10,000 products failed, the failure rate for that customer would be 100 per cent.

Planning, feedback and decision making on TQM is long term, often extending at least ten years into the future. A series of middle range plans of between three to five years are formulated to assist in meeting the long-term business plan and strategic themes.

One of the main TQM planning activity is the deployment of the President's annual management policy plan (developed from the company's long-range and mid-term plans) to all levels of the organizational hierarchy, i.e. policy deployment. This process provides the skeleton for TQM and helps to turn strategic intent into an annual operating plan. This plan is made available to group companies at the beginning of a fiscal year. The deployment is carried out, in the first place, by the plant managers to their respective manufacturing divisions, and then successively the plant manager's policy is deployed by each section/department manager to their area of responsibility through to foreman and line operators. The deployment is usually in terms of QCD. Figure 3.1 is an illustration of the policy deployment system from a manufacturer of ceramic products.

* M7 = affinity diagrams, relations diagram, systematic diagrams, matrix diagrams, matrix data analysis methods, process decision program charts and arrow diagrams.

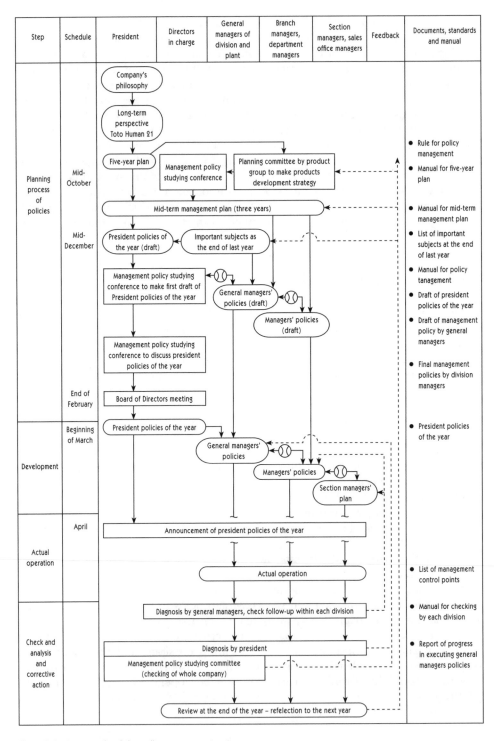

Figure 3.1 An example of the policy management system
Source: Toto Ltd, Chigasaki Works, Chigasaki City, Japan

Each plant manager develops his or her annual policies, improvement targets and plans for every section and department of the plant(s), which are within his or her remit of responsibility to meet the President's policy. The plant manager decides the annual policy for the plant, what key problems they need to tackle in relation to the President's policy. The policy is based on the long-range business plan, long-range plan for the plant's operation, the improvements which need to be made (taking into account an evaluation of the previous year's activities and performance), production forecast and schedules, and reports from departmental managers. This policy is fully discussed and debated with each section manager in relation to their annual policies and plans for departmental activities, until a final target is agreed along with the methods and means to reach the goal. For example, the plant manager may suggest to a section manager a target of 5 per cent improvement and the section manager may reply with a suggestion of 2 per cent, this process continues until a target is agreed with which all parties agree is feasible within the time frame of the plan. The assessment of capability, setting and agreeing of targets and establishing the means is conducted through discussion and consensus – what the Japanese term 'play catch' or 'catch ball'. It is usual to set yearly and half-yearly improvement plans and targets. The section manager then agrees with each of his foremen the activities, plans and targets for their group, who in turn agrees roles, targets, methods and improvement activities with each operator. Each division keeps a register of the improvement action agreed with staff.

In this way, the improvement activities of an organization are focused on carrying out projects to meet these policies. This ensures integration and the internalization of objectives. Every employee understands their manager's policy and, therefore, knows what to do and that everyone is working in a common and unified direction to achieve the goals of the business. In addition, employees understand the issues which are important to the company, helping to facilitate relations between the different sections of the business.

There is a set time-scale (usually six to eight weeks) for this deployment activity to be cascaded down through all organizational levels. In each company, the policy deployment commences at a set time in the calendar year. The long negotiations which are involved in the deployment helps to ensure consensus, and that there is a genuine commitment at all levels to meet the agreed targets.

The control and review of policies are necessary to compare actual to planned performance, identify gaps, problems and root causes, determine countermeasures, and recognize and reward achievement:

- The President's diagnosis
- Plant manager and section manager diagnosis and monthly review of plant activities
- Discussion of achievements and improvements at plant conferences on QCD
- For each section, their daily management and records in terms of clarity of the section's function in the organization and the role of each person, clear points of control, activities for improvement, standardization and taking corrective action

The PDCA cycle is extensively used in all these diagnoses, see figure 3.2. The results of these activities are reflected in the following year's policy, and assist in improving the process of deployment.

Figure 3.2 The plan-do-check-act cycle
Source: Dale and Cooper (1992)

It is usual for the plant manager to audit, on a quarterly basis, the progress being made by each section to achieve its improvement objectives, and for the section manager to undertake a diagnosis of his or her section at quarterly and monthly intervals. It is usual for the line operators to carry out a self-estimation of their achievements on a scale of 1 to 5, against the agreed target. This written assessment is commented upon by the foreman and is followed up by a personal interview and where appropriate, methods and plans are revised. The foreman then reports to the section manager on his or her achievement, the outstanding problems and the priority actions to be taken. This reporting procedure is continued up through the organizational structure. If there is low achievement against the target, a full and frank discussion will take place with all concerned to determine the reasons for this, and to decide the corrective actions to recover the situation.

In some organizations, the process of policy management deployment is also subject to diagnosis by outside experts, e.g. JUSE consultants and/or university professors. Any reports relating to the diagnosis are subjected to an in-depth examination. It is argued that it is the process of the deployment which is important, and not just the results.

It is usual for each section to have a visible display of this policy deployment, as part of their visible management system. Figure 3.3 illustrates the key points of the typical format of such a display. The left-hand side of the chart shows the tree of policy deployment from the plant manager down to the level of each section. Each section makes their own plans for improvement based on existing problems. The overall rate of imperfection for each section is related to the different processes with information being provided on individual problems. A proportion defective (p) control chart is used to monitor the rate of imperfection against the set target. The right-hand side of the chart displays annual improvement targets, for quality, cost, delivery, safety and morale. A slogan relating to the improvement is displayed on the board at the head of the problem to be solved. The names of the workers who are responsible for the various activities relating to the policy deployment are also

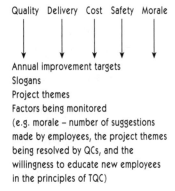

- President policy and annual theme
  ↓
- Plant manager's policy, annual theme for the plant and improvement targets
  ↓
- Section manager's policy and improvement targets
  ↓
- Statement of major projects
  ↓
- Current rate of non-conformance and targets for improvement
  ↓
- Data collected using the seven QC tools
  ↓
- Improvement monitored using a proportion non-conforming units chart (*p* chart)

Quality Delivery Cost Safety Morale

↓   ↓   ↓   ↓   ↓

Annual improvement targets
Slogans
Project themes
Factors being monitored
(e.g. morale – number of suggestions made by employees, the project themes being resolved by QCs, and the willingness to educate new employees in the principles of TQC)

Figure 3.3   Key points of the visual display of policy deployment for a section
Source: Dale and Cooper (1992)

displayed. All these plans include a number of provisions for the involvement of employees in the improvement process. Positioned at right angles to the board and completing the policy deployment 'corner' are pictures of typical imperfections in the section together with an improvement book. This book logs each improvement which has been made, and helps to promote standardization. It also helps to serve as a point of reference for people on what type of improvements have been made in the past. For the manufacturing department, some organizations keep the specific details of the deployment within the relevant offices, posting only the specific key actions, responsibilities and measures on the shopfloor policy deployment. This way focuses employees' attention on the specifics, rather than the elaborate details.

Within each section, there is an effort to solve, each year, at least two major projects; these projects are registered as themes and are derived from the policy deployment. This is in addition to the activities of any QC, i.e. a small voluntary group of employees from the same work area which meet on a regular basis under the leadership of their supervisor to solve problems relating to the work activities of their department. In European companies, there is a tendency by departments to try to solve too many problems at the same time and, as a consequence, the improvement effort tends to be too thinly spread.

In European companies, the job of the CEO is a lonely one. It is often the case that respective MDs, plant managers and other middle managers filter out information to the CEO. In Japan, the policy deployment and its visible display at shop floor level not only ensures that the President has a window on what is happening in each section of each division under his control, but that every person is clear on the details of the President's policy and what is required, by both their section and themselves, to make the necessary contribution to achievement of overall policy. The discipline of policy deployment and the agreement at each organizational level of achievable targets ensures that the energy of line operators is directed in the same direction as section managers and likewise up to the level of the President; a spiral upward movement.

There is little doubt that the policy deployment method facilitates the attainment of corporate goals and facilitates the operation of the organization in a systematic manner. It also assists in integrating the improvement process with organizational long-term strategic plans and actions arising from challenging for the Deming Application Prize and the more recently introduced Japan Quality Award (equivalent to the MBNQA and EQA).

It is clear that, with the attention and resources being committed to policy deployment in Japan, European companies have much to gain by studying how best they may use this method; see Akao (1991) and chapter 5 for further details of policy deployment.

The total commitment and leadership of senior management on a long-term basis is a point which is always stressed by the Japanese as being a key point for successful TQM activities. The role of senior management includes these activities:

- Ensuring that the entire organization is committed to TQM and establish corporate quality systems
- Continuously, promoting TQM activities
- Motivating employees
- Involvement in quality-related education and training
- Participating in activities such as:

  - membership of the committee for quality planning
  - QA meetings for design and manufacture of quality into the product
  - quality audit, improvement and corrective action meetings – and diagnosis of the improvement activities of site locations. In relation to these audits and diagnosis, senior management study, prior to the actual visits, information on factors such as the quality improvement plans, targets, achievements and problems. This data is provided by the TQM Promotions office. The role of this department is discussed later; see pages 61–2.

Research and Development (R&D)

In the situation in which product life cycles are shortening while competition is intensifying, Japanese companies believe that (R&D) is the main means of helping them to sustain their competitive edge, and this is the major focus of their efforts. They invest heavily in R&D, and vigorously pursue new product development, with the aim of achieving maximum profits from new products before competitors enter the market. They typically have a focused strategy to develop products which will feed into company performance and profitability within a prescribed time frame. Japanese companies are engaged in short-term and long-term R&D. The long-term R&D tends to relate to materials development, and how to combine and integrate different types of technologies. The less innovative short-term R&D is geared to the development of new product features and process development (i.e. incremental product improvement). It is also interesting to note that, in what European companies may regard as the maintenance department, it is not unusual to witness R&D being undertaken in machine technology using in-house expertise and/or through collaboration with external specialists. The Japanese companies also tend to engage in pure research as opposed to leasing this to universities. It must be said that they do rely on existing technologies, but are extremely good at improving the details.

Their aim is to bring an increasing number of attractive high-value added products to the market, in the shortest possible time. This is seen to be a key issue, and is one to which they commit considerable time and resources. Product life cycles in Japanese markets are becoming shorter and shorter, and there is an ever-increasing demand from the market-place for new products. Considerable efforts are concentrated on reducing the cycle time for product development. The Japanese market is forever looking for products with more unique features, and there is a never-ending demand for new products. Japanese companies believe that if they produce standard products with only a minimum of diversification, they will not survive in the market-place. Some Japanese companies have combined the functions of R&D and marketing to facilitate the creation of new market demands, to develop their present market share and to exploit technology know-how.

Japanese companies have a systematic approach to R&D, and this helps to reduce the time from conception of an idea to market launch. They have a huge R&D database on their accumulated experiences from product development to full-scale production from which their designers can draw to satisfy customer needs. This typically contains a variety of information on aspects such as design features, QFD carried out on previous products, product development concepts, design for manufacturability, FMEA, FTA, STA, reliability, and the product shapes and features which appeal to customers. This is the result of many years of accumulated experience. The database provides them with a competitive advantage by enabling them to produce new designs and products at a faster and faster rate. This is something which European companies will find hard to emulate. Japanese companies thrive on their reputation for leading-edge technology, and corporate prestige is measured in terms of the R&D activity.

The R&D project team steers the product concept through the various stages from R&D through development to trial production and, ultimately, full-scale production. The process for new production introduction is usually well developed and clearly outlined. Therefore, the R&D team ensure that the design intent is being planned into the product and helps the production areas to understand the product. In addition, the team assist with operator training and deal with problems as and when they arise during each stage of the manufacturing process. The attention to detail in this type of activity and the closeness of inter-functional communication is particularly impressive. A common view is that the research laboratory is the teacher, and the factories are the students. The R&D centres tend to select and prove the equipment before it is used by the factory in full-scale production.

At one research centre, it was clear that, as a supplier of components to the automotive industry, they were developing advanced electronics for use in automotive components and, in turn, these developments are driving design developments in the major motor manufacturers. In general, the reverse is true in the European motor industry, with the supplier manufacturing to an OEM's design and carrying out little development work of their own.

The Motivation for Starting TQM

A general view among European industrialists is that all Japanese companies have been operating to the principles of TQM since the early 1960s; this is a popular misconception. A number of Japanese companies have only introduced TQM within the last ten years or so. This reflects, to some degree, the priorities of the Ministry of International Trade and Industry (MITI) in developing Japanese industry.

These are the major motivations and associated problem points:

- Environmental, national and business factors and changing circumstances such as: the second oil crisis, exchange rate of the yen, slow economic growth and severe competition
- A lack of effective long-range planning
- An organizational emphasis on defensive mechanisms
- The new products which were launched not achieving their sales target values
- A need to develop new products which are attractive to the market-place – in the past, the tendency was to carry out formal and technological development rather than listening to the real needs of customers
- Slow growth in sales and market, leading to stagnation of the business
- Concerns about how to achieve the long-term plan of the organization and the President's plan on QCD
- Complacency with current profits and a failure to recognize the seriousness of the situation
- The written and verbal experiences of companies who were already practising TQM, in particular, those companies who had received the Deming Application Prize and are a major customer of the company in question
- Organizational, conceptual and business weaknesses:
    - Lack of advanced planning for quality
    - Lack of liaison between development, design and manufacturing departments
    - Emphasis on manufacturing for quantity, without sufficient regard for quality
    - Management policies which were not universally understood throughout the organization
    - A poor approach to the solution of problems
    - Poor morale of workers
    - Only stop-gap measures employed to cope with customer claims
    - Chronic defects in the manufacturing process
    - Problems at production start-up due to insufficient pre-production planning

It is worthy of mention that the reasons are similar to those found in European companies, as outlined in chapter 1. Whenever a Japanese company has faced a crisis of any kind, they have turned to the introduction of TQM as a principal pillar for their management activities.

Here are the priority actions in the introduction of TQM:

- Promotion of policy management
- Planning the introduction of new products in a more effective manner

- Building in QCD at source, and putting in place a company structure for quality assurance and daily control
- Developing stable processes

The introduction of TQM in Japanese companies has not been problem free; they have encountered similar problems to their Western counterparts in the introduction and advancement of TQM – see also chapter 12:

- Committing the requisite time and resources which are required to bring improvement activities to a satisfactory level
- Involvement of senior management in the improvement process
- Making effective use of quality management tools and techniques

These are the factors which Japanese companies consider as the key for success in the introduction of TQM:

- The President and senior executives must exercise strong leadership. These top managers must find out what their middle managers' views are on TQM and obtain their ideas on improvement projects and targets.
- Starting with the President, a good level of TQM education and training must be given at all levels of the organization, and this must be put into practice and repeated using the PDCA cycle.
- Top and middle management must take the responsibility for training their subordinates in TQM.
- It is important that middle managers are committed to TQM and provide effective leadership. (See chapter 2, pages 48–9.)
    - Maintaining close relationships between different divisions in the organization
    - Communicating concepts and ideas vertically down the organization
    - Educating employees about making quality their first priority
    - Spreading the concept of continuous quality improvement throughout the organization
- There is a need to develop effective QA procedures.

Organizing and Planning for Quality

Japanese companies take a total approach to the assurance of quality, from product planning through to sales and services. They usually have a TQM Promotions Office at their head office and, sometimes, at each plant. As the name suggests, it is used to promote TQM, through a variety of activities:

- Establishing a TQM policy
- Education and training (inside and outside the organization)
- Promoting standardization
- Facilitating QCs and cross-functional teams
- Involvement in steering committees
- Ensuring that all company employees, suppliers and distributors have the same TQM aims

- Analysing and co-ordinating improvement activities
- Communicating and exchanging data with suppliers

The Japanese are great advocates of the lateral management of major functions, and typically have committees dealing with QA, development, cost, delivery, supply, policy, and standardization. For example, a typical improvement committee will meet three or four times each year, and will establish improvement policies and deal with issues such as the organizational activities of QCs and how to develop the skills of employees. A QA committee will analyse, catalogue and discuss any day-to-day problems, non-conformance problems in the field and make decisions on how to resolve problems.

The manufacturing department is responsible for maintaining quality and, in this respect, it is usual to find inspectors reporting to the manufacturing manager. The QA department are responsible for these things:

- Providing guidance to manufacturing and other sections in terms of problem analysis and developing improvement plans
- Evaluation of product quality performance
- Audits of the manufacturing division
- Product and audit inspections
- Quality-related training
- Ensuring that people follow up the plans which have been decided by the TQM promotion office or TQM committee, and assisting in cascading these plans down to all levels in the organization hierarchy

In large organizations, there is usually a corporate QA department (CQAD). For example, this is the role of the CQAD at a major manufacturer of electronic products:

- To give guidance on TQM to all companies within the group
- To set a long-term and medium-term policy for the manufacturing divisions
- Quality education and training
- Quality auditing
- To maintain a quality performance system for each division, and to grade divisions according to performance
- To assess whether the product is easy to use
- To determine if the product is safe, if used incorrectly
- To carry out inspections of their own products on a component-by-component basis
- To examine packaging
- To carry out endurance tests
- To undertake comparative studies and evaluation of their own and competitors' products, and other tests to anticipate problems before they occur
- To undertake lifestyle research
- To study how to produce readable instruction manuals

To reach a consensus on the promotion of TQM activities and to increase the level of corporate awareness of TQM and exchange quality-related information, regular meetings are held between corporate and plant QA departments.

The GM of each division is responsible for TQM and the TQM promotion office and QA department work together to facilitate continuous and company-wide improvement. Each section and division is responsible for QCD planning at source. They submit a report on their improvement activities to the QA department; the QA department then compiles a report for the TQM promotion office which, in turn, is passed to the President for consideration in his annual audit of the division. This report typically covers specific improvements, goals and achievements, explanation of achievements and/or shortfalls, projects undertaken, feedback data, state of health of cross-functional teams, and customer satisfaction. The annual audit by the President involves him going around the offices and plants to evaluate their TQM activities. This is the purpose of the audit:

- To check that improvements are being made against the plan
- To demonstrate to employees that the President is committed to TQM
- To share ideas and future plans with employees and to obtain their thoughts
- To assess the use of statistical methods
- To enable employees to report their achievements to senior management

The Japanese hold the view that QA in all aspects of their business is the central core of TQM, and without effective QA procedures to support the communication of company requirements, TQM is difficult. QA is part of the Japanese style of thinking. Consequently, intensive effort is devoted to the assurance of quality on a day-to-day basis. All the companies visited had charts and diagrams which outlined, in considerable detail, their basic QA system and procedures.

When problems occur, they are analysed in detail using a defect analysis sheet. Everything is itemized in considerable depth and they pay incredible attention to the smallest of detail. The Japanese place great emphasis on finding out exactly where and why they are doing things wrong. The usual procedure is to put into place some temporary countermeasure to gain control of the situation while investigation is made into the root cause of the concern. This is followed by individual and then systematic reoccurrence prevention measures. They are very careful not to repeat any failures made in the past, and make continual reference to various failure recurrence prevention check lists. The Japanese are fanatical about taking precautions with regard to QA. When anything unsatisfactory is detected, it is fed back to the appropriate upstream stage and preventive actions are taken to counteract the trouble. They have tremendous discipline and this appears to be inbred into their behaviour, both at work and home.

The emphasis is on source control and discipline. For example, a transformer manufacturer emphasizes the theme of: 'If you do not observe such and such factor, mistakes will happen.' (with graphical details of the mistakes being displayed). A number of other typical activities are employed for source control:

- QA tables (e.g. control plans) for in-company and sub-contractors work
- Design review to prevent any failure on the part of designers
- The production of operating procedures by the foreman and line operators
- Standards and instructions for daily control

A variety of aids are provided to ensure that operators have all the help required to get it right the first time and to prevent errors from occurring:

- Check sheets
- Operating instructions
- Product identification cards
- Mistake-proof devices
- Process operation sheets
- Defect analysis sheets
- Features and parameters to which attention is required
- QA tables
- Machine vision systems

At a furniture manufacturer, to promote process management and control at source, every line worker produces a working instruction entitled *What I know about my job – the knack of doing my job*; these are displayed at appropriate prominent places. In a transformer manufacturer, chalk boards were available at strategic places in the factory, and are used by employees to develop quality improvement ideas.

The Japanese companies tend to use all the seven quality control tools, QC7* – see Ishikawa (1976) and chapter 14 for details – together and visibly display the results on a quality control notice board (termed an MQ station). In this way, they are not only listening to the process but taking action to improve it, and this combined use of the seven quality control tools facilitates problem resolution and improvement action. Each section in a Japanese company has an MQ (manufacturing quality) station which is a base point for TQM activities. It is usual for workers to gather at the station to consider quality issues and to exchange information on the PDCA cycle.

In recent times, considerable use has been made of SPC by Western companies; however, it is rare to see quality control charts used in conjunction with the other six quality control tools. This is a lesson to be learnt from the Japanese.

In planning for quality from the R&D and design stages, considerable attention is given to listening to the voice of the customer, and a variety of means are employed for this purpose. In the stages of planning and production preparation, trial production and full-scale production and field experience, detailed notes are kept of any problems encountered and the countermeasures which have been put into place. In addition, a detailed report is produced at the end of the new product introduction process. It is a normal part of the Japanese management style to take detailed notes of any concerns encountered and countermeasures implemented during planning, production preparation, volume production and field experience. These detailed notes of knowledge are collected and filed to provide an extensive database. These notes are always referred to and used in the planning of new products and during various investigations. All the necessary preparations are made in advance of actual production and considerable resources are committed to this activity. In European organizations, production preparation is usually rushed, in the hope that any problems can be corrected later. Even if notes are made they are often not analysed and used to prevent reoccurrence of concerns in future products.

In the development and design stage, engineers from the QA and inspection department take-up residency in the development and design department. This is termed the 'resident engineer' system and what we, in Europe, term concurrent

---

* QC7 = cause and effect diagrams, histograms, check sheets, Pareto diagrams, control charts, scatter diagrams and graphs.

engineering or simultaneous engineering. The designs are evaluated for potential difficulties at the volume production stage. Consideration is given to the preventive measures used for troubles experienced in the past, and an efficient means of production to ensure design quality. In the production preparation stage, engineers from the development and design department take-up residency in the Manufacturing and QA departments (the 'resident engineer' system). This is to ensure design intent is fully translated into following processes, to feed in know-how obtained during the design and development stage and to promote the implementation of countermeasure against troubles, including mistake-proofing; for details of mistake-proofing, see Shingo (1986). These cross-functional teams facilitate the process of simultaneous/concurrent engineering, encourages a problem-solving orientation, develops diversified skills and improves communication which not only reduces the time for product development and production preparation, but also ensures that the designs are suitable for manufacture and reduces the number of late and costly engineering changes.

Major suppliers also join in at the design stage; they are called 'guest designers'. This activity recognizes that the supplier is the product specialist and helps to ensure that his expertise is used to identify improvements early in the design cycle. Suppliers are also encouraged to suggest cost levels for their products.

To help to assure product quality, there is feedback and/or feed forward of quality information in production planning, product design, evaluation of prototype products, pre-production planning, purchasing, quality audit, evaluation of pre-production products, volume production, inspection, evaluation of the products from volume production and sale and field service operations. The objective is to build in quality at each step, before sending work to the next process. There is total collaboration and co-operation between R&D, technical, QA and manufacturing departments to eliminate problems and ensure that processes are mistake-proof. This is facilitated through the use of cross-functional teams.

To identify defects early on in the design process and to assure the quality of design, it is usual to use techniques such as design reviews, design of experiments, QA meetings, QFD, FMEA, FTA, quality audits and reliability tests. In the production preparation phase, the production engineers endeavour to predict failures for the process and to take collective action before machine and process sequences are finalized. FMEA and process capability studies are employed to assist with this. It is usual to carry out a process capability study every time new production facilities are used, when a new design is produced on existing facilities, and in the mass production of established products.

In all the companies visited, the housekeeping was immaculate, and factories and offices are clinically clean. The general impression is of a working environment which is comfortable and in harmony with employees. For example, a visit around a steel mill involved the mission members wearing white gloves, which when discarded were hardly discoloured. When touring the photosetting department of a printing company, members had to tie plastic covers over their shoes. Little dust was found on window ledges in any of the organizations visited. The Japanese companies believe in having clear gangways. Any necessary equipment relating to the process is put onto racking which is located on an outside wall. It is not uncommon to see the space between the gangway and the outside wall painted green to represent grass, and potted plants placed on the painted area. The discipline of cleanliness and housekeeping is a prerequisite for effective QA, and this should be pursued more vigorously by European companies. However, many European companies do not spend sufficient effort to define and quantify their housekeeping requirements. It is accepted that the condition of housekeeping is the responsibility of the employees local to the area and is maintained by them. A variety of aids were used to promote housekeeping under what is termed the 5 Ss – five Japanese words all starting with 's':

- *Seiri*: organization – separating what is required from that which is not
- *Seiton*: neatness – arranging the required items in a tidy manner and in a clearly defined place
- *Seiso*: cleaning – keeping the surrounding area and environment clean and tidy
- *Seiketsu*: standardization – clean the machinery and equipment according to laid down standards so as to identify deterioration
- *Shitsuke*: discipline – follow the procedures which have been laid down

The 5S evaluation form used by NSK–RHP (Aerospace) is given in figure 3.4.

Nissan Motor Manufacturing (UK) refer to this form of housekeeping as the 5 Cs:

- Clean out – determine what is necessary and unnecessary, and dispose of the latter
- Configure – provide a convenient, safe and orderly place for everything, and keep it there
- Clean and check – monitor the condition of the area during cleaning
- Conformity – develop the habit of routinely maintaining cleanliness
- Custom and practice – train people in the disciplines of the 5 Cs

NSK–RHP (Blackburn) use the acronym of CANDO: cleanliness, arrangement, neatness, discipline and orderliness.

Management of Improvement

It was crystal clear from the presentations made by the Japanese managers and technical specialists that they form part of a totally committed management team who are enthusiastic, enjoy work and are vigorously working on continuous improvement in pursuit of perfection. They clearly believe in the future, and have a long-term vision of where their respective company is heading. The Japanese companies visited exhibit the typical profile of high growth. For example, one company during the last three years had experienced an increase in sales of 21 per cent, the new products to sales ratio had increased by 25 per cent, and labour productivity had improved by 50 per cent. Most companies were planning to increase sales by 20 to 25 per cent over a period of three years.

The Japanese management articulate very effectively what they are doing, and have considerable confidence that the strategy and course of action they are pursuing is right. This confidence is based on a detailed understanding of the true situation, based on statistical data from extensive ongoing monitoring activities. The aim of each company is to be the market leader and best in class whereas, in the West, the majority of companies appear satisfied with second or third place. The Japanese

Item # and description	5S Evaluation Form	Item Score (0–5)	What is the team doing to improve to next level?
1. Removing unnecessary items	All items not required for performing operations are removed from the work area, only tools and products are present at work stations.		
2. Storage of cleaning equipment	All cleaning equipment is stored in a neat manner; handy and readily available when needed.		
3. Floor cleaning	All floors are clean and free of debris, oil and dirt. Cleaning of floors is done routinely – daily at a minimum – posted schedule.		
4. Bulletin boards	All bulletins are arranged in a neat and orderly manner. No outdated, torn or soiled announcements are displayed.		
5. Emergency access	Fire hoses and emergency equipment are unobstructed and stored in a prominent easy-to-locate area. Stop switches and breakers are marked or colour-coded for visibility.		
6. Items on floor	Work-in-process, tools and any other material are not left to sit directly on the floor. Large items such as tote boxes are positioned on the floor in clearly marked areas, identified by painted lines.		
7. Aisleways – markings	Aisles and walkways are clearly marked and can be identified at a glance; lines are straight and at a right angles with no chipped or worn paint.		
8. Aisleways – maintenance	Aisles are always free of material and obstructions; nothing is placed on the lines, and objects are always placed at right angles to the aisles.		
9. Storage and arrangement	Storage of boxes, containers and material is always neat and at right angles. When items are stacked, they are never crooked or in danger of toppling over.		
10. Equipment – painting	All machines and equipment are neatly painted; there are no places in the plant less than two metres high that are unpainted.		
	Subtotal pg 1		

Figure 3.4 5S evaluation form
Source: NSK-RHP (Aerospace)

Item # and description	5S Evaluation Form	Item Score (0–5)	What is the team doing to improve to next level?
11. Equipment – cleanliness	All machines and equipment are kept clean by routine daily care.		
12. Equipment – maintenance	Controls of machines are properly labeled and critical points for daily maintenance checks are clearly marked. Equipment checksheets are neatly displayed and clean.		
13. Equipment – storage	Nothing is placed on top of machines, cabinets and equipment; nothing leans against walls or columns. Guards and deflectors are used to keep chips and coolant from falling to the floor.		
14. Documents – storage	Only documents necessary to the operation are stored at the work stations and these are stored in a neat and orderly manner.		
15. Documents – control	All documents are labelled clearly as to content and responsibility for control and revision. Obsolete or unused documents are routinely removed.		
16. Tools and gages arrangement	Tools, gages and fixtures are arranged neatly and stored, kept clean and free of any risk of damage.		
17. Tools and gages convenience	Tools, gages and fixtures are arranged so they can be easily accessed when changeovers or setups are made.		
18. Shelves and benches – arrangement	Arranged, divided and clearly labelled. It is obvious where things are stored; status and condition is recorded.		
19. Workbench and desk – control	Kept free of objects including records and documents. Tools and fixtures are clean and placed in their proper location.		
20. 5S control and maintenance	A disciplined system of control is maintained at the highest possible level. It is the responsibility of everyone to maintain this system and environment.		
	Subtotal pg 2 + Subtotal pg 1		
	Total	÷ 20 =	5S Score

Figure 3.4 Continued

improvement activities tend to have a single title, banner or umbrella, e.g. Total Productive Maintenance (TPM) – for details, see Nakajima (1988a) – TQM, JIT, under which various initiatives are brought together as an integral part of the company's business plans and translated into a company-wide effort. This helps to give their improvement activities and teams a clear focus. In European companies, the initiatives being pursued often tend to be segmented and somewhat fragmented, and are the responsibility of individual departments and people. There is also the tendency for people to be on the lookout for the next concept to replace the one which is current.

The Japanese have developed an organizational culture and management style which, based on the evidence of their investments and success in world-wide production facilities, can operate successfully anywhere. Their success is not simply a matter of national culture; this is but one factor. The key lies in their ability to create an organizational culture within an environment which is conducive to continuous improvement. The saturation of the Japanese markets, the strength of the yen, high labour costs and the aggressive sales drive of individual companies with expectations of higher and higher sales will cause Japanese companies to seek an increasing number of off-shore manufacturing bases.

In many European manufacturing companies, if a small number of key people leave, there is a danger that the improvement process will first stagnate and then finally degenerate; see chapter 12. Whereas, the Japanese appear to have moved to a situation of what might be classed as autonomous improvement. All employees manage for themselves the improvement effort which proceeds in a common direction with each person accepting ownership for the improvement. They appear to have developed a standardized method of managing companies and the improvement process, a method that can be applied to most cultures. They are expanding on a world-wide basis so as to maintain their high sales-growth, and most have made a series of moves to internationalize their base of operation.

Through their involvement with individual initiatives, QCs and/or through the suggestion scheme, supervisors and operators are constantly engaged on problem prevention and improvement activities. They also pay keen attention to machinery and equipment quality through the application of TPM. In Japanese companies, operators can stop the production line, using what is known as a helpline, if they are experiencing any kind of quality problem or if they cannot keep up with the production rate. When problems arise emergency teams assist the operator to rectify the situation. There are regular meetings between operators, supervisors and technical specialists to discuss problems and improvement actions. In Western companies, when problems occur there are usually a number of organizational layers between spotting the problem, its solution and recovery of the situation. It is worth pointing out that Japanese manufacturing managers operate in a more favourable environment than their Western counterparts. Japanese companies have a bias toward manufacturing, in general and engineering, in particular. Companies employ huge numbers of engineers. The majority of European manufacturing companies employ insufficient numbers of engineers and consequently have not the resources to solve problems. Every Japanese manager with whom discussions have been held realizes that manufacturing is the key to their national economy. Work occupies the collective consciousness of the Japanese people and there is a general realization that their future depends on it.

Japanese managers and technical specialists exhibit a caring attitude towards production and what is happening on the factory shop floor. Senior and middle managers spend a considerable amount of time on the shop floor to see what is happening. They ask about results and problems; they give advice and help to create good habits through leadership (management by walking about). There is a tendency in European companies for senior managers to isolate themselves in their office and to fail to have regular contact with those involved with the production of products and delivery of services. Senior European managers should ask themselves the question: What is the purpose of my office?

The Japanese invest in equipment, technology and process improvement, without having to worry about short-term payback periods, they know that this will be beneficial over the longer term. This also applies to investing in a period of recession. This willingness to invest must be a considerable feature in the motivation of their managers and engineers. In the main, the investment is to reduce labour costs. Over the last 30 years or so, the Japanese have considerable proof of the wisdom of this policy. The typical payback period for equipment is three to five years, compared to the one year which is typical in European companies; interest rates for borrowing money are also lower. In European companies, the production personnel are usually required to specify a break even production volume and, in relation to the investment in new equipment, it is common requirement to make the justification over a three-shift operation.

European manufacturing management frequently complain that their engineers always want sophisticated computer equipment and software for the projects which they are undertaking. By contrast, while they make extensive use of CAD/CAM systems, Japanese engineers concentrate a considerable amount of their improvement effort on doing the simple things well. A considerable amount of the equipment employed by Japanese companies is relatively basic. The key factor is not the equipment itself, but how it is used to improve manufacturing efficiency. It is always remembered that the equipment is only required to support manufacturing and improve efficiency. All the Japanese companies visited had their own internal machinery manufacturing division, and a vast amount of the equipment seen in their plants is customized. The proprietary equipment is often employed to eliminate waste and transportation between processes, and to facilitate good internal logistics.

The Japanese are never shy in sharing the results of their improvement activities with Western visitors, as tables 3.1 and 3.2 show.

Table 3.1 Improvement activity of a semi-conductor manufacturer

Goals	Achievements in three years
Equipment	85% utilization
Manufacturing cost	50% reduction
Failure rate	10% reduction
Production	Two fold improvement
Suggestions	Four per person each month
Accidents	Zero

Table 3.2 Improvement activity of a temperature controller manufacturer

Function	Before JIT, Upgrade, Manufacturing Process (JUMP)	After JUMP
Production lead time	3 days	2 days
Inventory		
parts	30 days	3 days
WIP	12 days	8 days
finished product	5 days	2 days
Workforce	13	6
Space	20m^2	12m^2

Visible Management Systems

Japanese companies place considerable emphasis on ensuring their operating data is visible on the factory shop floor. They believe that everyone in the company benefits from an open information system. It is not regarded as a status symbol as is typically the case in European organizations. A complete range of information, in a variety of formats, is displayed usually in simple, locally developed formats. This data assists managers, technical specialists, engineers and operators to manage their processes more effectively; it facilitates the process of continuous improvement, and identifies and publicizes the improvements. It is a common communication mechanism to keep employees in touch with what is happening; it provides a focus to help concentrate efforts; it indicates to people when events are not going to plan, and provides warning signals of all kinds of different events. Display devices are often created by operators and first-line supervision. In some cases, the display is related to a specific manufacturing section (e.g. who is responsible for specific activities, TPM achievements, QC members and projects and a skill matrix, including the picture of operators) and, in others, it is related to a particular topic (e.g. policy deployment, mistake-proofing, QCs, education and safety). Here are some examples of this visible management system:

- A display of the activities of QCs in terms of where they are located in the factory, current projects, achievements and membership
- One company, as part of a campaign to improve the plant safety performance, displayed on a noticeboard the safety actions to which each operator had committed themselves together with their picture.
- In a software engineering department, a board displayed against each work station, the name of the software engineer and the job on which he/she is currently working.
- In a metal part punching department, the process instructions of jobs which were scheduled to be started at various times during the day were hung on a rack against a time-scale from 0830 to 1930.
- A schematic layout in the sub-assembly and assembly areas of one organization indicated the flow of work and, using different colours, the zone position of different types of operators and their role. The following system was used:

red – full-time employees; brown – casual employees; blue – operators responsible for the supply of parts; and yellow – employees who come to assist
a section who have fallen behind their scheduled production target.

- The main steps of a JIT system in terms of its purpose, targets, activities, and
  achieved improvements was displayed on a noticeboard.
- A complete wall of one plant was covered in charts relating to a variety of
  issues, including details and pictures of improvements which have been made,
  safety achievements and performance, attendance statistics, quality issues, suggestions, production targets, QC activities and TPM activities.
- Another company hung on racks at the side of machines a series of large cards
  which operators had produced to train their peers on specific aspects of TPM.
- In a refrigeration unit assembly line, quality control check-sheets were displayed at each work station indicating the product characteristics to which
  attention is needed, the important processes in terms of quality, and the self
  inspections and tests to be carried out.
- In one organization, a number of sub-assembly areas were supplying assembly
  lines, across a gangway. Each sub-assembly area and line had scheduled production targets for specific times of the shift along with actual production
  achieved. If production was going according to schedule a grey card was
  displayed across the gangway, if production was two units behind schedule a
  red card was used.
- In a staff meeting room at the CQAD of a major electronics company, on the
  walls they displayed various data relating to their product performance in
  comparison to that of competitors, and the problems which are currently
  being experienced by users of their products.

There is little doubt that this sharing and diffusion of information helps to ensure
that everyone is working together for the good of the company, and will inevitably
reduce organizational conflict. There is a total openness about concepts such as
TQM, TPM and JIT. Everybody in the company knows why a particular concept is
being used, the strategies and objectives, techniques employed and successes and
failures; this facilitates team spirit. In a number of companies, the information
displayed indicated that the improvement objective was to reduce the number of
operating staff in a production section. Any staff affected in this way are transferred
to other sections and to subsidiaries. For example, in one company, operators are
sometimes transferred to the sales function.

The pump manufacturing division of a mechanical engineering company suffers
considerable seasonal fluctuation with some 65 per cent of production output scheduled between October to March. Middle and first-line management, together with
the company labour union, make plans on how to adjust the workload of people
in the manufacturing, assembly and engineering areas in both the slack and busy
periods. A matrix showing the movement and activities of people in these periods
is communicated and displayed. For example, during the slack period, employees
are moved between manufacturing, assembly and engineering to improve their skills
and knowledge, maintenance, mistake-proofing, standardization, and improvement
activities are carried out, jigs are produced and trial manufacture is conducted on
parts currently purchased. Employees also go to customers and dealers to assist with
the selling of the product and listening to what they have to say about the product
and service. These two examples emphasize the flexibility of the Japanese worker. All

the companies visited stressed this point and said workers accepted job rotation and movement from one job to another very readily. This job flexibility and job rotation helps to eliminate departmental boundaries, which are often a major stumbling block to improvement activities, and diffuses new technologies, approaches and systems to every corner of an organization. Most workers are in multi-skilled groups and able to do all jobs in this areas. There are no detailed job descriptions and the salary is paid for the person and not the job. Japanese companies firmly believe in developing generalists, and not specialists. The system of lifetime employment and single company labour unions obviously facilitates flexibility, job rotation and long-term education and training programmes.

Involvement of People

There is a clear recognition in Japanese companies that their greatest asset is manpower, and all employees are encouraged to participate in continuous improvement activities. In more than one company visited, it was said that, because of the lifetime employment situation, they were always searching for ways to motivate and revitalize their staff. The usual means was through QCs, suggestion schemes, other small group activities, a variety of presentations, job rotation, and continuous education and training.

QCs and suggestion schemes provide the main mechanisms and motivation for involving everyone in an organization in continuous improvement. Considerable importance is attached to these two activities; they are viewed as complementary activities and it is claimed that there is no friction. QCs can submit suggestions and also have their projects evaluated by the scheme. A variety of recognition and award schemes, contests and prizes are in place for recognizing employees' efforts and to provide direct rewards. Great kudos is attached to these awards. The quantity and quality of suggestions are seen to be important and to reflect the department manager's ability to create an environment that is conducive to improvement.

Suggestion schemes

The following is typical of the operating characteristics of their suggestion schemes.

A suggestion is submitted and evaluated the same day by the foreman of the section, the person making the suggestion gets a sum of 100–300 Yen. If the suggestion is considered to have potential, it is evaluated by the assistant section and section manager or the QC committee who evaluate how many points it is worth. Alternatively more data can be requested from the proposer and the second proposal is evaluated in the same way. The formal acceptance and payment are, in general, made within one month of a suggestion being presented. The suggestions can be spiralled up to receive monthly, six monthly and annual commendations; this involves a presentation by the proposer to explain his/her idea. The following are the values of the awards given to suggestions by one company.

1st grade	10,000 Yen
2nd grade	5,000 Yen
3rd grade	3,000 Yen
4th grade	2,000 Yen
5th grade	1,000 Yen

Quality circles (QCs)

Without exception, all the organizations visited had thriving QC programmes involving a large proportion of the total workforce. According to JUSE, some 5.5 million workers are members of a QC, equating to 10 per cent of the Japanese workforce. QCs are applied as follows:

- Production areas
- Non-production areas – high level, managed
- Non-production areas – low level, supervised

In general, QCs are employed for reasons of education, communication, improving the environment, changing attitudes, etc., and not to reduce costs.

QCs can be considered as a natural part of Japanese working life and, in this respect, it is perhaps not advisable to compare them with the use of QCs by Western organizations. Within each section, the line workers are involved with their foreman in making day-to-day improvements in their routine work activities. They do not appear to separate out, as is the case in the West, QC activities and day-to-day work activities; it is one unified improvement effort. QCs generally tackle projects which are related to their section's improvement objectives for meeting the President's, plant manager and section manager policies and they tend to be managed by the section manager. The organizations did stress that QCs, while essential, are but a small part of their quality improvement process. In discussions with Dr Noguchi (Executive Director, JUSE) on this matter, he reports that the quality management experts have differing views as to the effectiveness of QCs in solving an organization's quality problems: Ishikawa claimed 30–35 per cent; Juran claimed 15–20 per cent; and Deming, 5 per cent.

In most Japanese companies, all non-managerial employees belong to a QC. There is some suggestion that membership is not voluntary with considerable peer pressure to be involved. The effectiveness of QCs is usually assessed at annual or six-monthly intervals, at which time good performance is recognized.

During the last few years, the Japanese companies have been making changes to the way in which QCs are operated. These changes have come about as the popularity of QCs has spread out within the country and as a result of pressure from the labour union. These are the changes identified:

- If QCs meet outside of work time, they are paid.
- A project carried out by a QC can be submitted through the suggestion system and a monetary reward made to each QC member. The money received is usually allocated for recreational facilities, education and training, social activities, etc. for the general development of the group. There appears to be little difficulty in acknowledging the ownership of a suggestion either by an individual or a group.
- In the manufacturing areas, it is expected that each working zone has a QC.
- Each QC is expected to complete a set number of themes, usually two, each year.
- While the QC members can select their own themes, it is expected that they submit this to the section manager for approval.
- The QCs are managed. The section manager will check the progress of the themes undertaken by QCs and, if they are behind schedule with their projects,

he will step in and assist them. The QCs have themes which are related to their section's improvement activities derived from the policy deployment process.

- Each QC is required to submit a written report to the section manager when they have completed a project. The manager comments on the report and signs to say that it has been completed satisfactorily along with suggestions to improve the future efficiency of the QC.
- The way that QCs are operated by the Japanese companies is more akin to the quality improvement team concept followed by Western companies, and not to the typical text book definition. In most cases, an engineer is available to assist QCs with difficult projects.

Here are some typical objectives of QCs and suggestion schemes in the organizations visited:

- QCs
  - To provide opportunities for self-improvement of knowledge and skills through co-operative team efforts
  - To create a rewarding work environment
  - To create a workplace where total participation in quality control is a reality

- Suggestion schemes
  - To improve the power to work and individual abilities
  - To promote friendly and healthy human relations among all employees and to vitalize activities
  - To improve the company structure and operations

There is a considerable effort to create a work environment in which staff are active participants. Employees are treated as human beings and not as tools; and they go to considerable lengths to promote harmony between personnel and technology.

Education and Training

Japanese companies believe that everyone in an organization must understand TQM, and that this can only be achieved by education and training. They take a long-range view of quality education and training, and tend to have a master training schedule and curriculum to develop the skills of all their employees. The schedule recognizes the different training requirements of people in different functions and levels in the organizational hierarchy; see figure 3.5 for an example of such a matrix. Senior managers take a personal interest in the content of the training programme of their organization.

Most of the TQM training is aimed at engineers – for example a 30-day course taken as 5 days each month for 6 months – and the general view in a Japanese company is: 'If an engineer does not understand TQM then he is not an engineer.'

Education and training programmes are developed to promote an awareness of TQM and to increase each person's knowledge and skills. Japanese companies take the view that the most important factor in TQM is the education of people, and the

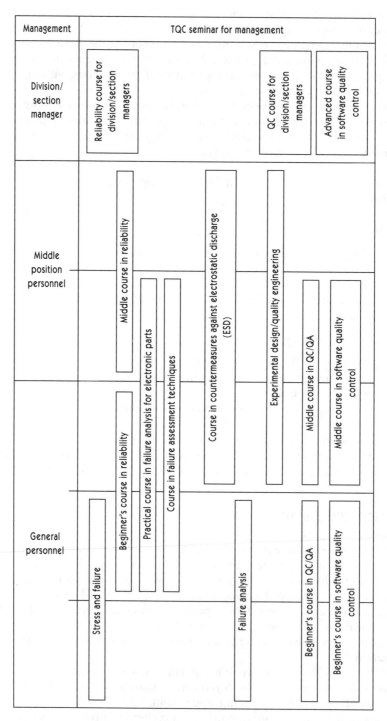

Figure 3.5 Education system for TQC
Source: Omron Corporation, Kusatsu-City, Japan

point is made that education and training acts as a key motivator for the pursuance of improvement. The majority of companies encourage their employees to suggest the professional training they wish to undertake. The Japanese firmly believe that better education makes for an improved worker. In one company's training programme, two machine operators were undertaking CAD/CAM training and the plant director had enrolled for a course on gas welding techniques.

The Japanese companies do not develop specialists such as quality engineers. Their aim is to give everyone a knowledge of the principles and techniques of TQM and, consequently, there is a clarity of understanding with everyone being involved in improvement activities. It should also be noted that new employees receive formal TQM training within a short time of joining a company.

Here is an outline of the training given at supervisory level by a mechanical engineering organization:

- Self development
- Effective use of time
- Education of subordinates
- Labour and personnel management
- Safety and health management
- Enhancement of production efficiency
- Understanding costs
- Quality consciousness/tools and techniques
- Process control
- Maintenance
- Environmental control

Both the breadth and depth of this company's supervisor training programme are worthy of comment. For example, in the section on 'Understanding costs', the supervisors are given detailed information on both fixed and variable costs in their area, plus an understanding generally of everything in a production operation that influences costs, e.g. assembly line balancing. The depth of knowledge would be unusual at much more senior levels in European organizations. The breadth of training is illustrated by the information given on what would generally be regarded as other people's jobs. In this way, the supervisors are given a total picture of business operations. The majority of the training material is in the form of checklists that the supervisor is expected to go through before, and after, taking action.

In general, European companies give little real training at supervisor level. By contrast, Japanese companies regard supervisors as the first level of management and give them the skills to match this responsibility. All senior managers have been through the same training and so have shared knowledge and beliefs. This approach has tremendous power.

Everyone in a Japanese organization is trained to use the seven quality control tools, and there was ample evidence (as displayed on the quality noticeboards discussed earlier) that these tools were well developed during all stages of production. A variety of training is given in techniques, and presentation and leadership skills to deepen TQM consciousness among employees and to improve their problem-solving ability. The most intensive training is given to design and production engineers.

In European companies, people are usually trained by one company, often then moving on to another company which benefits from the training and development already done. European companies must be willing to adopt a broad-minded approach and expect to gain as much as they lose from this turnover of people skills; otherwise, there is a danger that investment in education and training will be inhibited. This also frequently results in a failure to develop training strategies; rarely do European companies set improvement objectives for training programmes.

In Japan, the quality training programme is typically carried out by staff from corporate and divisional quality departments, engineers, invited lecturers from outside the company and by institutions such as JUSE. For example, JUSE offer 25 different courses which deal with TQM and these are attended by a range of people from Presidents and top management to line workers. Between 600 and 800 people are undergoing TQM in any one day at JUSE and, currently, some 40,000 take their courses. There has been a fourfold increase in the number of delegates since 1980, following the second oil crisis, and a tenfold increase since 1960. Currently, some 300 courses are held each year, and they are updated annually. Almost without exception, the instructors carry out an audit to assess the effective use of newly acquired skills by the people they have trained.

Because of the lifetime employment practices of large Japanese organizations, it is possible for them to invest heavily in a long-term programme of education and training and retraining to develop their employees' capabilities. A programme of initial training prepares them for work with the organization in terms of mission, philosophy, systems, procedures and job skills. The fact that all new employees, from junior to senior high school and university, begin employment in an organization at the same time each year helps the organization of the training and forms the basis for relationships which will last for a very long time.

Total Productive Maintenance (TPM)

The concept of TPM is now very much in evidence in Japanese companies. Nippondenso (a subsidiary of the Toyota Motor Group) has achieved considerable success with TPM, which every company in Japan is now trying to emulate. It combines preventive maintenance with TQM and employee involvement. It is clear that TQM and TPM are similar concepts, with the common goal of improving product quality. TPM is considered as an additional driver which is complementary to TQM.

Japanese companies are very much motivated by national prizes.

- The Deming Prize recognizes outstanding achievement in quality strategy, management and execution.
- The Japan Quality Medal is for companies who have won the Deming Application prize and can thereafter demonstrate five or more years of continuous improvement.
- The Japan Quality Award recognizes outstanding achievements in business excellence.
- The Ishikawa prize is for new methods or new systems for the modernization of management and achievement by their application.
- The Japan Institute of Plant Maintenance Award is for TPM.

These awards are perceived as being extremely prestigious. More than one company commented that the TPM award was the hardest of all the awards in Japan to achieve.

There was a range of different views, among the companies visited, on the meaning of TPM. The widest definition was that TPM encompassed the more narrow term of total prevention maintenance. Therefore, TPM is seen as a total method of management. Full details of TPM can be found in Nakajima (1988a, b). It was Nakajima who developed TPM by combining the key features of preventive, productive and predictive maintenance with TQM, QCs and employee involvement. However, in terms of actual maintenance procedures and systems, TPM contains nothing new.

At one company it was suggested that TQM is about 'how to' and TPM is concerned with 'why'. However, while a number of Japanese companies started TQM some 25 to 30 years ago, the majority of them have only become involved with TPM during the last decade. The consensus view among the companies is that, in their experience, TQM has only a limited influence on machine performance and, so, they have introduced TPM to focus on the machines. The condition of the equipment has a considerable influence on the quality of production output, and is a key element in manufacturing a quality product. The machine needs the input of people to keep it clean and to improve its efficiency and operation, thereby promoting a sense of 'plant ownership' by the operators and a feeling of shop-floor goodwill. This is the purpose of TPM.

TPM is a scientific company-wide approach in which every employee is concerned about the maintenance and the quality and efficiency of their equipment. The objective is to reduce the whole life cost of machinery and equipment through more efficient maintenance management and, as far as possible, to integrate the maintenance and manufacturing departments. Teamwork is a key element of TPM. By analysis of each piece of equipment, it focuses on reducing manufacturing losses and costs – i.e. the six major losses (breakdown, set-up/adjustment, speed, idling and minor stoppages, quality defects and start-up) – and establishes a system of preventive maintenance over a machine's working life. The emphasis of TPM is to improve the skills of operators in relation to machine technology, and to train and educate operators to clean, maintain and make adjustments to their machine. The training and education of operators is carried out by maintenance and engineering staff. In this way, machinery is kept at optimal operating efficiency. The 5Ss are essential activities in TPM, and they also promote visible management.

These are the main organizational characteristics of TPM:

- Integration of maintenance and production departments
- Small teams of operators/maintainers
- Training is undertaken to make operators feel like owners
- Good habits are developed

  - Cleaning becomes checking
  - Cleaning highlights abnormalities
  - Abnormalities are rectified
  - Continuous improvement of environment and equipment

In addition to QCs, the Japanese companies operate TPM circles made up of operators and maintenance staff which tend to focus on the production facility.

In a battery manufacturing company, the three-year TPM programme has the usual seven key steps:

1   Initial cleaning, to identify problems with equipment that are not noticed during normal operations
2   Countermeasures at the source of problems, to minimize accumulation of dirt and other contaminants, and to put in place improvements to make it easy to access parts of the equipment which need cleaning
3   Set maintenance, cleaning and lubrication standards for groups of equipment and carry out appropriate training
4   General inspection procedures and schedules
5   Autonomous inspection procedures and schedules
6   Orderliness and tidiness
7   Full autonomous maintenance

After each TPM step has been achieved, a TPM sticker is issued and placed on a machine. They started TPM to improve efficiency, quality, control and the ability of supervisors. Each employee is given a 20-hour education programme on TPM. The operating personnel devote some 8 to 10 hours of paid overtime each month to TPM activities, and produce TPM study sheets to educate and involve their peers. Twice a year, the best ideas are selected for an award. Silver stars are put on machines which have operated at 100 per cent efficiency during a period of two shift operation. The progress is measured using overall equipment effectiveness which relates to the sum of availability, performance and quality. Examples of TPM efficiency improvements are a 20 per cent increase in machine performance for the battery plate making line and 100 per cent increase on the battery assembly line.

Just in Time (JIT)

JIT is typically considered by Japanese companies as a key feature of TQM, and so it is worth mentioning how JIT is being developed. Most companies said that their systems were still being developed and each day they try to make progress to one-by-one production. The aim in all cases is to eliminate the seven mudas (wastefulness, or non-value added aspects):

- Excess production
- Waiting
- Conveyance
- Motion
- The process itself
- Inventory
- Defects

This is to ensure that all actions carried out are adding value to the product. The typical cycle employed to eliminate waste is: identify waste, find the cause of waste, make improvements, and standardize the improvement to hold the gains. As part of this cycle, it is usual to ask 'why' five times.

These are the main factors currently surrounding the deployment of JIT by Japanese companies:

- Customer service
- Selective use
- TPM essential
- Pilot projects
- Reduced set-up times
- Selective use of Kanbans
- Flexible supply chains
- Logistics
- Supplier audits
- Dual sourcing
- Manufacturing technology
- Production system development

Customer service

The main purpose of JIT is not inventory reduction but improved delivery of products to customers. The first aim is to reduce waste, and the second is to reduce lead times.

Selective use

JIT is not applied universally to all products and components. The Japanese investigate each manufactured item and determine if JIT can be used. For example, the view was formed that the Japanese were finding that JIT was difficult to apply in the case of semi-conductor manufacture. To cater for fluctuating demand, they kept stocks of diffused wafers which were then customized.

TPM essential

TPM is crucial to the effective operation of JIT.

Pilot projects

When JIT is initially applied a production/assembly line is chosen as a pilot, where it is developed and refined before being extended to other production/assembly areas.

Reduced set-up times

Reduction in machine and process setting-up times is important. For example, on the lead oxide grid pasting line of a battery manufacturer, it previously took two operators 30 minutes to change the dies; this has now been reduced to one minute for one person.

Selective use of Kanbans

A variety of Kanbans are used – cards, small boxes, Kanban squares and lights. Kanbans are used in only certain parts of the production system; they are also used to order some parts from suppliers.

Flexible supply chains

A feature of the production system is that, if operator A is being supplied with product by operator B, and if they are not meeting the production schedule, B stops supplying the product and comes to their assistance. Some operators are dedicated to the supply of parts to manufacturing and assembly line personnel; others are responsible for coming to the production line and assisting with emergencies as and when they occur.

Logistics

At one company, most suppliers are located within 50–60km of the factory, some within 20km and others are at a much greater distance. The delivery frequency is dependent upon the quantity and varies from daily, every two days and every three days. Another company said they deliver three times a day to OEMs and, on average, their suppliers deliver twice a day to them. One company provides a three-month forecast to their suppliers and, each day, they pick from suppliers production lines and/or stores the parts they require. It is interesting to note that, at a wire harness manufacturer, the comment was made that 'like it or not we have to be a JIT supplier to Honda, Nissan and Toyota'. This comment is typical of that heard in European automotive component suppliers.

The suppliers tend to work to a specific scheduled delivery time on the day in question, and the supply is made in small lorries who make trackside deliveries. There is often a mix of parts from different suppliers on the same truck. This is also the case in the delivery of finished product to the customer. There is serious traffic congestion in Japan's principal cities, and this has no doubt been attenuated by the transportation of small amounts of goods at frequent intervals. Koshi (1989) claims that 43 per cent of motor vehicle traffic in Japan carries freight and proposes an underground network for the distribution of goods.

Supplier audits

Some parts are supplied direct to the line without inspection, while others are inspected. This decision is related to previous quality performance of the parts and the supplier's quality system. An audit to assess a supplier's quality system, manufacturing processes and parts quality is usually carried out. There are three types of audit – new supply audit, periodical audit and emergency audit. The results of incoming inspection and non-conformances found on the line are evaluated each month and fed back to suppliers. Information between customer and suppliers is regularly exchanged using computer-aided quality information systems. Quality improvements meetings are usually held once a month with the aim of improving the quality of supplied product. It is interesting to note that, in general, control charts and process capability data are only requested from suppliers when non-conformances occur. The considerable attention to the use of SPC by European companies is not seen in Japan. They only tend to use SPC when proving capability and when they are experiencing problems. The absence of 'visible' SPC is indicative of the progress made in quality improvement. If an organization has very capable processes a process capability index (C_{pk} value greater than 3) the ongoing use of charting may be considered as superfluous.

Dual sourcing

A mix of single and dual sourcing is employed by the companies visited and, in both cases, the relationships with suppliers are long-term. Among the reasons for dual sourcing was to keep some flexibility in a customer's dealings with its suppliers, competition in terms of QCD, to maintain a competitive edge, and the capacity of suppliers. It is usual to ensure that the largest volume of business goes to the supplier who performs best in terms of QCD. One manager, when questioned about the sourcing of wire harnesses by major Japanese motor manufacturers said: 'Of course Honda, Nissan and Toyota employ dual sourcing.' These three motor manufacturers divide their requirements between the company and their competitor depending on capacity, demand and schedule. At regular intervals, the company confirm their capacity to these three major customers.

Manufacturing technology

The Japanese are employing the same machinery and technology as their European counterparts. However, because of activities such as TPM, reduced setting-up time by use of single minute exchange of dies (SMED) – for details, see Shingo (1985) – and integrated materials handling their machine efficiency and effectiveness is much higher. All their machinery and equipment is not new. For example, at one company, they had die casting machinery which was over 15 years old. A number of their production system improvements have come from developing and applying small inexpensive customized equipment for the handling and transfer of parts between processes, processing itself and the application of mistake-proofing devices. In general, they employ modern production layouts without huge visible investments, that is apart from CAD, manufacturing and simulation systems.

Production system development

Here are some examples of the means employed by Japanese companies in developing their production systems:

- Product and cellular layout – they tend to change the layout to reflect changes in product mix
- The use of mixed model production and assembly lines
- The employment of cycle time conveyors
- To facilitate easy movement and production flow, operators standing at workstations
- Considerable efforts being made to smooth production in relation to volume, variety, and capacity; they carry out a number of iterations of the sales and production plan to achieve this; most organizations give their annual or six monthly production programme to suppliers; they are then issued with a more precise schedule three months before delivery and, with one month to the build programme, they are issued with the exact delivery schedule
- When human operation is more efficient and effective than machines, the Japanese will employ human effort – on a number of occasions, it was said that on some tasks people can work faster than machines.
- In assembly situations, jobs are kept together in kit form.

Summary

A number of simple facts can be learnt from the Japanese experience of TQM:

- TQM depends on a systematic approach which is applied consistently throughout the entire organization.
- There are no quick fixes for the TQM success of Japanese companies. Western executives are always on the lookout for the universal panacea; unfortunately, there are none. This search for the quick fix is often an irritation to the Japanese. Their success is the result of the application of a combination of procedures, continuous discussion, systems, tools, improvement actions and considerable hard work and dedication from all employees.
- Senior and middle managers must believe in TQM as a key business strategy and be prepared to stick with it over the long term, and to ensure that it is integrated with other strategies.
- There must be a permanent managed process which examines all products, service processes and procedures on a continuous basis, and developing the mindset in all employees that there is no ideal state. Self-assessment against criteria such as the Deming Application Prize, Japan Quality Award, MBNQA or the EQA is an invaluable means of assessing progress to ensure that an organization continues to win customers.
- Each person should take personal responsibility for the QA activities within their area of control and QA must be integrated into every process and every function of an organization.
- Planning for improvement must be thorough.
- Improvement is a slow incremental process. Companies should not expect quick and major benefits from the application of any single method, system, procedure and/or tool and technique. To be effective, the quality management tools and techniques must be used together, in particular, the original seven quality control tools.
- There must be a fanatical obsession to pursuing perfection, challenging targets, reacting quickly to problems to find out what went wrong and putting into place corrective action.
- The concept of TQM is simple; however, defining, introducing and fostering the process is a considerable task and requires total commitment from all employees.
- TQM is all about common sense. The Japanese put common sense into practice. They manage and apply common sense in a disciplined manner. In European companies, a typical saying is: 'You cannot teach common sense.' The Japanese have done just that.

References

Akao, Y. (eds) 1991: *Hoshin Kanri: Policy Deployment for Successful TQM*. Cambridge, Mass.: Productivity Press.

Dale, B. G. and Cooper, R. 1992: *Total Quality and Human Resources: An Executive Guide*. Oxford: BPI.

Freeman, M. G. 1996: Don't throw scientific management out with the bathwater. *Quality Progress*, April, 61–4.

Ishikawa, K. 1976: *Guide to Quality Control.* Tokyo: Japanese Productivity Association.

JUSE, The Deming Prize Committee. 1996: *The Deming Prize Guide for Overseas Companies.* Union of Japanese Scientists and Engineers, Tokyo, Japan.

Koshi, M. 1989: Tokyo's traffic congestion can be unravelled. *The Japan Times,* November 14, 5.

Mizuno, S. (eds) 1988: *Management for Quality Improvement: The 7 New QC Tools.* Cambridge, Mass.: Productivity Press.

Nakajima, S. 1988a: *Introduction to Total Productive Maintenance.* Cambridge, Mass.: Productivity Press.

Nakajima, S. 1988b: *TPM Development Program.* Cambridge, Mass.: Productivity Press.

Shingo, S. 1985: *A Revolution in Manufacturing: The SMED System.* Cambridge, Mass.: Productivity Press.

Shingo, S. 1986: *Zero Quality Control: Source Inspection and the Poka-Yoke System.* Cambridge, Mass.: Productivity Press.

chapter four

Levels of TQM Adoption

B. G. Dale and D. M. Lascelles

Introduction

From research work carried out world-wide on the subject of TQM by the UMIST Quality Management Centre, it is clear that the extent to which organizations have adopted and committed themselves to TQM as the ethos of the business is variable. Six different levels of TQM adoption (or lack of it) have been identified (see figure 4.1):

1 Uncommitted
2 Drifters
3 Tool pushers
4 Improvers
5 Award winners
6 World class

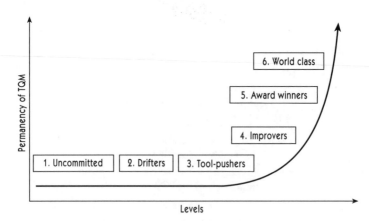

Figure 4.1 Levels of TQM adoption
Source: Lascelles and Dale (1993)

These levels of TQM adoptions were first derived by Dale and Lightburn (1992) based on empirical observation and, later, refined by Lascelles and Dale (1991). The descriptions underlying each of the levels have since been tested in a number of workshop sessions for senior management in America, Europe, Hong Kong and South Africa. The initial descriptions of each level have been refined and added to from this testing, and the current descriptions are reported in this chapter.

These levels are not necessarily the stages through which organizations pass on their TQM journey, rather they are characteristics and behaviour which organizations display at one point in time in relation to TQM. While there are obviously exceptions to these generalized descriptions, with some organizations midway between either of the six levels displaying hybrid characteristics and behaviour. It has been found that these six levels are a useful way of characterizing organizations and helping them to recognize symptoms and to develop plans for the future. This positioning has also been found useful in helping to understand the different perceptions of people, from a variety of hierarchial levels, of how they view the organization's TQM maturity. Some organizations, in using the levels as a TQM positioning model, have assigned a set of values (i.e. using a Likert type scale) to each of the statements which highlight the characteristics and behaviour for each level, thereby quantifying the perceived level of their TQM adoption.

The six levels are now described.

Level 1 – Uncommitted

Level 1 organizations are those who have not yet started a formal process of quality improvement and, in some cases, can be considered as being ignorant of TQM. Their quality initiatives are usually limited to gaining ISO9000 quality management system series registration and, perhaps, applying a few quality management tools and techniques, as a reaction to customer pressure. The extent to which both systems and tools and techniques have been applied is often directly related to the amount of time spent by the client representatives being on site and monitoring closely their use. The ISO9000 series of quality management systems will be seen by employees as a quality system, and not as a management tool. The Quality Department will be driving the quality management system, and the keeping of the ISO9000 series registration is totally dependent upon their efforts. The success of quality system audits by second and third party agencies will be viewed by senior management as an indication of the success of the company's quality initiative. The business will be operating in a detection mode (see chapter 1), but senior management believe a preventative approach is in place.

In this type of organization, much talk is likely to be heard on topics such as productivity gains, financial indicators, and ISO9000 series and other customer certificates of registration. TQM is seen both as an externally imposed contractual requirement and as an added cost – a twin threat to be avoided whenever possible. Quality is not given priority in terms of either managerial time or resource allocation. The focus will be on the product not on the process, and corrective and preventative action will not be taken intuitively but only in response to client/customer complaints. The priority is given to fire-fighting situations.

Problems are given support for their resolution, subject to the level of impact which they may have on sales turnover. In this respect, failures and non-conformances encountered prior to shipment of product will receive the greatest attention while those which have occurred after the product has been delivered and those problems which have arisen over a period of time will receive progressively less attention. It is also likely that the quality of design in terms of product service and process will not receive the necessary and appropriate attention at the right time.

Little investment in the education and training of management with respect to quality will have taken place, and managers consider themselves to be above this type of training. Consequently, senior managers in this type of organization are reluctant to take responsibility for, or to become involved in, improvement activities. Evidence of this lack of commitment usually surfaces strongly in an ISO9000 series implementation programme. It is usual to find that management makes time available at the beginning of the programme, but as it progresses the attention given will diminish, e.g. non attendance at meetings, failure to respond to requests for data, and not doing what they had agreed to do.

It is likely that this type of organization will have had some bad experience of TQM or one of its elements, in the form of a programme (i.e. QC, ISO9000 series registration, empowerment) and, consequently, the concept will have acquired a less than favourable reputation among the senior management team. Some managers will associate TQM with unreasonable demands on them and their time, and see it as a costly and bureaucratic system which will limit their autonomy.

Level 1 organizations are termed 'The uncommitted' because they have no long-term plan for continuous improvement, and are not convinced of its benefits. Their management, particularly at senior management level, are usually ignorant of the philosophy and values of TQM and, if they do have some knowledge of the concept, they may be sceptical as to its relevance for them and their business. Any knowledge that has been acquired has come through informal sources. They are not necessarily small, immature, unsophisticated or owner-managed organizations. Some 'household name' organizations are at this level and are often characterized by a long and successful trading history with little effective competition and a lack of customer pressure, i.e. market-niche products, protected markets and contracts assured which are subject only to the budgetary constraints of the client.

Here are the particular characteristics of level 1 organizations:

- An overwhelming emphasis and gearing of activity on return on sales and net assets employed, at the expense of other measures, both financial and non-financial
- Meeting output and sales targets is the major objective of the business, whatever the cost.
- There will be a lack of QA and behaviour regulating systems and, as a consequence, alternative methods will be employed to ensure that unrealistic production targets are met. These methods, more often than not, result in quality aspects of the job being discarded resulting in a high incidence of internal and external failure.
- A pervading attitude of short-termism as evidenced by frequent changes of priority, lack of investment in people, technology, research and development, and infrastructure and cost-cutting.
- The company is inward looking; its management style tends to be autocratic and is 'lean and mean', with senior management having sole discretion and decision making.

- The potential threat from the competition is not recognized.
- A number of negative elements are embedded in the organizational culture, e.g. 'them and us' attitudes, a limited view of 'on the job' expertise, inflexible working practices, job demarcation, little recognition of the potential of individuals, individuals are chastized in front of both their peers and subordinates and not given a chance to defend themselves, employees are required to wear identification tags to provide visual proof to management that they belong to a specific area, and managers enforce their ideas upon staff to a point where they are not allowed to think or deliver any inputs to the decision.
- The majority of employees have little concern for quality; it is seen as someone else's job and employees are not held responsible for the quality of their output. A typical scenario is that inspectors find the defects, and workers fix them.
- People hijack ideas and proposals from other employees to ingratiate themselves with management.
- When quality improvement proposals and suggestions for change are made, they are either squashed, not understood or changed to suit managements needs, and there is an unwillingness to instigate any real changes.
- One hundred per cent inspection is carried out on incoming materials, at key points during the production process, and on the finished product. The main focus of the activity is to measure conformance to specification and a considerable amount of activity revolves around the AQL concept.
- The data collected from tools such as checksheets and quality control checks tend to be left on file with no effort to identify trends or to highlight major non-conformances.
- Ineffective and inaccurate corrective action control procedures.
- A piecework system for operatives and inspectors, with payment made for non-conforming work.
- Any quality improvement initiatives tend to be 'bottom-up' and are product-related.
- The same problems reoccur with no formal procedures for pursuing long-term corrective action.
- Processes are not fully understood, documented and/or accessible.
- Employees are encouraged, when things go wrong, to make all efforts to 'cover their backs' and if blame can be passed to alleviate pressure then it is done without a thought for others. This type of action is condoned, if not, encouraged by management.
- Contact with customers is minimal.
- Suppliers are often blamed for quality problems, although the majority of the problems are of the company's own making.
- A lack of communication up and down the organization.
- Management and people are driven by fear and uncertainty. For example, in a plant of one of the UK's top performing companies (in profit terms), a defective batch of product was hidden from the plant director by the works manager and a production supervisor, so that it could be disposed of when the director was off-site. Other typical examples of this characteristic is the unwillingness of all levels of personnel to express their opinions and ideas in the presence of their manager/director.

It could be argued that such companies, which are often very profitable, do not need TQM when they seem to be doing very well without it. However, 'doing very well' is only for the time being and may not be a long-term phenomenon. Certainly, with rising costs due to inefficiency, they will in the future begin to suffer. Such uncommitted companies and their business philosophies are 'dinosaurs' belonging to another age; 'They are unlikely to survive the new economic age.' (Deming, 1982).

Level 2 – Drifters

Level 2 organizations will have been engaged in a process of continuous improvement for up to three years; they have followed the available advice and 'received wisdom' on TQM. The management team will be taking stock of the progress made but it is also likely that initial enthusiasm will have worn off so that ways of reviving the process are under consideration. At this stage, those with a short-term view may be expressing disappointment that TQM has not lived up to their expectations, and asking these questions

- What comes after TQM?
- What do we need to concentrate on next?
- What is the next fad?
- Should we be using BPR?
- Should we use the EFQM model for business excellence?

This type of organization is susceptible to the latest fad, and this focus is to the detriment of developing an in-depth understanding of the fundamentals of key concepts. For example, in a utility, some management believed that quality was being introduced into their processes by re-engineering them; therefore, they considered that there was no need for an ISO9000 series quality management system.

Senior management perceive that the motivation of employees can be improved but this is being suffocated by their supervisors and managers. To facilitate this motivation, a form of empowerment programme is put into place, and some senior managers express the belief that this will replace TQM. It will also be assumed by senior management that – in spite of their lack of visible involvement in TQM, recognition for the improvements which have taken place and their failure to prioritize improvement activities – continuous improvement will be naturally self-occurring and self-perpetuating.

This type of organization may have followed a programme along the lines of Crosby's 14 steps (1979); see chapter 1. Having reached Step 14 – 'Do it all again' – they do not know what to do next and are wary of 'doing it again' because the initiative taken to date has not been perceived as universally successful throughout the organization. In the case of a service, commercial or public-sector organization, they may have started with a customer care programme, perhaps in a blaze of publicity. It is not unusual to find organizations at this level seeking to employ the philosophy of one of the other quality management experts – a typical comment being 'We started with Crosby and are now viewing the Juran video tapes to see if his philosophy is suitable for our next step forward' – or to be considering the use of the EFQM model, taking the line: 'This is evidence of our commitment to TQM'.

There is a danger that this type of organization enters a cycle of programme renewal and decline, moving in ever-decreasing circles of false starts, waning enthusiasm, frustration and disappointment.

These are the characteristics of level 2 organizations:

- Continuous improvement is still perceived as a programme, not a strategy, or a process and will have a low profile within the organization. It will not be integrated with business and departmental objectives.
- There is no plan for deployment of the TQM philosophy throughout the organization. Communication is limited, and TQM does not penetrate to shop floor and office levels.
- Management are overly susceptible to outside interventions and are easily distracted by the latest 'fads' which are put out to management under various guises (i.e. a quality fashion victim).
- Management have undue high expectations of ISO9000 quality management system series registration, and fail to distinguish between meeting a particular standard and TQM. It is also likely that the procedures of such a system will be cumbersome, and control and disciplines engendered by the system will have been allowed to slide, and documents have become obsolete, resulting in a superficial application. While there is a belief that staff should work within the system, management cannot accept that they themselves need to accept the same disciplines. Consequently, at first-line supervision and operator levels, they tend to be driven by day-to-day actions and quotes, rather than compliance to quality management system requirements.
- The quality department has a low status within the organization.
- Continuous improvement activities are little more than cosmetic 'off-line' motivation programmes, with little impression on the company's organizational structure, internal relationships, and overall business direction.
- There is inadequate reporting of defects and inaccurate and/or inappropriate feedback, and there is a lack of clarity on what the real non-conformances and defects are.
- The softer aspects of TQM will have been promoted without the underpinning and mastering of the QA basics.
- Any teamworking is superficial, and departments only tend to co-operate to lay the blame on another department. Considerable infighting, rivalry and 'politics' exists between departments.
- A programme of QCs will have been attempted as a means of developing employees, and middle management told that they are judged by the number of QCs that are in operation. The initial QCs will have flourished, after which they will have floundered, and by now virtually died.
- No real changes in corporate culture have been made since the start of the TQM initiative. The activities associated with TQM are not given time to come to fruition before they are discarded and replaced with others.
- There is a reasonably high degree of suspicion and scepticism about TQM by management and staff, with a number of senior and middle managers not accepting the concept of TQM. Those at an operating level see TQM as another short-term tool to squeeze more productivity out of them.
- There are gaps in people's understanding of TQM and what it is, and, in addition, some key elements of the improvement process will have been

treated superficially. This will not have been helped by an uncoordinated training programme. A typical scenario is the awareness of TQM which exists at the lower levels of the organization, and understanding of the benefits is turned into frustration because they are not given the support of senior management, due to management's lack of knowledge of the concept and understanding of the seriousness of the situation facing the organization.

- There is a wide gulf between levels of the organizational hierarchy in their perceptions of TQM, benefits achieved and progress to-date.
- Self-assessment has been performed against one of the recognized award models, but the areas for improvement identified have not been addressed by developing a time-scaled plan of action. The focus of the self-assessment exercise is likely to have been on scoring mechanisms – 'scoring points' and impressing customers and suppliers – and not on how to facilitate improvement; it is perceived by many in the organization as being of little practical value. There is an overwhelming desire to win a Quality Award, mainly for PR and marketing reasons.
- A fear of failure and uncertainty pervades the organization, and there is the view that TQM will be sidelined in the medium term.

Level 2 organizations are termed 'The drifters' because they drift, without a clearly defined baseline, from one programme to another in a stop-start fashion, with concepts, ideas and initiatives being reborn and relaunched under different guises. Management teams try a variety of approaches, often in response to the latest trend, consultancy input, what they perceive will impress customers and what has been gained from conference presentations and discussions with other companies. A change of approach may be sparked off when a senior manager who has been a protagonist of the TQM philosophy and a particular line of thinking leaves the organization. Individual initiatives may be very creative because the managers are intelligent and articulate people, and some will be genuinely committed to and enthusiastic about TQM. However, while they are unable or unwilling to place quality improvement within a strategic business framework, it will not yield the desired long-term results.

Level 3 – Tool Pushers

A level 3 organization has more operating experience of continuous improvement than a drifter, usually between three to five years. They typically will have ISO9000 quality management system series registration and/or have met the requirements of the Quality system standard of one or more of the major purchasers. They employ a selection of quality management tools and techniques such as SPC, the seven basic quality control tools, QCs, DPA, FMEA and mistake-proofing, use a variety of quality improvement groups, and may be in the process of extending their knowledge of some of the more advanced techniques such as DOE, QFD and the seven management tools.

It is not uncommon to find that the training on tools and techniques has been aimed at persons who cannot propagate their further use and application; hence, the knowledge is contained. The system certification and use of tools and techniques will usually have been prompted and forced by a customer-driven initiative or based on the initiatives of individual employees. In some cases, the tools and techniques will not have been implemented in a strategic and systematic way, but reactively and when necessary. An increasing number of organizations at Level 3 are also looking to the criteria of the TQM and performance and business excellence models of MBNQA (US Department of Commerce, 1998) or the EFQM (1998) to provide an indication to senior management of what is involved in TQM and to give some direction and structure to their improvement process; the quantitative assessment of progress being perceived as of particular benefit.

A detailed examination of the QA procedures, quality planning systems and the use of quality management tools and techniques reveals that, in the main, they are being employed with an almost militaristic mindset, i.e. exacting and stringent quality requirements have been set by the customer and, as a result, a regulative approach has been built around fulfilling them.

If the organization is owned by an off-shore parent company, it is likely they will have made an attempt to address the annual themes in their officially submitted business plans and will have responded to the improvement initiatives put out by regional and corporate headquarters. However, there will be the lack of master plan to integrate and sustain the various initiatives which have been downloaded by headquarters to the various operating businesses.

There are a number of level 3 organizations who have purchased a particular quality improvement tool, e.g. the Juran video training tapes, and then followed the recommended advice: training by module, establishment of problem-solving teams, project by project improvement, etc. However, even though some of these teams have been highly successful, after a period of up to two years, the impetus of this type of training has been lost and the Juran training methodology have fallen into disuse. Such companies buy tools, training packages, programmes, etc. and disregard them once the novelty has worn off; they, fail to realize the potential afforded by the tool by neglecting to link it into a continuous improvement strategy. It is often the case that the tool itself is then blamed as 'ineffective' when, in reality, it was its incorrect application which caused it to fail.

Here are the characteristics of level 3 organizations:

- They are forever looking for the latest panacea for a 'quick fix'. This has happened with QCs, SPC, FMEA, DOE, QFD and benchmarking, The MBNQA, EFQM model and BPR are now being used in this way by many organizations.
- Not all members of the senior management team are committed to TQM; those that are will probably not understand its full implications, with con-siderable variability in their knowledge of the subject. The different inter-pretations placed on the concept are sometimes wanted and built upon by management to disguise their lack of commitment to TQM. Some of these senior managers do not see it as their responsibility to facilitate improvement; they have a 'what is in it for me?' attitude. This surfaces in the form of auto-cratic and negative behaviour particularly in the sales/marketing and finance functions. They have a tendency to delegate TQM responsibilities to the Quality Department – customer complaints, issues revolving around adminis-tration errors (i.e. pricing, invoicing, duplication of orders, over and under supply), and chairing ISO9000 series management review meetings. Middle managers may say all the right things, but they remain unconvinced, in their own minds, of the value and strategic importance of TQM, and demonstrate

this by their day-to-day actions. In their area of responsibility, they give priority to systems and techniques which they consider will have more short-term impact than TQM. These apparently conflicting priorities are communicated through their actions and comments to first-line supervision and operators, where the understanding of TQM and continuous improvement is usually patchy.

- The continuous improvement effort is concentrated in the manufacturing/operations departments with other departments remaining less involved in the improvement efforts. The tools and techniques will be in a reasonable state of health in those areas most effected by customer audits. The Quality Department is usually the main driving force of the improvement process, and company employees perceive the department owning QA and quality improvement. There will also be a perception within the Quality Department staff that they themselves own the continuous improvement process.
- A certain amount of inter-departmental/functional friction and lack of communication is likely to be evident.
- Detailed quality procedures are in place and the focus is on control of what exists now. The emphasis is on solving current, rather than future, problems.
- A quality management information system will exist but the data provided by the system will not be used to its full potential.
- Meeting output targets is the key priority of the majority of managers, with conflict between the manufacturing/operations and QA departments.
- Short-term results regarding product output and quality are expected, resulting in reactive problem solving and a neglect of long-term root cause process improvement actions.
- The management style is reactionary.
- Organizations have acquired a reputation for their products and services, but their processes have considerably potential for improvement.
- There are repeated claims from some parts of the organization that TQM is not working, with a tendency to dwell on old practices as being more effective.

This type of organization finds it very difficult to sustain the momentum of its improvement initiatives and is continually on the look-out for new ideas and quick fixes to deploy. The practice followed is often to replace those quality management tools and techniques which have been found to require considerable effort and disciplined application to make them work. The fire-fighting culture tends to suppress those techniques which need more effort to use and apply them successfully. A level 3 organization gives the right kind of signals and presents the requisite image to its customers and suppliers, but under the surface a 'fire-fighting' culture remains, which is not really committed to TQM.

There are a number of similarities between level 2 and level 3 organizations, in that TQM has not effected the pervading organizational culture or achieved significant business results. The difference lies in the way in which organizations react to this, with level 2 organizations trying a new overall approach, while level 3 organizations merely turn to another tool or technique within the context of the same overall approach. Level 3 organizations more commonly have well developed quality management systems, and tend to be concentrated in the manufacturing sector.

Level 4 – Improvers

Level 4 organizations will typically have been engaged in a process of continuous improvement for between three to eight years and, during this time, made important advances. They understand that TQM involves cultural change and have recognized the importance of customer focused continuous improvement. The CEO and members of the senior management team have committed themselves to total quality through leadership and their own personal actions. They will have formulated a strategy for TQM, in conjunction with the other business strategies, and have implemented a good deal of it. It is at this level that TQM begins to have a real impact on business performance.

Here are the characteristics of level 4 organizations:

- A policy deployment and problem-solving infrastructure in place, together with a robust and pro-active quality system.
- A high degree of closed-loop error prevention through the control of basic production/operation and/or service processes.
- A long-term and company-wide education and training programme.
- Process improvement activities exist throughout the organization, with people looking to improve activities within their own sphere of influence, on their own initiative.
- The importance of employee involvement through a variety of departmental and cross-functional teams and other means is recognized, communicated and celebrated.
- Benchmarking studies have been initiated and the data is used to facilitate improvement activities.
- A 'leadership culture' is starting to emerge, with some strong quality improvement champions.
- Trust between all levels of the organizational hierarchy exists.
- The preoccupation with 'numbers' is less than in 'drifters' or 'tool pushers'.
- The 'hype' which is usually associated with TQM is replaced by an acceptance of good management principles and practice.

In level 4 organizations, TQM is still, however, dependent on a small number of key individuals to sustain the drive and direction of the improvement strategy. There is a danger of lost momentum and failure to 'hold the gains' if key managers or directors leave, mergers of businesses, organizational restructuring takes place or the economic environment and trading conditions become difficult. This has been the case for a number of organizations during times of recession, where the long-term nature of TQM and its benefits have been discarded at the expense of short-term 'survival'.

Level 4 type organizations are termed 'The improvers'. They are moving in the right direction and have made real progress but still have some way to go. TQM is not internalized throughout the organization and the process of improvement is not self sustaining, with organizations still vulnerable to short-term pressures and unexpected difficulties. The results of improvement projects are not all effectively utilized for improvements, and such initiatives are heavily dependent upon the individuals driving them. It is also likely that the change in culture is relatively slow and some contradictory signals are sent out, e.g. people empowerment versus control mechanisms. An overall strategy which pulls all the islands of improvement together is not fully in place and concerns will also be expressed by management with respect to resources, in particular, time. In 'improvers', the more complex quality management techniques must be implemented carefully, and they should be handled by employees who are able to understand them; otherwise, people will be overwhelmed and the technique rejected.

The next step forward involves the management and co-ordination of quality improvement across entire streams of processes – the point at which quality improvement starts to become total. Process stream improvement and benchmarking activities of key processes may take five to ten years to mature sufficiently, so it is unlikely that the kind of cross-functional culture required to move up to level 5 will emerge in less than five years; it is more likely to be around ten years. At this stage of development, TQM will be a focal point but will not necessarily have attained prime strategic importance.

Level 5 – Award Winners

To date, there have been over 200 winners of the Deming Application Prize, Japan Quality Award, the MBNQA and the EQA.

In their research on the long-term management issues of continuous improvement, Williams and Bersch (1989) conclude that strong world class quality-related competitiveness can only be achieved when an organization has reached the stage of being able to compete for these top quality awards. Because the challenge is so formidable they estimated that probably only 150 or so companies have reached this level of quality. Bertsch and Williams (1997) in discussions with Dale have suggested that:

> It is now impossible to estimate with any accuracy how many companies are beyond level 5 in your model. This is primarily for two reasons. Firstly due to the tremendous expansion of Total Quality (TQ) over the past ten years especially in South East Asia where information sources are scarce and often unreliable. And secondly because we are now coming to the view that many companies are practising the basic TQ principles at a high level and yet have never realised that such a thing as TQ exists. To them, such principles are just about effective management. So they never take part in TQ surveys or competitions, apply for Quality Awards or join TQ societies and networks, etc. and are therefore difficult to track down . . .

Level 5 organizations are therefore termed 'The award winners'. Not all organizations reaching this level have actually won an internationally recognized or national quality award but they have reached a point in their TQM maturity where the kind of culture, values, trust, capabilities, relationship and employee involvement in their business required to win such an award have been developed – a point at which continuous improvement has become total in nature.

Here are the characteristics of level 5:

- A leadership 'culture' exists throughout the business that is not dependent on the commitment and drive of a limited number of individuals; all employees are involved in improvement.
- A number of successful organizational changes have been made.

- Business procedures and processes are efficient and responsive to customer needs.
- The organization has effective cross-functional management processes and achieved process stream improvements that are measurable.
- Strategic benchmarking is practised at all levels, in conjunction with an integrated system of internal and external performance measurement.
- A more participative organizational culture exists than before TQM was initiated.
- Powers of decision making are relinquished by management to people at lower levels of the organizational hierarchy in varying degrees.
- TQM is viewed sincerely by all employees as a way of managing the business to satisfy and delight customers, both internal and external.
- Perceptions of key stakeholders (i.e. people, customers and society) of organizational performance is surveyed and acted upon to drive improvement action.

However, although they may appear to form part of an elite, level 5 type organizations have not necessarily achieved 'World Class' status. The attainment of level 5 status marks the end of an organization's TQM apprenticeship and signifies that the organization has the capability and the potential to make an impact at the highest level, world-wide.

Level 6 – World Class

This level is characterized by the total integration of continuous improvement and business strategy to delight the customer. Williams and Bersch (1989) claimed in 1989 that less than ten companies world-wide, all Japanese, have reached this stage. Smith (1994), in a chapter of his book termed *Becoming World Class*, says: 'Perhaps 50 organisations worldwide earn the world-class label.' However, in discussing numbers, the points made by Bertsch and Williams under the discussion of award winners should be noted.

An indication of world class quality performance is that a company can apply for the Japan Quality Medal five years or more after they have received the Deming Application Prize. This, according to JUSE (1998), is 'when it has been determined that an applicant company's implementation of CWQC has improved substantially beyond when it won the Deming Application Prize'. They go on to say: 'By setting the goal apply for the Japan Quality Medal when companies receive the Deming Application Prize, they can expect to prevent their CWQC from becoming stale and sluggish. In this way they can further develop their CWQC practices.' The Japan Quality Medal has currently been awarded on just 18 occasions (1998 data). While a clear indicator of TQM maturity, this award is not the sole qualification for level 6 status.

Closer to home The Royal Society for the encouragement of Arts, Manufacturers and Commerce, Inquiry Tomorrow's Company (1995) points out that there are too few world class companies in the UK and insufficient such companies are being created. In discussing the approach of Tomorrow's Company, this point is made:

The companies which will sustain competitive success in the future are those which focus less exclusively on shareholders and on financial measures of success – and instead include all their stakeholder relationships, and a broader range of measurements in the way they think and talk about their purpose and performance.

The characteristics of such a company, which it is claimed can compete at world class levels, are examined in the Inquiry:

- Defining and communicating purpose and value
- Developing and applying a unique success model
- Placing a positive value on relationships
- Working in partnership with stakeholders
- Maintaining a strong licence to operate

The relative small number of organizations which have truly reached level 6 epitomize the TQM concept. TQM is concerned with the search for opportunities to improve the ability of the organization to satisfy the customer. By this stage of TQM maturity (which will have probably taken more than ten years after its initiation), the organization is continuously searching to identify more product and/or service factors or characteristics which will increase customer satisfaction. The focus of its TQM strategy is on enhancing competitive advantage by increasing the customer's perception of the company and the attractiveness of the product and/or service. This constant drive to enhance customer appeal through what the Japanese call 'Miryokuteki Hinshitsu' ('quality that fascinates') is integral to the concept of continuous improvement. Just like the concept of TQ itself 'Miryokuteki Hinshitsu' is a vision, a paradigm and a value framework which will condition an entire organizational culture.

The never-ending pursuit of complete customer satisfaction to satisfy latent requirements is a personal goal of everyone in the organization and an integral part of their everyday working lives. TQM is no longer dependent on top-down drives to improve motivation and deploy the policy, but it is driven laterally throughout the organization. Kanter's terminology (1989) of 'PAL' – pooling, allying and linking across organizations, is useful here; she describes organizations who pool resources with others, ally to exploit opportunities and link systems in partnerships. Those organizations who PAL while seeking continuous improvement of processes and customer satisfaction are typical of level 6.

Customer desires and business goals, growth and strategies are inseparable; TQ is the integrative and self-evident organizational truth. The vision of the entire organization is aligned to the voice of the customer in such organizations. TQ is the single constant in a dynamic business environment – it is a way of life, a way of doing business – for all 'world class' organizations.

In summary, these are the characteristics of world class organisations:

- Company values are fully understood and shared by employees, customers and suppliers.
- Each person of the organization is committed, in an almost natural manner, to seek opportunities for improvement to the mutual benefit of everyone and the business.
- Dependability is the emphasized throughout the organization.
- The right things are got right first time and every time in every part of the company.
- Waste is not tolerated.
- The key processes of the organization are aligned to create common and shared objectives, and to facilitate an environment conducive to improvement.

- There is total willingness and inherent capability to predict and respond to changing market conditions and customer needs and requirements.
- They constantly compete, and win, against the best world-wide.

Attaining level 6 status is not the end, for none of the levels described here represents a 'steady state'. In particular, 'world class' status is often attainable for only a few years, and it is dangerous for an organization to become complacent and blinkered to environmental changes. It is possible for organizations to 'slip' to levels 5, or even lower.

Summary

TQM is a strategy for change in an environment where the accepted paradigms are subject to constant challenge. It is a strategy concerned with developing an organizational culture in which people are able to meet these challenges and realize the opportunities of change. The six levels described in this chapter are intended as a positioning model to aid organizations in identifying their weaknesses and addressing them, as part of the continual challenge of continuous improvement throughout the organization. The characteristics underpinning the six levels are also helpful in highlighting different perceptions of progress with continuous improvement at different levels of the organizational hierarchy of a firm. The characteristics of the more advanced adoptions should also provide the requisite inspiration to those less advanced to highlight the type of issues to which attention needs to be given.

References

Bertsch, B. and Williams, R. T. 1997: Personal discussion, 8th May.

Crosby, P. B. 1979: *Quality is Free*. New York: McGraw-Hill.

Dale, B. G. and Lightburn, K. L. 1992: Continuous quality improvement: why some organisations lack commitment. *International Journal of Production Economics*, 27(1), 57–67.

Deming, W. E. 1982: *Quality, Productivity and Competitive Position*. Cambridge MA.: MIT Press.

EFQM (European Foundation for Quality Management). 1998: *Self-Assessment 1998 Guidelines for Companies*. Brussels: EFQM.

JUSE, Deming Prize Committee, 1998: *The Deming Prize Guide for Overseas Companies*, Tokyo: Union of Japanese Scientists and Engineers.

Kanter, R. M. 1989: *When Giants Learn to Dance*. London: Simon and Schuster.

Lascelles, D. M. and Dale, B. G. 1991: Levelling out the future. *The TQM Magazine*, 3(2), 125–8.

Lascelles, D. M. and Dale, B. G. 1993: The Road to Quality. Kempston, Bedford: IFS Ltd.

Smith, S. 1994: *The Quality Revolution: Best Practice from the World's Leading Companies*. Oxon: Management Books.

The Royal Society for the Encouragement of Arts, Manufacturers and Commerce. 1995: *RSA Inquiry Tomorrow's Company*. London: RSA.

US Department of Commerce, 1998, *Malcolm Baldrige National Quality Award 1998 Criteria for Performance Excellence*, Gaithersburg: National Institute of Standards and Technology.

Williams, R. T. and Bertsch, B. 1989: *Proceedings of the First European Quality Management Forum*, European Foundation for Quality Management, 163–72.

part two

The Business Context of TQM

The purpose of this part of the book is to introduce the reader to some activities which have an influence on TQM in a business context.

Policy deployment is the Western translation of 'hoshin kanri' which is the Japanese strategic planning and management process involving setting direction and deploying the means of achieving that direction, with appropriate involvement at all levels of the organizational hierarchy. Chapter 5 reviews the history and concept of policy deployment and proposes a policy deployment model. It is argued that this model will enable an organization to deploy its vision, mission, goals, objectives, targets and means more effectively.

Chapter 6 discusses the importance of designing for quality, and the management issues involved in this process. The line taken is that quality, reliability and durability cannot be inspected into a product or service; these characteristics must be designed in during the upstream processes. The chapter, drawing on a range of relevant and useful British Standards, explores how organizations should take a systematic approach to design.

Quality-related costs commonly range from 5 to 25 per cent of an organization's annual sales turnover, depending on the 'industry' and the way in which they manage quality. The reduction of costs is an important part of any business plan. Chapter 7 explains why quality costs are important to management, defines quality costs and outlines how to identify, collect, analyse, report and use them to best advantage. The typical pitfalls in quality cost collection are also aired.

chapter five

Policy Deployment

R. G. Lee and B. G. Dale

Introduction

An increasing number of organizations, as part of a strategic planning approach to continuous improvement, are starting to use policy deployment. It has been found that this concept is an excellent means of engaging all employees in the business planning process and focusing an organization on the vital few objectives (VFO) to achieve business results. According to Newcomb (1989), policy deployment 'helps create cohesiveness within a business that is understood throughout the company; it provides a structure with which to identify clear organisational goals'.

In the late 1980s, the concept of policy deployment was little known outside of Japan. Dale recalls taking Japanese TQM Study Missions of European executives and management consultants to leading exponents of TQM in Japanese manufacturing industry in 1988 and 1989 and, it was clear, that when the concept of policy deployment was introduced by the Japanese host organization, this was something new to the Study Mission participants. This prompted Dale (1990) to write an introductory piece on the concept.

Policy deployment is the Western translation of 'hoshin kanri' which is the Japanese strategic planning and management process involving setting direction and deploying the means of achieving that direction; PDCA is used extensively in the process. The concept was developed in Japan in the early 1960s to communicate a company's policy, goals and objectives throughout its hierarchy. It was the Bridgestone Tire Company in 1962 who conceived the concept; see Akao (1991) and Kondo (1997). The company visited the Deming Application Prize winners and, in 1965, published a report which described the best practices and put forward ideas to resolve the perceived problems by the use of policy deployment. By 1975, hoshin kanri was widely accepted in Japan, proving to be effective in motivating employees and uniting them in their respective improvement processes as Japanese companies moved to increase 'their overall strength and character' (Kondo, 1997).

By the early 1980s, hoshin kanri began its journey across the Pacific Ocean on a wave of Deming Application Prize winning Japanese subsidiaries such as Hewlett–Packard's YHP Division and Fuji–Xerox. MBNQA and EQA winning companies started to use policy deployment successfully in the early 1990s, linking medium to long-term policy to annual plans to achieve significant improvements in business results. Woll (1996) outlines the benefits of the use of hoshin planning by three American organizations:

> Analog devices, for example, identified new product sales as one of its hoshins three years ago and was able to go from shipping $125 million in new products in 1995 to shipping $300 million in 1996. One Hewlett–Packard product group realized $8.4 million in manufacturing cost reductions within one year. Teradyne reports that hoshin planning helped them to ensure that its more than 1,000 active quality improvement teams work on meaningful activities that are aligned with its business goals.

There is little empirically researched academic literature on policy deployment, despite its popularity in large multi-nationals with Japanese subsidiaries; see Lee and Dale (1998). van der Wiele et al. (1996) say 'In recent times policy deployment has been a topic in which organisations have shown an increasing interest' but 'it is still not a well known technique in many companies' which is 'typical of those organisations who are not very well advanced in their quality management activities'. However, having made this point, it should be said that it features as a topic in texts such as Imai (1986) and Juran (1964); the latter was probably one of the first contributors to the development of the policy deployment concept.

This chapter reviews the concept of policy deployment and proposes a policy deployment model based on Mulligan's et al. (1996) catch-reflect-improve-pass (CRIP) process. The model, based on research described in Lee and Dale (1999), demonstrates how policy deployment, business results and self-assessment are inextricably linked into the PDCA cycle of business operations, and it is argued that this will enable an organization to deploy its vision, mission, goals, objectives, targets and means more effectively.

Definition: Policy Deployment

Hoshin kanri was developed in Japan to communicate a company's policy, goals and objectives throughout its hierarchy; its main benefit is to focus attention on key activities for success. Kano (1995) provides some background on the difficulties in the English translation of the term making the point that 'a considerable semantic gap exists between the English policy and the Japanese word hoshin'. A literal translation of hoshin kanri provides an insight into its concept (Total Quality Engineering, 1997):

> Hoshin = a compass, a course, a policy, a plan, an aim;
> Kanri = management control, care for;
> Together = 'management control of the company's focus'

The popular term 'policy deployment' is often used interchangeably with hoshin kanri. While the translation is useful as an insight and, in particular, attention should be drawn to the 'management', 'control' and 'focus' as elements, there are a number of widely varying definitions of hoshin, hoshin kanri, management by policy and policy deployment which expand the concept:

- Watson (1991): 'Perhaps the most accurate term for hoshin kanri would be target-means deployment.'
- Total Quality Engineering (1997): 'A system of forms and rules that encourage employees to analyse situations, create plans for improvement, conduct performance checks, and take appropriate action.'
- Integrated Quality Dynamics (1997): 'A one-year plan for achieving objectives developed in conjunction with management's choice of specific targets and means in quality, cost, delivery, and morale' or in 'catch-phrase' form: 'Hoshin = Target + Means'.

While these definitions offer variations on the themes of plans, targets and means, the most comprehensive and more 'encompassing' definition, and one that emphasizes the importance of the PDCA cycle and feedback, is that of Mizunode quoted in Eureka and Ryan (1990):

> Deploy and share the direction, goals, and approaches of corporate management from top management to employees, and for each unit of the organisation to conduct work according to the plan. Then, evaluate, investigate and feedback the results, or go through the cycle of PDCA continuously and attempt to continuously improve the performance of the organisation.

The most significant point to draw from the preceding definitions is that they 'interpret' hoshin kanri and often fail to mention feedback. Interpretation of hoshin kanri into policy deployment by the Western writers often leads to a watering down of the concept and, although 'catch-phrase' versions may make western management's job easier, it can lead to inadequate application of the method and unsatisfactory results.

What is Policy Deployment?

Kendrick (1988) provides one of the earliest Western articles on policy deployment, discussing how it was used by the Florida Power & Light Company to reshape the corporate objective-setting process to conform to customers needs. However, one of the first articles by a Western author to summarize the Japanese approach to policy deployment was produced by Dale (1990). He said: 'Policy Deployment within a process of long-term planning is one of the features of "the approach" to TQC by Japanese companies.' He described the deployment of the presidents annual management policy plan through the organizational hierarchy. It was a process of developing plans, targets, controls and areas for improvement based on the previous level's policy and an assessment of the previous year's performance. The plans and targets are discussed and debated at each level until a consensus on plans and targets is reached, along with the methods for meeting the goal – he called this 'play catch' now more commonly known as 'catchball'. Once agreement has been reached at all levels, in a strictly controlled six- to eight-week policy deployment period, individual, plans, targets, control points, improvement areas and corrective actions are recorded and, perhaps more importantly, predominantly displayed around the workplace. Control of the deployment process and subsequent implementation of the policies is conducted through quarterly, monthly, weekly and daily reviews depending on the level of the individual involved. Dale (1990) says the PDCA cycle 'is extensively used in these diagnosis' and that 'the discipline of policy deployment and agreement at each level' ensures everyone is working in the same direction.

The concept of policy deployment as providing a bridge between the corporate 'plan' and the 'do' steps in continuous improvement is re-emphasized by Robinson (1994) who says that at Harris Semiconductor (USA), the process:

> . . . embraces the concept of empowerment as a balance between alignment of activities to the goals and the freedom people have to take action. The ultimate purpose of this process is to empower people to make meaningful improvements.

More recently, Kondo (1997) described hoshin kanri as 'a system of management in which the annual policy set by a company is passed down through the organisation and implemented across all departments and functions'. There are a number of elements in Kondo's article which are key to the Japanese approach, support Dale's (1990) description of the process, and which are often overlooked or underplayed by those describing Western systems of policy deployment. Here are the key points made by Kondo (1997):

- Policy deployment is effective in motivating employees.
- The aim of the process is 'give and take'.
- For a top-down approach to work, senior manager's have to be highly respected.
- Results are checked by means of individual managers' control items.
- The process is an important strategy for allowing top managers to exercise leadership.
- Policy is not determined only by short-term considerations.
- Top management must 'lead the way in whipping up everyone's energy and enthusiasm'.
- The purpose of the top management audit is to find and solve problems, discover and build on strengths, and standardize and institutionalize improvements.
- If management audits are carried out in the wrong way, there is a danger they will become superficial and ritualistic.
- It is important for top managers to talk directly to ordinary workers.

These are the most important policy deployment concepts to be drawn from the writings of Dale (1990) and Kondo (1997):

- Leadership
- Communication
- Control
- Review

Also, that there are four stages:

- Policy setting
- Policy deployment
- Policy implementation
- Evaluation and feedback

However, despite the defined process and benefits to be gained from effective policy deployment, even in Japanese companies, there are some fundamental problems with its application. Kogure (1995) defines them thus:

1 Ambiguity of relations between goal and policy
2 Unfitness of content of management policy between superiors and sub-ordinates on matters pertaining to ratio of abstractness and concreteness

In the first case, Kogure (1995) describes the problems as distinguishing between policies and goals, the order in which they are issued and how they relate to each other. In the second case, Kogure (1995) discusses how there is an imbalance between content of policy and level of issuer – the higher the policy issuer, the more abstract the policy should be, and the less concrete, and that it is the role of the subordinate to develop plans and not policy. He describes four patterns:

1 Management policies of superior and subordinates are both quite abstract and deployment of policy is carried out only perfunctorily.
2 Content of superior manager's policy is too concrete.
3 A gap between the superior manager's policy and the subordinates manager's policy is quite conspicuous, because the former is too abstract and the latter is to concrete.
4 The matching subordinate manager's policy to the superior manager's policy is very appropriate and policies are deployed properly from top to bottom.

Pattern 4 is where true policy deployment occurs; however, as Kogure (1995) states, patterns 1, 2 and 3, and especially pattern 1:

. . . Frequently appear at the beginning stage of introducing TQC; however, sometimes these patterns still remain even in companies advanced in applying TQC, because employees in these companies have no full knowledge of how to balance abstractness and concreteness when deploying policy.

What Policy Deployment is Not

At first glance, policy deployment looks very similar to MBO; and, as Akao (1991) and Fortuna and Vaziri (1992) highlight, hoshin kanri was initiated by the emergence of MBO in Japan. However, although there are some similarities, there are more significant differences; Eureka and Ryan (1990) refer to hoshin kanri as MBO done right. From the work of Akao (1991) and Fortuna and Vaziri (1992), similarities and differences between policy deployment and MBO are revealed; see table 5.1.

Policy deployment is not a solution to all planning problems, but a process which enables managers to plan effectively and translate those plans into actions. Further-more, although Integrated Quality Dynamics (1997) consider the description of hoshin kanri as policy deployment as 'not the best translation' – they describe hoshin as a one-year plan with targets and means and that hoshin management is not only 'deployment' – their 'myths' are worth repeating:

Hoshin myths

- Hoshin is part of QFD
- Hoshin is only for the top management of an organization
- Hoshin is the corporate policy
- Hoshin is following the direction of the shining needle

Hoshin management myths

- Hoshin management is part of QFD
- Hoshin management works successfully only in Japanese organizations
- Hoshin management is strategic planning
- Hoshin management can be implemented without any other TQM methods and systems
- The key to successful hoshin management is deployment of targets
- When implementing hoshin management the start point is to determine the corporate vision.

These 'myths' offered by Integrated Quality Dynamics offer valid insights to misconceptions perpetuated by some writers on the subject. Policy deployment is not just about corporate philosophy and management jargon, it provides a positive process which engages all employees in the cycle of planning, implementing, and reviewing policy.

In terms of this, the authors list what policy deployment is not:

- An excuse to pay lip service to employee feedback during the catchball process
- An opportunity for 'empowered' employees to take decisions without adequate direction, support, checks and balances
- A permit for managers to abdicate their responsibility for the plan and the results

Table 5.1 Main similarities and differences between policy deployment and MBO

SIMILARITIES
- Self-determination of goals
- Attainment of goals
- Setting continuously higher goals
- Improvement in performance
- Self-evaluation of results
- Co-ordination, discussion, and exchange of ideas
- Inducement of creativity and morale improvement

DIFFERENCES
Policy deployment
- focuses on a general improvement plan for the organization, and not on an individuals's performance
- ensures an individual's goals are congruent with company objectives
- encourages employee participation in objective setting rather than acquiesce to a superior's bidding and direction
- focuses on timely and relevant feedback, not an annual or bi-annual review of progress
- focuses on the process of getting there, how the objectives will be met and what actions an individual must take
- emphasizes process and quality tools and techniques to solve problems
- encourages the formulation of management items
- encourages the establishment and implementation of TQM
- emphasizes customer focus and quality of products and services

The Policy Deployment Process

Policy deployment works on two levels to manage continuous improvement and achieve business results: strategic objectives and daily control of the business. The key features of the process are now examined.

5–10 year vision

A challenging customer-focused vision, pertinent to people at all levels and appropriate for the next five to ten years, is required. According to the Goal/QPC

Research Committee, (1994) a draft of the vision should be given to the organization for a reality check, and then communicated to everyone at all levels. Unfortunately, this is easier said than done, as visions are generally created at top management level and any reality check is likely to receive middle management filtering of employee comments to prevent unfavourable views reaching top management, i.e. the 'sponge' effect. The most effective way of overcoming this problem is to gather accurate information on the company, its customers, competitors and market, and then to hold workshops between top management strategists and employees without the middle management interference, i.e. to play catchball without middle management. However, this method needs to be treated with caution, because it is not usually a good approach to ignore middle managers.

Mid-term 3–5 year objectives

Translating the vision into mid-term objectives, together with the broad means to achieve them is the next step. Wood and Munshi (1991) suggest that the objectives should be prioritized and, from this, the critical ones are selected with a focus on a small number (maximum three) of breakthrough objectives. Then, the means are determined by which the objectives will be achieved and the objective and means are cascaded through a catchball discussion. The process of catchball provides the opportunity to ensure commitment to objectives at each hierarchical level, and produces an organization which is focused and committed to the same goals. However, these medium goals, as extensions of past performances, are of little value without analysis of critical problems, current practices and changes inside and outside the company. Mulligan et al. (1996) say a holistic perspective is required, including 'business objectives; environmental conditions; resources constraints; and definitions of core business processes'.

Annual plan and objectives

Annual, short-term objectives are determined from the mid-term goals and the annual plans should be actionable and specific. This one-year plan includes targets, means and measures that each manager will work on during that year. Goal/QPC Research (1994) say it is necessary to choose a small number of targets areas on which to focus (six to eight maximum), and that half of these should be related to the manager's participation in the strategic plan; the other half should be related to the critical process of the person's regular job. However, Mulligan et al. (1996) suggests that departments should have only three or four goals, so line management can have the appropriate level of focus and resources assigned. Nevertheless, regardless of the number of objectives, all must be measurable with monthly numerical targets, and the reasons for selection must be compelling and obvious (Watson, 1991). Furthermore, they should be owned by the organization through the process of catchball. Moreover, the plan, objectives, and targets should not be constrained at management level, but cascaded down to each individual team or employee.

The NSK–RHP Bearings, Blackburn Foundry's top-level policy deployment annual plan is shown in figure 5.1; this has been developed from the RHP Bearings European Division policy deployment plan. An example of a breakdown of this into an environmental policy is shown in figure 5.2.

blackburn challenge 98

Our aim is to defy inflationary pressures in all areas of our business. Our measure of success will be – achieving profitability at an output level of 7000 housings a day.

NSK-RHP blackburn – *Hoshin Kanri* 1998

We will all take ownership for achieving Profitability Without Volume

Strategies

* Through the application of Teamworking, involving everyone in Kaizen and CANDO activities, we intend to develop Total Productive Maintenance (TPM) in all areas of the site.

* The achievement of Target 160 actions will ensure we achieve profitability in 1998.

* Through achievement and maintenance of standards – ISO9002, ISO14001, BS8800 & IIP we will ensure Customer/Neighbour/Employee satisfaction.

Enablers

* Improve our productivity performance through,
  – key machine productivity status displayed throughout the factory – on line OEE's
  – all key machines taken to TPM stage 3 by Q2 and to stage 5 by Q3
  – key machine breakdown history (6 months) input to MAINPAC by Q4
  – 80% of our people involved in TPM activities by Q4

* Improve our cost performance by,
  – breaking down the factory into natural work groups, identifying all cost elements and setting targets for reduction
  – displaying sample housing costs at each stage of the production process to increase the cost awareness of our people
  – involving the Kaizen TPM Teams in the implementaiton of all *Target 160* activities

* Improve our customer/neighbour/employee satisfaction by,
  – maintenance of ISO9002 and ISO14001 working to improve our audit compliance
  – promoting a positive effect on the environment both inside and outside of our business
  – improving our employee's health standard and well being through achievement of BS8800
  – raising the skills level of our people in line with the business needs through IIP and application of our training plans, working always towards accreditation of the training to NVQ standards

blackburn mission

Our aim is to give unrivalled stakeholder satisfaction – by ensuring product conformance, on time delivery, minimal environmental impact and competitive costing. Always developing our people to their full potential and involving them to ensure their safety and well being.

	Objectives	Targets
Quality	Reduce Incident Of Audit None Compliance	–50%
	Reduce Customer Complaints	–50%
	Conformance To Specification	Fdry 97.6% M/c 99.2%
	Reduce Ferrybridge Returns	0.05%
Cost	Reduce Casting Cost	£2.07
	Reduce Expenditure Cost	–10%
	Reduce Labour Cost	–10%
Delivery	Improve Schedule Adherence	TBA
	Foundry & Machine Shop	TBA
People	Validation Of Skills Levels	40%
	Personal Development Reviews	1/year
Health & Safety	Achieve BS8800	Q4
	Reduce Lost Time Accidents	–50%
	Reduce Accident Incidents	–50%
	Introduce Smoking Policy	Q3
Environment	Reduce Waste	–10%
	Reduce Energy Usage	–10%
	Hold An 'E' Day	June 98

Danny McGuire
(Plant Manager)
Issue Level 1:1

Figure 5.1 NSK-RHP top-level policy deployment annual plan
Source: NSK-RHP Blackburn Foundry

NSK-RHP *blackburn* Environmental Policy 1998

'Breaking the Mould' to ensure our ENVIRONMENTAL future.

Strategies

➢ Through the Continuous improvement cycle, we will develop strategies to reduce our energy usage.

➢ Through our philosophy of **'Cost Down'** we will identify all waste and set out a programme to eliminate, minimise, recycle or make good use of all waste within the site.

➢ Through improved communications, we will involve our people, customers, suppliers, neighbours, regulatory bodies and other interested parties in minimising our impact on the environment.

Enablers

➢ Establish Programmes and systems for pollution prevention – specifically carry out trials to establish viable alternative products for solvent based paints and rust preventatives.

➢ Ensure compliance with all relevant environmental laws and legislation to which our organisation subscribes.

➢ Work with our local authority to ensure compliance with the Environmental Protection Act.

➢ Use the TMC process for setting and reviewing environmental targets and objectives.

➢ Inform, instruct and train our people in environmental issues, thereby ensuring continuous environmental awareness with the use of competency based training plans.

➢ Build on our 'best practice' recognition for incorporating environmental issues into existing management systems.

➢ Through communications and teamwork, involve our people to minimise our impact on both local and global environment.

➢ Contribute to the reduction of global warming through the reduction of, reuse of or recycling of all waste.

Objectives

Quality	Set up review meetings with local Environmental Officer to agree compliance with all legislative regulations, e.g. EPA.
Cost	Install bulk storage of paint, amine and resins by Q4 98 Target 10% energy & waste disposal reduction CAPEX proposal for site sub-metering Q4 98
Delivery	Audit waste disposal suppliers annually Deploy environmental TMC to work groups
People	Introduce formal start-up and shutdown procedures across site, complete Q2 98 Specific environmental issues to be posted on notice boards and briefed as necessary. Site to have an Environmental open day for employee's children during 1998.
Safety	Test and refine all Emergency Procedures. Complete ALL environmental aspects assessments Q1 98 Reduce Pollard noise levels to below 85 dec.
Environment	Investigate re-use of waste coolant, proposal by Q3 98. Carry out trials on alternative Rust Inhibitors, proposal by Q2 98 Install abatement equipment – amine

Danny McGuire
(Plant Manager)
Issue Level 1:1

Figure 5.2   NSK-RHP environmental policy
Source: NSK-RHP Blackburn Foundry

Deployment/roll down to departments

Clear, disciplined action plans with direction for improvement, what is to be measured, and the processes to be improved are generated through a continuous catchball between all levels and around chosen targets. Corporate and division/department planning cycles should be synchronized, and annual plans should present a prioritized set of actionable tasks, designed to achieve breakthrough in critical areas (Wood and Munshi, 1991). A significant aspect of policy deployment is the extent to which the targets and means initiated at the top level are extensively modified through negotiation by the creativity of the lower levels through bottom-up feedback. This involvement of everyone results in full ownership and understanding of the plan at all levels of the organization. The goal of catchball is to prevent sub-optimization; local optimization may have to be forsaken for the optimization of the interests of the company as a whole, even if this appears to rebuff the concept of 'empowerment' which pervades modern companies. Ideally, policy deployment should be a shop-floor process, with no off-site management retreats and/or staff-level planning. Once the goals, objectives and plans have been agreed, they should be openly displayed in the work area adjacent to the progress charts that are tracking achievement and targets.

Execution

The actionable tasks, following the deployment phase, should be taken up by team and individuals, departmentally and cross-functionally, depending on the task. When using the cross-functional approach, it is essential to identify the lead department to determine responsibility and supervision for the task. The team/individual should have a clear statement of target and means, and follow a PDCA cycle, with periodic checks from senior management (Wood and Munshi, 1991).

Progress review (monthly and quarterly)

The progress reviews stress the importance of self-diagnosis of targets and process. Problems should be identified, and corrective action implemented. Again, the PDCA is built into the policy deployment process, and regular checking will assure continuous improvement and reduce costs.

Annual review

Wood and Munshi (1991) suggest that the review process focuses on:

- achievements of the past year;
- lessons learned in the past year;
- the gap between goals and achievements in the past year;
- root cause analysis of the problems;
- environmental factors;
- future plans for the organisation.

This forms the basis of policy deployment for the succeeding year, the check being undertaken at the start of the cycle. However, one important review should not be forgotten: the review of the policy deployment process itself, to learn from the mistakes made and improve it for the following year.

Mulligan et al. (1996) say that the most tangible aspects of policy deployment is the four sets of reports that support the organization's planning process:

1 Hoshin plan summary

- Articulated objectives
- Objective owners
- Long- and short-term goals
- Implementation strategy
- Specific improvement focus

2 Hoshin action plan

- Detailed links between core objectives and implementation initiatives

3 Hoshin implementation plan

- Records progress as the plan is implemented
- One plan for each objective
- Incorporates task ownership, and milestones and due dates

4 Hoshin implementation review

- Charts post-implementation results relative to company goals
- Competitive benchmarks
- Accepted world-class benchmarks

A Check–Reflect–Improve–Scrutinize–Pass (CRISP) Approach to Policy Deployment

From an analysis of the research carried out into the policy deployment process of a 'world class' organization undertaken by Lee, and observations of the use of policy deployment by a variety of organizations, including Japanese manufacturing companies based in the UK, it is clear that the key to ensuring the effectiveness of the process is leadership and communication.

In the literature on policy deployment, there is consistent reference to cascade and catchball as essential elements of policy deployment. However, based on research and practical experience, while deployment is the area where management can have the most impact, they often fail to deliver what is necessary. The cascade process does not work because line managers fail to communicate with their teams in an effective manner, due to their lacking the time, the skills or the management style. Catchball fails to work because employees do not see the results of the process, and it becomes overreliant on individual management style. Policy deployment can be viewed in the form of a wheel, as shown in figure 5.3, with business results at the hub, targets and means as the spokes, and catchball as the rim. What is required is an effective application of the PDCA cycle, as described by Akao (1991) and Kondo (1997), throughout this policy deployment wheel, not just in name but in action.

Mulligan et al. (1996) make a valid and astute observation: 'The image of catchball involves a group of children passing a ball (idea) amongst themselves while

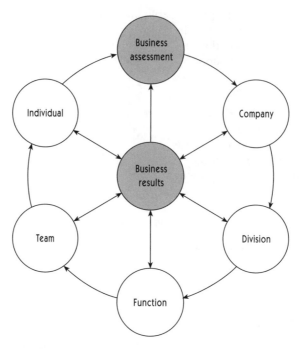

Figure 5.3 The policy deployment wheel

standing in a circle.' They go on to say that an alternative mnemonic 'CRIP' embodies the catchball concept more clearly. CRIP stands for check, reflect, improve and then pass the idea. Preferably, no one should pass on the idea immediately upon receipt, without first improving it. In this way, they believe a consensus is achieved with maximum participation and minimal conflict. However, more importantly, it prevents 'passing-the-buck' and, combined with PDCA, it can be used throughout the policy deployment process to monitor progress and continued relevance of objectives. Indeed, this whole cycle can become CAPD, when policy deployment begins with annual self-assessment, and the monitoring cycle begins with the 'check' step to ensure goals remain viable and appropriate; see Akao (1991).

One solution to the 'management' problem encountered with policy deployment is for organizations to adopt the CRISP approach. This is a development of the mnemonic CRIP, as briefly described by Mulligan et al. (1996) in relation to their discussion of hoshin kanri as a strategic planning method. CRISP stands for check, reflect, improve, scrutinize and then pass. The addition of 'scrutinize' to CRIP is an innovation which would solve the problems of unsatisfactory, incomplete policy deployment, management lack of commitment and attention to the process which, from our research, it is believed are the main issues. Furthermore, as well as being a useful mnemonic, the word CRISP has the added advantage of instilling the idea of a brisk, decisive manner to the way in which the process is conducted.

Essentially, CRISP entails each individual and team catching the policy, reflecting and improving upon it, but, before passing the policy up and down the hierarchal chain, having their work scrutinized by the previous level to ensure the reflection and improvement are in line with the original policy; see figure 5.4. This is the all important 'check' aspect in the PDCA cycle which often does not occur in an

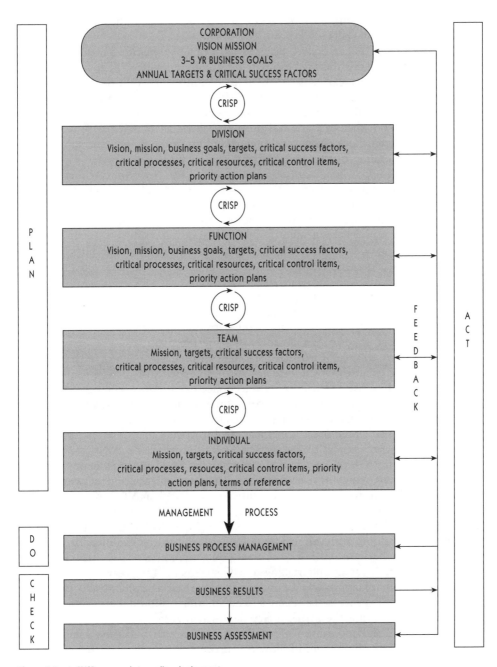

Figure 5.4 A CRISP approach to policy deployment

organization's deployment process. Although, at first sight, this approach may appear to add unnecessary bureaucracy to policy deployment and to extend the process time-frame, the addition of scrutiny does not have to be a viewed as a burden, because the CRISP approach has several advantages:

- Senior managers are required to demonstrate, and use, their leadership and communication skills.
- Senior managers can ensure that the right policy is being cascaded down the chain by checking their subordinate's planning activities.
- Senior managers can ensure there is commonality of policy deployment throughout the organization, that policy deployment is pervasive and that the whole organization is pulling together as one team in the same direction.
- Cross-functionality of plans and purpose will be facilitated.
- Managers can check employees' understanding of the policy, through scrutiny of their planning output and terms of reference.
- Middle and first-line managers are required to perform catchball-cascade because their team's plans and terms of reference will be checked by senior managers and middle managers respectively.
- Managers are required to communicate effectively in a team forum to ensure they meet senior management's scrutiny requirements.
- Managers would not be able to 'pass the policy deployment buck' without tailoring it, in conjunction with their team, because of senior management scrutiny.
- Managers would have an opportunity to demonstrate their leadership skills to senior managers throughout the process.
- Leadership and communication skill gaps can be identified, and personal development programmes organized during the process.
- Teams and individuals will see the catchball process in action when they are involved in scrutiny of the next level's improvement of their objectives.
- Teams and individuals will 'buy-in' to policy deployment when they see management using their feedback, become involved in its scrutiny, and have plans and objectives linked to company goals.
- It provides a 'closed-loop' for policy deployment.

The CRISP approach does not necessarily elongate the policy deployment process, if it is done efficiently. Much of the work should be done pre-policy deployment, with individuals and teams working cross-functionally to draft their VFO, plans and roles, responsibilities and objectives, after carrying out a self-assessment against a recognized model for business excellence, such as EFQM or MBNQA. In this manner, the pre-policy deployment work will form the basis of the catchball feedback up the chain, and form the framework for the final policy deployment activities. If CRISP is executed correctly, after undertaking a self-assessment, the workload during the policy deployment phase should be reduced. If the self-assessment and pre-policy deployment CRISP process has been successful, there should be no surprises or major reworks following the actual policy deployment.

An example of the application of a CRISP approach to policy deployment in a typical business unit (BU) would follow this process:

1 Prior to receiving the policy from the corporate organization, following self-assessment, each team/individual in the BU would go through a cross-functional process of defining their prioritized VFO, drafting plans and their terms of reference (TOR) for the following year. This would be fed up the chain through the BU using CRISP. Each higher level would catch the input from the subordinate teams/individuals, reflect upon it, improve upon it by

co-ordinating all cross-functional inputs, give the results of the improvement back to the originating teams/individuals for scrutiny to ensure that the original sense has not been subverted, and then pass it on to the next level. Finally, the general manager (GM) of the BU would pass on the BU prioritized VFO to the corporate organization for incorporation into their planning process.

2   On 'catching' the corporate organization's VFO, the senior management team, led by the GM, would reflect upon it in relation to the BU VFO they had already determined, noting complimentary and conflicting points. The senior management team would then improve the corporate organization's VFO using the previously determined BU VFO to produce the final version. The senior management team would pass their improved and BU specific VFO back to the corporate organization for scrutiny to ensure that the original sense of the deployed policy had not been distorted. On confirmation from the corporate organization that the BU VFO are acceptable, the senior management team would pass on the BU prioritized, cross-functionally co-ordinated policy – via the appropriate communication channels – to subordinate teams.

3   At the next function level, the team of line managers, led by a senior manager, would 'catch' the BU policy. The function team would reflect upon this policy, led by a senior manager who would show where their original input to the BU policy has been used to determine the BU VFO (highlighting catchball) and how the BU VFO are linked to the corporate organizations VFO. The team would then improve upon the BU VFO by linking their original and draft VFO to the BU VFO and determining a revised set of function specific VFO. Again, before the line managers deployed this policy to their teams, the function VFO would be passed back to the senior management team for scrutiny to ensure the interpretation and improvements were valid, that there were no cross-functional conflicts, and that the senior management's direction had been followed at the function level. As part of this scrutiny, the senior management team would check function, vision, mission, goals, objectives, targets, critical processes, resources, priority action plans, critical control items, and terms of reference (TORs). On passing scrutiny, the function line managers would communicate the deployed policy to their teams.

4   At team level, a similar process to the function level would occur and, finally, this would be deployed down to an individual level as necessary.

Following the successful use of the CRISP approach to policy deployment, each individual and team should see how their original input to the planning process, following self-assessment, has been used to generate the VFO and how their role is linked to the company policy. In this way, each employee will possess TORs that they have developed with their manager and are specifically tailored to support the VFO. They will also have a vision, mission, goals, objectives, targets and means that they have contributed to, and can understand in terms of their work and the company policy. Most of all, they will have played their part in policy deployment, been involved in catchball and bought in to the process.

The CRISP approach is a generic management technique which can be applied to any organization involved in a communication and feedback process; a model which shows the CRISP approach applied specifically to policy deployment is provided at figure 5.4. The model highlights how the PDCA cycle overlays the business process;

that using a CRISP approach policy is deployed throughout the company; and following the policy deployment process, how business process management results and self-assessment is linked to this cycle.

Summary

To ensure that the policy deployment process is effective, everyone in an organization needs to have proactive involvement in the cascade and catchball process, and this should be led by the senior management team. BUs and departments need to prioritize and co-ordinate their VFOs in an effective manner and, then, use these to identify and prioritize the processes which need to undergo improvements.

During the PDCA cycle of policy deployment, managers should focus on the 'check' rather than the 'act', which employees should be empowered to do. However, this check should not be used as an excuse for management to neglect their responsibility to inspect their subordinate's work. One method of ensuring that the cascade and catchball of policy deployment is effective and closed loop, is to adopt the CRISP approach as already described and to encourage managers to demonstrate effective leadership and communication.

Throughout the policy deployment literature – e.g. Dale (1990), Akao (1991), Hill (1994), Kondo (1997) there is a constant emphasis on the PDCA cycle in strategic planning and daily control. CRISP strengthens the catchball process which represents the PDCA cycle between organizational levels, and facilitates Kogure's (1995) 'pattern 4' of policy content and level of issuer, by forcing managers to conduct policy deployment and to have their activities scrutinized before passing the improved targets and means up or down the hierarchy. At each management level, they are having their work checked by superiors and checking their subordinates (and vice versa) and, in this way, allowing everyone to exercise and demonstrate leadership and commitment.

Hoshin kanri or policy deployment is simply PDCA applied to the planning and execution of a few critical strategic organization objectives. It is an essential element of TQM, and is slowly being acknowledged by authors such as Lascelles and Peacock (1996) and van der Wiele et al. (1996) as an essential link with self-assessment. Although policy deployment is best used by sophisticated organizations that are a long way down the TQM road, the authors believe that fundamental elements such as catchball can be used by less advanced companies to develop leadership and employee involvement, and to lay the foundation for future use of the full policy deployment approach.

References

Akao, Y. 1991: *Hoshin Kanri: Policy Deployment for successful TQM*. Cambridge, MA: Productivity Press Inc.

Dale, B. G. 1990: Policy deployment. *The TQM Magazine*, December, 321–4.

Eureka, W. E. and Ryan, N. E. 1990: *The Process-Driven Business: Managerial Perspectives on Policy Management*. Dearborn: ASI Press.

Fortuna, P. M. and Vaziri, K. H. 1992: *Orchestrating Change: Policy Deployment, Total Quality: A Manager's Guide for the 1990s*, The Ernst and Young Quality Improvement Consulting Company, Kogan Page, London.

Goal/QPC Research Committee. 1994: Hoshin planning: a planning system for implementing total quality management. In H. I. Costin (ed.), *Readings in Total Quality Management*, London: Dryden Press.

Hill, D. 1994: Policy deployment (Hoshin Kanri) in Durham, *Philips Quality Matters*, ISS56, Philips Elections, Eindhouen, The Netherlands, 11–13.

Imai, M. 1986: *Kaizen: the Key to Japan's Competitive Success*. New York: Random House Business Division.

Integrated Quality Dynamics, (1997), TQM: Hoshin, http://www.iqd.com:80/hoshin.htm

Juran, J. M. 1964: *Managerial Breakthrough*. New York: McGraw Hill.

Kano, N. 1995: A perspective on quality activities in American firms. In J. D. Hromi (ed.), *The Best on Quality: Targets, Improvements*, Milwaukee: ASQC Quality Press, Vol. 6, Ch. 16.

Kendrick, J. J. 1988: Managing quality: Lighting up quality. *Quality*, 27(6), 16–20.

Kogure, M. 1995: Some fundamental problems on Hoshin Kanri in Japanese TQC. In J. D. Hromi (ed.), *The Best on Quality: Targets, Improvements, Systems*, USA: Milwaukee, ASQC Press, Vol. 6, Ch. 23.

Kondo, Y. 1997: The Hoshin Kanri – Japanese way of strategic quality management. *Proceedings of 41st Congress of the European Organization for Quality*, Trondheim, Norway, June, Vol. 1, 241–50.

Lascelles, D. and Peacock, R. 1996: *Self-assessment for business excellence*. Maidenhead: McGraw Hill Book Company.

Lee, R. G. and Dale, B. G. 1998: Policy Deployment: An Examination of the Theory. *International Journal of Quality and Reliability Management*, 15(5), 520–40.

Lee, R. G. and Dale, B. G. 1999: Policy deployment: modelling the process. *Proceedings of the Institution of Mechanical Engineers*, (under consideration)

Mulligan, P., Hatten, K. and Miller, J. 1996: From issue-based planning to Hoshin: different styles for different situations. *Long Range Planning*, 29(4), 473–84.

Newcomb, J. E. 1989: Management by policy deployment. *Quality*, 28(1), 29–30.

Robinson, R. 1994: Goal deployment: getting everyone aiming at the same target. *Tapping the Network Journal*, 5(3), 8–11.

Total Quality Engineering 1997: *Hoshin Planning*, http://www.tqe.com:80/tqehelp/hoshin.html

van der Wiele, A., Williams, A. R. T., Dale, B. G., Carter, G., Kolb, F., Luzon, D. M., Schmidt, A. and Wallace, M. 1996: Quality management self-assessment: an examination in European business. *Journal of General Management*, 22(1), 48–67.

Watson, G. 1991: Understanding Hoshin Kanri. In Y. Akao (ed.), *Hoshin Kanri: Policy Deployment for Successful TQM*, Cambridge, Mass.: Productivity Press.

Woll, T. 1996: Mutual learning has corporations sharing good ideas. *Boston Business Journal*, 16(41), 22–3.

Wood, G. R. and Munshi, K. F. 1991: Hoshin Kanri: a systematic approach to breakthrough improvement. *Total Quality Management*, 2(3), 213–26.

chapter six

Designing for Quality

B. G. Dale

Introduction

Any product or service competes according to performance, appearance, price, delivery, reliability, durability, safety and maintainability; all of these depend fundamentally upon the design. Three factors are of fundamental importance to those responsible for developing a new product, and to those who will be responsible for using or operating the product:

1 Performance – will the performance of the product meet the expectations and needs of the end user?
2 Cost – what will be the cost, not only of developing and producing the product, but also of operating and maintaining and eventually disposing of it? (life cycle cost)
3 Timescale – will the product be available when required?

The customer's satisfaction with a product, and the reputation of the product and of its supplier, depends to a considerable degree on how well these factors are managed and harmonized during the various phases of the product life cycle.

Quality, reliability and durability cannot be inspected into a product, they must be designed in by the effective and accurate translation of customer requirements into practical designs and specifications that permit production, maintenance and servicing to be technically and economically feasible. The role of the design function is to translate customer requirements from the product/design brief into practical designs and specifications for materials, product and processes.

Failure, in the design stage, to take full account of environmental conditions, or simple errors of judgement can have far reaching consequences; the same is the case with respect to a design error reaching production undetected. All the evidence from bodies such as the Design Council indicates that the performance and appearance of many products could be substantially improved which, in turn, helps to increase

---

* This chapter is based on Dale and Oakland (1994).

market appeal and reduce production costs. A poorly designed product may damage a company's reputation, particularly if the product is unreliable, unsafe or difficult to maintain and repair. In general terms, these determine the quality of a design:

- The degree to which the functional requirements have been expressed in the design
- The degree to which the specification requirements have been realized
- The degree to which the design permits rational production and marketing
- The efforts made to attain a reasonable life (or failure rate) with low maintenance costs
- The speedy feedback of new experience and quality troubles

Senior management must integrate their business objectives into design, development, production/operations and marketing to ensure quality. To manage design effectively, some information needs to be known:

- What business is the organization in?
- What are the quantified targets for growth and profitability?
- What is the identity and market position being sought?

This information should be communicated to, and understood by, all concerned. BS7000-1 provides useful guidance on the management of product design.

This chapter explores the key activities of the design function, and highlights the importance of the design activity in TQM.

Design Planning and Objectives

Responsibilities must be assigned for various design duties to activities inside and/or outside the organization. The need to identify, and to control, design interfaces with other functions cannot be overemphasized. Designers need to be creative, but their work should be controlled where it affects others. It is also essential that the design team is not isolated from other disciplines; in particular, operations, QA, engineering and marketing.

The need for a design and development programme will depend upon the nature and complexity of the specified requirements. The programme generally consists of a breakdown of the design processes into separate elements; this can be presented as a chart showing the different activities against a time-scale, with key events and design reviews indicated. The extent of each phase, and the stages at which design reviews take place, may depend upon the product or service application, its design complexity, the extent of innovation and technology, the degree of standardization and similarity with previous designs.

In addition to customer needs, the designer should give consideration to the requirements relating to safety, environmental and other regulations, and should adequately define characteristics important to quality. The designer must not prescribe irrational tolerance limits in the specification. At the same time, the tolerances should represent the requirements that may exist for interchangeability. Here is a common argument used for the setting of 'tight' tolerances by the design function: 'If we set realistic tolerances the production/operations function will only claim that they cannot hold them. Therefore, if they are set deliberately tight at the outset, it will not matter if they are subsequently relaxed.'

The Main Stages in Design and Development

The design and development stage normally follows a chronological sequence and is presented in four stages:

1 Conceptual design
2 Embodiment design
3 Detail design
4 Design for manufacture

See figure 6.1 taken from BS7000-1. These stages are now described in brief.

Conceptual design

This is the stage of the design process in which ideas and working principles for the product are conceived. Such ideas only need to contain that detail necessary to define the essential elements of the idea or concept.

Embodiment design

This stage lays the foundation for detail design through a structured development of the concept. At the conclusion of this stage, most areas of design uncertainty should

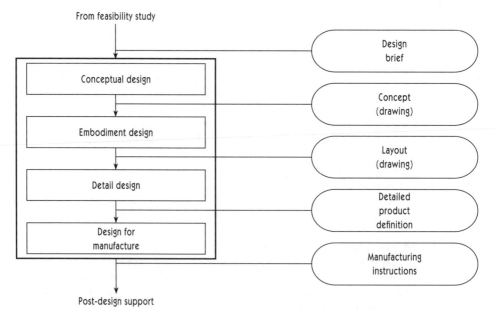

Figure 6.1 Idealized design process
Source: BS7000-1 (1993)

have been resolved, and much of the development and model testing carried out. The output will be in the form of data sufficient for full-scale models to be made, if required, and detail design to be undertaken. It is appropriate to conduct a design review at the completion of this stage.

Detail design

In this stage, the final details of the design are completed. Lack of adequate attention to detail design can lead to many problems, including delays in the design process and final designs that fail to meet the design brief. A design review at, or during, the completion of this stage is essential.

Design for manufacture

The completion of the detail design will not necessarily result in instructions suitable for the manufacture of the product; some important procedures are necessary:

- Control of the interface design (the design of multiple component products by teams needs controls to ensure compatibility of, and interface between, components without detriment to product performance)
- Control of manufacturing instructions (also known as configuration control)
- Checking the manufacturing instructions

These features enhance the quality in product design and should be considered from the conceptual stage:

- Avoiding unnecessary complexity – an easily manufactured product/component gives rise to less risk of process error, additional costs and quality-related troubles and where appropriate, existing and proven components of known cost and reliability should be used
- Avoiding unnecessary variety – if components are designed and specified for common usage, this results in longer production runs of fewer different parts with economic and quality advantages
- Avoiding unnecessary costs
- Minimizing or eliminating features known to cause quality troubles

Design, Maintainability and Safety

The responsibility for satisfying the product brief – with a product that can be produced at a cost and which allows a profitable return on investment – rests primarily with the designer. Cost is just as much an attribute of the design specification as are performance, appearance, reliability, life, and safety, and is an essential factor to be satisfied by the optimum design solution. A design that fails to meet its cost specification is no better than one that fails to satisfy its performance requirements. Whatever organizational approach is adopted to achieve more economic designs, it will ultimately depend on people. An additional benefit of management cost control is that it requires the co-operation of all departments and, thereby, opens up more channels of communication and opportunities for co-operation. Cost reduction must be a totally integrated activity and, increasingly, the designers' job is one of co-ordination, and integration, of the sometimes conflicting interests of all departments.

The designer is responsible for the achievement of operational requirements, including maintainability requirements in design within the usual constraints of schedules and costs. To satisfy these requirements, maintainability should be specified at the beginning of the design process and maintainability studies, as appropriate, should be performed during this process. Figure 6.2 illustrates the way in which maintainability studies and their sequences relate to design tasks.

BS6548-2 provides guidance on studies, which should be carried out during the design phase, and on the relationship of these studies to maintainability and maintenance support tasks. The purpose of maintainability studies is to assist design decision making, to predict the quantitative maintainability characteristics of an item, and to help in the evaluation of alternative design options. Maintainability studies should be developed, and integrated with the design process to meet the stated system operational requirements. To ensure that these requirements are met, maintainability studies should be carried out during all phases of design, and their results should provide inputs to decision making.

Maintainability analysis, an integral part of maintainability studies, is a process which translates operational requirements into detailed qualitative and quantitative maintainability requirements and design criteria. It provides inputs to the design process by means of documentation under these headings:

- Specific maintainability requirements to be met in the design
- Design guidelines and checklists to ensure that the required maintainability features are included in the design
- A summary of basic maintenance functions and support requirements

Maintainability analyses are involved in iterative design trade-off studies, a number of which may be required before the optimum design is selected. They should also be used to evaluate the extent of achievement of the maintainability design requirements.

At the outset of the design process, national and international legal requirements that may place constraints on designs and designers must be identified. These are not only concerned with the aspect of health and safety of material but also with the avoidance of danger to persons and property when material is being used, stored, transported, or tested. There is an increasing amount of legislation which places certain constraints on designs and which must be taken into account prior to the production of products and services for sale. In the UK, the Consumer Protection Act (1987) has introduced a major legal requirement for product safety and product liability and BS8800 is increasingly being used by organizations in developing a safety management system.

It is necessary for the design function to recognize factors that may have concealed danger potential. As far as possible, such elements should be eliminated from the design or be in accordance with 'fail safe' principles. The increasing use of new materials and 'performance' specifications can also present certain safety problems for designers.

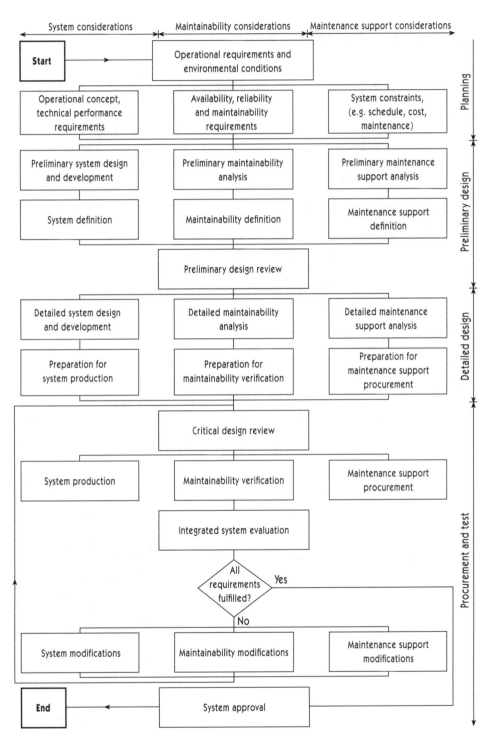

Figure 6.2 Maintainability studies in the design process
Source: BS6548-2 (1992)

Design and Standardization Philosophy

The time span between a good, practical idea and the manufacture of a marketable product will always be uncertain, and many products have reached the market place too late. The BS7000 series is about using a methodology to improve the systematic design, development, market research, planning and development of the manufacturing process; used as an audit tool and *aide-mémoire*, it can help in the design process. One of the key factors in the management of product design is the drafting and management of clear, accurate and comprehensive specifications.

The earliest point at which component, material or even manufacturing process, standardization can be applied is at the design stage. Involving standardization as a function in new designs can result in constructive suggestions that are unlikely otherwise to be made.

Standardization is the result of the compromise between the opposing forces of customer demand and economic necessity. It is now a prime requirement in economic design and production. Further, it must be a principal aim carried right through a company's organizational structure. The aims and results of standardization are shown in figure 6.3, from PD3542.

Standardization, in its broadest sense, is the discipline of using the minimum number of different materials and parts for the maximum application, produced by the most economical manufacturing processes, of the appropriate quality to give reliable and acceptable performance at minimum cost. It is an essential tool for organizations which diversify to spread the risk over a wider sector of the market since, if control is not applied, the increased variety of materials can undo the beneficial effects.

Unnecessary design variations cause variation in the use of operational resources, in the purchase and storage of materials, the operation of processes and, indeed, in managerial and design work. Since variations of one kind or another may have crept

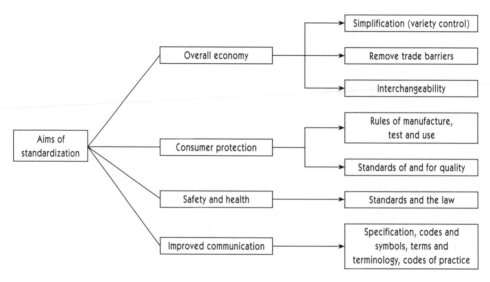

Figure 6.3 Aims and results of standardization
Source: PD3542 (1988)

into a company's products or services, processes, and procedures over a period of years, they are not always easily eliminated unless external influence is brought to bear. The majority of new designs are evolved rather than invented, and an organization cannot afford to keep on 'rediscovering the wheel'. As the rate of new discovery and the depth of past experience increases, so does the importance of recording and retaining the best practices to ensure consistency in approach and methods used in the future.

As the user, as well as the creator of materials, the designer is expected to incorporate those features and parameters which have an assured availability and quality. It is important that national and international standards are incorporated at company level. The person in the company responsible for standards can assist the designer by obtaining background information on the relevant standards and ensuring that this information is communicated effectively.

The ideal situation is when an organization offers a product or service in which all components are identical and are all generated in an identical manner. There are many products and services that, while having similar functions, must be offered in a range of forms, sizes, or capacities, while others may have a generic similarity but perform different tasks. There are also products and services that are dissimilar in character but may contain common features.

It is important that the company policy on the use of external and internal standards is clear. Management has a duty to guide the designer in these respects and it can do this by means of codes of practice on the design policy to be followed. The scope and benefits of standards in design are listed here.

- To employ a reliable design control policy to satisfy ISO9001
- To provide a facility capable of recording key aspects of product design, so taking full advantage of previously used techniques in the evolution of new ones
- To ensure that unproved new parts and methods do not proliferate while, at the same time, not inhibiting exploitation of technological developments
- To simplify the communication of the necessary technical requirements to the production department and to improve project scheduling

Designers have a significant role in the effective use of standards:

- To implement international, national and company standards as a means of complying with market requirements and health and safety legislation
- To initiate product standards which make good design and economic production/operations activities
- To consolidate existing designs and to allow the free movement of design services to other areas
- To implement the setting of quality and reliability standards
- To maintain the effective use of existing resources and deployment of capital on new process equipment

The Standards Manual

Standards are of importance to companies as a means of removing barriers to trade, of achieving economies in production/operations, of regularizing procedures, and of specifying performance and quality. Furthermore, standards are sometimes referred to in legislation, either in contractual use or in trade descriptions. In every organization, there is a need to establish standards that will harmonize with, and make use of, relevant national and international standards, and which will improve productivity through better design, reduced variety, improved quality and lower unit costs.

It is necessary to document these standards so that they are available for reference, to classify them according to their subject and type, and to publish them in a company standards manual. The scope of the manual may include all areas of company activity, covering materials, bought out items, manufactured parts, design practices, quality and inspection procedures, and production/operations processes.

The primary purpose of a company standards manual is to communicate standards information so as to derive the available benefits.

- Control of unnecessary variety
- Improved management control
- Improved QA
- Provision of a central source of information
- Promotion of value engineering
- Provision of on-the-job reference information
- Clarification of responsibilities
- Improved product or service safety
- Information for training new staff
- Uniform interpretation of policies
- Auditing of procedures
- Visible proof of standardization and organization
- Demonstration of the company's quality system to customers

Although most companies recognize the need for standardization, they sometimes have no form of standards manual and, in many cases, there is little evidence that standards exist. In such situations, 'quick fixes' are applied and no long-term corrective measures are put in place, which may result in the same problem occurring at some future date.

Variety Control

Considerable costs can be incurred by a lack of attention to variety control at the design stage. The introduction of each new part, material, or method will be reflected by increased costs in design, production/operations planning, purchasing, stores, inspection, assembly, etc.

Some sophisticated methods exist for classifying and coding materials, parts, and commodities so that they can be retrieved at a later date. This avoids the introduction of new parts or materials, where satisfactory ones exist. The cost of such systems, and their degree of sophistication, should be weighed against the benefits, which may depend to some extent on the size, complexity and type of industry or operation. In most cases, the use of a simple classification system can separate items or materials that are likely to be repeated. The cataloguing and coding of materials and parts also has the advantage that the code can be used instead of the full description.

The scope and benefits of variety control in the design department may be summarized:

- Provision of standardized data to reduce design time
- Provision of a standards handbook as a training aid and a source of basic standards to maintain continuity of design
- Coding and cataloguing of all materials and parts including purchase specifications for reliable identification
- Design and control of company coding systems to avoid duplication and ambiguity
- Formulation of design and manufacturing specifications to clarify work instructions
- Technical information service and advice on national and international standards to reflect the state of the art

Variety reduction is sometimes confused with variety control. The former is a retrospective operation to reduce existing variety; this can be expensive because of the effect on existing designs, specification, planning layouts and materials. Even with the best means of variety control, periodic exercises of this kind may still be needed, because of the development of production or operational facilities, modification to the product or service range, company mergers or supply difficulties.

Value Engineering

The technique and philosophy of value engineering on a product/service being designed, or value analysis on an existing product/service, is based on simple concepts, but its effective use can be realized only through the co-ordinated effort of a team of specialists. There are six steps to all value engineering exercises:

1 *Selection* of the product or service, part, or sub-assembly or component for investigation: The product/service or operation under study must offer a benefit. Identification of high absolute cost outputs, comparison with competitors' products, or a sudden material price rise or shortage can all aid selection.

2 *Information*: this stage involves collection of all the relevant facts about the product, part or service, e.g. design criteria, production/operations methods, detailed costs, customer usage, expected product/service lifetime, and maintenance. It requires the fullest co-operation of all those involved in the design, production/operations, QA, and marketing of the product or service.

3 *Analysis*: the next step is to analyse the functions the product/service performs, to rank these in order of priority and to assign, as accurately as possible, the costs attributable to each function. A grid or matrix may be used for this function/cost analysis. The purpose is to identify items of poor value for further investigation.

4 *Speculation* on ways of improving poor value items requires a broad knowledge of alternative design strategies, materials and production/operations techniques. Although this activity may be called brainstorming, brainwriting, creative or lateral thinking, it is important that such thinking includes more mundane,

but equally vital, ideas such as standardization of materials or parts, elimination of unnecessary variety, grouping of components or service elements, etc.

5   *Evaluation*: most effort is normally expended at this stage because the reward for the correct evaluation of a good idea can be considerable, and the penalty for a mistake can be even greater. Detailed information is required on the performance, cost and availability of alternative materials or methods required. Similarly, the dependence of costs on tolerances, grade, size, shape, level of service, quantities, etc. must be ascertained.

6   *Implementation*: if the value engineering investigation has been an integrated company activity then this stage will be relatively simple. Monitoring of the results is, in any event, a necessary final step in the value engineering exercise.

Here is a convenient *aide-mémoire* for the steps in value engineering:

- What is it?
- What does it do?
- What does it cost?
- What else will do the job?
- What does that cost?

Whatever the precise techniques, value engineering is much more than cost reduction. Value, measured in terms of quality, performance and reliability at an acceptable price or, in other words, customer satisfaction and customer delight is the overall aim.

Design Qualification and Validation

It is important that the design process provides periodic evaluation, including an analysis of the reliability implications of all parts, materials and processes of the design at significant stages in its development. Such evaluation can take the form of analytical methods, such as FMEA (discussed in chapter 17), and FTA, as well as inspection or test of prototype models or services and actual output samples. The amount and degree of such examination is related to the risks identified in the design plan. Independent evaluation may be employed, as appropriate, to verify original calculations, provide alternative calculations or to perform tests. To provide statistical confidence in the results, an adequate numbers of samples must be examined by testing, checking or inspecting. The tests can include these activities:

- Evaluation of performance, durability, safety, reliability and maintainability under expected storage and operational conditions
- Inspections to verify that all design features are as intended and that all authorized design changes have been accomplished and recorded
- Validation of computer systems and software

Fault tree analysis (FTA)

FTA is concerned with the identification and analysis of conditions and factors which cause or contribute to the occurrence of a defined undesirable event, usually one which significantly affects system performance, economy, safety or other required characteristics. It is suitable for the analyses of single failure modes involving complex failure logic and redundancy.

The fault tree is an organized graphical representation of the conditions or other factors causing or contributing to the occurrence of a defined undesirable event, referred to as the 'top event'. The tree is in a form which can be understood, analysed and, as necessary, rearranged to facilitate the identification of important information:

- Factors affecting the reliability and performance characteristics of the system, e.g. component fault modes, operator mistakes, environmental conditions and software faults
- Conflicting requirements or specifications which may affect reliable performance
- Common events affecting more than one functional component, which would cancel the benefits of specific redundancies

FTA is basically a deductive (top-down) method of analysis aimed at pinpointing the causes, or combinations of causes, that can lead to the defined top event. The analysis is mainly qualitative but, depending on certain conditions, it may also be quantitative. There are several reasons for performing FTA independently of, or in conjunction with, other dependability analyses:

- The identification of the causes or combinations of causes leading to the top event
- The determination of whether a particular system reliability measure meets a stated requirement
- The demonstration that assumptions made in other analyses, regarding the independence of systems and non-relevance of failures, are not violated
- The determination of the factor(s) which most seriously affect a particular reliability measure, and the changes required to improve that measure
- The identification of common events or common cause failures

The fault tree is particularly suited to the analysis of complex systems comprising several functionally related or dependent sub-systems with different performance objectives. This is especially true whenever the system design requires the collaboration of many specialized technical design groups.

These are the principal benefits of the FTA techniques:

- It gives the designers an insight into the structure of the system.
- It is possible for the analyst to produce a list of all possible serious component fault combinations, some of which may not have been considered by the designers, including any single point failures.
- It permits the effects of external factors beyond the control of the designers to be analysed (such as human error and weather).
- When the relevant data are available, the probability of the top event and, hence, possibly the system reliability or availability can be estimated.

These are the main limitations of the FTA techniques:

- The analysis can be time consuming.
- It has to be repeated for each top event.

For these reasons, it is often the case that only those top events that are judged to occur most commonly, or those judged to have more important safety implications, are analysed.

Design Review and Audit

Purpose and organization

A design review can be defined as a formal, documented and systematic critical study of a design proposal by specialists who are not necessarily engaged in the design process. The participants at the design review generally include representatives of all functions affecting quality as appropriate to the phase being reviewed. This review is different from a project progress meeting, which is primarily concerned with time and cost. The prime objective of a design review procedure is to provide a preventive evaluation to identify and to anticipate problem areas and inadequacies, and to initiate corrective actions to ensure that the final design and supporting data meet customer requirements; it can also encourage constructive participation of an optimum design.

At the conclusion of each phase of the design development cycle, a review of the design should be conducted:

- Preliminary reviews at the time of product or service concept and planning proposal, bid, or request for funds, and also when a contract or authorization is received
- Intermediate reviews when the following are completed: block or function diagram, flow design, equipment design, styling, and development model tests
- Final reviews when material lists and specifications are complete, or when pre-production units are tested and analysed

The extent of design review, the methods to be used and the composition of the review team will depend upon the nature of the product/service application, its design complexity, the degree of standardization, the state of the art, the competence of the design originator and the degree of similarity with past proven designs.

Following completion of a review, it is usual for a final report to be submitted to the responsible executive to summarize the recommendations made and any modifications subsequently incorporated in a design. However, the final authority for design decisions rests with the designer and his/her design manager.

BS5760-14 provides useful advice on design reviews and is commended as an essential complement to the BS7000 series.

Elements of design reviews

It is useful to establish a checklist of factors for the design review. As appropriate to the design phase and product or service, these are typical of the elements to be considered:

- Items pertaining to customer needs and satisfaction

    - Comparison of customer needs expressed in the product/service brief with specifications for materials, products or services and processes
    - Validation of the design through prototype tests
    - Ability to perform under expected conditions of use and environment
    - Considerations of unintended uses and misuses
    - Safety and environmental compatibility
    - Compliance with regulatory requirements, national and international standards, and corporate practices
    - Comparisons with competitive designs
    - Comparison with similar designs, especially analysis of internal and external problem history to avoid repeating problems

- Items pertaining to product specification and service requirements

    - Reliability, durability, serviceability, and maintainability requirements
    - Permissible specification tolerances and comparison with process capabilities
    - Product/service acceptance/rejection criteria
    - Ease of assembly and installation, storage needs, shelf-life, and disposability
    - Benign failure and fail-safe characteristics
    - Aesthetic specifications and acceptance criteria
    - FMEA and FTA
    - Ability to diagnose and correct problems
    - Labelling, warnings, identification, traceability requirements, and user instructions
    - Review and use of standard materials or parts

- Items pertaining to process specifications and service requirements

    - Producibility of the design, including special process needs, mechanization, automation, assembly and installation of components
    - Capability to inspect and check out the design, including any special inspections and check requirements
    - Specification of materials, including approved supplies and suppliers, as well as availability
    - Packaging, handling, storage and shelf-life requirements, especially safety factors relating to incoming and outgoing materials or items

Design verification

Design verification may be undertaken independently or in support of design reviews by applying these methods:

- Alternative calculations, made to verify the correctness of the original calculations and analyses
- Testing, e.g. by model or prototype tests or trials of the service
- Independent verification, to verify the correctness of the original calculations and/or other design activities

Design audit

It is usual to carry out a critical examination of the design so as to ensure that there will be an acceptable level of reliability and maintainability in operational use. This audit is carried out by staff who are independent of the design process, and should cover all activities from the design concept to testing, installation, operation, degradation of performance in service, and maintenance. The audit will help to identify any design weaknesses requiring modifications but should not offer a solution; this is the province of the designer.

Design baseline and production/operations release

The results of the final design review need to be appropriately documented in specifications and drawings that define the design baseline. The total document package that defines the design baseline will require approval at appropriate levels of management affected by, or contributing to, the product or service. This approval constitutes the production/operations release and signifies that the design can be realized.

An objective of the design process is to produce clear and comprehensive data that contains the information necessary for purchasing, production/operations, inspection, tests, checks and maintenance; this data usually consists of specifications and instructions. Procedures are also prescribed for the identification and revision status of design documents, records of changes made and their distribution, control and recall.

Product Testing and Measurement

Testing is a normal part of any product development for reasons such as: improvements in performance, function and quality and optimization of clearances. It is usual to include an analysis of materials and processes proposed in the design during the design and development phase, with regard to the known reliability and producibility of such parts. If innovation in materials or techniques is proposed, then the desirability from both design and operational stand points should be analysed and/or tested to justify adoption in preference to established alternatives.

Although tests to destruction are neither possible nor feasible with certain products, one of the more successful ways of ensuring the quality and, in particular, the reliability of systems, equipment, and parts is through R&D. With this, attempts are made to simulate actual operational and environmental conditions on a test basis, the samples of product or operations being representative of the envisaged or actual product or service. When used in the preventative rather than the assessment sense, development can be beneficial, especially where the QA function is working in conjunction with design and development functions to monitor and feed-back the necessary data as a basis for future modifications.

The methods of measurement, check and test, and the acceptance criteria applied to evaluate the product, service, and processes, during both the design and production/operations phases need to be specified. Here are the parameters:

- Performance target values, tolerances, and attribute features
- Acceptance and rejection criteria
- Test, check and measurement methods, equipment, bias and precision requirements, and computer software considerations

Evaluation of the Design Process

An evaluation of the actual product design process should be carried out to establish whether the plans made to achieve the objectives set out in the design brief were adequate, whether estimated times and costs were accurate and whether the general management of the product design function was satisfactory. A review of the progress of the design project will reveal areas where improvements can be made for the next product design venture. The evaluation of the design process should examine both company procedures and those that are specific to the project; it is essential to record data during the progress of the project to assist the evaluation.

The person responsible for the design function should answer these questions when evaluating a specific design activity:

- Were all the objectives achieved?
- Was the planning comprehensive?
- Was the work completed within the planned time?
- Were the costs of the activity within the budget?
- Were the design staff understretched or overstretched?
- Were training needs identified?
- Were recruitment needs identified?
- Were the procedures specific to the project adequate? Did they interface properly with the standard procedures?

Document (or Design) Change Control and Feedback

It is necessary for an organization to have in place a procedure for controlling the release, change and use of documents that define the design baseline and for authorizing the necessary work to be performed to implement changes that may affect the product or service during its entire life cycle. All design modifications made after the design has reached the point of release for production/operations are regarded as changes. These also should be governed by design change control measures, if the achieved and demonstrated reliability is not to be unacceptably reduced by later design changes made for non-reliability reasons; the later in the process the change is made, the more costly it will be. The use of QFD (discussed in chapter 15) helps to reduce the number of design and document changes.

In industries where innovation, redesign, and product improvement are continuously practised, control of changes is of critical importance to product or service quality and reliability. However, it should not be forgotten that the main reason why organizations face problematical engineering changes is that the design was a problem to begin with.

Rarely, if ever, does a product go onto the market without some engineering changes being effected during its initial introduction phase. In the launch of a new product design, essential design changes usually arise in the development and manufacture stages. Dale (1982) gives these reasons for design and document changes:

- To make the product work, to help the product to achieve its specification, to make it possible to manufacture it, etc.
- To take advantage of improvements in manufacturing technology during the product's life cycle
- To meet the need to improve the life, quality conformance, reliability, maintainability, serviceability, safety, attractiveness, etc. of the product
- To reduce production costs, to facilitate changes in supplier, to improve the flexibility of sourcing, to reduce distribution costs, etc.

One unavoidable cause of design changes is the permanent loss of supply for a component or material. A single source manufacturer may discontinue the production of a part or a type of grade of raw material from an overseas source may become unavailable owing to political events.

The design (or document) change procedure should provide for various necessary approvals, specified points and times for implementing changes, removing obsolete drawings and specifications from work areas, and verification that changes are made at the appointed times and places.

There are a number of factors to consider in design change procedure:

- How the change is to be classified
- The subject of interchangeability
- The structure, organization and responsibility of the design change committee
- When the change is to be implemented
- The change procedure itself, along with the relevant documentation

Balcerak and Dale (1992) have carried out research into design change control, the main findings of their work are summarized here:

- Engineering changes can be usefully and objectively classified by two separate criteria, namely type (which indicates the impact of the change on the various departments of the company) and grade (which indicates the urgency with which a change should be processed).
- For each engineering change, it is the responsibility of the engineering change committee to answer two questions: Is the engineering change commercially justifiable? If it is, then when should it be implemented?
- Six determinants of engineering change effectively were identified: market forces; drawing office work; availability of replacement parts or raw materials; stock run out; availability of replacement tools; and tool wear.
- All but the simplest engineering changes require more than one determinant to be considered, when deciding the optimum effectivity date.
- Feedback from manufacturing areas, essential to the success of an engineering change procedures, provides information on the status of individual changes, a measure of the performance of the engineering change procedure, and experience, based upon which effectivity estimating can be improved in the future.

It is important that the experience gained from previous designs and user experience is employed in current and future designs. For this to be effective, accurate notes need to be kept, all data analysed, and the analysis fed back so that the necessary corrective action can be planned and implemented. To facilitate this, a procedure is often established to encompass recording, reporting, analysis and distribution of information gained during production or operations, assembly, installation, commissioning, servicing and field use. There must be a constant evaluation of the situation throughout the life of the product/service not just during the stages of development.

Summary

This chapter has argued the importance of design as a means for organizations to sustain their competitive edge. It has made the point that the market-place is now very demanding in terms of its design requirements. There is also pressure to reduce the time taken from conception of an idea to the launch of a product/service to the market-place. Consequently, the design process needs to become smarter and more proactive. This can be facilitated by the use of a number of quality management tools and techniques such as QFD and FMEA, as well as the traditional methods of value engineering and design reviews.

There is a need for organizations to adopt a systematic approach to design, and the key elements of this have been examined in the chapter. It is also important that design is not pursued in isolation from other disciplines. Concepts such as simultaneous engineering should be used to ensure that a team approach to design is followed, and that the views and inputs from other functions are sought and listened to.

References

Balcerak, K. J. and Dale, B. G. 1992: Engineering change administration: the key issues. *Computer-Integrated Manufacturing Systems*, 5(2), 125–32.

Dale, B. G. 1982: The management of engineering change procedures. *Engineering Management International*, 1(3), 201–208.

Dale, B. G. and Oakland, J. S. 1994: Designing for quality. In B. G. Dale and J. S. Oakland, *Quality Improvement Through Standards*, in conjunction with the British Standards Institution, Cheltenham: Stanley Thornes, 99–134.

chapter seven

Quality Costing*

B. G. Dale

Introduction

This chapter defines quality costs and explains why they are important to management. It also outlines how to determine, report and use quality-related costs.

Ideas of what constitute quality costs have changed rapidly in recent years. Whereas only a few years ago the costs of quality were perceived as the cost of running the QA department and the laboratory, plus scrap and warranty costs, it is now widely accepted that they are the costs incurred in designing, implementing, operating and maintaining a quality management system, the costs involved in introducing and sustaining a process of continuous improvement, plus the costs incurred owing to failures of systems, processes, products and/or services. Quality costs arise from a range of activities (such as, the functions of sales and marketing, design, R&D, purchasing, storage, handling, production planning and control, production/operations, delivery, installation and service) make, in some way, a contribution to these costs. Suppliers, sub-contractors, stockists, distributors, agents, dealers, and especially customers can all influence the incidence and level of these costs.

Quality-related costs commonly range from 5–25 per cent of a company's annual sales turnover or operating costs in public sector type operations, depending on the 'industry' and the way in which the company manages quality and the improvement process. Of this cost, 95 per cent is expended on appraisal and failure. Reducing failure costs by eliminating causes of failure can also lead to substantial reductions in appraisal costs. Quality costs may be reduced to one-third of their current level by the use of a cost-effective quality management system (Dale and Plunkett, 1990).

Definition and Categorization of Quality Costs

The importance of definitions to the collection, analysis and use of quality costs cannot be over-stressed. Without clear definitions, there can be no common understanding

* Barrie Dale is indebted to the late Dr Jim Plunkett for the use of some of his research findings to be used in this chapter.

or meaningful communication on the topic. The definition of what constitutes quality costs is by no means straightforward, and there are many grey areas where production and operation procedures and practices overlap with quality-related activities. Quality costs may be regarded as a criterion of quality performance – but only if valid comparisons can be made between different sets of cost data. Clearly, the comparability of sets of data is dependent on the definitions of the categories and elements used in compiling them. If definitions are not established and accepted, the only alternative would be to qualify every item of data so that at least it might be understood, even though it may not be comparable with other data. The value of much of the published data on quality-related costs is questionable because of the absence of precise definition and lack of qualification.

Many definitions of quality-related costs are in fairly specious terms. Admittedly, there are difficulties in preparing unambiguous acceptable definitions and in finding generic terms to describe tasks having the same broad objectives in different cases. It should also be appreciated that problems of rigorous definition arise only because of the desire to carry out costing exercises. Consideration of quality in other contexts (e.g. training, supplier development, design and engineering changes, and SPC) does not require such sharp distinction to be made between what is quality-related and what is not. However, there is ample practical and research evidence in the literature to show that, even when collecting costs, collectors do not feel constrained to stick to rigorously defined elements. By and large, collectors devise their own elements to suit their own industry and/or particular situation. The result is a proliferation of uniquely defined cost elements which preclude comparisons between data from different sources.

Accounting systems do not readily yield the information needed, as it is presently defined and rigorous definitions of quality activity elements are necessary only for costing purposes. Thus, there is an apparently absurd situation of defining elements in a way which makes them difficult to cost. Given that accounting systems are unlikely to change radically to accommodate quality costing difficulties, there should be greater consideration of the accounting aspects when defining quality cost elements. However, the use of activity-based costing (ABC) systems should make it easier to gather quality-related costs. In simple terms, ABC breaks down products and services into elements called 'cost drivers' (e.g. machine set-up), and, for each cost driver, an overhead rate is determined. The cost drivers are then added together for a particular product or service. This results in more accurate product costs, since costs are not just related to volume of production but to the environment (e.g. variety, change, complexity) in which they are produced. Details of ABC are provided by Innes and Mitchell (1990) and Cooper and Kaplan (1991). These systems are used to enable more accurate calculations of product costs, and tend to focus on values at an activity level. This enables the quality cost associated with an activity to be more easily obtained. It also aids the inspection of the detailed activity analysis and consideration of the cost drivers affecting these activities. ABC is of particular benefit in identifying costs in non-manufacturing areas. A process management structure in which a manager is responsible for a complete process, regardless of functional structures, is also an aid to the identification, collection and reporting of quality cost data.

Overambition or overzealousness may prompt people, including management consultancies, to try to maximize the impact of quality costs on the CEO and members of the senior management team. Consequently, they tend to stretch their definitions to include those costs which have only the most tenuous relationship with quality. This attempt to amplify quality costs can backfire. Once costs have been accepted as being quality-related, there may be some difficulty in exerting an influence over the reduction of costs which are independent of quality management considerations. It is not always easy to disown costs after one has claimed them, especially if ownership is in a 'grey area' and no one wants them. In relation to this point of overambition, these questions are posed:

- Is the typically quoted figure of quality costs as 25 per cent or so of annual sales turnover or operating cost realistic?
- What is the basis for figures which are frequently quoted in excess of this 25 per cent?
- What are likely reactions of senior management when the calculated quality costs are less than this figure? For example, figures of this order of magnitude tend to be remembered by senior management. If the calculated quality costs for their organization turns out to be less than this figure, there is sometimes a tendency for them to believe they have nothing to worry about in terms of continuous improvement; clearly, this is a dangerous assumption.
- What can be said to executives whose response to this claim of 25 per cent is along the lines: 'If the organization is incurring costs of this magnitude, how are we managing to survive?'

Definitions of the categories and their constituent elements are to be found in most standard quality management texts. Detailed guidance is given in specialized publications on the topic BS6143-2, Campanella (1999), Dale and Plunkett (1995) and Grimm (1987).

The widespread use and deep entrenchment of the prevention-appraisal-failure (PAF) categorization of quality costs (Feigenbaum, 1956) invites analysis of the reasons for it. After all, arrangement of data into these categories is usually done for reporting purposes, after the collection exercise. It adds nothing to the data's potential for provoking action, except perhaps by facilitating comparison with earlier data from the same source (and even this may not be valid because of their relationship to current warranty costs, where these are included, to other current costs).

However, there are some general and specific advantages to be gained from the PAF categorization. Among the general advantages are that it may prompt a rational approach to collecting costs, and it can add orderliness and uniformity to the ensuing reports. These are the specific advantages of this particular categorization:

- Its universal acceptance
- Its conferral of relative desirability of different kinds of expenditure
- Most importantly, it provides keyword criteria to help to decide whether costs are, in fact, quality-related or basic work (e.g. essential activities in producing and supplying a company's products and/or services) and, in this way, it helps to educate staff on the concept of quality costing, and to assist with the identification of costs.

The last-mentioned point may explain why earlier literature on the subject – e.g. Feigenbaum (1956), and ASQC (1974) although this booklet has now been withdrawn – defines the term 'quality costs'. Matters are judged to be quality-related if they satisfy the criteria set by their definitions of prevention, appraisal and failure.

However, as TQM has developed, the need to identify and measure quality costs across a wider spectrum of company activities has arisen, and the traditional PAF approach is, in some respects, unsuited to the new requirement. These are among its limitations:

- The quality activity elements as defined do not match well with the cost information most commonly available from accounting systems.
- There are many quality-related activities in grey areas where it is unclear in which category they belong, although this is not detrimental to the process of cost collection, provided the decision making is consistent.
- In practice, the categorization is often a post-collection exercise done in deference to the received wisdom on the topic.
- The categorization seems to be of interest only to QA personnel.
- It is not an appropriate categorization for the most common uses of quality-related cost information.

In these circumstances, a broader categorization which measures only the cost of conformance and the cost of non-conformances, as in Crosby's (1979) philosophy, is gaining recognition. The principal arguments in its favour are that it can be applied company-wide and that it focuses attention on the costs of doing things right as well as the costs of getting them wrong. This is considered to be a more positive all round approach which will yield improvements in efficiency. In theory, all costs to the company should be accounted for under such a system. In practice, departments identify key-result areas and processes against which to measure their performance and costs. Details of one such process cost model are incorporated into BS6143-1.

Machowski and Dale (1998), in reporting the main findings of a questionnaire survey which assessed, with in an organization involved in the design and manufacture of telecommunications equipment, the level of understanding of quality costing in a cross-section of employees, together with their attitudes and perceptions of the concept, concluded that:

> The respondents had a better understanding of the price of conformance and price of non-conformation categorisation than the traditional PAF model. This should be noted by those cost collectors deciding on the best ways of categorising quality costs and seeking alternatives to the traditional PAF model. The main advantage of the broader POC and PONC categorisation is that it can be applied company-wide and focuses attention on the cost of doing things right as well as the costs of getting them wrong.

Here are some other alternatives:

- Controllable and uncontrollable
- Discretionary and consequential
- Theoretical and actual
- Value adding and non-value adding

Clearly the prospects for success of a costing system will depend on how well the system matches and integrates with other systems in the company and the way that the company operates. Categorization of costs so that they relate to other business costs, and are easy for people to identify with, must have distinct operating advantages. From observations of quality departments at work, it is suggested that a supplier–in-house–customer categorization would have such advantages. Another such practical alternative (Nix et al., 1993), based on investigations carried out into one company's total cost of ownership of supplied parts is: attaining, possessing and sustaining costs. However, whatever categorization is preferred, there is no escaping the need to decide what is quality-related and what is not. In attempting to do so, there are no better passwords than prevention, appraisal, and failure (despite their limitations as cost categories).

When defining and categorizing costs, it is important to try to define the quality activity elements to align with the business activities of the company and to fit in with existing costing structures. Warranty cost is an example of just such an element. Clearly, it is quality-related; it is part of the business agreement between a company and its customers, and the company must make financial provisions to meet its possible liabilities under the agreement.

In the matter of definitions of quality and their ease of costing, accountants have a preference for definitions which are confined to meeting specification. Open-ended definitions such as 'fitness for purpose' admits too many intangibles and make costing more difficult. If, say, 'fitness for purpose' is the quality objective, it must be met through suitable specifications and detailed requirements; the cost collectors must not be left in the difficult situation of trying to decide what parameters affect the product's or service's suitability for its purpose.

Collecting Quality Costs

Purpose

These are among the main purposes of collecting quality-related costs:

- To display the importance of quality-related activities to company management in meaningful terms, i.e. costs
- To show the impact of quality-related activities on key business criteria, e.g. prime cost, and profit and loss accounts
- To assist in identifying projects and opportunities for improvement
- To enable comparisons of performance with other divisions or companies to be made
- To establish bases for budgets with a view to exercising budgetary control over the whole quality operation
- To provide cost information for motivational purposes at all levels in the company

There is little point in collecting quality-related costs just to see what they may reveal. Establishing the purposes of the exercise clear at the outset can go a long way towards avoiding pitfalls and unnecessary work.

Pursglove and Dale (1996), in a study of the setting up of a quality costing system in an organization involved in the manufacture of PVC-based oil coatings and moulding compounds, provide an interesting angle in making the case for quality costing. First, they give these reasons why no attempt had previously been made by management to gather quality costs:

- A lack of understanding of the concept and principles of quality costing among the management team
- An acute lack of information and data
- The profitable nature of the business

They go on to relate the reasons why the new MD, whose only experience of a quality costing system was at his previous company, decided to set-up a quality costing system, and quote him, saying:

> This system was perceived as 'making good sense of the data gathered' and he particularly liked the way that the costs were expressed as a percentage of raw material usage costs.

This was the justification for setting up a quality costing system:

- Quality problems with the company's main business account, resulting in the return of significant amounts of material and subsequent claims
- Inadequate methods of measurement and control of materials through the production process
- Ineffective control over raw material ordering
- Amount of non-conforming finished product

Pursglove and Dale (1996) go on to say that:

> It was hoped by senior management that the quality costs system would help to identify the areas of costs and highlight those on which to focus improvement effort. Another objective was to set and monitor departmental targets in order to promote and manage reductions in the main costs.

Strategies

Clearly, the strategy to be adopted will be influenced by the purpose of the exercise. If, for example, the main objective is to identify high cost problem areas then approximate cost data will suffice. If the CEO and members of the senior management team already accept that the organization's cost of quality is within the normally quoted range and are prepared to commit resources to improvement, there is no point in refining the data. If, on the other hand, the objective is to set a percentage cost reduction target on a particular aspect of the company's activity, it will be necessary to identify all the contributing cost elements carefully, and to ensure that corrective action produces real gains and does not simply transfer costs elsewhere. If the intention is only to take a snapshot from time to time as a reminder of their magnitude, the strategy will be to identify and measure large ongoing costs.

Another aspect which needs to be considered is whether to collect and allocate costs on a departmental or business unit basis, or across the whole company. In some cases, analysis at company level is inadequate as the problems would be set out in terms too global to generate ownership at departmental or process level. On the other hand, analysis at too detailed a level would lead to a trivialization of problems.

These types of issues will also have a bearing on the definition and identification of cost elements. The incidence of such diverse objectives with their differing requirements serves to reinforce the case for a rational approach in which the purposes of the exercise are clearly established at the outset. However, whatever the purpose of the exercise, key elements in any strategy are to involve the Finance and Accounting department right from the outset and to start with a pilot exercise on an important operation, process or department. An example of how such a strategy was developed in a manufacturer of coatings is given by Pursglove and Dale (1995).

Scope

As mentioned earlier, deciding the scope of the exercise in the sense of agreeing what should be included under the quality-cost umbrella may be far from straight-forward; there are many 'grey areas'. For example, there are those factors which serve to ensure the basic utility of the product, guard against errors, and protect and preserve quality, e.g. the use of design codes, preparation of engineering, operations, technical and administrative systems and procedures, capital premiums on machinery and equipment, document and drawing controls, and handling and storage prac-tices. Whether such factors give rise to costs which may be regarded as being quality-related is a matter for judgement in individual cases.

Often there are activities, usually of a testing or running-in type, where it is unclear whether it is a peripheral quality activity or an integral and essential part of the production/operations activities. For example, if the state of the technology is such that a manufacturer cannot be certain of making a product which is fit for purpose, without actually testing each unit and showing it to be so, is the cost of the test a quality-related cost?

Problems of categorization may arise for costs generated by functions other than quality and production/operations. Examples are the contributions of purchas-ing and supplier development to supplier quality assessment, QA, and development and the activities of engineering design departments involved with concessions and design modifications prompted by quality considerations. Quantifying, classifying and costing such inputs is difficult, but they can amount to significant expenditures.

These are the kinds of problems which will need to be addressed when deciding the scope of the exercise. Because each case is different, it is not possible to offer general solutions other than to suggest that if there is serious doubt, the cost should not be defined as being quality-related where it is unlikely to be amenable to change by quality management influences. Other suggested criteria are that an item or activity is quality-related when spending less on it will possibly result in an increase in failure costs and spending more on it will possibly result in a decrease in failure costs. It is always better to underestimate rather than overestimate the costs of quality.

Cost collection

When establishing a cost collection procedure for the first time, four important points need to be noted:

1 There is no substitute for a detailed thorough examination of the operating processes in the beginning. Modifications to the procedure may be made later, in necessary, with hindsight and as experience of applying the procedure grows.

2 People will readily adopt ready-made procedures for purposes for which they were not intended if they appear to fit their situation. Hence, it is very important that the 'first-off' should be soundly based.

3 Procedures should be 'user friendly', i.e. the information needed should be readily obtainable from a relatively small number of sources. Nothing inhibits information gathering so much as have to gather it from a large number of sources. It is strongly recommended that the system used to collect quality costs should be made as automatic as possible with minimum intervention of the cost owners.

4 The accounts department must be involved right from the start.

The methodology adopted by an organization for the collection of costs must be practical and relevant in that it must contribute to the performance of the basic activities of the organization. Here are some approaches to quality cost collection:

- Use the list of cost elements in BS6143-2 as a guide
- Identify potential elements of cost from the literature
- Develop a list of elements from company-specific experience
- Use Semi-structured methods

  - By using education seminars, presentations, questionnaire and brain-storming techniques, it is possible to identify elements of cost specific to a department, or business unit, or process.
  - The process cost model outlined in BS6143-1 can be used to identify POC and PONC for each department. The use of a semi-structured method of collecting quality costs is described by Machowski and Dale (1995) on a study undertaken on the engineering change process of a telecommunication equipment manufacturer.

The elements identified can be based on people's activities and/or material waste.

It is most important that quality-cost collection guidelines are developed. For example, apportioning staff time to a particular quality-cost category, how to allocate an activity into different cost categories, what to include in a particular element, losses caused by sub-standard products/services, etc.

Management accountants are always under pressure to produce all sorts of costs and, if quality costing is to be successfully stouted in a company, they need to be convinced that there is some worth in the exercise.

Quality-cost information needs to be produced from a company's existing systems. It is easier to develop a quality costing system in a 'greenfield' situation as opposed to attempting to break into an established system. A common fallacy is that larger companies have accounting systems from which it is relatively easy to extract quality-related costs. Often such companies have large immutable accounting systems and practices imposed by a head office and have little flexibility to provide quality costs. On the other hand, smaller companies are less likely to have a full-time professionally qualified person responsible for management accounting. Some of the difficulties in obtaining quality-cost data are related to organizational structures and with the accounting system. For example, it has been found on more than one occasion that, in a functional structure, there is no real incentive to report and reduce costs of quality and, in relation to the accounting system, ABC has been found to be useful in identifying cost of quality in non-manufacturing areas.

A noticeable feature of accounting systems is the greater accountability the nearer one is to the production/operations areas. This has implications for the cost collection exercise because a number of quality costs are incurred close to the production/ operations area. Hence, the accountability bias is in the quality-cost collector's favour. A factor working in the opposite direction is the involvement of personnel from a wide spectrum of functions. It is important that the quality costing exercise does not concentrate purely on the production/operations; a considerable amount of non-value added activity and waste is incurred in the non-producing or service functions.

When seeking to measure costs under quality-related headings, it is sometimes easy to overlook the factor that the task is primarily a cost collection exercise and that these exercises have other, different, criteria to be considered which are sensibly independent of the cost topic. Plunkett and Dale (1985) suggest an appropriate set of criteria for any cost collection exercise:

- Purpose
- Relevance
- Size of costs
- Ease of collection
- Accuracy of data
- Potential for change
- Completeness

A set of back-up criteria like these can often provide a useful way out of the dilemma about whether particular activities and costs should be included in a costing exercise.

Some Cost Aspects of Manufacturing Industry

There are a number of cost aspects – hidden in-house quality costs, scrap and rework, appraisal costs and warranty costs – which occur in manufacturing industry which warrant discussion. Commercial organizations, and those providing a service, will have their equivalents of these types of costs.

Hidden in-house quality costs

Hidden quality costs occur in two forms:

1 Those owing to in-built inefficiencies in processes and systems
2 Activities which are clearly quality-related but do not carry a quality tag

There are many in-built inefficiencies such as excess materials allowances, excess paper and forms, excess production/operation starts, poor material utilization, deliberate overmakes and production overruns. These, are sometimes not regarded as costs, but may in fact have their origins in engineering, technical, manufacturing and operating inefficiency. The same may also be true of the provision of standby machines, equipment and personnel, additional supervision, some safety stocks and items, and other contingency items. Similarly, excess and selective fitting owing to variability of machined parts is often an accepted practice. This can be considerably reduced or even eliminated by the use of SPC and design of experiments.

Phua and Dale (1997), in an examination of overmakes in a small company manu-facturing complex high technology PCB for the aerospace and defence industries, identified a number of company practices such as two panel loading, step and repeat factors and an outdate overmake planning grid which contributed to the excessive number of overmakes being manufactured and put into inventory as stock boards. The implementation by the company of a number of improved planning measures reduced the number of overmakes by one-third.

Another type of in-built inefficiency, frequently encountered in the packaging industry, is where customers change, at the last moment, their order requirements on the packaging manufacturer. In this situation, the manufacturer usually do their very best to respond to prevent a line stop situation at the customers and incurs additional costs due to this exceptional service response, which will not be recovered from the customer.

Snagging facilities to avoid stopping production in line manufacturing are a form of in-built inefficiency. Many people would reason that, because systems are imperfect, it is necessary to provide contingency facilities, such as snagging areas, and that their operating costs are just another built-in burden. However, there is no reason why the principle of accountability should not apply and the function responsible for the failure (purchasing, stores, planning, etc.) made accountable for the cost.

Inattention to maintenance of process performance may result in built-in costs by acceptance of lower levels of capability and more non-conformances than are necessary. Maintenance budgets are frequently decided on an arbitrary or general experience basis without taking due regard of the particular process needs. Maintenance should be preventive in the sense of prevention of non-conformances rather than preventing breakdown. Failure to do this is tantamount to building in unnecessarily high levels of non-conformance with consequential in-built costs. The use of techniques such as SPC and TPM will draw attention to changes in capability and cause maintenance work to become more process oriented than machine oriented.

Major activities in the second category are concessions, modifications and engineering changes. It is suspected that, in many companies, concessions are an expedient way of maintaining production schedules and that little account is taken of the disadvantages incurred in deciding to overlook non-conformances. Not least among these are proliferation of paperwork and lax attitudes towards quality and its improvement among managers, supervisors and operatives. In fact, frequent concessions on non-conforming goods are a positive disincentive to operators and first-line supervision to get it right first time.

In many companies, goods passed on concession do not feature in quality reporting systems because they have escaped the company's defect reporting system. In some companies, goods are supposed only to be passed on concession if they cannot be rectified. It is often easier to find reasons why goods cannot be rectified than it is to rework them. Hence, concession systems may become an engineering/technical expediency or, equally, they may be seen as a production expediency to avoid impediments to output or delays in delivery.

To anyone investigating costs in manufacturing industry, striking features are the large amount of time and money spent on modifications and engineering changes, and an apparent acceptance they are facts of engineering life that one must learn to live with. Thus they might justifiably be categorized as in-built costs. The costs, though hidden, are believed to be substantial and, quite apart from the costs of personnel directly involved, there can be serious implications for inventory and even impediments to output if modifications and changes are not kept to a minimum or processing the modifications or changes becomes protracted.

There is need for a new set of specific definitions and elements to help to determine the cost associated with these types of activities.

Other examples of hidden costs are provision of 'clean areas' and 'protection' for components and assemblies, segregation, marking, and handling of scrap, movement of goods for inspection purposes, the activities of purchasing and accounting personnel in dealing with rejected supplies, the effects of order-splitting (for quality reasons) on planning and manufacture, and the costs of machine downtime for quality reasons.

Scrap and rework

These costs are collected and reported in most companies. They frequently are regarded as important costs which feature in companies' business decisions. Yet the economics of scrapping or rectification are by no means clear in many companies.

The first difficulty is the valuation to be placed on scrapped goods. Some popular views encountered are that the value should be the factory selling price, the market price, the raw materials price or the materials cost plus the cost of processing to the point of scrapping, or the materials cost plus 50 per cent of the cost of processing, irrespective of the point of scrapping. These different bases will obviously give rise to very different valuations. The second difficulty is that the decision about whether to scrap or rework is often taken by personnel who do not have access to the financial information necessary to make an economic choice and, in any case, the economics will vary depending on workload, urgency of delivery, etc. It will often be found that scrap vs rework decisions are based primarily on ease of rework and output and delivery targets rather than on cost.

The practice, found in some organizations, of deducting from quality costs the income from sales of scrap is to be discouraged because it makes the overall quality cost appear to be better than it really is. Also, the type and quantity of scrap sold at a particular time may bear no relation to current production.

Appraisal costs

Though appraisal costs cover a wider range of activities, the majority of the expenditure is on in-house inspection and test activities. Opinions differ about whether testing is an appraisal cost. Carson (1986) is positive that testing is about detecting defects, that it is an appraisal cost, and that there is an onus on the manufacturing department to 'get it right first time'.

Testing is effectively proving the fitness-for-purpose of the product in one or more respects. There may well be cases where such testing ought not to be necessary, but is, and hence incurs a quality cost. However, in many cases, the state of the technology may be such that testing is unavoidable. A manufacturer may be unable to give guarantees without testing the product; he may be unable to secure insurance cover without testing, and it may be a contractual requirement of the customer. In the end, the decision whether to test may be taken out of his hands, whatever he thinks he can achieve without testing. Whether testing is a quality-related – or a purely production activity – is a matter to be decided in individual cases.

The economics of appraisal are not known in most companies. High costs of failure are apparently used to justify inspection and its frequency, without any attempts being made to determine the true economic balance. It is somewhat surprising that the economics of inspection are not well established and widely known, considering that inspection-oriented approaches have predominated in manufacturing industry for many decades. There is evidence of the potential for cost reductions by drastic reductions in inspection forces, apparently without loss of quality; see, for example Kohl (1976) and Richardson (1983). It is expected that there would be little change in first-off inspection unless the capability of machines and tools to sustain tolerances was improved, but that the patrol and final inspection activity can be reduced through SPC. This is all part of the change of philosophy from detection to prevention, as discussed in chapter 1.

Warranty costs

Warranty costs are usually met from a provision set aside for the purpose. Care needs to be taken when determining costs from changes in provisions because the provision may be used to meet some other charge or may be topped-up from time to time with arbitrary amounts of money. Hence, it is necessary to know about all the transactions affecting the provision.

Reporting Quality Costs

Quality cost reporting is not yet widely accepted as one of the normal activities in reporting of quality performance. Duncalf and Dale (1985) report that only 36 companies out of 110 respondents to a questionnaire survey of quality-related decision making claimed to collect quality costs and, of these, there were few that collected them across all the categories of prevention, appraisal and failure.

An important consideration in the presentation of quality-related costs are the needs of the recipients, and it may be worth presenting information in several different formats:

- Weekly reports of costs of scrap and rework may be of greatest value to shop floor supervisors.
- Monthly reports of total costs highlighting current problems and progress with quality improvement projects would be suitable for middle management.
- Total costs and costs on which to act are needed by senior managers.

While selective reporting of this kind has its merits, it should always be done against a background of the total quality-related cost. Ideally, quality cost reports should show opportunities for cost savings leading to increased profits or price reductions.

For maximum impact, quality costs should be included in a company's cost-reporting system. Unfortunately, the lack of sophistication of quality-cost collection and measurement is such that it does not allow quality-cost reporting to be carried out in the same detail and to the same standard as, for example, the production/operations and marketing functions. Reporting of quality costs is, in the main, a sub-section of the general reporting of quality department activities and, as such, loses its impact. Often, quality reports do not separate out costs as an aspect of quality which is worthy of presentation and comment in its own right. This usually results in cost information not being used to its full potential. Separating costs from other aspects of quality, and discussing them in the context of other costs, would improve the clarity of reports and help to provide better continuity from one report to the next.

Good standards of reporting are essential if the costs are to make an impact and provoke action. Managers are like everyone else in wanting easy decisions to make. Having costs, which are the basis of business decisions, tangled up with technical information makes the data less clear than it could be and may provide a reason to defer action. The manager's problem should not be to disentangle and analyse data; it should be to decide whether to act, choose which course of action to pursue and ensure provision of the necessary resources. Problems, possible solutions and their resource requirements should be presented in the context of accountability centres which have the necessary authority to execute the decisions of the senior management team.

Many manufacturing companies make goods for stock and it may be many months, or possibly years, after manufacture that a product goes into service. This raises the issue of comparability (or even relevance) of categories of cost one with another. Much has been written about definition, categorization, and reporting of quality costs, and the implication is always that the reported costs are concurrent and relevant to each other. Clearly, prevention costs should have a bearing on appraisal and failure costs, and expenditure on appraisal may influence the magnitude and distribution (between internal and external) of failure costs, but not necessarily concurrently. In some industries, the time lag arising between action and effect are such that concurrent expenditures on, say, prevention and warranty, bear no relation whatever to each other. Reporting only concurrent costs in isolation can be misleading and it is perhaps worth considering, in some cases, contemporary costs as well as concurrent costs.

The long intervals which may occur between manufacture and receipt of warranty claims can have some special implications for cost reporting. Warranty costs in any period may bear no relation to other quality costs incurred in the same period, and should not be reported in the same context. To include them can distort considerably the quality performance of the company or department as depicted by the levels and ratios of quality-related costs. The delays may also mean that the causes underlying the failures leading to the claims may no longer be a problem.

One of the maxims of cost collecting seems to be that, in general, costs need to be large to hold attention. This creates something of a dilemma for the cost collector because large costs are often insensitive to changes. However, the collector cannot omit large costs, concentrating instead only on smaller costs which may readily be seen to change. Hence, cost groupings need to be chosen carefully so that cost reductions achieved are displayed in such a way that both the relative achievement and the absolute position are clearly shown. Another dilemma arises from the fact that one-off estimates do not change and that there is no point in collecting costs which do not change.

The format for the collection of costs should make provision right at the outset for all those elements and cost sources which are thought to be worth collecting. The creation of a quality-related cost file, integrated with existing costing systems but perhaps with some additional expense codes, should not present many problems. As stressed earlier, it is important to make provision in the file for collecting data which is not readily quantifiable even though it may take a long time to obtain satisfactory returns on a routine basis.

When reporting costs at regular intervals, it is important to ensure that sets of data remain comparable. If additional cost elements are introduced as an organization becomes more experienced in quality costing, these must be reported separately until an appropriate opportunity arises to include them among related costs. It is also worth coding each cost element to indicate its source and status, e.g. accounting records, calculation from standard data, calculation through surrogates, average rates, and estimates.

Presentation of costs under prevention, appraisal, and internal and external failure, as advocated by BS6143-2 and Campanella (1999), is the most popular approach, albeit with different cost elements appropriate to different industries, whether manufacturing, commercial or service-related. This format is favoured by quality managers perhaps because, on the face of it, it forms a quality balance sheet for the quality management function with prevention equivalent to investment, appraisal to operating cost, and failure to losses. This categorization of costs is of interest and some value to quality managers, but less so to other functional managers on the grounds that they do not relate directly to the activities of the business.

The influence of senior management is vital in the reporting of quality costs. If there is no pressure to reduce costs against mutually agreed targets then the reporting will become routine and people, quite naturally, will devote their efforts to what they believe are the most important events. It is important that senior management develop a quality-cost reduction strategy.

Uses of Quality Costs

According to Morse (1983):

> The potential uses of the information contained in such a (quality cost) report are limited only by imagination of management.

Many of the uses can, however, be grouped into four broad categories:

1 Quality costs may be used to promote product and service quality as a business parameter.
2 They give rise to performance measures.
3 They provide the means for planning and controlling quality costs.
4 They act as motivators.

Promoting quality as a business parameter

This first use is usually interpreted as gaining the attention of higher management by using their language, i.e. money, but costs can also be used to show that it is not only the quality department that is involved in quality, that everyone's work can impinge on quality and that it is indeed an important business parameter – especially if the influences of suppliers and customers are made clear. Clearly, knowledge of quality-related costs will enable decisions about quality to be made in an objective manner.

Giving rise to performance measures

This second use includes a wide variety of activities:

- *Trend analyses* to show changes in costs or cost ratios with time
  Diagnosis of the cause of change can often prompt pilot exercises in the use of specific tools and techniques.
- *Pareto analyses* to identify quality improvement projects
  This is the quickest route to the exploitation of quality cost data.
- Identification of *investment opportunities*
  Progressive companies are always looking for profitable ways to invest in quality improvement projects and initiatives, but their task is made very difficult by the lack of data and understanding of the economics of investment in quality. While it may be axiomatic that prevention is better than cure, it is often difficult to justify investment in prevention activities. To some extent, such investments are regarded as acts of faith. Little is known, and nothing has been published, on the appropriate levels and timing of investments, payoffs or payback periods. However, there are many opportunities for investment in prevention, with consequential real cost savings. Employing qualified experienced staff, encouraging continuing education and providing training are examples of investment in personnel. Investment in supplier quality development activities is claimed by many companies to pay handsome dividends (Galt and Dale, 1990).
  Of more direct interest to engineers and technical personnel are the possibilities of effective savings through investment in tooling, equipment and machinery and mistake proofing devices; for details of mistake-proofing, see Shingo (1986). Poor standard of tools are frequently responsible for non-conforming product, and the extra costs of providing a higher standard of tooling is often a worthwhile investment. Quality considerations also enter into the selection of machinery and equipment inasmuch as a premium is paid for machine tools with the potential to achieve a capable process, thus avoiding failure costs and, maybe, some appraisal costs. Kaplan (1983) takes this line of argument further when he suggests that if manufacturing costs decrease as quality increases (and there is evidence of this), then the financial justification for new capital equipment, including robots, should include the savings in manufacturing cost from achieving a lower incidence of defects.
- *Performance indicators* and *quality efficiency indexes*
  Business efficiencies are commonly analysed and expressed using a variety of criteria (mostly financial). Maintenance and improvement of quality are not among the criteria used. Quality managers' efforts to persuade fellow managers and directors of the value of continuous improvement to a company are often frustrated by a lack of well-known and accepted indices or standards. Some companies have developed measures for the purpose of internally monitoring improvement, but no general guidelines or methods of calculation exist which would readily allow a company to assess its standards against a norm or other companies' performances.
  The most popular comparative measure against which quality costs are measured is gross sales, followed by manufacturing or operating cost and value added. Other useful bases are hours of direct production labour, units of product, and processing cost. It is widely held that single ratios do not tell

the whole story and may always need to be considered alongside other ratios. BS6143-1 recommends that at least three comparison bases should be used, and urges care and caution in the selection of bases. Other useful guidance is given by Campanella (1999) and Feigenbaum (1991).

Quality-cost data may also be used to assist with vendor rating. Winchell (1987) lists 'visible' and 'hidden' quality costs. These items are included in the visible quality costs category:

- Receiving or incoming inspection
- Calibration of measuring equipment
- Qualification of supplier product
- Source inspection and control programme
- Purchased material reject disposition (material review)
- Purchased material replacement
- Rework of supplier-caused rejects
- Scrap of supplier-caused rejects

The visible costs, if tracked, are perhaps most significant because they can be good indicators of problem areas.

These are hidden quality costs:

- Those that are incurred by the supplier at his plant
- Those incurred by the buyer in solving problems at the supplier's plant
- Those costs which usually are not allocated to suppliers, but are incurred by the buyer as a result of potential or actual supplier problems – including loss of business from customers who do not come back

In much of the foregoing, it is implicit that placing costs on activities and quality management data somehow enhances the underlying data and shows something which might otherwise not be revealed. While enhancement of data in this way may be useful, it may not always be necessary. Sometimes, only translating numbers into costs is sufficient to provoke action (Richardson, 1983). Similarly, the mere collection of data may provoke investigative action. In one case study (Dale and Plunkett, 1995), it was only when the company began to collect quality costs and analyse its warranty payments that it became aware that its policy of automatic payment of warranty invoices for less than £1,000 was being seriously abused by customers. By the simple expedient of a knowledgeable person checking all invoices over £400, many tens of thousands of pounds were saved. Perhaps, more importantly, word soon spread the message that invoices were being checked and the incidence of attempted abuse reduced rapidly.

A means of planning and controlling quality costs

This third use of quality costs is widely mooted in the literature. Costs are the bases for budgeting and eventual cost control. Contributions from the quality fraternity tend to see establishment of quality-cost budgets for the purpose of controlling costs as the ultimate goal which may be achieved after accumulating a loss of data over a long time in pursuit of quality improvements of specific cost reductions.

Campanella and Corcoran (1983) drawing on ASQCs (1974) *Quality Costs – What and How* (now withdrawn) – summarize the uses of quality costs for budgeting thus:

> Once quality cost elements have been established and costs are being collected against them, you can generate a history with which to determine the average cost per element. These averages can serve as the basis for future quotes and 'estimates to complete'. Budgets can be established for each element. Then, going full circle, the actuals collected against these elements can be used to determine budget variances and, as with any good system of budget control, action can be taken to bring variances into line.

However, Morse (1983), giving an accountant's view, is not so positive:

> After quality cost information has been accumulated for several periods, it may be possible to budget certain quality costs.

These views appear to reflect the general situation that the quality management fraternity are much more optimistic about the potential for achieving fairly sophisticated uses of quality costs than are accountants. Also, despite the popularity of the topic with contributors to the quality literature, there are relatively few examples of its application to quality costing.

In the research experience of UMIST, the state of development of quality costing in most companies is not advanced enough to establish budgetary control over quality costs other than within the quality department.

Quality costs as motivators

Quality costs can be used for motivational purposes at all levels in a company. Costs have been used traditionally to motivate senior managers to become interested and to take part in the promotion of quality. As companies move towards TQM, the use of costs as a motivator becomes more widespread. Thus, for example, costs of scrapped goods are displayed to line supervision, operatives and clerical staff because they can see the relevance of them to their work. It is found that this group of people respond positively in terms of increased quality awareness, improved handling of the product, housekeeping disciplines, etc. Although the costs may be relatively small in company terms, they are usually large in relation to operatives' salaries. Thus a strong impact is made, in particular, when poor trading conditions result in restrictions being placed on salary increases and even freezes or reductions imposed, without disclosing sensitive cost information.

While it is clearly important to make good use of quality-related costs, it is equally important to avoid misuse of them.

- It must be remembered that in some industries quality costs are not susceptible to conventional cost reduction techniques and quality may not be compromised to save money, e.g. where there is a possibility of severe loss of life or ecological disaster. Only in those situations where the consequence of failure is merely loss of profit, is a manufacturer in a position to trade-off quality expenditure against potential loss of profit resulting from product failures (Cox, 1982).
- Costs alone must not be used to determine an optimum level of quality as suggested by 'economic cost of quality' models which appear everywhere in

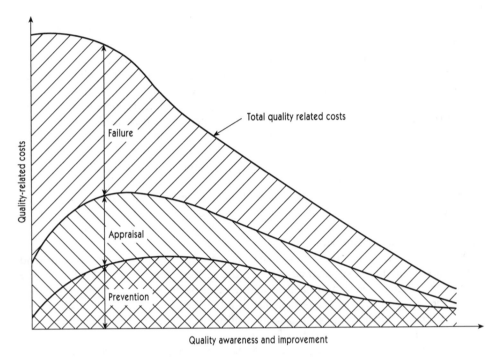

Figure 7.1 Increasing quality awareness and improvement activities
Source: BS6143-2 (1990)

the literature. Such models have been heavily and widely criticized in recent years. For example, Plunkett and Dale (1988) have observed that, though well-intentioned in warning against extravagance in pursuing quality, the models are only notional and do not reflect actual experience. Many of the published models are ambiguous, inaccurate and misleading. While there is no objection to trying to optimize quality costs, quality should not be compromised. Quality should be determined by customer requirements, not optimum quality costs. The real dangers are that the taking cognisance of the model will inhibit the development of TQM and quality improvement in the company, and that the company will perhaps settle for a standard of quality which is less than what their customer requires. The form of the model shown at figure 7.1 from BS6143-2, resembles real situations much more closely than the classical optimum quality-cost models which are usually portrayed in quality management and production and operations management text books.

• Comparisons with other cost data should be avoided. Comparisons should only be made after it has been shown that the data are genuinely comparable, i.e. sources, computation, accounting treatment, and reporting methods are identical.

Summary

The value of cost data should not be underestimated. Costs are a most effective way of drawing attention to, and illuminating, situations in ways that other data cannot.

It has been found that even the most rudimentary attempts at quality costing have been beneficial in identifying areas of waste and trends in quality improvement performance. It should also not be forgotten that quality costs are already being incurred by an organization, the whole purpose of the quality costing exercise is to identify these 'hidden costs' from various budgets and overheads. The objective is to allocate these indirect costs to a specific cost activity.

Unfortunately, the whole process of definition, collection, reporting, and use of quality-related costs is not yet well enough developed to be used in the same way as many other costs. A major influence in this is, undoubtedly, the solid entrenchment of the PAF categorization of quality-related costs. The potential uses of cost data derived from elements defined via this categorization are restricted and do not fit well with companies' day-to-day operating modes and experience. Nor do they lend themselves to sophisticated business uses. However, even with restricted potential, there is still much to be gained, as shown in this chapter. Sizes and proportions of costs can be used successfully as criteria for deciding whether to act, what resources should be committed, priorities to be allocated, etc.

As things stand now, the most widely accepted and used categorizations and definitions of quality-cost elements cause the definition–collection–reporting–use process sequence to be definition-driven, with companies making the best use they can of the outcome. However, companies should be looking for more effective ways of using quality cost data; perhaps taking a different approach to the categorization and definition of costs will assist with this.

However, what is more important is to make the process sequence dynamic. Use is the most important part of the sequence, but at present there is little or no feedback from uses to definitions. There is a need for use-driven definitions which will, in turn, affect the collection and reporting stages. The system can then become dynamic, changing as business requirements change. It is a task which needs to be tackled jointly by accountants and the manager responsible for quality in the company. The question to be answered is: How can cost information be used to improve the company's quality status, keeping in mind that quality status is determined by customers, supplier performance and in-house quality management?

References

ASQC, 1974: *Quality Costs – What and How*, American Society for Quality Control, Wisconsin, USA. This booklet has now been withdrawn, and the material included in Campanella (1990).

Campanella, J. (ed.) 1999: *Principles of Quality Costs: Principles, Implementation and Use.* Milwaukee: ASQC Quality Press.

Campanella, J. and Corcoran, F. J. 1983: Principles of quality costs. *Quality Progress*, 16(4), 17–22.

Carson, J. K. 1986: Quality costing – a practical approach. *International Journal of Quality and Reliability Management*, 3(1), 54–63.

Cooper, R. and Kaplan, R. 1991: Profit priorities from activity based costing. *Harvard Business Review*, 69(3), 130–5.

Cox, B. 1982: Interface of quality costing and terotechnology, *The Accountant*, June 21, 800–801.

Crosby, P. B. 1979: *Quality is Free*, New York: McGraw Hill.

Dale, B. G. and Plunkett, J. J. 1990: *The Case for Costing Quality.* London: Department of Trade and Industry.

Dale, B. G. and Plunkett, J. J. 1995: *Quality Costing* (2 edn). London: Chapman and Hall.

Duncalf, A. J. and Dale, B. G. 1985: How British industry is making decisions on product quality. *Long Range Planning*, 18(5), 81–8.

Feigenbaum, A. V. 1956: Total quality control. *Harvard Business Review*, 34(6), 93–101.

Feigenbaum, A. V. 1991: *Total Quality Control*. New York: McGraw Hill.

Galt, J. D. and Dale, B. G. 1990: Customer–supplier relationships in the motor industry: a vehicle manufacturers perspective. *Proceedings of the Institution of Mechanical Engineers*, 204(D4), 179–86.

Grimm, A. F. 1987: *Quality Costs, Ideas and Applications, Vol. 1*, Milwaukee: ASQC, Quality Press.

Innes, J. and Mitchell, F. 1990: *Activity Based Costing: a Review with Case Studies*. London: The Chartered Institute of Management Accountants.

Kaplan, R. S. 1983: Measuring manufacturing performance: a new challenge for managerial accounting research. *The Accounting Review*, 58(4), 686–705.

Kohl, W. F. 1976: Hitting quality costs where they live. *Quality Assurance*, 2(2), 59–64.

Machowski, F. and Dale, B. G. 1995: The application of quality costing to engineering changes. *International Journal of Materials and Product Technology*, 10(3–6), 378–88.

Machowski, F. and Dale, B. G. 1998: Quality costing: an examination of knowledge, attitudes and perceptions. *The Quality Management Journal*, 5(3), 84–95.

Morse, W. J. 1983: Measuring quality costs. *Cost and Management*, July/Aug, 16–20.

Nix, A., McCarthy, P. and Dale, B. G. 1993: The key issues in the development and use of total cost of ownership model. *Proceedings of the 2nd International Conference of the Purchasing and Supply Education Group*, University of Bath, April, 247–54.

Phua, L. and Dale, B. G. 1997: The effects of overmakes on company performance. *IEE Proceedings*, 144(2), 57–62.

Plunkett, J. J. and Dale, B. G. 1985: Some practicalities and pitfalls of quality-related cost collection. *Proceedings of the Institution Mechanical Engineers*, 199(B1), 29–33.

Plunkett, J. J. and Dale, B. G. 1988: Quality costs: a critique of some 'economic cost of quality models'. *International Journal of Production Research*, 26(11), 1713–26.

Pursglove, A. B. and Dale, B. G., 1995: Developing a quality costing system: key features and outcomes. *OMEGA*, 23(5), 567–75.

Pursglove, A. B. and Dale, B. G. 1996: The influence of management information and quality management systems on the development of quality costing. *Total Quality Management*, 7(4), 421–32.

Richardson, D. W. 1983: Cost Benefits of Quality Control – A Practical Example from Industry. *BSI News*, Oct 1983.

Shingo, S. 1986: *Zero Quality Control: Source Inspection and the Poka-Yoke System*. Cambridge, Mass.: Productivity Press.

Winchell, W. O. (ed.) 1987: *Guide for Managing Supplier Quality Costs*. Wisconsin: American Society for Quality Control.

part three

The Introduction of TQM

The introduction, development and advancement of TQM is central to many of the themes examined in *Managing Quality*. The purpose of this part of the book, after setting out a framework which can be used to introduce TQM, is to explore in detail the issues of service quality, HR and supplier development which need to be taken into account in the introduction of TQM concepts and practices into an organization. Sustaining the effectiveness of TQM is far from easy and the final chapter, chapter 12, examines the issues to which attention needs to be given.

Chapter 8 – A Framework for Introducing TQM
Chapter 9 – Managing Service Quality
Chapter 10 – Managing People in a TQM Context
Chapter 11 – Supplier Development
Chapter 12 – Sustaining TQM

Chapter 8 presents a framework to assist with the introduction of TQM. The material draws together a number of issues which need to be considered in its introduction and development. The structure of the framework consists of four main sections – organizing, using systems and techniques, measurement and feedback, and changing the culture. The framework has been used by a number of organizations in both the public and private sectors, and in manufacturing and service industries to introduce the basic element and practices of TQM.

Chapter 9 examines the implications for service quality in a changing business environment. It explores definitions and characteristics of services, the service quality GAP model, dimensions of determinants of service quality, measurement of service quality, customer service and service encounters, and service delivery processes and the role of personnel.

Chapter 10 argues that a number of organizations have not achieved the success they expected with TQM because they failed to give sufficient attention to the so-called 'soft' aspects of TQM. It is also pointed out that HR considerations are dealt with in a limited way by the TQM literature. The chapter goes on to review the need to consider these issues and, drawing on recent research, outlines the key role that the HR function can play in the development and success of TQM.

Organizations cannot consider TQM in isolation; they need to involve their customers and suppliers in the improvement process. Chapter 11 outlines the importance and role of supplier development in TQM, and the need to develop long-term collaborative business partnerships between customer and supplier. It identifies the typical barriers in supplier development, and draws on best practice to outline how organizations should start and advance the partnership concept.

Most organizations will encounter problems and obstacles in the introduction and development of TQM. If they are aware of what these are, they can agree actions to steer around or minimize them. Chapter 12 explores some of the typical problems in sustaining TQM. Also presented is an audit tool by which organizations can assess if they are experiencing the factors which can have a negative impact on the sustainment of TQM.

chapter eight

A Framework for Introducing TQM*

B. G. Dale

Introduction

This chapter presents a framework for the introduction of TQM. It is divided into four main sections, all of which need to be addressed once the motivation for TQM has been identified. The motivation will set the overall strategic direction of TQM, and influence the relevant importance of each part of the framework. The foundation of the framework is 'organizing' and the two pillars which form its structure are the use of 'systems and techniques' and 'measurement and feedback'. 'Changing the culture' is something which must be considered at all stages, including the initial organizing activities; it primarily results from the other initiatives described, interacts with them throughout the process, and will evolve with the organization's operating experience of TQM. People, both as individuals and working in teams, are central to TQM; without these skills and endeavours, continuous improvement will simply not occur. The framework integrates the various aspects of TQM, from 'soft' approaches (such as teamwork, employee development and human relations) to the use of 'hard' techniques (such as SPC and FMEA). A diagrammatic representation of the framework is given in figure 8.1 and a summary of its features in table 8.1.

The framework provides on indication of how the various aspects of TQM fit together and is particularly useful for many organizations:

- Those who are taking their first steps on the TQM journey
- Those with ISO9000 series registration, who require some guidance and advice on what to do next
- Those attempting to develop improvement plans and controls across a number of sites
- Those with less than three years operating experience of TQM

* Barrie Dale acknowledges the contribution of Dr Ruth Boaden to the development of the framework described in this chapter. He also wishes to thank the Directors and Managers who have commented on earlier versions of this chapter, in particular, he wishes to thank the past and current Associates of the UMIST TQM Multi-Company Teaching Company Programme for their invaluable suggestions in the development of the framework.

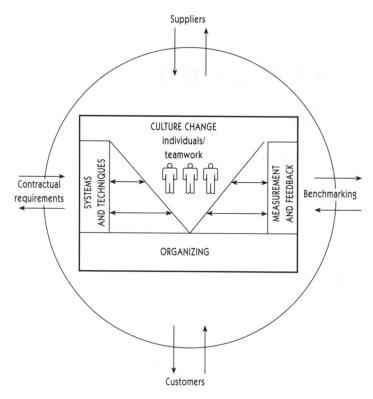

Figure 8.1 The TQM framework
Source: Dale and Boaden (1993)

The framework is not a 'how-to' guide for TQM. There are a considerable number of such guides outlining a step-by-step approach to TQM; these guides usually have a set starting point and follow one single route. The framework is a means of developing and presenting plans in a non-prescriptive manner; it is a guide to action and *not* things to be followed in a slavish manner. In this way, it allows organizations to choose an appropriate starting point and course of action, and to develop TQM and the improvement process at a pace which suits their business situation and available resources. If used in the correct manner, the framework ensures that there are adequate mechanisms in place to enable continuous improvements to take place. At this stage, they can turn to the use of self-assessment methods against a recognized model to identify strengths and weaknesses in their approach; for details of self-assessment, see chapter 22.

The framework was initially developed as a theoretical tool, from the UMIST research experience. The details of the framework as presented here have been based on its use by the senior management teams of a number of major manufacturing companies and a number of service organizations, in both private and public environments. In addition, the framework has been used in syndicate exercises by some 300 people from a wide variety of manufacturing and service organizations, in America, Europe, Hong Kong, South Africa and the UK. With its solid research base and practical testing and application, it is a very robust framework.

Table 8.1 TQM framework: a summary

Organizing	Systems and techniques	Measurement and feedback	Changing the culture
Long-term strategy for TQM formulated and integrated with other strategies; improvement plans developed	Identification of applicable tools and techniques at each stage of continuous improvement	Key internal and external performance measures identified, defined and developed	Assess the current status of organizational culture before developing plans for change
Definition of quality, TQM and continuous improvement developed and agreed	Training in the use of tools and techniques, for the right people at the right time	Ongoing discussion with customers about expected performance	Recognize the ongoing nature of culture change, and the need to outline specific changes
Choice of approach to TQM	Identification of other systems and standards that may be required by customers or legislation	Means for celebration and communication of success and teamwork developed	Recognize the role of people as an asset
Identification of sources of advice	Use of a formal quality system	Benchmarking, once improvement is under way	Plan change consistently and incrementally
Stages of improvement activity identified, taking the starting point into account	Identification of key business processes and improvement based on these processes	Consideration of the link between results from improvement and rewards	To minimize conflict, consider the inter-relationships of all activities within the organization
Executive leadership and commitment to TQM		Means of assessing the progress towards world-class performance considered, e.g. EFQM or MBNQA models	Identify factors which indicate that culture is changing
Vision and mission statements and values developed and communicated to all members of the organization			Consider the national and local culture
Decide the means by which TQM will be communicated			
Formal programme of education and training for all members of the organization			
Organizational infrastructure established to facilitate local ownership of TQM			
Teamwork established as a way of working and part of the infrastructure			

Organizing

This foundation stage is concerned with the motivation for starting TQM and a process of continuous improvement (which will influence the TQM approach adopted), and the resultant strategies, plans and means necessary to introduce and develop the process. The appropriate time to introduce TQM must also be considered, as should communication down and across the organization of what TQM is, why it is being adopted and what will be involved, including the cost and required resources.

It is also useful to consider the problems and obstacles likely to be encountered in the introduction of TQM and to agree actions to avoid or minimize them; see chapter 12 for details of typical difficulties and obstacles. Similar examples are also provided by Bunney and Dale (1996), Crofton and Dale (1996), Dale (1991) and Dale and Lightburn (1992).

In planning this stage, full use should be made of pilot schemes, whether they are in relation to the use of a technique such as SPC or the operation of improvement teams. In this way, problems can be resolved on a small scale and experiences fed back and reacted to *before* development and advancement of the issue under study.

The key actions in this stage are listed in the first column of table 8.1, and are explained further here.

A clear long-term strategy for TQM should be formulated and integrated with other key business strategies, departmental policies and objectives. This includes the development of a quality policy and quality strategy. The aim should be to integrate them with the long-term plans of the business. Any short-term strategy which the organization needs to pursue (e.g. to cater for rapid turnover of staff, market downturns, exchange fluctuations and supply difficulties) should be consistent and integrated with the long-term strategy. The strategy must then be developed into a series of improvement plans and objectives for each department and function, and also for those areas and aspects of the business which have been identified as requiring improvement, and methods of monitoring and assessment developed. Such plans will also result from the other three sections of the framework and from actions and initiatives which are independent of it. The methodology of policy deployment (Dale, 1990; Akao, 1991) is important in this respect; details are given in chapter 5.

A common organizational definition for quality, TQM, and other terms used as part of the continuous improvement process, should be developed, agreed and communicated in simple and non-technical language, after discussion. Consideration should also be given to the term (i.e. TQM, total quality performance, business excellence, world class, customer first, business improvement or continuous improvement) used to describe the improvement initiative or indeed whether a term is required. The development of a glossary of quality-related terms should be considered; useful guidance is provided in ISO8402 and BS4778-2. A lack of such definitions can hamper the progress of TQM; it will also help to prevent misunderstanding, competing views and different interpretations being made by the various functions and levels within the business and also with customers and suppliers, improving communication both inside and outside the business. Without clear definition, it is difficult to deliver what is espoused as quality. In particular, many people have difficulty in understanding the difference between TQM and QA.

The approach to TQM should be decided. This will depend on the existing culture of the organization, as well as the preferences of senior management, but is an important element in its success. Whichever TQM approach is adopted, it should be flexible and capable of fine tuning to suit the business needs and objectives of the organization. Some of the available options were explored in chapter 1.

The organizations and people (internal and external) who can be sources of advice on the approach to TQM, and its introduction and development, should be identified. Such advice may also be required to develop the quality management system to meet the requirements of the ISO9000 series and/or QS9000 and the application of particular tools and techniques. Useful expertise is often available within the organization. Such people know the internal workings of the organization, its processes and the unique problems which exist. This expertise should not be overlooked. It is always beneficial to combine internal expertise with external consultants knowledge and skills. In service organizations, which have large numbers of relatively small locations, or those manufacturing organizations which have a variety of operating sites spread across a country or throughout a number of countries, it is recommended that a 'directory of resources and experiences' is compiled to encourage co-operation and mutual assistance.

Stages of improvement activity should be identified at the outset, taking into account the starting point of the organization, the motivation for TQM and the tools and techniques which may be applicable. For example, Newall and Dale (1991) identified six stages of an improvement process – awareness, education and training, consolidation, problem identification and improvement planning, implementation of quality plans and assessment. A formal project planning methodology, which requires the identification of milestones and their ongoing monitoring, is also a vital tool at this stage.

Executive leadership, tangible commitment and support should be recognized as being crucial at all stages; see chapter 2. Such commitment should be demonstrated in actions:

- Allocating time to understanding and involvement in TQM
- Being visible and accessible ('management by wandering about')
- Holding discussions with people at the operating level of the business
- Providing words of encouragement and advice
- 'Quality' placed at the top of every business meeting agenda
- Identification of key performance measurements
- Use of tools and techniques in their everyday work activities
- Developing personal action plans
- Seeking feedback on their style of management
- Acting as a mentor to improvement teams
- Attending training sessions
- Writing articles on TQM in the company newsletter
- Ensuring that any decisions made are consistent with the agreed plans and objectives
- Exhibiting a passion for TQM

There is no magic formula for achieving such commitment, although the characteristics of good leaders are currently being researched with the aim of identifying appropriate management guidelines for the future. Useful guidance is currently provided by Bass (1985), Kotter (1990), Maxwell (1993, 1995), and Townsend and Gebhardt (1997a).

Vision and mission statements which are concise and understandable to all employees should be developed, displayed and communicated in company-unique language. It is also important to outline what needs to be done to make these statements and the associated company values become a reality, including the benefits that will accrue from TQM and how it will affect the way employees go about their jobs. The format and timing of education/awareness raising events should also be outlined. The influence of the historical culture of the organization, its people, processes, technology, products/services and the views of its current senior executives must not be underestimated in this process.

It is important that everyone in the organization can identify with the vision and mission statements; this will help to unite and focus employees on where the organization is heading. Employees must feel that the vision statement is achievable. Regular assessments should also be carried out to see whether employees believe that the organization is moving closer to achieving the objectives outlined in these statements.

Communication is a key component of TQM and management cannot communicate too much on issues relating to TQM and the improvements made. The communication should be based on common sense, be two-way, use jargon-free language and be consistent in the approach adopted. It must be good enough to win the 'hearts and minds' of all employees. The means of communication should include both written and verbal mediums in both group and individual mode (e.g. noticeboards, whiteboards, news sheets, booklets, team meeting minutes, team briefings, senior management 'state-of-the-nation' briefings, breakfast and birthday meetings and e-mail). Communication must be by example with management doing what they say must be done and they must assess, on a regular basis, to ensure that the messages they wish to portray are getting through. It also means that management must listen and act upon the views of those they manage.

A formal programme of education and training should be established. It is important to build the skills of employees and this programme should involve basic job skills and process training, including induction, TQM awareness, customer care, and training in the use of tools, techniques and systems. It must provide a common message and encompass the whole organization, starting with the senior management team and members of the TQM Steering Committee. The training should also aim to identify potential improvement projects.

The development of a training matrix, as in figure 8.2, helps to ensure that needs and capabilities are identified along with the current level of awareness of TQM, quality systems, tools and techniques, etc. Training records also need to be maintained. The training matrix should be reviewed whenever an appraisal is carried out. Consideration should also be given to the concept of a 'learning organization', this would require an internal library of information and the appropriate training aids to be set up.

An organizational infrastructure should be established which will ultimately facilitate local ownership of TQM. Direction should be provided by the TQM steering committee, but the time it sometimes takes for people to accept such ownership for TQM and continuous improvement should not be underestimated. Actions include deciding the membership of the committee, role and meeting frequency, setting up, as appropriate, local steering groups, identification of improvement co-ordinator (full-time or part-time), facilitators and team leaders along with clear definitions of

Person and function	Type of course and duration		
	General awareness	Specific (e.g. FMEA)	Degree of difficulty
Senior management			
Clerical			
Operator			

Figure 8.2 TQM training matrix

their roles, ensuring the means by which the actions developed by improvement teams can be carried through and agreeing budgets. In some companies, it may be more appropriate for TQM steering committee type issues to be discussed as an agenda item as part of the Management/Board of Director meetings. Research by Boaden and Dale (1993) has shown that full-time support is essential to get the process going and to establish a central pool of expertise, particularly in service or multi-site manufacturing organizations. However, it is important that the improvement structure does not duplicate the existing management structure. If it does, then questions must be asked about the latter. It is also recommended that the current organizational structure is assessed in terms of its suitability for starting and sustaining TQM.

Teamwork should be established and become part of the organization's method of working. In the first place, it is suggested that a review is undertaken of any teams which are already established, in conjunction with their previous and current projects. Following this, taskforces/project teams and cross-functional improvement teams should be established to address the major problems facing the organization, followed-up by the setting-up of departmental improvement teams.

Systems and Techniques

This pillar of the framework involves the development of a quality management system to provide the necessary controls and discipline, and the standardization of improvements. It also involves the use of quality management tools and techniques to, for example, aid quality planning, listen to the 'voices' of customers, capture data, control processes, make improvements, solve problems and involve people. Key actions at this stage are shown in the second column of table 8.1, and are explained further here.

The tools and techniques applicable at different stages of the improvement process should be identified. The areas/projects for the application of these tools and the conditions (organizational and people) necessary for the successful application of each tool and technique have to be identified. In the first place, consideration should be given to identifying tools and techniques with which employees are familiar, and those which are in regular use. Tools and techniques should be classified as core and optional, depending on their nature and impact and the environment in which they are being applied, e.g. manufacturing or service.

The right type of training targeted at the right people should be developed; it should emphasize why, how and the benefits of the use of tools and techniques. Many studies (Payne and Dale, 1990; Dale and McQuater, 1998) have demonstrated that the right type of training helps to stop the misuse of tools and techniques, e.g. SPC being applied in the wrong areas, only part characteristics being measured, used only for control purposes, lack of reactive disciplines, etc. When tools and techniques have been used incorrectly, an additional set of problems in the introduction of TQM is created. Suitable training packages on tools and techniques should be developed and customized to the organization – this is perceived to be very important in some situations, e.g. Public Services. There is no correct 'formula' for training, since each organization will be starting from a different position and will have different needs, audiences, topics and views on the delivery mechanisms; however, the superior performing companies have well-developed, cyclical formal training programmes for TQM, and have mechanisms in place for determining the effectiveness of the training.

Any other systems and standards which may be required as part of future contractual or legislative requirements, or simply to compete in certain markets should be identified and implemented. If relevant systems and standards are integrated with the improvement initiative, it is less likely that the organization will have conflicting priorities and policies, and confusion will be less. Examples include ISO14001, BS8800, Investors in People, Citizen's Charter, the Management Charter Initiative, National Vocational Qualifications (NVQs), Environmental and Responsible Care programmes, and Hygiene requirements. Ethical, social and political issues also have to be considered.

The use of a formal quality management system should be considered, if one is not already in place. If such a system is already in use, then some evaluation of its contribution to TQM is vital; the objective should be to improve continually, to strengthen the quality system and to ensure that any improvements are built into the system. The requirements outlined in the ISO9000 series offers a good starting point.

Process analysis and improvement should be a continual part of the organization's improvement process. The focus should be on processes, such as business planning and control, and order generation, rather than functions within the organization. Process analysis gives emphasis to the centrality of quality throughout the business process and also focuses attention on customer and supplier relationships. Once key business processes have been identified along with their process owners, rationalization, simplification and identification of key performance measures can occur. This forms the basis for improvement and, despite the difficulties of implementing such improvements when significant organizational restructuring may be necessary, it can yield significant business results.

Measurement and Feedback

This pillar of the framework enables the 'voice of the customer' to be translated into measures of performance with which the organization can identify, and on which it can improve. It also deals with internal measures of performance, supplier assessment and development and rewards and recognition. Key actions at this stage are shown in the third column of table 8.1, and are explained further here.

Key internal and external performance measures should be identified and defined, to assess the progress being made with TQM, and to ensure that customers are satisfied. The measurement process involves a two-way flow of information between the organization and its customers and suppliers, and these parties should be consulted as part of the process of deciding what measurements to make. There are two key questions which need to be addressed in relation to feedback:

- To whom is it made?
- What level of detail is provided?

When traditional financial and accounting type data measurement criteria are evaluated in terms of their relevance to TQM, it is often found that many of the existing indicators are inaccurate, unfocused, unconnected and seen as an end in themselves, and therefore obsolete. Care must be taken to ensure that appropriate measures are developed, defined clearly and used. The chosen performance measures should help to facilitate the integration of TQM into the business processes of the organization and encourage all employees to focus on the key business and quality issues. It is suggested that an organization considers the use of the 'balanced scorecard' method. This method employs performance measures that contains different viewpoints and perspectives, typically representing customers, internal processes, continuous improvement and financial.

The performance indicators must be monitored, displayed and communicated through debriefing sessions on a regular basis, thereby sharing the information with all employees. This also assists with renewing commitment when the improvement process starts to stagnate:

- If we cannot express what we know in numbers, we don't know much about it.
- You cannot manage what you do not measure.

People are encouraged when they are able to see the results of their activities and efforts on key results areas and measures. This also applies to qualitative evidence such as photographs of shop floor and office areas before and after a campaign to improve housekeeping. It is also useful to feed back data on typical mistakes and what long-term corrective action has been taken to avoid them being made again; any goals and targets established as part of this should be achievable. It is important to build results and corrective actions into improvement plans and to standardize the improvements across the organization. Senior management must recognize that gathering data for external measures is time consuming, and extra resources may well be needed.

Assessment of supplier performance and feedback of any measurements along with corrective actions is also a key feature of this pillar of the framework.

Discussion with customers (internal as well as external) about the performance expected, their needs and expectations using a variety of techniques, should be undertaken. This must be an ongoing exercise to ensure that gaps between actual performance and customer needs and expectations are identified and analysed, and actions put in place for closing the gap. In going about this exercise, it is also important to assess the relationship between the sales and marketing functions, and the strengths of each. The main objective of all this is to build a partnership with customers, to develop customer loyalty and hence to build competitive advantage.

Issues have to be considered:

- How well the organization is meeting customer expectations
- How well the organization responds to customer's comments
- The chief causes of concern to customers
- The main complaints from customers
- Suggestions the customer might have for improvements
- How the organization rates against the competition
- Whether the data which has been collected is actually used to generate improvements which benefit the customer

In some organizations, it may be necessary to initiate suitable systems for identifying customer needs. Customers must also be encouraged and invited to challenge the organization who are delivering the product or service. The trend is for increasing the level of contact with customers (internal and external), and such 'moments of truth' occur far more frequently in commerce, public organizations and service type situations than in manufacturing organizations; see chapter 9. Many systems exist to identify customer needs:

- Customer workshops
- Client service centres
- Panels and clinics
- Focus groups
- Customer interviews
- Market research
- Surveys – mail (including electronic), telephone, comment cards, point of purchase
- Trialing the service and/or product
- Field trials of new products
- Using 'test' consumers and mystery shoppers
- Product launches
- Field contacts

There must be a methodology and system for analysing and feeding back the data gathered from customers by such means, i.e. customer service measurement; the same applies to data on competitors.

Goodman et al. (1996) report eight common pitfalls identified by Technical Assistance Research Programs Inc. (TARP) that undermine the integrity and value of customer feedback. These pitfalls are useful to keep in mind in tackling the issue of customer feedback data:

- Inefficient and costly data collection
- Inconsistent classification schemes
- Old data
- Analysis in a vacuum
- Analysis without priorities
- Analysis that is not actionable
- Ineffective presentation of data and findings
- Failure to track the impact of corrective actions resulting from the voice of customer process

A considerable amount of useful guidance on understanding customer needs is provided by Gale (1994), McCarthy (1997) and Vavra (1997).

Means of celebrating and communicating success with TQM should be considered, and methods developed for recognizing the efforts of teams and individuals. The issue of ownership for TQM is linked to providing adequate recognition, rewards and incentives for quality efforts and, in this way, the message that quality is a strategic concern is reinforced. Two quotes are worthy of mention:

- 'What gets measured gets done.' (Anders Scharp, former CEO, Electrolux)
- 'What gets rewarded gets repeated.' (Anne Vant Haaff, former corporate Quality Manager, KLM)

Publishing successes is an effective means of communicating how people have tackled improvements. It helps to build up in people's minds that beneficial changes have started to take place, things which, at one time, appeared impossible are now possible; it also helps convert the cynics – with published evidence of success, they cannot say TQM is not working. Nothing succeeds like success.

Companies struggle in deciding how to recognize the efforts of teams and individuals for a job well done; often they fail to think through the implications of their decisions in an adequate manner. Recognition and communication of success can be facilitated in a number of ways:

- Quality news sheets
- Teambriefs
- Quality action days
- Team competition/celebration days
- Quality conferences
- Presentations by the President and/or CEO
- Supplier award days
- 'How are we doing' boards
- 'Thank you' notes
- Small tokens of appreciation such as mugs, pens, meals, certificates and trophies
- Publicity in the company newsletter
- Personal thanks
- Applause
- Special functions, e.g. dinner, get-togethers, overseas trips, use of the company resources for personal use
- Allocation of shares in the company
- Recognition of performance by customers

Personal 'thank you' and 'praise' notes from senior management are often seen as a more genuine recognition than buying people through money. Townsend and Gebhardt (1997b) presents some useful examples of successful recognition programmes which provide a range of thought provoking ideas.

In some organizations, people do not welcome individual recognition as they are made to feel uncomfortable by their peers but, in others, tokens of recognition are warmly desired and appreciated. To help in deciding the most appropriate way to celebrate success, it is recommended that views from employees are sought and the methods tailored to suit the needs of both the situation and employees.

Benchmarking should be considered once the organization has taken some steps to improve quality. The benchmarking of a small number of strategic processes helps employees to see the need for changes and thereby gives impetus to the improvement process. The concept of benchmarking is a proven technique for assisting companies with a process of continuous improvement. Internal performance and practices are compared with those of other companies, including the superior performing companies, in a bid to develop, improve and achieve best practice that lead to superior performance; see Camp (1989; 1995) and chapter 19 for details.

Linking rewards to improvement activities and results must be considered, although it is controversial. Financial payment for participation in improvement activities should be discouraged, in particular, those schemes relating to the individuals, but perhaps not overlooked. Continuous improvement should be a natural part of every person's job but people at different levels of the organizations have widely differing expectations of what improvement means to them personally and the company. There is a view, however, that 'links to pay and promotion may still be the most tangible proof that top executives take total quality seriously'; see Troy (1991). An IDS Study (1991) concentrated on those incentive schemes in which quality or customer service are major determinants of bonus payments. It concluded that few companies have sought 'to make a direct link between quality or customer service targets and then payment'. The study did go on to describe how Rank Xerox, Elida Gibbs, Scottish Widows, Companies House, British Steel and 3M have linked bonus payments in this way.

If there is pressure within an organization for financial payment, perhaps it could be approached through a Japanese style suggestion system (see chapter 3) or along the lines of the Improvement Opportunity Scheme as described by Piddington et al. (1995). Organizations and individuals have different perceptions of the value of suggestion schemes. Here are two common complaints:

- 'We did not get any feedback so we are not going to make any more suggestions.'
- 'The response time to the suggestion was too long.'

Means of assessing the progress of the business towards world class performance should be used. For example, The MBNQA Criteria for Performance (US Department of Commerce, 1998) and the EFQM (1998) Model for Business Excellence should be considered; see chapter 22.

Changing the Culture

Organizations attempt to change culture for different reasons. Changing the culture is a key element in TQM and has wide-ranging implications for the whole organization; it requires the introduction and acceptance of individual, group, and organizational change. TQM provides the opportunity to make and influence behaviour and attitudes which have real effects on internal and external relationships and the way the organization conducts its business.

Culture change is not just relevant to TQM, although the increased emphasis on customers and their needs makes some form of culture change a must for most organizations. There is, however, a shortage of information and guidance for companies looking for ways to change, plan and facilitate culture change. The change of culture must be planned to avoid ambiguity and to facilitate improvement; managers must learn to lead change, and useful advice is provided on this issue by Atkinson (1990), Kanter et al. (1991), Schein (1985) and Tichy (1983). The current status from both management and employee perspectives should be established before firm plans for change are developed.

It is not possible to identify key actions for this stage, but there are a number of features which should be considered. These are listed in the fourth column of table 8.1 and explained further here.

An assessment, from both management and employee perspectives, of the current status of the organizational culture should be undertaken before firm plans for change are developed. Senior management must be prepared to resolve conflicts, and cope with resistance to change which is identified in the assessment; the personal values of staff and their expectations sometimes present a problem.

Culture change must be recognized as ongoing, rather than a prerequisite to the introduction of TQM. Some degree of culture change in terms of senior management commitment and leadership and provision of adequate resources must, however, take place prior to, and as part of, the organizing stage. For example, the effective use of tools and techniques, developing the quality management system to meet the requirements of the ISO9000 series, teamwork, the impact of successful improvement projects, presentations, recognition, effective channels of communication, etc. are all activities which can contribute to culture change. Of course, other activities will contribute to the culture change process – e.g. improving the environment in terms of provision of uniforms and safety shoes, team meeting rooms and lockers – but may not connect directly with TQM and the improvement process. The crucial factor is a recognition of these activities and their contribution to culture change. In planning any changes, it is useful to develop thinking along these lines:

- 'Where are we now?'
- 'Where do we want to be?'

Middle management must be involved in the planning process, since the burden of change falls on them.

The role of people within the organization should be recognized. The way that these people are treated is vital, since they are an intellectual asset whose value to the organization can be increased by careful nurturing, or decreased by poor management. It should also be recognized that most organizations comprise people of differing ages, background, skills, abilities, levels of enthusiasm, levels of flexibility and ability to accept change; in some industries, tradition is very deep rooted and this presents a specific set of resistance to change difficulties. If culture change is to be successful, these people-based factors must be taken into account. The means of developing and involving people must be identified; a skills audit is a useful starting point for this. The Investors in People programme provides useful advice on people development.

Change should be planned and take place in a consistent and incremental manner. Experience indicates that if the change is too great and unplanned, the organization will revert back to the *status quo*. Clear and public displays of key indicators and 'how are we doing data' help to ensure that the changes which are made are real and that no slippage occurs. While there may also be some unexpected outcomes, they are no substitute for planned change.

The planned changes must be outlined in specific terms and, where possible, qualified against a time-scale. Employee attitude surveys, customer surveys and internal customer–supplier workshops are also useful for identifying culture change indicators. Here are some examples of possible changes:

- Creating a single-status environment and harmonizing conditions, eliminating other traditional status symbols, such as reserved car parking spaces, different types of dining facilities, different terms and conditions of employment (i.e. move blue collar sick pay towards that of staff) and other forms of demarcation (i.e. seasonal gifts being shared rather than going to individuals)
- Reducing the number of organizational levels
- Delegating decision making and the responsibility for taking actions down to the lowest possible level, thus spreading the power base
- Senior managers meeting employees of all levels on a regular basis
- Teaching managers to adopt a listening, consulting and learning style of leadership
- Enabling every employee to visit a customer and other parts of the business
- Arranging operator exchange programmes
- Arranging for operators to 'brief' customers during customer visits to the sites
- Developing a requirement for senior management to spend a specified amount of time with people at the operating level of the business
- Requiring the CEO to attend one meeting of each active quality team on an annual basis
- Training managers to act as trainers
- Changing the payment system to one which recognizes issues such as the team, acquisition of skills, flexibility, etc.
- Replacing supervision by leadership, and giving staff more freedom to get on with the job
- Introducing the concept of 'associates' rather than employees
- Making it possible for operators to move between jobs within the business
- Introducing cross-functional team activity
- Providing opportunities for management to listen to the views of staff and customers and to develop a listening and learning style of leadership
- Encouraging staff to tell management where they are going wrong – it is important to put into place a mechanism for ensuring that this happens, and providing guidance to staff in how to go about it, and to management on how to handle such feedback
- Changing to a cellular type organization
- Recognizing and respecting people's contribution to the business
- Providing financial education for everyone

The grid shown in figure 8.3 can be used to classify the degree of difficulty of each change and its effects.

Teamwork is an important facilitator in culture change, but organizations must ensure that the organizational infrastructure can adapt to the changes which teamwork will bring. The operating characteristics of the teams to be employed in TQM should be defined and communicated; see chapter 21. It is also essential that participants in teams and other improvement activities are volunteers, not 'conscripts'.

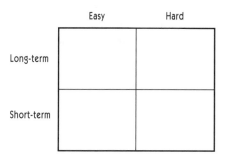

Figure 8.3 Culture change grid

The interrelationships of all activities in the organization, and the way in which they contribute to the overall quality of service and product provided should be identified, so that conflict is minimized and TQM becomes part of the way in which the business is run. Such conflict typically arises at middle management level, where the impact of strategic initiatives meets the problems of day-to-day running of the organization. In any large organization, there will be a variety of initiatives going on at one time, many of which will affect staff directly (e.g. installation of new computer systems, development of IT, introduction of Manufacturing Resources Planning (MRP II), cost-cutting exercises, marketing promotions), and these may indirectly contribute to the quality of product and service provided. It is important that management and staff understand the relationship between these and formal improvement initiatives; otherwise they may be perceived as being in conflict, and thus not achieve the desired outcomes. A case in point is the strain on resources, resulting in people not attending quality team meetings.

Factors which indicate that TQM has started to change culture should be identified. Without such factors, it is difficult to know whether culture change is taking place, and the concept may be undermined by 'lack of results'. Here are some factors that indicate that culture is changing:

- People see for themselves the need for tools and techniques.
- Motivators and champions start to emerge from various parts of the organization.
- People talk processes and not functions.
- Changes to procedures and systems are easier to make.
- People are not afraid of expressing their views.
- People show a positive response to recognition.
- Employees are viewed by senior management as an asset, and not as a cost.
- People volunteer to take on tasks which previously would have involved considerable negotiations between management and unions.
- Shop stewards assist management to explain new procedures.
- People ask for their setting-up activities to be video taped so as to reduce the machine down time.
- Ideas and suggestions start to flow from the shop floor.
- People show a willingness to serve others.
- Team meetings are scheduled outside of the shift team, without pay.
- Improvement teams ask management to suggest project themes.
- The distinction between the 'manager' and the 'managed' becomes hazy.

- Senior management shift their attention from TQM to concentrate on other things, but improvement activities continue.
- Continuous improvement continues in the face of organizational instability.

In planning for change, thought needs to be given to the culture of a country and its people. A national culture is a set of shared values, beliefs and behaviours which binds people into a relatively cohesive group; however, there may be sub-cultures within countries, i.e. local cultures. Details of national culture are provided by Hofstede (1984) in terms of four dimensions – power distance, uncertainty avoidance, individualism and masculinity:

- Companies in Hong Kong are characterized by paternalistic leadership, power, distance and, to some degree, risk avoidance by employees. In Hong Kong, there is also a tendency for Chinese people not to be open in reflecting opinions and ideas; they tend to look first for personal monetary reward and benefits. Such attitudes can be in conflict with culture change which is a longer-term process.
- In South Africa, there are a number of issues which have to be considered such as the political/union situation, the use of traditional leaders in an ethnic sense, the inherent suspicion of management by the workforce as a result of historical and political reasons, the characteristics of both first and third world cultures and concepts, racial integration of personnel by means of positive assertive actions, and the eleven official languages.

In addition, the culture of different industry types, which are often quite strong, needs to be taken into account.

Use of the Framework

The framework should be used as part of an eight-stage process:

1 Review the organization's adoption of TQM to date. This should include a presentation by senior management on the progress to date and future plans. The grid shown in figure 8.4 can be used for pinpointing the current position; The features of the four first four levels of the TQM adoption model (see chapter 4) – 'uncommitted', 'drifters', 'tool pushers' and 'improvers' – are also of help in positioning an organization. This stage can comprise a TQM awareness session if the business is relatively immature in their adoption of TQM.

2 Customize the framework to suit the individual organization. In the first place, a full presentation of the framework is made to the participants. If the framework is being developed for a single organization, the senior and middle managers are divided into syndicate groups and tasked to consider the features of each section of the framework and to customize it to suit the individual organization and its business. If the framework is being used in an open workshop session, and the participants are from manufacturing industry, the syndicate groups can be organized either by size of organization or type of industry. If they are from a mix of sectors, they can be organized by sector, e.g. manufacturing, transport, financial, public sector, healthcare.

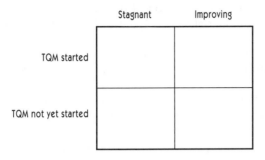

	Stagnant	Improving
TQM started		
TQM not yet started		

Figure 8.4 TQM grid

Culture Change Section	Yes	In part	No
Commitment			
– Senior management	●		
– Visibility		●	
Current status			
– Questionnaire			●
Employee involvement	●		
Training and people Development			
– Customer appreciation	●		
– Appraisals/objectives	●		
– Skills audit		●	
Conditions of employment			●
People environment		●	

Figure 8.5 TQM framework: feature assessment

3 Present and debate the customized framework. A spokesperson from each syndicate group makes a presentation on the framework they have developed, with the features of each group's framework being debated in open forum. In the case of a single company, a consolidated framework is developed, based on what has been agreed in the discussion arising from the open forum. If the syndicate group comprises a number of different companies, the participants can take the framework back to their own organization and then either debate the framework with their management team (and add or delete features as appropriate) or repeat the syndicate exercise as a single management team.

4 Assess which features of the framework are already in place. Self-audit surveys and internal and external indicators can be employed. A number of methods of measurement can be used, for example, ranking each feature on a 1–6 scale or the use of a yes, no, in-part classification. Figure 8.5 shows an example of this.

5 Prioritize the features which are not already in place. This should be done in accordance with the overall strategy and business plans of the organization. In some cases, an organization may wish to accept this generic framework as it stands, thereby skipping steps 2 and 3. The way that this had been handled is

to present the organizing section of the framework to the management team and for them to undertake steps 4 and 5 above. This is repeated for the other three sections.

6 Develop plans to introduce the prioritized features of the framework identified in the previous stage. The plans should have a start and finish date, with detailed actions, milestones, resources and responsibilities.

7 Communicate the details of the framework and the plans derived from it down through the organization. This helps to gain acceptance. The framework should also be communicated to suppliers and customers.

8 Identify any potential problems in putting the plans developed at stage 6 into place. Here are some of the typical problems encountered:

- Lack of structure and how to formalize the existing organization in relation to current management roles and responsibilities
- Lack of trained personnel
- Definition of terms, e.g. customer response time
- Conflict of barriers
- Traditional attitudes
- Time conflicts/constraints
- Constructing a real and meaningful mission statement which can be owned.

The format shown in table 8.2 can be used as part of this process.

Table 8.2 TQM framework: organizing section

Features Vision			Plans			
What will it look like?	What does it involve?	What is the current situation?	What needs to be done?	Who is going to do it?	What is going to be done?	What are the obstacles/issues?
1						
2						

Summary

These are the outcomes derived by those organizations who have used the framework:

- Developing the framework provides a mechanism for debating TQM and continuous improvement strategies, plans, actions and initiatives, and helps to generate a common level of understanding and to reconcile views and opinions. It also assists management in identifying the factors which can slow down the process of improvement (e.g. inconsistent objectives, insufficient involvement and ownership, lack of data, lack of operator involvement, failure to complete projects, break-up of improvement teams, etc.) and helps to pinpoint and eradicate weaknesses in the current TQM approach of the organization.
- The framework, once developed and customized, becomes a reference point for current and future improvement initiatives. It builds on the quality initiatives

already in place, and guides the organization's development of TQM in a formal manner.

- Use of the framework requires all members of senior and middle management to be involved in the planning process, thereby developing ownership of the resultant plans. The prioritizing of the framework features in conjunction with business and commercial needs against a time-scale helps to ensure that TQM is part of the business planning process and integrated with other strategies.
- The framework provides a means of communicating, in the organization's own language, what is involved with TQM, and it provides the essential logic of why the organization is adopting and progressing TQM and what is involved. It ensures that discussions on improvement are both structured and specific.
- In a multi-site operation, the framework provides a common approach and language for all businesses, and those likely to be acquired in the future. In this way, it avoids confusion with common suppliers and customers, and it presents a consistent approach and TQM image to both employees and the market-place. It helps to understand what each site has achieved in relation to TQM, assists in taking policy decisions – e.g. individual or common vision and mission statements, specific sites taking the lead role in piloting training programmes, quality management tools and techniques – shares common experiences and highlights the availability of resources, mutual assistance, training, expertise, experiences, etc. It also helps those businesses who are less advanced, in terms of TQM, to discuss in a coherent manner common issues of interest with those more advanced, i.e. the common language and approach helps to facilitate 'technology' transfer.
- It provides the means for the local management committee and/or the TQM Steering Committee to assess the progress made by businesses against the plans developed and ensures that issues are followed through. In undertaking this task, problems can be identified and appropriate countermeasures can be developed.
- It can be used not only to assess the maturity of TQM but to audit whether certain features of the framework are firmly in place. In this way, the next set of priorities can be identified.
- The correct use of the framework ensures that an organization puts in place the key features of TQM and a process of continuous improvement. Many of these fundamentals are encompassed in the 'TQM packages' offered by consultants. Thus an organization who feels they need some 'outside' assistance, can introduce and start a process of improvement without necessarily going to the expense of employing a management consultant. The use, if any, of a consultant could come later in the process when more specialized and detailed advice is required.

References

Akao, Y. (ed.) 1991: *Hoshin Kanri: Policy Deployment for Successful TQM*. Cambridge, Mass.: Productivity Press.

Atkinson, P. 1990: *Creating Culture Change*. Bedfordshire: IFS Ltd.

Bass, B. M. 1985: *Leadership and Performance Beyond Expectations*. New York: Free Press.

Boaden, R. J. and Dale, B. G. 1993: Managing quality improvement in financial services: a framework and case study. *The Service Industries Journal*, 13(1), 17–39.

Bunney, H. S. and Dale, B. G. 1996: The effect of organisational change on sustaining a process of continuous improvement. *Quality Engineering*, 8(4), 649–57.

Camp, R. C. 1989: *Benchmarking: the Search for Best Practices that Lead to Superior Performance*. Milwaukee: ASQC Quality Press.

Camp, R. C. 1995: *Business Process Benchmarking: Finding and Implementing the Best Practices*. Milwaukee: ASQC Quality Press.

Crofton, C. G. and Dale, B. G. 1996: The difficulties encountered in the introduction of total quality management: a case study examination. *Quality Engineering*, 8(3), 433–9.

Dale, B. G. 1990: Policy deployment. *The TQM Magazine*, 2(6), 321–4.

Dale, B. G. 1991: Starting on the road to success. *The TQM Magazine*, 3(2), 125–8.

Dale, B. G. and Boaden, R. J. 1993: Improvement framework. *The TQM Magazine*, 5(1), 23–6.

Dale, B. G. and Lightburn, K. 1992: Continuous quality improvement: why some organisations lack commitment. *International Journal of Production Economics*, 27(1), 57–67.

Dale, B. G. and McQuater, R. E. 1998: *Managing Business Improvement and Quality: Implementing Key Tools and Techniques*. Oxford: Blackwell Business.

EFQM (European Foundation for Quality Management) 1998: *Self-Assessment 1998 Guidelines for Companies*. Brussels: EFQM.

Gale, B. T. 1994: *Managing Customer Value*. New York: The Free Press.

Goodman, J., De Palma, D. and Broetzmann, S. 1996: Maximizing the value of customer feedback. *Quality Progress*, December, 35–9.

Hofstede, G. 1984: *Culture's Consequences*. Sage Publications. California.

IDS (Incomes Data Services) 1991: Bonus schemes: Part 2. *IDS Study No. 492*, October, London.

Kanter, R. M., Stein, B. A. and Jick, T. D. 1991: *The Challenge of Organisational Change*. New York: Free Press.

Kotter, J. P. 1990: *A Force for Change: How Leadership Differs From Management*. New York: Free Press.

Maxwell, J. C. 1993: *Developing the Leaders Within You*. Nashville: Nelson.

Maxwell, J. C. 1995: *Developing the Leaders Around You*. Nashville: Nelson.

McCarthy, D. C. 1997: *The Loyalty Link: How Loyal Employees Create Loyal Customers*. New York: John Wiley and Son.

Newall, D. and Dale, B. G. 1991: The introduction and development of a quality improvement process: a study. *International Journal of Production Research*, 29(9), 1747–60.

Payne, B. J. and Dale, B. G. 1990: Total quality management training: some observations. *Quality Forum*, 16(1), 5–9.

Piddington, H., Bunney, H. S. and Dale, B. G. 1995: Rewards and recognition in quality improvement in what are the key issues. *Quality World Technical Supplement*, March, 12–18.

Schein, E. H. 1985: *Organisational Culture and Leadership*. Oxford: Jossey-Base.

Tichy, N. M. 1983: *Managing Strategic Change: Technical Political and Cultural Dynamics*. New York: John Wiley and Sons.

Townsend, P. L. and Gebhardt, J. E. 1997a: *Quality in Action: 93 Lessons in Leadership, Participation and Measurement*. New York: John Wiley and Son.

Townsend, P. L. and Gebhardt, J. E. 1997b: *Recognition, Gratitude and Celebration*. Menlo Park, CA: Crisp Publication.

Troy, K. 1991: *Employee Buy-in to Total Quality*, R–97, New York: The Conference Board.

US Department of Commerce. 1998: *Malcolm Baldrige National Quality Award, 1998 Criteria for Performance Excellence*, National Institute of Standards and Technology, Gaithersburg, USA.

avra, T. G. 1997: *Improving Your Measurement of Customer Satisfaction*. Milwaukee: ASQC Quality Press.

chapter nine

Managing Service Quality

B. R. Lewis

Introduction

Managing service quality is concerned with understanding what is meant by service quality, what its determinants are and how they may be measured, and identifying the potential shortfalls in service quality – how they might arise and how they can be prevented. Responsibility for quality service lies with operations, marketing, HR and other management – working together within an organization.

Service quality issues have been of academic and practitioner interest to marketers (in particular) for more than two decades, resulting from the increasing importance of the services sector in the economy – to include both public and private, profit and non-profit organizations. This covers industries such as financial services, health care, tourism, professional services, government, transport and communications – where the focus of business activity is on 'services' rather than 'products'.

Services are characterized as being different from products along a number of dimensions which have implications for the quality of service provided to customers.

- Services are typically intangible. There is usually little or no tangible evidence to show once a service – for example, investment advice, or consultation with a doctor – has been performed.
- The production and consumption of many services are simultaneous; the service may not be separable from the person of the seller, and the customer may be involved in the service performance, e.g. legal advice. Thus, the service process, including staff at the customer interface, becomes integral to service quality.
- Related to this is the notion of heterogeneity: variability often exists in services as a function of labour inputs and non-standardization of delivery, and so the use of quality standards in the conventional sense is more difficult.
- Many services cannot be stored to meet fluctuations in demand – e.g. a doctor's time, purchase of shares in a privatization issue, and a hotel room – and so companies need to develop systems to manage supply and demand.

Further to this, as product and process quality and TQM have become prime concerns in the manufacturing sector, is the acknowledgement that service is critical for all organizations and that, in the manufacturing sector, quality is related not only to the product itself but also to all aspects of its supply and delivery through the non-manufacturing functions and, often, after sales use/service. Customer service and service quality is now a focus for any corporate or marketing strategy and high levels of service are typically seen as a means for an organization to achieve a competitive advantage. Consequently, it is clear that the service quality concepts and frameworks developed for the services sector, are applicable to all organizations and that attention needs to be focused on products/services, their production and delivery, together with all those personnel who are instrumental to quality service.

In this chapter, some comments will be made on the changing business environment which has implications for service quality. The focus will then turn to defining service quality, measurement of service quality and the role of personnel in service delivery. The final sections are concerned with the service delivery process, the need to monitor service quality, and the development of service recovery strategies.

The Service Environment

Environmental trends which impact on service and quality issues relate to consumers' awareness and expectations, technological developments, and competitive elements.

Consumers, be they individuals, households or businesses, are more aware of the alternatives on offer (in relation to both services/products and to provider organizations) and rising standards of service; so, their expectations of service and quality are elevated and they are increasingly critical of the quality of service they experience. Expectations are what people feel a service/product should offer and relate to the company and its marketing mix, both the traditional elements (product, price, place and promotion), and the extended elements of physical evidence, process and people; see Booms and Bitner (1981). The physical environment includes tangible clues which might be essential (e.g. computers in a travel agency) or peripheral (e.g. decor and uniforms) to a service being bought. The service process is also critical: if systems are poor (e.g. breakdown of computer access to customer accounts in a bank), employees are blamed and consumers perceive poor quality service. Personnel are also integral to the production of a service as already mentioned and, although their degree of contact with the customer varies, all have a contribution to make.

Advances in technology (e.g. management information systems (MISs), marketing information systems to include customer databases, bankers automated clearing system (BACS) and tourism reservation/booking systems) make a major contribution to facilitate customer–company exchanges and increase levels of service. Increased mechanization and computerization can de-personalize service(s) but also result in increases in speed, efficiency, accuracy and improved service(s). The other side of the coin is that depersonalized service could lead to less customer loyalty; but, generally, high 'tech' and high 'touch' go hand in hand, better personal service with enhanced technological efficiency. Technology can free employees' time and allow them to concentrate on the customer and to enhance customer–staff interaction. Technology should not replace people in the provision of service(s).

In addition, the business environment is increasingly complex and competitive as a result of economic conditions, legislative activity – e.g. deregulations in financial services and air travel, and the Citizens' Charter in the UK public sector – and widened customer choice and sophistication. Corporate reaction has been, on the one hand, to emphasize operations and financial efficiency, and/or more focused product and market strategies. In addition, they may have an appreciation of the importance of customer service and quality, and the possible opportunities for attaining differentiation and achieving a competitive edge by providing superior service, i.e. service quality is seen as a mechanism to achieve pre-eminence in the market place and the battle for market shares and, so, becomes a factor in strategic planning.

Benefits of good service

Without a focus on service quality, organizations will face problems and complaints from both employees and customers, and associated financial and other costs. Further, a proportion of dissatisfied customers will complain and tell others, generating adverse word-of-mouth publicity and possibly accusations of blame between personnel in the organization; and some customers will switch to competitors. With a service quality improvement process, an organization can expect a number of benefits.

- The most often mentioned benefit is enhancing customer loyalty through satisfaction. Looking after present customers can generate repeat and increased business, and may lead to the attraction of new customers from positive word-of-mouth communication. This is significantly more cost effective than trying to attract new customers; see, for example, Rosenberg and Czepiel (1984).
- A number of organizations highlight the additional benefits of increased opportunities for cross-selling; see Lewis (1990). Comprehensive and up-to-date product knowledge and sales techniques among employees, combined with developing relationships and rapport with customers, enable staff to identify customer needs and to suggest relevant products.
- In relation to employees, benefits may be seen in terms of increased job satisfaction and morale and commitment to the company, good employer–employee relationships, and increased staff loyalty; these all contribute to reducing the rate of staff turnover and the associated costs of recruitment, selection and training activities. Further to this, Heskett et al. (1994), in their service-profit chain, model the impact of employee satisfaction and performance and employee loyalty and retention, on customer satisfaction and retention, and organizational success.
- In addition, good service quality enhances corporate image and may provide insulation from price competition; some customers will pay a premium for reliable service quality. Overall, successful service quality leads to reduced costs (of mistakes, operating, advertising and promotion) and increased productivity and sales, market shares, profitability and business performance.

Defining Service Quality

At this point, it is useful to introduce the concept of 'service encounters', which may also be referred to as 'moments of truth' or 'critical incidents'; see Albrecht and Zemke (1985) and Czepiel et al. (1985). A service encounter is any direct interaction between a service provider and customers, and may take varying forms. For example, a bank customer wishing to make an account enquiry may choose between an interaction with an ATM (automated teller machine), or with a bank employee by telephone phone, letter or face-to-face in a branch: every time a customer comes into contact with any aspect of the bank and its employees he or she has an opportunity to form an impression of the bank and its service. Service encounters have a high 'impact' on consumers; the quality of the encounter is an essential element in the overall impressions and evaluation of the quality of service experienced by the customer.

Service encounters also have an impact on employees in relation to their motivation, performance and job satisfaction, and their rewards. Consequently, all organizations need to manage their service encounters effectively for the benefit of customers and employees, and for the achievement of corporate goals. This concept is developed further by Lewis and Entwistle (1990), who illustrate the variety of encounters which may prevail and which together impact on customer service and quality.

Service quality is variously defined, but essentially is to do with meeting customer needs and requirements, and how well the service level delivered matches customers' expectations. Expectations are desires/wants (i.e. what we feel a service provider should offer) and are formed on the basis of previous experience of a company and its marketing mix, awareness of competitors and word-of-mouth communication.

Consequently, service quality becomes a consumer judgement and results from comparisons by consumers of expectations of service with their perceptions of actual service delivered; see Gronroos (1984) and Berry et al. (1985; 1988). If there is a shortfall, then a service quality 'gap' exists which providers would wish to close. However, one needs to bear in mind two points:

- Higher levels of performance lead to higher expectations.
- To find expectations greater than performance implies that perceived quality is less than satisfactory, but that is not to say that service is of low quality. Quality is relative to initial expectations – one of the issues to take into account when measuring service quality.

The concept of service quality gaps was developed from the extensive research of Berry and his colleagues (Parasuraman et al., 1985; Zeithaml et al., 1988). They defined service quality to be a function of the gap between consumers' expectations of a service and their perceptions of the actual service delivery by an organization; and suggested that this gap is influenced by several other gaps which may occur in an organization:

Gap 1: Consumer expectations – Management perceptions of consumer expectations

Managers' perceptions of customers' expectations may be different from actual customer needs and desires, i.e. managers do not necessarily know what customers (both internal and external) want and expect from a company. This may be remedied by market research activities (e.g. interviews, surveys, focus groups and complaint monitoring) and better communication between management and personnel throughout the organization.

Gap 2: Management perceptions of consumer expectations – Service quality specifications actually set

Even if customer needs are known, they may not be translated into appropriate service specifications, due to a lack of resources, organizational constraints or absence of management commitment to a service culture and service quality. The need for management commitment and resources for service quality cannot be over-stated.

Gap 3: Service quality specifications – Actual service delivery

This 'service performance gap' occurs when the service that is delivered is different from management's specifications for service, due to variations in the performance of personnel – employees not being able or willing to perform at a desired level. Solutions are central to HR management and will be returned to later in this chapter.

Gap 4: Actual service delivery – External communications about the service

What is said about (the) service in external communications is different from the service that is delivered, i.e. advertising and promotion can influence consumers' expectations and perceptions of service. Therefore, it is important not to promise more than can be delivered (or expectations increase and perceptions decrease), nor fail to present relevant information. Success in this area requires appropriate and timely information/communication both internally and to external customers.

Gaps 1–4 together contribute to consumers' expectations and perceptions of actual service (gap 5). Organizations need to identify the gaps prevalent in their organization, determine the factors responsible for them, and develop appropriate solutions.

Dimensions of service

Dimensions of service quality are diverse and relate to both a basic service package and an augmented service offering (Gronroos, 1987). A basic or core service product might be hotel accommodation, with associated services which are required to facilitate consumption of the core service (e.g. hotel reception and check-in) and supporting services which are not required but may enhance the service and differentiate it from competition (e.g. a restaurant in a hotel). The augmented service offering includes how the service is delivered (process) and the interactions between a company and its customers:

- The accessibility of the service, e.g. the number of hotel receptionists and their skills and hotel design
- Customer participation in the process, e.g. the need to fill in forms
- The interactions between employees and customers, systems and customers, and the physical environment and customers

Dimensions of service (quality) have been discussed for nearly 20 years. Gronroos (1984) referred to the technical (outcome) quality of service encounters (i.e. what is received by the customer), and the functional quality of the process (i.e. the way in which (the) service is delivered) which, typically, includes the attitudes and behaviour, appearance and personality, service mindedness, accessibility and approachability of customer contact personnel. In addition, there exists the corporate image dimension of quality which is the result of how customers perceive a company, and which is built up by the technical and functional quality of its service(s). This model was later synthesized with one from manufacturing which incorporated design, production, delivery and relational dimensions of quality; see Gummesson and Gronroos (1987).

Other key contributors have been Lehtinen and Lehtinen (1982), who referred to process quality (as judged by consumers during a service) and output quality (judged after a service is performed). Edvardsson et al. (1989) presented four aspects of quality which affect customers' perceptions.

1 *Technical quality*: to include skills of service personnel and the design of the service system
2 *Integrative quality*: the ease with which different portions of the service delivery system work together
3 *Functional quality*: to include all aspects of the manner in which the service is delivered to the customer to include style, environment and availability
4 *Outcome quality*: whether the actual service product meets both service standards or specifications and customer needs/expectations

However, the most widely reported set of service quality determinants is that proposed by Parasuraman et al. (1985; 1988). They suggested that the criteria used by consumers that are important in moulding their expectations and perceptions of service fit ten dimensions:

1 *Tangibles*: physical evidence
2 *Reliability*: getting it right first time, honouring promises
3 *Responsiveness*: willingness, readiness to provide service
4 *Communication*: keeping customers informed in a language they can understand
5 *Credibility*: honesty, trustworthiness
6 *Security*: physical, financial and confidentiality
7 *Competence*: possession of required skills and knowledge of all employees
8 *Courtesy*: politeness, respect, friendliness
9 *Understanding*/knowing the customer, his needs and requirements
10 *Access*: ease of approach and contact

These ten dimensions vary with respect to how easy, or difficult, it is to evaluate them. Some, such as tangibles or credibility, are known in advance but most are experience criteria and can only be evaluated during or after consumption. Some, such as competence and security, may be difficult or impossible to evaluate, even after purchase. In general, customers rely on experience properties when evaluating services. Subsequent factor analysis and testing by Parasuraman et al. (1988) condensed these determinants into five categories (tangibles, reliability, responsiveness, assurance and empathy) to which Gronroos (1988) added a sixth dimension – recovery.

Service providers should also consider the contribution of Johnston et al. (1990) and Silvestro et al. (1990) who investigated service quality in UK organizations and identified fifteen determinants which they categorized as hygiene, enhancing, or dual threshold factors.

- *Hygiene factors* are those which are expected by the customer. Failure to deliver these will cause dissatisfaction: cleanliness in a restaurant, train arrival time, confidentiality of financial affairs, lack of queues and return of phone calls.

- *Enhancing factors* lead to customer satisfaction but failure to deliver will not necessarily cause dissatisfaction, e.g. bank clerk addressing you by name and the welcome received from a waiter in a restaurant.
- *Dual threshold factors* are those for which failure to deliver will cause dissatisfaction and delivery above a certain level will enhance customers' perceptions of service and lead to satisfaction, e.g. explanation of a mortgage service including repayment level, interest charges, payback period and other relevant conditions.

Zones of tolerance

Consumers' expectations with respect to dimensions of service are generally reasonable; for example, they expect luggage to arrive with them on an aircraft, and planes to arrive on-time most of the time. They also expect basics; for example, from a hotel in terms of security, cleanliness, and being treated with respect. However, expectations vary depending on a host of circumstances and experiences, and they also rise over time. Further, experience with one service provider (e.g. a hotel, or a doctor) can influence expectations of others (e.g. a banker, or a lawyer).

In addition, consumers have what Parasuraman et al. (1991a) refer to as 'zones of tolerance', the difference between *desired* and *adequate* expectations. The desired level of service expectation is what they hope to receive, a blend of what 'can' and 'should' be, which is a function of past experience. The adequate level is what they find acceptable based in part on their assessment of what the service 'will be', the 'predicted' service; it also depends on the alternatives which are available. Tolerance zones vary between individuals, service aspects and with experience, and tend to be smaller for outcome features than for process dimensions. In addition, if options are limited or non-existent (e.g. choice of general practitioner services, rail and airplane routes or hotels) desires may not decrease but tolerance levels may be higher; conversely, if many alternatives are available (e.g. choice of restaurants in a city), it is easy to switch and tolerance zones are more limited. Further, expectations are higher in emergency situations (e.g. the theft of a cheque book or loss of credit card) and when something was not right the first time.

Measurement of service quality

Parasuraman's dimensions of service provided the basis of the 'Servqual' questionnaire (Parasuraman et al. 1988), which was designed to measure service quality, i.e. the comparison between consumers' expectations of service (E) with their perceptions of actual service delivered (P). This is a 22-item scale with reported good reliability and validity which can be used to better understand service expectations and perceptions of consumers. The original scale items were of this form:

Service expectations (E):
'Customers should be able to trust bank employees.'
'Banks should have up-to-date equipment.'
Strongly agree . . . Strongly disagree
1   2   3   4   5   6   7

and perceptions (P):
'I can trust the employees of my bank.'
'My bank has up-to-date equipment.'
Strongly agree . . . Strongly disagree
1   2   3   4   5   6   7

The authors claimed that Servqual is a measure relevant to a broad spectrum of services and is based on their five generic service quality dimensions: reliability, responsiveness, assurance, empathy and tangibles. Further, they suggest that Servqual may be used to track service quality trends and improve service, categorize customers, compare branches/outlets of an organization and compare an organization with its competitors. However, it is limited to current and past customers because respondents need knowledge and experience of the company.

The dimensions of service quality have been investigated by both theorists and practitioners, together with associated measurement tools. In particular, a host of research studies have used Servqual and/or examined various aspects of the methodology. A number of criticisms have emerged, which are summarized by Smith (1995) and Buttle (1996).

In response to some of the criticisms, Parasuraman et al. (1991b; 1993; 1994) have continued to defend Servqual over other methods of evaluation of service quality, for its practical and diagnostic value. In their revised Servqual (Parasuraman et al., 1991b), a number of changes were introduced:

- Changing negatively worded statements to a positive wording
- Respondents are now required to indicate 'what an excellent service would provide' rather than 'what firms in an industry should provide'
- Changing some of the items
- Assessing the relative importance of Servqual's five dimensions by asking respondents to allocate 100 points between the five dimensions

In all, several conceptual, methodological and interpretive issues surround Servqual and its use, and there is a current debate as to whether the perceptions measure alone can predict overall measures of service quality as effectively as $P–E$ scores.

Additional measurement issues include: consideration of scaling techniques; the evidence that not all service quality dimensions are equally important; and that attributes and importance may change over time. A further concern relates to timing of measurement: before, during or after a particular service encounter. Finally, customers' assessments are generally with regard to routine service encounters: organizations also need to consider non-routine encounters.

So, there remains considerable challenge for both academics and practitioners to refine the methods used to identify and measure appropriate dimensions of service quality and the gaps which exist for organizations.

Industry examples

The author has been involved in a number of projects focused on dimensions of service quality. For example, Lewis (1990) assessed the expectations and perceptions of bank and building society customers with respect to 39 service quality criteria; a number of service quality gaps came to light, together with evidence of rising expectations. A related project (Lewis, 1991), an international comparison of retail customers of banks in the US and UK, provided evidence of cultural differences in attitudes and behaviour which impact on expectations and perceptions of service quality. Further, relationships between banks and small businesses were investigated by Smith (1990), and key areas of service were found to relate to bank personnel, organization and structure of the banks, pricing policies and product offerings.

In the tourism industry, Lewis and Owtram (1986) researched purchasers of package holidays with respect to expectations and anticipated benefits (prior to travel) and satisfactions/dissatisfactions (after their holidays). In another study (Lewis and Sinhapalin, 1991), dimensions of service quality were assessed by executives and passengers of an international airline, and a number of gaps were apparent between passengers' expectations and perceptions, and between management concerns as compared with customer needs.

Further, an investigation in the manufacturing sector (Lewis and Craven, 1995) was focused on the relationships between a major supplier and its business customers (also manufacturers), with dimensions of service quality relating to products, the organization and operations/systems:

- Products, e.g. quality of products, record of technological innovation, range of products, technical specifications, product availability
- The organization and its personnel, e.g. reputation, previous experience, helpful personnel, technical support, after sales service, location of supplier, communication/response times
- Operations/systems, e.g. delivery reliability and speed, ease of contact, administrative efficiency, and electronic aspects of ordering

The Role of Personnel in Service Delivery

Having assessed customer needs, organizations must set standards/specifications and systems for service delivery to include the relevant dimensions of customer service, i.e. to avoid gap 2. This implies a requirement for management commitment to a service culture and service quality, and the allocation of appropriate resources – in relation to products, systems, environment and people.

The subsequent challenge is to ensure that the service delivered meets the specifications set. This depends on the performance of all employees who must be able, and willing, to deliver the desired levels of service. Employees' contributions in meeting customer needs – and thus influencing customer perceptions of service – cannot be overstated, and success depends on the development of enlightened personnel policies for recruitment and selection, training, motivation and rewards for *all* employees – both customer contact and back-room staff.

Internal marketing

An understanding of the concept of internal marketing is central to personnel policies. Internal marketing views employees as internal customers and jobs as internal products (Berry, 1980), and a company needs to sell its jobs to employees before selling its service to customers, i.e. satisfying the wants of internal customers upgrades the capability to satisfy the needs of external customers. Gronroos (1981) refers to three objectives of internal marketing:

1 *Overall*: to achieve motivated, customer conscious and care-oriented personnel
2 *Strategic*: to create an internal environment which supports customer-consciousness and sales mindedness among personnel
3 *Tactical*: to sell service campaigns and marketing efforts to employees – the first market-place of the company – via staff training programmes and seminars.

Berry (1981) developed the concept in terms of the possibilities for market research and segmentation. He suggests that organizations should carry out research among employees to identify their needs, wants and attitudes with respect to working conditions, benefits and company policies. Further, he indicates that people are as different as employees as consumers and might be segmented in a number of ways. For example, with respect to flexible working hours which leads to increased job satisfaction, increased productivity and decreased absenteeism. In addition, 'cafeteria benefits' could be appropriate with respect to health insurance, pensions, holidays, etc. – the notion being that employees use 'credits' (a function of salary, service, age, etc.) to choose their benefits.

The concept of internal marketing has been researched by Varey (1996), who studied the origins, nature, scope and application of the concept, and considered how it might be developed to take greater account of the social and non-economic needs and interests of people working in an organized enterprise. From extensive review of the literature in various disciplines, organizational case studies, expert academic opinion and in-depth interviews with managers, some limitations of the popular concept of internal marketing were addressed, and consideration given to the structural impact of internal marketing which leads into a presentation of a broader conception of internal marketing. A number of themes offering a contribution to this broader conception were identified:

- Marketing-oriented service employee management
- Organization as an internal market
- Internal marketing as a social process
- The individual person in an internal market
- A relational perspective on communication
- Empowerment

Personnel policies

Personnel issues are addressed by Lewis and Entwistle (1990) who develop the concept of service encounters to include encounters or relationships within the organization, at all levels and between levels – which contribute to the quality of service delivered to the final customers. This includes relationships between customer contact and back-room employees, operations and non-operations staff, and staff and management at all levels and locations.

Successful personnel policies include recruitment and selection of the 'right' people. Key characteristics for employees to perform effectively may relate to process and technical skills, interpersonal and communication skills, flexibility and adaptability, and empathy with the customer. It is also vital to identify the training needs of new and present employees with respect to technical and interpersonal dimensions and, also, to consider employment conditions, i.e. employees' wants and attitudes with regard to working conditions, benefits and welfare. This is typically undertaken via a training audit. Subsequently, training programmes may be developed to provide product, company and systems knowledge and, also, interpersonal and communication skills. Zeithaml et al. (1988) in relation to gap 3 indicate that success will depend on these elements:

- *Teamwork*: evidenced by a caring management and involved and committed employees
- *Employee–job fit*: the ability of employees to perform a job

- *Technology–job fit*: Are the 'tools' appropriate for the employee and the job?
- *Perceived control*: For example, do employees have flexibility in dealing with customers? If not, stress levels may rise and performance decrease.
- *Supervisory control systems*: based on behaviours rather than 'output quality'
- *Avoidance of role conflict*: for employees in satisfying employees' expectations of the company and expectations of customers
- *Avoidance of role ambiguity*: Employees should know what is expected of them and how performance will be evaluated and rewarded.

A number of these elements have been researched by Lewis (1990) among employees of banks and building societies in the UK who provided opinions with respect to internal service encounters and relationships, perceptions of customer service in their organizations, training for customer service, and areas for service quality improvement. Overall, a number of deficiencies were found with respect to personnel initiatives and customer service training activities. A project by Lewis and Koula (1995) was also focused on gap 3, and comparisons were made between senior management and employees' opinions in a European bank with respect to service quality and personnel issues and activities.

A recent project by Lewis and Gabrielsen (1998) included a survey of front-line employees in a number of banks. The research objectives included the identification of organizational variables which affect the service quality process, and the survey of employees focused on attitude and opinion statements pertaining to organizational culture and internal working environment, the role of management, role perception, training, organizational structures, evaluation and rewards, and service recovery. The findings stressed the need for, and importance of, management concern for the organizational culture, the acknowledgement that HR are an intrinsic part of the service and quality delivered, and that the potential of employees (to be customer aware, innovative, and to use initiative) needs to be enhanced/maximized with appropriate leadership.

Customer service training programmes are typically designed to move a company to a service-oriented culture by breaking down barriers and improving internal communications. Several advantages are seen:

- Creating an atmosphere of all working towards a common goal
- Understanding the work of others
- Encouraging all staff to have responsibility and authority for achieving corporate objectives – which includes empowering employees to exercise judgement and creativity in responding to customers' needs

Employees also need to be supervised, and systems set to monitor and evaluate their performance – e.g. using product knowledge tests, or mystery shoppers – and satisfaction. In addition, organizations have a variety of recognition and reward schemes for excellent employees: customer service awards may be financial or not, and may involve career development.

Service Delivery

In relation to service delivery, organizations need to avoid gap 4, i.e. a failure to deliver the service as promised. Once a company has successfully assessed customer needs, translated them into service systems and standards, and recruited and trained employees, it must them manage its 'promises'. Quality systems are of benefit to help ensure this. Further, a company needs appropriate advertising and promotion so that the service offered in external communications matches the service that the organization is able to deliver. Advertising and promotion affects customers' expectations and perceptions of the delivered service and so it is important not to promise more than can be delivered, i.e. realistic communications are needed so as not to increase expectations unnecessarily and decrease perceptions of quality; the hotel which advertised 'there are no surprises' was deemed to be overpromising.

Monitoring service quality

A critical element in any service strategy is for a company to have, in place, systems to measure and monitor success. These include research and evaluation among employees and customers, using focus groups, discussions, surveys and interviews, and sometimes mystery shoppers and 'control' branches. Collection and analysis of customer complaints and complementary letters is often also valuable and, for some organizations, key indicators are provided by service guarantees and recovery activities.

Many, if not most, service providers now make promises and/or offer guarantees with respect to products/services, delivery and aspects of performance. In the private sector, these may be an element in a company's competitive armoury:

- Marriott hotels offer cash compensation if difficulties are not resolved in 30 minutes.
- A Pizza delivery becomes free after a certain time delay.
- UK organizations providing financial services publicize their Codes of Practice including, for example, their *Promises to Students.*

A significant activity of the recently privatized utilities in the UK has been the development and promotion, for competitive and consumer-oriented reasons, of their service guarantees.

- Norweb Distribution has 18 guaranteed standards of customer service, together with published performance targets and success rates.
- North West Water publicizes its 30 'Commitments to You' – their promises with respect to the service(s) that households can expect.
- British Telecom's *Commitment to Customers* comprises performance guarantees (and levels of compensation if they are not met) together with publicized quality of service targets – for example, promising to repair faults within a specified number of hours.

In addition, the Citizens' Charter has spurred the development of various service charters:

- The National Health Service has a *Patients' Charter* with ten guaranteed Patients' Charter Rights (promises) relating to the provision of health care, access to information and information on quality standards, together with national and local charter standards.
- Local authorities have Charters of Rights.

- The Royal Mail has a Customer Charter – with published performance standards and targets.
- The Department for Education has a Parents' Charter – outlining parents' rights on what they can expect.

Hart (1988) summarizes key considerations relating to service guarantees. Some aspects of service and customer satisfaction cannot be guaranteed, such as unconditional on-time arrival of aeroplanes, and so guarantees must be realistic. A good service guarantee is unconditional; it is easy too understand and communicate; it is easy to invoke and easy to collect on. It should also be meaningful, in particular with respect to payout which should be a function of the cost of the service, seriousness of failure and perception of what is fair, e.g. 15-minute lunch service in a restaurant or a free meal. Ideally, a service guarantee should make everyone in the company focus on good service, and examine service delivery systems for possible failure points.

Service failure and service recovery

To turn to service failures and customer complaints, service providers now realize that only a small proportion of dissatisfied customers complain, so that complaint data are not a true reflection of the extent of customer dissatisfaction. The reasons why dissatisfied people keep quiet are discussed by Goodman et al. (1986) and Horovitz (1990):

- Fear of hassle or too much trouble to complain
- No one being available to complain to or there being no easy channel by which to communicate disquiet
- No one caring and anyway 'it will not do any good'
- Not knowing where to complain
- Customers attributing themselves as a source of service problems by their failure to perform in the creation of the service

Hart et al. (1990) discuss the additional costs of replacing customers over those of trying to retain customers who may be dissatisfied. There is also evidence (Hart et al., 1990) of customers who complain and who then receive a satisfactory response subsequently being more loyal to an organization, more likely to buy other services products, and more likely to engage in positive word-of-mouth communication.

Organizations should strive for zero defects in their service delivery – to get things right the first time (Reichheld and Sasser, 1990). Consequently, many companies develop service quality systems which tend to be rigid with sophisticated techniques and structured personnel policies – to try to provide consistent high quality service. However, all service organizations will find themselves in situations where failures occur in their encounters with customers with respect to one or more dimensions of service quality, and where they need to deal with customer dissatisfaction and complaints. For example, problems do occur (e.g. bad weather may delay an airline flight, or employees may be sick and absent) and mistakes will happen (e.g. a hotel room not ready on time, a dirty rental car and a lost cheque book or suitcase).

Service failures have been investigated by several researchers – e.g. Johnston (1994) and Armistead et al. (1995) – and relate to problems in the service organization (e.g. with regard to employees, equipment and systems), those which may be customer induced, and those which are a result of actions of other organizations.

The actions which a service provider takes to respond to service failures are referred to as service recovery. Service recovery is defined by Armistead et al. (1995) as 'specific actions taken to ensure that the customer receives a reasonable level of service after problems have occurred to disrupt normal service', and by Zemke and Bell (1990) as 'a thought-out, planned, process for returning aggrieved customers to a state of satisfaction with the organization after a service or product has failed to live up to expectations'. The response from an organization to service failures needs to be the result of a conscious, co-ordinated, effort of the firm to anticipate that service flaws will occur, and to develop procedures, policies and human competencies to deal with them.

When something does go wrong, what do customers expect from the service firm? Zemke and Bell (1990) and Zemke (1994) concluded from their research these customer expectations for service recovery:

- To receive an apology for the fact that the customer is inconvenienced
- To be offered a 'fair fix' for the problem
- To be treated in a way that suggests the company cares about the problem, about fixing the problem, and about the customer's inconvenience
- To be offered value-added atonement, i.e. compensation, for the inconvenience

Service recovery is 'emotional and physical repair': organizations need to fix the customer first and then fix the customer's problem.

Critical to the service recovery process is the empowerment of front-line employees. It is essential to give personnel the authority, responsibility and incentives to identify, care about and solve customer problems and complaints; to allow them to use their judgement and to act with respect to the best solutions to satisfy customers. The personnel implications are highlighted by Schelesinger and Heskett (1991): empowerment is seen to lead to better job performance and improved morale – it is a form of job enrichment, evidenced by increased commitment to jobs and reflected in attitudes towards customers. Knowing that management has confidence in employees helps to create positive attitudes in the work place and good relationships between employees, and between employees and customers.

A number of research studies have focused on service recovery. For example, Johnston (1994) produced, from customer anecdotes, a list of factors that led to satisfactory recovery, e.g. attention, helpfulness, care, responsiveness, communication and flexibility. These would appear to be intrinsic to the actions found by Armistead et al. (1995), in a survey of managers across the services sector, to be most effective in satisfying customer complaints, e.g. immediate and speedy response, listening, courtesy, caring and honest responses, getting it right and solving the problem, and financial compensation.

A recent study by Lewis and Spyrakopoulos (1999) has investigated service failures and service recovery strategies used by banks to respond to these failures. A survey questionnaire was developed to measure customers' perceptions about the magnitude of service failures and the effectiveness of service recovery strategies. Service failures related to banking procedures, mistakes, employee behaviour and training, technical failures and omissions of the banks; and were found to vary in importance and some were more difficult to deal with satisfactorily than others. Different service recovery strategies – e.g. corrections, compensation, apologies and explanations – were more effective for particular failures. Further, customers with long relationships and higher deposits with their banks were more demanding with respect to service recovery.

Overall, service recovery may be seen as not just solving problems after they have occurred, but as focusing on critical service encounters and anticipating possible failure points. Ideally, an organization should identify potential problems and develop strategies for response to and solution of such difficulties. A review of academic evidence – e.g. Hart (1988) and Hart et al. (1990) – and practitioner opinions – e.g. Mason (1993) – leads to a number of requirements for an effective service recovery programme:

- Educate the customer and encourage complaints. Make it easy to complain and offer service guarantees.
- Monitor service process, detect and track failures, and analyse complaint data. Use the findings to improve service quality, and to prevent failures and dissatisfaction from happening again.
- Train, empower and facilitate employees to recover. Service recovery typically involves interpersonal interaction and communication skills, and knowledge skills, with implications for HR management.
- Show management commitment. Employees need to be supported by senior management who have a commitment to absolute customer satisfaction.

Summary

Today, the business environment is characterized by changing customer expectations, technological and product advances, legislative and political developments, and economic and competitive conditions which contribute to an increasing emphasis on service quality for all organizations – in both the services and manufacturing sectors. Managing service quality necessitates an integrated approach from operations, marketing, HR and other key managers/areas of a business.

Organizations need clearly defined service strategies with top management commitment and leadership. They need to understand their service encounters (both internal and external to the company) and potential failure points, and to avoid service quality shortfalls or gaps. This can be achieved by researching both service personnel and customers, identifying key dimensions of service quality, and developing appropriate service quality initiatives. Successful service strategies will include emphasis on products/services, delivery systems and procedures, technology, and personnel – their skills and commitment to the organization and its customers.

The outcome of a successful service strategy will be satisfied and retained employees and customers with consequent benefits to the organization. Increasingly, the links between customer retention and profitability are evident; see, for example, Heskett et al. (1994) and Buttle, 1996). There is a growing awareness of the 'lifetime value' of retained customers in terms of the revenues and contributions earned from a long-term relationship, i.e. the longer the association between company and customer, the more profitable the relationship for the company.

References

Albrecht, K. and Zemke, R. 1985: *Service America: Doing Business in the New Economy*. Homewood, Illinois: Dow Jones-Irwin.

Armistead, C. G., Clark, G. and Stanley, P. 1995: Managing service recovery. In P. Kunst and J. Lemmink (eds) *Managing Service Quality*, London: Paul Chapman Publishing, 93–105.

Berry, L. L. 1980: Services marketing is different. *Business*, 30(3), May/June, 24–9.

Berry, L. L. 1981: The employee as customer. *Journal of Retail Banking*, 3(1), 33–40.

Berry, L. L., Parasuraman, A. and Zeithaml, V. A. 1988: The service–quality puzzle. *Business Horizons*, July–August, 35–43.

Berry, L. L., Zeithaml, V. A. and Parasuraman, A. 1985: Quality counts in services too. *Business Horizons*, 28(3), 44–52.

Booms, B. H. and Bitner, M. J. 1981: Marketing strategies and organisation structures for service firms. In J. H. Donnelly and W. R. George (eds) *Marketing of Services*, Chicago: American Marketing Association, 47–51.

Buttle, F. 1996: *Relationship Marketing: Theory and Practice*. London: Paul Chapman.

Czepiel, J. A., Solomon, M. R. and Surprenant, C. F. 1985: (eds) *The Service Encounter: Managing Employee/Customer Interaction in Service Businesses*, Lexington, Mass.: Lexington Books.

Edvardsson, B., Gustavsson, B. O. and Riddle, D. I. 1989: An expanded model of the service encounter with emphasis on cultural context, *Research Report 89:4*, CTF Services Research Centre, University of Karlstad, Sweden.

Goodman, J. A., Marra, T. and Brigham, L. 1986: Customer service: costly nuisance or low cost profit strategy?. *Journal of Retail Banking*, 8(3), 7–16.

Gronroos, C. 1981: Internal marketing – an integral part of marketing theory. In J. H. Donnelly and W. R. George (eds) *Marketing of Services*, Chicago: American Marketing Association, 236–238.

Gronroos, C. 1984: *Strategic Management and Marketing in the Service Sector*. Chartwell-Bratt, UK.

Gronroos, C. 1987: *Developing the Service Offering – A Source of Competitive Advantage*, Helsinki: Swedish School of Economics & Business Administration, September.

Gronroos, C. 1988: Service quality; the six criteria of good perceived service quality. *Review of Business*, 9(3), Winter, 10–13.

Gummesson, E. and Gronroos, C. 1987: Quality of products and services: a tentative synthesis between two models, *Research Report 87:3*, Services Research Centre, University of Karlstad, Sweden.

Hart, C. W. L. 1988: The power of unconditional service guarantees. *Harvard Business Review*, 66(4), July–August, 54–62.

Hart, C. W. L., Heskett, J. L. and Sasser, W. E. 1990: The profitable art of service recovery. *Harvard Business Review*, 68(4), July–August, 148–56.

Heskett, J. L., Jones, T. O., Loveman, G. W., Sasser, W. E. and Schlesinger, L. A. 1994: Putting the service profit chain to work. *Harvard Business Review*, 72(2), March–April, 164–74.

Horovitz, J. 1990: *Winning Ways: Achieving Zero Defect Service*. Cambridge, Mass.: Productivity Press.

Johnston, R. 1994: *Service Recovery: an Empirical Study*. Warwick: Warwick University Business School.

Johnston, R., Silvestro, R., Fitzgerald, L. and Voss, C. 1990: Developing the determinants of service quality. In E. Langeard and P. Eiglier (eds) *Marketing, Operations and Human Resources Insights into Services*, Aix-en-Provence: 1st International Research Seminar on Services Management, IAE, 373–400.

Lehtinen, U. and Lehtinen, J. R. 1982: *Service Quality: a Study of Quality Dimensions*, Working Paper, Service Management Institute, Helsinki, Finland.

Lewis, B. R. 1990: Service quality: an investigation of major UK organisations. *International Journal of Service Industry Management*, 1(2), 33–44.

Lewis, B. R. 1991: Service quality: an international comparison of bank customers' expectations and perceptions. *Journal of Marketing Management*, 7(1), 47–62.

Lewis, B. R. and Craven, P. 1995: The role of customer service in buyer–seller relationships: evidence from the industrial gases market. *Interaction, Relationships and Networks, Proceedings of the 11th IMP International Conference*, 7–9 September, Manchester 762–786.

Lewis, B. R. and Entwistle, T. W. 1990: Managing the service encounter: a focus on the employee. *International Journal of Service Industry Management*, 1(3), 41–52.

Lewis, B. R. and Gabrielsen, G. O. S. 1998: Intra-organisational aspects of service quality management. *The Service Industries Journal*, 18(2), April, 64–89.

Lewis, B. R. and Koula, S. 1995: Service quality and internal marketing: an investigation in financial services. *Proceedings of the BAM Annual Conference*, 11–13 September, Sheffield, 385–97.

Lewis, B. R. and Owtram, M. T. 1986: The growth of international tourism and package holidays. In B. Moores (ed.), *Are They Being Served?*. Oxford: Philip Allan Publishers.

Lewis, B. R. and Sinhapalin, D. 1991: Service quality: an empirical study of Thai airways. In *Quality Management in Services*, Brussels: EIASM, May, 16–17.

Lewis, B. R. and Spyrakopoulos, S. 1999: Service failures and recovery in retail banking: the customers' perspective. Under revision for *International Journal of Bank Marketing*.

Mason, J. B. 1993: The art of service recovery. *Retailing Issues Newsletter, Center for Retailing Studies*, Texas A&M University, 5(1), June, 1–4.

Parasuraman, A., Berry, L. L. and Zeithaml, V. A. 1991a: Understanding customer expectations of service. *Sloan Management Review*, 32(3), 39–48.

Parasuraman, A., Berry, L. L. and Zeithaml, V. A. 1991b: Refinement and re-assessment of the ServQual scale. *Journal of Retailing*, 67(4), Winter, 420–50.

Parasuraman, A., Zeithaml, V. A. and Berry, L. L. 1985: A conceptual model of service quality and its implications for future research. *Journal of Marketing*, 49, Fall, 41–50.

Parasuraman, A., Zeithaml, V. A. and Berry, L. L. 1988: SERVQUAL: a multiple item scale for measuring consumer perceptions of service quality. *Journal of Retailing*, 64(1), Spring, 14–40.

Parasuraman, A., Zeithaml, V. A. and Berry, L. L. 1993: More on improving service quality. *Journal of Retailing*, 69(1), 140–7.

Parasuraman, A., Zeithaml, V. A. and Berry, L. L. 1994: Re-assessment of expectations as a comparison standard in measuring service quality: implications for further research. *Journal of Marketing*, 58, January, 111–24.

Reichheld, F. E. and Sasser, W. E. 1990: Zero defections: quality comes to services. *Harvard Business Review*, 68(5), September–October, 105–11.

Rosenberg, L. J. and Czepiel, J. A. 1984: A marketing approach to customer retention. *Journal of Consumer Marketing*, 1(1), 45–51.

Schelesinger, L. A. and Heskett, J. L. 1991: Breaking the cycle of failures in service. *Sloan Management Review*, 32(3), Spring, 17–28.

Silvestro, R. and Johnston, R. 1990: *The Determinants of Service Quality – Hygiene and Enhancing Factors*. Warwick: Warwick Business School.

Smith, A. M. 1990: *Quality Service and the Small Business–Bank Relationship*, MSc thesis, Manchester School of Management.

Smith, A. M. 1995: Measuring service quality: is ServQual now redundant?. *Journal of Marketing Management*, 11(1–3), January–April, 257–76.

Varey, R. J. 1996: *A Broadened Conception of Internal Marketing*, unpublished PhD thesis. Manchester School of Management, UMIST.

Zeithaml, V. A., Berry, L. L. and Parasuraman, A. 1988: Communication and control processes in the delivery of service quality. *Journal of Marketing*, 52, April, 35–48.

Zemke, R. 1994: Service Recovery. *Executive Excellence*, 11(9), September, 17–18.

Zemke, R. and Bell, C. R. 1990: Service recovery: doing it right the second time. *Training*, 27(6), June, 42–8.

chapter ten

Managing People in a TQM Context

A. Wilkinson

Introduction

This chapter is concerned with the HR issues relating to TQM. It argues that, while TQM does have far reaching implications for HR, this is dealt with in a rather limited way by the conventional TQM literature. Too much is labelled as motivation and training, while the remainder is dumped in the black box marked culture. Indeed, it is also argued that HR practice has significant implications for TQM. This chapter raises a number of issues which need to be addressed and argues that, until senior management and TQM practitioners take on board some of these considerations, TQM will not fulfil its potential.

TQM – The HR Problem?

The 1980s and 1990s have produced strong evidence that TQM has not achieved its objectives (Hill and Wilkinson, 1995). Major problems identified are an over emphasis on quality and not enough on total (Kearney, 1992), too much emphasis on processes and not enough on results (Garvin, 1991) and a failure to achieve changed attitudes and culture (Wilkinson et al., 1998). Systems and procedures driven TQM, where the focus is on the production process, conformance to requirements and achieving zero defects, has been criticized for being inward looking and bureaucratic, less concerned with producing 'quality' goods as to conforming to internal procedures. HR issues are often not deemed very significant with employees taking a role of following clearly laid down instructions.

However, central to this chapter is the 'human factor': however brilliant a strategy TQM is, it needs to be implemented, and this depends on people. A failure to change attitudes and culture can be partially attributed to the neglect of HR policies in the organization and a failure to align the HR policies with TQM to ensure integration. This is due partly to a lack of understanding of the issues involved, but also due to the emphasis quality professionals place on systems rather than the individual (Waldman, 1994).

The Two Sides of TQM

TQM has both 'hard' and 'soft' sides. The former may involve a range of tools and techniques, including SPC, and the basic quality management tools. The soft side of TQM is concerned with HR and cultural change. Central to this is creating customer awareness. Thus, in manufacturing companies, programmes may be run to show the workforce the end product of the material they handle and arrange for them to meet customers. In service organizations, such programmes represent an attempt to change the corporate culture towards a more customer-oriented approach, and there is a major emphasis on customer-care programmes. Such programmes can be seen as an educative process aimed at 'commercialization'. There are important implications for the workforce in the message that 'quality is everyone's business', as organizations are urged to move away from supervisory approaches to quality control towards a situation where employees themselves take responsibility for quality and are 'empowered' to deliver quality to customers both internal and external to the organization. The soft side thus puts the emphasis on the management of HR: a well-trained and motivated 'quality' workforce is more likely to contribute to organizational success. However, TQM writers tend to have a rather unitary view of the organization and, hence, some barriers to change are underplayed (Wilkinson and Witcher, 1991; Wilkinson, 1992). There is little acknowledgement that there may well be tensions between the production-oriented 'hard' aspects of TQM (which tend to emphasize working within prescribed procedures) and the 'soft' aspects (which emphasize employee involvement and commitment). Seddon (1989) argues that the waning of employee support for TQM (after early enthusiasm) can be attributed to management's focus on the 'hard' measurable aspects such as costs and production performance and the relative neglect of the 'soft' aspects: management gives insufficient attention to examining the underlying values and resulting behaviour of employees, with the result that there is a failure to achieve the 'cultural change' which is necessary if TQM is to be successfully implemented. Furthermore, Powell (1995) goes so far as to suggest that competitive advantage comes more through tacit behaviour and imitable factors (such as open culture, employee involvement and executive commitment), than the factors (such as benchmarking and process improvement) more commonly associated with TQM. There is growing evidence as the positive impact of best practice HRM on organizational performance (Pfeffer, 1994).

In this chapter, some of the soft issues which remain undeveloped within the TQM literature are examined. These issues of HRM and industrial relations, employee involvement, organizational culture and personnel practices are four which have arisen from a number of research projects examining links between TQM and HR issues; see Wilkinson et al. (1991), Wilkinson et al. (1992), Marchington et al. (1993), Wilkinson et al. (1998), Godfrey and Wilkinson (1998), Godfrey et al. (1998).

TQM, HR and Industrial Relations

Oakland (1989) states that:

> TQM is concerned with moving the focus of control from outside the individual to within; the objective being to make everyone accountable for their own performance, and to get them committed to attaining quality in a highly motivated fashion. The assumptions a director or manager must make in

order to move in this direction are simply that people do not need to be coerced to perform well, and that people want to achieve, accomplish, influence activity and challenge their abilities.

Each of the quality gurus places a rather different emphasis on the people-management aspects of the system (Dale and Plunkett, 1990; Oakland, 1989; Marchington, 1992; Coyle-Shapiro, 1993). For Crosby, Juran, and Taguchi, the role of employees in continuous improvement is minimal. While Crosby (1979) recognizes a need for quality awareness to be raised among employees and for more personal concern to be generated, his approach suggests that employees should be encouraged to communicate to management the obstacles they face in achieving their improvement goals. Moreover, he rejects outright the redesign of work, regarding work itself as a secondary motivator to how employees are treated.

Juran, in fact, argued in the 1940s that the technical aspects of quality control were well covered and 'an understanding of the human situation associated with the job will go far to solve the technical problems; in fact such an understanding may be a prerequisite to a solution'. However, he saw little role for ordinary shopfloor employees, with the primary responsibility with quality professionals and, to a lesser extent, middle management, although he warned against exhortation. His emphasis is on training and top management leadership (Juran, 1989). More recently, he has begun to discuss the notion of self-supervising teams arguing that the 'winning' quality companies have began to develop these concepts (Juran, 1991).

Taguchi (1986) argues that quality is achieved by minimizing variance; his methods have been concerned with enabling quality to be designed into a product or process – thus quality and reliability is pushed back into the design stage where they belong. He has little to say about HR issues.

Deming (1986), Feigenbaum (1983), and Ishikawa (1985) offer a rather more positive approach to people management. Deming is critical of exhortations, slogans and targets. In particular, Deming (1986) has criticized the notion of zero defects as a motivational programme:

> Eliminate slogans, exhortations and targets for the workforce asking for zero defects and new levels of productivity. Such exhortations only create adversarial relationships as the bulk of the causes of low quality and low productivity belong to the system and thus lie beyond the power of the workforce.

While Deming has been known for his advocacy of statistical techniques, he also believes that employees should be trained to spot defects, and to improve quality; they should be offered rewarding and challenging jobs and he argues (Deming, 1982) for the creation of high trust relations.

> Posters like these (zero defects) never helped anyone do a better job. What is needed is not exhortations, but a road map to improvement.

However, Deming's advocacy of rewarding and challenging jobs does not encompass a radical redesign of work. Central to his philosophy is 'pride in workmanship', subsequently refined as 'joy in work'. The implicit rationale is that, if individuals enjoy work, their motivation will be intrinsic, rather than extrinsic with the former being a prerequisite for continuous improvement. 'Joy in work' seems mainly to encompass the removal of obstacles preventing individuals from accomplishing the best possible job (Coyle-Shapiro, 1993).

Feigenbaum (1983) also argues that workers need a good understanding of what management is trying to do: 'improvement can only be achieved by everyone's participation' and the workforce must have a good understanding of management aims. 'Quality control begins with education and ends with education.' This is seen to be achieved through teamwork. Ishikawa (1985) places a strong emphasis on the internal customer and hence stresses the importance of employees being involved; he points out that Western companies need to overcome their professional 'expert' culture, suggesting that employees may be unwilling to co-operate given a lack of organizational consensus. Ishikawa (1985) writes of respect for humanity as a management philosophy. In his view,

> Top Managers and Middle Managers must be bold enough to delegate as much authority as possible. That is the way to establish respect for humanity as your management philosophy. It is a management system in which all employees participate from the top down and from the bottom up, and humanity is fully respected.

Thus TQM has important implications for people management. If quality is to be 'built in' rather than inspected, quality must be the responsibility of all employees rather than specified departments. TQM proponents have highlighted the need to increase the involvement of all employees in monitoring their own work with the aim of constantly maintaining and improving quality 'getting it right first time', and removing the need for retrospective quality checks (Crosby, 1979). The aim is for zero defects rather than an 'acceptable' quality level. TQM is also said to minimize the costs of poor and uncertain quality because it is a way of making everyone improve the quality of their work. Every person has a common focus, based on the customer, so that people with different jobs, abilities and priorities are able to communicate in pursuit of a common organizational purpose (Wilkinson and Witcher, 1991).

In short, TQM is supposed to place a greater emphasis on self-control, autonomy and creativity, expecting active co-operation from employees rather than mere compliance with the employment contract (Wilkinson et al., 1991). According to Hill (1991a): 'The task of top management is to design a structure and establish a culture that will maximise the effective participation of all employees in the pursuit of quality.' This is seen as a long-term process by most of the quality gurus of between five and ten years' duration.

The principles underlying certain versions of both TQM and HRM theory have some common themes. Both emphasize commitment, self-control and trust, and take McGregor's Theory Y view that workers are, if given responsibility will be motivated and committed and hence identify with company goals. (Theory X was the traditional view of workers as essentially lazy and hence needing close monitoring and control.) The HRM literature emphasizes that people are a key asset. In summarizing the HRM philosophy, Guest (1987, p. 512) states the case thus:

> Because they are the most variable, and the least easy to understand and control of all management resources, effective utilisation of human resources is likely to give organisations a significant competitive advantage. The human resource dimension must therefore be fully integrated into the strategic planning process.

However, most of the academic research has shown wide gaps between the theory of HRM and the practice with few organizations appearing to have achieved full blown

HRM, most companies adopting rather more *ad hoc* approaches (Storey, 1992; 1995).

TQM seems to require wholesale organizational changes and a re-examination of production/operations methods and working practices, and this has implications for industrial relations. However, the whole question of the problems faced in implementing TQM at a working level is neglected by the literature, and there is little systematic discussion of the conditions necessary for such an approach to be successful. Indeed, the quote from Oakland (on page 199) seems to imply implementation is unproblematic for management, and unitarism – a perspective based on assumptions that the organization comprises a group of people with a single set of values and loyalty and with management's 'right to manage' seen as rational and legitimate – is an underlying theme. Implementation is seen as a matter of motivation, with the correct attitudes being instilled by simple training programmes and education. Possible conflicts of interest are not addressed.

These issues are ignored in most texts on TQM – Oakland's standard work does not mention trade unions at all – and not understood by many organizations. However, unions are likely to be a countervailing source of power and loyalty. Moreover, while the literature suggests that persuading workers to take responsibility for QA and improvement, and adjusting traditional job roles requires simply a dose of motivation and training, these are issues which (certainly in the manufacturing sector) involve issues of job control and working practices and possibly monetary issues as well. Thurley and Wirdenius (1989) are surely right to point out that:

> . . . managers need to be reminded that the commitment of employees to production system objectives will depend on the acceptability of objectives as legitimate and the perceived justice of the arrangements governing employee work.

These are more fundamental issues than the usual 'teething problems' of the management of change because of fear of the unknown.

In one study, TQM in its early stages was regarded as essentially management policy and outside the union sphere of influence. However, while TQM at business strategy policy level was not seen as a union concern, TQM as implemented throughout the organization was. Thus, as TQM worked down the organization, industrial relations issues were increasingly involved. For example, workers in a machine tool company investigated by the author wanted additional payments because of their enhanced role in QA. Such issues may be more limited in the service sector where a high degree of managerial prerogative extended over issues concerning the management of staff (Wilkinson et al., 1992). Industrial relations considerations may also be important where TQM is associated with a programme of job losses or the intensification of work. Furthermore, trade unions may be concerned that TQM could marginalize the union as a communications channel, at the same time strengthening the sense of commitment to what might be seen as 'managerial' objectives. Thus a concern of unionists is that it 'can undercut the very basis of trade unionism by seeking to teach workers that redress to problems lay solely in individual not collective action' (Coyne and Williamson, 1991).

Nor should it be assumed that the workforce would necessarily welcome TQM. While it may be seen as facilitating a greater say in the way they work and the ability to influence their work environments, it may also be seen as increased responsibility and therefore pressure. A typical comment of employees is that they do not have the time. Furthermore, it is one thing for workers to be encouraged to come up with ideas, but it is entirely another that they should be expected to do so (Dawson and Webb, 1988). The failure of TQM is usually attributed in the literature to either technical difficulties – e.g. a lack of training or inadequate resource support – or the fact that it is not fully integrated into management strategy and practice. However, there may be more fundamental problems relating to the different conceptions of management and the workforce, with management seeing it as a set of 'neutral' techniques and tools like any other but, as Deming (1986) points out, the system is often seen as repressive by workers. While workers may find it difficult to challenge the logic of management action in principle, the workforce almost invariably inter-pret, evaluate and react towards managerial initiatives and, in their own way, 'audit' their introduction and operation.

Employee Involvement

A number of the TQM gurus advocate employee involvement in decision making – see, in particular, Deming (1982), Feigenbaum (1983) and Ishikawa (1985) – and this is reflected in the standard texts. Oakland (1989) writes of 'total involvement':

> Everyone in the organisation from top to bottom, from offices to technical service, from headquarters to local sites must be involved. People are the source of ideas and innovation and their expertise, experience, knowledge and co-operation have to be harnessed to get these ideas implemented.

Employee involvement is thus fundamental to TQM ideas, both in terms of an educational process and also more direct involvement in quality issues and how it relates to the job, although this is a long way from shared power or workers control as industrial relations writers see it (Marchington et al., 1993).

Three separate but integrated elements make up the participative structure of TQM. First, is the educative process at corporate level. This may be through a number of vehicles: papers, videos, briefing, 'walking the talk', etc. For example, at a fibres plant, workers attended workshops which provided them with some insight into what the manufacturers made out of the product they were given. Some manu-facturing organizations have posters and signs on the shopfloor stressing that 'Cus-tomers make paydays possible' and 'The next person you pass your work to is your customer', etc. However, some of these initiatives can backfire: Ben Hamper's account (1992) of his time at General Motors (GM) includes a story of how, as part of the quality initiative, a man dressed up as a cat – 'Howie Makem' – to patrol the shopfloor and urge workers to produce better quality. At GM, workers found it all too easy to see the gap between the rhetoric and the reality, and, indeed, there were suggestions that if there was a quality cat, there should also be a quantity cat since this was the other god that GM worshipped. Second, there may be changes in the organization of work. This may involve organizing work units into cells, the creation of semi-autonomous work groups, or some less fundamental restructuring, which involves the removal of inspectors, with workers taking responsibility for QA. Third, committees, QCs, quality improvement or action teams which may be established on an *ad hoc* basis to solve particular problems or may be more permanent fixtures. These may be either based on the work group or cross-functional in structure. Like QCs, however, TQM tends to offer involvement in a rather limited way since it is largely confined to the operational process. It does not then extend involvement over wider issues of corporate strategy.

The emphasis on teamwork pervades the quality literature. According to Hill (1991a, b), teamwork offers real opportunities to bring about more collegial relationships within the managerial group, a decline in resistance to change due to sectional interests and less organizational rigidity. Oakland (1989) argues that:

> ...much of what has been taught previously in management has led to a culture in the west of independence, with little sharing of ideas and information. Knowledge is very much like organic manure, if it is spread around, it will fertilise and encourage growth, if it is kept covered, it will eventually fester and rot.

He further argues that teamwork devoted to quality improvement, changes the independence to interdependence through improved communications, trust and free exchange of ideas, knowledge, date and information.

Juran's (1988) notion of self-control suggests that responsibility for quality be assigned to those who control the quality of what they do. This is said to improve motivation by encouraging employees to find satisfaction in their own work. Furthermore, the supervisory climate is meant to support this with fear of failure discouraged in favour of a search for failure. As Deming has argued, a drive through fear is counterproductive. Individuals blamed for mistakes are unlikely to search for them to put right and, thus, key systems failures will not be addressed. Thus, teams take responsibility, loosening the strain on individuals (Wilkinson and Witcher, 1991). TQM theory suggests that individuals and teams should have the power to improve their quality and this must represent real authority and the ability to regulate what they do. They must not take on responsibility for something that is beyond their control. Semi-autonomous work groups can help create the conditions for self control, as advocated by Juran. 'The concept of self-regulation of task activities has not only been demonstrated to sustain effort but, more importantly, has contributed to self-development. In turn, this may reduce employees' dependence on tasks assigned by superiors (Robertson et al., 1992). Thus, not only might the utilizing of HR in this way assist in the implementation of TQM but it should develop the self-confidence and competence of those involved. Research evidence from writers outside the quality field (e.g. Hackman and Oldman, 1976) suggest that these attributes are key causal variables in determining levels of performance, motivation and job satisfaction.

Robertson et al. (1992) argue that, given the right setting, employees will generally welcome the opportunity to contribute to quality improvement. However, in creating the right 'setting' for these activities, a number of principles are important (French and Caplan, 1973).

- The change process must not be used as a manipulative tool, e.g. employees advice is sought, but subsequently ignored.
- The decisions to be made should not be seen as trivial because this may undermine the motivation of those involved.
- The activities undertaken must be relevant both to the needs of workers and the quality improvement process.
- Workers involved, must have the authority to implement any decisions made (Robertson et al., 1992).

Participative decision 'making' is more likely to be accepted by those affected by it, and it is associated with higher satisfaction and may also lead to higher quality decisions (Bass, 1990).

Teamworking, at its best, involves employees willing to undertake a range of tasks, irrespective of job title, so as to meet customer requirements. There may be an absence of formal job descriptions and *all* employees (especially managerial staff) are prepared to be flexible when needed. This is sometimes referred to as 'working beyond contract' or a 'can do' state of mind. It is exemplified by the idea that workers have two jobs; one is to do their designated task, the other is to search for continuous improvements and changes (Morton, 1994).

In recent research, the author and his colleagues examined an organization where cell-based teamworking had been developed to the extent that it was viewed as the standard way of working with the teams having a great deal of autonomy, largely controlling task allocation, monitoring of attendance, health and safety issues and, to a lesser extent, the flow of production. The teams were responsible for choosing the areas to measure (within certain guidelines) and setting their own year-on-year improvement targets. Some of the more advanced teams also had responsibility for the recruitment and training of temporary staff as well as controlling overtime levels (Godfrey et al., 1998).

However, there is a considerable degree of ambiguity about TQM in practice – while the language is about increased involvement, there is also a strong emphasis on reinforcing management control. TQM shifts the focus of responsibility for quality to the people who actually do the work and makes extensive use of teams and other participative groups. The emphasis is on mixing people and functions to create empathy, to tackle the roadblocks which are always bound to arise in the implementation of planning and the service to the external customer. As such, it could represent a transformation from traditional authoritarian top-down decision making to task-oriented ideals: a shift from sophisticated control mechanisms to a system premised on worker commitment and where there are flatter structures and participative managers and workers. Its premise is clearly anti-expert (in the conventional sense that of professional or hierarchical expertise) in that all staff can/must contribute. If done properly, this requires a degree of participation which represents a major adjustment to the corporate culture and style of managing for most UK-based organizations; see chapter 12.

However, in the sense that quality methods of working emphasize monitoring and control (with the difference that workers do it themselves), TQM ideas can also be used to reinforce a management style rooted in Taylorism. In this sense, TQM is not simply a matter of the top telling the middle what to do with the bottom of the organizational hierarchy, but it may also seem to rank-and-file workers as a way of getting the bottom to take responsibility as well (Wilkinson and Witcher, 1991).

There are thus potential contradictions between increased employee influence over management decision making, and the limited impact of employee involvement upon underlying organizational structures (Marchington, 1992).

Finally, middle management need to be given more attention: TQM has implications which can affect the organization's traditional power culture because it is about empowering people to improve systems (thus bottom up) but this may be unsettling. Thus, as Giles and Starkey (1987) point out,

> ...quality is about power sharing-about giving power to the customer and to subordinates. If you allow people to influence you, you give up expert power. But people build up their reputations with expert power. To give it up goes against the organisations power culture.

In many of the organizations we have researched, it is clear managers are unwilling to relinquish power. Clearly, TQM is likely to require new propensities, attitudes and abilities. Bradley and Hill (1987) have argued that the burdens involved in operating participative management are usually ignored by its advocates so that, while the language of teamwork may be widespread, the reality is that, in practice, it can be little more than exhortation. As Schuler and Harris (1992) say: 'If middle managers were not included in designing the quality improvement programme in the first place, and if they are neither trained adequately nor offered sufficient incentive to change, they can be expected to resist the change process.' Placing responsibility for implementing TQM in the hands of those whose future is threatened by TQM is likely to shape the manner and enthusiasm in which they perform, and is clearly a major issue. The concerns of supervisors have been well documented. Fears of job security, job definition and additional workloads may mean withholding support and damaging the quality initiative (Klein, 1984).

Organizational Culture

If TQM, as Oakland (1989) maintains, 'is a way of managing the whole business organisation to ensure complete customer satisfaction at every stage, internally and externally', then TQM could be a way to change corporate culture to manage change in a more customer responsive manner. Achieving cultural change is central to what TQM is about.

Williams et al. (1991) state the case thus:

> Culture influences what the executive group attends to, how it interprets the information and the responses it makes to changes in the external environment. Culture is a significant contributor to strategy analysis and the development of strategy. Since culture influences what other members of the organisation attend to, how they interpret this information and react, it is a significant determinant of the success of strategic implementation. Culture influences the ability of the organisation both to conceive and to implement a new strategy.

In the long term, there is a necessity for the introduction of both quality systems and a quality culture to facilitate the quality process. A quality culture has been defined as 'a culture that nurtures high-trust social relationships and respect for individuals, a shared sense of membership of the organisation, and a belief that continuous improvement is for the common good' (Hill, 1991a). The links between culture change and total quality ideas have attracted much attention in the popular management literature. Yet, 'despite the growing awareness of cultural issues, comparatively little attention has been paid to the practical, day to day processes involved in creating, managing and changing organisational culture' (Williams et al., 1991).

Thus cultural change, in practice, is problematic. While TQM may be seen as an answer to the problem of larger companies suffering 'from rigid hierarchies which isolate top management, confine middle management to administrative roles and frustrate operational and supervisory management in their decision making' (Thurley and Wirdenius, 1989), TQM alone may not be able to overcome all these problems. The corporate culture of the organizations and existing ways of doing things might be too strong for TQM. Indeed, existing ways of doing things constitute the main barriers to TQM's successful adoption in the first place. Thus, it may be that rather than viewing TQM as a process for changing organizations, conversely organizations must change to accommodate TQM! (Wilkinson and Witcher, 1993). That is, quality management is often introduced so as to operate within existing structures and cultures rather than being used as a vehicle to transform them. Thus, the emphasis is on how to make existing processes work better rather than to alter those processes in the first place.

Moreover, as Hill (1991a) argues, the mechanisms which quality gurus suggest are necessary to convince people of quality management, tend to be training, education and leadership. This is seen as an adequate set of tools with which to create the appropriate corporate culture.

> All the literature on TQM indicates that to be successful TQM requires a cultural change. That's usually where the literature stops. In pursuit of cultural change, organisations will invest heavily in educational programmes, in old fashioned management development methods and so on. Often the strategy is one of hit and miss (Seddon, 1990).

Indeed, some writers on quality matters have effectively disregarded culture altogether as something to be addressed, and suggested it is essentially an outcome of TQM activities (Dotchin and Oakland, 1991). However, Hill argues that the work of Organizational Behaviour academics is of relevance to an understanding of culture. Thus Schein (1985) believes that structure, systems and procedures are important, but secondary, mechanisms of change, with the primary tools being leadership and education together with the 'more coercive levers of persuasion available to top management by virtue of their command of organisational power, namely the deployment of organisational rewards and punishments'. Thus, in the next section, our attention is turned to HR policies.

HR Policies and Practices

If the soft side is TQM is accorded importance, then it is clear that a re-examination of existing HR policies is required. The 'quality of people' is vital with quality within the HRM model seen broadly, incorporating quality of work, quality of workforce (including investment in training and development) and quality of treatment of the workforce by management (Guest, 1987).

There are a number of critical HR issues:

- Training
- Education and communication
- Selection
- Appraisal
- Pay
- Harmonization
- Employment security

Training

Technical training (tools and techniques) predominates in TQM texts but there is less emphasis on the necessary soft skills – e.g. teamwork – which may also be required. Moreover, with the looser more flexible organization, there are fewer explicit guidelines/rules/regulations and this puts a greater emphasis on the use of interpersonal skills to motivate staff. Yet there is evidence both of a lack of off-the-job training and management development, and of managers' desire for human relations skills (Scase and Goffee, 1989).

Commitment to learning seeks to ensure continuing training and development for all employees. It demonstrates employer willingness to encourage and facilitate employee development rather than just providing specific training to cover short-term crises. Different types of measure can be employed, ranging from fully-fledged 'learning companies' through to Employment Development Asssistance Programmes, and task-based and interpersonal skills training.

Education and communication

These are dealt with at length in the TQM literature. However, the evidence suggests that senior management commitment expressed merely through vision and mission statements is inadequate. The 'levers' at the disposal of Personnel may be more powerful in providing clear messages of change and may take the quality message beyond the talking stage.

Selection

Recruiting high quality, committed and appropriate staff to the organization is central to the achievement of quality. Competencies are often sought at the selection stage include trainability, flexibility, commitment, drive and initiative. Recruitment methods need to attract a pool of high-quality candidates, with a comprehensive induction programme representing the final stage of successful selection. The development and maintenance of the desired culture requires that the new recruits are open to working in that culture. Japanese implants have been noted for the time and effort they take to screen potential employees, often even for attitudes as much as the appropriate skills; this recognizes that attitudes are deep rooted and difficult to change in the short term (Marchington and Wilkinson, 1996).

Appraisal

Deblieux (1991) argues that performance appraisal has a key role to play as a primary tool to communicate to managers whether quality standards are being met. Furthermore, under TQM, the customer (internal or external) is regarded as supreme; it thus seems a logical step to include customer evaluation of managerial performance in their overall appraisal. However, it seems few organizations which have adopted TQM do this formally for either internal or external customers, although there is a growing use of 'mystery shoppers' whereby an individual, either a company employee or someone contracted in, poses as a customer, monitors and reports on their experience to senior managers. These are some examples of organizations using internal customers, often a manager's subordinates, to evaluate their manager's commitment to TQM. There are difficulties here, though, with evidence from the USA that managers are using their own survey data of customer satisfaction with their unit's performance to verify and, if necessary, challenge the surveys and ratings of senior managers (Snape et al., 1993).

Pay

It seems likely that companies will abandon pay policies which reward sheer volume of output. The quality management literature assumes employees are keen to participate in the pursuit of quality improvements with little concern for extrinsic reward. However, some companies have linked a bonus to customer service or quality. These include Scottish Widows, British Steel (with delivery to time measures) and Rank Xerox. Hill (1992) argues that more reinforcement is needed rather than mere 'propaganda and trinkets'; see chapter 8 for details of reward and recognition. There is also a view that group schemes such as performance-related pay with its individual emphasis may militate against the ideas of co-operation and teamwork espoused by TQM.

Harmonization

This is also seen as an important component of the new approach. This would include common terms and conditions – e.g. sick pay and hours of work – as well as the more symbolic one of shared canteen and car parking. This would certainly be consistent with the ideas of Deming.

Employment security

This is one way in which employers can demonstrate to employees that they really are their 'most important resource'. Unlike some of the other 'best practices', this one has to be qualified slightly. It does not mean that employees can stay in the same job for life, nor does it prevent the dismissal of staff who fail to perform at the required level. Similarly, a major collapse in the market which necessitates reductions in the labour force should not be seen as undermining this principle. The principal point about this practice is that it asserts that job reductions will be avoided, wherever possible, and that employees should expect to maintain their employment with the organization. A key factor which facilitates the achievement of employment security is a well-devised and forward-looking system of HR planning and an understanding of how organization may be structured to achieve flexibility. It is perhaps summed up best by the view that workers should not be treated as a variable cost, but rather viewed as a critical asset in the long-term viability and success of the organization (Marchington and Wilkinson, 1996).

Most of the studies on best practice HRM conclude that there needs to be horizontal integration (Marchington and Wilkinson, 1996), i.e. the policies must be mutually reinforcing and not adapted on a 'pick and mix' basis. Indeed, Pfeffer (1994) argues that there needs to be an 'overarching philosophy' that 'provides a way of connecting the various individual practices into a coherent whole'. Without an overriding philosophy, policies are undermined and diluted (Godfrey and Wilkinson, 1998). In recent research undertaken at UMIST, this was a typical view of employers: ·

- Employees are to be developed, informed and given greater responsibility.
- Management style should be open, friendly and participative.
- Teamworking, both cell-based and cross-functional should be the normal way of working.

The vision is of a committed and capable workforce, working in teams and requiring little in the way of direct external control. This common vision needs to be evident across all levels of management and, in particular, it must be shared by all senior managers.

The acceptance of such a common vision will pre-determine much of company activity and attitudes in the areas of TQM and the management of HR. It results in an acceptance of the importance of the HR dimension of TQM. The presence of an overall management vision influences the HR practices implemented, but also the way they are implemented. Where this common vision is missing, managers often had difficulty describing the type of company culture they would like to see, and employees complained about inconsistencies in management approach and a lack of commitment to TQM from senior management. Without this overall vision or strategy, there is a lack of direction in TQM and HR policies, and they both may fail to link in to business strategy. Moreover, there is also a lack of urgency in changing HR policies which conflict with TQM, and business strategy decisions may be taken which conflict with the TQM initiative.

However, simply referring to a common vision is insufficient, as there must also be understanding. In one organization, a manager complained that there had, in the past, been 'commitment without understanding'. There was a tendency for managers to say what they thought they should say without actually understanding the implications behind it. This led to inconsistent management behaviour and actions that conflicted with the espoused company values, e.g. putting extreme pressure on employees to increase production because they were falling behind target. This common vision can be reinforced by management training and the appraisal system. If the performance of managers is appraised solely on output and cost factors, then these will be deemed to be the most important aspects of management behaviour. At one site, a production manager was achieving high output figures through an autocratic management style with minimum employee involvement. His 'success' was rewarded with no direct challenge to the fact that his style failed to match the espoused management approach. The end result was that other managers were inclined to copy his style and the attempt to increase employee involvement and introduce teamworking at the site failed.

As well as having an overall vision, there also needs to be an infrastructure which links HRM, TQM and business strategy. This is provided through the development of a strong policy deployment process which is designed to ensure the senior management policy plan is deployed to all levels of the organization thus facilitating the management vision (Godfrey and Wilkinson, 1998).

Based on research at UMIST funded by the EPSRC, an audit tool was developed to facilitate self-assessment of HR policies and practices. It follows the people management structure of the EFQM Business Excellence Model; see table 10.1. It is not intended to score criteria but to provide a basis for an informed discussion of organizational policy. These are the key concerns (Dale et al., 1998):

- Reducing 'them and us' barriers between managers and employees
- Increasing the commitment of employees

Table 10.1 An audit tool to facilitate self-assessment of HR policies and practices

	Reducing 'us and them' barriers	Increasing commitment	Improving performance	Rewards and incentives	Employee involvement
Section 1: Planning and improving human resources					
1a Aligning HR and business strategy					
1b Employee surveys					
1c Single status and harmonization					
1d Rewards and employment security					
1e Innovative work organizations					
Section 2: Sustaining and developing capabilities					
2a Identifying and matching competencies					
2b Managing recruitment and career development					
2c Training plans					
2d Evaluating training					
2e Developing employees through work experience					
2f Developing team skills					
Section 3: Performance management					
3a Aligning targets					
3b Reviewing and updating targets					
3c Appraisals					
Section 4: Involving and empowering employees					
4a Encouraging participation					
4b In-house ceremonies					
4c Empowering people					
4d Recognition system supports involvement					
Section 5: Communications					
5a Identifying communication needs					
5b Sharing information					
5c Evaluating communication					
5d Effective communication structures					
Section 6: Caring for employees					
6a Health and safety and environmental issues					
6b Other benefits					
6c Social and cultural activities					
6d Employee facilities and services					

- Improving the performance of employees
- Dealing with incentives and rewards
- Increasing employee involvement

The emphasis on HR issues implies that the Personnel Department should have an input. Recognition of the significance of HR issues in principle is, by itself, inadequate. In her classic work, Legge (1978) points out that:

> ... the personnel management considerations involved in production, marketing and finance decisions were not so much overruled as went by default. In other words, non specialists, while formally recognising the importance of effective utilising human resources, lacking as they did the expertise to develop a systematic view of what this entailed in terms of personnel strategies and actions, in practice tended to underestimate the importance of the human resource variable in decision making on issues that were not explicitly personnel management.

Thus, Giles and Williams (1991) point out: Personnel people have much to offer quality management. They are guardians of key processes such as selection, appraisal, training and reward systems, which go right to the heart of achieving strategic change. In research carried out for the Institute of Personnel Management, it was suggested that there were five phases or areas of intervention (Marchington et al., 1993).

The first stage at which the personnel function may make a contribution is in the shaping of TQM initiatives at the formulation or developmental phase. Personnel people may be able to play a creative role here, in terms of the philosophy behind TQM and its degree of integration with current organisational practice and ethos. Of course, much depends upon the existing influence of the function, and its ability to gain access to senior levels of decision making within the organization. Assuming this to be the case, here are some are examples of areas in which interventions may be made:

- Preparing and synthesizing reports from other organizations which have experience of TQM
- Assisting with choices about the TQM approach to be adopted
- Influencing the type of TQM infrastructure to be adopted
- Shaping the type of organization structure and culture appropriate for the introduction of TQM
- Designing and delivering senior management development courses which create the right climate for TQM

The second area in which the personnel function can make a contribution is at the implementation phase of the TQM process. At this stage, a crucial facilitating role can be played by personnel professionals in ensuring that TQM is introduced in the most effective manner, and that all employees are aware of its potential within the organization. These types of activity may be undertaken:

- Training of middle managers and supervisors in how to develop the TQM process with their staff
- Training of facilitators, mentors and team members in interpersonal skills and how to manage the TQM process

- Designing communication events to publicize the launch of TQM
- Consulting with employees and trade union representatives about the introduction and development of TQM
- Assisting the Board to adapt mission statements and prepare quality objectives for dissemination to staff and customers

Having shaped and implemented a new TQM initiative, the personnel function can play an effective part in attempting to maintain and reinforce its position within the organization. Interventions in the third area are designed to ensure that TQM continues to attract a high profile and does not lose impetus. The contribution can be in these areas:

- Introducing or upgrading the TQM component within induction courses
- Ensuring that training in TQM techniques and processes continues to be provided within the organization
- Redesigning appraisal procedures so that they contain criteria relating to specific TQM objectives
- Preparing/overseeing special newsletters or team briefs on TQM
- Assisting quality improvement teams or suggestions schemes to work effectively and to produce ideas

The fourth area in which the personnel function may be able to make a contribution to TQM is at the review stage, either on a regular (perhaps annual or biennial) basis or as part of an ongoing procedure for evaluating progress. These are the kinds of interventions which may be employed:

- Contributing to or leading the preparation of an Annual TQM report
- Assessing the effectiveness of the TQM infrastructure – steering committees, quality service teams, improvement groups, etc.
- Preparing and administering employee attitude surveys on TQM
- Benchmarking the effectiveness of the organization's TQM with that of competitors or employers in other sectors/countries
- Facilitating the operation of internal reviews using criteria such as the EFQM or the MBNQA models

Fifth, and to some extent in conjunction with each of the above contributions, personnel functions can apply TQM processes to a review of its own activities, along the lines of that undertaken by the internal contractors analysed in the previous section. The precise list of practices obviously depends on the organization and function involved, but here are some of the more typical ones:

- Preparing offer and contract letters within a specified time
- Advising staff on their terms and conditions of employment
- Evaluating training provision on an annual basis
- Preparing and disseminating absence and labour turnover data to line mangers on a monthly basis
- Providing advice on disciplinary matters within a specified, and agreed, time period

It is not assumed that the more of these which are undertaken, the better. Indeed, employing such a strategy might result in poorer performance because resources are spread too thinly or the function comes to be seen as the purveyor of the latest fads and fashions which are irrelevant for organizational needs. The key question must be: How can the function continually improve its contribution to quality management initiatives and organizational success? Personnel and HR managers may therefore wish to develop an audit of their contributions based on these questions:

- What is our current contribution to TQM within these areas of activity?
- How is our contribution perceived by other people in the organization?
- What might be done to enhance our contribution to TQM?

Summary

TQM comprises both hard production/operations-oriented and soft employee relations-oriented elements and, while TQM proponents have tended to emphasize the 'hard' aspects of the theory, there is some attention paid to 'softer' issues.

However, involvement and cultural issues are dealt with in a somewhat cursory way, and industrial relations and HR practices are ignored. There needs to be both a general improvement of the HR variable, with employees seen as a resource to be developed rather than a cost to be controlled, and integration with TQM within the organization. Until a closer alignment between the ideas and practices of TQM and HRM takes place, it is unlikely that TQM will achieve its aims.

These points should be considered:

- TQM and HRM practices should be integrated.
- Middle management and supervisory concerns should be addressed; they are key actors in the TQM process.
- Culture is a complex concept and not easily manipulated. In attempting to change culture, senior management should utilize a wide array of 'tools'.
- The context of change should be considered. TQM introduced in a climate of recession, and associated with job losses and intensification, is likely to be perceived in a negative way by employees.
- Issues of power and conflict need to be addressed rather than ignored or dealt with only when they openly obstruct the programme.
- The Personnel Department has an important role to play in all these areas, and can make a contribution to TQM at a number of phases.

References

Bass, B. 1990: *Bass & Stodghill's Handbook of Leadership: Theory, Research and Managerial Applications.* New York: Free Press.

Bradley, K. and Hill, S. 1987: Quality circles and managerial interests. *Industrial Relations,* 26, Winter, 68–82.

Coyle-Shapiro, J. C. 1993: The quality guru's working paper. Unpublished paper.

Coyne, G. and Williamson, H. 1991: New Union Strategies. Liverpool: Centre for Alternative Industrial and Technological Systems and MTUCURC.

Crosby, P. B. 1979: *Quality is Free.* New York: McGraw-Hill.

Dale, B. G. and Plunkett, J. J. (eds) 1990: *Managing Quality*. 1st edn. Hemel Hempstead, Herts: Phillip Allan.

Dale, B. G., Godfrey, G., Wilkinson, A. and Marchington, M. 1998: Aligning people with processes. *Measuring Business Excellence*, 2(2), 42–6.

Dawson, P. and Webb, J. 1988: New production arrangements: the totally flexible cage? *Work, Employment and Society*, 3, 221–38.

Deblieux, M. 1991: Performance reviews support the quest for quality. *HR Focus*, November 3–4.

Deming, W. E. 1982: *Quality, Productivity and Competitive Position*. Cambridge, Mass.: MIT Press.

Deming, W. C. 1986: *Out of the Crisis*, Cambridge, Mass.: MIT Centre for Advanced Engineering Study.

Dotchin, J. and Oakland, J. C. 1991: Theories and concepts in total quality management. *Proceedings 2nd European Quality Conference for Education, Training and Research.*

Feigenbaum, A. V. 1983: *Total Quality Control* (3rd edn) New York: McGraw-Hill.

French, J. and Caplan, R. 1973: Organisational stress and individual strain. In A. J. Marrow (ed.), *The Failure of Success*, New York: AMACOM.

Garvin, D. 1991: How the Baldrige Award really works. *Harvard Business Review*. November–December, 80–93; see also Debate January–February 1992, 126–47.

Giles, E. and Starkey, K. 1987: The Japanization of Xerox new technology. *Work and Employment*, 3(2), 125–33.

Giles, E. and Williams, R. 1991: Can the personnel department survive quality management?, *Personnel Management*, April, 28–33.

Godfrey, G. and Wilkinson, A. 1998: *Adopting Best Practice HRM in a TQM Context*. Working Paper, Manchester School of Management, UMIST.

Godfrey, G., Wilkinson, A., Marchington, M. and Dale, B. 1998: *Vision, Deployment and Practice. TQM and HRM in Manufacturing*. Quality Management Centre Occasional Paper, Manchester School of Management, UMIST.

Guest, D. 1987: HRM and industrial relations. *Journal of Management Studies*, 24(5), 503–22.

Hackman, R. & Oldman, G. 1976: Motivation through the design of work: test of a theory. *Organisational Behavioural and Human Performance*, 16(2), 250–79.

Hamper, B. 1992: *Rivethead*. London: Fourth Estate.

Hill, S. 1991a: How do you manage a flexible firm? The Total Quality Model. *Work, Employment & Society*, December, 397–415.

Hill, S. 1991b: Why quality circles failed but total quality might succeed. *British Journal of Industrial Relations*, 29 December, 541–68.

Hill, S. 1992: People and quality. In K. Bradley (ed.) *People and Profits*, Aldershot: Gower.

Hill, S. and Wilkinson, A. 1995: In search of TQM. *Employee Relations*, 17(3), 8–25.

Ishikawa, K. 1985 (translated by D. J. Lu): *What is Total Quality Control? The Japanese Way*. Englewood Cliffs, NJ: Prentice-Hall.

Juran, J. M. (ed.) 1988: *Quality Control Handbook*. New York: McGraw-Hill.

Juran, J. M. 1989: *Juran on Leadership for Quality*. New York: Free Press.

Juran, J. M. 1991: Strategies for world class quality. *Quality Progress*, 24(3), 81–5.

Kearney, A. T. 1992: *Total Quality: Time to Take Off the Rose Tinted Spectacles*. Bedfordshire: A. T. Kearney and TQM Magazine.

Klein, R. 1984: Why supervisors resist employee involvement. *Harvard Business Review*, September–October, 87–95.

Legge, K. 1978: *Power Innovation and Problem Soluing in Personnel Management*. New York: McGraw-Hill.

Marchington, M. 1992: *Managing The Team: A Guide to Successful Employee Involvement*. Oxford: Basil Blackwell.

Marchington, M. and Wilkinson, A. 1996: *Core Personnel and Development*, London: IPD.

Marchington, M., Wilkinson, A. and Dale, B. 1993: *Quality and the Human Resource Dimension, The Case Study Report in Quality and the Human Resource Dimension*. London: Institute of Personnel Management.

Morton, C. 1994: *Becoming World Class*. London: Macmillan.

Oakland, J. S. 1989: *Total Quality Management*. London: Heinemann.

Pfeffer, J. 1994: *Competitive Advantage Through People*, New York: Free Press.

Powell, T. C. 1995: Total quality management as competitive advantage: a review and empirical study. *Strategic Management Journal*, 16(1), 15–37.

Robertson, I., Smith, M. and Cooper, M. 1992: *Motivation: Strategies, Theory and Practice*. London: Institute of Personnel Management.

Scase, R. and Goffee, R. 1989: *Reluctant Managers*. London: Unwin.

Schein, E. H. 1985: *Organisational Culture and Leadership*. Oxford: Jossey-Bass.

Schuler, R. and Harris, D. 1992: *Managing Quality: the Primer for Middle Managers*. New York, Mass.: Addison-Wesley.

Seddon, J. 1989: A passion for quality. *The TQM Magazine*, May, 153–7.

Seddon, J. 1990: A successful attitude. *The TQM Magazine*, January, 81–4.

Snape, E., Redman, T. and Bamber, G. 1993: *Managing Managers*. Oxford: Blackwell.

Storey, J. 1992: *Developments in the Management of Human Resources*, Oxford: Blackwell.

Storey, J. (ed.) 1995: *Human Resource Management*. London: Routledge.

Taguchi, G. 1986: *Introduction to Quality Engineering*. New York: Asian Productivity Organisation.

Thurley, K. and Wirdenius, H. 1989: *Towards European Management*. London: Pitman.

Waldman, D. 1994: The contributions of total quality management to a theory of work performance. *Academy of Management Review*, 19(3), 511–36.

Wilkinson, A. 1992: The other side of quality: soft issues and the human resource dimension. *Total Quality Management*, 3(3), 323–9.

Wilkinson, A. and Witcher, B. 1991: Fitness for use? Barriers to full TQM in the UK. *Management Decision*, 29(8), 46–51.

Wilkinson, A. and Witcher, A. 1993: Holistic total quality management must take account of political processes. *Total Quality Management*, 4(1), 47–56.

Wilkinson, A., Allen, P. and Snape, E. 1991: TQM and the management of labour. *Employee Relations*, 13(1), 24–31.

Wilkinson, A., Marchington M., Ackers, P. and Goodman, J. 1992: Total quality management and employee involvement. *Human Resource Management Journal*, 2(4), Summer, 1–20.

Wilkinson, A., Redman, T., Snape, E. and Marchington, M. 1998: *Managing Through TQM: Theory and Practice*. London: Macmillan.

Williams, A., Dobson, P. and Walters, M. 1991: *Changing Culture*. London: Institute of Personnel Management.

chapter eleven

Supplier Development

B. Burnes and B. G. Dale

Introduction

The quality of purchased supplies are crucial to a purchasing organization's products and services and, consequently, to its success in the market-place. In many cases, bought-in components and services can account for some 70–80 per cent of the final cost of a product; therefore, it is clear that suppliers are critical to the cost base of the purchaser. Many major European companies, following the example of Japan, have, during the last decade or so, started to encourage their suppliers to develop their quality management systems, adopt a continuous improvement philosophy, eliminate non-value added activity, improve their manufacturing systems, use lean manufacturing techniques, become more flexible and responsive, and pursue cost down activities.

This process of the customers working together with their suppliers to effect these changes is given a variety of names: supplier development, co-makership, partnership sourcing, customer-supplier alliances, and proactive purchasing. This variety of names, and the way different organizations interpret them and the process, has led to much confusion about both the meaning and practicality of the partnership approach to purchasing. This chapter, based on Burnes and Dale (1998), examines the key issues in sustainable partnerships under the main headings of long-term issues of partnership, barriers to developing partnership, conditions of partnerships, the issues to be considered in partnership, the process of partnership and the potential difficulties. The chapter concludes with a list of dos and don'ts when developing partnerships.

Long-term Issues of Partnerships

The traditional open-market bargaining approach to customer–supplier dealings has been based on the assumption that the parties involved are adversaries who have differing objectives and are engaged in a win–lose contest based upon tough negotiations and cost under-cutting. This approach focuses on negative issues and is characterized by uncertainty which can seriously undermine rather than reinforce competitiveness.

Partnership demands a new form of relationship. It means working together towards common aims and aspirations, based on the principle that both parties can gain more through co-operation than conflict. Partnerships are characterized by mutual trust and commitment, integrity, integration, co-operation, honesty, a willingness to be open and to declare problems, and to work together to find answers, the sharing of data and ideas, improvements and best practices, clearly understood responsibilities, collaborative R&D, and a desire for continuous improvement of the product and service. In many respects, this form of relationship has similarities with a vertically integrated firm but without the difficulties of managing a complex business across different types of technologies and processes.

To develop a viable long-term business relationship, considerable changes in behaviour and attitude are required in both the customer and supplier organizations, and this needs to be fostered. Customers need to be prepared to develop plans and procedures for working with suppliers and commit resources to this. For their part, suppliers have to accept full responsibility for the quality of their shipped product; they should not rely on the customer's receiving inspection to assess whether it meets their requirements. As a prerequisite of partnership, both parties have to reach an agreement on how they will work together, what they want from the relationship and how to resolve any problems which may arise. To ensure that the relationship is sustainable, it is important that the objectives of the agreement are examined and discussed on a regular basis.

Here are the typical benefits of developing a long-term business partnership:

- Reduction and elimination of the inspection of supplied parts and materials
- Improved product and service quality, and delivery performance and responsiveness
- Improved productivity, increased stock turns and lower inventory carrying cost and reduced costs per piece
- Value for money purchases
- Security and stability of supplies
- Transfer of ideas and expertise between customer and supplier and dissemination of best practice
- Joint problem-solving activities, with the customer providing assistance to the supplier to help to improve processes, leading to easier and faster resolution of problems
- Integration of business practices and procedures between customer and supplier
- A comprehensive customer–supplier communications network to ensure the supplier is provided with early access to customer future designs and manufacturing plans and being kept informed of changing customer requirements – this assists with the planning of workloads and would typically open up wider channels than those in the traditional relationship where the buyer and sales representatives would be the main point of contact
- Customer and supplier being more willing and open to examine their processes to look for improvements
- The supplier contributing to the customer's design process, undertaking development work and monitoring technological trends – this can lead to new innovative products

- Help to develop sustainable growth of the supplier in terms of investment in equipment and manufacturing resources – related to this is the reputation and credibility in the market-place which arises from the relationship
- Exposure of the supplier to new tools, techniques, systems and business practices
- Provision by the customer of an advisory service to suppliers in terms of training, equipment and operating methods

Barriers to Developing Partnership

Developing partnerships is not without difficulties. Lascelles and Dale (1990) have carried out research which reveals that certain aspects of the customer–supplier relationship can act as a barrier to supplier development:

- Poor communication and feedback
- Supplier complacency
- Misguided supplier improvement objectives
- Lack of customer credibility
- Misconceptions regarding purchasing power

Poor communication and feedback

In general, communication and feedback between customer and supplier is not good. Sometimes, it is even so bad that the parties do not even realize how poor they are at communicating with each other. The main dissatisfaction expressed by suppliers relate to technical specifications and requirements, the lack of consultation on design and product engineering issues and changes to the delivery schedule. There are some strong indications that not all dissatisfied suppliers actually communicate their dissatisfaction to the customer.

Supplier complacency

Suppliers being unconcerned about customer satisfaction. There are two types of measurement relating to a customer's satisfaction with the quality of supplies.

- Reactive measures

  - Failure data, e.g. non-conformity analysis, customer rejections, warranty claims
  - Customer assessment rating and audit reports
  - Verbal feedback from meetings with customers
  - Contractual requirements outlined in the customers' vendor improvement plans

- Proactive measures

  - Customer workshops and forum meetings
  - Market research
  - Benchmarking key processes
  - Competitor evaluation
  - Reliability analysis
  - Advanced quality planning

Misguided supplier improvement objectives

Customers are often not sure what they want from supplier improvement initiatives, and can underestimate the time and resources required to introduce and develop partnerships. There also appears to be a dilution and distortion of the quality message as requirements are passed down the supply chain. For example, when faced with demands to improve quality from customers, first tier suppliers usually react by implementing specific tools and techniques required by the customer. In turn, the supplier then insists that their own suppliers use the same tools and techniques but fail to understand that these are only fully effective within the context of an organization-wide approach to continuous improvement.

Lack of customer credibility

Suppliers need to be convinced that a customer is serious about continuous improvement. This requires the customer's behaviour and attitudes to be consistent with what they are saying to suppliers. Here are some examples of how a credibility gap may emerge:

- Purchasing and supplies management practices such as a competitive pricing policy, frequent switches from one supplier to another, unpredictable and inflated production schedules, last-minute changes to schedules, poor engineering design/production/supplier liaison, over-stringent specifications, inconsistent decisions made by supplier quality assurance (SQA) personnel, abuse of power by SQA personnel and the use of 'loss of business' as a bargaining ploy in negotiating a reduction in price. It is not uncommon for a customer to talk quality to its suppliers and then act quite differently by relegating quality to secondary importance behind, for example, price and meeting the production schedule
- The TQM and business excellence image which major purchasing organizations attempt to create in discussions with suppliers are not reflected in practice when supplier personnel visit their own manufacturing sites
- A customer has accepted non-conforming items over a long period of time, even if unwittingly, and then criticises the supplier for supplying non-conforming materials
- There may be a lack of a strategy for dealing with the tooling used for supplied parts. For example, a supplier may report to the customer that the customer-supplied tooling is reaching the end of its useful life. The customer then asks the supplier to carry out some minor refurbishment as a short-term measure, the supplier advises against this but is pressurized to do the repairs. When non-conforming parts are found in batches from the 'patched-up' tooling, the supplier acquires quality performance demerits
- The customer fails to react positively to supplier concerns about design issues and are prepared to let the supplier carry the consequences.
- Failure to respond to a supplier's request for information and to provide advice on queries
- The use of supplied components without them passing the initial sample approval procedure

- When the customer's SQA personnel are fooled by the camouflage measures, fakes and ruses employed by a supplier in an assessment of a vendor's quality system
- The supplier being forced to hold stocks to cover their customer's inadequate scheduling and poor systems control

Misconceptions regarding purchasing power

Purchasing power is a major issue in the buyer–supplier relationship. Lack of purchasing power is a commonly cited reason for the lack of success in improving supplier performance. The general view is that a purchaser's influence on its suppliers varies with its purchasing power, and the greater this is, the more effective will be its SQA activities. These power imbalances can cause uneven levels of commitment in the relationship.

Purchasing power alone is no guarantee of improving supplier performance. Companies with considerable purchasing power may well improve the quality of purchased items but will not necessarily achieve lasting benefits or motivate their suppliers to internalize the benefits of a process of continuous improvement to satisfy all their customers.

Conditions of Partnership

One of the key points which stands out is the wide diversity of partnership arrangements which have developed within the UK over the last decade. Though, as might be expected, there is a marked contrast between the public and private sectors, there is an equally marked contrast within the private sector. This is neither surprising nor any cause for alarm. The main driving force behind the move to customer–supplier partnerships has been the establishment of Japanese transplants in Europe, especially the UK. However, it has to be recognized that the conditions under which European customers and suppliers operate are markedly different than those in Japan. In Japan, many large organizations have dedicated suppliers – companies who only supply them. This has led to the phenomenon, in the motor industry for example, where it is not just Toyota vying with Nissan and Honda for supremacy but the entire Toyota supply chain battling against the Nissan and Honda supply chains. These are clearly not the conditions which operate in the UK and the rest of Europe.

In the UK, dedicated suppliers are few and far between. The best and most competitive suppliers will be dealing with most, if not all, the main companies in their industry. These suppliers will work closely with a particular customer to develop a product, process or service. The way that this is done varies but includes obtaining a supplier's input on product development and sharing product planning and development data with suppliers. However, the benefit to that customer is likely to be short lived because, in a commercial environment, the supplier has to offer this same type of R&D activity to its other customers to retain their business. On this theme of development and the concentration on core competencies by the major customers, it is clear that many UK customers and suppliers are now abandoning adversarial relationships in favour of more co-operative partnerships. They are attempting to fit these to their circumstances and needs, rather than merely copying what worked for Japanese companies in Japan; this is the right thing to do.

Nevertheless, it does mean that customers and suppliers are having, in a relatively short space of time, to learn, adopt and adapt an approach to purchasing which has taken Japanese companies over forty years to develop. Quite rightly, different companies, industries and sectors are developing partnerships in their own way to meet their own needs and circumstances. However, it must be recognized that no one enters into a partnership with their suppliers or customers out of any altruistic motive or wish to be 'nice' to them. Partnerships are driven by hard-headed business objectives, mainly the need to achieve/maintain competitiveness in an increasingly global and hostile business environment. For example, even partnership suppliers are being told that, for an increasing amount of business, they are expected to cut costs. Therefore, it has to be recognized that customer–supplier partnerships are not an easy option or some sort of panacea. This is particularly the case where a supplier is expected to meet the global requirements of its major customers. Underlying the rhetoric of partnership are difficult choices not only about whether to enter into partnerships and the the type to be adopted but also, and perhaps more importantly, the internal upheavals this requires for most organizations.

The Issues to be Considered in Partnership

Burnes and Whittle (1998) show the steps that organizations need to go through to decide whether to undertake a partnership initiative. However, even when organizations have examined all the issues involved and decided that the partnership approach is for them, they should not attempt to rush into building new external relationships and mechanisms until they are sure that the internal equivalents are appropriate and effective. In particular, senior management should complete these tasks first:

- Outline clear objectives for the partnership initiative and ensure that those involved understand what they are and are committed to the ideals.
- Develop a strategy and plan to accomplish these objectives.
- Establish a procedure for deciding which suppliers to involve.
- Ensure that the philosophy of the organization is in line with, or can be realigned to, the partnership approach to purchasing, especially the need for teamwork.

Though the above will not necessarily be easily achieved, in the first instance, perhaps the most critical task will be for the organization to refocus and restructure those aspects of its own operations which are crucial to effective supplier performance. In effect, what is required is for it to put its own house in order before it asks its suppliers to do the same. In particular, the increasing complexity of the task of obtaining conforming supplies at the right time, at the right price and every time suggests that the conventional form and organization of the purchasing management function may no longer be adequate. Traditional staff structures based on tight functional groups have resulted in compartmentalized attitudes to suppliers which hinder supplier development. Companies will need to restructure their purchasing, quality and engineering departments to ensure that they have the right skills in dealing with suppliers, and that functional accountability and logistics are adequate for the task of supplier development. It is also important to establish a multi-functional teamwork approach to purchasing.

To be effective, partnership requires well-trained personnel capable of working with suppliers to achieve the objectives which have been agreed; in effect, these personnel act as change agents. Purchasing and other staff who, where necessary, liaise with suppliers will need to understand the capabilities of suppliers' processes and systems and have a good working knowledge of the philosophy, principles, techniques of improvement and shopfloor procedures. It is also important that a customer's staff can speak the same language as their suppliers counterparts, whether these be in production, quality, design, finance or sales activities. Embarking on an action plan for partnership with insufficient regard to the needs of the purchasing organization's skills is likely to result in frustration and, possibly, eventual failure of the initiative.

It is also important that the most effective mechanism and linkages for communication and feedback are used. Typically, purchasing, quality, design, engineering/technical and production personnel all talk to suppliers but with no single functional area accepting total responsibility for the quality, cost and delivery of the bought-out items. The need for clear accountability and co-ordination is a crucial factor in ensuring that channels of communication between them are effective and that suppliers receive a consistent message. Importantly, it must be clear who will be responsible for all negotiations and communications for current and future business with each supplier.

For a company with many suppliers and bought-out items, it may take several years to introduce and develop an effective process of partnership. It has to be recognized, however, that not all suppliers will welcome, or be capable of accepting, this form of approach. Some, for whatever reason, will prefer to maintain a more adversarial approach. Though, in the longer term, a process of supply base reduction will eliminate many of these, others may well remain. It will also be the case that while a few suppliers may be world class, the majority will need to improve if they are to meet the company's expectations. Therefore, most companies will find that they will need to adopt different practices with different suppliers. Probably, in the majority of cases, a partnership approach based on a commitment to supplier improvement will be the order of the day. On the other hand, with those suppliers whose performance is already world class, it may be the customer who finds itself being improved. However, with some suppliers, relationships may well remain antagonistic.

Therefore, before starting a process of partnership, a company will need to review its supplier base and identify those suppliers with whom it needs to work with in the long term, and the type of relationship it will be able to establish. As it will not be possible to launch a partnership approach with all its suppliers at once, the company will need to establish a mechanism for selecting the initial group of suppliers. One approach is to concentrate on new products, product and process modifications and new vendors. Another approach involves the use of Pareto analysis (see chapter 14) to focus priorities by ranking bought-out components and materials according to some appropriate parameter, e.g. gross annual spend.

To assist their suppliers, some major organizations have documented the fundamental requirements for the control of quality and achievement of improvement, some have even produced explanatory booklets; *QS9000*, as discussed in chapter 13, is a good example of this. These organizations make it is a condition of the purchase order agreement that suppliers' products comply with these requirements.

Assisting suppliers to improve their performance is important; however, it must be recognized that the delivery of non-conforming product from a supplier can often be attributed to an ambiguous purchasing specification and poorly detailed customer requirements. Purchasing specifications are working documents used by both customer and supplier and must be treated as such. The content of material and product specifications have become highly standardized, and usually include such features as functional physical characteristics, dimensional details, reliability characteristics, methods of test and criteria for acceptance, conditions of manufacture, installation, storage and use, and so on. The purchasing department should review the accuracy and completeness of purchasing documents before they are released to suppliers. It is good practice to send these documents to the quality department for their comments prior to transmission to the supplier.

It is also important to recognize that, just as suppliers can learn from customers, the reverse also applies. Suppliers are knowledgeable in their own field of operation and should be given every opportunity to provide a design input to the preparation of the specification. With the reduction in specialist technical staff in many customer organizations, this is now a common occurrence. Suppliers will be more likely to accept responsibility for defects and their associated costs if they are involved in the design of the product or formally agree with the customer the specification and drawing for the part to be produced. This supplier input to the design process is a key factor in cost avoidance and reduction, and helps to reduce the product development lead time.

One outcome of partnerships is that an increasing number of major purchasing organizations are awarding more long-term contracts and contracts for the life of a part. Strategic sourcing – i.e. single or dual sourcing – is considered by many writers and practitioners to be a complementary policy. This will inevitably contribute to the reduction in the size of organizations' supplier bases. The reduction in the supplier base can result in many benefits:

- Less variation in the characteristics of the supplied product
- Increases in the amount of time the customer's QA and purchasing personnel can devote to vendors
- Improved and simplified communications with vendors
- Less paperwork
- Less transportation
- Less handling and inspection activity
- Fewer accounts to be maintained and, thus, reduced costs for both parties

It is easier to develop a partnership relationship if the suppliers are in close proximity to the customer. Consequently, a number of customers are now reversing their international sourcing strategies to develop shorter supply lines and are recommending that suppliers set up operations close to their main manufacturing facilities. Closeness is also a vital element in the use of a JIT purchasing strategy.

The Process of Partnership

Having put its own house in order and selected suitable suppliers for inclusion in their partnership programme, the next step is for the purchasing organization is to involve the selected suppliers and to obtain their commitment. This entails communicating to suppliers what is required, and reaching an understanding with them on a set of common objectives.

The most practical way of setting about this task is to hold presentations to suppliers covering issues such as these:

- The approach being taken to partnership
- What is expected of suppliers and what assistance they can expect from the customer
- The quality system standard to be used
- How suppliers' performance will be assessed, how the results will be communicated, and what assistance will be provided to help suppliers to improve

Presentations to suppliers can be held either on the customer's premises or at individual supplier's sites. A supplier conference and/or presentation must give those involved an opportunity to air grievances and discuss problems in an open and honest manner, and must be aimed at establishing a climate of co-operation and commitment.

Once a supplier's senior management team have agreed to participate in the partnership process, it is usual for the purchasing organization to visit the supplier's factory and carry out a formal vendor approval survey. The objective of the survey is to assess the supplier's suitability as a business partner including the identification of strengths and weaknesses, awareness of continuous improvement mechanisms and cost effectiveness of collaboration. The survey is a multi-disciplinary task which, in a number of cases, involves the customer's purchasing, quality, engineering and technical personnel. The survey should cover areas such as controls, processes and capabilities, workshop environment, plant, technology, R&D, quality systems, staff attitudes, responses, tooling, and planning and administrative systems.

As part of its audit, a customer must assess the supplier's commitment to advanced product quality planning (APQP). A useful summary of APQP, which consists of five phases – plan and define the programme, product design and development, process design and development, product and process validation and feedback, assessment and corrective action – is provided by Thisse (1998). APQP commences with a joint review of the specification and classification of product characteristics, and the production of an FMEA. The supplier should prepare a control plan to summarize the quality planning for significant product characteristics. This would typically include a description of the manufacturing operation and process flows, equipment used, control characteristics, control plans, specification limits, the use of SPC and mistake-proofing, inspection details, and corrective and preventive action methods. The supplier would then provide initial samples for evaluation, supported by data on process capability on the key characteristics identified by both parties, plus test results. Following successful evaluation of initial samples, the supplier is now in a position to start a trial production run followed by routine volume production.

Once the customer has assessed the adequacy of the supplier's policies, systems, procedures and manufacturing methods, and the supplier has been able to demonstrate the quality of its shipped product, the goods inward inspection of suppliers can be reduced considerably; in some cases, down to the ideal situation of direct line supply. At this point, 'preferred' or 'certified supplier' status can be conferred on the supplier. Many companies now also operate a supplier award scheme to recognize excellent supplier performance.

This assessment should not be a one-off exercise. An increasing number of major purchasing organizations will audit all their suppliers at regular intervals. This is to ensure that suppliers systems, processes and procedures are being maintained and improved. The frequency at which each supplier is reassessed is dependent on several factors:

- The supplier's performance
- The status awarded to the supplier
- The type of item being supplied
- The volume of parts being supplied
- The occurrence of a major change at the supplier, e.g. change of management, change of facilities and process change
- The supplier's request for assistance

The partnership process is ongoing aimed at building an effective business relationship based on openness – a relationship which demands a greater and quicker exchange of information between both parties. During the early days, the parameters of the new relationship are never completely clear to either both party, and it takes time to work out ground rules which are suitable for both of them. A number of major purchasing organizations have introduced electronic ordering and purchasing with their key suppliers and, even, the electronic sharing of product data. The more that can be done to transfer data in digital format the better, in terms of error reduction and improved communication. This linking of information systems and processes can often test the strength of the relationship, in particular, when incompatibilities in customer and supplier systems are discovered. The electronic data exchange relates to quality, technical requirements and specifications, schedules, manufacturing programmes, lead times, inventory management, and invoicing. Suppliers are obliged to communicate any changes to materials, processes or methods that may affect the dimensional, functional, compositional or appearance characteristics of the product. Customers are obliged to provide sufficient information and assistance to aid development of their suppliers' approach to continuous improvement. In some cases, this extends to joint problem-solving and cost-reduction activities. When the relationship has developed from problem solving to problem avoidance, it indicates that relationship has passed a major hurdle.

It is argued by writers such as Fruin (1992) and Morris and Imrie (1992) that the benefits of partnership are best achieved by spreading the concept to all members of the value-added chain from raw material to end product. This is perhaps best handled by a supplier association. Such an association is usually taken to be a group of first-level suppliers and a particular customer. This is a loose grouping who share knowledge and experience for the purpose of continuous improvement down the supply chain. This is characteristic of the Japanese supply chain where it is also usual for first tier supplier to develop their own supplier associations. Fruin (1992) points out that 'the Toyota Motor Corporation has three regional supplier associations and Nissan Motor has two'. These forms of co-operative supplier networks are now starting to develop in Europe. For example Morris and Imrie (1992) describe a network in place at Lucas Girling, and Hines (1992) describes how the Welsh Development Agency, through their 'Source Wales' initiative, has assisted Llanelli Radiators to form a supplier association.

Potential Difficulties of Operating Partnerships

In a partnership which is regarded as a success by both parties, everyone wins. If only one party is considered the winner, as is the case with typical adversarial purchasing arrangements, there can be no basis for a partnership. A partnership is about a long-term relationship between a customer and a set of suppliers, to reduce total costs all round, develop and maintain a competitive position and to satisfy the end customer. It is important that the partnership is lived in the way it is articulated and talked about. This is far from easy and their are many potential obstacles.

Based on our practical and research work, here are the main difficulties usually experienced in developing a partnership approach:

- An overemphasis on cost reduction and piece price down, rather than the total cost of acquisition
- Variations in the approaches of individuals and a general lack of cohesion
- A perceived lack of understanding by the customer of the business implications of its actions, e.g. sudden and large-scale changes in production level and work mix, changes in priorities, and a failure to stick with delivery schedules
- Poor and inconsistent communication
- An unwillingness by customers to reciprocate openness with the suppliers
- Poor reliability of information and systems
- Inadequate project management
- A tendency for the customer to blame all the problems which are encountered on the supplier
- Inability to respond to things which have gone wrong and to resolve the problem
- Failure to respond to suggestions and ideas for improvement
- A lack of understanding from the customer of a supplier's constraints and problems
- A customer asking the supplier to do things which they themselves have not achieved
- A lack of understanding of the minor problems which undermine the credit-ability of the customer
- A mismatch between what is requested and the existing infrastructure

Summary

Suppliers are now recognized as an essential part of any organizations competitive-ness. There are two major reasons for this: greater global specialization and changes in the nature of competition. Effective partnership requires purchasing organizations to treat suppliers as long-term business partners, and this necessitates a fundamental shift from the traditional adversarial buyer–supplier relationship. Properly imple-mented partnership will help to reduce costs and increase market share to the benefit of both parties, together with technology transfer issues surrounding product, pro-cess, practices and systems. However, the nature and mechanisms of partnership must be related to the particular circumstances and needs of those involved. In conclusion, the following dos and don'ts developed from the work of Galt and Dale (1990) will help both customers and suppliers to establish the type of partnership that is most appropriate for them.

- *Do* look at ways of reducing the size of the supplier base. By reducing incom-ing material, component and sub-assembly variability, outgoing product and service quality will improve.

- *Do* ensure that, in support of the supplier development process and its various stages, your staff and those in the customer organization use the appropriate engineering quality tools. These tools include SPC, the seven quality control tools, the seven management tools, FMEA, FTA, QFD, design of experiments; the tools also facilitate design for manufacturability and cost avoidance.
- *Do* involve suppliers in new product development and investigate the full range of ways of achieving this.
- *Do* encourage suppliers to despatch only conforming product, thereby eliminating the need to carry out duplicate testing and inspection on incoming goods.
- *Do* award long-term contracts to key suppliers who have shown commitment and improvements so as to demonstrate the tangible benefits that can arise from a long-term relationship.
- *Do* consider implementing an assessment and rating scheme to select and measure the performance of suppliers. Poor selection will lead to increased costs as other suppliers are sought to compensate for the deficiencies of the one chosen without due care.
- *Do* develop procedures, objectives and strategies for communicating with the supply base.
- *Do* treat suppliers as partners, thereby establishing trust, co-operation and dependence.
- *Do* ensure that the staff dealing with suppliers act in a consistent and courteous manner and match actions to words.
- *Do* respond positively to suppliers requests for information.
- *Do* develop and decide upon mutually agreed purposes and values that define the relationship and measure its success. The approach by the customer must be seen by the supplier as helpful, constructive and of mutual benefit.
- *Do* decide and agree on the best means of communication and the provision of reliable information and monitoring a constructive dialogue. This requires defined points of communication to be established.
- *Do* listen and be receptive to feedback, and be willing to share information and ideas and to discuss problems. Discover and respond to functional perceptions, in both customer and supplier, of the state of the partnership.
- *Do* provide education to raise awareness of the partnership approach and specific training for the new skills required.
- *Do* be honest about the state of the partnership, and avoid complacency.
- *Do* ensure that customer and supplier organizations are sufficiently knowledgeable about each others business, products, procedures, systems and how the respective organization's worked.
- *Do* remember a flexible and open approach is crucial, with the encouragement of positive constructive criticism.

- *Don't* begin partnership unless senior management understand what is involved and that they support the concept.
- *Don't* overlook the fact that senior management commitment, in both customers and suppliers, to the ideals of partnership is necessary along with their active participation in the process, including understanding its importance. Management must recognize that it is not a 'quick fix' solution to achieve cost reduction.

- *Don't* treat suppliers as adversaries.
- *Don't* keep suppliers short of information.
- *Don't* buy goods on price alone. Ensure other criteria such as quality and delivery performance, R&D potential, competitive manufacturing and engineering excellence are also taken into account.
- *Don't* constantly switch suppliers.
- *Don't* accept non-conforming goods.
- *Don't* talk quality but act production schedule and price per piece.
- *Don't* forget that the initial samples procedures is a key factor in receiving conforming supplies.
- *Don't* forget that the customer and supplier must be prepared to add value to each other's operations, through reducing costs, identifying opportunities for improvement.
- *Don't* forget that the move to partnering usually takes longer than expected.
- *Don't* overlook the fact that the principles and values of partnership must be cascaded to all relevant levels in the customer and the supplier and must be fully accepted, in particular, by those staff at the day-to-day contact point.
- *Don't* forget that the effectiveness of the partnership must be measured and monitored.
- *Don't* forget that developments affecting both parties should be carried out with mutual consultation.
- *Don't* assume that there will be no problems; ensure that suitable counter-measures are ready to address the obstacles encountered.

References

Burnes, B. and Dale, B. G. (eds) 1998: *Working in Partnership: Best Practice in Customer–Supplier Relations.* Aldeshot, Hauts: Gower Press.

Burnes, B. and Whittle, P. 1998: Supplier partnerships: assessing the potential and getting started. In Burnes and Dale (1998, ch. 6).

Fruin, W. M. 1992: *The Japanese Enterprise System, Competitive Strategies and Co-operative Structures.* New York: Oxford University Press.

Galt, J. and Dale, B. G. 1990: Customer supplier relationships in the motor industry: a vehicle manufacturers perspective. *Proceedings of the Institution of Mechanical Engineers,* 204(D4), 179–86.

Hines, P. 1992: Materials management for the 21st century: Llanelli Radiators Supplier Association. *Logistics Today,* March–April, 19–21.

Lascelles, D. M. and Dale, B. G. 1990: Examining the barriers to supplier development. *International Journal of Quality and Reliability Management,* 7(2), 46–56.

Morris, J. and Imrie, R. 1992: *Transforming Buyer–Supplier Relationships.* London: MacMillan Press.

Thisse, L. C. 1998: Advanced quality planning: a guide for any organisation. *Quality Progress,* February, 73–7.

chapter twelve

Sustaining TQM*

B. G. Dale

Introduction

TQM is a long-term process. It can take an organization up to ten years to put the fundamental principles, practices, procedures and systems into place, create an organizational culture that is conducive to continuous improvement and change the values and attitudes of its people. It requires considerable effort and intellectual input by the senior management team, and a clear strategic direction and framework. It is also unfortunate that misconceptions abound with regard to what TQM and quality improvement are, and how to achieve them. Therefore, it is little wonder that the vast majority of organizations do encounter problems in their continuous improvement efforts; see chapter 10. In recent times, there have been a number of reports – Boyett et al. (1991), Develin and Partners (1989), Harari (1997), Kearney (1992), The Economist Intelligence Unit (1992), Miller (1992), on a survey by Ernst and Young, Naj (1993) and Tice (1994) – outlining the lack of success of some TQM initiatives and the problems which have been encountered. However, the vast majority of such reports, based on questionnaire surveys, contains flaws in the interpretation of the findings since they usually do not define what they mean by TQM.

This chapter describes the main issues which impact on the sustaining of TQM; 'sustaining' in this context means the maintaining of a process of continuous improvement. The issues have been grouped into five categories: internal/external environment, management style, policies, organization structure and process of change. The categories and issues are summarized in table 12.1.

The issues described have been identified from work carried out over a period of three years on an EPSRC funded project (Dale and Boaden, 1991). They were initially identified from fieldwork carried out in six organizations (12 sites) and then refined and developed by reference to relevant theories, in the form of a TQM sustaining

* Barrie Dale acknowledges the contribution of Dr Ruth Boaden, Mr Mark Wilcox and Ms Ruth McQuater to the material contained in this chapter. He also acknowledges the support of the EPSRC for their funding of research contract GR/H.21499.

Table 12.1 TQM sustaining categories and issues

Environment	External:
	a. Competitors
	b. Employee resourcing, development and retention
	Internal:
	a. Customer focus
	b. Investment
	c. The 'fear' factor
Management style	a. Industrial relations
	b. Management/worker relationship
Policies that may conflict with TQM	HRM
	Financial
	Maintenance
	Manufacturing
Organization structure	a. Positioning of the quality function
	b. Departmental, functional and shift boundaries
	c. Communication
	d. Job flexibility and cover
	e. Supervisory structure
Process of change	a. Improvement infrastructure
	b. Education and training
	c. Teams and teamwork
	d. Procedures
	e. Quality management system
	f. Quality management tools and techniques
	g. Confidence in management

audit tool (TQMSAT); for more detail, see Dale et al. (1997). The issues reflect a variety of perspectives of business operation, including continuous improvement, organizational behaviour, HRM, industrial relations and the labour process. The objective of the TQMSAT is to identify the issues that impact on the sustaining of TQM. The issues are investigated by discussion of aspects of the organizations under each of five categories. The TQMSAT does not prescribe 'solutions' to the issues raised. The use of the information revealed is organization-dependent, but it has most commonly been used as an input to planning the advancement of the improvement process, sometimes as part of self-assessment against one of the internationally recognized models of business excellence, i.e. MBNQA or EFQM. The TQMSAT is primarily intended for use by a skilled interviewer who is knowledgeable in TQM, but can be used in self-assessment mode depending on the level of openness and trust in the company. The TQMSAT has been validated and tested at seven manufacturing sites: four first-line automotive component suppliers (UK, USA, Germany and Spain), a manufacturer of bearings and two packaging manufacturers; one example of this testing is provided by Kemp et al. (1997). Examples are used from each of these seven case studies to outline and highlight the issues underlying each of the five sustaining categories. However, before describing each of the categories and the examples, the development and methodology of the TQMSAT is outlined.

TQMSAT: Development and Methodology

The majority of the self-assessment methods and audit tools which are in common use focus on the review of an organization's activities and results against a predetermined model, framework or system standard; see Lascelles and Peacock (1996) and Conti (1997). In this way, progress made by them to meet a specification of business excellence can be assessed. Such assessments are, in general, focused on looking for positive factors, although organizational weaknesses are also identified. For example, in using the EFQM model strengths and areas of improvement are identified for each of the 33 criterion; see chapter 22.

The TQMSAT is different in that it is looking for a specific set of predetermined negative factors; that is, those factors identified from the research which have been seen to have a detrimental effect on the sustaining of TQM. Companies are often reluctant to face up to failures because they usually require actions which have far-reaching effects, but the TQMSAT forces companies to address these types of issues. It can also be argued that focusing on the negative issues is probably the best way to understand the strengths and weaknesses of TQM within an organization. However, during the interview process carried out to determine if the negative issues are in place, some areas of strengths are also identified.

In five of the organizations where the audit tool was tested, self-assessment against either the MBNQA or EFQM models was taking place at the same time. The feedback from the collaborating organizations was that the findings from use of TQMSAT made a useful input to the collection of data with respect to some of the criterion, in particular with obtaining views from a cross-section of the organization.

Figure 12.1 shows the key skeps in using the TQMSAT. The TQMSAT should be used by either an outside agency such as a management consultant or by an organization in self-assessment mode. If it is being used by an outside agency, a plant tour is recommended to gain an insight into the improvement initiatives in operation, the process and technology being used and the general operating environment of the business. It is also recommended that historical information such as reports and presentations are collected and analysed.

Interviews, which should last for about one hour each, are conducted with between 10 to 20 people, depending on the size of the organization, from a cross-section of the organizational hierarchy. The time needed for each interview will depend on the person's position and knowledge of the company, it needs to be kept flexible to enable areas of the audit to be dealt with in depth. In deciding the selection of people to be interviewed, some consideration should be given to the inclusion of TQM champions, since the negative influences are likely to have been identified by them. The person being interviewed should be informed of the purpose of the interview at least one week prior to it taking place. The interviewee should be encouraged to seek views from their area on the issues which people believe are affecting the sustaining of TQM. Using the guidelines provided, the interviews should explore the issues which comprise each of the five sustaining categories. In this way, the questioning draws out the history and background which may be inhibiting TQM and highlights areas to be improved. Some of the issues can be explored in greater or less detail, depending on the person being interviewed and their knowledge of the business and TQM. By discussing these issues with a variety of people, most of the factors which impinge on the sustaining of TQM will be

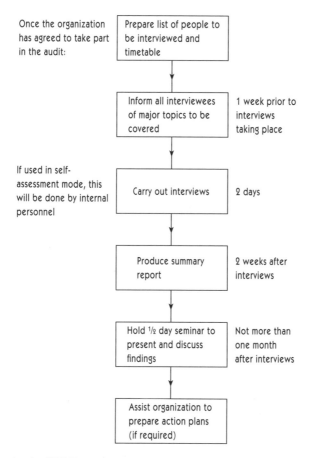

Once the organization has agreed to take part in the audit:

Prepare list of people to be interviewed and timetable

Inform all interviewees of major topics to be covered — 1 week prior to interviews taking place

If used in self-assessment mode, this will be done by internal personnel

Carry out interviews — 2 days

Produce summary report — 2 weeks after interviews

Hold ½ day seminar to present and discuss findings — Not more than one month after interviews

Assist organization to prepare action plans (if required)

Figure 12.1 Key steps in using TQMSAT

uncovered. A small number of questions are given under each of the five categories as examples for each of the issues. The questions have been prepared in TQM jargon-free language and, in this way, should have universal understanding, irrespective of the approach taken to TQM. These questions have proved useful in unlocking the thought processes of the interviewee and hence to facilitate a discussion about the degree of difficulty caused by the issues being explored. Questions can, of course, be developed and tailored to suit the organization under examination and also the person being interviewed. The strength of TQMSAT is in the categorization of issues; the individual questions asked are not of themselves significant.

Once the interviews have been completed, a summary report outlining the findings for each of the issues should be produced. A half-day seminar should then be held to feed back and discuss the findings, and assist the organization to develop an action plan to overcome the difficulties identified. The people attending the seminar should include all the employees who have been interviewed. In presenting the findings, it should be remembered that it is the perceptions of people with respect to difficulties which are being reported, if senior management believe the perceptions to be incorrect then they need to consider how they can change the perceptions.

The interpretation of results is crucial. As the line of questioning is essentially 'negative' to draw out positive action plans for the future, it is important that the outcomes which are reported do not encourage the semantics of blame. The 'problem' statement should be explained as the relatively 'easy' bit, the solutions take longer and need full continued participation and co-operation of everyone and not just management, who it is easy to blame for all the problems identified.

Category 1 – Internal/External Environment

A common method to distinguish between the internal and external environment and its influencing factors is to use the strength, weaknesses, opportunities and threats (SWOT) framework.

According to Wheelan and Hunger (1988), opportunities and threats are viewed as external variables:

> The *external environment* consists of variables (Opportunities and Threats) that exist outside the organisation and are not typically within the short-term control of top management.

Strengths and weaknesses are part of the internal environment:

> The *internal environment* of a corporation consists of variables (Strengths and Weaknesses) within the organisation itself that are also not usually within the short-term control of top management.

The point of making these distinctions is that there are a number of environmental variables which are often outside the direct control of managers, although they can affect a business through the perceived negative and destabilizing effect which they have, both on employees and the improvement process. Therefore, managers need a knowledge of these variables, so that they can, where possible, plan around them. The factors in this sustaining category are therefore split into external and internal environment.

External environment: Competitors

This relates to the ability of the organization to understand and to react to the threat posed by competitors (e.g. building a state-of-the-art plant in greenfield conditions and competing directly with the organization for its current customers), and to compete in global markets which have high technical, quality and performance standards, and measures, and involve new technologies.

Here are some typical questions.

- Can you identify which companies and/or products comprise the competition?
- What is your knowledge of the competition, in terms of quality performance and technology employed?
- How is data on the competitors collected and analysed?
- How is data on the competitors communicated to non-management employees?
- What concerns do you have about the competitors?
- Where is the company's advantage in the market place vis-à-vis the competitors and from the point of view of its suppliers?

In a bearings manufacturer, its main competitors are known to employees, but there was a genuine interest in having more data about them. It was felt that this would stop some employees becoming complacent and alert others to the threat. There was some concern about the competition, but this did not appear to be a major worry although there was an awareness that some orders had been lost. There was a strong view that the company had a good name in the industry and this gave them a competitive advantage. The biggest weakness was recognized to be delivery performance. It was felt that, if the competition focused their attention on reducing lead time, this would result in a loss of market share.

External environment: Employee resourcing, development and retention

The inability to recruit and retain employees of sufficient calibre to maintain an organization's growth can threaten the strategic direction of the business. New employees, in particular, in the case of the recruitment of a relatively large number over a short time frame, have also to be integrated into the improvement culture of the organization, otherwise they can have a disruptive effect on the improvement process. Another factor in this issue is the retention of employees and the efforts made by management to develop them.

Here are some typical questions.

- What difficulties do you have in recruiting employees of the right calibre?
- In which type of skill/function do you experience recruitment difficulties?
- What difficulties do you experience in retaining key personnel?
- What external labour supply problems exist that could affect the business?
- What policies and procedures to you have to develop employees?
- What are the main reasons people give for leaving?

One of the packaging manufacturers experiences no difficulty in recruiting people of sufficient calibre. However, in some functions, the training given to people has increased their market potential and they have moved to competing organizations to improve their salary and job prospects.

In some cases, the development of people is taking place through training and increasing job flexibility. Much of this stems from departmental heads' initiatives, rather than a company policy. The development through formal training courses was recognized and these are regarded as plentiful, typified by the comment 'people seem to do lots of courses'. In other cases, little development of people has taken place, e.g. new operators being recruited on a six-month contract and just used as an extra pair of hands.

Internal environment: Customer focus

Meeting the needs and requirements of customers is the main thrust of TQM. It is important to have measures in place to assess how well the products and services meet the customer requirements, and to identify their future needs. In some organizations, TQM is not introduced for these reasons and the motivation for introducing TQM needs to be assessed.

Here are some typical questions.

- What methods do you use to ensure that you are the supplier of choice of your customers?
- How do you ensure that you meet the needs and requirements of your customers?
- What type of feedback do you receive from the customer?
- What are the weaknesses in how you deal with the customer?
- Is the internal customer concept recognized?
- Is the TQM initiative perceived to be a good thing?
- Is TQM seen as an imposition and resented?
- Is TQM seen as long term, or as a fad?
- What do you believe are the major factors motivating quality improvement?

The Spanish automotive component supplier are extremely well-focused on their major customers – SEAT and VW – and were proud of their quick reactions to responding to meet their needs and requirements. The positive feedback from customer second party audits and surveys was perceived as an indication that their performance, in the eyes of the customer, is along the right lines. The practice of customer visits by operators is well entrenched. For example, the marketing manager, when making visits to SEAT, usually takes operators with him, and members of the assembly cell have spent time on the assembly line at SEAT observing how the connector assembly was fitted to the end product. These visits have helped to build up confidence among the operating staff.

There is good knowledge of the internal customer concept among the operators, e.g. when they encounter a non-conformance with a part, they have no hesitation in going to the supplying process and discussing the problem with them. However, this concept is less well understood in the non-manufacturing departments.

Internal environment: Investment

The willingness of a business to finance new machinery and equipment, to invest in education and training, recruitment and to improve the fabric of buildings and the associated environment, can affect TQM in many ways. Adequate resources to meet the business plans and improvement actions that have been developed are also needed, as well as positive responses to improvement team suggestions to implement the findings from their projects.

Here are some typical questions.

- Are you satisfied with the level of investment in the business?
- Are the investments made by the right people?
- Who is consulted about the investment?
- Have the investments made been worthwhile?
- Is the investment, which has been made, recognized by employees?
- Are you satisfied with the way in which investment priorities are determined?
- What is the market share-market growth profile of the organization?
- To what extent do non-management employees understand the process of investment decision making?
- What feedback is given to non-management employees about the progress of ongoing investment decisions?

In one of the two packaging manufacturers, the majority of people interviewed had a lot to say about the apparent unwillingness to invest in new machinery. This was claimed to influence confidence in the future of the business and employee morale. The perceived reason for the lack of investment was considered to be the relatively low levels of profitability which is a common occurrence in the first quarter of each year and the policies of the plc. Some people were aware of what was required to obtain investment through the capital equipment request process, others less so. There was also a lack of feedback regarding the progress of the investment requests. The general view is that the investments made were prudent and the benefits were clearly evident. However, it is felt that the company could be penny wise and pound foolish in terms of ongoing investment in machinery, e.g. a cheaper equivalent of belting specified by the manufacturer being purchased which, in the long term, increased the cost of maintenance. It was also considered that more could be done in getting the views of the users of equipment prior to its proposed acquisition.

Internal environment: The 'fear' factor

The 'fear factor' or loss of control describes the uncertainty felt by employees about their future. It may be caused by plant closures within the group, redundancies, restructuring, relocation, low volume of work within a business, merger and take-overs, and a lack of trust between managers and the workforce. The type of corporate control used – strategic planning, financial control and strategic control – can also influence this factor, as can morale. Where the 'fear' factor is present a survival/pro-tectionist attitude may develop with short-term decisions taken on a reactive basis.
   Here are some typical questions.

- Does the 'fear factor' exist in your organization? If so, describe it, and where and when it occurs.
- What major organizational changes (e.g. takeovers and mergers) have taken place recently?
- How have these changes affected the long-term improvement plans of the business?
- Is the change process seen as threatening?
- Have management been open, direct and honest in communicating issues relating to change?
- What plant closures, redundancies or restructuring have there been recently?
- To what extent have these type of events caused uncertainty/insecurity among the employees?
- How is this uncertainty/insecurity being managed and how are people being involved and contributing to the change?

This factor is firmly in place at the German automotive component supplier. Typical of the view was 'if we cannot reduce wages and salaries the plant will close and the equipment will be transferred to Spain and England'. The fear factor is attenuated because of the increase in the unemployment rate in Germany and the lack of experience of the majority of German people with this level of unemployment. There was a good slice of realism typically expressed by the comment: 'Germans cannot live as well as we have done in the past.' Senior management have used the fear factor to encourage people to increase their efforts. Another example of the 'fear factor' was some employees putting roadblocks in front of those at a lower level in the organization who are taking the initiatives to make improvements, expressed in terms of being worried about 'stepping on people's area of responsibility'. When ideas are not followed up and projects not completed, there is little explanation given to the people who have taken the initial initiative.

Category 2 – Management Style

This category distinguishes between macro and micro levels, and implications of management style, using the sub-categories of industrial relations and management/ worker relationships respectively. The former defines the way in which a business manages employee relations, as outlined typically by Fox (1974) and Marchington and Parker (1990). The latter concerns the attitudes, values and interpersonal skills of managers and supervisors, and their interaction with their subordinates.

Industrial relations

As already outlined in this book one of the basic tenets of TQM is that managers and workers share the same objectives. This management style has been described as unitarist by Fox (1974). Writers such as Burrell and Morgan (1979) developed Fox's work to define two alternative styles: pluralist and radical. To sustain TQM, the shift from a radical or a pluralist management style to a unitarist position is necessary. However, this transition is often problematic and the path is potentially strewn with conflict, in particular, where there is existing trade union recognition and collective bargaining procedures in place. Three categories of industrial relations are summarized here (Morgan, 1986).

1   A 'unitary' management style emphasizes a sense of teamwork and pulling together and having common goals for all employees.
2   A 'pluralist' management style recognizes the 'rights' of individuals and groups. Procedures for collective bargaining are in place and mechanisms used via trade union representatives.
3   The 'radical' concept of industrial relations is based on the notion of opposing class interests. The organization is seen as overtly political, where managers and workers strive to achieve incompatible goals.

The relationship between management and the workforce at the manufacturer of bearings was not adversarial, and there was an effort on both sides to work together; the point was made that they had been clear of industrial relations disputes for many years. However, there was still a considerable degree of 'them and us' in play, brought about by previous decisions and actions, false starts, and changes in senior management. There was also a feeling that some people, albeit a minority, would reject anything put forward by management.

Management/worker relationship

This issue centres around the notion of trust and discretion within the relationship. TQM is often said to lead to high trust/high discretion roles and relationships through the use of teamwork in all its various forms within a process of continuous and company-wide improvement. Self-managing work groups, empowerment, increased participation and the involvement of employees in decision making are related factors. The management/worker relationship is also concerned with the potential confusion and contradictions in management style resulting from a style based on scientific management with low trust/low discretion (Taylor, 1964). Even where companies believe that they have moved away from such a style, remnants of the principles are often found to be embedded in the operating practices of the organization.

At the UK-based automotive component supplier the 'them and us' situation was only evident in the relationship between project managers and the shop floor, in terms of the initiation of new products. It is claimed that project managers were not willing to seek or listen to ideas from the operating level of the business, and, when suggestions had been made, there was often no feedback to operators. It was also felt that the senior management team should be seen more on the shop floor. Recognition and rewards for commitment to improvement was also raised in probing this issue with personal 'thank-you' notes and 'pats on the back' from managers emerging as the key responses.

Category 3 - Policies

It is not unusual to find policies within the organization which conflict, are inconsistent with, or overlap with, TQM. Here are some typical policies:

- In HRM, if the policy is to pursue individualistic practices supported by the reward system, this undermines the teamwork ethos of TQM. Other aspects of HRM policies, which may conflict with TQM, include the level of salaries in relation to the type of work done, lack of transparency of salaries across the organization, perceived discrimination in relation to reward and effort, a complex salary grading structure, performance-related pay, and levels of salaries relative to those within the geographical area. Other examples of conflicting HRM policies include a lack of consistency in applying appraisal systems, performance assessment and discrimination between shop floor and staff on issues of sickness and leave of absence.
- Financial policies that encourage short-term decision making and business results to maintain stock market credibility and benefits to shareholders. These prevent managers pursuing the longer-term objectives of TQM.
- Maintenance policies which, due to a need to reduce costs, limit the amount of work carried out on planned maintenance. This, in turn, impacts on the performance of the machinery and its ability to produce conforming product.
- Manufacturing policies that focus and encourage output rather than quality performance and customer satisfaction. This focus also has a detrimental effect on training (which, as a consequence, may be perceived as unnecessary or time wasting) and the holding of improvement team meetings.

Here are some examples of such policies identified at one of the packaging manufacturers.

- Human resources (HR)
  - The policy of part-time contracts – while considerable emphasis is made by management to explain the reasoning behind this policy, the communication needs to be reinforced and maintained
  - The operating of the staff appraisal system and, in particular, ensuring consistency between employees

- Production
  - Maintaining production output and quality, in terms of conforming product – when under pressure to meet production targets there is a temptation to increase the machine running speed on the corrugator even though this is known to have a detrimental impact on board quality
  - The pressure to meet production targets – this also had an adverse effect on the meetings of quality teams; while the company are prepared to pay people to meet in teams after their shift ends, the view expressed by employees is that they wish to hold their quality team meetings in company time. A comment which encapsulates this view is 'if the company cannot make available the time for us to meet during normal working hours, why should we give up our time to the company'
  - The time which people have available – if a person is involved in a quality team, there is a perception that they are short of work in their day-to-day job and, consequently, they will be given more work to do

- Maintenance
  - There was a view that maintenance was not given the attention it deserved and, since the machinery was a key determinant of quality, this conflicted with TQM.

Category 4 – Organization Structure

This category is concerned with the issues that arise from the way in which a business is structured and includes functions, roles, responsibilities, hierarchies, boundaries, flexibility and innovation. Structure has been defined by Wilson and Rosenfield (1990) as:

> the established pattern of relationships between the component parts of an organisation, outlining both communication, control and authority patterns. Structure distinguishes the parts of an organisation and delineates the relationship between them.

Positioning of the quality function

The size and role of the quality function within the organization, and its relation to other departments, influences the deployment of the quality policy and its integration with other aspects of the organization. The principles which underpin TQM – everyone taking personal responsibility for QA, pursuing continuous improvement in their day-to-day work activities and being reorientated towards the customer, see chapter 1 – pose a problem for the positioning of the quality function. The quality department can detract people from practising these types of principles by retaining responsibility for continuous improvement. On the other hand, it is often charged with implementing the quality policy which involves managing the process of change, providing guidance to departmental heads and 'empowering' employees.

Here are some typical questions.

- What position does the quality manager/director have in the organization? Who reports to them and how do they relate to other functions, especially production.
- Is the quality function in a position to develop and influence business policy and changes in the business?
- Do you consider that the role and responsibilities of the quality department are understood?
- Can the quality manager/quality director help to influence a change in the business to make the environment more conducive to improvement?
- To what extent is the quality manager/director responsible for quality, or have they delegated this responsibility to line managers?
- How much do individuals take responsibility for their own QA and quality improvement?

At the bearings manufacturer, there were some different views about the degree to which people had accepted responsibility for ownership of QA and quality improvement and had 'pride' in their job. A lot of discussion centred around production and inspection responsibilities. Overall, only in a minority of cases did people hold the view that final inspection would take the responsibility for product quality. It was also felt that the quality department should work more closely with the engineering and production departments to give advice and guidance on the more preventative aspects of quality management.

Departmental, functional and shift boundaries

The boundaries and barriers which are built up between departments, functions and shifts are obstacles to teamwork and cross-functional/inter-departmental working and co-operation. These barriers are often a legacy of the hierarchical structures and bureaucracies established under scientific management which promoted functional foremen and specialists. They typically lead to empire building and a lack of understanding of other departments which hinder the sustaining of TQM.

Here are some typical questions.

- How much of a problem are departmental barriers and empire building in the organization?
- Which departments do you consider to present the most barriers?
- How do these barriers affect cross-functional co-operation and communication?
- What steps are being taken to break the barriers down?
- Are people sympathetic to what is involved in jobs undertaken by others?
- To what extent are there problems between shifts?
- To what extent are cross-functional teams in operation?

At the bearing manufacturer, the departmental barriers issue was perceived as a major problem in both a physical and mental sense, described as 'hand grenades thrown over the wall'. There was also a lack of sympathy by some people of what was involved in the jobs undertaken by people outside their immediate departmental function:

- 'I do a better job than you.'
- 'My skills are higher than yours.'
- 'I have pride in my work but it is just a job to them.'
- 'We are doing our job right. Why is this not the case with you?'

The view was expressed that the Service Departments were more inclined to help production when things were going smoothly and not when problems were being experienced. The fact that a number of the procedures in the Service Departments were set up when the company employed more people was given as a potential cause of a lack of responsiveness.

The main problems in relation to shift boundaries was the failure of one shift to accept the set-ups of another and that any difficulties resulted from person-to-person conflict rather than shift-to-shift conflict.

Communication

The issue here is the way in which communication is practised, both up and down and across the organization. The methods by which achievements are recognized and communicated is also examined.

Here are some typical questions.

- What evidence is there of a communication policy, e.g. newsletters, team brief, quality noticeboards?
- What is the predominant direction of transfer of information – up or down the organization?
- How effective is the flow of information in terms of two-way transfer?
- Are business objectives communicated so that the business plan is understood at all levels of the organizational hierarchy?
- Are individual and team objectives aligned to the business plan?
- What potential communication problems exist?
- What means are used to recognize and communicate the achievements of both individuals and teams?

In the German automotive component supplier, the general view was that people are told rather than being given the reasons for a particular course of action and situation, and that there is a lack of systematic information. This comment typifies this view: 'Why did management do it that way? Why did they take that course of action?' Senior management do not appear to communicate company objectives down through all levels of the organization for example, by, quarterly 'state-of-the-nation briefings' which can be used to explain to every employee the situation and the key decisions, and through team briefings.

Job flexibility and cover

This serves to highlight the reliability of a business on key people in specialized functions. Both numerical and task flexibility are important if a business is to respond to changing demand and circumstances.

Here are some typical questions.

- Which areas and skills are particularly vulnerable to problems if key people are unavailable or leave the company?
- What steps have been taken to encourage job flexibility?
- Is there a policy of succession planning in place within the organisation?
- What barriers are there to making the changes, e.g. trade union resistance, demarcation, working practices, protectionism?

The small size of the Spanish component supplier made them particularly vulnerable to this issue. They had a succession planning process in place and this was of some help as was training to increase flexibility.

Supervisory structure

This concerns the limitations of the traditional supervisory role, and the reorganization to a team leader type structure which is considered more suitable to improvement initiatives, in particular, at the operating level of the business.
Here are some typical questions.

- What types and levels of supervision exist?
- How do supervisors treat and deal with their staff on a day-to-day basis?
- What type of activities to supervisors undertake on a daily basis?
- To what extent do supervisors control or lead to gain employee commitment to continuous improvement?
- What features of a team leader type structure are in place, e.g. setting direction, steering, aligning people in the common direction, motivating, communicating?
- To what extent do supervisors, in the event of a crisis, revert back to the traditional supervisory role?

In the UK automotive component supplier, the team leader structure is reasonably well developed but the outcomes arising from the daily meetings held at the start of the shift between the team leader and the team, and those between the team leaders and the production manager, are not fed back to the respective teams. There is also little evidence of the team leaders attempting to align their people in an agreed common direction, or motivating and inspiring their staff. In addition, the training given to team leaders and the team is often not followed through and used.

Category 5 – Process of Change

These issues underpinning this category relate to the improvement process itself and/or are a direct result of some form of improvement activity and action. They refer to the training, coaching and development of employees (i.e. skills, attitudes and behaviours) as well as changes in organization structure and management style, and the adoption of new working practices which are required as part of the TQM initiative. Many of the issues in this category relate to the ability of management to implement change and integrate TQM into the working practices of the organization.
The process of change involved in integrating the philosophy of TQM into an organization is complex and wide ranging. If the process is to be effective, it requires the creation of an environment where employees are motivated to want to improve

on a continuous basis. If the managers cannot create this environment, then any systems, tools, techniques or training employed will be ineffective.

Improvement infrastructure

This considers the adequacy of the improvement infrastructure in terms of steering committee, co-ordinator and facilitators and assesses 'hype' versus real ownership.
Here are some typical questions.

- Is there a steering committee? Is its membership and role communicated across the company?
- Is there an improvement co-ordinator?
- What is her/her role?
- Are there designated improvement facilitators?
- If so, in which areas and functions?
- To what extent do the co-ordinator and facilitator possess the right type of skills and knowledge to undertake these types of roles?

In one of the packaging manufacturers, the full-time facilitator was seen as the key link in the improvement chain and his promotion is perceived to have weakened the improvement infrastructure and left a void, with a consequential loss of focus. There is a lack of knowledge about the TQM steering committee, its membership and role. While the role of the part-time facilitator is recognized, there are insufficient people taking on this role. It was found that the team leaders are not forceful; they need to feel they have the total backing of top management behind them and to exercise this support.

Education and training

This considers the appropriateness of the training programme in relation to the needs of the individual and the organization. It includes the design, delivery and evaluation of the programme.
Here are some typical questions.

- What type of training – job, management, TQM – have you had?
- Are you satisfied with the level of education and training opportunities which exist within the company?
- To what extent have you put the skills and knowledge acquired to use?
- Are the trainers effective?
- What coaching and counselling have you had from your immediate managers and functional staff to assist you in putting into practice the skills and knowledge acquired through training?

The standard training programme which is in place at the UK component supplier was recognized to be excellent. However, the mixing together on training courses of people from all levels of the organizational hierarchy was not effective and some scaling down of the range of levels attending a particular training course is needed. It is evident that refresher training is required from time to time. Attention is also required to the training which is required by individuals, and a systematic method put into place to identify these needs.

Teams and teamwork

This considers the health of teams and teamwork within the organization and the mechanisms in place to support and encourage teams.

Here are some typical questions.

- What type of improvement teams are in operation?
- How effective are these types of teams?
- What are the major reasons for the lack of success of teams?
- To what extent is teamwork practised as part of normal business activities?
- To what extent do you think teamwork is beneficial for you and the organization?
- What are your major frustrations about teams in general, and, in particular, with ones you have been involved with?
- To what extent is there a conflict between teams, rewards and putting forward ideas and suggestions for improvement?
- Do improvement teams prevent individuals from pursuing personal improvement initiatives?

In one of the packaging manufacturers, there have been a number of projects completed successfully through improvement team activity, and there was good support for the teamwork ethic. The value of the projects completed was recognized along with their value in increasing quality awareness. However, there have been cases in which teams have been less successful. These were given as the main reasons:

- Project findings accepted but not implemented
- Project terminated due to a lack of investment
- The team stopping meeting due to increased production pressure
- A lack of back-up and support

There are currently no teams in operation. They fizzled out when the improvement facilitator took up another post and production volumes increased.

Procedures

This considers the procedures, or lack of them, which are in place to counteract problems and abnormalities. The ability of people to understand and follow procedures, and the willingness of management to respond effectively to ideas and suggestions for improvement are also factors considered.

Here are some typical questions.

- To what extent do problems recur? If so, why?
- What sort of problems recur?
- How do you report any potential concerns which you have?
- How are these concerns responded to?
- Is there any evidence of ideas and concerns being reported but nothing being done to correct and prevent them from recurring, i.e. the 'sponge' syndrome?
- What type of corrective and preventative mechanisms are in operation?

At the bearings manufacturer, problems tend to recur, in particular, at the operating level of the business. This tends to be brought about by people not being prepared to take the trouble to request changes to be made, the ineffectiveness of the short-term corrective actions taken, and the failure to standardize the changes.

Quality management system

This considers the effectiveness of the quality management system and the need to ensure that quality manual and procedure owners seek continuous improvements to the system. It also investigates the degree to which the system has been developed using a process management approach.

Here are some typical questions.

- Is the quality management system reactive or proactive?
- Are the procedures underpinning the system followed in everyday work activities?
- To what extent are the systems and procedures presented as processes?
- Are the processes independent of the organization?
- Are process owners identified?
- How can the quality management system be strengthened?

The quality management system of one of the packaging manufacturers tends to be reactive and the procedures cumbersome. For example, when an audit is being undertaken, it is claimed that 'people dust down the procedures, follow what is in the manual and then revert back to their normal way of doing things'.

Quality management tools and techniques

This issue considers the need for a planned approach to identify and apply quality management tools and techniques, and to integrate their use into the day-to-day operations of the business.

Here are some typical questions.

- What type of quality management tools and techniques do you use in your everyday work routines? And, in improvement teams?
- How do you decide which tools and techniques to apply?
- Why are tools and techniques used in your department?
- Which tools and techniques give the greatest impact?
- To what extent is there resistance to the introduction and use of tools and techniques?

The overwhelming view at the German component supplier was tools and techniques are not used in any systematic way, and a number of the ones in use tend to be used in static mode and are not well understood. There is also a failure by managers to use the tools and techniques in their day-to-day decision making.

Confidence in management

This considers the extent of confidence in senior management by both managers and workers. Lack of confidence can be brought about by many things:

- The lack of success of previous TQM initiatives
- The inability to see projects through to a conclusion
- Actions not mirroring promises
- Changes in management
- Conflicting priorities, that suggest that TQM is not as important as they previously suggested, among other things

This factor also considers the negative effects on sustaining TQM of those managers who are resistant to change and tend to suppress continuous improvement activities.

- How confident are you that management are serious about TQM?
- Is there stability at the top of the organization?
- Describe examples of areas where you have a lack of confidence and ask if these are in play within the organization.
- Is confidence in management growing or decreasing?
- How effective are management in prioritizing the various ongoing improvement initiatives within the organization?
- Do any people in the organization block improvement initiatives?
- Are you confident that management will reverse the attitudes and behaviour of the people who are resistant to improvement?

The considerable number of changes in senior management at the bearings manufacturer has led to a lack of confidence, attenuated by the style of some previous managers, and the inability to see projects and initiatives through to a satisfactory conclusion. This has led to a tendency to blame any problems on management and a certain degree of apathy. The current management team are suffering from the attitudes created by their predecessors. To build up confidence it was said that 'management must be seen to be straight-talking and their actions must always mirror their words'.

Summary

TQM is a long-term process which requires considerable dedication and hard work to achieve the vision; along the journey, there are many pitfalls to avoid and barriers to surmount. The typical pitfalls have been explored in this chapter and include: inadequate leadership, fear and resistance to change, lack of problem-solving skills, failure to complete projects, break-up of improvement teams, lack of resources devoted to continuous improvement, inadequate information and its analysis and poor communication. These pitfalls impact negatively on the sustaining of TQM and they have been grouped into the five categories of internal/external environment, management style, policies, organization structure and the process of change and developed in the form of a TQMSAT. These categories have been described along with their underlying issues.

Using the methodology outlined in the chapter, TQMSAT has been piloted at seven manufacturing sites. In each case, it was successfully able to identify a range of issues which had the potential to have a negative impact on the sustaining of TQM and has helped management to identify fundamental causes rather than just to see symptoms. The trialing of the tool indicates that its relevance and value depends on the status of TQM in the company at the time of its application.

References

Boyett, J., Kearney, A. T. and Conn, H. 1991: What's wrong with total quality management? Tapping the network quality. *Quality*, 3(1), 10–14.

Burrell, G. and Morgan, G. 1979: *Sociological Paradigms and Organisational Analysis*. London: Heinemann Educational Books.

Conti, T. 1997: *Organisational Self-Assessment*. London: Chapman and Hall.

Dale, B. G. and Boaden, R. J. 1991: *Total Quality Management: Integration and Development*. Swindon: Engineering and Physical Sciences Research Council.

Dale, B. G., Boaden, R. J., Wilcox, M. and McQuater, R. E. 1997: Total quality management sustaining audit tool: description and use. *Total Quality Management*, 8(6), 395–408.

Develin and Partners. 1989: *The Effectiveness of Quality Improvement Programmes in British Industry*. London: Develin and Partners.

Economist Intelligence Unit. 1992: *Making Quality Work – Lessons for Europe's Leading Companies*. London: The Economist Intelligence Unit.

Fox, A. 1974: *Beyond Contract: Work, Trust and Power Relations*. London: Faber & Faber.

Harari, O. 1997: Ten reasons TQM doesn't work. *American Management Association – Management Review*, January, 38–44.

Kearney, A. T. 1992: *Total Quality: Time to Take off the Rose-tinted Spectacles*, Bedfordshire: A. T. Kearney and the TQM Magazine.

Kemp, A., Pryor, S. and Dale, B. G. 1997: Sustaining TQM: A Case Study at Aeroquip Iberica. *The TQM Magazine*, 9(1), 21–8.

Lascelles, D. M. and Peacock, R. 1996: *Self-Assessment for Business Excellence*, Maidenhead, Berkshire: McGraw Hill.

Marchington, M. C. and Parker, P. 1990: *Changing Patterns of Employee Relations*. London: Harvester Wheatsheaf.

Miller, C. 1992: TQM's Value Criticized in New Report, 9 November, New York: American Marketing Association.

Morgan, G. 1986: *Images of Organisation*. London: Sage.

Naj, A. 1993: Some manufacturers drop efforts to adopt Japanese manufacturing techniques. *Wall Street Journal*, 1.

Taylor, F. W. 1964: *The Principles of Scientific Management*. Harper and Row.

Tice, L. 1994: Report card on TQM. *Management Review*, January, 22–5.

Wheelan, G. and Hunger, H. 1988: *Strategic Management and Business Policy*. 3rd edn. California: Addison Wesley.

Wilson, D. C. and Rosenfield, R. H. 1990: *Managing Organisation*. London: McGraw Hill.

part four

Quality Management Systems, Tools and Techniques

Quality management systems, tools and techniques are a fundamental part of an organization's approach to TQM. This part of the book deals with their use and application. In the individual chapters dealing with tools and techniques, each tool and technique is described together with an indication of their range of application and how they are constructed and deployed.

Chapter 13 presents an overview of quality management systems and argues that such a system is a key building block in an organization's approach to TQM. The review includes the fundamental purpose of a quality management system and the development of quality system standards. The ISO9000 series of quality management system standards are reviewed, including implementation issues and guidelines, the assessment and registration process and their benefits and limitations.

Chapter 14 opens by examining the role of quality management tools and techniques in the introduction and development of TQM. It then goes on to explore the issues which should be considered in selecting tools and techniques, and the typical problems found in their use and application. It describes a number of the basic quality control tools – check lists, flow charts, check sheets, tally charts and histograms, graphs, Pareto analysis, cause and effect diagrams, brainstorming and scatter diagrams. It then goes on to describe and outline the use of the seven management tools: relations diagram method, affinity diagram method, systematic diagram method, matrix diagram, matrix data analysis method, process decision program chart and the arrow diagram method. Departmental purpose analysis and mistake-proofing, which are not covered elsewhere in the book, are outlined. In all cases, the focus is on describing the tools and their uses, avoiding excessive detail on their construction. Examples of the tools and techniques are taken from a variety of organizations and situations.

Chapter 15 outlines the concept of QFD. The methodology is fully explained, in particular, the construction of the house of quality, and the planning, organizing and managing of QFD projects is reviewed. The benefits of QFD are examined and potential pitfalls identified and guidelines provided for its effective use.

Chapter 16 provides a review of DOE. It opens by describing the historical background of design of experiments before going on to explain details of the methods. The key steps in setting about undertaking an experimental design are explained in simple to understand language.

Chapter 17 gives an overview of the concept of FMEA together with its value as a planning tool to assist with building quality into an organization's products, services and processes. FMEA is described, along with the procedure. Drawing on experience from Allied Signal, the development of both design and process FMEA are outlined and guidance to effective use examined.

Chapter 18 provides an overview of SPC and its concepts. The main factors in the plan and design of a control chart are examined, and details of how to construct the more popular type of control charts are given. The issues involved with the implementation of SPC are described and typical problems encountered in the introduction and application of SPC are highlighted.

Chapter 19 outlines the history of benchmarking, summarizes the main types of benchmarking and gives an overview of the main steps in a formal benchmarking process. The main learning experiences from a number of diverse benchmarking projects carried out within North West Water are also explored in the chapter, mentioning success factors, difficulties and pitfalls.

Chapter 20 outlines the concept of BPR, traces its history and development, and examines how it complements TQM. The benefits and potential problems of BPR are reviewed, and guidance is given on how to set about a BPR project.

Chapter 21 deals with the use of teams and teamwork in TQM. The operating characteristics of project teams, QCs and quality improvement teams are outlined. A set of guidelines to help to ensure that teams are both active and effective is provided, along with a simple assessment methodology.

Chapter 22 deals with quality awards and self-assessment, and its role in the advancement of TQM. The chapters, drawing on a number of recent studies, examines the influence of TQM and business performance. The key points of the Deming Application Prize, MBNQA and EQA are reviewed. The various ways of undertaking self-assessment against a business excellence model is outlined. Drawing on a major European research study on self-assessment, the key learning lessons from the use of self-assessment by European business are highlighted.

chapter thirteen

Quality Management Systems

B. G. Dale

Introduction

This chapter opens by examining the concept of QA and the responsibilities of people within an organization for carrying out the activity. A quality system is defined and the background of quality system standards traced, the key features of the ISO9000 series are examined, implementation guidelines and issues outlined, the quality system assessment and registration reviewed, and the benefits and limitations highlighted. A model is also presented which outlines what is required for a small company to achieve ISO9000 series registration. Much has already been written about quality systems and standards – Dale and Oakland (1994), Davies (1997), Hall (1992), Jackson and Ashton (1993), Lamprecht (1992, 1993) and Rothery (1993) – and there are the standards themselves; therefore, this chapter is constrained to an overview of the key features and issues.

What is Quality Assurance (QA)?

QA is defined in ISO8402 as:

> ...all the planned and systematic activities implemented within the quality system, and demonstrated as needed, to provide adequate confidence that an entity will fulfil requirements for quality.

This, simply stated, means good management.

QA is often regarded to be discrete policing by the QA Department. This is not so. The ideal role of the department is to oversee the whole process of QA within an organization, to provide guidance and advice on the assignment of roles and responsibilities to be played by each function and person, and to address weaknesses in the system. QA needs to be an integral part of all an organization's processes and functions, from the conception of an idea and, then, throughout the life cycle of the product or service – determining customer needs and requirements, planning and designing, production, delivery and after-sales service. It is an integrated management system.

The objective should be that every person in the organization takes personal responsibility for the quality of the processes for which they are accountable. This includes treating following processes as customers, and endeavouring to transfer conforming products, services, materials and documents to them, monitoring quality performance, analysing non-conformance data, taking both short- and long-term action to prevent the repetition of mistakes, and feedforward and feedback of data. The emphasis should be on the pursuance of corrective and preventive action procedures and non-conformance investigation in a thorough manner with closed-loop effectiveness. It is also necessary for everyone to perform their tasks as defined by the quality system.

The main objective of QA is to build quality into the product and/or service during the upstream design and planning processes. QFD, FMEA, DOE, design reviews, design for manufacturability and quality audits, as part of an APQP process, are of considerable assistance in the pursuance of this goal.

QA, planned and managed along these lines, will strengthen an organization's TQM efforts.

What is a 'Quality System'?

A quality system is defined in ISO8402 as:

> . . . organisational structure, procedures, processes and resources needed to implement quality management.

The purpose of a quality system is to establish a framework of reference points, to ensure that every time a process is performed the same information, methods, skills and controls are used and applied in a consistent manner. In this way, it helps to define clear requirements, to communicate policies and procedures, and it improves teamwork.

There are three levels of documentation, hierarchical in nature, that are required of a quality system.

1 *Company quality manual*: This fundamental document provides a concise summary of the quality policy and quality system along with the company objectives and its organization. ISO10013 provides useful guidelines on the development and preparation of quality manuals.
2 *Procedures manual*: This describes how the system functions, structure and responsibilities in each department.
3 Work instructions, specifications, methods of performance and detailed methods for performing work activities

In addition, there should be a database (at level 4) containing all other reference documents, e.g. forms, standards, drawings and reference information.

The quality system should define and cover all facets of an organization's operation from identifying and meeting the needs and requirements of customers, design, planning, purchasing, manufacturing, packaging, storage, delivery, installation and service, together with all relevant activities carried out within these functions. It deals with organization, responsibilities, procedures and processes. Put simply, a quality system is good management practice.

A quality system, if it is to be comprehensive and effective, and cover all these activities and facets, must be developed in relation to a reference base against which its adequacy can be judged and improvements made. This reference base is a 'quality system standard'.

A documented quality system which embraces quality management objectives, policies, organization and procedures and which can demonstrate, by assessment, compliance with the ISO9000 series of quality system standards or that of a major purchaser, provides an effective managerial framework on which to build a company-wide approach to a process of continuous improvement.

The Development of Quality System Standards

Irrespective of the approach taken to TQM, and the quality management maturity of the organization, a business will need to demonstrate to customers that its processes are both capable and under control, and that there is effective control over procedures and systems. This pressure for proof that systems and procedures are in place, and working in an effective manner, led to the development of quality system standards. The origins of this can be traced back to the 1950s when the US Department of Defense and the UK Ministry of Defence (MOD) saw a need for a unified quality system for their suppliers.

The early standards were provided by major purchasers to their suppliers. These standards were customer and sector specific, and were designed to be used in contractual situations in the industries for which they were designed and operated; the standards had a strong bias towards inspection activities. Each purchaser developed individual methods of assessment, which involved visiting the supplier to examine the degree to which their operating procedures and systems followed the requirements of the standard. This method of assessment is called second-party certification.

Most of the current quality system standards evolved from military standards, e.g. the American Military Standard – MIL-Q-9858A, the NATO Allied Quality Assurance Publications (AQAPs) and the Canadian Standards Association – CSA-Z299. There has also been a considerable contribution to formalized QA procedures by NASA, the controlling body for the US space programme, the US Polaris submarine programme and the Canadian nuclear power generating industry. There has been considerable co-operation by the USA, Canada and the UK in relation to quality system development. A UK standard for quality systems was first published in 1973 by the Procurement Executive of the UK MOD as defence standards – the DEF-STAN O5–21 series. These were virtual copies of the US-derived NATO AQAPs used by NATO in defense procurement, which were based on MIL-Q-9858A. The AQAP standards (AQAP 1–14) addressed the problem of achieving consistency and total product interchangeability in the supply of standardized weapons and ammunition coming from many different suppliers and intended for the different national military units which make up NATO. The MOD used the DEF-STAN O5-21 series to approve potential suppliers and audit current suppliers in contractual situations. It was a requirement that a supplier developed their quality system to meet the clauses set out in these standards for them to be included on the list of MOD assessed contractors. These standards became the basis for contracts with the MOD from April 1973 onwards. One principle is that the prime contractors must conduct audits of their own suppliers in line with the requirements of these standards. The

O5-21 series were withdrawn in 1985, and MOD assessments were carried out using the AQAP standards. From September 1991, the MOD have, in the main, relied on third-party assessment against the ISO9000 series of standards. They only assess suppliers/contractors who are outside the current scope of the accredited certification bodies. This type of situation relates to specific military applications such as aircraft construction, ammunition and explosives, packaging and software. A new set of defence standards (the 05–90 series, 05–91 to 05–95) which includes the ISO9000 series plus special military purchase requirements are used to audit suppliers in contractual situations.

In 1972, the BSI published BS4891. *A Guide to Quality Assurance* which set out recommendations on organizations for, and the management of, quality and was intended as a guide to companies developing their quality management system; this standard was withdrawn in 1994. This was followed in 1974 by the issue of BS5179 – a three-part standard *A Guide to the Operation and Evaluation of Quality Assurance Systems* – which was withdrawn in 1981 after being superseded in 1979 by the first issue of BS5750.

During the mid-1970s, there was a proliferation of quality system standards produced by a variety of second- and third-party organizations. The Warner report (1977), *Standards and Specifications in the Engineering Industries*, stressed the need for a national standard for quality management systems, to reduce the number of assessments with which suppliers were being subjected to by their customers. It pointed to the shortcomings and fragmented nature of the British system of standards. It was recommended that British standards be produced to provide the single base document for quality systems. Subsequently in 1979, the BSI issued the BS5750 series of quality management system standards.

It was the BSI who formally proposed the formation of a new technical committee to develop international standards for assurance, techniques and practices (ISO/TC 176); this committee is responsible for developing and maintaining the ISO9000 family of standards. Some 20 countries participated in the development of the ISO9000 series. In 1987, the series of international standards on quality management systems were first published by the ISO. This 1987 version of the standards, while reflecting various national approaches and international requirements, was based largely on the 1979 version of the BS5750 series and the eight or so years of UK user experience, mainly in manufacturing industry and the CSA Z299 series. The text of these international standards was approved as suitable for publication as a British standard without deviation – BS5750: Parts 0–3 and extended in 1991 to services and software as Parts 8 and 13. The ISO9000 series has been revised and reissued in the summer of 1994 and approved as a British standard, the BSENISO9000 series. This revision was meant to be interim involving minor changes pending a full revision; ISO standards are meant to be revised every five years. The Phase 1 revisions were undertaken with the aims that no new requirements were introduced and that the standards should be clarified to aid implementation and assessment. The revision is part of a broader programme, resulting from a long-term strategy adopted by ISO/TC 176 and termed *Vision 2000*; see PD6538. The draft versions of the revised 2000 standards are now under consideration and the four primary standards will be:

- ISO9000 *Quality Management Systems – Concepts and Vocabulary*
- ISO9001 *Quality Management Systems – Requirements*

- ISO9004 *Quality Management Systems – Guidelines*
- ISO10011 *Guidelines for Auditing Quality Systems*

The ISO9000 series were adopted by CEN and CENELEC as the EN29000 series, thus harmonizing the approach to quality systems among the European community. They have perhaps had the most significant and far-reaching impact on international standardization of any other set of standards. An excellent account of the historical background of the ISO9000 series is provided by Spickernell (1991).

Government initiatives

In July 1982, a White Paper was published on *Standards, Quality and International Competitiveness* (HMSO, 1982) which suggested that to maintain standards, certification bodies should be accredited by a central agency so as to uphold the standards of the certification bodies. The National Accreditation Council for Certification Bodies (NACCB) was the national statutory body established in June 1985 with the task of assessing the independence, integrity and technical competence of leading certification bodies applying for Government accreditation in four areas – approval of quality systems, product conformity, product approval, and approval of personnel engaged in quality verification. At the same time, the National Measurement Accreditation Service (NAMAS) was set up to deal with laboratories. NAMAS was formed by the amalgamation of the British Calibration Service and the National Testing Laboratory Accreditation Service (NATLAS), also in 1985. In August 1995, and in response to market demand, NACCB and NAMAS merged to create a single accreditation authority: the UK Accreditation Service (UKAS). The objective is to bring economies of scale and improved efficiency to UK accreditation. Accreditation, which is awarded in the UK by the Secretary of State for Trade and Industry, allows a certification body to demonstrate their competence and independence. To be eligible for accreditation, third-party certification bodies are required to meet criteria outlined in three standards:

1 BS7511 for certification bodies issuing certificates of product conformity
2 BS7512 for certification bodies certificating that suppliers' quality systems comply with appropriate standards, normally ISO9001, 9002 and 9003
3 BS7513 for certification bodies certificating the competence of personnel

This set of standards helps to promote confidence in the way in which product and quality system certification activities are performed, and in the accreditation systems and bodies themselves. From the accreditation granted, it will be clear whether the body is accredited for quality system assessment only, and in which fields, or whether it has the additional qualification of being accredited to certificate conformity of product.

Those companies who have been assessed by an accredited certification body can use the symbol of a gold crown (signifying Government) and gold tick (signifying approval) if the scope of certification applied for falls within the scope of accreditation of the accredited certification body.

The Department of Trade and Industry (DTI) through their National Quality Campaign – initiated as a result of the White Paper (HMSO, 1982) – and 'Managing into the 1990s' programme, actively encourages British industry to consider more seriously its approach to quality management; one of the methods advocated is registration to the ISO9000 quality management system series. The DTI issue a central register of 'quality assured companies' which lists the firms whose quality management system has been approved by major users or independent third party assessment bodies; this means the investigation is done by an independent organiza- tion, unrelated to buyer or seller. The register also describes the assessment standard used – the ISO9000 series or its equivalent and details of the certification body.

Acceptance of the ISO9000 series of standards

Major industrial purchasers, in particular within the motor industry, have their own system standards and procedures for assessing their suppliers systems. These stand- ards, because they tend to be specific, are often more demanding, in certain areas, than the ISO9000 series.

The use of the ISO9000 series has not been accepted and used universally across the UK motor industry, but this situation is moving ever close, in particular with the development of QS9000. The Society of Motor Manufacturers and Traders Limited in their booklet *Quality* Systems and the Motor Industry (SMMT, 1990) issued a quality policy statement which

> recommends that member and non-member companies recognise and take account of approvals to BS5750/ISO9000/EN29000 Quality Systems Standard as a minimum when contracting work out and buying in supplies. It is strongly recommended that all UK automotive industry companies obtain approvals as applicable to this standard through accredited third party certification.

The Chrysler Corporation, Ford Motor Company and General Motors Corporation have produced a common quality system assessment standard: QS9000. This standard, on which development work was started in 1988, was first released in August 1994, with a world-wide version in February 1995. It harmonizes the separate quality system standard requirements of these three companies and will reduce the current level of duplication in terms of information requested from suppliers leading to economic advantage. The first section of QS9000 aligns itself with the 20 elements of ISO9001. The QS9000 are regarded as supplementals to ISO9001 and are prescriptive in detail. Here are some examples:

- APQP shall be in place, supported by a multi-disciplinary approach for decision making.
- Trends in quality, operational performance, current quality levels and customer satisfaction shall be determined and documented. These should be compared by competitive analysis and/or benchmarking and be reviewed by management.
- FMEA shall be used.
- Capability studies are mandatory, and minimum capability indices are stipulated.

The second section (sector-specific) contains additional but common and harmonized requirements of Chrysler, Ford and General Motors covering the production part approval process, continuous improvement, identification of key product and process parameters, process capability performance and measurement system studies on product and process parameters, and development of control plans. Sixteen typical examples are cited of areas of such activities together with fourteen techniques/methodologies to support them. The third section addresses customer specific additional and non- general requirements.

Registration to ISO9001, ISO9002 or ISO9003 is a useful foundation leading to the development of a quality system to meet the independent system requirements of customers. A number of major purchasers use this registration as the 'first-pass' over a supplier's quality system. They will take the ISO9000 series as the base, and only assess those aspects of the system which they believe are important; for example, those clauses which are not covered in the ISO9000 series; customers often require the supplier to have additional features to the series supplanted within the system or those clauses without sufficient detail to the satisfaction of the customer. On the other hand, many major customers are not prepared to accept a supplier's ISO9001, ISO9002 or ISO9003 registration and wish to carry out a full assessment of their quality system.

- Dale and Plunkett (1984), reporting on a study carried out in 12 fabricators, found that most were subjected to about six audits a year.
- Singer et al. (1988), in a study of the impact of quality assurance on 13 suppliers to the nuclear industry, found that most companies are audited four or more times each year.
- Galt and Dale (1991), in a study of the supplier development programs of a cross-section of 10 UK-based organizations, found that five of the firms studied relied totally on their own evaluation of suppliers, three considered it to be a good starting point and only two accepted third-party recognition as being adequate for their supplier evaluation purposes. They go on to say: 'It was clear that most of the firms considered their own quality standards to be above those required for the ISO9000 series registration.'
- Boaden et al. (1991), reporting on a recent study of TQM in the UK construction industry, make the point: 'One of the main arguments put forward for the ISO9000 series of standards is that it will help to reduce second-party assessments, the responses indicate that this has not happened in the construction industry; clearly a disappointment.'

It is clear from these four studies and, at the time they were carried out, that a number of organizations were not prepared to accept the approvals and certification of recognized bodies which have been awarded to suppliers with whom they are dealing; a company may be approved to ISO9001, ISO9002 or ISO9003 but some of its customers still intend to audit them on a regular basis. However, this situation is now changing as companies operating on a global basis have become registered to the ISO9000 series and, in turn, are encouraging the same of their suppliers and also as confidence grows in third-party schemes. The seventh cycle of the ISO Survey of ISO9000 and 14000 certificates awarded worldwide (ISO, 1997) reveals that, up to the end of December 1997, at least 226,349 ISO9000 series certificates have been awarded in 129 countries world-wide.

The ISO9000 Series of Standards: An Overview

In simple terms, the objective of the ISO9000 series is to give purchasers an assurance that the quality of the products and/or services provided by a supplier meets their requirements. The series of standards defines and sets out a definitive list of features and characteristics which it is considered should be present in an organization's management control system through documented policies, manual and procedures, which help to ensure that quality is built into a process and that it is achieved.

Among other things, it ensures that an organization has a quality policy, procedures are standardized, defects are monitored, corrective and preventive action systems are in place, and that management reviews the system. The aim is systematic QA and control. It is the broad principles of control, in general terms, which are defined in the standards, and not the specific methods by which control can be achieved. This allows the standard to be interpreted and applied in a wide range of situations and environments, and allows each organization to develop its own system and then test them out against the standard. However, this leads to criticisms of vagueness.

The original BS5750 series was developed primarily by the engineering sector of industry, and, consequently, many of the terms and definitions are engineering based. Therefore, they require interpretation for the specific needs of individual organizations, and this has led to problems in some sectors of manufacturing industry and in the majority of non-manufacturing organizations. For example, Owen (1988) writing from the chemical industry is critical of the standard for being too orientated to the engineering industry and Oliver (1991) expresses the view that it 'uses language that the construction industry does not use and, by and large, does not understand'.

Despite these types of difficulties, it has been applied in a wide variety of manufacturing situations and registration is being received in an increasing number of non-manufacturing environments – banking, consumer, education, financial services, gardening, hotel and catering, legal, local authorities, marketing services, recruitment, transport and travel agencies.

The series of standards can be used in three ways:

1 To prove guidance to organizations, to assist them in developing their quality systems
2 As a purchasing standard (when specified in contracts)
3 As an assessment standard to be used by both second-party and third-party organizations

Functions of the standards and their various parts

The ISO9000 series consists of five individual standards (ISO9000, ISO9001, ISO9002, ISO9003 and ISO9004) divided into four parts:

1 Guidelines
2 Model for QA in design, development, production, installation and servicing
3 Model for QA in production, installation and servicing
4 Model for QA in final inspection and test

The standards have two main functions. The first function is an introduction to the series and this identifies the aspects to be covered by an organization's quality system. The guidelines contained in ISO9000 and ISO9004 gives guidance in quality management and their application. The second function is to define, in detail, the features and characteristics of a quality management system that are considered essential for the purpose of QA in contractual situations, for three main different types of organization, depending upon the services they offer. Organizations usually register for one of these categories:

• Design, development, production, installation and servicing – ISO9001
• Production and installation, and servicing – ISO9002
• Final inspection and test – ISO9003

The guidelines – ISO9000 (Parts 1–4) and ISO9004 (Parts 1–4)

ISO9000 *Guidelines for Selection and Use* and ISO9004 *Guidelines for Specific Applications* (which are considered as one part of this series of standards) consist of a number of parts and are intended only as guidelines. They cannot be used as reference standards with which to assess the adequacy of a quality management system. These two parts are more reader friendly than ISO9001, ISO9002 and ISO9003. Organizations embarking on the development of a quality system to meet the requirements of ISO9001, ISO9002 or ISO9003, should find ISO9000 (Parts 1–4) and ISO9004 (1–4) of considerable help in the initial stages where an overview is needed.

- *ISO9000–1* is a guide and starting point to the use of other standards in the series. A thorough understanding of its content is essential if the series of standards are to be interpreted and used correctly.
- *ISO9000–2* is a guide for the interpretation and application of ISO9001, ISO9002 and ISO9003. This guidance document is useful to organizations in understanding the requirements of these three standards. It is structured in line with ISO9001 and needs to be read in conjunction with that part of the ISO9000 series with which compliance is sought.
- *ISO9000–3* sets out guidelines to facilitate the application of ISO9001 to organizations developing, supplying and maintaining software.
- *ISO9000–4* is a guide to dependability – i.e. reliability, maintainability and availability – programme management and covers the essential features of such a programme.
- *ISO9004–1* is a guide to good quality management practice and, in this, it provides more detail than ISO9001, ISO9002 and ISO9003. It also contains reference to a number of quality aspects, e.g. quality risks, costs, product liability and marketing, which are not covered in the same level of detail in ISO9001, ISO9002 and ISO9003. Considerable emphasis is placed throughout on the satisfaction of customer needs and requirements.
- *ISO9004–2* gives guidance and a comprehensive overview for establishing and implementing a quality system specifically for conditions encountered in the service sector.
- *ISO9004–3* provides guidance on quality system elements for processed materials, which are typically provided in bulk.
- *ISO9004–4* gives guidelines for quality improvement, covering concepts, principles, methodology, and tools and techniques.

With respect to auditing the ISO9000 series contains three standards.

- ISO10011–1 provides guidelines for auditing a quality system and for verifying the ability of the system to achieve defined objectives.
- ISO10011–2 gives guidance on the education, training, experience, personal attributes and management capabilities to carry out an audit.
- ISO10011–3 provides guidelines for managing quality system audit programmes.

Detailed definition of features – ISO9001, ISO9002, ISO9003

ISO9001 *Model for Quality Assurance in Design, Development, Production, Installation and Servicing* covers circumstances in which an organization is responsible for conceptual design and development work, and/or where it may be required to cover post-delivery activities such as commissioning and servicing. It contains 20 elements and is the most comprehensive in scope.

ISO9002 *Model for Quality Assurance in Production, Installation and Servicing* covers circumstances where an organization is responsible for assuring the product and/or service quality during the course of production or installation only. This part consists of 19 elements, excluding design control.

ISO9003 *Model for Quality Assurance in Final Inspection and Test* is used when conformance to specified requirements can be assured solely at final inspection and test, as in the case of a distributor. This contains 16 of the elements of ISO9001 excluding design controls, purchasing, process control and servicing.

Principal clauses in ISO9001

The 20 principal clauses in ISO9001 together with key factors of the quality system are given below. The ISO9002 standard includes all the clauses of ISO9001 apart from design control while the ISO9003 standard does not include the clauses of design control, purchasing, process control and servicing.

1 *Management responsibility*

- Corporate quality policy development, definition statement, organizational goals, aims and objectives, deployment, implementation, communication, understanding and review
- Organization, structure, resources, trained personnel, responsibility and authority
- Management representative
- Management review and reporting of the system to ensure its effectiveness, including policy and objectives

2 *Quality system*

- Documentation and implementation of procedures and instructions
- Quality manual: the first part of the manual should describe how the company operates; the second part should list the requirements of various standards against which registration of approval may be sought and references the procedures to satisfy these requirements
- Quality planning, quality plans, work instructions, inspection instructions, etc.

3 *Contract review*

- Definition and documentation of customer (internal and external) needs and requirements, including records
- Contract and tender compatibility
- Quality planning
- Capability of compliance with requirements
- Amendment to contract

4 *Design control*

- Design and development planning, including statutory and regulatory requirements

- Identify and allocate resources
- Organizational and technical interfaces
- Definition and control of design inputs, outputs and interfaces
- Design verification to confirm outputs meet input requirements
- Design validation
- Review, approve, record and control design changes

5 *Document and data control*

- 'Document' (in the form of any type of media) needs to be defined
- Formal review and approval of documents by authorized personnel
- Correct issues of necessary documents available at appropriate locations
- Obsolete documents removed or assured against intended use provided suitable documentation is maintained
- Changes to documents are authorized and recorded

6 *Purchasing*

- Suppliers/sub-contractors evaluation, and monitoring of performance and capability
- Records of acceptable suppliers
- Formal written definition of requirements and specification
- Verification of sub-contracted product by the customer, if required in the contract

7 *Control of customer-supplied product*

- Verification, storage and maintenance of 'free issue' or customer-supplied material for use on their order

8 *Product identification and traceability*

- Unique and positive identification of material, parts and work-in-progress from receipt and through all stages of production, delivery and installation
- Demonstrated traceability and its recording as, and to the extent, specified

9 *Process control*

- Identifying and planning the processes
- Process control procedures, where their absence would adversely affect quality
- Monitoring of key characteristics and features during production
- Process definition and qualification
- Processes carried out under controlled conditions
- Criteria for workmanship, including illustrations, written standards and samples
- Provision and control of equipment
- Maintenance of equipment to ensure process capability

10 *Inspection and testing*

- Established procedures
- Goods receiving inspection and testing, or other means of verification
- In-process inspection and testing

- Final inspection and testing
- Inspection and test records, including responsibilities

11 *Control of inspection, measuring and test equipment*

- Control, calibration and maintenance of equipment needed to demonstrate compliance with requirements
- Consideration of other measurements needed
- Calibration procedures and processes defining equipment, location, methods of checking, acceptance criteria, etc
- Documentation and calibration records
- Traceability to reference standards, where applicable
- Handling and storage

12 *Inspection and test status*

- Identification of inspection and test status (i.e. untested, tested, checked, reject, meets the requirements) throughout all processes
- Confirmation that tests and inspections have been carried out
- Authority for release of conforming product

13 *Control of non-conforming product*

- Identification and control to prevent unauthorized use
- Segregation of non-conforming materials, parts and products, where practicable
- Review and decide on appropriate remedial action (e.g. destroyed, repaired, reworked or regraded)
- Reinspection

14 *Corrective and preventive action*

- Procedures, routines and reporting of customer complaints and product non-conformities
- Detection, investigation and analysis of causes
- Elimination of causes and abnormalities
- Corrective action control
- Preventive action to analyse and eliminate potential problems
- Assignment of responsibilities
- Changes to procedures, working instructions

15 *Handling, storage, packaging, preservation and delivery*

- Methods and equipment which prevent product damage, preservation, segregation, and deterioration
- Maintenance of product integrity
- Use of designated storage areas to prevent damage and/or deterioration
- Receipt and delivery of items into and out of storage
- Procedures to ensure that the product is packed to prevent damage throughout the entire production to delivery cycle

16 *Control of quality records*

- Adequate records relating to inspections, tests, process control, etc. to demonstrate achievement of product quality and effective operation of the quality system

- Traceability and full history
- Retention time for records
- Storage, retrievable, legibility and identification
- Method of disposition when no longer required

17 *Internal quality audits*

- Audit plan, verification, responsibility, and auditor independence
- Procedures to ensure that the audit method is clear
- Compliance with the documented system
- Reporting of discrepancies and results to personnel responsible for the area audited
- Assessment of the effectiveness of actions taken
- Review and implementation of corrective action by management to bring activities and the quality system into agreement with the planned arrangements

18 *Training*

- Assessment and identification of needs
- Provision of the required training
- Written job responsibilities and specification
- Determining degree and method of competency
- Planned and structured training programme
- Training records

19 *Servicing*

- Contractual specification
- Procedures for performing and verifying that needs and requirements are met

20 *Statistical techniques*

- The use of samples to determine product and service quality
- Identifying the need for statistical technique
- Process capability determination, acceptability and certification
- Product characteristic verification

The set of requirements outlined in ISO9001 can be supplemented for specific industries or products by 'QA specifications', 'QA guidance notes' and 'codes of practice' which provide more detail.

It is worth mentioning that ISO14001 *Environmental Management Systems: Specification with Guidance for Use* shares many common management principles with the ISO9000 series and a number of organizations are considering how they may develop their quality management system as a basis for environmental management (Wilkinson and Dale, 1998).

Implementation Guidelines for the ISO9000 Series of Standards

At this point in the chapter, it is useful to quote the guidelines, with some development by the author, advanced by Long et al. (1991) based on their research into the application and use of the ISO9000 quality system series in small- and medium-sized enterprises; the guidelines are also applicable to larger organizations.

- An organization should be clear on the reasons for seeking ISO9001, ISO9002 or ISO9003 registration. Implementation for the wrong reasons will prevent the organization from receiving the full benefits. In addition, it may be found that implementing and maintaining the requirements of the chosen standard is a burden, in terms of costs and extra paperwork, with no compensating benefits. ISO9001, ISO9002 or ISO9003 registration must therefore not be sought just to satisfy the contractual requirements of major customers or for marketing purposes. Indeed, when most competitors have ISO9000 series registration there is little marketing advantage and, in many markets, it is now an order to quality criterion.

- The development of a quality system to meet the requirements of ISO9001, ISO9002 or ISO9003 should be managed as a project, with the identification of key steps, milestones and time-scales. This will prevent progress being sporadic and variable.

- Prior to a programme of ISO9000 series implementation, it is important that an internal quality audit is conducted of the existing quality system against the appropriate part of the standard, by a qualified auditor. This will determine the initial status of the company's quality management system, enable management to assess the amount of work required to meet the requirements of ISO9000 series and also to plan for systematic implementation of the standard. Without this knowledge, the above-mentioned project planning process would be impossible. It is important that a realistic time-scale is established, because if it is set too tight there will be a tendency to do things artificially and this will result in considerable time spent later in debugging the system. On the other hand, if set too long, there may be a tendency to do little in the initial period. Involvement of the appointed management representative during the quality audit is essential.

- For those organizations developing a quality management system for the first time, a steering committee should be established comprised of all the heads of departments and chaired by the CEO. This type of representation is essential to gain cross-functional support for the project and to help to ensure the smooth development and implementation of the system. Participation and commitment from all the heads of departments is essential to gain employee support for the project, and this will help to ensure the smooth implementation and subsequent maintenance of the standard. In extremely small companies, where there is little or no second-tier management, the wholehearted commitment and involvement of the CEO is critical and essential.

- The ISO9000 series should be considered as the minimum requirement. Without a documented quality management system, there is neither basis nor connected reliable data to monitor the process of quality improvement. Organizations should, however, aim to have a quality system which surpasses the standard's requirements, with new quality initiatives built into the system, as illustrated in figure 13.1. A quality system which meets the requirements of ISO9001, ISO9002 or ISO9003 should in no sense be regarded by senior management as the pinnacle of their quality management achievements. All it says to the outside world is that the organization has controls, procedures and

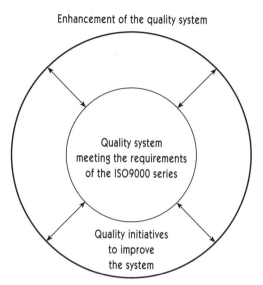

Enhancement of the quality system

Quality system
meeting the requirements
of the ISO9000 series

Quality initiatives
to improve
the system

Figure 13.1 Quality system development

disciplines in place. The organization should treat ISO9000 series registration as a precursor to developing their approach to TQM.

- There is a need to create a conducive environment for the development of a quality system which meets the requirements of the ISO9000 series. This can be achieved by the formulation of organizational quality policy and quality objectives. The responsibility of executives in the establishment, maintenance, and development of the ISO9000 series cannot be understated. The total commitment and leadership of senior management to the process of quality system registration to ISO9001, ISO9002 or ISO9003 is vital; only they can deliver the resources and co-operation of appropriate personnel and provide the necessary direction. The CEO while accepting ultimate responsibility, has, as one would expect, to delegate a variety of tasks. Senior management must not only understand the principles of the ISO9000 series but should ensure that the quality policy is implemented and understood by all employees, and that everyone in the organization has quality improvement objectives for their jobs. They also need to react positively to the actions resulting from quality audits.
- Training at all levels within the company is required on the importance of product and service quality, in general, and the reasons for the quality system and its benefits, in particular. This will help to facilitate the right type of behaviour, attitude and values of employees towards the ISO9000 series, and will encourage total participation. It only provides the opportunity to answer any questions which employees may have about the standard and the process, and the reasons for registration. A systematic approach to quality, education and training will reduce resistance to change and other obstacles. An element of this awareness can occur if the initial audit is well explained and sympathetically carried out, explaining the reasons for recommendations.
- Once all the above steps have been taken, the organization is in a position to commence developing its system to meet the requirements of the ISO9000

system series. Accurate procedures including operating and working instructions are required. These procedures must be practical, workable and easily implemented. Wherever possible, they should document what employees are currently doing; they are most likely then to continue in the same way and fulfil assessment requirements naturally. Only where the standard would suggest that some modification is required should they be introduced. In writing the procedures, it is worthwhile to keep in mind how to demonstrate to the auditor that the ISO9000 series requirements have been fulfilled. The personnel who are given responsibilities for writing the procedures must be familiar with the requirements of the ISO9000 series and be fully conversant with the procedures they are drafting. The use of consultants and management specialists to write procedures is less desirable; they are less likely to understand fully all the activities of the company. It is often found that when procedures are written in 'ivory towers' and then pushed into the working environment as required mandates, this leads to two main problems. First, there is the confrontation of changing the way the people work without any perceived gain and benefit. Second, when a formal assessment of the system is due, there is an intense period of activity when people start to check the system and work to the procedures to ensure that they pass the audit. Also with respect to this, it is helpful to document the procedures before trying to improve it, unless the change is easy to make. The use of consultants to write procedures also skips over the positive factor of employee involvement and the related communication issues; the 'ownership' of the processes by those operating them is lessened. This also happens when there is an overuse of technology aids in producing the procedures. The procedures as they are being developed and/or documented need to be checked to see that they meet the requirements of the ISO9000 series and how they impact on other procedures, systems and activities.

- The quality management system must become an integral part of the management process. When it is treated in this way, it will ensure that business improvements are incorporated into the system.

Quality System Assessment and Registration

When the organization has written the necessary procedures and instructions, and developed its quality system to meet the requirements of that part of the ISO9000 series for which registration is sought, these key activities need to be accomplished.

- Train and educate staff in the workings and operation of the system and test out the procedures which have been developed. Education and training is a key determinant of people following procedures, completing the appropriate documentation, taking corrective action seriously, providing timely and accurate information, and being aware of their responsibilities. In some companies, plans for training are supplemented by people's involvement for which departmental achievements are rewarded. For example, snapshots of audit requirements undertaken by an ISO9000 series implementation team and recognition of performance given by rewards such as mugs, writing blocks, pens, etc.
- Arrange for a pre-assessment of the system to be carried out by a suitable qualified person.

- Decide the most appropriate time to go for assessment.
- ISO9000 series registration is conferred by certification bodies who have, in turn, been accredited in the UK by UKAS. The list of accredited certification bodies should be consulted and a 'supplier audit' of them carried out. It is important to establish the scope of the certification body's approval, their fee structure, relevant experience and knowledge in the organization's field of work, reputation, current workload, etc. Goodman (1997) lists 12 tips for choosing a certification body and this serves as a useful checklist.
- Apply to the chosen accredited certification body who will then supply an information pack. Upon completion of the necessary forms, the certification body will provide a quotation and details of fees. After agreeing a contract, the appropriate documentation (including the quality manual) is then sent to the certification body to check compliance against the standard. In general, a certification body will usually want to see proof that the quality system has been in effective operation for a period of six months. However, this depends on the size of the company and the maturity of its quality management system.
- If the documentation reaches the standard, some certification bodies proceed to the on-site assessment for a preliminary review (pre-audit assessment). At this stage, the company is able to make appropriate modifications and establish corrective actions to take account of the assessors' initial findings and comments.
- The formal assessment involves an in-depth appraisal of the organization's quality management system for compliance with the appropriate part of the standard. This is carried out by a small team of independent assessors appointed by the certification body and under the supervision of a registered lead assessor; these assessors should be knowledgeable in the organization's field of activity. If the assessors discover a deviation from the requirements or identify a non-compliance with the documented procedures, a discrepancy report is raised. At the end of the assessment, the non-conformances are reviewed and the assessors make a report on their recommendations, this includes a verbal report to management by the lead assessor. The recommendation can be unqualified registration, qualified registration and non-registration. Any non-compliance with the appropriate part of the standard must be rectified, within a prescribed time, before approval is given.
- Once registered, the certification bodies have a system of routine surveillance. The frequency of these surveillance visits varies with the certification body but is generally twice a year. The certification body have the right to make these visits unannounced. The registration usually covers a fixed period of three years, subject to the regular surveillance visits. After three years, a quality system reassessment is made. However, the main approach these days are continuous assessment visits of which there are a minimum of two per year. Continuing assessment is planned so that the cumulative effect over a two-year cycle results in a complete audit of the quality system. This not only reduces the cost of registration but also minimizes the inconvenience caused to the organization. The continued compliance with the requirements of the standard is confirmed in writing following the site visit.

Long et al. (1991) from their research into the implementation of the ISO9000 series have identified four factors that determine the time taken by organizations to implement the standard.

1 The status of the quality system prior to seeking ISO9001, ISO9002 and ISO9003 registration, determined by the presence, or otherwise, of activities which are in accordance with one of these three standards, and their existence in a documented form: when few activities are in place and/or activities are not documented then more time is required first to document and then to develop the system to meet the appropriate requirements

2 The complexity of the company – in terms of work locations, products manufactured, services offered, type of production and the type and number of production processes and operating instructions – with increasing complexity more procedures and work instructions are required to be documented

3 The priority given by management to implementing the requirements of the standard and the time they are prepared to set aside for the activity from their normal day-to-day work responsibility affects the progress of implementation – this is especially the case when there are no full-time personnel responsible for QA

4 The existence of a conducive environment, required for the implementation and development of the standard: resistance to change, lack of understanding about product and service quality and poor attitudes among employees toward quality improvement are major obstacles in implementing the requirements of the chosen standard

ISO9000 Series Registration: A Model for Small Companies

McTeer and Dale (1996) have developed a model which outlines what a small company needs to do to achieve ISO9000 series registration. The model, which is shown in figure 13.2, consists of three domains (motivation, information and resources)

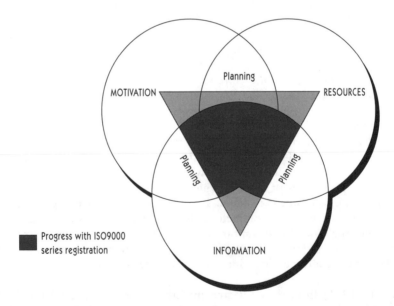

Figure 13.2 An active quality management system regime
Source: McTeer and Dale (1996)

and planning and, by examining the interaction between them, highlights how progress towards ISO9000 series registration can be enhanced or diminished. The dynamics of the model require that the four domains are raised from their latent state through internal and external motivations. As the factors inflating or deflating the domains strengthen or weaken, so the rate of progress towards installing a quality management system to meet the requirements of ISO9000 series increases or decreases. It is argued that progress by a company towards ISO9000 series registration is only made when the demands of motivation, information and resources occlude. The union of only two domains is insufficient to generate sufficient momentum to promote progress towards registration and, if all the domains are sufficiently deflated, the progress to ISO9000 is halted. Drawing on the paper by McTeer and Dale (1996), the model is now described.

Motivation

In a small company's journey from a primitive quality management system to attaining registration to the ISO9000 series, the degree of motivation can be regarded as the most important driving force. The degree of motivation can be influenced, positively and negatively, by both internal and external factors. The most powerful motivating force is demand from customers, in particular large ones, for registration and the fear of losing orders; this ensures that the momentum to introduce an ISO9000 series quality management system is maintained. Head office pressure and the impact of senior management are also factors influencing the degree of motivation, e.g. in making appropriate resources available. The motivation is also affected by employee attitudes and behaviour. Antagonism or apathy from employees towards the company's endeavours to ISO9000 series registration makes it difficult to progress quality management system development.

In addition to the primary forces, there are a number of secondary forces, including, the enhancement of company status in the market-place, the urge to gain a commercial advantage, and advertising opportunities.

Information

As well as educating the company's quality management system champion to the requirements of the ISO9000 series, education and training on quality management system principles and practices must also be given to appraise the workforce of what is required from them. This can help to alleviate or avoid many of the problems associated with the acceptance of new working procedures, practices and disciplines. The solution for many companies is to employ management consultants to ensure that the detailed requirements of developing an ISO9000 series quality management system are achieved and this can help to overcome many of the problems of comprehending the requirements of the standards. By strengthening the reservoir of quality management knowledge, the quality management system champion is better able to communicate effectively with their consultant and better placed to understand the problems and pitfalls of introducing a quality management system. In this way, delays in the process of documenting the system, nugatory work and over documented and bureaucratic quality manuals can be avoided.

If a company is already able to build upon established QA and quality control procedures (no matter how basic), this also helps to speed things up. Failure to raise the level of quality awareness and understand the demands of the ISO9000 series leads to confused, frustrated and neglected employees, and poorly briefed managers, who will tend to restrict the progress towards ISO9000 series registration.

Resources

Three resources are significant: time, finance and availability of personnel.

In failing to make or allocate time to the process of introducing a quality management system, programmes will slip, leading to suspension or abandonment as other more urgent tasks appear and take precedence. Time and the availability of personnel are closely coupled. If the quality management system champion is able to delegate work to staff or a management consultant, time pressures can be eased. Extra resources devoted towards the development of a quality management system are also instrumental in increasing the pace of progress.

In small companies, there is usually little slack time available in the owner or managing director's day-to-day work activities to dedicate to the development of a quality management system. Further, there is a shortage of staff time to assist in this process and the problem becomes more acute as the number of employees in the company diminish. Unless compensated by a greater stimulus to produce a quality management system, a lack of time or conflicting priorities will delay or lead to termination of progress. Also, for many small companies, the budgeting for the process of introducing, and then maintaining, an ISO9000 series system requires some minor restructuring of finances.

Planning

Planning is crucial to the successful introduction of an ISO9000 series quality management system. Only by formulating a sensible plan, which details a timetable of achievable events, milestones and target dates, will a company succeed in this objective. This includes recognizing the need for education and training, additional skills, the use of external resources and, in some cases, the need to appraise company employees of the need for ISO9000 series registration. This domain is seen as both the magnet which draws the motivation, information and resources domains together, and provides the glue that binds them.

Only by drawing together motivation, information and resources can progress be made towards the installation of a quality management system to meet the requirements of the ISO9000 series. Figure 13.2 illustrates the situation when the pursuit by a small company towards ISO9000 series registration is advancing and maturing, the three elements are overlapping and locked together by the planning element. The size of the area of occlusion between these four elements provides a portrayal of the intensity of a small company's progress towards acquiring ISO9000 series registration.

Benefits and Limitations of the ISO9000 Series of Standards

Since its introduction, the ISO9000 quality system series has been widely accepted throughout the world. A number of *benefits* are claimed for the system:

- A reduction in errors, customer complaints and non-conforming products, services and costs and the retention of customers
- Elimination of the number of audits and assessments and also a reduction in the time taken by customers to audit the system, leading to a saving in resources need for such activities
- Improved controls, discipline – e.g. preventing the use of short cuts and duplication of activities – procedures, documentation, communication, dissemination and customer satisfaction, quicker identification and resolution of problems, ensures consistency – i.e. the job is done the same way, time after time – increased quality awareness, in particular, from those departments and people who traditionally perceived 'quality' not to be their major concern
- Identification of ineffective and surplus procedures and documents and other forms of waste
- A better working environment

For details, see various BSI literature, Atkin (1987), Bulled (1987), Collyer (1987), Dale and Oakland (1994), DeAngelis (1991), Ford (1988), Hele (1988), Long et al. (1991), Marquardt et al. (1991), Perry (1991), Rayner and Porter (1991) and SMMT (1990).

A survey carried out by PERA International and Salford University Business Services Limited (1992) of 2,317 firms who had completed a Quality Consultancy Project under the DTI Enterprise Initiative prior to 31 December 1990 found these benefits:

> Overall, 89% of all clients surveyed believed that the introduction of quality management systems had a positive effect on their internal operating efficiency.
>
> Some 48% of firms claimed increased profitability, 76% improved marketing and 26% improved export sales – all attributed the effect to the introduction of quality management systems.

A survey carried out in 1993 by Research International Ltd for Lloyds Register Quality Assurance (1993) assessed the impact of the ISO9000 series on British business. Some 400 managers from companies of varying size and industrial type were interviewed. These were among the main findings:

- Of companies which have gained ISO9000 series registration 89 per cent said it met or exceeded their expectations.
- Eighty-six per cent of companies said registration had improved management control, 69 per cent said it had increased their efficiency and productivity, and 40 per cent claimed it had reduced their costs.
- Disappointment expressed about the ISO9000 series was relatively low. Only 3 per cent reported that it had increased their paperwork and 6 per cent said gaining approval was too costly.

Since then, there have been numerous surveys (Vloeburghs and Bellens, 1996) in various parts of the world. A survey by Buttle (1996) which claims to be 'the most comprehensive national omni-sectoral survey into the impacts of ISO9000 on UK business' obtaining data from 1,229 organizations found, using factor analysis, that the three most important benefits sought from certification are: profit improvement, process improvement and marketing benefits. The survey also pointed out widespread willingness to recommend the ISO9000 standards to other firms.

On the other hand, a number of *difficulties, problems and shortcomings* have been reported and discussed:

- Deciding what constitutes design and development work and thereby selecting whether to apply for ISO9001 or ISO9002 registration
- Deciding whether registration be sought for the whole company or just one unit/division/site/premise or even a specific operation carried out on one site or certain defined activities, as in the case of local authorities
- Applicability of the standards to certain situations
- Interpretations of various sections of the standard and understanding the requirements of the standards
- Terminology used
- Lack of flexibility and perceived restrictions on creativity
- Lack of relevance to the real needs of the business, resulting in a view of bureaucracy gone mad and a 'why bother' attitude from people at the operating end of the organization
- A lack of direction in relation to SPC
- Weaknesses in some of the requirements and omissions which are crucial to continuous improvement, such as the lack of detail to the leadership required, people involvement and customer satisfaction
- The time and resources needed in writing procedures and training and retraining staff in the requirements of the ISO9000 series and the internal auditing of the system
- The bureaucracy involved in documentation and accreditation and the lack of mutual recognition of certificated bodies between countries
- The cost involved in achieving ISO9000 series registration and then maintaining the registration (This applies, in particular, to small companies. The cost comprises the additional workload incurred by company personnel in writing the procedures, managerial time, increased paperwork, etc., the fee of the management consultancy (if a consultant is used to assist with the process of registration) and the certification body's fees.)
- Perceived by small companies to be applicable only to large companies
- In some cases, in particular sales/service situations, the rigour and applicability of the standards are perceived as restrictive and barriers to providing a flexible and responsive service to customers

Details are given by Association of British Certification Bodies and the NACCB (1994), BSI Policy Committee for Small Businesses (1994), Brennan (1994), Campbell (1994), Commerce (1994), Dale and Oakland (1994), Hersan (1990), Jennings (1992), Long et al. (1991), Oliver (1991), Owen (1987), Owen (1988), Rayner and Porter (1991), Sayle (1987) and Whittington (1989). Some of these reported difficulties have been eased by the 1994 revision of the ISO9000 series in terms of clearing up the ambiguity regarding implied requirements, consistency of clause numbering between ISO9001, ISO9002 and ISO9003, process control requirements and the emphasis given to preventive action and the provision of advice for small businesses (e.g. *ISO9000 for Small Businesses* (BSI, 1997)). In addition, a number of the certification bodies have introduced a special service of assessment and surveillance to reduce the cost of ISO9000 series registration to small businesses. The fee structure of such services has been developed to help smaller businesses.

Seddon (1997) has launched almost a one-man crusade against the ISO9000 series and his recent book provides some interesting reading of views of what he considers to be the damage inflicted on companies that adopt and implement the requirements of this series of standards.

The subject of the ISO9000 series of standards, when raised at conferences and symposiums, almost always leads to heated debate. Analysis of the ensuing discussion reveals that there are a small group of people who are firm believers in 'the system' and, diametrically opposed to them are an equally small group who are antagonistic towards the system. The vast majority of people take the centre ground. This group have no strong views one way or the other and, in the main, their respective organizations are registered to the relevant part of the ISO9000 series, because it is a contractual requirement of customers. They report that some of the benefits outlined above have been received and it is considered an aid to marketing. Many managers outside the quality function see ISO9000 series registration as a bureaucratic system and take the view 'Let's get the certificate on the wall for 3 years and then do it all over again'. Irrespective of the views expressed, the ISO9000 series is here to stay.

What follows now is an overview of the benefits and limitations of the ISO9000 series. The data is based on the type of discussions mentioned above, supplemented with comments made by directors, managers and technicians on the Ford Motor Company three-day SPC training courses for suppliers held at UMIST, various discussions with executives, consultants during the course of the UMIST TQM research, both on a national and international front, and comments made by executives on early drafts of this chapter.

A quality system is a fundamental pillar in an organization's approach to TQM and it helps to ensure that any improvements made are held in place; see figure 13.3. However, ISO9000 quality system series registration is not a prerequisite for TQM. Some organizations, in particular those from the non-manufacturing sector, have analysed and improved their systems and working practices and then have gone straight to TQM.

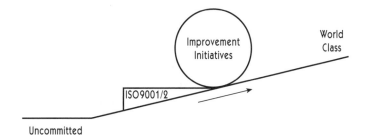

Figure 13.3 Quality improvement and the ISO9000 series

The guidance provided in the 20 clauses of ISO9001, and the independent assessment surveillance, is an indisputable aid in developing and maintaining the procedures, controls and discipline required in a quality management system. The system should help to ensure that more people within the organization are touched by quality and, in this way, quality awareness is raised. The ISO9000 series does, however, tend to encourage the separation of a business into areas that complete the recording of requirements and those areas which do not. For example, functions such as Finance, MISs and HR are little affected, except for training requirements. It is TQM which stimulates the business by creating the understanding that all its component parts have customers, that waste must be systematically eliminated, and that improvement is a continuous process. To help to eradicate these weaknesses relating to the separation of functions BSI QA introduced, in 1991, company-wide registration to extend quality system accreditation to the whole of the company (core businesses as well as supporting functions); see Perry (1991) for details.

The UMIST TQM research experience indicates that, in most companies, it is not easy to involve every function and person in taking responsibility for their own QA and to make quality improvements in the processes for which they are responsible; see Lascelles and Dale (1993). The ISO9000 series of standards, albeit limited in respect of the point made above, can assist in making this happen.

> It is a contractual requirement of many customers that their suppliers are registered to the ISO9000 series of standards, registration is also required to get on bid lists. Once a company has become registered, it is more than likely that it will ask its suppliers, distributors and providers of service to do the same, setting into motion a chain reaction, or what might be classed as a form of pyramid selling. Therefore, in many sectors of industry and Government procurement agencies, it is necessary from a marketing viewpoint, and, without it, a company will simply not receive orders. In much of the world, it is now a prerequisite condition to doing business. An increasing number of long-standing suppliers to companies have been told by them that they must have ISO9000 quality system series registration to continue to be a supplier. This is in spite of the supplier being the supplier of choice for a considerable period of time. Once ISO9001, ISO9002 or ISO9003 registration has been achieved an organization cannot afford to lose it.

Suppliers have a habit of doing what their customers want and many organizations have achieved ISO9001, ISO9002 or ISO9003 registration to provide documented proof that they have an adequate quality system in place, just to satisfy the demands of their major customers. This may not produce the required improvement ethos naturally and any gains made will be short-lived if registration is perceived as a contractual condition rather than a foundation for ongoing improvement. Some suppliers also use it to demonstrate to customers (actual and potential) that they are committed to quality and have achieved what they often call 'the right level of quality'.

> A system based on the ISO9000 series provides only the foundation blocks; registration to the relevant part of the ISO9000 series should be viewed as the minimum requirement, and the objective should be to develop and improve the system in relation to the needs of the organization. An organization does not achieve superior performing company status merely by ISO9001, ISO9002 or ISO9003 registration. The winners will be those who have a dedicated commitment to company-wide improvement through continuous self-assessment of what they do.
>
> The preparation of systems, procedures, working instructions, etc., to meet the requirements of the ISO9000 series, will have a beneficial affect on a company's performance in terms of improved process yields, reduced levels of non-conformance, improved management control, etc. However, the underlying mechanisms of the ISO9000 series are such that they will tend towards a steady-state performance. The ISO9000 series of standards are designed to produce consistency both in actions, products and services. An organization can have a consistent performance with a high level of non-conformance. In the words of one Executive: 'ISO9000 is an excellent system for telling us where we have produced rubbish.' The achievement of consistency while meritious, leads to the goal and, once achieved, can result in complacency.

The question, 'Does the quality system reflect the needs of the customer?', should forever circulate in minds of senior management.

Only if there is strong leadership and a written commitment to improvement in the management review of the system will an improvement cycle be triggered. Some organizations have done this by building on and widening their quality systems management review meetings which deal with issues such as quality audit, corrective and preventive action; production rejections, concessions and corrective actions; waste levels; supplier performance/concessions; customer complaints; and market trends and requirements, into monthly steering meetings for quality improvement. In this way, the quality system is integrated into the quality improvement process; it is not uncommon to find they are operated in parallel.

Having an ISO9000 series certificate of registration does not, as a matter of course, imply that non-conformities at all stages of the process will not occur. The standard is not prescriptive as to the means of prevention. Detection methods which rely very heavily on inspection techniques, human or mechanical, would appear to satisfy the standard in many aspects. This may be an acknowledgement of the fact that there are many processes where, given the state-of-the-art technology, it is not possible to achieve 'zero defects'. The standard clearly indicates that corrective and preventive actions procedures should be established, documented and maintained to prevent recurrence of non-conforming product, and that the system is maintained and developed through the internal audit and management review, but there is a lack of evidence to suggest that improvement is an explicit criterion by which ongoing registration is monitored. In general, the ISO9000 series tends to measure the effectiveness of documentation, paperwork and procedures (the requisite assessments are often termed a paperchase); this leads to the claim that they encourage bureaucracy and a complex process of documentation.

Experience indicates that the ISO9000 series has a limited impact on the total improvement operation of an organization simply because it does not go to the root cause of problems. Most problems are resolved at branch level and this is a failure in a number of businesses.

By way of a comparison, the Ford Motor Company require their suppliers to demonstrate ongoing improvements in their quality system and processes, and these improvements are assessed by documentation, reports and visits by Ford personnel to the supplier. However, there is no published data about inter- and intra-industry comparisons. There is also no evidence that companies who are registered to ISO9001, ISO9002 or ISO9003 exhibit a better quality performance and have a more positive approach to continuous and company-wide quality improvement than those who are not registered.

Some people are confused about the relationship between the ISO9000 series and TQM. They are not alternatives; a quality system is an essential feature of TQM. However, some organizations see ISO9001, ISO9002 or ISO9003 registration as the pinnacle of their TQM achievements and no plans are laid for building on this registration; a small number of people even believe that improvements driven through internal audits of the ISO9000 series will lead their organization to TQM. As previously mentioned, registration often results in a sense of complacency, in particular, after successful third-party assessment of the system.

It should be obvious from the above discussion that ISO9001, ISO9002 or ISO9003 registration, or for that matter any other quality system registration or certification or approvals, will not prevent a supplier from producing and delivering non-conforming products and/or services to its customers. The standards are a specification for the management of quality and there is clear distinction between registration and capability; this fundamental fact needs to be recognized. Product and/or service quality is determined by the individual organization and its people and processes, and not by a quality system standard.

Proof of this difference is provided from an investigation carried out by Judy Mone of the initial samples submitted by some 300 suppliers to the Leyland Daf assembly plant. It was a contractual requirement of the then Leyland Daf organization that all its suppliers are registered to the ISO9000 series or its equivalent, but she found that over 30 per cent of initial samples did not conform to requirements; see Mone et al. (1991) for details.

Many organizations and executives have inflated views of the ISO9000 series; these are often picked up from the hype generated by those selling advisory services. These views can lead to high expectations of what the standard can achieve which, in the long term, may do it a disservice. There are some typical comments (not referenced and attributed to individuals):

- Quality recognition of the ISO9000 series from a National accredited certification body is prized nationwide because it is known to be difficult to achieve the high standards required by their impartial testing procedures.
- . . . it will give the car-buying public a guarantee of complete satisfaction or their money back. What it aims to achieve is the world's coveted benchmark of quality: BS5750. . . . it is a standard that is recognized as being truly superb and is a move that no other rival car maker can afford to ignore.
  How can it be coveted and difficult to achieve when many thousands of companies in the UK have already met this requirement?
- Such and such a company are the first in their industrial sector to obtain the prestigious ISO9001, ISO9002 or ISO9003 registration – tremendous achievement, very proud to have achieved to the registration, the most significant event in the company's history, breaking new ground for quality, etc., etc. (write-up and picture in the local paper).

To the informed, what these motherhead statements and platitudes are saying is that the organization has taken the first step down the TQM journey.

Summary

A quality system is one of the key building blocks for an organization's TQM activities. The ISO9000 generic series of quality system standards defines and sets out a definitive list of features and characteristics which should be present in an organization's quality management system through documented policies, manual and procedures, whatever the product manufactured or offered, or the service provided, or the technology used. In this way, sound advice is provided on how an organization may develop a quality system.

In addition to incorporating the clauses of the ISO9000 series, a quality system design must maximize ownership, allow flexibility without loss of control, enable it to be developed to cope with changes in the business and capture improvements and, above all, it must be 'user friendly'.

Seeking registration for the wrong reasons and a system which is too inflexible and bureaucratic are some of the major pitfalls. Registration to the ISO9000 series will improve an organization's systems, procedures and processes but, on its own, will not deliver continuous and company-wide improvement. To make best use of the ISO9000 series, it is important that the implementation is carried out in the right spirit and for the right reasons. This is an area in which management commitment is vital. The solution to many of the reported difficulties, shortcomings and criticisms against the standard lies in the hands of an organization's senior management team. The saying 'you only get out what you put in' is so relevant to the ISO9000 series and it is so important that the system is seen as being alive. All too often, the ISO9000 series system is left solely in the hands of the Quality Department.

Registration to the ISO9000 series of standards is not the only way to achieve QA; neither is it a prerequisite for TQM. It is, however, becoming necessary to have the appropriate registration to do business at both a national and international level and, in this respect, it is a key marketing tool. It is the fear of loss of business and substitution in the market-place that have caused many organizations to attain ISO9000 series registration. The ISO9000 series provides a common benchmark for good quality management system practice which is recognized throughout the world. An organization which is registered to the appropriate part of the series should be working in an organized, structured and procedural way with defined methods of operating.

It is important that organizations do not view ISO9000 series registration as their pinnacle of success in relation to QA. It only provides the basic foundation blocks; they must have strategies and business plans in place to move on and cater for areas which are not addressed by the standard, and develop to TQM. This is particularly important in smaller businesses who, in a number of cases, attain ISO9000 series registration and have no interest and vision to developing further their quality management activities.

References

Association of British Certification Bodies and the NACCB. 1994: *Quality Systems in the Small Firm: A Guide to the Use of the ISO9000 series.* London: National Accreditation Council for Certification Bodies.

Atkin, G. 1987: BS5750 – practical benefits in the factory', *Works Management*, November, 38–42.

Boaden, R. J., Dale, B. G. and Polding, E. 1991: A state-of-the-art survey of total quality management in the construction industry, *Research Report to the European Construction Institute*, Loughborough.

Brennan, S. 1994: Death or honour, *Commerce Magazine*, April, 8–9.

BSI 1997: *ISO9000 for Small Businesses.* London: British Standards Institution.

BSI Policy Committee for Small Businesses. 1994: *The Application of BS5750 to Small Business: Initial Report.* London: BSI.

Bulled, J. W. 1987: BS5750 – Quality management, systems and assessment. *General Engineer*, November, 271–80.

Buttle, F. 1996: An investigation of the willingness of UK certificated firms to recommend ISO9000. *The International Journal of Quality Science*, 1(2), 40–50.

Campbell, L. 1994: BS5750: What's in it for small firms. *Quality World*, March, 377–9.

Collyer, R. 1987: BS5750 and its application. *Polymer Paint Colour Journal*, 177(4191), 318–20.

Commerce, C. 1994: BS5750, *Commerce Magazine*, May, 16–18 (2nd edn).

Dale B. G. and Oakland, J. S. 1994: *Quality Improvement Through Standards* (2nd edn). Cheltenham: Stanley Thornes (Publishers).

Dale, B. G. and Plunkett, J. J. 1984: A study of audits, inspection and quality costs in the pressure vessel fabrication sector of the process plant industry. *Proceedings of the Institution of Mechanical Engineers*, 198(B2), 45–54.

Davies, J. S. 1997: *ISO9000 Management Systems Manual*. New York: McGraw Hill.

DeAngelis, C. A. 1991: ICI advanced materials implements ISO9000 programs. *Quality Progress*, 24(11), 49–51.

Ford, E. 1988: Quality assured fabrication. *The Production Engineer*, October, 36–8.

Galt, J. D. A. and Dale, B. G. 1991: Supplier development: a British case study. *International Journal of Purchasing and Materials Management*. Winter, 16–22.

Goodman, S. 1997: Tips on how to choose your certification body. *Quality World*, February, 114–15.

Hall, T. J. 1992: *The Quality Manual: the Application of BS5750, ISO9001, EN29001*. Chichester: John Wiley.

Hele, J. 1988: BS5750/ISO9000 and the metals processor. *Metallurgia*, March, 128–34.

Hersan, C. H. A. 1990: A critical analysis of ISO9001. *Quality Forum*, 16(2), 61–5.

HMSO 1982: *Standards, Quality and International Competitiveness*, Government White Paper, Cmnd 8621, HMSO.

ISO 1997: *The ISO Survey of ISO9000 and ISO14000 Certificates (seventh cycle)*. Geneva: ISO.

Jackson, P. and Ashton, D. 1993: *Implementing Quality Through ISO9000*. London: Kogan Page.

Jennings, G. M. 1992: ISO9001/ISO9002 – use, misuse and abuse. *Quality Forum*, 16(2), 61–5.

Lamprecht, J. L. 1992: *ISO9000, Preparing for Registration*. New York: Marcel Dekker.

Lamprecht, J. L. 1993: *Implementing the ISO9000 Series*. New York: Marcel Dekker.

Lascelles, D. M. and Dale, B. G. 1993: *Total Quality Improvement*. Bedford: IFS Publications.

Long, A. A., Dale, B. G. and Younger, A. 1991: A study of BS5750 aspirations in small companies. *Quality and Reliability Engineering International*, 7(1), 27–33.

Marquardt, D., Chove, J., Jensen, K. E., Petrick, K., Pyle, J. and Strahle, D. 1991: Vision 2000: the strategy for the ISO9000 series standards in the 90s. *Quality Progress*, 24(5), 25–31.

McTeer, M. M. and Dale, B. G. 1996: How to achieve ISO9000 series registration: a model for small companies. *Quality Management Journal*, 3(1), 43–55.

Mone, J., Hibbert, B. and Dale, B. G. 1991: Initial samples and quality improvement: a study, *Proceedings of the Sixth National Conference on Production Research*, Hatfield Polytechnic, Bell and Bain, September, 459–63.

Oliver, B. 1991: Further thoughts on ISO9000. *Quality News*, 17(3), 122–3.

Owen, F. 1988: 'Why quality assurance and its implementation in a chemical manufacturing company. *Chemistry and Industry*, August, 491–4.

Owen, M., (1987), Ford, SPC and BS5750, *Quality News*, 12(12), 323.

PERA International and Salford University Business Services Ltd. 1992: *A Survey of Quality Consultancy Scheme Clients, 1988–1990*. London: The Enterprise Initiative, DTI.

Perry, M. 1991: *Company-Wide Registration: A Foundation for Total Quality*. Milton Keynes: BSI Quality Assurance, British Standards Institution.

Rayner, P. and Porter, L. J. 1991: BS5750/ISO9000: The Experiences of Small and Medium Sized Firms. *International Journal of Quality and Reliability Management*, 8(6), 16–28.

Research International Ltd and Lloyds Register Quality Assurance. 1993: *BS5750/ISO9000: Setting Standards for Better Business*. London: Lloyds Register Quality Assurance.

Rothery, B. 1993: *ISO9000*. Aldershot, Hants.: Gower Press.

Sayle, A. J. 1987: ISO9000 – progression or regression. *Quality News*, 14(2), 50–3.

Seddon, J. 1997: *In Pursuit of Quality: The Case Against ISO9000*. Oak Tree Press. Middlesex.

Singer, A. J., Churchill, G. F. and Dale, B. G. 1988: Supplier quality assurance systems; a study in the nuclear industry. *Proceedings of the Institution of Mechanical Engineers*, 202(B4), 205–12.

SMMT 1990: *Quality Systems and the Motor Industry*. London: SMMT.

Spickernell, D. G. 1991: The path to ISO9000, *Third Business Success Seminar*, November, London: BSI.

Vloeburghs, D. and Bellens, J. 1996: Implementing the ISO9000 Standards in Belgium. *Quality Progress*, June, 43–8.

Warner, F. 1977: *Standards and Specifications in the Engineering Industries*. London: NEDO.

Whittington, D. 1989: Some Attitudes to BS5750: a study. *International Journal of Quality and Reliability Management*, 6(3), 54–8.

Wilkinson, G. and Dale, B. G. 1998: Manufacturing companies attitudes to system integration: a case study examination. *Quality Engineering*, 11(1), 249–56.

chapter fourteen

Tools and Techniques: An Overview

B. G. Dale and P. Shaw

Introduction

To support, develop and advance a process of continuous improvement, it is necessary for an organization to use a selection of tools and techniques. Some of these tools and techniques are simple (sometimes deceptively so) while others are more complex. There are a considerable number of tools and techniques; these are perhaps the popular and most well known:

- Flow charts
- Check lists
- The seven quality control tools QC7*
- Quality costing
- SPC
- FMEA
- FTA
- DOE
- QFD
- The seven management tools M7*
- DPA
- Mistake-proofing
- Benchmarking

Tools and techniques have different roles to play in continuous improvement and, if applied correctly, give repeatable and reliable results. Here are some of their roles:

- Summarizing data and organizing its presentation
- Data collection and structuring ideas

* QC7 = check sheets, histograms, graphs, pareto diagrams, cause and effect diagrams, scatter diagrams, and control charts.
* M7 = affinity diagrams, relations diagrams, systematic diagrams, matrix diagrams, matrix data analysis, process decision program charts and arrow diagrams.

- Identifying relationships
- Discovering and understanding a problem
- Implementing actions
- Finding and removing the causes of the problem
- Selecting problems for improvement and assisting with the setting of priorities
- Monitoring and maintaining control
- Planning
- Performance measurement and capability assessment

A number of the tools and techniques in the above list have a separate chapter in the book devoted to them. This chapter provides an overview of the tools and techniques which are not given such coverage, but are likely to be used in an organization's improvement process. The focus is on describing the tools and their uses, and avoids detail on construction. Where appropriate, guidance for further reading is provided for those who may wish to extend their knowledge of a particular tool or technique. A deliberate attempt has been made to choose examples from a variety of situations to give the reader a flavour of their applicability in a wide number of situations.

Selecting Tools and Techniques

Potential users must always be aware of the main uses of the particular tool and technique they are considering applying. There is often a danger of using a tool and technique in a blinkered manner, almost expecting it to solve the problem automatically.

When selecting tools and techniques, there are two factors which organizations should keep in mind:

1 The application of any tool and technique in isolation without a strategy and plan will only provide short-term benefits. If tools and techniques are to be effective over the longer term, appropriate employee behaviour and attitudes are needed.
2 No one tool or technique is more important than another – they all have a role to play at some point in the improvement process. It is a mistake to single out one tool or technique for special attention and to become overreliant on it; the Japanese make the point that a warrior should never have a favourite weapon. A common saying used to emphasize this is: 'If you only have a hammer, it is surprising how many problems look like nails.'

A number of companies use tools and techniques without thinking through the implications for TQM or how the concept will be developed and advanced within the organization. This can give rise to misconceptions and misunderstandings which eventually become barriers to progress. Many companies who use tools and techniques as the springboard to launch an improvement process usually single out a specific tool or technique, sometimes at random, and apply it with undue haste without giving sufficient thought to the issues:

- What is the fundamental purpose of the technique?
- What will it achieve?

- Will it produce benefits if applied on its own?
- Is the technique right for the company's product, processes, people and culture?
- How will the technique facilitate improvement?
- How will it fit in with, complement or support, other techniques, methods and quality management systems already in place, and any that might be introduced in the future?
- What organizational changes, if any, are necessary to make the most effective use of the technique?
- What is the best method of introducing, and then using, the technique?
- What are the resources, skills, information training, etc. required to introduce the technique successfully?
- Has the company the management skills and resources, and the commitment to make the technique work successfully?
- What are the potential difficulties in using the technique?
- What are the limitations, if any, of the technique?

It is important for managers to address these questions when considering the introduction of any tool or technique. Unfortunately, some managers are always looking for tools and techniques as a quick-fix solution to the problems facing their organization at a particular point in time. In general, management teams that are 'technique reactive' tend to be unclear on the concept of TQM. They often confuse the implementation of a particular technique with TQM and tend to use the technique as an end in itself rather than as a means to an end.

If the management team is preoccupied with specific techniques, and lacks an adequate understanding of TQM and the improvement process, the risk is that tools and techniques are picked up and discarded as fashion changes; an analogy can be made to a magician producing balls out of the air or pulling rabbits out of a hat; see figure 14.1. When this happens, and a tool or technique fail to meet expectations, disillusionment sets in and the company experiences considerable difficulty convincing its employees that it is serious about improvement. This, of course, has an adverse effect on the use of techniques in the organization in the future. One of the main reasons that companies fall into this trap is that they have unduly high expectations of the benefits arising from the use of a single tool or technique which stem from the lack of clarity and in-depth understanding of it. Much of this is a result of the publicity and selling which often accompany a specific tool or technique. In general, on its own, a single tool or technique may simply indicate or signify the presence of a problem which must be identified and resolved to produce only a small incremental improvement. It is only as a result of the cumulative effect of a series of tools and techniques within a TQM approach that the organization starts to see long-term benefits from its improvement endeavours; see figure 14.2. Therefore, organizations should resist the temptation to isolate the benefits arising from any one tool or technique.

Motivation for the use of any particular tool or technique is a key factor in the success of its implementation. They could be those specified as a contractual requirement by a major customer, they may be what management believe the market-place will be expecting in the future, or the view may be taken that their use will give the organization an edge over its competitors. We have found (Dale and Shaw, 1990) that, when a major customer insists on the use of a specific technique as a contractual requirement of its suppliers, two phases can be identified in its use.

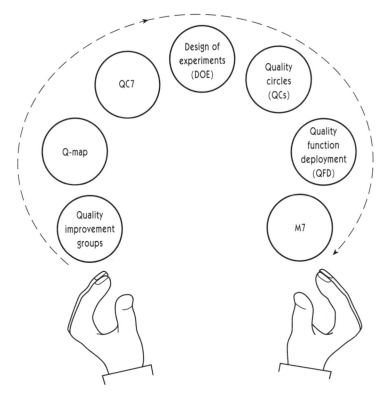

Figure 14.1 The use of quality management tools and techniques
Source: Dale and Cooper (1992)

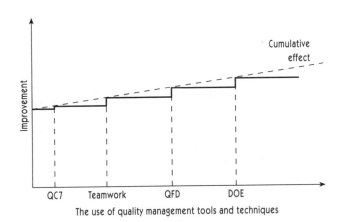

The use of quality management tools and techniques

Figure 14.2 Incremental improvement through the use of quality management tools and techniques
Source: Dale and Cooper (1992)

1 The technique is applied by the supplier simply to satisfy the demands of the customer so as to maintain the business. To emphasize this, they point out a case in which SPC was used on a process for a particular customer's product and when other customers' product were made on the same process, SPC was not used. During this phase, the supplier often resorts to a number of camouflage measures, fakes and ruses to convince the customer that the technique is being applied effectively and beneficially. The emphasis in this phase is on satisfying the customer's paperwork requirements. This phase is wasteful of time and resources, but suggests that suppliers appear to need this phase to develop their own awareness and understanding of the technique which is being applied.

2 The second phase begins when the supplier's management team starts to question how they might best use the technique to enhance the company's competitive position. This is when real improvements begin to occur. They also point out that motor industry suppliers appear to have reached this phase in a shorter period of time with FMEA than they did with SPC, and suggest that this is due to the learning experience and also the depth of intellectual demands of each technique. Those organizations using techniques such as SPC for the sole reason of satisfying the quality system audits of major customers are missing the direct benefits of the correct use of the technique and also the opportunity that it affords to launch a process of continuous improvement. The danger in adopting this approach is that the improvement process goes only as far as the customer requires.

Because of the variety of starting points and motivations for improvement, it is not possible to identify a universal implementation plan detailing the order in which specific techniques should be used by an organization. However, one piece of advice is that organizations should start with the simpler techniques, such as the checklists, flowcharts and QC7. Simple tools and techniques can be just as effective as the more complex ones. In the West, there is a tendency to ignore the simple tools and to use tools and techniques in isolation; the Japanese companies tend to use QC7 together and give high visibility to the results. In this way, they are not only listening to the process through control charts, but taking action to improve it. This combined use of QC7 facilitates problem resolution and improvement action.

Difficulties and Issues Relating to the Use of Tools and Techniques

Research carried out by Dale et al. (1998) into the difficulties relating to the use of tools and techniques discovered that the critical success factors relating to the successful use and application of tools and techniques could be grouped into four main categories:

1 Data collection
2 Use and application
3 Role in improvement
4 Organization and infrastructure

They also identified a number of issues which relate to the difficulties experienced with all tools and techniques, including management support, user understanding, integral approach, discipline and application. A number of issues which relate to specific tools and techniques were also highlighted, including level of complexity, visual display, initial investment and overall status of TQM.

Building on this initial work, Dale and McQuater (1998) have identified five main influences on each of the four success factors; see figure 14.3.

1. Experience
2. Management
3. Resources
4. Education
5. Training

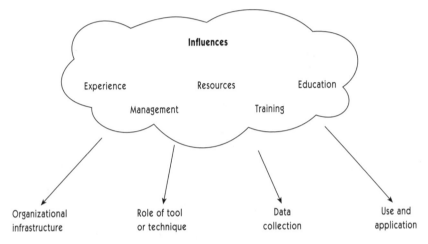

Figure 14.3 The effects of influences on continuous improvement
Source: Dale and McQuater (1998)

Based on these influences, an assessment methodology has been developed for identifying potential difficulties that impinge on the effective use of tools and techniques in an organization, and for providing a diagnostic analysis. The methodology, described by Dale and McQuater (1998), consists mainly of an assessment grid, a questionnaire and semi-structured interviews. These approaches can be used separately as well as in combinations, depending on the organization's objectives for carrying out the assessment. The Assessment Grid which can be used on its own to undertake a 'health check' of potential areas for concern is reproduced in figure 14.4.

Flow Charts

Process mapping (sometimes called 'blue printing' or process modelling), in either a structured or unstructured format, is a prerequisite to obtaining an in-depth understanding of a process, before the application of quality management tools and techniques such as FMEA, SPC and quality costing. A flow chart is employed to provide a diagrammatic picture –, often by means of a set of established symbols, showing all the steps or stages in a process, project or sequence of events – and is of considerable assistance in documenting and describing a process as an aid to examination and improvement.

(a)

Please indicate on the grid ONLY the techniques and tools you recognize. For those that you have recognized, if you use them for **any** purpose, not only for quality-related matters, please tick the box marked use.

Example	Recognize	Use
QC7		
Cause and effect	✔	
Check sheets		
Control charts		
Graphs/charts	✔	✔
Histograms	✔	✔
Pareto analysis	✔	✔
Scatter diagrams	✔	

	Recognize	Use
QC7		
Cause and effect		
Check sheets		
Control charts		
Graphs/charts		
Histograms		
Pareto analysis		
Scatter diagrams		
M7		
Affinity diagrams		
Arrow diagrams/critical path analysis		
Matrix data analysis methods		
Matrix diagrams		
Process decision programme chart		
Relation diagrams		
Systematic diagrams/tree diagrams		
Techniques		
Benchmarking		
Brainstorming/brainwriting		
Departmental purpose analysis		
Design of experiments (Taguchi)		
Failure mode and effects analysis		
Flow charts		
Force field analysis		
Problem solving methodology		
Quality costs		
Quality function deployment		
Questionnaire		
Sampling		
Statistical process control		
*		
*		
*		
*		
*		

* Add any company–specific techniques and tools not indicated on the list

(b)

Please complete the grid ONLY for the techniques or tools you indicated on the recognition and use grid. Do not attempt to fill it in its entirety. They may be occasions when some of the categories cannot be allocated a score; in that case insert 9 (not applicable)

Score out of 5 in each of the categories where:

1 = No value

2 = Low value (e.g. little used, not understood, little or poor training, etc.)

3 = Some value (e.g. basic understanding, small benefits, basic training, etc.)

4 = High value (e.g. good understanding, some benefits, reasonable training, etc.)

5 = Very high value (e.g. complete understanding, excellent benefits, effective traing, etc.)

9 = Not applicable or no training

For example: *Pareto analysis*	Importance 5	Relevance 4	Use 2	Understand 3	Application 3	Resources 2	Management 1	Training 1	Benefit 4
	Importance	Relevance	Use	Understand	Application	Resources	Management	Training	Benefit
QC7									
Cause and effect									
Check sheets									
Control charts									
Graphs/charts									
Histograms									
Pareto analysis									
Scatter diagrams									
QC7									
Affinity diagrams									
Arrow diagrams/critical path analysis									
Matrix data analysis methods									
Matrix diagrams									
Process decision programme chart									
Relation diagrams									
Systematic diagrams/tree diagrams									
Techniques									
Benchmarking									
Brainstorming/brainwriting									
Departmental purpose analysis									
Design of experiments (Taguchi)									
Failure mode and effects analysis									
Flow charts									
Force field analysis									
Problem solving methodology									
Quality costs									
Quality function deployment									
Questionnaire									
Sampling									
Statistical process control									
Other techniques, tools, systems									
For example:									
ISO9000 series									
Quality operating system QS9000									
Other awards (e.g. EQA)									

Figure 14.4 An assessment grid for a 'health check': (a) recognition and use grid; (b) application grid

Source: Dale and McQuater (1998)

A chart, when used in a manufacturing context, may show the complete process from goods-receiving through storage, manufacture, assembly to despatch of final product or simply some part of this process in detail. What is important is that each 'activity' is included to focus attention on aspects of the process or subset of the process where problems have occurred or may occur to enable some corrective action to be taken or countermeasure put into place.

Traditionally, charts (called process charts) have employed conventional symbols to define activities such as operation, inspection, delay or temporary storage, permanent storage and transportation, and are much used by operations and methods and industrial engineering personnel; see Currie (1989) for details. In more recent times, they have witnessed considerable use in BPR; see chapter 20.

There are a number of variants of the classical process flow chart, including those tailored to an individual company's use with different symbols being used to reflect the situation under study. What is important is not the format of the chart and/or flow diagram, but that the process has been mapped out – with key inputs, value-adding steps and outputs defined – and that it is understood by those directly involved and responsible for initiating improvements. Analysing the data collected on a flow chart can help to uncover irregularities and potential problem points. It is also a useful method of dealing with customer complaints, providing traceability by establishing the point in the customer/supplier chain where a break or problems has occurred, its potential cause and corrective action. In a number of cases, processes are poorly defined and documented. Also, in some organizations, people are only aware of their own particular aspect of a process; process mapping helps to facilitate a greater understanding of the whole process, and it is essential to the development of the internal customer/supplier relationship. Figure 14.5 is an example of flow charting for the process of non-conformance identification and preventive action.

A specific kind of process mapping – quality management activity planning (Q-map) – was developed by Crossfield at the Allied Signal plant in Skelmersdale. It is used to map out and analyse organizational procedures to examine what needs to be done, by whom and when, i.e. 'As-is' to 'as-desired'. The methodology is described in detail by Crossfield and Dale (1990), who outline how Q-map has been applied successfully in modelling major aspects of Allied Signal's QA systems and procedures, including incoming inspection of material, initial sampling of goods, gauge control/planning, advanced quality planning, new product introduction, implementation of SPC, supplier certification, final view inspection, skip lot sampling, customer initial sample inspection reporting, warranty analysis, and FMEA. It cuts through the complexities of procedural mapping by simple graphical analysis. Each area of interest starts with one 'activity box' which identifies the inputs, outputs, resources required and constraints that apply to that interest. Figure 14.6 is a typical example of Q-map.

Here are the main steps in constructing a flow chart:

- Define the process and its boundaries, including start and end points.
- Decide the type and method of charting and the symbols to be used, and do not deviate from the convention chosen.
- Decide the detail with which the process is to be mapped.
- Describe the stages, in sequence, in the process, using the agreed methodology.
- Assess if these stages are in the correct sequence.
- Ask people involved with the process to check its veracity.

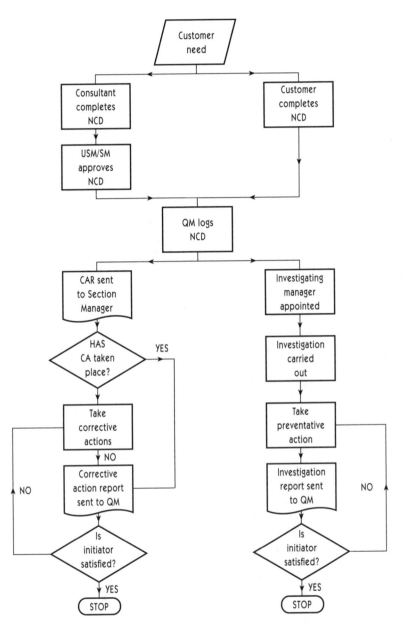

Figure 14.5 Flowchart: non-conformance identification and preventative action process

Check Lists

Check lists (sometimes called inspection or validation check lists) are used as prompts and aids to personnel. They highlight the key features of a process, equipment,

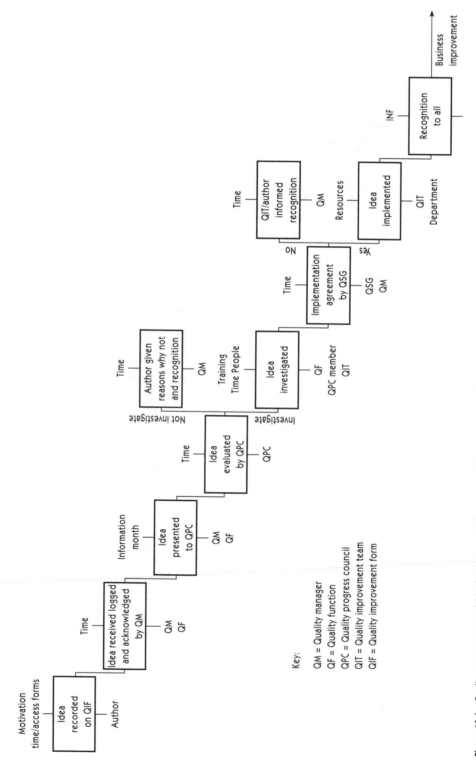

Figure 14.6 Quality management activity planning: quality improvement idea-customer needs awareness

system and/or product/or service to which attention needs to be given, to ensure that the procedures for an operation, housekeeping, inspection, maintenance, etc. have been followed. Check lists are also used in audits of both product and systems. They are an invaluable aid for QA and, as might be imagined, the variety and style and content of such lists are immense. Table 14.1 is used in the internal audit of the quality management system.

Table 14.1 Checklist – ISO9001

Document/record		QM-13 Ref
Quality Manual (QM-13) Boiling Water Treatment Feed Manual Cooling Water Treatment Feed Manual Pre-treatment Feed Manual Plant and Equipment Schedule	Maintained with all revisions	Para. 1.2.3
Customer service reports All filed at regional office and consultant's home office in client's files, separated and in chronological order	Countersigned by client Checked and initialled by unit sales manager Dates of visit/last visit Highlight non-conformities Stock levels Control limits	Para. 3.5 Para. 7.1.2
Quality plans Inside front cover of client's files at regional offices and consultant's home office	Must be reviewed on a minimum 12-month basis Checked and initialled by unit sales manager Plant, programme frequency of visits, etc.	
Non-conforming letters retained in client's files and also in a separate file or at least summary log	Issues as and when non-conforming situations are noted and as per guidelines reference interpretation of results	Para. 3.3
Client's files	Quotations/proposals containing quality plans Customer service reports Sales orders Laboratory reports, technical service reports boiler reports, etc. Non-conforming letters Complaints Audits	Para. 2.5 Para. 3.1 Para. 4.0 Para. 3.6 Para. 3.7 Para. 5.0 Para. 3.4
Calibration records	Held by consultant and regional offices Retain for five years Audit by unit sales manager every six months	Para. 3.2
Complaints	Follow procedures in Quality Manual (QM-12) Retain copies in client's files and also separate file for complaints Retain for five years	Para. 5.0
Home office audits	Once per year by unit sales manager	Para. 1.2.3
Random audits	Unit sales manager to make every six month for each consultant	Para. 3.7 (v)
Training records	Retain for five years	Para. 4.0 Para. 7.0

Here are the basic steps in constructing a checklist:

- Study the activity for which the checklist is to be drawn up.
- Drawing on observations of the process, discussions with operatives, and appropriate working instructions and procedures, construct the checklist.
- Walk the checklist through the process by following what happens at each stage.
- Ask the person who is carrying at the process to check its accuracy.
- Display it next to the process.
- Assess its use in practice.

Check Sheets

These sheets or forms are used to record data. The check sheet is a simple and convenient recording method for collecting and determining the occurrence of events. The events relate to non-conformities, including the position in which they appear on the non-conforming item (when used in this way they are sometimes referred to as a 'measles' chart or defect position or concentration diagram or areas for concern chart), non-conforming items, breakdowns of machinery and/or associated equipment, non-value adding activity or, indeed, anything untoward which may occur within a process. Check sheets are helpful in following the maxim of 'no checking or measurement without recording the data' and are effective in making the first attack on a problem.

They are prepared, in advance of the recording of data, by the operatives and staff being affected by a problem. Check sheets, in table, process, diagram or picture format, are extremely useful as a data collection device and record to supplement attribute quality control charts. The data from a check sheet provide the factual basis for subsequent analysis and corrective action. There are many different kinds of check sheets; figure 14.7 is an example of a check sheet.

Check item	Week no. Day						
	1	2	3	4	5	6	7
Warp board							
Board delamination							
Surface defect							
Incorrect board spec.							
Incorrect print density							
Shouldering							
Incorrect ink weight							
Off square feeding							
Print mis-registration							
Split bends							
Deep slots							
Narrow slots							
Ink smudging							

Figure 14.7 Check sheet: gluing/stitching department
Source: Rexam Corrugated North East Ltd

These are the main steps in constructing a check sheet:

- Decide the type of data to be illustrated. The data can relate to the number of defectives, the percentage of total defectives, the cost of defectives, the type of defective, process, equipment, shift, business unit, operator, etc.
- Decide which features/characteristics and items are to be checked.
- Determine the type of check sheet to use, i.e. tabular form or defect position chart.
- Design the sheet. Ideally, it should be flexible enough to allow the data to be arranged in a variety of ways. Data should always be arranged in the most meaningful way to make best use of it.
- Specify the format, instructions and sampling method for recording the data, including the use of appropriate symbols.
- Decide the time period over which data is to be collected.

Tally Charts and Histograms

Tally charts are a descriptive presentation of data which help to identify patterns in the data. They may be used as check sheets with attribute data (pass/fail, present/absent) but are more commonly used with measured or variable data (e.g. temperature, weight, length) to establish the pattern of variation displayed, prior to the assessment of capability and computation of process capability indices; see chapter 18 on SPC for details. Tally charts are regarded as simple or crude frequency distribution curves.

Statisticians tend to construct histograms rather than tally charts but, for general analysis purposes, they are more or less the same. A histogram is a graphical representation of individual measured values in a data set according to the frequency or relative frequency of occurrence. They take measured data from the tally sheet and display its distribution using the class intervals or value as a base – it resembles a bar chart with the bars representing the frequency of data. The histogram displays the distribution of data and, in this way, reveals the amount of variation within a process and/or other factors such as edited data and poor sampling techniques. There are a number of theoretical models which provide patterns and working tools for various shapes of distribution; the distribution most often encountered is called normal or Gaussian. Others may be skewed, bimodal, isolated island, etc.

Table 14.2 shows a tally chart and figure 14.8 is a histogram constructed from the data collected on the tally chart.

There are several ways of constructing histograms depending upon whether the data are discrete or continuous, whether they are single or grouped values, and whether there is a vast amount of data. The following guidelines are given for the treatment of continuous data of sufficient quantity that grouping is required:

- Subtract the smallest individual value from the largest.
- Divide this range by 8 or 9 to give that many classes or groups.
- The resultant value indicates the width or interval of the group. This should be rounded for convenience, e.g. 4.3 could be regarded as either 4 or 5 depending upon the data collected.
- These minor calculations are undertaken to give approximately 8 or 9 group class intervals of a rational width.

Table 14.2 Tally chart: effluent analysis – pH

pH	Frequency	Total
4.75–5.25		0
5.25–5.75		0
5.75–6.25	I	1
6.25–6.75	IIII	4
6.75–7.25	ЖН III	8
7.25–7.75	ЖН ЖН III	13
7.75–8.25	ЖН ЖН III	14
8.25–8.75	ЖН ЖН II	12
8.75–9.25	IIII	4
9.25–9.75	III	3
9.75–10.25	I	3
10.25–10.75		1

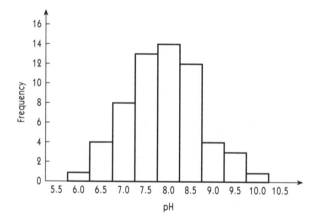

Figure 14.8 Histogram: effluent analysis – pH

- Each individual measurement now goes into the respective group or class.
- Construct the histogram with measurements on the horizontal scale and frequency (or number of measurements) on the vertical scale.
- The 'blocks' of the histogram should adjoin each other, i.e. there should be no gaps unless there is a recorded zero frequency.
- Clearly label the histogram and state the source of the data.

Graphs

Graphs, be they presentational (i.e. to convey data in some pictorial manner) or mathematical (i.e. one from which data may be interpolated or extrapolated), are used to facilitate understanding and analysis of the collected data, investigate relationships between factors, attract attention, indicate trends and make the data memorable. There is a wide choice of graphical methods available – line graphs, bar charts, pie charts, Gantt chart, radar charts, band charts – for different types of application.

Figure 14.9 shows a line graph which illustrates right first time production; figure 14.10 show a bar chart showing the same date and figure 14.11 is another bar chart, giving the reasons for quality control failure.

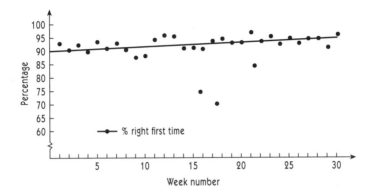

Figure 14.9   Scatter plot: 'Right first time' production

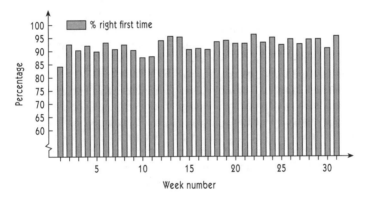

Figure 14.10   Bar chart: 'Right first time' production

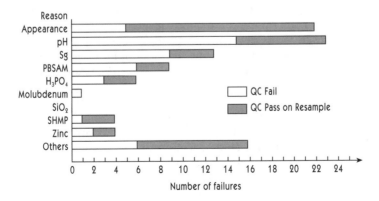

Figure 14.11   Reason for QC failures

These issues need to be considered in the construction of graphs:

- Using clear titles and indicating when and how the data was collected, i.e. the theme of the graphs and the source of data.
- Ensuring that the scales are clear, understandable and represent the data accurately.
- When possible, using symbols for extra data to provide clarity of explanation.
- Always keeping in mind the reason why a graph is being used, i.e. to highlight some information or data in strikingly and unambiguous way; anything which facilitates this objective is desirable.

Pareto Analysis

This technique is employed for prioritizing problems of any type, e.g. quality, production, stock control, sickness, absenteeism, accident occurrences and resource allocation. The analysis highlights the fact that most problems come from a few of the causes; it indicates what problems to solve and in what order, e.g. 'Juran's (1988), vital few and trivial many'. In this way, the improvement efforts are directed toward areas and projects that will have the greatest impact. It is an extremely useful tool for condensing a large volume of data into a manageable form, and in helping to determine which problems to solve and in what order. A Pareto diagram can be considered as a special form of bar chart, comprising a simple bar chart with a cumulative percentage curve overlaid upon it.

The analysis was labelled 'Pareto' after a nineteenth-century Italian economist Wilfredo Pareto who observed that a large proportion of the country's wealth was held by a small proportion of the population; hence, the generalized term or expression, 'the 80/20 rule'. Lorenz, early in the twentieth century and based on these observations, produced a cumulative graph for demonstrating the dominance of the '20%'. Juran, in the 1950s, using a similar analogy observed that a large proportion of quality problems were attributable to a small number of causes, i.e. 80% of the rejections are caused by 20% of the defect types.

The technique involves ranking the collected data, usually via a check sheet, with the most commonly occurring problem first and the least last. The contribution of each problem to the grand total is expressed as a percentage, and cumulative percentages are used in compounding the effect of these problems. The ranking of the problems is usually in terms of occurrence and/or cost – just because one defect type happens more frequently than another it does not necessarily mean that it is the costliest or the one that should be tackled first. The results are often presented in two ways: the ranked data as a bar chart and the cumulative percentages as a graph. Figure 14.12 shows such an analysis of the reasons for returned goods.

Pareto analysis, while simple in terms of its construction, is extremely powerful in presenting data; by focusing attention on the major contributor(s) to a quality problem it generates attention, efforts, ideas and suggestions to hopefully gain a significant overall reduction in these problems. It is not a 'once and for all' analysis. If used regularly and consistently, the presentational part of the technique is extremely useful in demonstrating continuous improvement made over a period of time.

Here are the basic steps in constructing a Pareto diagram:

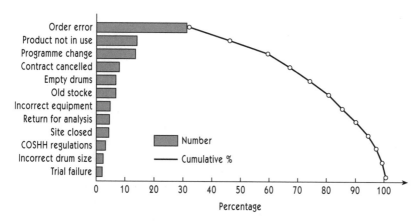

Figure 14.12 Pareto analysis: reasons for returned goods

- Agree the problem to be analysed.
- Decide the time period over which data is to be collected.
- Identify the main causes or categories of the problem.
- Collect the data using, for example, a check sheet.
- Tabulate the frequency of each category and list in descending order of frequency. (If there are too many categories, it is permissible to group some into a miscellaneous category, for the purpose of analysis and presentation.)
- Arrange the data as in a bar chart.
- Construct the Pareto diagram with the columns arranged in order of descending frequency.
- Determine cumulative totals and percentages, and construct the cumulative percentage curve superimposing it upon the bar chart.

Cause and Effect Diagrams

This type of diagram was developed by Ishikawa (1986) to determine and break down the main causes of a given problem. Cause and effect diagrams are often called Ishikawa diagrams and sometimes 'fishbone' diagrams because of their skeletal appearance. They are usually employed where there is only one problem and the possible causes are hierarchal in nature.

The effect (a specific problem or a quality characteristic/condition) is considered to be the head, and potential causes and sub-causes of the problem, or quality characteristic/condition to be the bone structure of the fish. The diagrams illustrate, in a clear manner, the possible relationships between some identified effect and the causes influencing it. They also assist in helping to uncover the root causes of a problem and in generating improvement ideas.

They are typically used by a QC, quality improvement team, Kaizen team, problem-solving team, etc., as part of a brainstorming exercise to solicit ideas and opinions as to the possible major cause(s) of the problem and, subsequently, to offer recommendations to resolve or counteract the problem.

It is important to define the problem or abnormality clearly, giving as much detail as possible to enable the identification of potential causes. This can be quite a difficult task, and the team leader must assume responsibility for defining a manageable problem – if it is too large it may need sub-dividing into a number of sub-problems – to ensure that the team's efforts and contributions are maximized in a constructive manner. There are three types of diagrams:

1 In the *5M cause and effect diagram*, the main 'bone' structure or branches typically comprise machinery, manpower, method, material and maintenance – the 5Ms. Often teams omit maintenance, and hence use a 4M diagram; others may add a sixth M (Mother Nature) and so use a 6M diagram. The 4M or 5M or 6M diagram is useful for those with little experience of constructing cause and effect diagrams and provides a good starting point in the event of any uncertainty. In non-manufacturing areas, the 4Ps (policies, procedures, people and plant) are sometimes found to be more appropriate.

    As with any type of cause and effect diagram, the exact format is not so important as the process of bringing about appropriate countermeasures for the identified and agreed major cause(s) for the problem.

2 The *process cause and effect diagram* is usually used when the problem encountered cannot be isolated to a single section or department. The team members should be familiar with the process under consideration; therefore, it is usual to map it out using a flowchart and to seek to identify potential causes for the problem at each stage of the process. If the process flow is so large as to be unmanageable, the sub-processes or process steps should be separately identified. Each stage of the process is then brainstormed and ideas developed using, for example a 4M/5M/6M format. The key causes are identified for further analysis.

3 The *dispersion analysis cause and effect diagram* is usually used after a 4M/5M/6M diagram has been completed. The major causes identified by the group are then treated as separate branches and expanded upon by the team.

Figure 14.13 shows an example of a cause and effect diagram for a non-value added work analysis carried out by a purchasing department.

Cause and effect diagrams are usually produced via a team approach and involve these basic steps:

- Define with clarity and write (in a box to the right-hand side) the key symptom or effect of the problem. Draw a horizontal line from the left-hand side of this box.
- Ensure that every team member understands the problem and, then, develop a clear problem statement.
- Decide the major groupings or categories for the causes of the effect; these form the main branches of the diagram.
- In a brainstorming session with all group members, speculate on causes of the effect and add these to the branches or sub-branches of the diagram.
- In a following session, discuss the causes and analyse them to determine those which are most likely to have caused the effect.
- Rank the most likely, or major causes of the problems, in order of importance. This can be done by Pareto voting; 80% of the votes should be cast for 20% of the causes. (If, for example, there are 35 causes, using the figure of

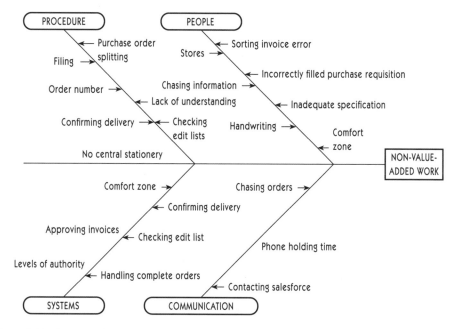

Figure 14.13 Cause and effect analysis: purchasing department non-value-added work analysis
Source: Grace Dearborn Ltd (1990)

20% this gives each member 7 votes to allocate to what they believe are the causes of the effect.)

- Gather any additional data needed to confirm the key causes.
- Decide upon improvement plans, actions, tests and experiments to both verify and address the key causes.

The conventional cause and effects diagrams have been developed and refined by Ryuji Fukuda (1990) at Sumitomo Electric; these are termed cause and effect diagrams with addition of cards (CEDAC) – the cards being used to reflect the teams continually updated facts and ideas.

Brainstorming

Brainstorming, a method of free expression, is employed when the solutions to problems cannot be deduced logically and/or when creative new ideas are required. It is used, as highlighted in the above discussion on cause and effect diagrams, with a variety of quality management tools and techniques.

Brainstorming works best in groups. It unlocks the creative power of the group through the synergistic effect – e.g. one person's ideas may trigger the thoughts of another member of the group – and, in this way, stimulates the production of ideas. It can be employed in a structured manner (in which the group follow a set of rules) or in an unstructured format (which allows anyone in the group to present ideas randomly as they occur).

Here are some factors to be considered when organizing a brainstorming session:

- Prepare a clear and focused statement of the problem.
- Form a group and appoint a leader/facilitator. A team will always produce a greater number of ideas than the same number of individuals working in isolation.
- Elect someone to record the ideas as precisely and explicitly as possible. Ideally, this is shown on a flipchart or on a white board to maintain a visible and permanent record.
- Review the rules of brainstorming, i.e. code of conduct:
  - Each member in rotation is asked for ideas.
  - A member can only offer one idea in turn.
  - The ideas are stated in as few words as possible.
  - Where a member has no ideas, they say 'pass'.
  - Strive for an explosion of ideas and build on the ideas of other group members.
  - Accept all ideas as given and record them. Questions are only asked to clarify issues.
  - No criticism, discussion, interruptions, comments or judgement are allowed.
  - Ideas are not evaluated during the brainstorming session.
  - Good-natured laughter and informality is encouraged, to enhance the environment for innovation activity.
  - Exaggeration maybe used since it adds humour and often provides a creative stimulus.

- Review the problems encountered in brainstorming, to prevent or to minimize their occurrence:
  - Attempting to evaluate ideas during brainstorming
  - Criticism of individuals and a lack of cohesion among group members
  - A person trying to play the role of an 'expert'
  - A tendency to state 'solutions' rather than possible 'causes'
  - Arguments
  - Side discussion and members trying to talk all together
  - Members shouting out ideas when it is not their turn
  - Poor management of the process, e.g. leader dominating the group
  - Sessions being too long
  - Failure to use flipcharts, whiteboards, etc. to display the data visually
  - Omission of ideas – the person noting the ideas suppressing those with which they disagree

- As ideas are suggested, write these down so that they can be seen by all members of the group.
- Allow the ideas to incubate for a period of time before they are evaluated.
- Determine the best ideas by consensus – this can be done in a number of ways: majority voting or polling, Pareto voting, paired comparisons, ranking on a scale of say 1 to 10, or each team member ranks the items in order of priority with 5 points given to the first idea and 3 and 1 points respectively to the second and third ideas, etc.

There are a number of variations on the classical brainstorming method:

- With *brainwriting*, each person writes down ideas on cards and these cards are placed to the right of the person. After a defined period of time and when stimulation is needed, a person takes cards from their left and uses the data on the card to both develop the idea and encourage new ideas.

- With *braindrawing*, when stimulation is needed, each person does a drawing of an idea and passes it to another person in the group who continues the drawing.

Scatter Diagrams and Regression Analysis

Scatter diagrams or scatterplots are used when examining the possible relationship or association between two variables, characteristics or factors; they indicate the relationship as a pattern – cause and effect. For example, one variable may be a process parameter – e.g. temperature, pressure, screw speed – and the other may be some measurable characteristic or feature of the product, e.g. length, weight, thickness. As the process parameter is changed (independent variable), it is noted together with any measured change in the product variable (dependent variable), and this is repeated until sufficient data have been collected. The results, when plotted on a graph, give a scattergraph, scatterplot or scatter diagram. In very simple terms, variables that are associated may show a linear pattern; those that are unrelated may portray an obvious or non-linear random pattern. An example of a linear scatter plot of an effluent analysis for solids/chemical oxygen demand is given in figure 14.14.

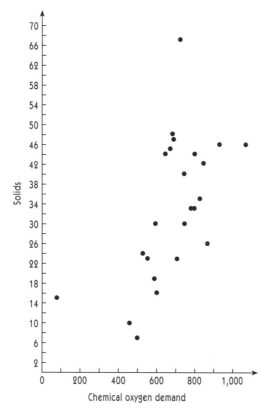

Figure 14.14 Scatter plot: effluent analysis – solids/chemical oxygen demand

Analysis should concern itself with the dispersion of the plots and if some linear, or known non-linear, relationship exists between the two variables. In this way, the scatter diagram is a valuable tool for diagnosis and problem solving. Regression analysis would subsequently be used to establish not only the equation of a line of 'best fit', but provide the basis for making estimates or predictions of, say, the product variable for a given value of the process parameter. In this way, it is possible to reduce the amount of data which is measured, collected, plotted and analysed.

How valid, or reliable, such estimates are, is largely a function of the degree of correlation which exists between the two variables (if indeed only two variables are under consideration), and whether the estimates are interpolated (i.e. from within the range of collected data) or extrapolated (i.e. outside that range).

Where there are more than two variables, multivariate regression analysis should be used; however, a good background of statistical knowledge is required to undertake this analysis.

The Seven Management Tools

Most of the so-called 'seven new management tools' of quality control have seen previous use in other than TQM applications, e.g. value engineering and value analysis, CPA, PERT, organizational analysis, so the choice of the term 'new' is unfortunate. These tools were developed by the Japanese to collect and analyse non-qualitative and verbal data, in particular, from sales and marketing, and design and development activities. In Japanese companies, these tools are typically used by QC in sales and design areas and in QFD. It is usual to find some of the tools used together (e.g. a systematic diagram being produced from the data contained in an affinity diagram). A brief description follows; a full description of these tools is outside the scope of this chapter – however, they are covered in detail by Mizuno (1988), Ozeki and Asaka (1990) and Barker (1989).

1: Relations diagram method (relationship diagraph or linkage diagram)

This is used to identify, understand and clarify complex cause and effect relation-ships to find the causes and solutions to a problem and to determine the key factors in the situation under study. They are also employed to identify the key issues to some desired result. Relations diagrams are used when the causes are non-hierarchic and when there are multiple interrelated problems; they tend to be used when there is a strong feeling that the problem under discussion is only a symptom. They allow the problem to be analysed from a wide perspective because a specific framework is not employed; hence they allow for the use of multi-directional rather than linear thinking. Relations diagrams can be considered to be a more free and broader version of a cause and effect diagram. Figure 14.15 shows an example in relation to the handling ability of a 'shrink bag' project.

Here are the major steps in constructing a relations diagram:

- The central idea problem or issue to be discussed is described clearly and accepted by those concerned.

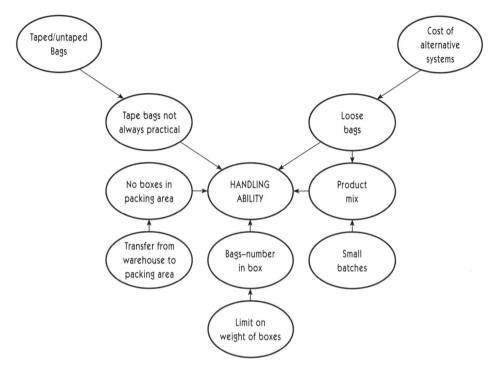

Figure 14.15 Relationship diagraph: shrinkbag handling ability

- Issues, causes and related problems which are believed to be affecting the central problem(s) are identified. These are written, in summary form on cards: one issue, cause or problem per card.
- The cards are then placed around the central problem/issue in a cause and effect relationship. This is done by placing the card believed to have the strongest relationship closest to the central problem/issue; other cards are ranked accordingly.
- The cause and effect cards are enclosed within rectangles or ovals, and arrows are used to highlight which causes and effects are related; the relationships is indicated by arrows pointing from cause to effect. The key cause and effects are emphasized by double lines, shading, etc.
- Appropriate revisions are made to the diagram.
- The resulting diagram is analysed for principle causes.

2: Affinity diagram method (KJ method)

This is used to categorize verbal and language data about previous unexplored issues, problems and themes which are hazy, uncertain, large, complex and difficult to understand, thereby helping to create order out of chaos. It is used in conjunction with, or as an alternative to, brainstorming and is useful when new thoughts and ideas are needed. This diagram uses the natural affinity between opinions and partial data from a variety of situations to help to understand and to structure the problem. It tends to be a creative, rather than a logical, process. The diagram helps to organize data, issues, concerns and ideas for decision making, and to reach solutions about previously unresolved problems. Figure 14.16 shows an example for the typical difficulties encountered in new product formulation.

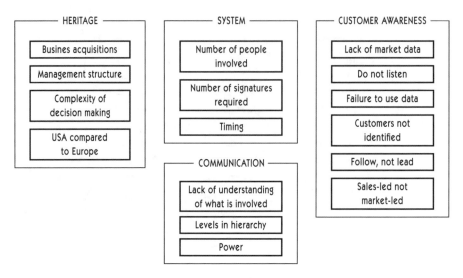

Figure 14.16 Affinity diagram: typical difficulties encountered with new product formulation

Here are the basic steps for developing an affinity diagram:

- Decide and clarify the theme, issue or opportunity.
- Collect whatever data is currently available on the theme. This could involve interviews with relevant personnel, customers, suppliers, etc., an examination of previously made notes and reports, brainstorming, encouraging people to express opinions, etc.
- Each idea, note, need, etc. is written on a card or 'Post-It' note.
- The card is placed in a random fashion on the table, board, wall or whatever means is being used to display the data.
- Those cards with related ideas are placed together and separated from the remaining cards. This development of related issues and natural clusters is often done by the team members moving the cards around the board in an atmosphere of silence. The idea of this is to allow the more creative right-hand part of the brain to be used. Team discussion can help to develop the individual statements, ideas, etc. on the cards within the cluster. Each group of cards are given a title which reflects the characteristics of its group; the group of stacked cards is then treated as one card. This group card is usually termed the affinity card.
- This process is repeated until all ideas are clustered within different groups.
- The group affinity cards, usually around 5 to 10, are arranged in a logical order and broad lines drawn around them.

3: Systematic diagram method (tree diagram)

This is used to examine, in a systematic manner, the most appropriate and effective means of planning to accomplish a task ('How to') or solving a problem; events are represented in the form of a root and branch relationship. It displays, in increasing detail, the means and paths necessary to achieve a specific goal or to clarify the component parts which lead to the root cause of a problem. They are used when the causes that influence the problem are known, but a plan and method for resolving the problem have not been developed. They can also be useful when a task has been considered to be simple but has run into implementation difficulties. A systematic diagram is usually used to evaluate several different methods and plans for solving a problem and, thereby, assisting with complex implementation. They are used to identify dependencies in a given situation and to search for the most suitable improvement opportunities, and when there are major consequences for missing key tasks. Figure 14.17 shows an example in relation to a project to eliminate waste.

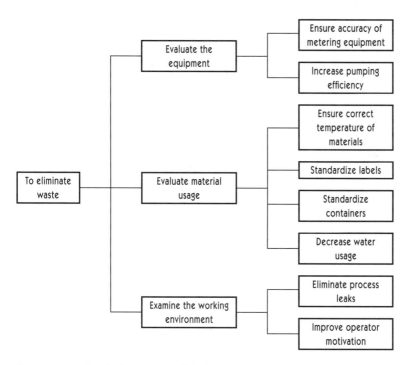

Figure 14.17 Systematic diagram: waste elimination

These are major steps in constructing a systematic diagram:

- The problem to be solved or task to be accomplished is written on a card. The card is placed on the left-hand side of the board, table, wall or what other means is being used to display the data.
- The primary methods and tasks to accomplish the objective or primary causes of the problem are identified. A typical question used in this identification is: 'To achieve the objective, what are the key means?' Each of these methods, tasks, etc. are written on a card and placed directly to the right of the problem statement. In this way, the first level of a root and branch relationship is created.

- Each primary method, task, idea, cause, etc. is treated as the objective and the previous step repeated with these secondary methods, etc. placed to the right of the ones to which they relate; in this way, forming the tertiary level. This process is then repeated until all the ideas are exhausted. It is unusual to go beyond four levels in development of the means.
- Working back from the right-hand side of the completed diagram through the levels, the relationship between objectives and means, or problem and causes is checked to ensure that the means and causes are each related to the objectives and problem respectively: 'Will such and such objective be accomplished if a particular method or task is implemented?'

4: Matrix diagram method

This is used to clarify the relationship and connecting points between results and causes or between objectives and methods and, by the use of codes, to indicate their relative importance and the direction of the influence. The diagram is also useful to draw conclusions between consequences and their causes. They are used when there are two sets of factors and methods which may have no relationship with each other, and when a cumulative numerical score is needed to compare or item to another. The factors are arranged in rows and columns on a chart with the intersections identifying the problem and its concentration; the intersecting points are the base for future action and problem solving. Seeing, in a graphical manner, the complete problem or picture and its essential characteristics and the actions which may impact on the problem is of considerable help in developing a strategy for solving the problem and in prioritizing present activities. Symbols are used to depict the presence and strength of a relationship between sets of data. There are a number of types of matrix diagrams – e.g. L-type, T-type, Y-type – each having a specific range of applications. Table 14.3 shows the structure of an L-type matrix for use by the purchasing department in eliminating non-value added work.

Table 14.3 L-type matrix: eliminating non-value-added work – purchasing department

Key function	Incorrect completion of forms	Sorting invoicing errors	Levels of authority	Chasing suppliers	Inadequate specification	Chasing information
Procedure						
Systems						
People						
Communication						

These are the major steps in constructing a matrix diagram:

- Decide the format of the matrix – L-type, T-type, C-type – and the characteristics, tasks, problems, causes, methods, measures, etc. to be mapped and displayed.
- Deciding how to arrange the problems and their causes. For example, an L-shaped matrix may be used for relating customer needs and design features. The customer needs are listed in the rows and the design features relating to each need are listed in the columns.
- Define and specify the symbols which are to be used to summarize a relationship.

- The relationships between, say, the needs and features or problems and causes, etc. are identified and discussed, and symbols used to indicate the strength of the relationship where a column and row intersects.
- Review the completed diagram for accuracy.

5: Matrix data analysis method

This is used to quantify and arrange the data presented in a matrix diagram in a clear manner. It is a numerical analysis method and employs techniques such as multivariate analysis.

6: Process decision program chart (PDPC) method

This is used to select the best processes to obtain the desired outcome from a problem statement by evaluating all possible events, contingencies and conceivable outcomes that can occur in any implementation plan. Considering the system as a whole, it is used to anticipate unexpected events and to develop plans, counter-measures and actions for such outcomes. It is used to plan each possible chain of events than need to occur when the problem or goal is unfamiliar, new or unique, in particular, when the stakes of potential failure are high. In this, it is similar to FMEA and FTA. However, it is claimed to be more dynamic than these two methods since the relationship between the initiating condition/event and terminating condition/event has been thought out and mapped. It is based on a systematic diagram and uses a questioning technique of, for example, 'What could go wrong?', 'What are the alternatives?' and the listing of actions or counter-measures accordingly. The PDPC has no prescribed set of rules. Figure 14.18 shows an example in relation to a bottleneck engineering problem.

These are the key steps in constructing a process decision program chart:

- Describe the problem.
- Identify the issues, anticipated results, likely undesirable outcomes, alternative solutions and approaches.
- Determine the relationships between the issues, solutions and desired goal. These relationships and events are arranged in chronological order, and indicated with arrows.
- In the event of a new problem, additional data, etc. that occurs, without prior warning, during the course of events, the process is reviewed and changes made to reflect the new set of conditions.

7: Arrow diagram method

This method applies systematic thinking to the planning and execution of a complex set of tasks. It is used to establish the most suitable plan, to schedule for a series of activities in a project, and to monitor its progress in an efficient manner so as to ensure adherence to the schedule. Arrow diagrams are necessary to describe the interrelationship and dependencies of tasks within a job or project which is complex. They are deployed at the implementation planning stage of a project. The sequence of the steps involved, and their relation to each other, are indicated by an arrow and, in this way, a network of activities is developed. This method, its form of construction, calculations and identification of critical path are well known and used in project

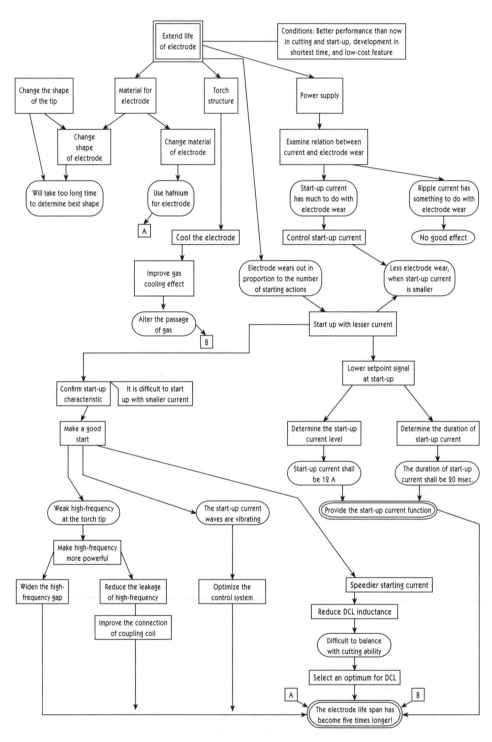

Figure 14.18 An example of a bottleneck engineering problem solved by the PDPC method
Source: Daihen Corporation

management in relation to CPA and PERT. Figure 14.19 shows an example of an arrow diagram constructed by quality improvement facilitators for a Quality Notice Board project.

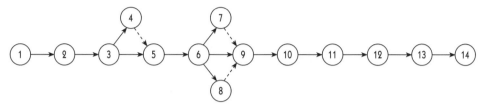

Activities Key

  1–2 Choose locations

  2–3 Assign responsibilities (deleted: facilitators will action)

  3–4 Determine size and configuration of displays needed

  3–5 Consider health and safety implications of potential locations

  5–6 Establish public relations departments' stock of displays and their avaiability

  6–7 Determine method of display (free-standing/wall-mounted)

  6–8 Determine preferred 'editorial content' of displays

  6–9 Action update of display contents

 7–12 Obtain costings for additional/alternative displays

 9–10 Source initial display items (e.g. graphs, photos, successes)

10–11 Agree format and action the 'design a logo' competition

11–12 Arrange for displays to be sited/mounted

12–13 Review cost implications

13–14 Seek verbal feedback from site employees

Figure 14.19 Arrow diagram: project quality notice boards-project management

These are the key steps in constructing an arrow diagram:

- Identify all the activities needed to complete the plan.
- Decide the feasible sequence of the activities – which activities must precede certain activities (consecutive activities), which activities must follow an activity (consecutive activities) and which activities can be done at the same time (concurrent activities).
- Arrange the diagram from left to right according to the above logic with each activity represented by an arrow.
- The beginning or end of an activity or group of activities is called an event or node. Represent these as circles at the tail and head of an arrow. Number the events in the same order as the activities occur.
- Indicate the time required for each activity, under the appropriate arrow.
- Analyse the network to find the critical path and to establish in which activities there is free time (float). This is achieved by determining the earliest and latest event times.

Departmental Purpose Analysis (DPA)

DPA is a structured quality management tool. Perhaps its main value is facilitating the internal customer – supplier relationship, determining the effectiveness of departments, and extending the quality improvement initiatives to non-manufacturing areas. The concept of DPA originated at IBM (Lewis, 1984). These are the key features of DPA:

- A departmental task analysis is undertaken to determine what a department needs to be achieve to meet the company objectives. In this way, a department's objectives are aligned to company objectives, and this helps to ensure uniformity of opinion on both departmental and company objectives.
- DPA identifies, in a clear manner, the purpose, roles, responsibilities and total contribution of a department to adding value to an organization's activities; non-value adding work is highlighted.
- DPA identifies the workload of departmental staff and the current utilization of skills.
- DPA describes the relationship between a department and its internal customers and suppliers.
- DPA provides the basis for applying and establishing performance measures by which a department can ensure that it is focusing on satisfying the needs and expectations of its internal customers. From the measurements, improvement objectives and targets can be agreed with all those concerned.
- DPA identifies interdepartmental problems which can be the subject of a cross-functional team.

Part of a DPA of a Sales Office is shown in tables 14.4 and 14.5.

Mistake-proofing

The mistake-proofing technique is used to prevent errors being converted into a defect. The concept was developed by Shingo (1986), and is based on the assumption that no matter how observant or skilled people are, mistakes will occur unless preventative measures are put in place. Shingo argues that using statistical methods is tantamount to accepting defects as inevitable, and that instead of looking for and correcting the causes of defective work, the source of the mistake should be inspected, analysed and rectified. He places great emphasis on what he calls 'source inspection', which checks for factors which cause mistakes, and then using Poka-Yoke or mistake-proofing devices to prevent their reoccurrence.

Mistake-proofing has two main steps: preventing the occurrence of a defect, and detecting the defect. In short, the purpose is to stop processes from operating when conditions exist that will lead to defects. The system is applied at three points in the process:

1 In the event of an error, prevent the start of a process.
2 Prevent a non-conforming product from leaving a process.
3 Prevent a non-conforming part being passed to the next process.

The mistake-proofing technique employs the ingenuity and skills, not only of the engineers and/or technical specialists, who may develop and fit the devices, but also of the operators who have first identified the cause for the mistake and then

Table 14.4 Departmental purpose analysis: sales office main tasks – suppliers

Task	What is the input?	Who provides it?	Is it right?	How can it be modified?
Taking of orders	Phone calls, telexes, fax messages, ansafone, postal orders	Clients, salespersons, unit offices	In the main yes, but some aspects such as packaging sizes, address detail, order numbers, are sometimes given with the assumption we know what is missing.	Personnel placing orders could be more explicit with details. Some detail could be checked at unit offices prior to passing to sales office. Ansafone could be replaced by the Wang electronic mail system.
Processing orders	Computer via VDUs and internal sales office order input form	Sales office	Yes, within our abilities and constant interruptions by phone calls and visitors, which by causing distractions, can lead to errors.	A CSP is in the system to assist with efficiency. Sales department could specify if the checking of product programme is required as some require it and others do not.
Answering enquiries and liaison with shipping & transport, warehousing & customer stores	Phone calls to engineering technical, purchasing, production, credit control, customer stores, shipping & transport and warehousing	Clients, unit offices & salespersons	Generally yes, but clients sometimes require miracles, are annoyed and sometimes abusive if they do not get them.	Sales office is manned 9 a.m.–5 p.m. Technical back-up and stores are often not available during the working day. Warehouse is unmanned after 4 p.m., which makes transport ineffective as they can only answer in the main based on information from the warehouse.
Daily booked order figures	Edit list	Computer Department	Yes	Computer could produce the same data but would have to run in parallel for one year while it built up a year's record.
Outstanding order list – Chemicals	Computer listing 106	Computer Department	No	Glassware & reagents should be on engineering list. Due date is required.
Outstanding order list – Engineering	Computer listing 109	Computer department	No	Glassware & reagents should be on this list, not on chemical list.
New account raising	Orders	Clients, Salespersons, Unit Offices	No	Sales office often get passed around in obtaining territory numbers; responsible sales units/offices should know their own prospects.
Process confirmatory orders	Postal orders	Clients, Unit Offices, Salespersons	No	These are confirmatory to verbal instructions. They are not required from unit offices and sales persons.

Table 14.5 Departmental purpose analysis: sales office main tasks – customers

Task	What is the output?	Who receives it?
Processing orders	A Works order set	Warehouse, stores, production control, purchasing & manufacturing plants
Answering enquiries and liaison with shipping & transport, warehousing & customer stores	Fast, accurate response	Clients, unit offices, salespersons, credit control, transport & stores
Daily booked order figures	Accurate booked sales figures	Sales management and Operations Management
Outstanding order list chemicals	That all booked orders are progressed to invoices	Sales office
Outstanding order list engineering	That all booked orders are progressed to invoices	Sales office
New account raising	The facility to process client orders	Sales office
Process confirmatory orders	Processed client orders	Sales office
Ordering and progress of engineering bought out items	Purchase requisitions and progress sheet	Engineering and purchasing departments
Price list maintenance	Special price lists	Sales office and sales management
Forward order diary	Orders raised to client's requirements	Sales office
Water treatment service and supervisory contracts	Memos annotated with account numbers and account special instruction facility displaying contract	Sales office and accounts department

participated in the corrective action measures. In Japanese companies, QC are very active in developing and using mistake-proofing devices. The devices may be simple mechanical counters which ensure that the correct number of parts are fed into a machine; they may be cut-off switches, limit switches or float switches which provide some regulatory control of the process or operation, and thereby stopping a machine or process automatically. They may be devices which prevent a part being incorrectly fed into the machine, assembled incorrectly, fabricated incorrectly, or placed incorrectly into fixturing. In other words, the assumption is made that, if the part can possibly be fed in wrongly, etc. it will be – unless some preventative measure is taken. This is the essence of mistake-proofing. It is usual to integrate the mistake-proofing device and signal with some audible, visual display or mimic diagrams and/or warning light to indicate that something has gone wrong.

Dale and Lightburn (1992), based on their research into mistake-proofing in a European motor industry supplier, offer some guidelines to organizations approaching the development of mistake-proofing:

- Mistake-proof at the earliest possible opportunity, certainly at the development stage and before any pre-production activities are undertaken.

- Involve manufacturing and quality department personnel in the R&D activity, and ensure that there is a forum for the discussion of manufacturing and design problems and their interfaces; cross-functional teams, and concurrent and simultaneous engineering should facilitate this.
- The design and process FMEA, analysis of customer reject returns, warranty claims, field failure reports, in-house scrap and rework, and inspection data should help to pinpoint potential problems that could be resolved by mistake proofing.
- It is much easier to mistake-proof new products than to develop devices for existing products.
- A team approach should be taken to study potential problems and the likely causes of mistakes, and the development of mistake-proofing ideas and devices. The team should be multi-disciplined and involve operators. Customers should also be involved, because this helps to build up relationships and provides concrete proof that long-lasting improvement actions are being taken. However, some suppliers are sensitive to their problems being exposed to customers.
- There should be some basic training in the principles, techniques, applications, and use of mistake proofing, as well as other activities like problem solving and team building.
- To broaden the experience to mistake-proofing techniques and applications, information should be shared with other companies using the concept.

Summary

Irrespective of the TQM approach chosen and followed, an organization will need to use a selection of tools and techniques to assist with the process of continuous improvement. It is recommended that the more simple tools and techniques such as QC7 are used in the beginning and to ensure that the tools and techniques which are currently employed are used effectively, before attempts are made to introduce other tools.

A planned approach for the application of tools and techniques is necessary. The temptation to single out one tool or technique for special attention should be resisted and, to derive maximum benefit from the use of tools and techniques, they should be used in combination. It should be recognized that tools and techniques play different roles, and management and staff should be fully aware of the main purpose and use of the tools and techniques they are considering applying in the organization; if this is not the case, they could well be disappointed if the tools or technique fails to live up to their expectation. It is also important to understand the limitations of how and when tools and techniques can best be used.

The tools and techniques should be used to facilitate improvement, and be integrated into the way the business works, rather than being used and viewed as bolt-on techniques. The way the tool or technique is applied, and how its results are interpreted, are critical to its successful use; a tool or technique is only as good as the person who is using it.

Tools and techniques, on their own, are not enough; they need an environment and technology which is conducive to improvement and to their use. An organization's CEO and senior managers have a key role to play in the effective use of tools and techniques:

- Developing their knowledge of the tools and, when appropriate, using them in their day-to-day activities and decision making
- Being fully aware of the main purpose and use of the particular tools and techniques which are being applied
- Delegating responsibility for their promotion to suitable individuals
- Maintaining an active interest in the use of tools and the results
- Endorsing expenditure arising from the education and training required and the improvement activities resulting from the employment of tools
- Recognizing and rewarding those employees who utilize tools and techniques in their day-to-day work activities

References

Barker, R. L. 1989: The seven new QC tools. *Proceedings of the First Conference on Tools and Techniques for TQM*, Bedford: IFS Conferences. 95–120.

Crossfield, R. T. and Dale, B. G. 1990: Mapping quality assurance systems: a methodology. *Quality and Reliability Engineering International*, 6(3), 167–78.

Currie, R. M. 1989: *Work Study*. London: Pitman.

Dale, B. G. and Cooper, R. 1992: Total Quality and Human Resources: An Executive Guide. Oxford: BPI.

Dale, B. G. and Lightburn, K. 1992: Continuous quality improvement: why some organisations lack commitment. *International Journal of Production Economics*, 27(1), 57–67.

Dale, B. G. and McQuater, R. E. 1998: *Managing Business Improvement and Quality: Implementing Key Tools and Techniques*, Oxford: Blackwell Publishers.

Dale, B. G. and Shaw, P. 1990: Failure mode and effects analysis in the motor industry: a state-of-the-art study. *Quality and Reliability Engineering International*, 6(3), 179–88.

Dale, B. G., Boaden, R. J., Wilcox, M. and McQuater, R. E. 1998: The use of quality management techniques and tools: an examination of some key issues. *International Journal of Technology Management*, 16(4,5,6), 305–25.

Fukuda, R. 1990: *CEDAC: a Tool for Continuous Systematic Improvement*. Cambridge, Mass.: Productivity Press.

Ishikawa, K. 1986: *Guide to Quality Control*. Tokyo: Asian Productivity Organisation.

Juran, J. M. 1988: *Quality Control Handbook*. New York: McGraw Hill.

Lewis, L. 1984: *Quality Improvement Handbook*. Havant, Hants.: IBM.

Mizuno, S. 1988: *Management for Quality Improvement; the Seven New Q.C. Tools*. Cambridge Mass.: Productivity Press.

Ozeki, K. and Asaka, T. 1990: *Handbook of Quality Tools*. Cambridge, Mass.: Productivity Press.

Shingo, S. 1986: *Zero Quality Control: Source Inspection and the Poka Yoke System*. Cambridge, Mass.: Productivity Press.

chapter fifteen

Quality Function Deployment (QFD)

I. Ferguson and B. G. Dale

Introduction

The QFD methodology was developed in Japan at Kobe Shipyard, Mitsubishi Heavy Industries as a way to incorporate knowledge about the needs and desires of customers into all stages of the design, manufacture, delivery and support of products and services. It arose out of a need to achieve simultaneously a competitive advantage in QCD. These, along with people and environmental factors, are the key performance measures of superior performing Japanese companies, and such organizations use QFD as a matter of course in design and new product development.

To take the conception of the product or service into reality requires choices of many aspects of product or service design, which means 'trading off' the high performance of one aspect of the design with another, so that the product will be successful for the business and also in the market. This requires good reliable benchmarked information available from several areas:

- Customer needs
- Functionality
- Costs and capital
- Reliability
- Reproducibility
- Manufacturing needs to satisfy postulated quantities per time period

These are critical demands of any design, and how well each separate demand is integrated within the whole determines the success of the product in meeting its horizons.

QFD is a technique which is used, in the first place, for translating the needs of customers and consumers into design requirements, being based on the philosophy that the 'voice of the customer' drives all company operations. In turn, these are translated into component parts and processes which are necessary for producing the end product. Consequently, the final product is one that has been driven by the voice of the customer. In carrying out activities, it uses a number of information collection, dissemination and decision-making techniques.

QFD is well suited to manage the integration of the techniques in the design process with its related matrices and focus on business and customer needs. Within the business plan, its function is to translate the needs of the customer and consumer into product and process design, and – through the related matrices of capital, cost and reliability – assure that the 'best choice' of parameters (such as functionality, reliability and reproducibility) are met. It employs a step-by-step approach from customer needs and expectations through the four planning phases:

- Product planning
- Product development
- Process planning
- Production planning through to manufactured products and delivered services

The technique of QFD seeks to identify those features of a product or service which satisfy the real needs and requirements of customers (market or customer required quality). A critical part of the analysis is that it takes into account discussions with the people who actually use the product:

- What do they feel about existing products?
- What bothers them?
- What features new products should have?
- What is required to satisfy their needs, expectations, thinking and ideas?

QFD is a systematic procedure which is used to help build in quality into the upstream processes and also into new product development. It thus helps to avoid problems in the downstream production and delivery processes and, consequently, shortens the new product/service development time. The concept helps to promote proactive rather than reactive development.

Figure 15.1 shows the close relationship that QFD, functional analysis, FMEA, FTA and DOE have with each other. Each technique provides information for the design process, to bring the required outputs to a reality.

Here are some of the major decisions which have to be made before QFD can be used:

- Deciding which functions and personnel should be represented on the team and who is to be the team leader – this applies, in particular, at the product planning stage
- Overcoming the usual issues of team members saying they are too busy to attend team meetings, so that the team fails to meet on a regular basis – the need for good teamwork practices should also be recognized as a critical element in the success of the QFD exercise
- Ensuring that the supporting tools and techniques of quality management are in place before QFD is used

This chapter now goes on to outline some of the fundamentals of QFD.

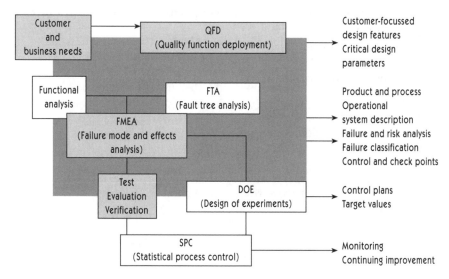

Figure 15.1 Integration and relationship of techniques
Source: Ian Ferguson Associates

Understanding Customer Needs

The voice of the customer is the cornerstone of QFD. Therefore, an important issue in carrying out a QFD exercise is to determine who actually is the customer and what is the market sector. The external customer can include companies in the supply chain, distributor, wholesaler, retailer and the consumer. However, as outlined in chapter 1, it should not be forgotten that there are also customers inside the organization, e.g. the related subassembly, manufacturing process, and those affected in the supply chain. It is important to identify the customer chain or hierarchy, as each level will have its own particular needs and bias. This hierarchy needs to be understood and, where necessary, allowed for in their interpretation with respect to the design. A list of needs from each level of the hierarchy will usually show some area of conflict and a decision on a trade-off, if any, will need to be made. The customer and consumer groups who are to be involved in the QFD exercise should be targeted, with factors such as type of users, age groups, areas and social factors being considered. A plan should be formulated for gathering the data in terms of the categories of customers to be contacted, resources needed for gathering the data and the methods to be used. There are a variety of methods for understanding customer needs, and preference should be given to the use of diverse, meaningful data. To talk and listen to the customer is paramount to understanding their real needs and requirements; therefore, of the three methods of achieving this, as outlined below, the preferred method is direct contact with the customer.

1   Direct contact with the customer
   • Customer questionnaires
   • Face-to-face discussions with customers
   • Consumer contact

2 Failure-related information (showing where customer needs are not being met)
- Field-failure data
- Warranty returns
- Customer complaints
- Consumer association reports

3 Surveys
- Market surveys
- Dealer information
- Trade shows
- Test marketing
- Product reports, as typically reported in trade magazines
- Product to market share trend information
- Competitive data

In using these methods for understanding customer requirements, here are some typical issues which need to be considered:

- What is wrong with the product and/or service?
- Which performance features delight the customer?
- When, by whom and how is the 'if only . . .' term used?

It is usual to express the customer needs in their original words and, then, to translate them into the technical language of the organization. Working with the original statements of the consumers and customers can be difficult; however this offers more insight into their needs and requirements. The reason for this is that they have not been forced to make a choice between the predetermined options that are inherent in a structured questionnaire type approach. These original statements will typically relate to a mixture of desires, problems, potential solutions to problems, dissatisfactions and negative statements as well as important items not stated. However, some interpretation of the customer's words will, at times, be necessary. The sorting of these often confusing statements, so that the wishes of the customer are understood, is crucial to the realization of a design which meets their needs and requirements. Affinity and tree diagrams – see chapter 14 – are extremely useful in facilitating this task.

As outlined above, by assembling customer needs in a systematic manner, three levels of customer expectation may be identified:

- The basic functional expectation
- The expectation of performance
- The unexpected items

However, it must be said that, in endeavouring to meet the objective of delighting the customer, conflicting issues often arise and some trade-offs need to be made in a logical manner.

Organizations which use QFD in an effective manner do so to identify product and service features (including additional features) which customers will find attractive and to help to 'charm and delight them'. It uses the customer voice to prioritize important from not so important features, and to separate generic from special features. In this way, differentiating quality characteristics, features and/or technical advantages can be established between the organization and its competition. These requirements, features and specifications which are identified can then be translated into design requirements as part of the product-planning phase and subsequently deployed through the other three phases to ensure that what is delivered to the customer truly reflects his or her wants or needs. In this way, it provides the mechanism to target selected areas where improvement would enhance competitive advantage.

QFD Road: The Main Steps

Stage 1: Product planning

These are the main objectives of the product planning phase:

- To identify customer requirements
- To determine competitive opportunities
- To determine substitute quality characteristics
- To pinpoint requirements for further study

In this way, it enables a complete picture – with a customer focus – to be taken of product and/or service.

An example of the 'house of quality' derived from the product planning phase of QFD is shown in figure 15.2. In simple terms, there are ten key elements of the product planning stage:

- The project
- Customer needs
- Customer priorities and competitive comparisons and planned improvements
- Design features or requirements
- The central relationship matrix – the whats vs hows
- Relative weights of importance
- Design feature interactions
- Target values
- Technical comparisons
- Service information and special requirements

The *project* to be studied in product development should be identified and defined by senior management, and the decision made to use QFD. The scope of the project should be clearly outlined, including targets, operating constraints and time-scales. Following on from this, a clearly defined mission statement should be produced, and a team formed. At this stage of the project, it is useful to create a business model which includes market definition and size, product life history, competitive products and prices, projected sales, prices and costs, and the estimated capital requirements and likely payback.

Customer needs: Gathering the voice of the customer can be done in the ways described earlier in this chapter: by formal questionnaires, focus clinics, direct questioning, listening in a prepared environment, etc. The information gathered in this way can be entered into a chart similar to that shown in figure 15.3, complete with

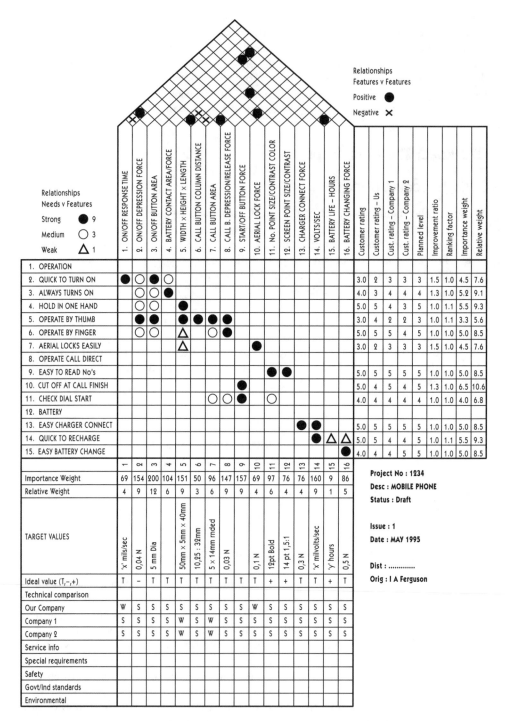

Figure 15.2 House of quality
Source: Ian Ferguson Associates

Customer classification EXTERNAL/INTERNAL	Voice of customer Actual information	Why needed	What	Who	When	Where	How
SOCIO ECONOMIC GROUP AGE SEX	SPOKEN or WRITTEN WORDS	The answer to: WHY do you want, need this product?	The answer to: WHAT is or will it be used for?	The answer to: WHO uses or will use it?	The answer to: WHEN do or will customers use it?	The answer to: WHERE do or will customers use it?	The answer to: HOW is or will the product be used?
1							
2							
3							
4							
5							

Figure 15.3 Gathering the voice of the customer and interpreting it into customer needs

Source: Ian Ferguson Associates

full information of why the product is needed, for what purposes, who uses it and when, and where and how it is used. This information provides the basis for more easily translating the customer's voice into customer needs which can be satisfied by design features. For example, 'Mainly men in the UK will use the mobile phone while on the move' will translate into the needs for that group of customers as a requirement: one-handed operation of the phone, including the ability to dial and hold from the same hand. The phone will then conveniently have design features of the width and depth of the mobile phone, button areas and depression forces, etc., see figure 15.2.

Once the customer statements have been produced and further rationale provided in terms of the why, what, who, etc. using the format shown in figure 15.3, this gives additional insights into the customer needs and market niche requirements. In relation to the case of the mobile phone, these statements and their back-up information now require bringing to a single and individual customer need from which a design feature can be developed with a target value assigned to it in order to satisfy the need. Thus, for example, 'using the mobile phone while on the move' has a special connotation with mobile phone size and depression forces as shown in figure 15.2.

A tree diagram and a fishbone diagram (see chapter 14) are useful tools for developing these customer needs to their lowest level. For further analysis and cross-referencing purposes, it is convenient to summarize the various needs into the lowest categories as shown in figure 15.4. Not only does this give assurance that the basic functional needs of the customer are understood, but those that are considered are the key performance, safety, reliability, and cosmetic related needs.

In some cases, it is necessary to understand the relationship between the various groups of customers and where, and when, and how frequently each group is involved with the particular need attributed to the product. Such analysis work can easily be drawn up from the information contained in figures 15.3 and 15.4.

The customer needs (whats), taken from the customer logic tree, and the means of satisfying them (i.e. the design features (hows)) are then entered in the house of quality (figure 15.2) from a table (see table 15.1) designed to ensure that each need has a design feature that can have a target value assigned to it.

The customer needs are those that are considered to be a priority of the customer; these are on a scale of 1 to 5 with those that are rated from 3 to 5 considered as important. The appropriateness to the particular house of quality will be taken into account, as will those unexpected or unusual needs, whatever their priority. In

Table 15.1 Customer need, design feature and target value matrix

	Customer needs	Design features	Target value
1	Quick to turn on	On/Off response Time	'x' mil.secs
		On/Off button area	5 mm dia
2	Always turns on	On/Off depress force	'y' N
		Battery contact force	'z' N
3	Hold in one hand	Width × length × height	50 × 5 × 40 mm
4	Operate by thumb	Call button area	14 mm dia

Source: Ian Ferguson Associates

Customer reference	Statement			Basic	Performance	Esteem	Safety	Reliability
	Level 1	Level 2	Level 3					
1								
2								
3								
4								
5								

Figure 15.4 Developing customer needs from analysis of customer statements
Source: Ian Ferguson Associates

determining customer needs, it is also important to establish a product and customer hierarchy as each level will have its own particular needs and bias. A list of needs from each level will usually show some areas of conflict and a decision on a trade-off, if any, will need to be made.

Customer priorities and competitive comparisons and planned improvements are the key to prioritization and decision making on critical design features, which will be a common thread throughout all the stages of the QFD process.

The columns in figure 15.2 are used as follows:

1   *Degree of importance*: Information gathered during customer surveys together with team knowledge is the key for grading each 'need' on a scale of 1 to 5 with 5 being the most important.

2   *Our company rating*: Listed here is an objective view of the company's standing against each customer need from the perception of the customer on a scale of 5 to 1 with 5 being very good and 1 being poor. As much information as can be obtained from impartial sources should be used in this analysis.

3/4   *Competitors' rating*: Similar sources as used in 2 will obtain this information for the major competitors. Benchmarking should be used to supplement the information acquired in this way.

5   *Planned level*: This is the company's strategy for the new or modified product, influenced by competitive issues and strategic policy objectives.

6   *Improvement ratio*: This is obtained by dividing the planned level by the company rating.

7   *Sales point*: A maximum of 1.5 is given for a strong marketing feature down to 1.0 for the expected features. Only 2 or 3 such points should feature in this analysis. It is in this analysis that 'excitement' qualities are taken into consideration.

8   *Importance weight*: This is the result of multiplying the degree of importance by the improvement ratio and by the sales point.

9   *Relative weight*: This figure is obtained by taking each importance weight as a percentage of all the weights.

Design features or requirements provide is a very challenging step for engineers. The key is to look for characteristics, features and technical requirements that express the customers' needs, rather than finite design specifications. This assists in examining the best option for a number of criteria.

The central relationship matrix – the whats vs hows: The centre block of the house of quality shown in figure 15.2 represents the relationship strength of each customer need with every design feature. The solid circle symbol representing a strong relationship, the open circle a medium relationship, and the triangle a weak relationship. These relationships are usually equated to numerical numbers of 9, 3, and 1 respectively. The difference between them representing a means of emphasizing a design feature that is very important to one that is less so.

If there is no relationship between a customer need and a design feature, this will be highlighted by an empty row, indicating that the need will not be satisfied. On the other hand, if there is no relationship between a design feature and a customer need, this will result in an empty column, indicating that the design feature is not necessarily required from a customer perspective.

Relative weights of importance: this calculation indicates the strength of each design feature required in relation to other design features, the priority from the customer's perspective of the need that created the design feature. To achieve these two parts, the weight of importance of each design feature is the product of the relative weight of the customer need and the particular relationship that has been designated in the central matrix.

Design feature interactions: each design feature needs reconciling with other design features. This is recorded in the roof of the house of quality. Its purpose is to relate the interactions to the proposed target values of design features. A positive relationship is an opportunity to reduce a value that may help to reconcile an interacting negative relationship. Negative relationships require determined design alternatives to weaken the relationship; they are potential sources of conflict and QA problems.

Each design feature should have a *target value* assigned to it in order, which can act as a benchmark in the choice of design concepts at a later stage in the process. The target value will normally be best in class and one that will satisfy the customer to the point of delight. The values are not design specifications and could well be enhanced as the QFD process proceeds. They will certainly be equal to or better than any competitively benchmarked design. These target values may be modified in the light of the information contained in the roof of the house. The reconciliation between relationships is helped by declaring the feature that is a constraint and adjusting the other value according to its ideal value.

Technical comparisons are made with the design features, both from the company's existing product range and also those of the competitive ones which are under investigation.

The comparisons may be made on some form of quantitative scale or on a 'Same', 'Better', and 'Not so good' type basis. Reference will be made to competitive designs where the feature has a higher assessment and, if this cannot be bettered, it should be adopted. The customer's evaluation of the company's product and that of its competitors should also be considered. In theory, the engineer's technical evaluation and the customer's evaluation should agree. If this is not the case then the target value chosen is not perceived as the best one.

Service information and special requirements: service information affecting design features from warranty, complaints, field failures, defect records, internal quality costs, product performance, etc. is recorded. The purpose of this is to ensure that concepts and design work later in the process will eliminate these faults. Safety items, special regulatory items, and environmental issues affecting any design feature are also recorded. The purpose of this is that any concept or product definition must be seen to satisfy these requirements.

Deploying Customer Needs into Product and Process Definition

Figure 15.5 highlights some of the aspects which need to be taken into account, in particular, the main linkages.

Stage 2: Product design, concurrent to a degree with Stages 3 and 4

The product planning carried out in stage 1 enables a variety of critical design features to be derived which reflect the needs of the customer. This second stage

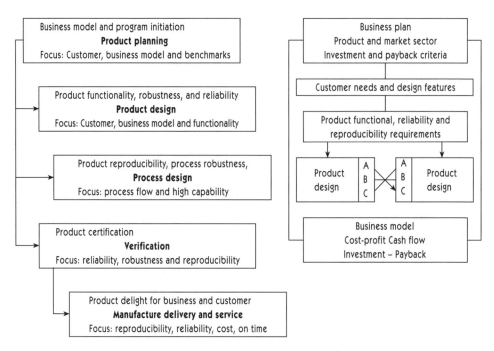

Figure 15.5 Customer needs deployed into product and process definition
Source: Ian Ferguson Associates

involves translating the stage 1 design features into component part design features or characteristics.

One aspect of the power of QFD is to enable the customer-derived design features to be reconciled with the product functional requirements. In addition to this, QFD demands that all the relationships between functional requirements and part features are understood. A part feature that is required to carry out many functions will be more of a risk, in the accomplishment of its task, than a part feature with only one function to perform.

The output of this stage is a set of target values for part features. These values – together with other sets from the customer-derived design features, reliability engineering, and process design characteristics from stages 3 and 4 – form a standard by which any concept of product design, existing or new, may be judged as to whether or not it meets all the required criteria.

The final task of stage 2 is to prioritize the part characteristics of the chosen concept from a customer's point of view. This should ensure that process designers are in no doubt as to those features which must be reproduced to a high capability in the manufacturing processes. A product design is not a design if it cannot be manufactured. Accordingly, product concepts leading to designs are, at this stage, subjected to processability, risk and cost analysis. Product design decisions are best taken concurrently with process design decisions, see BS7000-1 for further details.

By deriving critical design characteristics of both product and process design the QFD process is ideally suited to provide critical functions that should be treated as part of the FMEA process of risk analysis, see figure 15.6.

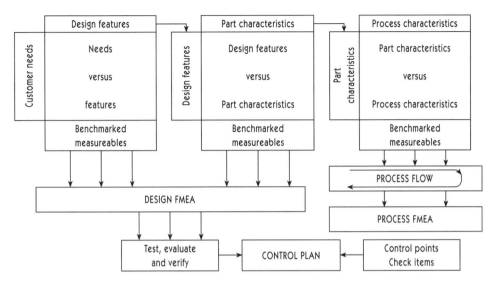

Figure 15.6 Quality function deployment and reliability
Source: Ian Ferguson Associates

Stage 3: Process design, concurrent to a degree with stages 2 and 4

This third stage ensures that the part characteristics identified as a priority are related to process characteristics, whose target values will ensure their reliability and reproducibility. The process design – which may be an existing process, an existing process with additions and modifications, or a completely new process – will be the subject of intense cost and risk analysis.

The output of the stage will be a prioritized list of process characteristics which the production operating system of stage 4 will be capable of reproducing with a high degree of capability.

Stage 4: Manufacturing operating systems

The purpose of this stage is to ensure that operational production planning uses those systems which are complete, reliable and which will give the high capability requirements that have been identified in stage 3. This involves areas such as operational specifications and control plans, training, preventative maintenance, gauging methods, audit inspections and SPC.

This section has just provided an overview of the mechanics of QFD. For those wishing to develop their knowledge of QFD, see Akao (1990), Bossert (1991), Ferguson (1992, 1995), Eureka and Ryan (1988) and QFD Symposium Transactions: 1990 to 1998.

The Benefits of the Four-stage Approach

The four-stage integrated approach outlined above – with the customer needs and priority ratings reflected at each stage by the use of integrated importance weights

– ensures that what is being moulded, machined, coated, filled, assembled, etched, etc. at the manufacturing stage, will more than meet the customers' needs and requirements when they receive the product. This is a sound basis for advanced quality planning.

The analysis is progressive and can be stopped at any of the four stages. However, the experience from the Japanese companies is that the greatest benefit is derived when all stages are completed, and the process is carried out in an integrated manner. Each stage obviously has a use and a value of its own, but one stage by itself is limited in its impact with the customer. Thus the stage 1 house of quality is extremely useful in understanding customer needs and properly identifying their key priorities. The needs are then developed into design features and provide an excellent opportunity to assess target values chosen in comparison with customers' perception and competitive products. However, if the product and process design work thereafter is not integrated, all the knowledge and understanding which has been generated can lead to the development of a product with reliability or cost problems.

A multi-disciplinary team is used to prepare the QFD. The membership of the team is likely to change depending on the stage of QFD being addressed. A number of the seven new quality control tools (i.e. relations diagram, affinity diagram, matrix diagram and systematic diagram) are also used to assist with the QFD process.

Difficulties Associated with QFD

Here is a summary of the main difficulties which are typically experienced with QFD:

- Determining who is the customer and identifying their needs, in particular, when the market is new, the customer is not certain of what they want, and knowledge of the market is sketchy – also, related to this, reconciling the various customer needs at various levels in the supply chain
- A belief that QFD cannot begin until customer needs have been totally defined, leading to a loss of momentum
- Customer information gathered by Marketing Department alone, causing difficulty for engineers to interpret the customer needs
- Deciding which chart format best suits the project under consideration
- The development of matrices which are too large
- Failure to extend QFD past the product planning stage thereby missing the integration of best performance with reliability and cost
- Mixing of whats with hows and hows with whats
- Skipping some of the steps and failing to pay attention to detail
- Not addressing fully the issues arising from analysis of the various matrices
- No internal feedback of the findings
- Too wide a scope of project, causing difficulty of focus
- A desire by engineers to arrive at a design specification too soon, thereby closing out other potential worthwhile options
- Non-attendance at meetings, and shifting priorities

Here are some issues which can help to overcome the difficulties:

- Team-based training on the project being tackled, followed up by regular facilitation by an outside expert
- A logical system of collecting customer information
- Adequate analysis undertaken over the complete range of customer needs
- Using the expertise of team members to overcome any inertia in identifying customer needs and requirements
- Making full use of relevant data on warranty claims, field failures, previous products and competitive data so as to develop target specifications
- Ensuring that the QFD charts and matrices are incorporated into the organization's systems and used on an ongoing basis
- Refining the analysis by sharing the data with customers and any subsequent discussions which may take place

Implementation of QFD

These are the key steps in the effective implementation of QFD.

- Management issues

  - The process must be driven by senior management.
  - Appropriate resources and the provision of training need to be allocated and actioned by management.
  - Appoint a steering committee and a QFD champion.
  - Use a project management system to act as a communication vehicle.

- Project issues

  - Select the first project with a limited time frame and a good chance of an early success.
  - Establish a time frame for the project from the outset, and keep to it.
  - Have a clear project definition and objectives and always have them in view; it is also important to identify any project limitations and operating constraints. This helps to create a focus on what is being done.
  - Develop a clear market definition and business model.
  - Provide a glossary of terms used in the QFD process.

- The QFD team

  - Train as a team, using as many as company specific examples as possible.
  - Establish a core team, which is multi-disciplined, of 5–7 people.
  - Hold regular team meetings with a short time duration.
  - Do detailed work outside the meeting and use the meeting for analysis, and decision making. It is important that each member of the team is prepared to make a significant time commitment to the project.
  - One of the cornerstones of QFD is the customer's voice – it is best for all the team to be part of the data collection process which is involved in listening to that voice.
  - It takes longer, but consensus decisions generally work best.
  - Team energy can be created by paying attention to direction, structure, project management and human issues.

- Methods of working
  - Do as much concurrent work as possible, e.g. competitive benchmarking with existing product and process designs.
  - Create a planning matrix of customer needs to decide what should go into a house of quality; some items will be better achieved by traditional means.
  - Keep a realistic perspective on the detail entered about customer needs. Focus on the important, the difficult, and the new.
  - Try to ensure that the house of quality is kept to within an approximately 30 × 30 matrix.
  - Use customer's voice and benchmarks as major decision makers to achieve best in class.

Summary

The QFD process provides a powerful structure for product and process develop-ment. When used in an effective manner, it can bring a correct customer focus to designs that will perform to a high degree of satisfaction with reliability and cost worthiness. It shortens the development cycle for the design, and results in fewer engineering changes. In this way, the product/service which the customer receives not only meets their needs but, if the customer interface has been done correctly, there can be unexpected product features which will cause delight and product loyalty. There will also be a common thread through all operations which is trace-able back to what the customer really wants.

The discipline of the various matrices used in QFD is to ensure that, apart from satisfying the customer, designs giving optimum performance, reliability and max-imizing the value-to-customer ratio are achieved. The application of clear objectives, logical thinking and analysis by the team using the QFD methodology as a frame-work, will help to achieve these goals. A by-product of this type of activity is that it promotes teamwork across functions and levels of the organizational hierarchy.

Understanding customer needs and the acceptable value to cost ratio is an effect-ive means of developing a product which will gain market share. The logical integ-rated planning disciplines involved with the QFD framework replaces the 'quick fix' approach to design and new product development. With perseverance to detail, QFD will help to bring products to market on time, which are best in class, and ensure product acceptability both from the market and producer.

The use of QFD is not a magic wand. It is a methodology and, by itself, it will not solve bad designs, eliminate waste, solve resource problems, prevent engineering changes being made, etc. It requires a realistic programme and an understanding that it needs considerable attention to detail. Moreover, management commitment, an adequate understanding of the technique, cross-functional teamwork, good train-ing, and an effective champion are vital ingredients for success.

References

Akao, Y. (ed.) 1990: *Quality Function Deployment: Integrating Customer Requirements into Product Design*. Cambridge, Mass.: Productivity Press.

Bossert, J. L. 1991: *Quality Function Deployment: A Practitioners Guide.* New York: Marcel Dekker.

Eureka, W. E. and Ryan, N. E. 1988: *The Customer-Driven Company: Managerial Perspectives on QFD.* Michigan: ASI Press.

Ferguson, I. 1992: Delighting the customer. *Manufacturing Breakthrough*, September/October, 277–84.

Ferguson, I. 1995: *Quality Function Deployment: Developing a Color TV.* Michigan: QFD Institute Transactions.

chapter sixteen

Design of Experiments (DOE)

I. Ferguson and B. G. Dale

Introduction

DOE are a series of techniques which involve the identification and control of parameters which have a potential impact on the performance and reliability of a product design and/or the output of a process with the objective of optimizing product design, process design, process operation, and limiting the influence of noise factors. The methodology is used when an analysis of the effect on system outputs of different values of design parameters is required. The objective is to optimize the values of these design parameters to make the performance of the system immune to variation. The concept can be applied to the design of new products and processes, or to the redesign of existing ones. These are the objectives:

- To optimize product design, process design and process operation
- To achieve minimum variation of best system performance
- To achieve reproducibility of best system performance in manufacture and use
- To improve the productivity of design engineering activity
- To evaluate the statistical significance of the effect of any controlling factor on the outputs
- To reduce cost

DOE techniques, in particular for process improvement, involve the identification and control of those parameters or variables (termed factors) which have a potential influence on the output of a process, choosing two or more values (termed levels) of these variables and running the process at these levels. Each combination of factors and levels or experimental run is called a trial. The basic idea is to conduct a small number of experiments with different parameter values and to analyse their effect on a defined output such as plating thickness. Based on the analysis, a prediction of system performance can be made.

This chapter explores some of the fundamentals and mechanics of DOE. Those seeking more knowledge of the topic should consult the specialists texts: Barker (1990), Bendell et al. (1990), Lochnar and Matar (1990) and Taguchi (1986) and the design of experiment course notes of Ferguson (1995).

Methods of Experimentation

Most people in business, to a greater or lesser, experiment in some way. For example, adjusting a variable to produce a desirable result, taking an action to discover a reaction and testing an hypothesis. There are a number of methods of experimentation – trial and error (the step-by-step method of changing one factor at a time), full factorial (i.e. the classical method) and fractional factorial. One of the objectives of industrial experimental design is to be confident that a difference in output attributable to a change in the level of a factor is significant in relation to any experimental error and other factors that were part of the experimental design.

Trial and error method

The trial and error method usually means unsystematic changes of factor levels using the experience of the experimenter(s) as the guiding principle. The first experiment is run with all the factors at the first chosen level and the results of the run are recorded. The second experiment is run by changing the first factor to its second option and again recording the results of the run. Then keeping this factor at that optimum level, variations are made to another factor to find its optimum with the other factors being kept constant, and so on. Assumptions are then made about the preference for the lower or higher levels for each of the factors. This approach is familiar and easy to use and understand. However, it is widely criticised not least for the fact that no information is provided about any interactions which may occur between any two of the factors tested and so reproducibility is poor. It is also inefficient, resource intensive and costly. In addition, it is not easy to hold, from experiment to experiment, the factors constant and this in itself creates variation.

Full factorial method

The full factorial approach is to consider all combinations of the factors which are being tested. In this way, all possible interactions between the factors are investigated to find the best combination. For example, three factors with two levels each (i.e. level 1 and level 2) would need 2^3 (= 8) trials, as shown in table 16.1.

Table 16.1   The full factorial method

Trial number	Control factors		
	A	B	C
1	1	1	1
2	1	1	2
3	1	2	1
4	1	2	2
5	2	1	1
6	2	1	2
7	2	2	1
8	2	2	2

Source: Ian Ferguson Associates

This may be feasible for a small number of factors and when experimentation is easy, but even with, say, seven factors at two levels, the minimum number of trials would be 2^7 (= 128). Despite the fact that both the main effects and interactions can be measured in a thorough and pure scientific manner, the time and costs associated with running such a large number of experiments is usually considered to be prohibitive and unrealistic in industrial situations. Also, much of information obtained from the trials would be from combinations of factors which are of little of practical value. This problem may be overcome by the use of fractional factorial designs.

Fractional factorial

To overcome the disadvantage of the number of trials necessary in a full factorial design, factional factorial designs are used where the chosen fraction of the full design gives an even and balanced spread throughout all the factors being studied. Typically a quarter of the 128 experiments required for seven factors at two levels would involve just 32 experiments.

It was three Englishmen who took the lead on this problem of experimental size: Fisher (1925) in the 1920s primarily in agriculture, and Plackett and Burman (1946) in process-orientated manufacturing in the 1940s. Their method of experimentation was to change several factors at the same time in a systematic way so as to ensure the reliable and independent study of the main factors and interaction effects. They constructed orthogonal arrays with a limited number of runs as a subset of the full factorial layout. The subsets are 'balanced' in terms that an even number of each level of each factor is tested during the running of the experiment, i.e. the array is balanced between columns rather than between trials. The technique of orthogonal arrays enables the size of the experiment to be reduced to a practicable level by carrying out only a fraction of the total number of combination of factors. However, in doing this, interaction information will be sacrificed. It is therefore important to use the technical knowledge of those involved in the experiment to ensure that this loss of information is relatively insignificant. A typical Fisher array is shown in table 16.2.

Table 16.2   A typical Fisher array

Runs	Factors						
	A	B	C	D	E	F	G
1	1	1	1	1	1	1	1
2	1	1	1	2	2	2	2
3	1	2	2	1	1	2	2
4	1	2	2	2	2	1	1
5	2	1	2	1	2	1	2
6	2	1	2	2	1	2	1
7	2	2	1	1	2	2	1
8	2	2	1	2	1	1	2

Source: Ian Ferguson Associates

It can be seen that, in the array, the columns represent the independent variables or factors to be studied and tested at one of two levels, and the rows represent the tests or experiments to be performed. In an experiment which has eight experimental runs (i.e. L_8), the first option or level of factor A, A_1 is tested four times, and the second option or level of factor A, A_2 is also tested four times. In addition to this, during the experimental run, the array tests all the combinations of options or levels of any two factors. Thus, A_1 is tested against both B_1 and B_2, as well as A_2 similarly testing B_1 and B_2. The other property that orthogonal arrays have, due to their full factorial heritage and balance, is the ability to study the effects of interactions between factors. The number of interactions that can be studied is dependent on the size of the array.

The simple analysis of an orthogonal array is done by averaging the responses that are applicable to the level of each factor. Therefore, in the Fisher array shown in table 16.2, factor A_1 is given by averaging the results obtained from running experiments numbers 1 to 4 and factor A_2 by averaging the results obtained from running experiments numbers 5 to 8. The difference between level 1 and level 2 of each factor is an indication of the significance of that factor in influencing the response measured. Generally, the larger the difference, the greater the significance.

Analysis of the orthogonal array enables the strength of each level of each factor to be measured, and their relative significance in influencing the designated output (e.g. bond strength) to be assessed. Analysis of variance is used to estimate the significance that any factor has in influencing the measured response in relation to 'error' (e.g. measurement and inconsistency in the setting of factor levels) in the experimental system.

The efficiency of these orthogonal arrays in addition to the L_8 already described, is further illustrated by the example of L_4 (3 independent factors at two levels and involving four experimental runs), L_{12} (11 factors at two levels and 12 experimental runs) and L_9 (4 factors at three levels and nine experimental runs. The experiments are not necessarily performed in the order of 1, 2, 3, 4. Instead, the preference is to perform them in random order, unless it is advisable that they be carried out in sub groups. Undertaking the runs in random order is the best way to protect the experiment from the occurrence of unforeseen changes.

The arrays suggested by Taguchi (1986) gives economies of scale and time in the cost of experimentation. They are also practical to use in a team environment; then maximum use is made of technical knowledge which exists within the team for detail such as the choice of factors, the setting of the levels, whether to study an interaction between factors, and not least the choice of responses of the experimental runs. There are a small number of orthogonal arrays or experimental designs that constitute a fundamental set of arrays; they are sometimes referred to as the 'cookbook'.

The following experiment outlines the concept of orthogonal arrays. It concerns part of the process used in the pharmaceutical industry in the manufacture of medicines in tablet form. To produce uniform tablets in terms of size and content, the initial process of mixing the drug solution and the carrying medium is paramount. It is vital that the particle size, the even distribution of the drug (content uniformity) and the moisture content are controlled with small variation around the target value prior to feeding into the tablet making part of the operation. The three measured responses are therefore particle size, content uniformity, and moisture content. Table 16.3 shows the layout of the experiment; the orthogonal array is an L_8. The results of each experimental run from the particular combination of the factors in

Table 16.3 Experimental layout – powder granulation

	Control factors	Level 1	Level 2
A	Mixing speed	High	Low
B	Drying temperature	High	Low
C	Chopping speed	Long	Short
D	Drying mechanism	Type A	Type B
E	Drying time	Long	Short
F	Mixing time	Long	Short
G	Solution addition rate	Fast	Slow

Source: Ian Ferguson Associates

Table 16.4 Results of experimental runs

	A	B	C	D	E	F	G	Particle size
1	High	High	Long	Type A	Long	Long	Fast	3.8
2	High	High	Long	Type B	Short	Short	Slow	4.5
3	High	Low	Short	Type A	Long	Short	Slow	5.3
4	High	Low	Short	Type B	Short	Long	Fast	4.9
5	Low	High	Short	Type A	Short	Long	Slow	4.4
6	Low	High	Short	Type B	Long	Short	Fast	2.9
7	Low	Low	Long	Type A	Short	Short	Fast	2.3
8	Low	Low	Long	Type B	Long	Long	Slow	3.6

Source: Ian Ferguson Associates

the run are given in table 16.4. The results of each experiment are an average from a satisfactory sample size.

The experiment will indicate the combination which gives the best result, but there may be a better combination; this is done by analysing the effect of each factor. The output or response of the relevant experiment where the information occurs is simply added up and averaged so that comparisons may be made between level 1 and level 2 of each factor. Comparisons of the relative difference between level 1 and level 2 and between each factor can then be made as to the significance of each factor in affecting the response or output of the experiment. An example of the calculations made is shown in table 16.5. The average of the experimental run is 3.96.

Because of the balanced construction of the orthogonal array, it is permissible to view the significance of each of the factors, relative to each other in terms of their effect on influencing the value of the output or response, in this case 'particle size'; see table 16.6. Thus mixing speed (A), solution addition rate (G), chopping speed (C) and mixing time (F) have the greatest effect in that order, and drying time (E) and drying temperature (B) are, in this example, of no relative significance at all. It is helpful to look at these effects graphically and in comparison with the factorial effect on the variation of the responses within the sample of each experimental run. The other useful property that the balance of the array gives is the additive effect of each of the main control factors in the value of the response, beyond the

Table 16.5 Response table – means

$$A1 = \frac{1}{4}(3.8 + 4.5 + 5.3 + 4.9) = \frac{18.5}{4} = 4.625$$

$$A2 = \frac{1}{4}(4.4 + 2.9 + 2.3 + 3.6) = \frac{13.2}{4} = 3.300$$

$$B1 = \frac{1}{4}(3.8 + 4.5 + 4.4 + 2.9) = \frac{15.6}{4} = 3.900$$

$$B2 = \frac{1}{4}(5.3 + 4.9 + 2.3 + 3.6) = \frac{16.1}{4} = 4.025$$

Source: Ian Ferguson Associates

Table 16.6 Analysis of the experiment

	A	B	C	D	E	F	G
Level 1	4.625	3.9	3.550	3.950	3.900	4.175	3.475
Levle 2	3.300	4.025	4.375	3.975	4.025	3.750	4.450
Difference	1.325	0.125	0.825	0.025	0.125	0.425	0.975

Source: Ian Ferguson Associates

Table 16.7 Analysis of the experiment

A2	Mixing speed	= 3.96 – 3.300 = 0.660
G1	Solution add. rate	= 3.96 – 3.475 = 0.485
C1	Chopping speed	= 3.96 – 3.550 = 0.410
F2	Mixing time	= 3.96 – 3.750 = 0.210
Total below average		= 3.96 – 1.765 = 2.195

Source: Ian Ferguson Associates

experimental average. In this example, particle size is required to be as small as possible. The effect below average is shown in table 16.7.

If the experiment has been conceived properly and shows variation in the results of the different combination of factors in each experimental run, it would be expected to see approximately half of the control factors having some additive effect on the output for a two-level array. The total below average, in this case, can now be used as a prediction of the result if the process is set up using a combination of factor level settings that reflect their best effect on the output; in this case A2, C1, F1 and G1. The other factors B, D and E can be set at the level where least cost is incurred. This may be B2 – lowest temperature, E2 – shortest drying time and perhaps either D1 or D2 according to the lower capital cost, or the lower operating cost.

As the orthogonal array is only a subset of the full factorial array (in this case 8 or 128), it is obligatory to conduct a confirmation run and to compare the results which are obtained with the prediction. The closer the confirmation run is to the prediction, the better has been the team thinking in the construction of the experiment in terms of: the response chosen, the factors affecting the responses, the levels chosen for the factors and their accurate setting, the measurement system and accuracy, considerations of interaction and uncontrollable factors that may affect the response.

From the analysis of the experiment, it is clear which level of each factor would be preferred for a desired output. By looking at what happened to the output when each factor was moved from level 1 to level 2, it can also be seen which factors have the greatest effect on the output. Where there is only a small difference the factor has little effect. On the other hand, where the difference in levels of a factor are greatest, this is the factor which is most significant. It is always helpful to present the results in graphical form, to facilitate the understanding of the data and its communication.

Taguchi: An Overview of his Approach

As mentioned earlier, DOE dates back to the work for agricultural research of Sir R. A. Fisher in the 1920s and historically required a great deal of statistical knowledge and understanding, which most industrial users of experiments found somewhat intimidating. Over the years, much effort has been devoted to simplifying the task of experimentation. In the late 1970s, the work of Genichi Taguchi on experimental design made what is regarded by many as a major breakthrough in its application. Taguchi is a statistician and electrical engineer who was involved in rebuilding the Japanese telephone system, and has been involved in applying DOE in the Japanese electronic industry for over 30 years. He promotes three distinct stages of designing in quality:

1 System design – the basic configuration of the system is developed. This involves the selection of parts and materials and the use of feasibility studies and prototyping. In system design, technical knowledge and scientific skills are paramount.

2 Parameter design – the numerical values for the system variables (product and process parameters – termed factors) are chosen so that the system performs well, no matter what disturbances or noises (i.e. uncontrollable variables) are encountered by the system (i.e. robustness). The objective is to identify optimum levels for these control factors so that the product and/or process is least sensitive to the effect in changes of noise factors and the changes that they make. The experimentation pinpoints this combination of product/process parameter levels. The emphasis in parameter design is on using low-cost materials and processes in the production of the system; it is the key stage of designing in quality.

3 Tolerance design – this is the third stage in the design process and is not to be confused with 'tolerancing'. The tolerance design process uses experimental design to investigate the effect on the variance of the output characteristic, of product design and process design.

- Product design involves choosing the upper specification limit (USL) and lower specification limit (LSL) around the nominals of key design parameters that have been prescribed by the parameter design study, and having done this, reconciling the choice of limits of the factors in the design that are predicted to cause most variation, with typically, the cost of reducing the tolerance gap, or the choice of more expensive materials.

- Process design involves choosing the USL and LSL around the nominals of key process factors that have been prescribed by the parameter design study, and having done this, reconciling the choice of limits of the factors in the process that are predicted to cause most variation, with typically the cost of reducing the tolerance gap, or the choice of more expensive methods.

Taguchi's approach addresses these:

- Determining the quality level, as expressed in his loss function concept
- Improving the quality level in a cost effective manner by parameter and tolerance design
- Monitoring the quality level using SPC; a feedback/feedforward closed loop system is also recommended

His 'off-line' approach to quality control is well accepted in the West, in particular, with the engineering fraternity but, inevitably, there are many criticisms of some of his statistical methods and rather surprisingly to the advocated philosophy; for details, see Gunter (1987) and Kackar (1985). What the critics seem to forget is that Taguchi's methods (i.e. engineering, experimental design and data analysis) have proven successful both in Japan and the West, and those organizations who have adopted his methods have succeeded in making continuous improvement; it is this which is important, and not the methods used. There is little doubt that his work has led to increased interest in a variety of approaches and methodologies relating to DOE. However, it should not be overlooked that a number of other people have made significant improvements with the other approaches to experimental design. The maxim to be applied should be: 'If it works for you, use it.'

Achieving Robust Design: Tile Manufacture Example

An interesting example of the principles of parameter design and robustness is provided by the case study of the Ina Seito company who manufacture tiles, wash basins and related products. This study was first published in the 1950s. In 1953, they purchased a new oven for a reputed $500,000. The operation and oven layout is illustrated in figures 16.1–3. The tiles are loaded into compartments in a carrier which is then transported through the oven on a conveyor belt. The heat to fire the tiles is provided by elements which are placed around the periphery of the tunnel kiln. Air circulates the heat around the oven. There are four different temperature zones in the oven through which the carrier of the tiles pass for different lengths of time. For convenience the oven carrier sections have been numbered: 01 to 09 and 11 to 16.

The commissioning trials for the new oven consisted of batches of normal production tiles sent through the oven at the usual known temperature conditions. Samples of tiles from each compartment were then measured for length, width, and warp. The results of measurements of length and width are displayed in histogram form in relation to specifications in figure 16.4. Those tiles in locations 11 to 16 are within specification and centred on the target value of 150mm, while the tiles in location

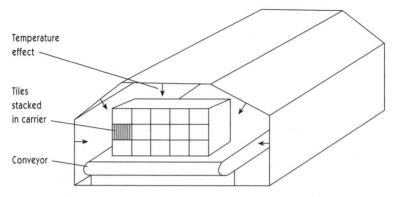

Figure 16.1 Tile manufacture: a reconstruction based on a 1953 problem of Ina Seito
Source: Ian Ferguson Associates

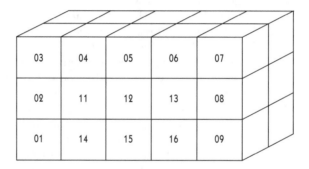

Figure 16.2 Location in oven carrier
Source: Ian Ferguson Associates

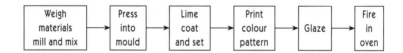

Figure 16.3 Production sequence
Source: Ian Ferguson Associates

01 to 09 have a wide distribution of size, with the average being below target value and outside the lower specification limit. They had been exposed to more heat through their position in the carrier and had experienced greater contraction in size.

The Japanese engineers decided that, rather than attempting to cure the cause, i.e. the effect of temperature and position, it would be more efficient and economical to accept the present conditions. Their strategy was to find a solution that would render the tiles robust to the effect of temperature and position. They decided to experiment with the formulation of the tile ingredients. As a means of comparison, some of the existing formulation is included as one of the options. The experimental matrix was an L_8 orthogonal array with each trial having a different

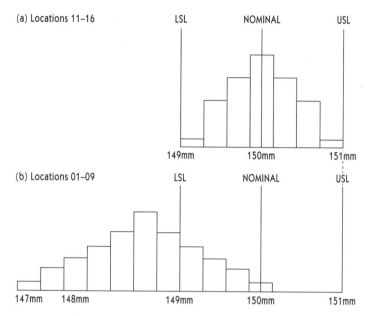

Figure 16.4 Tile manufacture: measured length and width prior to experiment
Source: Ian Ferguson Associates

combination of the ingredients; see table 16.8. After each experimental run measurements of length, width, bow and strength were taken; the results are shown in tables 16.9 and 16.10.

The choice of level of the various ingredients that made up the tile recipe was proven by the confirmation run to ensure that the length and width of the tile were acceptably close to the target value of 150mm, whatever the position of the tile in the oven carrier. There was a robustness in the final mixture of ingredients in relation to the effect of position and oven temperature.

Steps in Experimental Design

Based on Ferguson (1995) the key steps in designing and running a fractional factorial experiment are now outlined in brief:

Step 1: Define the project objectives

This information should be included in the definition of the project objectives:

- A background statement
- The goal to be achieved
- Why the experiment is being considered
- Clear objectives which will result in the goal being achieved
- The area of performance to be achieved
- Available and relevant background statistical information

Table 16.8 Case study – experimental design for tile manufacture

		Control factors	Level 1	Level 2
1	A	Quantity of lime	5%	1%
2	B	Additive particle size	Course	Fine
3	C	Quantity of clay	53%	43%
4	D	Clay supplier	S1	S2
5	E	Glazecoat thickness	Thick	Thin
6	F	Quantity of recycled material	4%	0%
7	G	Quantity of feldspar	5%	0%

Source: Ian Ferguson Associates

Table 16.9 Experimental layout and runs

	Control factors							Noise factor				Average	σ_{n-1}
	A	B	C	D	E	F	G	11....	16	01....	09		
1	1	1	1	1	1	1	1	147	148	147	145	147.5	1.517
2	1	1	1	2	2	2	2	145	146	145	148	146.2	1.169
3	1	2	2	1	1	2	2	153	152	149	153	151.8	1.941
4	1	2	2	2	2	1	1	151	151	154	154	151.8	1.722
5	2	1	2	1	2	1	2	148	147	148	145	147.3	1.211
6	2	1	2	2	1	2	1	149	147	146	150	147.7	1.633
7	2	2	1	1	2	2	1	147	147	145	146	146.5	1.049
8	2	2	1	2	1	1	2	148	147	146	147	147.5	1.049

Noise factor: N1 = Oven carrier locations 11–16
N2 = Oven carrier locations 01–09
Source: Ian Ferguson Associates

Table 16.10 Response table – mean

	Quantity lime A	Add part size B	Quantity caly C	Clay supplier D	Glazecoat thick E	Quantity RCM F	Quantity Fspar G
Level 1	149.333	147.167	146.917	148.292	148.625	148.542	148.375
Level 2	147.25	149.417	149.667	148.292	147.958	148.042	148.208
Difference	2.083	2.25	2.75	0	0.667	0.5	0.167
Rank	3	2	1	7	4	5	6
Significant level	5%	Fine	43%	S2	Thick	4%	5%
Response	149.333	149.417	149.667	148.292	148.625	148.542	148.375

Source: Ian Ferguson Associates

Step 2: Select critical characteristics

Critical characteristics affect performance. When the mathematical relationship is known between the setting of the characteristic and the performance level, usually by some method of experimental design, it is then possible to improve performance to a benchmark level. Typical critical characteristics are, for example, thickness of plating affecting the protection performance of the article, spring depression forces affecting the release forces available and component flexibility affecting assembly weights and strengths. This step should be undertaken by people who are knowledgeable about the process under investigation, using engineering and technical 'know-how' and supported by intuitive, empirical evidence. It is also useful to construct a critical characteristic hierarchy chart. From this, the interactive and dependent characteristics should be noted and the critical characteristics decided upon by asking some questions:

- Is there an accurate measurement system available, with a known acceptable capability of measurement?
- Are the critical characteristics 'pure' and energy related and not confounded? For example, in a central locking sub-system of a car, the electric motor which provides rotational torque to the plastic gear train which, in turn, provides linear motion to the rack and which provides the locking motion, is confounded if the linear motion is measured as a function of the revolutions per minute of motor spindle. This is an indirect relationship. The 'pure' and functional characteristic in this case is the torque applied to the gear train.
- Can the critical characteristics be improved in value by their controlling factors?

The output of the system should also be decided upon in terms of 'nominal the best' 'larger the better' or 'smaller the better'.

Step 3: Determine the issues that affect the critical characteristics

Brainstorming should be used to identify the issues that affect the critical characteristics. It is useful to think in terms of what would *not* create the characteristic, and what would happen if the characteristic were to be changed. From this exercise, an affinity diagram should be considered to group the items and to help to make sense of the data. It is also useful to arrange the items on a cause and effect diagram, adding appropriate items as relevant, with each item being rated on a scale of 1 to 10 for 'appropriateness' to the project objectives, e.g. technical, manufacturability, etc.

Step 4: Identify control factors and noise factors

From the factors affecting the performance defined in step 3, make two separate lists: the control factors and noise factors. A noise factor is something that either cannot be controlled or, for economic reasons, is not to be controlled, e.g. different batches of materials, parts and materials that are at the top and bottom specification limits, atmospheric conditions, etc. It is usual to categorize noise factors into three groups – external noise (variations in the manufacturing environment, e.g. ambient temperature and relative humidity), internal noise (variations due to deterioration, wear or ageing) and piece-to-piece noise (variations in parts manufactured to the same specification). A fundamental part of parameter design is to experiment with the control factors which are to be tested against the noise conditions likely to be experienced in practice. If it is economically possible, control factors are tested against individual major noise factors which, for the purposes of the experimental runs, only have to be controlled to their upper and lower limits, and are separated from

					1	2	3	4	
					1	2	2	1	N3
					1	2	1	2	N2
	A	B	C	D	E	F	G	1	1	2	2	N1

	A	B	C	D	E	F	G				
1	1	1	1	1	1	1	1	•	•	•	•
2	1	1	1	2	2	2	2	•	•	•	•
3	1	2	2	1	1	2	2				
4	1	2	2	2	2	1	1				
5	2	1	2	1	2	1	2				
6	2	1	2	2	1	2	1				
7	2	2	1	1	2	2	1				
8	2	2	1	2	1	1	2				

Figure 16.5   Using an orthogonal array for noises being studied
Source: Ian Ferguson Associates

the control factors in a simple outer array. If it is not economically possible to do this, then the sample size of the experiment should be increased and time/order randomization used, to take into account the extreme conditions of noise. For this reason, noise factors are controlled for the experimental runs only, and are separated from control factors in an outer array, see figure 16.5. To minimize the size of the experiment, it is usual to select a small outer array for the noise factors. Interactions between noise factors are of little interest so the choice of design is much simpler.

Control factors are factors which may be controlled during production, e.g. temperature, speed, tension, pressure and material type. The basic idea of parameter design is to be able to define control factor level settings that will ensure minimum variation of output under known noise conditions and to have the output distribution centred on a value that will be mutually acceptable to other critical characteristics affecting overall performance. Achieving these twin objectives gives what is sometimes called 'a robust design'.

To mix a noise factor with control factors during an experiment would defeat the purpose of achieving a robust design. If they are mixed, then decisions on the best level of control factors would be taken when their optimum level has been influenced by a factor which, in reality, cannot be guaranteed in normal production to be at the level which was used in the experimental runs, making accurate analyses impossible; 'confounded' is the usual term used to describe this situation.

Step 5: Select the control factors to be optimized during the experiment

From the list of control factors set out in step 4, select the control factors to be used in the experiment to influence the output or critical characteristic. The relative rating of the factors carried out in step 3 is a useful guide to this.

Step 6: Choose the orthogonal array and assign factors to columns, in the array

The choice of the orthogonal array depends on a number of conflicting demands:

- The likely costs of the experiment
- The number of control factors to be studied
- The number of levels of the various control factors
- Whether an interaction is to be studied
- Whether a screening experiment is to be used for differentiating between the vital factors and the less significant ones in terms of their influence over the specified response(s)

  This kind of experiment which may, if engineering knowledge demands it, study an interaction between two factors is usually run at two levels of control factor so as to screen a set of variables. It is an experiment in which those factors deemed not to be significant are discarded, and those deemed not to be significant are retained for future probing in a second experiment. This second experiment, which may be run at three levels of control factors, may consider interactions between control factors. When a large number of factors are being considered, the concept of performing a sequence of experiments in a step-by-step manner is a useful strategy to adopt.

- Whether the experiment is used for setting ideal levels for the significant factors
- Whether it is required to break the experimental design into smaller sets of runs, called blocks

  A typical reason for this is it is not possible to accomplish all the runs of the design at one time.

Sometimes what to allocate columns is not a straightforward decision, especially when interactions are to be studied. The orthogonal array is constructed in such a way that, say, column 3 will indicate whether the factor in column 1 and the factor in column 2 have an interaction or whether they are independent. If interactions are to be studied, a larger design is required, using different columns to study the main effects. If a factor is allocated to every column, this is termed a 'saturated' design; this is often the case in a screening experiment.

The facility for minimum change in a column is most useful when one of the factors being studied is inconvenient and difficult to change from one level to another, e.g. temperature in a process oven. On the other hand, other factors which are easily controlled, such as by adjustment of a lever or knob, have maximum convenience for change. It can be useful to rank factors for their difficulty of change on a scale of 1 (easy) to 5 (difficult). Apart from other reasons, this problem of convenience of change can also be helped by running the experiment in a random sequence.

In all the orthogonal arrays, column 1 has only one change between the levels of a factor as the experiment proceeds down the array. Thus in an L_8 array, column 1 has four trials at level 1 for the first consecutive four trials, and then four at level 2 for trials from number 5 to 8. Columns 2 and 3 in the L_8 array also exhibit a pattern of changing from one level to another. Column 2 has three changes during the eight trials, while column 3 has only two changes. Columns 4 to 7 do not exhibit such a convenient pattern of level change, with column 4 having seven changes if the experiment is run in the order of trial 1 to 8.

Step 7: Choose the levels of the control factors

Apart from any economic considerations, there are four main objectives in the choice of control factor levels:

1. To produce adequate differences between each level so that, as the experiment proceeds, the various combination of the factors, which are controlled by the orthogonal array, cause sufficient variation to enable the analysis to isolate the significant factors

    The reverse condition of too little difference between factor levels nullifies the strength of an experimental design.

2. To avoid an uneven balance between factor levels; otherwise any one factor becomes so significant that it 'swamps' out the effect of other factors

3. To choose a level for a factor such that it does not result in information which cannot be measured

4. To choose the levels for factors which are capable of being set to the chosen level during the course of the experiment

Step 8: Choose sample size

The main purpose of industrial experimental design is to make a product or process 'robust' to the variability caused by a variety of items that are not controlled or are uneconomic to control during the experiment, i.e. 'noises'. There are some examples:

- Parts used that are at the top and bottom of their specification limits
- Variability in the performance of machines used in a process
- Environmental aspects of cleanliness, temperature and humidity

To achieve a 'robust' design, it is necessary to be assured that these noises have an opportunity to influence the various control factor combinations governed by the orthogonal array. It is sometimes helpful to take the combination of control factors most likely to cause variation and then to generate sufficient responses from that combination so that the cumulative standard deviation results in a reasonably constant pattern around the average of the cumulative standard deviation. One way of doing this is to have a sufficiently large sample size to ensure that all the noises have impacted on the design.

This pattern – the signature of the combination of control factors – should vary for each experimental run. The differences in the signatures help to provide the answer to those control factors most susceptible to the effect of noise. The size of samples needed in this method depend upon the stability of the design and process, and the degree of accuracy required.

One way of reducing the sample size is to identify the highest and lowest level of the noise and to control this at these levels during the course of the experiment. The control factor combinations will then be tested once at the high level of noise and once at the low level of noise, with a sample size being typically reduced to as little as 5 at each noise level. This gives the full signature spectrum of the design and process caused by the noise factors in the various experimental runs. Design layouts for this system require the identified noises to be arranged in an array which will combine the highest and lowest levels of each of the noises.

If the high and low levels of noise are not used, care should be taken to see that the sample size is large enough to enable the noise in the system to have sufficient opportunity to act upon the control factors and influence the experimental output.

Step 9: Organize the experiment and carry it out

This is a multi-disciplined task, and involves considerable organization in scheduling the logistics required by the experiment and tracking the products involved. There are some typical decisions that need to be taken:

- Are the facilities available when required and will the environmental surroundings of the experiment be free from external disturbances?
- Who is overseeing the experiment?
- Have all those involved in running the experiment agreed to the experimental plan?
- Have the objectives of the experiments been fully explained to all those likely to be involved?
- Has an initial trial of one of the runs been done for affirmation?
- What will be the procedure employed if a trial run fails?
- Who is measuring and collecting the data?

Once the experiment has been conducted, it is necessary to analyse the data using appropriate signal-to-noise ratios and averages and interpret the results, examining relevant interactions. However, interactions tend to be unstable and are not preferred for reproducibility. A better strategy is to have some assurance that the critical characteristic, i.e. the output, is not confounded and then to find factors that can be directly controlled to improve the critical characteristics. Optimum conditions should be chosen and a prediction made for the results of the confirmation trial and run. A confirmation run should be carried out at the optimum settings to validate the conclusion. If a confirmation trial fails to produce the predicted result, it may be as a result of 'confounding'.

Step 10: Analyse the data

To fully understand the best settings for control factors, from the experiment data, the significance of each factor in relation to all the factors must be known. This includes the significance of each factor in influencing the output from both a variation and a location perspective. Coupled with this, it is necessary to understand what effect each factor has on the output distribution when set at the best setting in terms of robustness. There are four possibilities:

1 To minimize variation (reducing the spread of the distribution)
2 To change the location or average of the distribution
3 To minimize both the variation and to change the location of the distribution
4 To have little effect at all

The effective relative significance of each factor can be conveniently determined by the use of analysis of variance, which Taguchi (1986) extends into quantifying each factor and residual into a percentage contribution to variation.

To categorize each control factor into one of these four categories, the data of each experimental run is first summarized into both an average and standard deviation for that run. The average response for each factor, for both location and variation, is then calculated from these single experimental run figures, using the pattern of the orthogonal array to determine level 1 and level 2 etc. as set out earlier.

Apart from standard deviation, there is a choice of metric for determining the variation:

- Standard deviation
- Logarithmic transformation of standard deviation
- Taguchi's signal-to-noise ratios that combine location and variation into one relative metric

It should be noted that some information is lost by combining both location and variation into one metric; this approach may be useful in very sensitive designs. These ratios can also reflect the different requirements between output characteristics:

- Smaller is better, e.g. shrinkage, porosity and vibration
- Larger is better, e.g. weld strength, yield and product life
- Target is better, e.g. a dimensional characteristic such as diameter, length and width

For more advanced experimenters, Taguchi (1986) has recommended a variety of dynamic signal-to-noise ratios for situation where different inputs require a different output, for example, the turning radius for a car via the input of a steering wheel.

Whichever system is used for computing the significance and ability of a factor to influence variation, the resultant tables should show the two situations simultaneously, so that the final choice of setting will result in primarily reducing variation to a minimum, while defining means of adjusting the location to the ideal target value. Response graphs are very useful for achieving this. It is also recommended that a Windows™ based software package such as *Design of Experiments* by Total Quality Software (Nix and Ferguson, 1995) be used for this calculation work.

The case study given in tables 16.11–13 shows the use of analysing for variation as well as means when using design of experiments in a Taguchi style parameter design.

Step 11: Predict the result of the confirmation run

An orthogonal array is only a subset of the full factorial array, so it is necessary to confirm that the choice of factor level settings is the best choice and that it is repeatable. To do this, a prediction is made of the improvement over the average of the experimental output, whereby each significant factor adds to the whole improvement. A confidence limit may also be calculated for the given size of the confirmation run. In the case study given in tables 16.11–13 this is location and variation.

With this knowledge, a confirmation run is made, with the product or process design set with the control factors at the preferred level. The size of the confirmation

Table 16.11 Case study – release times for an anti-depressant compound

	Control factor	Level 1	Level 2
A	Mixing speed	Slow	Fast
B	Mixing temperature	High	Low
C	Interaction temp x speed		
D	Mixing time	Short	Long
E	Feed temperature	High	Low
F	Material type	Type A	Type B
G	Screen size	094	125

Notes: Responses: Particle size, % release per time period
Noise factor: 5 different runs at different times
Source: Ian Ferguson Associates

Table 16.12 Experimental layout and runs

	Control factors							Noise factor – Batch No.					Result	
	A	B	$A \times B$	D	E	F	G	B1	B2	B3	B4	B5	Avg.	Var.
1	1	1	1	1	1	1	1	1.50	1.51	1.49	1.49	1.48	1.49	0.011
2	1	1	1	2	2	2	2	1.53	1.52	1.53	1.52	1.51	1.52	0.008
3	1	2	2	1	1	2	2	1.47	1.46	1.46	1.44	1.45	1.46	0.011
4	1	2	2	2	2	1	1	1.42	1.42	1.43	1.44	1.42	1.43	0.009
5	2	1	2	1	2	1	2	1.61	1.59	1.54	1.63	1.55	1.58	0.038
6	2	1	2	2	1	2	1	1.71	1.69	1.70	1.69	1.68	1.69	0.011
7	2	2	1	1	2	2	1	1.55	1.53	1.58	1.53	1.52	1.54	0.024
8	2	2	1	2	1	1	2	1.45	1.46	1.45	1.45	1.44	1.45	0.007
											Experimental Average		1.52	0.015

Source: Ian Ferguson Associates

Table 16.13 Analysis leading to prediction of 1.49:0.004

	Mixing speed A	Mixing temp. B	Inter. $A \times B$	Mixing time D	Feed temp. E	Material type F	Screen size G
Variation							
Level 1	0.010	0.017	0.013	0.021	0.010	0.016	0.014
Level 2	0.020	0.013	0.018	0.009	0.020	0.014	0.016
Difference	0.010	0.004	0.005	0.012	0.010	0.002	0.002
Average							
Level 1	1.47	1.57	1.50	1.52	1.52	1.49	1.54
Level 2	1.57	1.47	1.54	1.52	1.52	1.55	1.50
Difference	0.10	0.10	0.04	0.00	0.00	0.06	0.04

Source: Ian Ferguson Associates

run needs to be sufficient to give confidence that it represents what will happen in reality.

Step 12: Interpret the confirmation run and decide if the project is finished

The confirmation run should reflect the prediction and confidence limits. If outside the limits, it is advisable to ask some questions:

- Were the control factors set as required for the whole of the run?
- Were the required procedures followed?
- What was the influence of the measurement capability?
- Were the noise factors allowed for in the experimental design?
- Has another factor more influence than expected? If this is suspected then the cause and effect diagram should be re-examined.
- Is an unstudied interaction between two or more factors influencing the output?

Finally, reference should be made to step 1 to decide if all the goals and objectives have been met and that the performance level is satisfactory.

Summary

This chapter has given an appreciation of the concept and practice of robustness, in both product and process design, as the cost effective way of reducing variation. Experimental design using a variety of matrices which suit different conditions is a key technique for understanding the effect of each controllable factor, be it a product or a process design, in minimizing variation while centring the output on a target value. It is a major technique in investigating quality problems.

The role of experimental design is to build quality into the upstream process by optimizing critical characteristics. A key aspect of experimental design is parameter design. This identifies what parameters are important in a design, be it a product or process, and where each one should be set to achieve minimum variation in a consistent and repeatable manner. Thus robust design experimentation is concerned with identifying as many factors as possible which will enable the system to perform as designed, whatever the various uncontrollable events or noise with which it has to contend.

Taguchi has raised the awareness of engineers and technical staff to the fact that many of the problems associated with design, production costs and process control can be resolved using experimental design and analysis methods. This contribution to both awareness and the knowledge base of the subject should not be overlooked.

References

Barker, T. B. 1990: *Engineering Quality by Design*. New York: Marcell Dekker.
Bendell, A., Wilson, G. and Millar, R. M. G. 1990: *Taguchi: Methodology within Total Quality*. Bedford: IFS Publications.

Ferguson, I. 1995: *A Practical Course in Parameter Design*. Birmingham: Ian Ferguson Associates.

Fisher, R. A. 1925: *Statistical Methods for Research Workers*. Edinburgh: Oliver and Boyd.

Gunter, B. 1987: A perspective on the Taguchi method. *Quality Progress*, June, 44–52.

Kackar, R. N. 1985: Off-line quality control, parameter design and the Taguchi method. *Journal of Quality Technology*, October, 176–209.

Lochnar, R. H. and Matar, J. E. C. 1990: *Designing for Quality: An Introduction to the Best of Taguchi and Western Methods of Statistical Experimental Design*. London: Chapman and Hall.

Nix, A. and Ferguson, I. 1995: *Design of Experiments Software Program*. Total Quality Software. Lincolnshire.

Plackett, R. L. and Burman, J. P. 1946: The design of optimum multifactorial experiments. *Biometrika*, 33(3), 305–25.

Taguchi, G. 1986: *Introduction to Quality Engineering: Designing Quality into Products and Processes*. Tokyo: Asian Productivity Organization.

chapter seventeen

Failure Mode and Effects Analysis (FMEA)

J. R. Aldridge and B. G. Dale

Introduction

This chapter provides an overview on the concept of FMEA and its value as a planning tool to assist with building quality into an organization's product, service and processes. The purpose of FMEA is described and the procedure for the development of both design FMEA and process FMEA outlined. In examining the use of FMEA, reference is made to the work carried out in developing the use of FMEAs at Allied Signal Automotive, Skelmersdale Operation. The plant is a manufacturing and assembly facility producing turbochargers for the automotive industry. The Company is the world's largest producer of automotive turbochargers, with a current market share of 50 per cent. The lessons learnt in the use of FMEA are fully examined in the chapter.

What is FMEA?

The technique of FMEAs was developed in the aerospace and defence industries as a method of reliability analysis. It is a systematic and analytical quality planning tool for identifying, at the product, service and process design stages, what potentially could go wrong, either with a product during its manufacture or end use by the customer or with the provision of a service, thereby aiding fault diagnosis. The use of FMEA is a powerful aid to advanced quality planning of new products and services and can be applied to a wide range of problems which may occur in any system or process. Its effective use should lead to a number of reductions:

- Defects during the production of initial samples and in volume production
- Customer complaints
- Failures in the field
- Performance-related deficiencies, although these are less likely if a detailed development plan is generated from the design FMEA
- Warranty claims

In addition, there will be improved customer satisfaction and confidence as products and services are produced from robust and reliable production and delivery methods. It has also relevance in the case of product liability.

There are two categories of FMEA: design and process.

1   A design FMEAs assesses what could, if not corrected, go wrong with the product in service and during manufacture, as a consequence of a weakness in the design. Design FMEA also assists in the identification or confirmation of critical characteristics.
2   Process FMEAs are mainly concerned with the reasons for potential failure during manufacture and in service as a result of non-compliance with the original design intent, or failure to achieve the design specification.

The procedure involved in the development of FMEA is progressive iteration. In brief, it involves the following steps:

- The function of the product, service and/or process is agreed, along with suitable identifications.
- Potential failure modes are identified.
- The effects of each potential failure are assessed and summarized.
- The causes of potential failure are examined.
- Current controls for the detection of the failure mode are identified and reviewed.
- A risk priority number (RPN) is determined; the details are provided below.
- The corrective action which is to be taken to help to eliminate potential concerns is decided.
- The potential failure modes in descending order of RPN are the focus for improvement action to reduce/eliminate the risk of failure occurring.
- The recommendations, corrective actions and countermeasures which have been put into place are monitored and reviewed for effectiveness.

The RPN comprises an assessment of occurrence, detection and severity of ranking and is the product of the three rankings:

1   The *occurrence* is the likelihood of a specific cause which will result in the identified failure mode and, based on perceived or estimated (in the case of process capability) probability, is ranked on a scale of 1 to 10.
2   The *detection* criterion relates, in the case of a design FMEA, to the likelihood of the design verification programme pinpointing a potential failure mode *before* it reaches the customer; a ranking of 1 to 10 is again used. In the process FMEA, the detection criterion relates to the existing control plan.
3   The *severity of effect* (on a scale of 1 to 10) indicates the likelihood of the customer noticing any difference to the functionality of the product or service.

The resulting RPN should always be checked against past experience of similar products, services and situations.

The requisite information and actions are recorded on a standard format in the appropriate columns. An example of a process FMEA from Allied Signal Automotive is shown in figure 17.1. The procedure used at the plant for design and process

Process Function Requirements	Potential Failure Mode	Potential Effect(s) of Failure	Sev	Class	Potential Cause(s)/ Mechanism(s) of Failure	Occur	Current Process Controls	Detec	R.P.N.	Recommended Action(s)	Responsibility & Target Completion Date	Actions Taken	Sev	Occ	Det	R.P.N.
Kit parts to the Assembly line	Incorrect parts used on build	Turbo failure	7		Wrong parts presented to the line at change over	2	Visual check by setter to the shop Packet. Introduced from the bulk issue area set up on the line Marking of the part number on the 'A' surface on Compressors to ID. Marking of the part number on the Turbine flange.	3	42							
Kit parts to the Assembly line	Contaminated parts	Turbo failure	7		Contaminated parts due to lack of cleanliness of holding containers, Organic material in spacer (GT)	2	Visual check, work instructions by Station describing method of Assembly	7	98	Introduce cleaning process for all the boxes, which the parts are presented to the line. Euroboxes 300mm × 200mm, 400mm × 300mm & 600mm × 250mm	LM, DN, PE, BW, mid December 1997	Quotes collected, Capital approval sanctioned Delivery 12 December 1997	7	2	3	42
Check cross over holes	Cross over hole not drilled	no oil flow Turbo failure	8		Broken drill, missed operation	5	Air Gauge on assembly 100% prior to build; work instructions by Station describing method of Assembly.	3	120	New poka yoked fixture provided for an 'in process' end of line check. Will pressure test the Centre Housing and check that the cross over hole is present. If OK a letter 'T' will be stamped.	PC, DC, MB Oct 1997	New end of line test fixture, pressure tests CH and checks for Cross over hole, being debugged at supplier to be on stream 1st Dec 1997	8	2	3	48
Affix label to Center Housing	Wrongly orientated to Customer requirements or on Wrong side of Center Housing	Unable to read the customer no on the engine, reject unit which customer will have to adjust label to correct orientation and record ppm	5		Process controlled by the operator and is capable of producing defects	4	100% Visual check by operators; work instructions by Station describing method of Assembly.	5	100	Design new fixture to mistake proof, by Interlocking the fixture to prevent Assembly. Will prevent the Stick Screws from being supplied with air on the detection of incorrect label orientation.	LM, AM, FW, 15 November 1997	Design and detail drawings being modified to suit CH with Backplate assembled	5	2	3	30
Affix label to Center Housing or Compressor Hsg	Incorrect data on label	Customer Dissatisfaction Could use the wrong turbo	7		Wrong input	2	Software provides for a checksum so that the data has to be inputted twice to verify; work instructions by Station describing method of Assembly.	5	70							
Affix label to Center Housing or Compressor Hsg	Label not properly affixed	label will fall off	5		Hole oversize from machining, stripped thread	4	100% Visual check by operators when recording the Serial Number on audit sheet; work instructions by Station describing method of Assembly.	3	60							
Affix label to Center Housing or Compressor Hsg	Label Missing	Unable to ID unit	5		Operation carried out incorrectly	4	100% Visual check by operators Serial Number recorded on audit sheet; work instructions by Station describing method of Assembly.	2	40							

Figure 17.1 Potential failure mode and effects analysis (process FMEA)

Source: Allied Signal Automotive

FMEA has been mapped using the Q-map technique – for details of Q-map see Crossfield and Dale (1990) – as shown in figures 17.2 and 17.3. The FMEA is a live document and should always be modified in the light of new information or changes.

From the design FMEA, the potential causes of failure should be studied, and actions taken before designs and drawings are finalized. Likewise, with the process FMEA, actions must be put into place before the process is set up. When used in the proper manner, FMEA prevents potential failures occurring in the manufacturing, producing and/or delivery processes or end product in use, and will ensure that processes, products and services are more robust and reliable. It is a powerful technique and a number of the well-publicized product recall campaigns could conceivably be avoided by the effective use of FMEA. However, it is important that FMEA is seen not just as a catalogue of potential failures, but as a means for pursuing continuous improvement. It should also not be viewed as a paperwork exercise carried out to retain business, because this will limit its usefulness.

The concept, procedures and logic involved with FMEA are not new; every forward thinking design, planning and production engineer and technical specialist carries out, in an informal manner, various aspects of FMEA. In fact, most of us in our daily routines will use subconsciously a simple informal FMEA. However, this mental analysis is rarely committed to paper in a format which can be evaluated by others and discussed as the basis for a corrective action plan. What FMEA does is to provide a planned systematic method of capturing and documenting this knowledge; it also forces people to use a disciplined approach and is a vehicle for obtaining collective knowledge and experience through a team activity.

In service-type operations, it is often the case that the first time an organization is aware that something has gone wrong with delivery of the service, is when customers complain. It is clear that a simplified version of FMEA would also be of benefit in non-manufacturing situations. A pilot study carried out at Girobank* within the Data Capture Services of the Headquarters Operations Directorate has confirmed that FMEA is of benefit in paper-processing type activities. The technique has since been incorporated into an interdepartmental improvement project to address sub-process improvement relating to a particular stream of work. One of the main benefits of process FMEA is that it has helped to address the complex internal customer–supplier relationship while improving sub-process procedures. The application of process FMEA is considered by the bank as a valuable improvement tool and will develop alongside other such tools with Girobank's ongoing training initiatives; see Gosling et al. (1992).

The FMEA technique is described in BS5760–5, major purchasing organizations – e.g. Ford Motor Company (1988), Jaguar Cars (1996) and the Garrett Automotive Group (1990) – have published their guidelines on FMEA, as have the Society of Motor Manufacturers and Traders (1989). It features as a subject in textbooks on quality and reliability management – e.g. Groocock (1986) and O'Connor (1991) – and there are a number of FMEA software programs available, which are designed on a hierarchy structure.

---

* The authors wish to thank Catie Gosling for the use of her material in describing the use of Process FMEA of Girobank.

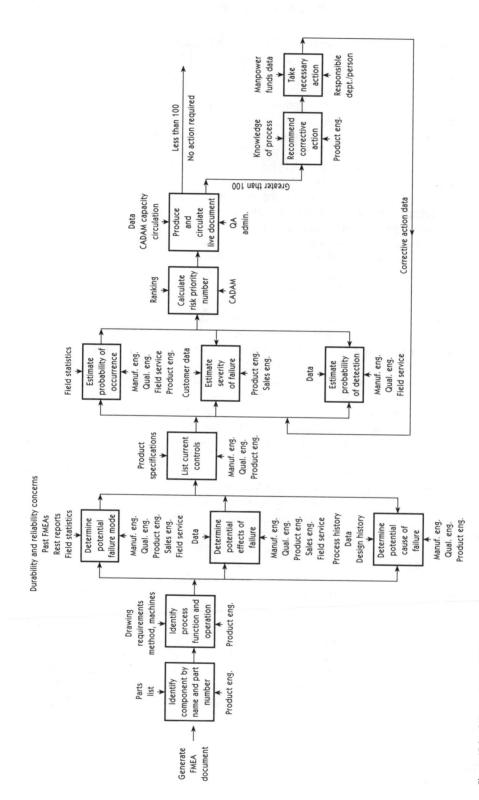

Figure 17.2 Q-Map – design FMEA

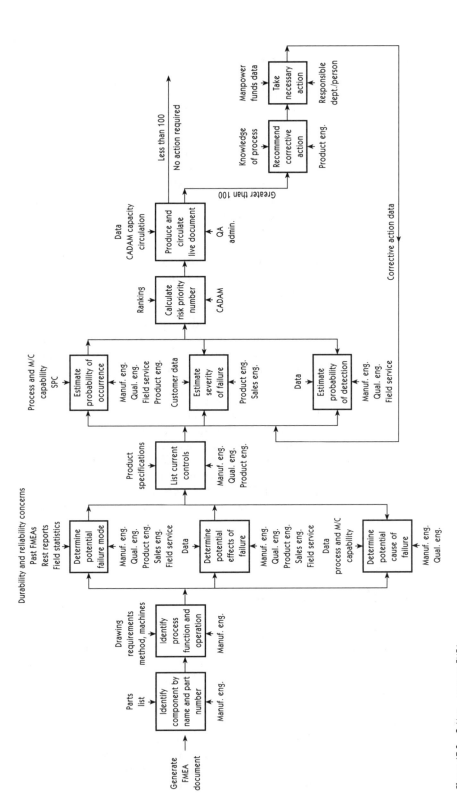

Figure 17.3 Q-Map – process FMEA

Development of a Design FMEA

For a design FMEA, the potential failure mode may be caused, for example, by an incorrect material choice, part geometry, or inappropriate dimensional specification.

The procedure then identifies the effects of each potential failure mode, examines the causes of potential failure and reviews current controls for the design FMEA, which usually include some form of design verification programme. In the case of a turbocharger, this includes items such as material pull tests, heat cycling tests of components subject to high temperature, life cycle fatigue tests to failure, static engine testing, and dynamic engine testing on development vehicles. With regard to the latter, these tests are often carried out by the customers as part of their overall engine/vehicle evaluation programme. Past experience on similar products is often used to verify the validity of certain component parts for a design.

The occurrence for a design FMEA is an estimate on a scale of 1 to 10 of the potential failure occurring at the hands of the customer, a ranking of 1 indicating that the failure is unlikely (typifying a possible failure rate of less than 1 in a million), and a ranking of 10 indicating an almost inevitable failure (typically 1 in 2).

The detection criterion rests on the likelihood of a current design verification programme highlighting a potential failure mode before it reaches the customer. A ranking of 1 indicates almost certain detection, and a ranking of 10 indicates that the current controls are very unlikely to detect the failure mode before despatch to the customer.

The severity of effect ranking is again on a 1 to 10 basis. A ranking of 1 indicates that the customer is unlikely to notice any real effect in the case of a vehicle on performance or the performance of the sub-system. A ranking of 10 implies that a potential failure mode could affect safe vehicle operation and or non-compliance with government regulations. A severity ranking cannot be altered by any means other than by redesign of a component or assembly; it is a fixed feature. Clearly, serious implications exist under product liability legislation – The Consumer Protection ACT (1987) – for high-severity rankings, and these high rankings must be addressed as a matter of urgency.

The activity following the evaluation of current controls is the determination of the RPN.

Development of a Process FMEA

In the case of a process FMEA, the potential failure mode may be caused by, for example, the operator assembling the part incorrectly or variation in the performance of the equipment or data entered incorrectly into a system by an operator.

The procedure then, as is the case of a design FMEA, identifies the effects of each potential failure mode, examines the causes of the potential failure mode, and reviews the current controls. For a process FMEA, the current controls might be operator-performed inspection or SPC information on the capability of the process.

The occurrence for a process FMEA is based again on a 1 to 10 scale with a ranking of 1 indicating that a failure in the manufacturing process is almost certain not to occur. This is based either on past experience of a similar process, both within the factory and in the field with the customer, typically identified by a high process capability value. Conversely, a ranking of 10 indicates that the failure is almost certain to occur and will almost definitely reach the subsequent operation or customer if countermeasures and controls are not put into place. An occurrence ranking of 10 suggests, and indeed demands, that corrective action be undertaken because it highlights a potentially incapable process.

Detection rankings for a process FMEA indicate for a ranking of 1 that the potential failure mode is unlikely to go undetected through the manufacturing process. A ranking of 10 suggests that current manufacturing inspection controls and procedures are unlikely to detect the potential failure mode in the component or the assembly before it leaves the factory, and that urgent corrective action is required. It is interesting to note that a successive inspection check (e.g. bolt torque conformance) does not result in the detection ranking being markedly reduced, it would still be assigned a ranking of between 7 and 10 since experience indicates that 100 per cent subsequent inspection is only capable of detecting 80 per cent or so of defects. The situation would be assessed differently in the case of automated inspection.

A much better method of detection is a successive check at a subsequent operation whereby the operator is unable to perform his/her operation unless the previous operation has been correctly executed. This can be achieved by designing fixturing in such a way that they will only accept conforming parts from a previous operation. Another method is to install error-proofing devices – for details see Shingo (1986) and chapter 14 – at source to perform the inspection automatically. Examples are the modification of fixturing with fouling plates to prevent mis-assembly or counting devices to dispense into a dish the correct number of bolts which the operator is made visibly aware of should any be missed.

The criterion for the severity of effect ranking is determined in a similar manner to that for a design FMEA.

The activity following the evaluation of current controls for a process FMEA is again the determination of the RPN.

Analysis of Failure Data

To apply FMEA effectively, it is necessary to obtain some real figures for the calculation of the RPN, in particular for internal and external failure rates. These can then be used for compilation of the occurrence ranking. This was achieved at the plant by analysing and summarizing external failure and internal reject data. External failure data are collated using computer aids by field service engineers. The data are obtained from visits to customers to review units which have failed, the disposition of which is determined, i.e. whether the failure liability is due to the plant, the customer or, in some cases, no fault is found. Internal process failure rates are collated weekly by the QA department. The data are obtained from rejection notes attached to non-conforming parts by production and inspection personnel.

It is important to realize that, if a process FMEA is being compiled for a new product, for which no internal or external failure rate history is known, then it is acceptable to use judgement on failure rates for a similar product. At the plant, an analysis was performed of the external failure rates over a five-year period using a spreadsheet program on a personal computer. These failure rates were then ranked highest to lowest, to identify the highest occurring items. The external data were then compared with the internal failure rate data and comparisons made to identify trends in which external and internal failure rates were correlated. When looking at external failure rates, a degree of caution needs to be exercised. In terms of the company's products, a guarantee is given, from the time a product is sold, to the end user. It is impractical to consider the previous year of warranty data only, since for many applications, particularly for the commercial diesel business, the completed vehicle may not be put into use for up to 18 months following the date of manufacture. Additionally, some customers are relatively slow in requesting visits for claims evaluation. This obviously leads to a distorted overall picture – which makes the five-year evaluation more realistic. Consideration must also be taken of any high occurrence failures attributable to one cause. Investigation should be undertaken to see if the cause has been eliminated and, if so, then these should be ignored. The emphasis should be placed on identifying the consistent patterns of regularly occurring effects of failure. These types of failure are the ones to which corrective action should be applied.

Recommended Actions for Design and Process FMEA

Following the determination of the RPN, it is usual to perform a Pareto analysis and to address the potential failure modes in order of decreasing RPN. Determining the figure for an acceptable RPN is really a matter of the application of commonsense. If 100 is assumed to be the acceptable maximum then this should be checked against past experience. The rule to be applied is to adopt a consistent approach for each of the rankings, and generally it will be found that the high RPNs are as expected. This takes the form of identifying recommended action(s) and assigning personnel to take appropriate improvement measures by a particular date, which should be before scheduled product release to the customer.

Following satisfactory completion of the actions, the RPN can be recalculated and, if below the agreed acceptable limits, then the corrective action can be assumed to be adequate. If this is not the case, then the design or process must be readdressed by appropriate corrective actions.

For a design FMEA, the potential failure causes must be studied before drawings are released to production status. In the case of the process FMEA, all the controls and measures to ensure design intent which are carried forward into the final product must be implemented. If this is not done properly then problems relating to identified failure modes will occur during manufacture. In the case of a new process, potential failure modes may be overlooked because of lack of experience. However, if this is discovered at a later date, these must be included in both process and design FMEAs for future consideration.

Background to the Use of FMEA at Allied Signal

While large OEMs in the automotive industry demand that FMEAs are prepared for their products, there is an almost irresistible temptation by suppliers just to use the FMEA as a paperwork exercise to retain the business. This unfortunately seems to be a commonplace activity within the European motor supplier industry; see Dale and Shaw (1990) for details. This state of affairs dulls the perceived value of the technique, since the lack of thought, plus the usual lack of practical and realistic corrective actions, can easily be spotted by an experienced supplier QA engineer.

This was indeed the early experience at the plant in the late 1980s. FMEA had been used as an activity that initiated from the QA Department to satisfy a number of customer supplier QA requirements. The use was not widespread among other departments within the organization, although some pressure from the Quality Manager and the Allied Signal Group had been put on the manufacturing engineering department to utilize the technique, and a number of manufacturing engineers had been trained in the use of FMEA via external courses. This had resulted in some marginal attempts in the use of the technique. However, little or no emphasis was placed on positive corrective actions to reduce potential failure modes. The design FMEAs were being compiled by product engineering in a similar manner to those by the QA Department – that is to say to satisfy customer demand.

This historical method of FMEA generation resulted in it being thought of, by those who had come into contact with it, as merely a window-dressing exercise; consequently, the full benefits of using the technique in a structured manner had been missed. From discussions with customers and engineering personnel, and also the findings of Dale and Shaw (1990), it is clear that this situation typifies the European motor industry and is still the case in the vast majority of suppliers.

These were the main deficiencies observed in the preparation and use of FMEA:

- The design FMEA was undertaken retrospectively and not early in the product development.
- The design FMEA was being completed singularly by the product engineer, with little or no input from experienced personnel of other functions.
- Design verification programmes were poorly documented; they were, however, generally executed in a reasonably satisfactory manner.
- The design FMEA was not made available to the manufacturing engineer as an aid to compiling the process FMEA and this was often used as an excuse as to why a process FMEA had not been completed.
- Problem areas identified by the FMEA were often not addressed adequately, or they were given unrealistic RPNs since it was perceived that this would worry the customer and perhaps jeopardize business. In fact, the customer often would identify these omissions during a quality system survey and in relation to a delivered non-conforming product.
- Recommended actions tended to be poorly identified or omitted, even when a high RPN identified that they were required.

Developing the Use of FMEA at Allied Signal

The responsibility for the preparation of the FMEA must be assigned to an individual who has a good working knowledge of the process or design. To obtain a meaningful working document, there must also be inputs from a variety of functions – e.g. quality engineering, supplier QA, purchasing, field service/warranty engineering, sales/application engineering – using a team approach. The selection of a team is a key feature in ensuring that the document is complete and that agreement is reached on proposed corrective actions for improvements. The people chosen to be members of the team should have the relevant experience, be well motivated and have the time to carry out the full range of tasks involved with FMEA.

Design FMEA

The initial preparation of the design FMEA is by the product engineer responsible for a particular project. The product engineer completes the first six columns of the FMEA form: part function and number, potential failure mode, potential cause of failure, potential effect of failure and current controls (design verification). This should be done when the first draft of a drawing or conceptual design is available, and not when the design has been converted into a development part, when it would be much more difficult to effect any major changes. A failure to observe this fundamental rule of 'think first, not do first' allows potential unnecessary mistakes to be made and costs to be incurred.

Once the product engineer has satisfactorily completed the form, the design FMEA team then meets to discuss the prepared FMEA by analysing, in turn, each part of the form. This procedure allows for any omissions to be included and for rankings to be assigned so as to calculate the RPN. Additionally, and most importantly, the adequacy of the design verification can be reviewed to prevent the potential failure mode from reaching the customer.

The key members for the design FMEA team are shown in figure 17.4. The sales engineer is the interface between the customer and the plant and provides most of the information on customers' needs and wants to the design FMEA. The quality engineer, in normal circumstances, would take the role of facilitator as the link for the administration of the FMEA into the computerized FMEA database. He (or she) also provides an input on the assessment of a particular design feature during the production process. The manufacturing engineer is an important member of the team and exerts a strong influence on development of the design in relation to design for manufacturability.

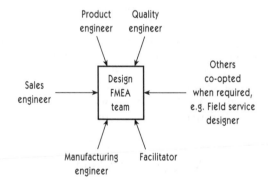

Figure 17.4 Structure of a design FMEA team

Field service engineers and designers are co-opted when required to provide a specialist or more detailed input to a design change or detailed product history based on field experience. This outline of the main activities played by the team members is also similar to that used for a process FMEA and is by no means conclusive. However, experience indicates that large teams are not as effective as small ones; a key factor in the preparation of the design FMEA revolves around total involvement and interaction of all team members.

The meetings to review a design FMEA are best kept to a fixed time of about one hour, and any material not covered during this time should be reviewed at a subsequent meeting. The essential ingredient for success is to hold regular meetings throughout the initial stages of product testing and verification. A meeting should be called to review the FMEA when any significant change is taking place, or if the outcome of a test, for example, proves the part to be incapable of meeting the design criteria.

Process FMEA

The process FMEA should ideally commence with the design FMEA available and to hand. In this way, the design intent can be transferred through to the manufacturing stage, before the purchase of any specific tooling and equipment, with an already determined process route and early enough to allow time to implement any specific controls to ensure product quality conformance. However, some organizations do not have the design authority and customers are not always prepared to make available the design FMEA.

The process FMEA team structure at the plant is shown in figure 17.5. The manufacturing engineer performs a similar task to that of the product engineer in the preparation of a design FMEA: the completion of the part name and number, the potential failure mode which, for the process FMEA, relates to a process failure caused by an incorrect machining or assembly operation, the potential effect of the failure which may relate either to a subsequent process or to its effect on the customer in service. The potential cause of failure can either relate to an error made at source or to a preceding operation and the current controls indicating both proposed manufacture and quality conformance measures.

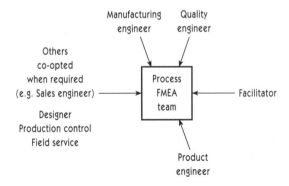

Figure 17.5 Structure of a process FMEA team

The process FMEA team proceeds in a similar manner to that for a design FMEA, by reviewing the FMEA form as prepared by the manufacturing engineer, adding any additional information, and determining the RPN on the basis of past experience, and then recommending corrective actions. These are reviewed at a later stage, when they have been tested on an initial sample batch. Examples of recommended actions for a process FMEA are typically the execution of a process potential capability study and the subsequent institution of SPC control for non-capable processes, improvement of tooling, additional operator instruction sheets, the use of mistake-proofing devices, application of successive check systems, and the commencement of a planned preventive maintenance programme.

The major difficulties of the process FMEA development have been an initial reluctance by the manufacturing engineering function to take a leading role in the preparation and use of FMEA. The reasons for this include a perceived lack of time to allocate to the use of the technique, ignorance of what the technique can do to improve the quality of the product and robustness of the manufacturing processes, and a certain scepticism of quality management techniques, since SPC, although in widespread use, has not been an instant cure for all quality ills as was naïvely thought by some management and staff.

These difficulties experienced are similar to the four main difficulties identified by Dale and Shaw (1990) in their study of the use of FMEA by automotive component suppliers:

- Time constraints in preparing FMEA
- Lack of understanding of the purpose of FMEA
- Lack of training
- Lack of management commitment

They go on to comment that 'these tend to be management and concept orientated difficulties rather than technical difficulties in the preparation of FMEA'.

The major factor affecting the adoption of FMEA and its development as an effective advanced quality planning technique, has been consistent pressure by the FMEA facilitator, pressure from the quality manager, and the onset of increased customer pressure for evidence of FMEA use. Today, some very worthwhile use is being made of the FMEA technique to readdress long-standing problem areas and, much to the surprise of some sceptics, has yielded a satisfactory solution.

Summary

The major driving forces to improve the design and process FMEA procedures at Allied Signal has been a combination of two factors:

- The use of a FMEA facilitator as a change agent identifying weaknesses in the procedure and suggesting methods for improvement
- The increasing requirements imposed by customers in the automotive industry for the use of the technique

As a final point, a few 'dos' and 'don'ts' are given which may help organizations to avoid some of the difficulties and traps typically encountered in the preparation and use of FMEA.

- *Do* develop a strategy for the use of FMEA.
- *Do* drive the implementation with the full support of senior mangers, it is the responsibility of the senior management to see that there is a positive attitude in the organisation to FMEA.
- *Do* ensure all personnel who are to be involved with the FMEA are made aware of the potential benefits arising from the procedure and the necessity for corrective action to be implemented if improvements are to be made.

- *Do* try to ensure that engineers feel that FMEAs are an important part of their job.
- *Do* make FMEA meetings short but regular throughout the early stages of the product life cycle.
- *Do* consider producing FMEA for product families, material categories, main assemblies and process routes (i.e. generic FMEA) rather than for each component.
- *Do* put into place a procedure for review/update of the FMEA, it should always be treated as a living document.

- *Don't* overlook the benefits of involving customers and suppliers in the preparation of FMEA.
- *Don't* start the FMEA process when the design has reached an almost fixed state, when changes will be that much harder to effect.
- *Don't* allow the preparation of FMEA to be carried out in isolation by one individual.
- *Don't* allow important failure modes to be dismissed lightly with comments such as, 'we've always done it like this', or 'that will involve a considerable investment to change', without considering the feasibility and cost of the change.
- *Don't* use the technique as just window dressing for the customer. There is little difference in the effort made when using FMEA in this way from that required when using it in the correct manner.

References

Crossfield, R. T. and Dale, B. G. 1990: Mapping quality assurance systems: a methodology. *Quality and Reliability Engineering International*, 6(3), 167–78.

Dale, B. G. and Shaw, P. 1990: Failure mode and effects analysis in the motor industry: a state-of-the-art study. *Quality and Reliability Engineering International*, 6(3), 179–88.

Ford Motor Company. 1988: *Potential Failure Mode and Effects Analysis: An Instruction Manual*. Brentwood: Ford Motor Company.

Garrett Automotive Group. 1990: *Guide to the Use of FMEA*, Torrance, California: Allied Signal Inc.

Gosling, C., Rowe, S. and Dale, B. G. 1992: The use of quality management tools and techniques in financial services: an examination. *Proceedings of the 7th OMA (UK) Conference, UMIST*, June, 285–90.

Groocock, J. M. 1986: *The Chain of Quality*. New York: John Wiley and Sons.

Jaguar Cars Ltd. 1996: *Instruction Guide to the Use of FMEA*. Coventry: Jaguar Cars Ltd.

O'Connor, P. D. T. 1991: *Practical Reliability Engineering*. Chichester: John Wiley and Son.

Shingo, S. 1986: *Zero Quality Control: Source Inspection and the Poka-yoke System*. Cambridge, Mass.: Productivity Press.

Society of Motor Manufacturers and Traders Limited. 1989: *Guidelines to Failure Mode and Effects Analysis*. London: Society of Motor Manufacturers and Traders.

chapter eighteen

Statistical Process Control (SPC)*

B. G. Dale and P. Shaw

Introduction

In recent years, SPC has become a fashionable buzzword in industry but the concept is not new; its roots can be traced back to the work of Shewhart (1931) at Bell Laboratories in 1923. The control charts in use today are little different from those developed by Shewhart to distinguish between controlled and uncontrolled variation. Also, in the late 1920s, Dudding, a British statistician, was carrying out work along similar lines to that of Shewhart. The BSI published two early standards on SPC: BS600, which was their first standard on quality control, and BS600R. SPC was used by American industry during World War II to assist with the quality control of war materials, and the now-defunct British Productivity Council produced, over 30 years ago, a film entitled 'Right First Time' which provides a vivid illustration of the use of SPC by a UK automotive manufacturer.

The 1980s witnessed a resurgence in statistical quality control, in general, and SPC, in particular. Many words have been written about it and a considerable number of training courses have been offered on the technique by a wide variety of organizations. The trend is such that it might appear to a casual observer that an entire industry has emerged to provide a myriad of consultation services on SPC.

What then has caused SPC to become such a popular technique among American and European manufacturing companies?

To answer this question, it is necessary to go back to the economic recovery of Japan after World War II. The Japanese, stimulated by the teachings of Deming (1982, 1986) quickly became skilled exponents of SPC. Western industrial managers who visited Japan during the late 1970s, seeking to learn the lessons behind the international success of the Japanese manufacturing companies, identified several key reasons for it. One of the most important was the significant use of statistical methods by employees at all levels of the organization, resulting in low piece-to-piece

---

* In preparing this chapter, the authors have drawn on their experience of working on behalf of the Ford Motor Company, since 1984. They have also drawn on the data contained in the Ford SPC instruction guide and the SPC course notes used on their 3-day course.

variability of their manufactured parts. Today, in the West, there is considerable interest in quality, and how it might be improved effectively and economically. It is the pursuit of continuous improvement that has promoted the revitalized interest in SPC.

The aim of this chapter is to give an overview of SPC and its concepts – both statistical and philosophical – to examine the issues involved with implementation, and to illustrate some typical problems encountered in the introduction and application of SPC.

What is SPC?

SPC is generally accepted to mean control (management) of the process through the use of statistics or statistical methods. Perhaps because of this generalized definition of SPC, or people's poor understanding of the subject, some misconceptions have arisen about its applicability and usefulness.

There are four main uses of SPC:

1 To achieve process stability
2 To provide guidance on how the process may be improved by the reduction of variation
3 To assess the performance of a process
4 To provide information to assist with management decision making

SPC is about control, capability and improvement, but only if used correctly and in a working environment which is conducive to the pursuit of continuous improvement, with the full involvement of every company employee. It is the responsibility of the senior management team to create these conditions; they must be prime motivators in the promotion of this goal and provide the necessary support to all those engaged in this activity.

It should be recognized at the outset that, on its own, SPC will not solve problems; the control charts only record the 'voice of the process' and SPC may, at a basic level, simply confirm the presence of a problem. There are many tools and techniques (see chapter 14) which guide and support improvement; in many instances, they may have to be used prior to the application of SPC, and concurrently with it to facilitate analysis and improvement.

Potentially, the application of SPC can be extensive. It is not simply for use in high volume 'metal cutting'; it can be used in most manufacturing areas, industrial or processing, and in non-manufacturing situations including service and commerce; see Owen (1993).

The Development of SPC

A brief history of SPC was presented in the introduction. What now follows are some perceptions of the development of control charts into the broader issues of SPC.

When first evolved, the control chart, using data which provided a good overall picture of the process under review, had control limits set out from the process average, which reflected the inherent variation of the process. A process with more variation, than another will have wider limits, i.e. the greater the variation, the wider the limits. This variation was established from an accurate review or study; consequently, the limits were deemed to reflect the actual 'capability' of the process. The charts so constructed were actually called 'charts for controlling the process within its known capability'. As the word 'capability' has, in the last decade, been taken to mean something slightly different, the charts tend now to be called 'performance-based' charts, i.e. to control the process within its known performance.

When this idea was discussed with potential users, the question was asked: What if the control limits are outside the specification limits? This resulted in the development of a chart where the control limits were set in from the specification limits. The distance by which these limits are set in is a function of the inherent variation in the process. Those processes with greater variation will have limits which are set in further from the specification limits than those with less variation. To reflect this, these charts were called 'modified' control charts or 'charts to control the process to specification limits'. These charts tend now to be called 'tolerance-based' charts. A further derivation of this type of chart is one where 'alternative modified limits' are used.

If an organization's quality objective is to produce parts or services to specification, the so-called tolerance-based chart may prove useful; signals are given to alert operational personnel of the likelihood of producing out-of-specification products. This type of chart does not encourage the pursuit of improvement in process performance.

Using the performance-based charts with limits which reflect the inherent variation of the process and having some statistical estimate of this variation, the objective is to establish its source(s) – perhaps using experimental design tools and appropriate tools and techniques – and to strive to reduce it on a continuous improvement basis. The consequence of this is that control limits should, over time, reduce; this reflects the reduction in process variation and thereby demonstrates an organization's commitment to continuous improvement. This reduction in variation is confirmed by increased values or measures of process capability.

This situation is where Western companies should be now, i.e. striving to reduce variation by using control charts to monitor their processes, and the data generated from the charts to pursue continuous improvement aggressively. If an organization is not using SPC in this manner, management need to evaluate their use of SPC critically and see what is going wrong.

Some Basic Statistics – Averages and Measures of Dispersion

Measures of Central Tendency

These are numerical values that tend to locate the middle of a set of data. There are many such measures of central tendency or 'average', some of which can be omitted from this discussion of SPC, leaving the arithmetic mean, median and mode.

- The *arithmetic mean* ($\bar{x}$) is determined by adding all the values together and dividing by the number of values. It can be distorted by extreme (rogue) values and, when calculated, it may not correspond to any one particular value in the set of data.

$$\bar{x} = \frac{\Sigma x}{n}$$

where: Σ means 'the sum of', and n is the number of values or sample size

- The *median* is the middle value in a group of measurements when they are arranged in order, e.g. from lowest to highest. Fifty per cent of the values are equal to or less than the median and fifty per cent are equal to or greater than the median – the midpoint.
- The *mode* is often interpreted as that part of the measurement scale where values occur most frequently, or the most commonly occurring value.

These averages or measures of central tendency give an indication of where most of the values tend to cluster. In the context of SPC, it is the arithmetic mean which attracts most attention, be it the mean of a sample, the mean of a series of samples or the mean of a series of sample means. This average may provide information about the accuracy or setting of a machine or a process, and may give an indication of how well a target or some nominal value is being achieved.

Measures of dispersion

These are numerical values that describe the amount of variability or spread that is found among data. This dispersion may be quite small or it may be large, so some measure of this is required. There are several measures of dispersion which can be used; the most common are the range and the standard deviation. The former is easy to calculate while the latter is a little more difficult. The range and/or the standard deviation give an indication of the variability of the data; they are measures of precision.

- The *range* (denoted by R) is the difference between the smallest and the largest values within the data being analysed. There may be circumstances where this simple approach can be troublesome, but provided some common sense is used, it can be regarded as an acceptable definition.
- The *standard deviation* (denoted by S, σ or $\hat{\sigma}$ depending upon the data under analysis) is a measure which conveys by how much, on average, each value differs from the mean.

Variation and Process Improvement

Products manufactured under the same conditions, and to the same specification, are seldom identical; they will most certainly vary in some respect. The variation which may be large or almost immeasurably small, comes from the main constituents of a process: machine, manpower, method, material, and Mother Nature. The measuring system itself may also give rise to variation in the recorded measurement; this is why repeatability and reproducibility studies are so important.

- *Repeatability* describes the closeness between results of successive measurements of the same characteristics carried out under the same conditions.
- *Reproducibility* is the closeness between the results of measurement of the same characteristic carried out under changed conditions of measurement.

An important means of improvement is the reduction of variation. SPC is a very useful tool because: given the capability of the measuring system, it ascertains the extent of the variation and whether it is due to special and common causes of variation; and process improvement is achieved by removal of either, or both causes. It should be stressed that while SPC, if properly used, will give an indication of the magnitude of the variation, it will not give the source. The efforts of management, technical, engineering, and management and site service activities should be directed at establishing the likely source(s) of variation and, more importantly, reducing it continuously. A number of management decisions are based on interpreting variations in data whether they be sales, output or financial and, if the variation is misinterpreted, it could lead to incorrect decisions being made. Therefore, it is important that managers improve their knowledge of variation and its causes.

The first step in the use of SPC is to collect data to a plan and to plot the gathered data on a graph called a control chart, see figure 18.1. The control chart is a picture of what is happening in the process at a particular time; it is a line graph. These data are then used to calculate control limits which are the main means of determining whether the process is in a state of statistical control. Once the process is rendered stable by the identification and rectification of special causes of variation, its process capability can be assessed. The next task is to reduce, as much as possible, the common causes of variation so that the output from the process is centred around a nominal or target value. This is a continuing process in the pursuit of continuous improvement. It is not the natural state of a process to be in statistical control, and a great deal of effort is required to achieve this status and a great deal more to keep it so. The amount of this effort and its focus is a function of senior management within their overall remit, consequently, engineering, economic and financial (*inter alia*) considerations must and do play their part in eliminating variation.

What are special and common causes of variation?

Special (or assignable) causes of variation influence some or all the measurements in different ways. They occur intermittently and reveal themselves as unusual patterns of variation on a control chart. Special causes should be identified and rectified and, hopefully, with improved process or even product design, their occurrence will, in the long term, be minimized. In the short term, their presence should be highlighted and a response programme established to deal with them. It is imperative, in the management and control of processes, to record not only the occurrence of such causes, but any remedial action that has been taken, together with any changes that may occur or have been made in the process. This provides a valuable source of information in the form of a 'process log', to prevent the repetition of previous mistakes and in the development of improved processes. Here are some typical special causes:

- Change in raw material
- Change in machine setting
- Broken tool or die or pattern
- Failure to clean equipment
- Equipment malfunction
- Keying-in incorrect data

Common (or unassignable) causes influence all measurements in the same way. They produce the natural or random pattern of variation observed in data when it is free

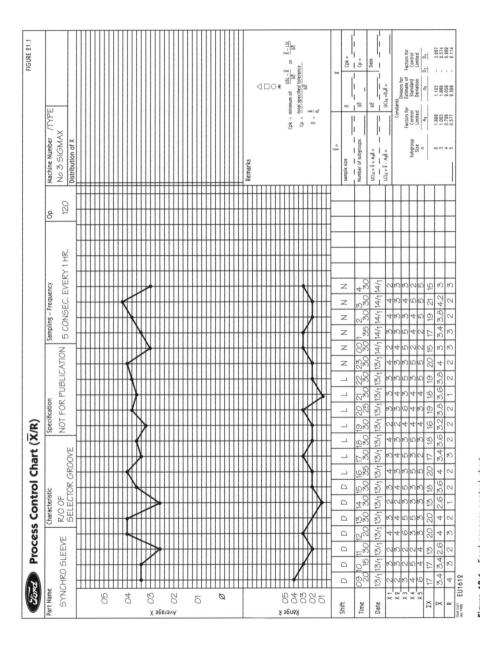

Figure 18.1 Ford process control chart

Source: Based on a format used by Ford Motor Company

of special causes. Common causes arise from many sources and do not reveal themselves as unique patterns of variation; consequently, they are often difficult to identify. If only common cause variation is present, the process is considered to be stable and hence predictable. Here are some typical common causes:

- Badly maintained machines
- Poor lighting
- Poor workstation layout
- Poor instructions
- Poor supervision
- Materials and equipment not suited to the requirements

In the pursuit of process improvement, it is important that a distinction is made between special and common cause sources of variation, because their removal may call for different types and levels of resources and improvement action. Special causes can usually be corrected by operational personnel – the operator and/or first-line supervisor. Common causes require the attention of management/engineering/technical/management services/site services personnel. Teams, comprising relevant personnel, are often set up to eliminate special and common causes of variation. Operational personnel often have a considerable knowledge of process parameters and, therefore, they should be included in such teams.

Variable and Attribute Data

Variable (or measured) data are the result of using some form of measuring system, e.g. vernier or pressure gauges, thermometer or odometer. The accuracy and precision of the measurements recorded is a function not only of the measuring system, but also of the personnel engaged in the activity. Therefore, it is essential to ensure the capability of the measuring system to minimize the potential source of errors which may arise in the data.

The measurements may refer to product characteristics (e.g. length, diameter, weight, torque or arrival times), or they may relate to process parameters (e.g. temperature, screw speed, pressure, shot weight, chemical analysis or ph). Control of process variables gives earlier feedback and leads to better diagnosis of the causes for variation than measurement of product characteristics.

Typically, the measurements may be labelled as $x_1, x_2, x_3, \ldots, x_{n-1}, x_n$ where n is the sample size or number of measurements collected. The (arithmetic) mean is given by

$$\bar{x} = \frac{\Sigma x}{n}$$

The range is given by

$$R = x_{largest} - x_{smallest}$$

The standard deviation is given by

$$S = \sqrt{\frac{\Sigma(x - \bar{x})^2}{n - 1}}$$

Attribute (or countable) data would be the result of an assessment using go/no-go gauges (as a proxy for measured data) or pass/fail criteria, e.g. conforming/non-conforming. It is important to minimize subjectivity when using the pass/fail type of assessment. To assist those employed in this activity, the boundaries of acceptance and rejection must be clearly defined. Reference standards, photographs, or illustrations may help in this regard and, where possible, the accept/reject characteristics should be agreed with the customer. It is also necessary to differentiate between non-conforming items or units and non-conformities. A non-conformity may be a blemish or presence of some non-preferred feature, e.g. a scratch on surface finish or some similar aesthetic characteristic; the product could still be useable but the occurrence would/may be a source of annoyance to the customer. The objective is to minimize, or eliminate, the source of these problems. A non-conforming item or unit is one which fails to meet the assessment criteria for one or a number of reasons; in other words, a non-conforming item may have one or several non-conformities.

With attribute data, again it is the 'average' which is the main source of interest, i.e. the number or proportion of non-conforming items or the number or proportion of non-conformities.

Data Collection

The objective of data collection is to form a good overall 'picture' of how a process performs. It is important that, before any study of the process is carried out, calibrated gauges which are adequate for the purpose are available as are reference standards or examples, and that all operational personnel fully understand what is going on and what is required of them.

A data-gathering plan (often referred to as a control plan) needs to be developed for collection, recording and the plotting of data on the control chart. The data collected should accurately reflect the performance of the process. These are the factors to be considered in the plan and design of a control chart:

- Whether the data is to be collected as variables or attributes
- The sample or subgroup size
- The frequency of collection
- The number of subgroups to be taken
- Sampling risks – the risk of a sample indicating that a process is out of control when it is not and, on the other hand, the risk that the sample fails to detect that a process is out of control
- Costs: of taking the sample, of investigation and correction of special causes, and of non-conforming output

Different data gathering plans may give different 'pictures' of a process, and there are many formal economic models of control charts. However, consideration of statistical criteria, and practical experience, has led to organizations formulating general guidelines for sample size and intervals between samples. In the automotive-related industry, it has led to the widespread acceptance (for variables) of a sample size of 5, a one-hourly sampling frequency, the taking of at least 20 subgroups as a test for stability of a process, and the use of three standard error control limits. To obtain a meaningful picture of process performance from attributes data, and to ensure that the statistical theory supporting the design of the control chart is valid, larger samples ($n > 25$) and more subgroups are often required.

There is nothing sacrosanct about these guidelines and, in selecting the sample size and frequency, some experimentation will, in general, be required. If other sample sizes are more appropriate, then they should be used. Whatever plan is developed, it must be able to show any changes in the process, so the general maxim of sampling is 'little and often'.

Different sampling methods will yield different kinds of information. If, for example, samples (or subgroups) of size 5 are taken every hour from a process, and each sample of 5 is the most recent pieces, it will give the 'latest news' of the process. In this case, any within-sample variation which is present is a measure of process variation.

A sampling frequency of once an hour may result in data which suggests a process is both in control and capable, yet some non-conforming parts may be produced. This situation would suggest that the variation is greater than is perceived and, hence, the sampling should be done more frequently. However, if output from the process did not have any non-conformance problems, it might be prudent to sample less frequently. What is important is that the data collected has helped to increase the knowledge about the process, and confidence has been built up in how it is likely to perform.

Control chart design must not only reflect a clear understanding or engineering/technical/operating knowledge of the process, but be such that those administering the chart (i.e. collecting the data and calculating and plotting data points) can do so with ease and confidence not only in what they are doing but what the 'voice of the process' (the chart) is saying to them. It is important that senior management realize that the control chart is a formal communication from the 'operator' to them about the state of the process; it can be regarded as their 'window' on the organization's operating processes.

Construction of Control Charts using Variables Data

Control charts using mean and range are the most popular variables charts in use, and they are now used to discuss the methods of control chart construction. Other types of variables charts include mean and standard deviation, median and range, moving average and moving range, and individual value and moving range.

There are four steps to control charting.

1 Calculate each sub-group average ($\bar{x}$) and range value (R). Plot this data on the chart.
2 Calculate the process average ($\bar{\bar{X}}$) and process mean range ($\bar{R}$). Plot these statistics on the chart as heavy broken lines.
3 Calculate and plot on the chart the control limits.
4 Analyse and interpret the control charts.

The process average, $\bar{\bar{X}}$ is the mean of all the sample means, and the mean range, $\bar{R}$ is the average of all the sample ranges. These are used to calculate control limits and are drawn on the chart as a guide for analysis. They reflect the natural variability of the process and are calculated using constants, appropriate to the sample size, and taken from statistical tables. Here are the formulae used:

- Mean control chart

    Upper control limit $(UCL_{\bar{x}}) = \bar{\bar{X}} + A_2 \bar{R}$

    Lower control limit $(LCL_{\bar{x}}) = \bar{\bar{X}} - A_2 \bar{R}$

    where A_2 is a constant derived from statistical tables and is dependent upon the sample size.

- Range control chart

    Upper control limit $(UCL_R) = D_4 \bar{R}$

    Lower control limit $(LCL_R) = D_3 \bar{R}$

    where D_4 and D_3 are constants derived from statistical tables and is dependent upon the sample size.

With small sample sizes there is no lower limit on the range chart.

It should be noted that the distance of the control limits from $\bar{\bar{X}}$ is a measure of the inherent variability of the process. High variability, as measured by $\bar{R}$, will give wide control limits; low variability will result in narrow limits. The limits simply reflect the performance of the process when the study data were collected.

If, however, the process mean $\bar{\bar{X}}$ is vastly different from the target or nominal value of the specification, it can be advantageous to set the limits out from this target value, after an adjustment to the process setting has been made. Provided care is taken in the interpretation of ongoing data, no fundamental objection can be made to this approach. These control limits (drawn on the chart as solid lines) are often called action limits, and are set at three standard errors or $A_2 \bar{R}$ from the reference value. The method is based on American practice and, in more recent times, has been embodied in BS7782 and BS7785. In a way, these control limits indicate the acceptable differences, which may occur at random, from the reference value $\bar{\bar{X}}$. If random variation only is present in the process, most (99.73 per cent) of the plotted values should lie within the boundaries when using action limits calculated on this basis. Assuming that there are no unusual patterns within the action limits, there is a low probability of points occurring outside the limits. Such points cannot be attributed to random variation – a special cause is deemed to be present.

To apply SPC to maximum advantage, it is essential to have a full statistical understanding of measures of location, measures of dispersion, the normal distribution, and distributions other than normal. These are well covered in the texts of Duncan (1986), Grant and Leavenworth (1996), Montgomery (1996), Oakland (1996), Ott (1975), Owen (1993) and Price (1984).

Interpreting a Variables Control Chart

The range and mean chart are analysed separately, but the patterns of variation occurring in two charts are compared with each other to assist in identifying special causes which may be affecting the process. The range chart monitors uniformity and the mean chart monitors where the process is centered. The range chart is the more sensitive to piece-to-piece variability, so it is usually analysed first.

The process shown in figure 18.2 is not in statistical control, as indicated by data falling outside the control limits. The responses to this condition should be noted.

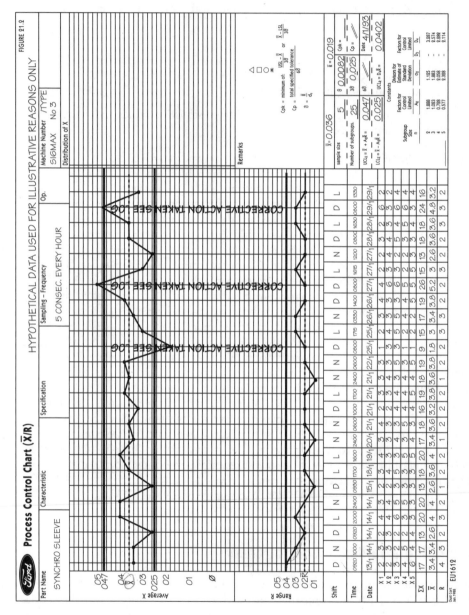

Figure 18.2 Control chart demonstrating 'out of control' condition

Source: Based on a format used by Ford Motor Company

The fact of the data being outside the control limits shows there are special causes present in the process. These are other indications of special causes, based on generalized statistical probability theory:

- A run of points in a particular direction, consistently increasing or decreasing – in general, seven consecutive points is used as the guide
- A run of points all on one side of the reference value $\overline{\overline{X}}$ or $\overline{R}$ – in general, seven consecutive points is used as the guide
- Substantially more or less than two thirds of the points plotted lying within the mid-third section of the chart – this might indicate that the control limits or plot points have been miscalculated or misplotted, or that data have been edited, or that process or the sampling method are stratified
- Any other obvious non-random patterns, e.g. 'saw tooth' and cyclic

All such special causes should be identified and eliminated. To assist in this activity, it is essential that operational personnel record, preferably on the control chart, all changes that may affect the process, e.g. a change in raw material, tool or die, fixture change, a change of operator, an addition of chemicals to a process, or shift change-over data.

A process that is not in control, or is unstable, is not predictable; to consider the capability of such a process is futile and incorrect.

Unlike the process shown in figure 18.2, that illustrated in figure 18.3 is clearly in statistical control as no special causes are manifested. When this is the case, the control chart can now be used for ongoing control because the process is expected to behave as it did when the study was carried out. If properly maintained, the chart will indicate to operational personnel when they need to do something to the process and, alternatively, when to do nothing. It discourages operators from interfering needlessly with the process. Overcontrol occurs when all deviations from the target are attributed to special causes. Undercontrol occurs when all deviations from the target are attributed to common causes. Either mistake, in general, introduces an extra element of variation into the process. Every time an adjustment is made when it should not have been, production may be lost. On the other hand, when an adjustment is not made when it should have been, the quality of the process output is jeopardized. Statistical control charts should be used to determine when it is appropriate to interfere with the process and when it should be left alone. The control chart should be displayed as close as possible to the process or activity in question. In this way, they have greatest value, providing an invaluable means of communication between operating personnel and management.

Construction of Control Charts using Attribute Data

To detect changes in process performance, control charts using attributes data generally require data from quite large sample sizes to obtain the same precision and accuracy as with variables data. For example, a sample or subgroup size of 25 or more is quite common. The subgroup size should be large enough to include several non-conforming items per sample. The subgroups need to be larger than for measured data, and it is often suggested that a minimum of 25 subgroups should be taken.

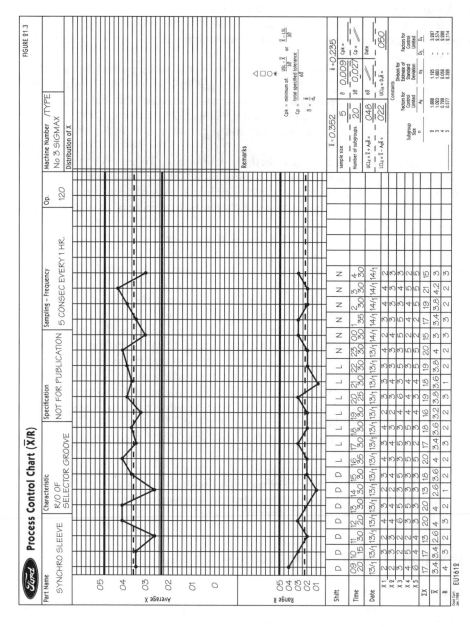

Figure 18.3 Control chart demonstrating 'in control' condition

Source: Based on a format used by Ford Motor Company

An argument in favour of inspection by attributes is that it is not such a time-consuming task as that for variables, so the sample size can be much larger. It is also less costly to undertake. For example, limit gauges or plug gauges are easier for operators to use than more sophisticated measuring devices. In those processes, where it is a natural or required part of the process or quality procedure to carry out a 100 per cent inspection or test, the sample size (i.e. the batch size) may well be very large. The same is true in the appraisal of paperwork procedures.

Experience shows that attribute data often exists in a variety of forms in an organization, although it may not be necessarily analysed statistically. The data may be in the form of existing inspection reports, write-ups on rework or rejected items, credit notes, mistakes made, but are not analysed in control chart format.

There are a variety of charts which can be used to organize attribute data so as to assist with process control. The choice of chart is dependent on whether the sample size is kept constant and whether the inspection criterion is a non-conforming item or a non-conformity within an item. The main types of attributes chart for non-conforming items are proportion/percentage (p) and number defective (np) charts; for non-conformities, they are proportion (u) and number (c) charts.

The collection and organizing of data is almost identical to that described for variables except that, for each sample, the number (or proportion or percentage) of non-conforming items or non-conformities is recorded and plotted. The reference value on attribute charts is the process average with the control limits set at three standard errors from the process average. For example, for a p chart the formulae are the process average ± 3 standard errors:

$$\text{Upper control limit (UCL}_p) = \bar{p} + 3\sqrt{\frac{\bar{p}(1-p)}{\bar{n}}}$$

$$\text{Lower control limit (LCL}_p) = \bar{p} - 3\sqrt{\frac{\bar{p}(1-p)}{\bar{n}}}$$

where $\bar{p}$ is the process average and $\bar{n}$ is the average sample size.

Sometimes the calculation of the lower limit will reveal a negative limit, so no lower limit will be used.

To use a p chart, effectively for process control, the sample size can vary but should not vary too much. An effective rule of thumb is that the sample size should be within ± 25 per cent of the average sample size ($\bar{n}$) established during the initial data collection phase.

It can be seen from the formulae that, apart from the statistical criteria in assuming three standard errors, the determinants in the control limits are a function of the process average (i.e. $n\bar{p}$, or $\bar{p}$, or $\bar{u}$, or $\bar{c}$) and the sample size, n.

The formulae for defining the control limits for these other types of attribute control charts can be found in most standard texts on SPC.

The interpretation of attributes data on control charts is similar to that mentioned earlier for variables data, but is worth noting:

- In terms of runs, many people use a run of eight consecutive points rather than seven as with variables data. The distinction should be of no consequence to most users.

- Runs of data points above the process average indicate a deterioration in the process, while a run below the process average indicates an improvement in process performance.
- Unless the sample size is very large, it is unlikely that there will be a lower control limit.

In terms of process improvement, activities should be generated to reduce the process average; this is sometimes referred to as 'the chronic state of the process'. To facilitate this, it is important that, in addition to recording and plotting the data points on the chart, additional data collection and its recording should be made as to the reason(s) why the item(s) was/were classified as non-conforming – this may be done for one reason or fault or for many faults. To bring about improvement, the cause(s) of rejected work has to be known, which can then be prioritized for remedial action or countermeasure implementation.

The control charts for non-conforming items and non-conformities are modelled using the Binomial and Poisson probability distributions, so some statistical knowledge of these distributions would enhance the users understanding of attribute control charts.

Construction and Interpretation of Control Charts

The following dos and don'ts developed from Dale and Shaw (1990) may help organizations to avoid some of the difficulties and traps encountered in the construction and interpretation of control charts.

- *Do* ensure that the data used to construct the initial control limits is a true reflection of process performance.
- *Do* use the data which are already available to assess the feasibility of using SPC in a particular situation, to determine the type of control chart to be used and to set up initial control limits. However, *don't* lose sight of the dangers of using historical data; examine the data closely and the means by which they were collected.
- *Do*, if there is some uncertainty about what can or cannot be measured, use attribute data as a short-term expediency and then develop to the use of variables data.
- *Do* ensure that control charts are kept simple.
- *Do* move the data collection upstream from product characteristic to process parameters.
- *Do* stand back from the data portrayed on the control chart and question what message they are giving. This will help to ensure that some of the fundamentals of control charting have not been ignored.
- *Do* use teams of appropriate personnel in each department to assist in the construction of control charts.
- *Do* try to understand what variation is, in general terms, and endeavour to understand its likely source(s) in specific terms about the process.
- *Do* use DOE to identify the key control factors in the process.

- *Don't* lose sight of the statistical theory on which control charts are based or the underlying logic of SPC.

- *Don't* be afraid to experiment with the control chart format, sample size, sampling frequency, and product characteristics and process parameters measured.
- *Don't* ignore potential relationships or correlation between product characteristics and process parameters.
- *Don't* be tempted to measure and control too many characteristics and parameters.
- *Don't* forget that the process can exhibit within-sample and between-sample variation.
- *Don't* worry about abandoning control charts which have been based on ill-conceived sampling procedures and making the decision to start afresh.

Process Capability

Because it is easier to understand, the capability of processes using attribute data is mentioned first.

With the $n\bar{p}$ chart (number of non-conforming items), it is usual to express the average number of acceptable items per sample as a percentage to quantify capability, i.e.

$$\left(1 - \frac{n\bar{p}}{n}\right) \times 100\%$$

With the p chart (proportion or percentage of non-conforming items), it is simply the average proportion of acceptable items expressed as a percentage, i.e.

$$(1 - \bar{p}) \times 100\%$$

With charts for non-conformities, c and u, it is somewhat meaningless to talk about capability; it is preferable to quantify the average non-conformities per sample or average proportion of non-conformities per item into a measure of 'defects per 100 units' (DHU).

- $\bar{c}$ is average number of non-conformities per constant sample size. This value should be translated into non-conformities per 100 items.
- $\bar{u}$ is average proportion of non-conformities per item. This value should be multiplied by 100 to give DHU.

Some organizations translate defects per unit (DPU) into parts per million (PPM), and from this an equivalent in terms of C_p and C_{pk} is obtained in general, these capability indices are reserved for measured data).

With measured data, the use of indices such as C_{pk}, in particular, and C_p has been in increasing use during the past decade, and it is for this reason that they are described.

The capability of a process is defined as three standard deviations on either side of the process average when the process is normally distributed. The C_p index is found as the result of comparing the perceived spread of the process with the appropriate specification width or tolerance band.

$$C_p = \frac{\text{total specified tolerance}}{\text{process spread}}$$

Today, customers are specifying to their suppliers minimum requirements for C_p; for example: $C_p \geq 1.33$; $C_p \geq 1.67$; or $C_p \geq 2.00$. In simple terms, this means is that all parts should lie comfortably inside the specification limits.

Given that the process 'spread' is equal to six standard deviations these should be noted:

- $C_p = 1.33$ implies the tolerance band of eight standard deviations, i.e. $\frac{8}{6} = 1.33$.
- $C_p = 1.67$ implies the tolerance band of ten standard deviations, i.e. $\frac{10}{6} = 1.67$.
- $C_p = 2.00$ implies the tolerance band of twelve standard deviations, i.e. $\frac{12}{6} = 2.00$.

It follows that:

1. the specification limits have to be wide – commensurate with excellent physical and functional requirements of the product, or
2. the process variation as determined by the standard deviation has to be small, or
3. both conditions (1) and (2) apply.

As the C_p index compares the 'spread of the process' with the tolerance band, it is primarily concerned with precision – it takes no account of the accuracy or setting of the process. It is for this reason that C_p is often defined as 'process potential' capability, i.e. what the process is potentially capable of achieving.

The C_{pk} index, however, take into account both accuracy and precision by incorporating in the calculations, $\overline{\overline{X}}$, i.e. the process (or grand) average. There are two formulae:

$$C_{pk} = \frac{\text{USL} - \overline{\overline{X}}}{3 \text{ standard deviations}}$$

where USL is the upper specification limit, or

$$C_{pk} = \frac{\overline{\overline{X}} - \text{LSL}}{3 \text{ standard deviations}}$$

and LSL is the lower specification limit.

It is customary to quote the smaller of the two values, giving the more critical part of the measurements distribution. Similar minimum requirements are often prescribed for C_{pk} as for C_p mentioned above.

Because C_{pk} indices assess both accuracy and precision, they are often defined as 'process performance capability' measures. That is, the C_{pk} gives an estimate of how the process actually performs – i.e. its capability – whereas the C_p gives an estimate of its potential, i.e. what it could do if the setting was on the nominal or target value of the specification.

In the calculation of both C_p and C_{pk}, it is necessary to know or obtain an estimate of the process standard deviation $(\hat{\sigma})$. The standard deviation can be estimated by using the formula:

$$\hat{\sigma} = \frac{\overline{R}}{d_2}$$

where d_2 is a constant derived from statistical tables and is dependent upon the sample size.

This exploits the relationship between the range and the standard deviation which was mentioned earlier in the chapter.

With reference to this, these points should be noted:

- $\overline{R}$ is the average within sample variation. There may be present in the process some considerable between sample variation which should be included in $\hat{\sigma}$. If this is not investigated, $\hat{\sigma}$ could be underestimated, hence any C_p or C_{pk} index will be overestimated.
- The indices implicitly assume that the data (measurements) when drawn out as a histogram or frequency distribution curve, give a reasonable approximation to the normal (or Gaussian) distribution curve. While many processes will offer data which comply with this, there are exceptions and some modifications in the calculations may be necessary.

The comments made on capability relate to data collected over a long term (many days or shifts) from a stable, in control and predictable process. Often short-term capability needs to be investigated, particularly for new products or processes; it may be required as part of supplier verification programme, i.e. initial sampling requirements or first article inspection. The time scale is then dramatically reduced to cover only a few hours run of the process.

It is recommended that data are collected in the same manner as for initial control chart study, but the frequency of sampling is increased to obtain as many samples (of size n) as possible to give a good picture of the process, e.g. about 20 samples of size n. Data are plotted on the control chart with appropriate limits, but these indices are calculated:

- P_p = preliminary process potential
- P_{pk} = preliminary process capability

The formulae is exactly as for C_p and C_{pk} but the minimum requirements may be higher; for example $P_p \geq 1.67$ i.e. 1.67 implies the tolerance band is ten standard deviations wide and the process 'spread' equals six standard deviations. ($\frac{10}{6} = 1.67$).

It should not be forgotten that all capability indices are estimates derived from estimates of the process variation ($\hat{\sigma}$). The reliability or confidence in the estimate of the process standard deviation is a function of these:

- The amount of data which has been collected
- The manner in which the data were collected
- The capability of the measuring system, i.e. its accuracy and precision
- The skill of the people using the measuring system
- People's knowledge and understanding of statistics

Implementation of SPC

Among the major manufacturers in the UK, the Ford Motor Company are considered to be the leaders in the promotion and use of SPC by using it in their own manufacturing plants, and in requiring their suppliers to demonstrate that their processes are in a state of statistical control and capable. To assist their supplier base in meeting the statistical requirements outlined in their Quality System Standard, Ford have established a number of Regional Training Centres in Britain, France, Germany, Spain and the Republic of Ireland. Each centre, using Ford-produced material, offers a three-day SPC course. The School of Management at UMIST is one of four such centres in Britain and the authors have been involved in this training activity since 1984. It is appropriate, therefore, when discussing how to start on SPC, to draw upon the guidelines established by Ford and the experiences acquired by the authors while assisting motor industry suppliers with the implementation of SPC. Some of the most important points are worth enlarging upon.

Awareness

Everyone in the organization should have some basic understanding of SPC and its use. People should not be frightened and intimidated by SPC; the tendency to overcomplicate the training should be avoided at all costs. The approach which is recommended is for employees to be exposed to a small amount of training followed by practice, and for this sequence to be repeated until adequate knowledge, skills and confidence have been built up.

The training and education programme should start with the senior management team and be cascaded down through the organizational hierarchy using appropriate modes of training at each level. If SPC is to be successful in the longer term, the awareness needs to start with senior management and they must take their obligations seriously, providing the necessary commitment, visible leadership and resources. Training for SPC must not be seen as being only for people at the lower levels of the organization.

The time interval between SPC training and the introduction of the technique should be kept to a minimum. The training must always be linked to projects.

Selection of a statistical facilitator

The role of the facilitator is that of a co-ordinator and a source of expertise on the subject of SPC and improvement methods. He or she plays a vital role in the establishment and continued success of SPC and continuous improvement in the organization. The point succinctly is made, in the Ford (1985) SPC course notes:

> The importance of selecting this individual is paramount to the success of the programme and must not be allowed to carry the negative stigma that many 'special' assignments do.

The facilitator requires good personal and technical skills; these are their typical responsibilities:

- To ensure that everyone in the organization is kept informed of progress and developments
- To assist with developing strategies to advance TQM and the process of continuous improvement
- To monitor progress in individual areas and assist people as and when required
- To arrange and monitor training on SPC and related techniques
- To initiate applications of SPC in areas/departments not currently using it
- To provide advice on all aspects of statistical matters relating to process improvement
- To assist with all aspects relating to the charting and analysis of data
- To participate in quality awareness and improvement meetings, workshops and user groups and liaise with the relevant steering committees
- To analyse available indicators – e.g. product and process history files – to provide, at regular intervals, a state-of-the-art picture of the benefits and savings achieved as a result of process improvement

In their guidelines, Ford (1985) recommend that the appointment of the facilitator should take place early in an organization's SPC programme. Dale and Shaw (1989) claim that companies who appoint a facilitator are less likely to experience difficulties with the introduction and application of SPC.

From this work of Dale and Shaw, it is possible to outline the profile of an SPC facilitator: the appointment is likely to be made from within the organization, the job will be in addition to the individual's normal workload, the individual will be of middle or senior management status and their discipline will be either quality or technical.

Setting-up a steering committee/arm for SPC

It is useful to establish a steering committee to oversee the programme and to develop a strategic plan for implementation. The main function of the committee should be to guide, plan, publicize and manage the progress of SPC and to develop diagnostic and improvement actions. This body will give continuity and structure to the programme and ensure that SPC is not dependent on a few people for its direction and future development, and will help to establish an improvement infrastructure. It also gives visibility to SPC and shows that management are serious in pursuing its application. To be effective, the steering committee needs to be active and to plan well ahead.

Selection of an area for a pilot programme

A number of organizations fall into the trap of trying to apply SPC to all areas/departments at the same time (the 'Big Bang' approach). It is not uncommon to find organizations setting weekly targets for the number of characteristics for which control charts are required to be constructed. If SPC is implemented too quickly and without proper planning, it is probable that many of the key elements necessary for success will be overlooked.

A better approach is to apply SPC in one area where the probability of success is high. This will allow an organization to check out its implementation planning thoroughly and enable it to gather feedback on all the likely pitfalls. Once SPC has been used successfully in one area, it is easier to extend its use to other areas and departments. The old adage – 'success breeds success' – should not be forgotten.

Difficulties Experienced in Introducing and Applying SPC

The purpose behind the application of SPC is straightforward – to reduce variation in process output, first by establishing whether or not a process is in a state of statistical control, and second, if it is not, getting it under control by eliminating 'special' causes of variation. Finally, SPC may be used to help reduce 'common' causes of variation.

However, a number of organizations do encounter problems in the introduction and application of SPC. In a recent study of the use of SPC by suppliers in the automotive-related industry, Dale et al. (1990) have reported on the main stumbling blocks which are typically encountered; these are shown in tables 18.1 and 18.2.

Table 18.1 Main difficulties experienced in the implementation of SPC

Difficulty	Score (N = 120)
Lack of knowledge/expertise on SPC	149
Poor understanding and awareness within the company of the purpose of SPC	136
Lack of action from senior management	118
Lack of SPC training for operators	106
Lack of knowledge of which parameters to measure and/or control	97
Difficulty in convincing people that SPC is beneficial	94
Negative reaction of operators	87
Negative reaction of senior management	85
Negative reaction of middle management	82
Negative reaction of line management	82
A general lack of encouragement	80
Lack of action from line management	78
Deciding which of the various charting techniques to use	74
Lack of SPC training for senior management	65
Lack of action from middle management	64
Lack of SPC training for line management	58
Poor communication between management and the shop floor	57
Lack of SPC training for middle management	47
Deciding whether to express data in an attribute or variables format	43
Literacy/numeracy of operators	42
Negative reaction of trades union	30
Literacy/numeracy of line supervision	11
Feedback of data	9
Lack of resources devoted to SPC	9
Difficulty in measuring key product characteristics	7
Small batch production	6
An inadequate computer system	5
Organization changes	5
Operators workload	5
Deciding on manual or computer-aided charting	5
Lack of appropriate gauges	3
Replacement of machinery	2
The nature of product non-conformities	1

Note: Respondents were asked to select and rank the five main inhibitors to the introduction of SPC. The score was awarded by allocating points of 5, 4, 3, 2 and 1 respectively to the first, second, third, fourth and fifth inhibitor given.

Table 18.2 The difficulties encountered in applying SPC

Difficulty	Score (N = 130)
Applying SPC to a particular process	139
Resistance to change	108
Deciding which characteristic and/or parameter to chart	93
Deciding which charting technique to use	85
Lack of management commitment	85
Lack of problem-solving skills	52
Time restraints	48
Poor understanding of SPC techniques	41
Lack of a company-wide training programme on SPC	35
Attitudes of the workforce	33
Poor understanding of the SPC philosophy	31
An inadequate computer system	3
Unrealistic specifications	3
Difficulty in demonstrating the benefits of SPC	3
Small batch production situation	3
Attitudes of first-line supervision	3
Incapable processes	2
Difficulty experienced in measuring product characteristics	2
Lack of feedback to the workforce	1
Lack of equipment to measure specific characteristics	1
Lack of appreciation of the disciplines necessary to support SPC	1

Note: Respondents were asked to select and rank the three main difficulties encountered in applying SPC. The score was calculated by allocating points of 3, 2 and 1 respectively to the first, second and third difficulty indicated.

Out of 158 respondents, 122 (77 per cent) indicated that they had experienced difficulties in introducing SPC, and 130 (82 per cent) said they had encountered difficulties with its application and development. These were the top three difficulties in introducing SPC:

- Lack of knowledge/expertise of SPC
- Poor understanding and awareness within the company of the purpose of SPC
- Lack of action from senior management

These were the three main difficulties in its application:

- Applying SPC to a particular process
- Resistance to change
- Deciding which characteristic and/or parameter to chart

Looking at the variety of difficulties outlined in tables 18.1 and 18.2, it is clear that organizations encounter a wide range of stumbling blocks in their endeavour to use SPC, indicating that there is no easy recipe for success. When the range of difficulties are studied, it is apparent that they can be categorized under two main headings:

- Management commitment
- Having the knowledge and confidence to use SPC successfully, including the willingness to experiment and adapt SPC to less well-publicized applications, e.g. small batch production runs and multi-product situations

It is clear that the majority of difficulties are caused by the lack of commitment, awareness, understanding, involvement and leadership of middle and senior managers. While SPC may be seen to be a bottom-up activity, used by people responsible for controlling a process, it needs management to take their obligations for improvement seriously if it is to be effective over the longer term. They need to devote more intellectual thought and day-to-day attention to SPC. It should not be treated merely as a source of control charts which management uses to present to their customers a picture suggesting they are doing something positive about quality improvement.

Dale and Shaw (1991), writing on the common issues and queries which organizations raise in relation to SPC, make the point that a number of people who are considering the use of SPC in their organization and those concerned with its implementation do not understand the fundamentals underlying the concept. They go on to say that there is still a degree of resistance in some industries to its introduction and use. Here is a profile of an organization which questions the use of SPC:

- The Board of Directors and senior management team are not devoting sufficient time and resources to TQM, in general, and SPC, in particular.
- There is a lack of corporate vision, mission, policies and values.
- Meeting the production schedule is the number one priority.
- The emphasis is on firefighting and not on quality planning and prevention-type activities.
- A lack of attention is devoted to the production preparation stage.
- Education and training is accorded a low priority, and is not properly assessed and monitored.
- The organization does not have an SPC facilitator.
- Emphasis is on the individual and not on teamwork.
- Engineers are divorced from the realities of the factory shop floor.
- The manufacturing function is not considered a top priority.

Summary

SPC, supported by the positive commitment of all employees in an organization within a framework of TQM, has proved to be a major contribution in the pursuit of excellence. It supports the philosophy that products and services can always be improved. However, it is a technique which, by itself, will do little to improve quality. It is basically a measurement tool and it is only when a mechanism is in place to remove 'special' causes of variation and to squeeze out of the process 'common' causes of variation that an organization will have progressed from simply charting data to using SPC to its fullest potential. Management commitment and leadership, a structured and ongoing training programme, and its correct use, is crucial to the success of SPC.

References

Dale, B. G. and Shaw, P. 1989: The application of statistical process control in UK automotive manufacture: some research findings. *Quality and Reliability Engineering International*, 5(1), 5–15.

Dale, B. G. and Shaw, P. 1990: Some problems encountered in the construction and interpretation of statistical process control. *Quality and Reliability Engineering International*, 6(1), 7–12.

Dale, B. G. and Shaw, P. 1991: Statistical process control: an examination of some common queries. *International Journal of Production Economics*, 22(1), 33–41.

Dale, B. G., Shaw, P. and Owen, M. 1990: SPC in the motor industry: an examination of implementation and use. *International Journal of Vehicle Design*, 11(2), 115–31.

Deming, W. E. 1982: *Quality Productivity and Competitive Position*. Cambridge, Mass.: MIT, Centre for Advanced Engineering.

Deming, W. E. 1986: *Out of the Crisis*. Cambridge, Mass.: MIT, Centre for Advanced Engineering.

Duncan, A. J. 1986: *Quality Control and Industrial Statistics*. Illinois: Richard D. Irwin.

Ford Motor Company 1985: *Statistical Process Control Course Notes*. Brentwood: Ford Motor Company.

Grant, E. L. and Leavenworth, R. S. 1996: *Statistical Quality Control*. New York: McGraw Hill.

Montgomery, D. C. 1996: *Introduction to Statistical Quality Control*. New York: John Wiley and Sons.

Oakland, J. S. 1996: *Statistical Process Control: a Practical Guide*. London: Heinemann.

Ott, E. R. 1975: *Process Quality Control: Troubleshooting and Interpretation of Data*. New York: McGraw Hill.

Owen, M. 1993: *SPC and Business Improvement*. Bedford: IFS Publications.

Price, F. 1984: *Right First Time*. Basingstoke, Hants.: Gower Press.

Shewhart, W. A. 1931: *Economic Control of Quality of Manufactured Product*. New York: D. Van Nostrand Co. Inc.

chapter nineteen

Benchmarking*

R. Love and B. G. Dale

Introduction

From the late 1980s onwards, there has been a growth of interest in the subject of benchmarking. This has been triggered by the success of the improvement methods used by the Xerox Corporation and by the development of the self-assessment methods promoted by the MBNQA and EFQM models for business excellence. Benchmarking, as it is known today, originated in Rank Xerox. It is now well documented – e.g. Camp (1989) – that when Rank Xerox started to evaluate its copying machines against the Japanese competition, it was found that the Japanese companies were selling their machines for what it cost Rank Xerox to make them. It was assumed that the Japanese produced machines were of poor quality; this proved not to be the case. This exposure of Rank Xerox's vulnerability highlighted the need for change.

The concept of benchmarking was popularized by the seminal work of Camp (1989), based on the experiences on Rank Xerox. In simple terms, benchmarking is an opportunity to learn from the experience of others.

- It helps to develop an improvement mindset among staff.
- It facilitates an understanding of best practices and processes.
- It helps to develop a better understanding of processes.
- It challenges existing practices within the business.
- It assists in setting goals based on fact.
- It provides an educated viewpoint of what needs to be done rather than relying on whim and gut feel.

Since the publication of this work of Camp (1989), many other books of a similar nature have been published: Codling (1995), Cook (1993) and Zairi and Leonard

* The authors wish to thank Heather Bunney and Mark Smith for their contribution to the benchmarking projects and material on which this chapter is based. They also wish to thank MCB University Press for allowing material to be extracted from the paper Love, R., Bunney, H. S., Smith, M. and Dale, B. G. 1998: Benchmarking in Water Supply Services: the Lessons Learnt. *Benchmarking for Quality Management and Technology*, 5(1), 59–70.

(1994). As pointed out by Zairi (1995), there has been a lack of research on benchmarking and any that has been conducted tends to concentrate on surveys of the concept. Apart from a small handful of papers – Hanson and Voss (1995), Leonard (1996) and Prasad et al. (1996) – there is little to prepare the people involved in carrying out a benchmarking exercise of the many issues which need to be faced and the means of resolving some of the main problems which are typically encountered.

Most organizations carry out what can be termed as informal benchmarking. This traditional form of benchmarking has been carried out for years, commencing with military leaders. This takes two main forms:

1   Visits to other companies to obtain ideas on how to facilitate improvement in their own organization
2   The collection, in a variety of ways, of data about competitors

This is often not done in any planned way; it is interesting but limited in its value, due to a lack of structure and clear objectives. To make the most effective use of benchmarking and to use it as a learning experience as part of a continuous process rather than a one-off exercise, a more formal approach is required.

There are three main types of formal benchmarking:

1   Internal benchmarking
2   Competitive benchmarking
3   Functional/generic benchmarking

Internal benchmarking is the easiest form of benchmarking to conduct. It involves benchmarking between businesses or functions within the same group of companies. In this way, best practice and initiatives are shared across the corporate business.

Competitive benchmarking is a comparison against the direct competitors within a company's market. It is often difficult, if not impossible in some industries, to obtain the data for this form of benchmarking as, by the very nature of being a competitor, the company is seen as a threat.

Functional/generic benchmarking involves comparison of specific processes with 'best in class' in different industries, often considered to be world class in their own right. Functional relates to the functional similarities of organizations, while generic looks at the broader similarities of businesses, usually in disparate operations. Usually, it is not difficult to obtain access to other organizations to perform this type of benchmarking. Organizations are often keen to swop and share information in a network or partnership arrangement, particularly when you offer no direct threat to the companies business or market share.

There are a number of steps in a formal benchmarking process. They are now briefly described; more detail can be found in Anderson and Petterson (1996), Camp (1989) and Camp (1995).

● Identify what is the subject to be benchmarked (e.g. the invoicing process), decide who will be in the team, the support they require (e.g. training, project champion), their roles and responsibilities, reach agreement on the benchmark measures to be used (e.g. number of invoices per day, per person), create a draft project plan and communicate with the required internal parties. The process chosen for benchmarking should have a significant impact on customer satisfaction and/or internal efficiency and management must be committed to improving the process.

- Identify which companies will be benchmarked from a set of selection criteria defined from the critical success factors of the project. Research potential partners and select the best partner(s).
- Develop a data collection plan. Agree the most appropriate means of collecting the data, the type of data to be collected, who will be involved and a plan of action to obtain the data, e.g. identify contacts in partnering organizations, the questionnaire(s) to be used and the composition, telephone surveys, site visits, etc.
- Tabulate and analyse data. Determine the reasons for the current gap (positive or negative) in performance between the company and the best among the companies involved in the benchmarking exercise. The gap is usually expressed in the form of a percentage.
- Estimate, over an agreed time frame, the change in performance of the company and the benchmark company so as to assess if the gap is going to grow or decrease, based on the plans and goals of the parties concerned.
- Define and establish the goals to close or increase the gap in performance. This step requires effective communication of the benchmarking exercise findings and gaining acceptance of the data. It is recommended that the audience for the communication and the means by which it is to be carried out – e.g. presentation, formal report, newsletter, noticeboard – should be chosen carefully.
- Develop action plans to achieve the goals. This step involves gaining acceptance of the plans by all employees likely to be affected by the changes.
- Implement the actions, plans and strategies. This involves effective project planning and management.
- Assess and report the results of the action plans.
- Reassessment or recalibration of the benchmark to assess if the actual performance/improvement is meeting that which has been projected. This should be conducted on a regular basis and involves maintaining good links with the benchmarking partners.

This chapter summarizes the main learning experiences from a number of diverse benchmarking projects carried out within the North West Water (NWW) part of the Utility Division of United Utilities.

Company Background

United Utilities is an international company primarily involved in the supply of drinking water, treatment of waste water, electricity distribution and supply. The company was formed in January 1996 following the merger of NWW and Norweb. It was England's first multi-utility company and is made up of five divisions. The Utility Division manages the two regulatory companies, NWW Ltd and Norweb Distribution.

The main responsibility of NWW is to provide waste water and water services to a population of nearly seven million people in the North West of England, servicing an area which covers 14,000km². They collect, treat and transport water to customer's taps, and take away and treat wastewater before returning it safely to the environment. North West Water run over 200 reservoirs, 150 water treatment works, 600 waste water treatment works, 960km of aqueduct, 40,000km of water mains and 30,000km of sewers.

As part of the company's approach to the management of excellence, three benchmarking projects were initiated by the Business Quality Group in early 1995. The purpose of these projects was to promote and trial the use of benchmarking as a business improvement methodology, thereby encouraging further benchmarking projects within the business. This was intended to be done by demonstrating to employees the process of benchmarking and, from this, provide tangible benefits and cost savings in three high visibility areas – i.e. customer services, operations and laboratory services – through identifying and then adapting and/or adopting external best practices. Benchmarking was also used to demonstrate how a TQM approach to solving a key business issue can deliver bottom-line improvements.

The benchmarking methodology adopted was a modified 10-step process outlined by Camp (1989); see figure 19.1. The benchmarking teams were encouraged by the Business Quality Group to follow each of the ten steps and to complete a benchmarking study record when each of the key phases of planning, analysis, integration and action had been completed.

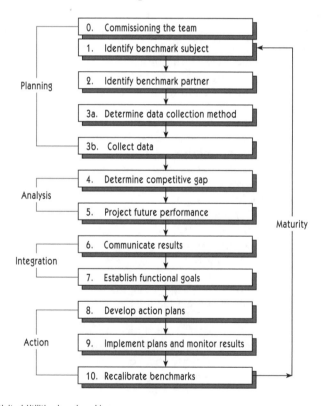

Figure 19.1 The United Utilities benchmarking process
Source: North West Water

While the '10-step' benchmarking process provides a good outline for benchmarking teams to follow, the ability to understand each of the steps and associated tasks requires some in-depth training. The decision to bring the benchmarking training 'in-house' and to train all team members using a case study approach was critical to the success of the projects. Indeed, as the benchmarking process has developed within the Utility Division, team members have not only received an initial two-day training programme but have also participated in a one-day 'kick-off' workshop involving the team, project leader and project sponsor to ensure that everyone has a clear understanding of the scope and processes involved in the project. The combination of these two events is believed to provide 'best practice' in benchmarking project start up procedures.

Why Benchmarking?

When NWW started to develop its formal approach to business quality and managing towards excellence, it was decided to undertake a minimum of three benchmarking projects each year. This was the logic underlying this decision:

- Through the mechanisms of a benchmarking project, process owners will focus on what needs to be improved and will be motivated to do so by exposure to the practices seen outside the organization.
- By focusing on high visibility key processes with the potential of a high return on investment, the methodology and practice of benchmarking would be encouraged in diverse areas of the business.
- People will be required to look outside of their current process and, through comparison with other organizations, see and recognize opportunities for improvement.
- Benchmarking should demonstrate to business unit management that current performance is not as good as initially thought, removing complacency and providing a platform for improvement.
- By focusing on processes rather than individuals, the traditional 'blame culture' would be removed.
- Benchmarking should increase the velocity of change from a public sector mentality approach to management and day-to-day work activities to that of industry leaders in the private sector. As part of this process, it was expected to breakdown insular attitudes and behaviour which, at the time, was found in some areas of the business.

In 1995/96, three benchmarking projects were each sponsored by a Director of NWW and facilitated by the Business Quality Group.

- The customer services project involved looking at the process of customer call handling with respect to such areas as the time taken to answer calls and query/complaint resolution performance.
- In laboratory services, the area addressed was the process of waste water sampling with consideration of the flow of information through the process, examining such factors as turn-around time of sampling, analysis, validation of results and archiving, as well as percentage completion rates.
- In relation to operations, it was the area of customer satisfaction within planned rehabilitation work (the process of digging up roads to replace and/ or repair water pipes causing a disruption to supply), examining aspects such

as communication with customers before, during and after work was carried out together with liaison with contractors.

From these three projects – and other more recent projects carried out in the areas of plant services, procurement, employee communications, customer strategy and legal services – it is possible to identify some of the key issues for success, some pitfalls and some lessons which have been learnt. This data is presented in the form of guidelines to other organizations which may help to ensure that benchmarking projects are successful.

Success Factors

Each of the projects chosen related to key business processes which not only impacted on customers but also had the potential for considerable improvement resulting in a return on investment for the time and resources devoted to benchmarking activities. Each benchmarking team, to a greater or lesser extent, talked to their business partners – i.e. customers and suppliers – when determining the key performance indicators (KPI) for their project.

In each project, the process was mapped to understand better what and how it was done. It was often found that, although it was generally thought everyone involved knew the process being mapped, it was not until the process was mapped 'warts and all' that people actually realized what happened in the process. This mapping also helped to communicate the subject area being benchmarked, helping to reflect what happens and it was found that this was much more effective than simply referring to a set of procedures. This process mapping helped to pinpoint the weak areas of the process, which is important before selecting benchmark partners. For example, with the customer services project, they were able to extrapolate meaningful data from their process, allowing them to determine their current position in relation to the partners benchmarked and where they were being outperformed; this also facilitated a concentration of effort on specific process areas.

At the outset of the data collection phase, it is helpful to consider how the raw data collected is going to be managed and analysed.

- What data is required to quantify the process in meaningful terms?
- How is the data going to be collected?
- Is it already available from another source?
- What do we want to know about the process that is currently not known?

It was also found beneficial to summarize the benefits of each benchmarking project into business, process and cost benefits for the area under consideration.

When contacting potential benchmarking partners, it is helpful to identify the specific areas of activities and the measurement of success which are to be discussed during the visit. It was found to be important to send out a pack of information to those organizations who, in principle, have agreed to participate in a benchmarking project:

- Covering letter including the reason for undertaking the benchmarking project
- Overview of the organization

- Details of the process being benchmarked, including KPIs and their definitions and descriptions – for example, the customer services call handling project included abandoned call rate, profile of calls in relation to peaks and troughs, staffing levels, number of customer services representatives available to take calls, number of calls dealt with by each customer services representative per day, average time to answer calls, call profile, service levels, percentage of enquiries dealt with in first call and percentage of repeat calls per customer on the same issue
- Benchmarking code of conduct to be signed by both parties
- Data collection plan
- Questionnaire seeking data from the benchmarking partner and a completed questionnaire by the benchmarking team reflecting the state-of-the-art of the process being benchmarked

The benchmarking teams rated and selected their partners on the basis of their critical success factors in terms of what was required to be achieved from the project, as well as such aspects as comparable size, structure, geography (where deemed appropriate), reputation with respect to product and service quality, and market position and segmentation using a criteria rating form to focus on the critical few.

The key findings from each benchmarking visit were related to an action plan with respect to what is or what has been implemented; this helped to ensure that the best practices identified were captured and acted upon. In addition, it was found to be important that the analysis identified common threads from the benchmarking visits. Simple graphical displays were used to communicate to all concerned the comparison of the KPIs of the process being benchmarked with that of the partners. This assisted with the acceptance of changes which needed to be made, as well as regular communication of progress which was built into the project plan after the completion of each phase, so that everyone concerned was up to speed before being presented with the project findings.

In the case of the laboratory services project, the process being investigated was large and incorporated many different variables and subprocesses, depending on the type of sample. This made it difficult to map and evaluate the process in an effective manner, e.g. to track performance measures, such as the time taken between each process step. In retrospect, the process was not sufficiently well defined to effectively benchmark; this was due to its broad nature, scope and size. Also, there were constraints placed on the project which had not been initially understood, such as the technology used in the process. Furthermore, while the team did look outside its own industry, initially only companies with laboratories were considered. As the flow of information through the process was being considered, this was perhaps too narrow an approach to selecting partners; companies who dealt primarily with the analysis and processing of data should have been considered more closely.

The major constraint encountered with the operations refurbishment project was only looking inside the water industry for benchmarking partners. As benchmarking is about breakthrough improvement and the implementation of best practices, looking within the industry is insufficient as often the 'best' at particular practices are from diverse areas. This has a tendency to happen with very specific benchmarking projects such as this and needs to be watched and the insular attitudes avoided, e.g. by thinking generically about what is being done rather than literally.

It is important to contact the benchmarking partners early, this can be more difficult than expected with respect to the time involved and identifying the right person(s). Desk research into the companies being considered as benchmarking partners should be undertaken before deciding on partners, although this does depend on time constraints and the type of project being tackled. It has been found useful to visit four to five organizations and that all the visits should take place within a period of one month. However, as the company is looking for high gains in the long term from benchmarking, it is worthwhile taking the time to ensure that the company being benchmarked is suitable for analysis.

After each visit to a benchmarking partner, it is important to detail what has been learnt. It was also found helpful to summarize what the organization is doing better than the benchmark partner in a report format, identifying key points and providing quantitative as well as qualitative data.

Difficulties and Pitfalls

For a benchmarking project to be a success, there are certain difficulties and pitfalls which must be avoided. Based on the projects undertaken, these are the most common ones:

- *Unrealistic assumptions* – when planning the actual project, realistic assumptions need to be made about the time required to complete the individual steps of the benchmarking project, the resources needed and the commitment of employees, other than the team members. The planning of the project needs to be as pragmatic as possible. It is also important to 'manage' the expectations at senior management in respect of quick results and instant benefits as well as their role in the benchmarking process.
- *The team members must be free to participate in the project* – the activities associated with the project should not become something else team members do as part of their normal working week; this will hamper progress and may seriously effect time-scales, commitment and, eventually, the findings of the project.
- *Lack of a contingency plan* – if the project plan is based on a single set of circumstances or conditions, it is extremely vulnerable to changes. It is essential that a contingency plan is prepared to support the implementation and to prepare for any unexpected major changes to the project. This contingency plan must be developed to cope with both favourable as well as adverse changes. If implementation is broken down into a number of sequential steps, then it must be possible to bring phase two forward if phase one took less time than was initially expected, just as phase two would be delayed if phase one took longer than expected.
- *Failure to update the plan* – too often the creation of a plan is seen as a means to an end. Instead, the plan should be considered as a living document which is based on certain assumptions (such as time, cost, resources, levels of commitment) and external factors (such as the benchmarking partners response and the time of year). These assumptions will almost certainly change over the period of a benchmarking project requiring the plan to be updated in terms of what is required and when. In any reconfiguration of the original project the assumptions should be taken into account and any changes which may be

required in them. For example, if the project is to finish on time, more money may have to be spent on resources than was originally estimated to achieve any results of significance.

- *Failure to communicate the plan* – communication of what has been done, what is currently being done and what is planned is vital to the success of a project. If people are not fully aware of what is expected of them, the type of information which has been gathered about best practice, how the benchmark information is to be used to initiate improvements and the changes that will result from the implementation of best practices found from the benchmarking project, then it is highly likely that the plan will fail. It is also important to consider what needs to be communicated and the detail, as well as how it should be done.
- *Inadequate project definition* – if the benchmarking team is not aware of why they are doing a particular project and their capability to change a process then the project will lack direction and focus, leaving them unsure of what to measure and what best practices they are looking for.
- *Inadequate process understanding* – when documenting a process which is being benchmarked, it is important that not only are the processes described but also each process step plus the main practices. When carrying this out, the question 'how do we know this?' should be asked a number of times – i.e. the 5 'why' approach – to validate what the team considers to be the process with those who are involved at each step. If this is not done, then it may lead to any conclusions drawn from the benchmarking study being invalid and of potential danger to the present process.
- *The team try to do everything themselves* – it is important that the team members do not become insular and try to do everything in relation to the project by themselves. At times, they will need to seek the advice and help of individuals who are not directly involved in the benchmarking project. This assistance may be in areas such as data collection, where the data which is required is already being collected by someone, either within a department or externally.
- *The subject area is too large* – unless the process is within the control of the team, and within their comprehension, then it is very difficult to both measure, in meaningful terms, what is done and ask the right questions of the benchmarking and business partners, e.g. customers and suppliers.
- *It seems like a good idea to use benchmarking*, i.e. the latest fad and fashion – benchmarking, just like any other quality management technique, when used inappropriately, will not achieve the expected benefits to the business. Therefore, a balance should be reached between the scope of the problem, the return on investment which is expected and the level of improvement. There is little point in spending considerable time, money and resources on benchmarking a process which will not affect customers in any significant way by bringing breakthrough improvement to business operation.

Key Learning Lessons

Based on the experiences of carrying out the three benchmarking projects this section summarizes what is considered to be the key role and functions of project sponsors, team leaders and team members. Each group of people should be familiar with the role and function performed by the others. These guidelines will provide a form of healthcheck of key considerations to be taken into account by organizations with respect to these type of roles.

Project sponsors should be clear that, when carrying out a benchmarking study, it is better to focus on a particular business process rather than the product or service. Businesses produce products and services but it is processes that provide the end product or service. By focusing on what is done, and how it is done, rather than just the end product, more tangible results of a breakthrough nature can be obtained from the study. It should not be forgotten that some managers and directors perceive benchmarking to be simply a competitive analysis of products, services, equipment, factory facilities and operating costs.

The teams should be assembled from a range of skills and areas of expertise from within the process to be benchmarked, with roles and responsibilities assigned at the start in accordance with these skills and responsibilities, e.g. data gatherers, communicators, etc.

The narrower the focus of the investigation the greater the chance of success. By focusing on a specific process which has a clearly defined start and end point, that is well documented and within the teams control to change, this increases the chances of not only learning more about what is presently done but also improves the understanding and appreciation of how other organizations do it better, e.g. faster, cheaper, and with a better quality service or product.

Management should be personally involved in the benchmarking process, and the project sponsor should encourage their involvement. It is important to be seen to do more than just evaluate the success or failure of a project at its various review stages. They should, particularly in the case of a project sponsor, become involved in the activities of the project, especially when benchmarking visits and the lessons learned from them are evaluated, so that they can understand more about the reasons for benchmarking and why the organization needs to adapt constantly and to adopt best practices. The sponsor is critical to ensure that the project is carried through to the implementation stage; projects often run in peaks and troughs and, on occasions, require someone to kick start it again.

It is useful for process 'experts' from outside the team to be involved in the preparation and validation of the questionnaire which will be used when determining who are to be the benchmarking partners and gleaning information from the eventual partners. These personnel would be made up of both those involved in the day-to-day running of the process and those who are either its suppliers or customers.

When presenting the results of a benchmarking project, it is useful if not only the improvements in areas such as customer satisfaction and reduced cycle time are defined but also measures such as financial and operational savings are offset against the cost of the project.

It is important to remember that it may not be feasible to emulate a world class organization's processes straightaway and, initially, it may be worthwhile benchmarking organizations which are best in class so that an understanding is achieved of the partners process, rather than being dazzled by it, wondering 'how do we get there?'.

The *team leader* is primarily responsible for the planning of the project and its management. It is useful at the start of each meeting to review the team's progress against the plan, particularly at the stages of collecting and analysing data, organizing visits to benchmarking partners, and recommending and implementing improvements to the process.

The team leaders communicate with people and the parties who are outside of the team members through the use of newsletters, bulletins on noticeboards, face-to-face discussions, general updates to those who are required to buy in to the project, and they undertake presentations, where appropriate, to individuals and departments who are crucial to successful implementation of the project findings.

Team members determine who are the customers and suppliers and hold discussions with them before deciding what are the success criteria and performance measures for the success of the project. The measures should be based around what customers/suppliers require, because these are where improvements will be most tangible.

The team members provide a 'picture' of the process, e.g. a flow chart, to focus ideas and data collection methodologies. By providing a picture of the process, it is easier to identify what is needed to know and where to concentrate understanding on what is currently being done.

The team members then describe the process, the process steps and the practice at each step to help to understand what is currently done and to provide a reference point for change in the process at a later date, e.g. this is what used to be done, this is what is currently done, this is why it was changed and this is the result of the change.

What can be measured needs to be balanced against what would be liked to be measured. It may be found that once the study has begun, there are certain areas of the process which should be measured for the purposes of understanding both what is done and what others do but, at present, this is beyond current capability. It is beneficial to understand why this is currently beyond capability and to do something about it before continuing with the benchmarking project. It should always be kept in mind, in particular, when carrying out a benchmarking visit, that the reason for benchmarking is to understand how other organizations and their people do things better.

Specific measureables are used in the process to analyse the performance gap. Simple tools such as a Z-chart (see figure 19.2) are used so that the position among partners can be demonstrated within the areas that have common measures, as well as demonstrating what is required to achieve these levels of performance.

Team members should think generically when looking at other organization's processes. It is important when considering partners to think outside of the current industry. In other words, who does what best, or is perceived to be the best, within the process being studied? This was a particular problem in the operations refurbishment project, because of the specific nature of the activities under consideration.

Not all benchmarking visits are appropriate. It is important when determining partners that only the relevant few organizations are visited where there is a possibility that something of significance will be learnt. If this is not given adequate consideration, visits can become very much hit and miss, and learning from others becomes a matter of luck rather than through a systematic structured approach.

Throughout the project, the team should be kept informed about what individual members are doing, both at an informal and formal level. Team meetings should always have an agenda which is circulated well before the meeting (this should be decided by the team in advance and not dictated to them) with minutes circulated within a few days of the meeting being carried out. As with any agenda, the items for discussion/action should be prioritized with appropriate times allocated to each item, just as would be expected in a project plan.

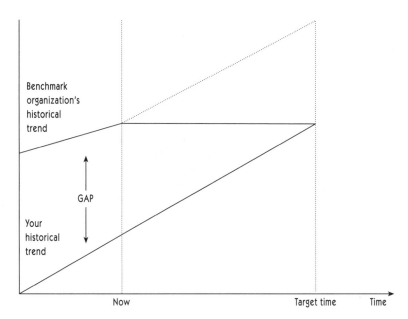

Figure 19.2 Gap analysis

A record of what has been done, how it was done, why it was done, should be kept for reference at a later date, when a report is being prepared or other benchmarking projects are being started. A benchmarking log book is useful for reference at a later date when producing the report.

Team members should remember to ask the question 'how do we know?' when assessing what is done and what other people do. Hard evidence is needed to back up any assumptions made about internal processes and those of other organizations, rather than assuming 'It sounds like a good idea so let's do it'.

Summary

Benchmarking is a technique for the continuous improvement of business processes. It is, therefore, important to ensure that the process of benchmarking is thought of in a similar vein; the objective is to improve continually the benchmarking process used for each project – by sharing successes, pitfalls, and failures of each project and, thereby, promoting continuous learning.

A benchmarking project is likely to generate other additional benchmarking projects within the process studied or with interfacing processes. A project, in addition to the savings generated, is also helpful in promoting understanding of key performance indicators and measures of quality; in other words, what do we need to have in place to understand what we do, how we do it, why we do it, and how well we do it.

The reasons for NWW undertaking a series of benchmarking projects were communicated across the organization:

- It solves problems which are important to the business rather than people pursuing 'pet' projects.

- It is based on a systematic approach and reality and not history or gut feel.
- Benchmarking projects are proactive rather than reactive.
- The results allow for controlled change rather than frantic catching up.
- They are focused on objective evaluation rather than subjective perceptions.

These are the main benefits achieved:

- Average annual savings of £1 million
- Identified where North West Water is in relation to the outside world
- Demonstrated the potential to improve key processes, thereby increasing motivation and facilitating the commitment to change – this is very important in the facilitating of improvement in a monopoly supplier environment
- Proved the usefulness of benchmarking as a concept and quality management technique
- Removed complacency and the 'not invented here' syndrome, e.g. 'they do that but we can't because we're different'

It became clear, as the benchmarking studies progressed, that while lots of organizations and people use the benchmarking jargon, much of the discussion relates to competitive analysis of product and equipment and *not* the benchmarking of processes. While the benchmarking concept is relatively simple, the difficulties involved in progressing a benchmarking project are not often realized. A case in point is step three in the benchmarking process 'identify best in class'; experience from this study indicates that it takes some degree of investigation and analysis to identify best in class organizations, particularly if the project has been ill-defined with no clearly identifiable process. The more unusual the process being benchmarked, the more difficult this becomes and the more difficult to identify meaningful generic data and questions. In specific processes such as the ones investigated as part of the operations refurbishment project, there is a tendency for the benchmarking team members not to be willing to look outside of their own industry sector by concentrating on the functionality of the process steps rather than thinking in terms of what we do, e.g. communicate positively, effectively and helpfully with our customers.

The experience of benchmarking at NWW indicates that it takes around six months to undertake and implement the findings of a benchmarking project. From the benchmarking projects undertaken, a number of key lessons have been learnt. These have been distilled in the form of success factors and pitfalls to be avoided. It is hoped that these will serve as guidelines to other organizations which help to ensure that any benchmarking projects are effective. The key roles of a project sponsor, team leader and team member have been identified as crucial for success. The guidelines outlined in this chapters can prove helpful to other organizations in communicating to these three groups of people what is expected of them.

It is clear from study of the benchmarking literature that much of the material is very similar. The tendency is to focus on issues such as the history of benchmarking, the process steps and general discussion of benefits and potential problems. There appears to be a sparsity of written material based on actual benchmarking experiences. The study reported in this chapter goes someway to extending the knowledge of the benchmarking concept.

References

Anderson, B. and Petterson, P. G. 1996: *The Benchmarking Handbook*. London: Chapman and Hall.

Camp, R. C. 1989: *Benchmarking: The Search for Industry Best Practice That Leads to Superior Performance*. Milwaukee: ASQC Quality Press.

Camp, R. C. 1995: *Business Process Benchmarking: Finding and Implementing the Best Practices*, ASQC Quality Press.

Codling, S. 1995: *Best Practice Benchmarking*. Basingstoke, Hants.: Gower Press.

Cook, S. 1993: *Practical Benchmarking: A Manager's Guide to Creating a Competitive Advantage*. London: Kogan Page.

Hanson, P. and Voss, C. 1995: Benchmarking best practice in European manufacturing sites. *Business Process Re-Engineering and Management Journal*, 1(1), 60–74.

Leonard, K. J. 1996: Information systems and benchmarking in the credit scoring industry. *Benchmarking for Quality Management and Technology*, 3(1), 38–44.

Prasad, S. Tata, J. and Thorn, R. 1996: Benchmarking maquiladora operations relative to those in the USA. *International Journal of Quality and Reliability Management*, 13(9), 8–17.

Zairi, M. 1995: The integration of benchmarking and BPR: a matter of choice or necessity? *Business Process Re-Engineering and Management Journal*, 1(3), 3–9.

Zairi, M. and Leonard, P. 1994: *Practical Benchmarking: A Complete Guide*. London: Chapman and Hall.

chapter twenty

Business Process Re-Engineering (BPR)

J. Macdonald and B. G. Dale

Introduction

BPR was popularized as a formal concept by the writings of Hammer (1990), Davenport and Short (1990) and Hammer and Champy (1993) but perhaps James Harrington (1987), with his emphasis on process improvement in action, was the real originator. The earlier work of Hammer (1990) and the later expanded version of Hammer and Champy (1993) tended to focus on corporate transformation, while the other influential text of Davenport and Short (1990) has a focus on business process redesign, linking the concept specifically to developments in technology and industrial engineering. Many of the first cases of BPR had a heavy focus on IT, to enable redesign implementation.

In recent times, BPR has emerged as the concept which enables an organization to take a radical and revolutionary look at the way in which it operates; references to it abound in management and technical publications. It has become popular in a short period of time, promising amazing results very quickly in relation to corporate and technological change, transformation and competitive pressures. Some writers – e.g. Born (1994) – regard it is a successor to TQM, making the point that, rather than continually improving a process, BPR challenges the need for a process. The protagonists of BPR argue that it, rather than TQM, is the concept which enables an organization to make the necessary step changes, originality and improvements to the business which will enable it to leapfrog the competition. On the other hand, writers such as Zairi (1996) and Harrington (1998) believe that BPR will soon fall out of favour with industrialists. There is an emerging view in the literature – e.g. Elzinga et al. (1995), De Toro and McCabe (1997) and Zairi (1997) – that Business Process Management (BPM) is a better option.

While TQM is based, in general, on continuous improvement in processes over a relatively long period of time, BPR emphasizes structural process redesign, process re-engineering and fundamental rethinking of the business; this leads to claims of producing faster returns in a relatively short period of time through its one-step solution to a problem. However, they are both philosophies to improve the performance of a business and, in the authors' view, continuous improvement should come first to provide the base for the more radical change and improvements generated by BPR. It should also not be overlooked that TQM also drives breakthrough improvements.

The underlying issues in BPR are not necessarily new, albeit the language is modern. The early material on the subject made little mention that the approach had its origins in other change initiatives. Its roots are to be found in scientific management (Taylor, 1911), the system theories proposed by Beer (1981), the breakthrough concepts through a process approach advocated by Juran (1964), benchmarking initiatives outlined by Camp (1989), the group technology concept pioneered by Burbidge (1963), work study concepts as typically outlined by Currie (1989), improvement initiatives in manufacturing systems proposed by Schonberger (1986) and modern information, communications and systems technology.

There is some confusion as to what constitutes BPR, what it covers, which initiatives it embraces, and its relationship with TQM. This is not helped by the variety of terms (e.g. business process improvement, business process redesign, business process re-engineering, core value driven process re-engineering, process redesign, business restructuring, new industrial engineering, process simplification and value management) which various writers use in their description of BPR, along with the associated imprecision in which the terms are used. However, most of the terms refer roughly to the same type of activity, pointing out that gains in performance can be achieved by taking a holistic and objective view of business processes.

The authors, along with writers such as Harrington (1995) and Kelada (1995), view TQM and BPR as a complementary and integral approach rather than in opposition; see Macdonald (1995a). In fact, many of the tools and techniques which have been proved and used in continuous improvement are employed in BPR projects, and a number of the principles and practices of BPR are very similar to those which underpin TQM. Our combined practical and research evidence points to the fact that those companies who have been successful in building continuous improvement principles into their business operation in an evolutionary manner have created the solid platform and environment on which to develop the concept of BPR. Those organizations starting with TQM will have a better understanding of processes, which is central to both TQM and BPR. Having learned how to change using the continuous improvement philosophy, they are more ready to deal with the more radical designing of new processes which is demanded by BPR. In general, it has been service industries and public sector organizations which have taken up the theme of BPR rather than manufacturing industry. It would be argued by managers in the service industries and the public sector that, without BPR undertaken as part of the natural management process of running a business, they would simply not have survived. In general, they have only relatively recently felt the winds of change.

As outlined in chapter 1, management have a tendency to be attracted to those initiatives which are easy to understand and which can give them fast results. Attracted by consultants promises of what BPR is about and what it can achieve, some managements have been led to believe that it has superseded TQM. The justification for including the chapter on BPR in this book is to help managers to identify the commonalities and differences. The aim is to present, in simple terms, what BPR means, its main approaches and methods, techniques employed and main principles and practices.

Approaches Used in BPR

The two main approaches employed in BPR are process redesign and process re-engineering, and these are both examined here. The approaches are based on taking a holistic and objective view of the core processes that are needed to accomplish specific business objectives, without being constrained by what already exists. BPR covers a range of activities that result in radical change, to either individual processes or to the total organization. The main differences between the two approaches are that the latter involves greater structural change and risk while the former is quicker, less costly to implement but with potential less benefit and improvement.

Business process redesign

Hammer and Champy (1993) point out that every re-engineering measure usually start with process redesign. Process redesign can be carried out in many different ways depending on the degree to which the process is to be changed; it usually takes the existing process(es) as the base. It concentrates on those core processes with cross-functional boundaries and is generally customer focused, with a view to process simplification, streamlining, mistake-proofing the process, efficiency and adaptability. It tends to seek answers to questions such as these:

- What is this process doing?
- What are the core competencies?
- What are the key elements?
- What are its key measurables?
- What are the main information flows?
- Is it adding value?
- Is it producing an output which fully meets customer requirements?
- How can it be improved?
- How can it be done differently?
- Who is the process owner?
- Can it be done by someone less skilled?
- Is the technology employed used to best advantage?
- Can new technology provide new solutions?
- Can activities be integrated?
- Can activities be done in parallel?

Process redesign has its roots in DPA – see chapter 14 – which originated at IBM in 1984. It also uses many of the techniques used in O&M and work study, but employs modern methods of IT to best advantage, in particular, for integrating process activities. The emphasis has been on relational databases, communication technology and networked personal computers to enable information to be shared and kept up-to-date, facilitating processes to be undertaken in simultaneous mode. Process redesign would be difficult to achieve without the formalized procedures arising from the application of a quality management system.

Business process re-engineering

Process re-engineering or new process design demands more imagination and inductive thinking, and radical change than process redesign; those charged with the implementation of a project should abandon their belief in the rules, procedures, practices, systems and values that have shaped the current organization. It raises and challenges assumptions such as make-or-buy decisions, structures, functional responsibilities and tasks, systems and documentation – e.g. supplier payment – elimination of specialist departments, etc. Hammer and Champy (1993) define re-engineering as:

> a fundamental rethink and radical redesign of business processes to achieve dramatic improvements in critical contemporary measures of performance, such as cost, quality, service and speed.

The approach is based on the view that continuous improvement is not sufficient to meet the organizational expectations for business development and change. Business process re-engineering seeks to make major fundamental, radical and dramatic breakthroughs in performance and is holistic in nature. The main focus is to ensure a 'clean slate' or 'greenfield' approach to processes, pinpointing that part of the organization on which to put the emphasis and highlighting the processes which add value. It is, however, not without risks, resources, time and costs which are associated with the efforts involved in a re-engineering project.

The concept is based on making best use of IT in terms of communication and information handling systems. It harnesses the enablers of technology and the release of the innovative potential of people to achieve breakthrough improvements, requiring a change from functional thinking to process thinking.

The Principles of BPR

Despite the difference in emphasis and terminology used by various authors, the principles and values remain relatively common. From publications such as Hammer and Champy (1993), Macdonald (1995a, b), Tinnila (1995) and Coulson-Thomas (1994), these are the main principles of BPR:

- Strategic in concept
- Customer focused
- Output rather than input focused
- Focus on key business processes
- Process responsibility and decisions at point where work is performed
- Cross-functional in nature
- Internal and external customer supplier relationships
- Senior management commitment and involvement
- Involves networking people and their activities
- Integrated involvement of people and technical aspects
- Clear communication and visibility
- Mindset of outrageous improvement
- People at all levels of the organization prepared to question the status quo in terms of technology, practices, procedures, approaches, strategies

A number of these principles are similar to those related to TQM as outlined in chapter 1.

Risks and Benefits of BPR

BPR projects tend to be across functional boundaries, eliminating functions, and processes and changing their boundaries. Consequently, there are a number of risks associated with BPR:

- If the wrong processes are selected for BPR, i.e. if they are not core, the impact to the business will then be limited on delivering value
- Inadequate analysis, planning and assessment, in particular, of current state analysis
- The resulting upheaval and costs may outweigh the savings, in particular, when the changes impact negatively on delivery schedules in terms of response and development times to customers
- The long cycle time needed to complete a project and produce beneficial results to a business
- Management and staff not providing the leadership and direction to the process, leading to projects failing to realize their potential
- People failing to take ownership for the initiative
- Excluding people from the lower levels of the organizational hierarchy in the design and building of new processes
- Lack of attention to the so-called 'soft issues'
- Misconceptions relating to downsizing and restructuring, creating resistance to change
- Destruction of teams and teamwork

There are a number of barriers that can inhibit radical change:

- Traditional management behaviour
- Opposition, due to fear of what the change might entail, in particular, during down sizing, delayering and outsourcing
- Lack of resources, time, commitment and 'belief'
- The investment required in IT and other systems

A related issue to risks and barriers is the issue of how an organization's culture can adopt to empowerment. Empowerment within an organization's process will have a direct impact upon process expectations and system design. This impact may be within the re-engineered process and also at the point where that process affects others.

Useful discussion on the lack of success with BPR projects is provided by writers such as Deakins and Makgill (1997), King (1994), Hall et al. (1993), Kennedy (1994) and O'Brien (1995).

The processes selected for BPR should be based on issues such as critical success factors, significance to the business, degree of process failure, customer concerns, volume of paperwork, long lead-time, controls, degree of firefighting activities and financial cost to the organization.

These are benefits of BPR:

- Increased customer focus
- Improved profitability
- Improved quality and control
- Improved corporate flexibility
- Increases speed of service delivery and responsiveness
- Improved measurability within the processes operation and the management of that information

Implementation of BPR

Chan and Peel (1998) have carried out research which points to the fact that BPR results from external factors (such as customers, competition and change) and by internal factors (including technology, efficiency, cost and strategic focus). In approaching implementation, these movitational factors or drivers should be taken into consideration.

The implementation of BPR requires a greenfield approach along the lines of: 'If we were to start this company now, with the knowledge we have, how would it be organized?' The focus is looking at completely new ways of accomplishing work, i.e. redesign from scratch. These are the key factors in the implementation of a success-ful BPR project:

- The project champion
- The steering committee
- Process design team
- Process owner
- Implementation team

BPR will involve a number of cross-functional issues and strategic decisions, thus the sponsor of a BPR project must be a senior manager. The tendency to appoint the IT Director or HR Director as the champion(s) of a BPR project, should be avoided because of the impact of technology on people. The *project champion* should establish the vision and goals, allocate resources, empower employees, hold employees account-able for activities they have been allocated, resolve functional and departmental conflicts, and communicate and champion change.

As with all major projects, it is recommended that a *steering committee* of appro-priate personnel is established. This will be its role:

- To define the improvement objectives and develop a vision statement for the process.
- To manage the project against the agreed time-scale.
- To provide resources and ensure that appropriate people are involved in the project.
- To ensure that the individuals involved have the right set of skills and techniques.
- To identify issues and resolve them.
- To challenge the *status quo* and continually ask the five whys.
- To resolve functional conflicts.

A *process design team* should comprise 6–8 members who have the appropriate skills, expertise and knowledge of processes and their analysis and measurement, facilitation and project management, IT and data handling, innovation and creative thought, and team building. Consultants and equipment suppliers often provide a useful supplement to the team. Depending on the project and size of the organization, some members of the team may have to be full-time. This is justified on the basis that whole parts of the business may be subjected to re-engineering, and the length of time which is needed to complete the project. The team must decide how to allocate tasks and whether to establish mini-teams to focus on subprocesses. They must also have regard for the potential effects that the processes redesign will have upon other existing processes.

This is the role of the team:

- To identify and map the current state of the existing processes involved in the project along with their related information flows
- To define and understand the existing processes
- To identify the critical processes
- To challenge all assumptions surrounding processes and how they have developed
- To accept no boundaries and demarcations
- To find breakthrough improvements
- To design the new processes
- To ensure that the people who will be affected are involved in the process
- To decide how the changes will be measured and assessed
- To pilot the changes and modify the design, as appropriate
- To remain customer focused throughout the whole of the redesign
- To present the recommendations to the project sponsor and steering committee
- To communicate on a regular basis with all those likely to be affected by the change

Once the process design teams recommendations have been accepted, the implementation phase can begin. This usually involves disbanding the team and the establishment of a *process owner*, responsible for the actual re-engineering and accountable for the process goals. The person should be a senior manager selected from the process design team. This is his or her role:

- To ensure that the plans are fully implemented
- To obtain and organize the necessary resources
- To select the implementation team
- To overcome any resistance to the changes
- To encourage people to follow the new ways of working
- To manage the new process
- To ensure that the goals are achieved

Implementation team: the team members are effectively the managers of the newly designed process; they will usually be drawn from the membership of the process design team.

BPR Methodology

There are four main phases of a BPR project – preparation, innovation and design, implementation and assessment.

These are the main activities in the *preparation* phase:

- Reviewing the strategic objectives of the business, because this will provide an indication of the need for BPR – from this review, the decisions will be taken to redesign the key processes of the organization in line with the business objective; it also involves the setting of objectives for others
- Choosing the BPR project – this will include establishing the team and educating its members in the fundamentals of BPR
- Mapping the strategic processes of the project as it is, concentrating on the big picture – the typical tools and techniques to assist with this are described in chapter 14
- Identifying and defining customer needs and requirements, and pinpointing which of the key processes have the greatest influence on the customer – this will involve customer surveys and the like
- Defining strategies that can match business needs and characteristics with customer requirements
- Through various activities, identifying the 'breakthrough' theme
- Obtaining steering committee approval for the ideas and developing clear objectives for the design team

The *innovation and design* phase involves these activities:

- Developing vision statements for the BPR project so as to represent an organization which has these characteristics:

  - Based on a customer orientated process
  - Products and services dertermined customer needs and requirements
  - IT services designed to empower employees to serve customers
  - One point of contact and a unified face to the customer
  - All employees clearly focused on the customer

- Encouraging the team to think outside of functions and processes and to forget boundaries, hierarchies, authorities and limits of current systems and technology
- Since the role of IT in providing the radical change is important, the IT department focusing their efforts on the processes which have been redesigned or re-engineered
- Being realistic on what BPR can achieve and ensuring that the initiative is integrated with other improvement initiatives and infrastructures, in particular, existing processes and their expectations
- Redesigning or re-engineering the selected processes
- Preparing the organization for the change and addressing important issues:

  - Restructuring the basic organization and reporting procedures
  - Redeployment planning
  - Payment and reward

The *implementation* phase involves these activities:

- Developing an implementation plan
- Implementing the new process design in pilot mode
- Agreeing the goals and objectives for the redesigned process and communicating them to all concerned
- Developing rational metrics for the newly designed process
- Addressing the cultural and people issues to support the smooth work of the re-engineered processes – this may require that the new process design be implemented in a number of phases, and will allow the people skills and other processes that affect the re-engineered process to develop at a effective speed and cost
- Emphasizing teamwork along the concept of the 'one-stop' shop using technology to share 'specialist' knowledge through 'generalist' team players
- Developing education and training programmes to provide specific skills for employees to fulfil their new role

Holding the gains involves these activities:

- Recognizing the change
- Managing the re-engineered business
- Managing the people dimensions
- Maintaining the change
- Exploiting the gains

Summary

The principles and practices of BPR have their base in other concepts such as TQM, workstudy, group technology, etc.; the same applies to the tools and techniques used in BPR. The authors are of the view that BPR is complementary to TQM, rather than being an alternative or in opposition. For example, TQM can help to 'hold the gains' achieved from BPR and can create an environment that will help to ensure the success of BPR projects. The claims that BPR is a successor to TQM should be dismissed.

There has been considerable debate on the key differences between BPR and TQM. In short, the former is based, in general, on radical and breakthrough change over a relatively short time period; the latter, in general, on incremental improvement over the longer term and working within existing framework systems and procedures by improving them. This distinction is outlined in pictorial form by Imai (1986). In the authors' view, aiming for large step changes makes a project riskier, more complex and also involves greater expense. Incremental change is safer and costs less. The simplicity of incremental improvement often overshadows the fact that, in practice, it requires effort and constant application to implement in an effective and efficient manner.

TQM and BPR do share common themes, such as a focus on customers, key processes, eliminating waste, benchmarking. One of the key differences is that BPR places more emphasis on equipment and technology and TQM more emphasis on people. BPR tends to concentrate on one process at a time using a project planning methodology, whereas TQM takes a more holistic view of the organization, building improvement into all its areas of operation. TQM acts as the foundation for an organization's day-to-day functioning and continual improvement that allows and supports the development of BPR as an effective business improvement tool. To enjoy the best out of both concepts, they should be combined and integrated together. As mentioned in chapter 12, TQM can sometimes stall and plateau, and other initiatives, within the overall framework of the approach, can often provide the spark to revitalize it. BPR could provide this type of excitement, but to do so it needs to be positioned within the broader TQM approach.

BPR requires dedication, acceptance of risk and considerable upheaval. It is important that an organization is clear on this because it is so easy to find them in conflict with the potential cost savings. Not every organization is capable of accomplishing the level of change required, but any organization that has the ambition to be the best cannot ignore BPR but must accept the challenge. Some industries, which operate in dynamic environments, are more akin to take on the risk associated with BPR than others where the disturbance of processes could have severe consequences. It is also important for organizations to be clear on whether they need business process redesign or the more radical process re-engineering.

Managers are central to the success of re-engineering projects and they must be prepared to change their role and power structures, and to provide the necessary leadership; see chapter 1.

References

Beer, S. 1981: *The Brain of the Firm*. Chichester: John Wiley.

Born, G. 1994: *Process Management to Quality Improvement*. Chichester: John Wiley.

Burbidge, J. L. 1963: Production flow analysis. *The Production Engineer*, 42(12), 742–52.

Camp, R. C. 1989: *Benchmarking: the Search for Industry Best Practices that Lead to Superior Performance*. Milwaukee: ASQC Quality Press.

Chan, P. S. and Peel, D. 1998: Causes and impact of re-engineering. *Business Process Management Journal*, 4(1), 44–5.

Coulson-Thomas, C. 1994: *Business Process Re-engineering: Myth and Reality*. London: Kogan Page.

Currie, R. M. 1989: *Work Study*. London: Pitman.

Davenport, T. H. and Short, J. E. 1990: The new industrial engineering: information technology and business process re-design. *Sloan Management Review*, 31(4), 11–27.

Deakins, E. and Makgill, H. H. 1997: What killed BPR? Some evidence from the literature. *Business Process Management Journal*, 3(1), 81–107.

De Toro, I. and McCabe, T. 1997: How to stay flexible and elude fads. *Quality Progress*, 30(3), 55–60.

Elzinga, D. J., Horok, T., Chung-Yee, L. and Bruner, C. 1995: Business process management: survey and methodology. *IEEE Transactions on Engineering Management*, 24(2), 119–28.

Hall, G., Rosenthal, J. and Wade, J. 1993: How does re-engineering really work. *Harvard Business Review*, November–December, 60–72.

Hammer, M. 1990: Re-engineering work: don't automate, obliterate. *Harvard Business Review*, 68(4), 104–12.

Hammer, M. and Champy, J. 1993: *Re-engineering the Corporation*. London: Nicholas Brealey.

Harrington, H. J. 1987: *The Improvement Process*. New York: McGraw Hill.

Harrington, H. J. 1995: *Total Improvement Management: the Next Generation in Performance Improvement*. New York: McGraw Hill.

Harrington, H. J. 1998: Performance improvement: the rise and fall of re-engineering. *The TQM Magazine*, 10(2), 69–71.

Imai, M. 1986: *Kaizen the Key to Japan's Success.* New York: Random House.

Juran, J. M. 1964: *Managerial Breakthrough.* New York: McGraw Hill.

Kelada, J. N. 1995: *Integrating Re-engineering with Total Quality.* Milwaukee: ASQC Quality Press.

Kennedy, C. 1994: Re-engineering: the human costs and benefits. *Long Range Planning*, 27(5), 64–72.

King, W. R. 1994: Process re-engineering – the strategic dimensions. *Information Systems Management*, 11(2), 71–3.

Macdonald, J. 1995a: *Understanding Business Process Re-engineering.* London: Hodder and Stoughton.

Macdonald, J. 1995b: Together TQM and BPR are winners. *The TQM Magazine*, 7(3), 21–5.

O'Brien, B. 1995: *Decisions About Re-engineering: Briefings on Issues and Options.* London: Chapman and Hall.

Schonberger, R. J. 1986: *World Class Manufacturing: the Principles of Simplicity Applied.* New York: Free Press.

Taylor, F. W. 1911: *The Principles of Scientific Management.* London: Harper and Row.

Tinnila, M. 1995: Strategic perspective to business process re-design. *Management Decision*, 33(3), 25–34.

Zairi, M. 1996: Uninspired by re-engineering. *Strategic Insights into Quality*, 4(1), 19–20.

Zairi, M. 1997: Business process management: a boundaryless approach to modern competitiveness. *Business Process Management*, 3(1), 674–80.

chapter twenty-one

Teams and Teamwork

B. G. Dale

Introduction

The development of people, and their involvement in improvement activities both individually and through teamwork, is a key feature in a company's approach to TQM. A key aspect of this is making full use of the skills and knowledge of all employees to the benefit of the individuals and the organization. There are a number of different types of teams with different operating characteristics, all of which can act as a vehicle for involving people in improvement activities. Some teams have a narrow focus, with members coming from one functional area, whereas others are wider and cross-functional dealing with the deep-rooted problems between internal customers and suppliers. The names given to the teams are varied – quality circles (QCs), yield improvement teams (YITs), quality improvement teams, continuous improvement teams, problem elimination teams, self-directed work teams, process improvement groups, task groups, SPC teams, error cause removal teams, corrective action teams, Kaizen teams and cross-functional teams – and are found in areas such as design, QA, costs, standardization, delivery and supply. There are also groups of people already working together, who are also involved in continuous improvement activity and form hybrids between two or more types of teams.

Japanese companies and their people are much more comfortable with the use of teams as part of their continuous improvement efforts than is usually the case in European companies. This may be because of the divisive nature of Western industry – 'them and us', 'management and unions', 'staff and hourly paid', 'headquarters and operating locations', 'what's-in-it-for-me', etc. It is often the case in European organizations that management will decide to launch some form of team activity as part of an improvement initiative; they will put the members together and expect the team to work in an effective manner without any form of training, coaching, direction, management attention, counselling or teambuilding. In such circumstances, it is little wonder that the team starts to flounder within a few months of its inception.

This chapter, which is based on the UMIST research on teams – e.g. Dale and Lees (1986), Manson and Dale (1989), Briggs et al. (1993), Boaden et al. (1991) and Dale and Huke (1996) – and practical experience of working with teams in many different types of organization, examines the role of teamwork in a process of continuous improvement and outlines the operating characteristics of project teams, QC and quality improvement teams. The key constituents of teams in terms of sponsor, facilitator, leader and member are outlined. A method for evaluating the health of teams is described. Some guidelines are also given which should help to ensure that teams are both active and effective.

The Role of Teams in Continuous Improvement

Teams have a number of roles to play as a component in a process of continuous improvement:

- Aiding the commitment of people to the principles of TQM
- Providing an additional means of communication between individuals, management and their direct reports, across functions and with customers and suppliers
- Providing the means and opportunity for people to participate in decision making about how the business operates
- Improving relationships, developing trust and facilitating co-operative activity
- Helping to develop people and encouraging leadership traits
- Building collective responsibility and developing a sense of ownership
- Aiding personal development and building confidence
- Developing problem-solving skills
- Facilitating awareness of quality improvement potential, leading to behaviour and attitude change
- Helping to facilitate a change in management style and culture
- Solving problems
- Imbuing a sense of accomplishment
- Improving the adoption of new products to the production line
- Improving morale
- Improving operating effectiveness as people work in a common direction and through this generating interaction and synergy

In 1993, ASQC commissioned the Gallup organization to assess employee attitudes on teamwork, empowerment and quality improvement. The survey of 1,293 adults focused on a variety of topics including extent of participation in quality teams, employee feelings of empowerment, and effects of technology and teamwork on empowerment. It was found that there was a high level of employee participation in quality improvement teamwork and there was considerable evidence which pointed to the positive effects of quality and teamwork on employee empowerment. It was also found that employees are very clear on the purpose of quality-related teamwork, under its multitude of names and that those employees participating in such teamwork are also more likely to receive training than those who do not participate.

Types of Teams

In the superior performing organization, teamwork is second nature. For example, the senior management work together as an effective team, managers of the various operating and functional units act as a team, people from different functions co-operate in the team activities which are needed in FMEA, SPC, simultaneous engineering, benchmarking, supplier development, ISO9000 quality management series registration and internal audits. In addition to teamwork within functions, it is common to find teams working together across the business. In some cases, e.g. Crosby methodology (1979), teams are hierarchial in nature – a corrective action team is formed on a directive from a quality improvement team. Unless effective teamworking and cohesion is seen at the top of an organization, it is unlikely that the managers will be able to encourage their employees to work effectively in teams. The superior performing organizations use a variety of ways to facilitate team building, improve relationships and to reinforce the teamwork ethic. For example Dale and Huke (1996), writing about their experiences in Hong Kong, give examples such as carnivals, team competitions, social and recreational activities, and entry into the dragon boat race competition. Having made the case for teams, it is important for the management of an organization to decide when and how to use teams, and what for.

There are a variety of types of teams with differing characteristics – in terms of membership, mode of participation, autonomy, problem selection, scope of activity, decision-making authority, access to information, problem-solving potential, resources, and permanency – which can be used in the improvement process. It is important that the right type of team is formed for the project, problem, or activity under consideration and that a working definition of the team is decided upon. The most popular types of teams are project teams, QCs and quality improvement teams.

Project teams

As already discussed in chapters 1 and 2, the drive to improve quality originates at the top of an organization. If senior management identify the main problems facing the organization, key improvement issues can be developed which are then allocated among their membership for consideration as a one-off project. The project owner then selects employees to constitute a team which will consider the improvement issue. The owner can either lead the team themselves or act as 'foster parent', 'sponsor' or 'guardian angel' to the team. Through participation in project teams, managers better understand the problem-solving process and become more sensitive to the problems faced by other types of teams. The senior management project team is one example of this type of team, but there are others. These are the typical characteristics of such teams:

- The objective has been defined by senior management.
- The team is led by management.
- It is temporary in nature.
- The project is specific and significant, perhaps addressing issues of strategic change and will have clear deliverables within a set time-scale.
- The team is organized in such a way to ensure it employs the appropriate talents, skills, and functions which are suitable in resolution of the project.
- The scope of activity tends to be cross-functional.
- Participation is not usually voluntary – a person is requested by senior management to join the team and this is done on the basis of their expertise for the project being tackled.
- Team meetings tend to be of long rather than of short duration, although they occur on a regular basis.

Quality circles (QCs)

QCs, when operated in the classical manner, have characteristics which are different from other methods of teamwork. They have been the subject of many books (Hutchins, 1985; Mohr and Mohr, 1983; Robson, 1984) and the focus of much research (Bradley and Hill, 1983; Hayward et al., 1985; Hill, 1986) almost to the exclusion of research on other types of team activity. A comparison of the Japanese operation of QCs to that of Western companies has already been made in chapter 3; however, it is suffice to say that QCs, in the classical sense, have not been too 'successful' in Western organizations. In the author's opinion, this is because they were introduced at a time in the West when organizations did not fully understand and practise the principles of TQM. A vast amount of experience was however acquired in the operation of QCs, much of which has been well documented. It is suggested that any organization wishing to develop effective teamwork and resolve some of the issues which arise in the operation of teams should consult the written wisdom on QCs, because they will find much good advice on facilitation, problem-solving skills, organization of meetings and maintaining the momentum.

A QC is a voluntary group of 6–8 employees from the same work area. They meet usually in company time, for one hour every week or fortnight, under the leadership of their work supervisor, to solve problems relating to improving their work activities and environment.

These are the typical characteristics of QCs:

- Membership is voluntary and people can opt out as and when they wish.
- Members are usually drawn from a single department and are doing similar work.
- All members are of equal status.
- They operate within the existing organizational structure.
- Members are free to select, from their own work area, the problems and projects which they wish to tackle – these tend to be the ones they have to live with every day; there is little or no interference from management.
- The QC members are trained in the use of the seven basic quality control tools, meeting skills, facilitation, team building, project management and presentation techniques, etc.
- Appropriate data collection, problem-solving skills and decision-making methods are employed by QC members to the project under consideration.
- Meetings are generally of short duration, but a large number are held.
- There is minimum pressure to solve the problem within a set time frame.
- A facilitator is available to assist the QC with the project.
- The solutions are evaluated in terms of their cost-effectiveness.
- The findings, solutions and recommendations of the QC are shown to management for comment and approval, usually in a formal presentation.
- The QC implements their recommendations, where practicable.
- Once implemented, the QC monitors the effects of the solution and considers future improvements.
- The QC carries out a critical review of all its activities related to the completed project.

Fabi (1992) has carried out a wide-ranging analysis of the literature published between 1982 and 1989 on QCs and, from this, has analysed 40 empirical studies undertaken on QCs. From examination of this work, using contingency factors, he has identified several factors which are critical to the success of QCs:

- Management commitment and support
- Involvement and support of employees and unions
- Training of members and leaders
- Organizational and financial stability
- Personal characteristics of the facilitator
- Individual characteristics of members
- External and organizational environments
- Organization readiness and implementation

There have been a number of derivatives of QCs resulting in teams operating under a variety of names but with very similar characteristics to QCs. A case in point are the quality service action teams (QSATs) operated by National Westminster Bank. They comprise small groups of staff to consider specific problems, topics and problems at local level, the intention is that every branch should have a QSAT; see Boaden et al. (1991).

Quality improvement teams

Teams of this type can comprise members of a single department, be cross-functional, and include representatives of either or both customers and suppliers. The objectives of such teams range across various topics but fall under these general headings:

- Improve quality
- Eliminate waste and non value-added activity
- Improve productivity

The characteristics of quality improvement teams are more varied than any other type of team activity:

- Membership can be voluntary or mandatory and can comprise of line workers, staff or a mixture of both. Some teams involve a complete range of personnel from different levels in the organizational hierarchy.
- Projects can arise as a result of a management initiative, a need to undertake some form of corrective action, a high incidence of defects, supplier/customer problems and an opportunity for improvement. It is usual to agree the project brief with management.
- The team is usually formed to meet a specific objective.
- In the first place, the team leader will have been appointed by management and briefed regarding objectives and time-scales.
- The team is more permanent than project teams but less so than QCs. In some cases, teams disband after a project; in others, they continue.
- Members are usually experienced personnel and well versed in problem-solving skills and methods.
- The team is self-contained and can take whatever action is required to resolve the problem and improve the process.

- The assistance of a facilitator is sometimes required to provide advice on problem solving, use of specific quality management tools and techniques and keeping the team activity on course. In most cases, a facilitator is assigned to a number of teams.

At Chesterfield Cylinders (a manufacturer of steel cylinders), this is the procedure and responsibilities for setting up a quality improvement team:

- The total quality steering group (TQSG) agrees the project for the team.
- The TQSG appoints one of its members to act as mentor for that team.
- The TQSG discusses possible candidates for team leader. The mentor then approaches the proposed team leader and invites him to lead the project.
- The mentor clearly identifies the problem to be addressed with the team leader.
- The mentor and the team leader agree the team.

Then, this is the mentor's role:

- To guide the team leader when required
- To monitor the team progress and ensure that the team is addressing the identified and agreed project
- To give support to the team leader when problems arise that cannot be resolved by the team leader
- To introduce outside expertise when required
- To report back to the steering group on team progress

Differences between Teams

Manson and Dale (1989) have carried out research on the differences between QCs and YITs (one type of quality improvement team) in one of the UK's largest printed circuit board (PCB) manufacturers. Table 21.1 has been developed from their work. It is recommended that when a company uses more than one type of team activity, they clearly identify the characteristics and operation of each type of team. For example, at Betz Dearborn Ltd Widnes (manufacturer of speciality chemicals for water treatment), in deciding which improvement approach to adopt, these three factors are taken into account:

1 Where the idea for the improvement originated
2 The strategic significance of the improvement
3 Whether the improvement affects more than one major area of the company's operation

Commonalities between Teams

In relation to the operating characteristics of any type of teams used in the quality improvement process, these two points should be noted.

Table 21.1 Differences between QCs and yield improvement teams

Feature	QC	YIT
Purpose	• Involve employees • Increase employee participation • Teambuilding • Develop people	• Improve process yields • Reduce scrap • Solve quality-related problems
Team building	• Will only solve problems if an effective team has been developed • Members work together • Operate by consensus	• Formed around a problem • Members are given specific tasks • Onus is on the individual • Peer pressure to perform • Goals, targets and achievements are established and assessed • Team develops around its achievements
Leadership	• Section members/first line supervisor • Members lack authority and power • Lack of access to functions, people, and information • Dependent on others for data and advice	• Production/section managers • Members are relatively senior • Independent
Problem-solving potential	• Limited • Minor problems • Limited skills	• Considerable • Major problems • Highly skilled
Project resolution rate	• Low	• High
Infrastructure	• Steering committee • Infrequent meetings • Lack of regular reporting of individual QC progress	• Steering committee • Monthly reports to Managing Director • Weekly reporting of leaders to steering committee

1 The key issue is not the name of the team activity, but rather the structure of the team, its operating characteristics, remit, accountability, and ability to resolve problems.

2 If management initiate any form of team activity, they have an implicit responsibility to investigate and evaluate all recommendations for improvement, implement all feasible solutions, demonstrate interest in the team's activities, recognize and celebrate success, otherwise, there is demotivation of team members.

Any type of team is composed of a number of key constituents, and requires more than an enthusiastic membership if it is to be successful. These guidelines are adapted from those developed by Betz Dearborn and Chesterfield Cylinders:

- Team sponsor
  - QSG member and a senior manager
  - Actively supports the team in its task, especially by contributing to the removal of road-blocks
  - Helps to resolve priority conflicts

- Mentor to the team leader
- Ensures that the team leader has the skills and training required to lead the team
- Acts as communications link between the team and TQSG and also with departments who are affected by the project
- Ensures that the team's activities are accepted by the department in which they are working, e.g. holds meetings with the area management, staff and operator to help to generate a total understanding of the project and the reasons for it
- Agrees a charter with the team, including objective, deliverables/outcomes, resources (team), boundaries and timeframe
- Ensures that other people and teams are not addressing the same project as the team
- Ensures that the team and its leader are responsible for the processes which interface with the chosen project
- Holds regular meetings with the team's facilitator

- Team facilitator

  - Helps the team mentor and team leader in establishing the team
  - Ensures that the right balance of skills is on the team and available to the team
  - Acts as coach to the team leader and assists with tasks as requested by the leader
  - Responsible for team progress and direction
  - Ensures all team members contribute
  - Responsible for communication from the team to the world outside the team
  - Communicates team road-blocks to team sponsor and helps to remove
  - Identifyes training needs of the team and provides and implements, as appropriate
  - Assists the team in preparing recommendations and presentations to management
  - Helps sponsor to resolve external resource/priority conflicts
  - Celebrates success with the team

- Team leader

  - Chosen by management or be appointed by the team; another issue to be considered is whether the role of team leader be rotated among team members
  - Organizes and sends out agenda
  - Ensures the team members are familiar with the protocol of team meetings
  - Ensures the team has a convenient place to meet
  - Consults with line managers on suitable times for team meetings
  - Starts the meeting on time and adheres to the agenda
  - Takes minutes
  - Collates data
  - At the end of the meeting, agrees the date and agenda for the next meeting
  - Communicates minutes and follow-up actions
  - An active contributor and listener

- Ensures that team members know what is expected of them
- Leads the definition and implementation of team processes
- Prepared to commit time to the project
- Responsible for team progress and direction
- Understands and is sympathetic to the various stages of development that teams go through, e.g. the forming-storming-norming-performing cycle developed by Tuckman (1965); these steps, in brief, are forming (get to know each other), storming (airing and resolving differences, building relationships and agreeing group goals), norming (establishing group norms, working together, defining individual and team goals, and developing the meeting, communication and work processes), and performing (effective teamwork)
- Identifies any training needs of the team and its members
- Provides regular verbal reports and copies of team minutes to the mentor about the progress of the team

- Team member

  - Clear on why they wish to become a member of a team, e.g. wish to solve problems and resolve concerns, improved access to information, increased involvement in decision making
  - Enthusiastic about the project; its resolution must be of direct benefit to them
  - A willing team member; not coerced into joining the team
  - Contributes relevant experience
  - Prepared to commit time outside of team meetings to collect data and carry out agreed actions
  - Takes responsibility, as requested, for follow-up actions
  - Respects the role of team leader
  - An active contributor
  - An active listener
  - Never afraid to say 'I don't understand'
  - Able to follow through actions
  - Respects the ideas and views of other members
  - Takes minutes as and when requested by the team leaders

Evaluation of Teams

It is not easy to evaluate the effectiveness of team-working, other than by the effectiveness of the actual solutions produced and improvements made. It is, however, important that the 'health' of a team is regularly assessed. These are observable characteristics of an effective team:

- Everyone is participating, making a contribution and is involved in actions and through this are achieving their personal potential.
- Relationships are open.
- Team members trust and respect each other.
- Members listen closely to the view of other members of the team and have an open mind and maintain a positive attitude.

- Everyone expresses their views, ideas and problems and all available means are used to support ideas.
- Members respect the operating procedures and principles of the team, and they own the team process.
- There is clarity of focus on the project being tackled and members know what is expected of them.
- The TQM team leader has the ability to translate ideas into action.

On the other hand, these are the usual characteristics of an ineffective team:

- Poor leadership
- Cliques, defensiveness, and closed minds within the team membership
- Downright hostilities, conflict, competition and lack of tolerance between team members
- Members not all participating in the activities of the team
- Limited communications between team members
- Insufficient attention to the team process
- No pride displayed in the team activity
- Members feelling they are being taken advantage of

Briggs et al. (1993) describe the aims of an audit, based on a semi-structured interviewing methodology, undertaken of the quality improvement teams operating at Staffordshire Tableware Ltd:

- What teams were involved
- Who comprised the membership
- How teams were operating
- What projects were being tackled
- How participants felt about the programme

They go on to say that the information gathered 'was used to create a picture of team activity for use as: an historical record, prior to an expansion of the programme, a feedback tool to improve team effectiveness and to plot a course for future development of the team programme.'

UMIST, in conjunction with Chesterfield Cylinders Ltd, have developed a 'team fitness check' which consists of a questionnaire completed by each member, the leader and the mentor of the team and then discussed and acted on by the team (and the management, if necessary). The idea for this team fitness check came from a Quality Circle Health Assessment developed in the mid-1980s by Eric Barlow at Philips (Hazel Grove). The questionnaire is shown in figure 21.1.

Team Competition

To formally recognize and celebrate team activity and encourage role model behaviour, a number of organizations hold an annual team competition/conference, usually held off-site, in which those team activities considered to be the best are presented. The judging committee of internal staff and external experts assess the team projects in terms of theme selection, problem analysis and solution, members' participation and contribution, results and benefits, and presentation.

1. Is your team meeting regularly?

Has not met for 6 months		Has not met for 3 months		Has not met for 6 weeks		Meets every 3 weeks
1	2	3	4	5	6	7

If you have scored 5 or less:

- Is it due to pressure of work?   Yes/No
- Is it due to a lack of resources?   Yes/No
- Is it due to company reorganization?   Yes/No
- Is it due to the non-availability of the leader?   Yes/No
- Is it due to the apathy of team members?   Yes/No
- Is it due to the meeting time?   Yes/No
- Is it due to shift patterns?   Yes/No
- Is it due to the team comprising of people from different shifts?   Yes/No
- Is it due to the availability of a convenient place to meet?   Yes/No
- Is the project too large?   Yes/No
- Is the project too difficult?   Yes/No
- Is it due to some members of the team not identifying with the project?   Yes/No

2. Is the level of attendance at meetings satisfactory?

Less than 50% of members attend		Less than 60% of members attend		Less than 80% of members attend		All members attend
1	2	3	4	5	6	7

If you have scored 5 or less:

- Is it due to work pressure?   Yes/No
- Is it due to members being off site?   Yes/No
- Is it due to people being instructed not to attend?   Yes/No
- Is it due to people having nothing to report?   Yes/No
- Is it due to people being involved in other committees, projects and teams?   Yes/No
- Is it due to a lack of interest in the project?   Yes/No

3. Are all members of the team involved in making decisions about the project and committed to resolving it successfully?

None committed		Less than 30% committed		Less than 50% committed		All committed
1	2	3	4	5	6	7

If you have scored 5 or less:

- Is it the nature of the project?   Yes/No
- Is the project sufficiently challenging?   Yes/No
- Is it the size of the project?   Yes/No
- Is it due to all members of the team not being associated with some elements of the project?   Yes/No
- Is it due to a lack of innovation?   Yes/No
- Is it due to a lack of commitment?   Yes/No
- Is it due to personality clashes within the team?   Yes/No
- Is it due to the size of the team?   Yes/No
- Is it due to lack of appreciation and recognition?   Yes/No

4. Is the team operating effectively?

Very ineffective						Very effective
1	2	3	4	5	6	7

If you have scored 3 or less:

- Is it due to the leader?   Yes/No
- Is it due to the team?   Yes/No
- Is it due to one member of the team?   Yes/No
- Is it due to one member of the team dominating the meeting?   Yes/No
- Is it due to a clique?   Yes/No
- Is it due to personality clashes between the leader and members?   Yes/No

– Is it due to decisions based on opinion and not fact?   Yes/No
– Is it due to not all members of the team being involved in its activities and associated decision making?   Yes/No
– Is it due to members not feeling part of the team?   Yes/No
– Is it due to a lack of structure and procedure?   Yes/No
– Is it due to the size of the team?   Yes/No
– Is it due to lack of skills?   Yes/No
– Is it due to a lack of adherence to team rules; do these need to be revisited?   Yes/No
– Is it due to a lack of a periodic review?   Yes/No
– Is it due to a lack of mission?   Yes/No

5. Are inter-meeting actions carried out satisfactorily?

Not at all   Very
satisfactory   satisfactory

1   2   3   4   5   6   7

If you have scored 3 or less:

– Is it due to a lack of leader coordination?   Yes/No
– Is it due to a failure to set priorities?   Yes/No
– Is it due to workload priorities?   Yes/No
– Is it due to lack of member commitment?   Yes/No
– Is it due to poor definition of activities?   Yes/No
– Is it due to lack of support from the mentor?   Yes/No
– Is it due to a lack of support from people outside the team?   Yes/No

6. Is the team receiving support from departments?

No support   Complete
whatsoever   co-operation

1   2   3   4   5   6   7

If you have scored 3 or less:
– Is it due to one or more departments?   Yes/No
– Is it due to management?   Yes/No
– Is it due to supervisors?   Yes/No
– Is it due to technical specialists?   Yes/No
– Is it due to lack of support from the mentor?   Yes/No
– Is it due to departments viewing the team as outside interference?   Yes/No
– Is it due to a lack of publicity about the team's activities?   Yes/No

7. Does the team require further training?

Yes   No

If YES, in which areas is training required?

8. Has the team received proper recognition of their activities?

No recognition   Complete
whatsoever   recognition

1   2   3   4   5   6   7

If you have scored 3 or less:

– Is it due to a lack of a personal 'thank you' from management?   Yes/No
– Are the current methods not sufficient?   Yes/No
– Are the current methods not suitable?   Yes/No

9. Do the members of the team regard the team as successful?

Not at all   Very
successful   successful

1   2   3   4   5   6   7

10. Summarize what actions you are going to take.

Figure 21.1   Fitness check questionnaire
Source: Eric Barlow at Philips (Hazel Grove)

With respect to the RHP Bearings' (manufacturer of industrial, precision and aerospace bearings) annual team competition, each site holds its own internal competition to decide which team will represent them at the annual competition. At the formal event, each team submits a project brief detailing issues such as team members, project objective and details, how the data was analysed, problem-solving approach used, results and outcomes, future opportunities. The team of judges makes assessment of each team using the scoring guideline shown in figure 21.2.

SCORING GUIDELINE

Teamwork	35 points

Did all the team members get involved?
Did they think and work outside the meeting time?
Did they share, care, support and develop?
Did they have regular meetings and reports?
Did they involve others when required?

Tackling the problem	30 points

How was the project selected?
Did they consider people impact, complexity, company benefit?
Did they set clear and challenging objectives?
Were the objectives in line with company policy?
Did they use a systematic approach, e.g. PDCA?
Did they use appropriate tools and techniques?

Solution/results	20 points

What was the degree of originality used?
Were all possible options considered?
Was an action plan shown for implementing the solution?
Are the objectives/plan being met?
Are results expressed in terms of objectives?
Are there other spin off benefits?
Are the results relevant to the customer or internal customer?
Was the result verified as effective and permanent by monitoring the implementation?

Presentation	15 points

Was it well planned and structured?
Did it emphasize the key points and justify the solution?

Figure 21.2 Scoring guideline
Source: RHP Bearings

It is usual to award a commemorative certificate to each member of a team making a presentation and a small financial reward – e.g. vouchers – to be spent together as a team activity such as a dinner, attendance at a sports event or theatre, holding of a picnic, attendance at a training event, to improve the working environment, etc. The winning team receive a similar certificate and reward but, in addition, an annual trophy of some kind.

Paul Monk, Managing Director of RHP Bearings, writing in the Company's Spring 1996 News Letter, which was devoted to the 1995 Team Competition, makes these comments:

The standard of entries to the competition gets better each year. This year surpassed what has gone before.

The Team Competition is symbolic. It is the crowning event in a year of good work and it represents the total quality ethic we embrace through involving all our people in order to improve the business results of our Company and make it a better place to work.

As a result of team working, scrap rates across the NSK–RHP group have halved in two years and productivity has increased by between 35% and 40%.

Guidelines for Developing Effective Teams

As outlined in chapter 1, a continuous improvement process will encounter periods of stagnation when nothing appears to be moving. This phenomenon is mirrored by teams whose members begin with high levels of energy but can quickly slump and suffer frequent troughs of inactivity.

To ensure that teams work effectively and efficiently, these factors should be taken into account:

- Management must commit themselves to nurturing and supporting teams. They need to release, on a gradual basis, authority and accountability and put in place a suitable organizational support structure.
- Prior to launching any form of team activity in relation to the introduction and development of TQM, it must be ensured that the appropriate awareness and education with regard to TQM has been undertaken.
- Each member must be clear about the aims and objectives of the team and its potential contribution to the day-to-day operations. The team should have specific goals, and an action plan and milestone chart for the project in hand, with completion dates related to the objective. This not only assists in setting boundaries on the project but helps the team to stay focused on the project in hand. All members of the team should benefit from the resolution of the project. The project must not be too large to discourage team members; an early success is vital.
- The team members must be trained in appropriate data collection, problem-solving, experimental and decision-making methods and the team must ensure that it uses the taught skills and methods effectively. The team should be confident in the use of the tools they have been taught and also be aware of any relevant new tools. Training should include project planning, team-building and team dynamics so as to provide an understanding of the behavioural needs which may determine team effectiveness and to assist members to feel part of the team. They must also be aware of which type of tools and methods work best for specific problems or situations.
- Special coaching and counselling should be provided to the team leaders because they are critical to a team's success. They must have the appropriate leadership skills in relation to the team.
- The team mentors must be seen to be actively supporting and contributing to the team. This applies, in particular, to requests for resources and support from key organizational functions.
- The team should be disciplined and should have and utilize a set method of problem solving based on fact and not opinion, along the lines of classic project

management. Some companies have developed a process which it is recommended that its teams should follow. However, it is recognized that some teams prefer a less structured approach to retain flexibility.

- There should be a set of rules and operating procedures that guide the meetings of the team. A project monitoring system also needs to be set up to ensure that the team is operating in an effective manner.
- Teams should meet on a regular basis and work to an agenda. Each meeting should be constructive, with a purpose, an aim and an achievable goal. The team must be led effectively in terms of direction, support, feedback encouragement, participation and keep minutes and record actions. The team must never leave a meeting without agreeing future actions, and the date and time of the next meeting.
- Once a team meeting has been agreed by its members, only in exceptional circumstances should the leader and any team member fail to attend the meeting.
- Periodic reports to management and the 'mentor' on team activities must be prepared. The results and decisions should be communicated accurately to the rest of the workforce. It is also important that management carry out a periodic review of each team's progress.
- People who are likely to be affected by the results of the project should be involved in the team activity.
- The team should receive appropriate recognition for successful improvements.
- The performance of the team on completion of a project should be evaluated and reviewed to see what worked, what did not and what could be done better, including the identification of training needs and pinpointing barriers. This feedback should be constructive; it is recommended that team members are counselled on how to give and receive feedback and thus to learn from each of their failures. It is sometimes useful to use someone from outside the company to evaluate team activity and to provide added impetus to the team.

Summary

Teamwork is a key element of any TQM approach. There are a variety of teams with different operating characteristics which can be used in TQM. The superior performing organizations employ a number of different types of teams. Different types of teams can be used at different stages of an organization's development of TQM. Some teams are drawn from one functional area of the business and have a narrow focus with perhaps limited problem-solving potential; other types of teams are wider and tend to be cross-functional. This chapter has concentrated on three types of teams – project teams, QCs and quality improvement teams – and describes their operating characteristics.

It is surprising how many organizations make a number of fundamental mistakes in establishing teamwork as part of their TQM approach:

- Teams are not given any training.
- The wrong type of team is established for the project being tackled.
- The team is structured in such a way that team members discuss their views on the cause of the problem and these ideas are then passed over to technical personnel and engineers to come up with a solution. The net result is team

members feel they have achieved nothing and become disaffected with the
team process.
- Too many teams introduced at one time, which the infrastructure cannot support.
- The leader is unaware of the importance of their role to the success of the team.

The setting-up of teams usually occurs within the first six months of introducing
TQM. To help organizations to avoid some of the common mistakes, guidelines are
outlined which should be considered prior to setting up any form of team activity.
However, even if the guidelines are followed, teams are likely to encounter periods of
stagnation when nothing appears to be happening. A means of assessing the health
of teams is proposed to help team members to overcome these periods of inertia and
maintain their performance and effectiveness. It is vital that teams learn from experience. It is also pointed out that it takes hard work and commitment to develop
effective teamworking.

Dale and Huke (1996) quote the Director of Materials of Maxtor (HK) Ltd who
likens teamwork to sport in making the comment:

In our business, team is of the essence with product life cycles getting shorter and shorter, if any
individual or department is not fully co-operating it is akin to a player in a sports team game dropping
the ball.

References

Boaden, R. J., Dale, B. G. and Polding, M. E. 1991: *The NatWest Route to Quality Service*.
Sheffield: Employment Department.
Bradley, K. and Hill, S. 1983: After Japan: The quality circle transplant and production
efficiency. *British Journal of Industrial Relations*, 21(3), 291–311.
Briggs, R., Palmer, J. and Dale, B. G. 1993: Quality improvement teams: an examination,
Proceedings of the Quality and Its Applications Conference, University of Newcastle-upon-
Tyne, September, 101–105.
Crosby, P. B. 1979: *Quality is Free*. New York: McGraw-Hill.
Dale, B. G. and Huke, I. 1996: *Quality Through Teamwork, Booklet No. 7*. Hong Kong
Government Industry Department.
Dale, B. G. and Lees, J. 1986: *The Development of Quality Circle Programmes*. Sheffield:
Manpower Services Commission.
Fabi, B. 1992: Contingency factors in quality circles: a review of empirical evidence. *Inter-
national Journal of Quality and Reliability Management*, 9(2), 18–33.
Hayward, S. G., Dale, B. G. and Frazer, V. C. M. 1985: Quality circle failure and how to
avoid it. *European Management Journal*, 3(2), 193–211.
Hill, F. M. 1986: Quality circles in the UK: a longitudinal study. *Personnel Review*, 15(3),
25–34.
Hutchins, D. 1985: *Quality Circles Handbook*. London: Pitman.
Manson, M. M. and Dale, B. G. 1989: The operating characteristics of quality circles and
yield improvement teams: a case study comparison. *European Management Journal*, 7(3),
287–95.
Mohr, W. L. and Mohr, H. 1983: *Quality Circles: Changing Images of People at Work*.
Massachusetts: Addison-Wesley.
Monk, P. 1996: *RHP News, Spring*, Newark: RHP Bearings Ltd.
Robson, M. 1984: *Quality Circles in Action*. Aldershot, Hants.: Gower Press.
Tuckman, B. W. 1965: Development sequence in small groups. *Psychological Bulletin*, 63(6),
384–99.

chapter twenty-two

Self-Assessment, Models and Quality Awards

B. G. Dale

Introduction

If a process of continuous improvement is to be sustained and its pace increased, it is essential that organizations monitor, on a regular basis, what activities are going well, which have stagnated, what needs to be improved and what is missing. Self-assessment provides this type of framework in generating such feedback about an organization's approach to continuous improvement. It helps to satisfy the natural curiosity of management as to where their organization stands with respect to the development of TQM. This method is now being given a considerable amount of attention by organizations throughout the world. The main reason for this increasing interest is the MBNQA which was introduced in the USA during 1987 and the EQA, introduced in Europe during 1991. These holistic models provide the mechanism for putting a score on the organization's current state of TQM development. The criteria of each award encapsulate a comprehensive business management model. There are many definitions of self-assessment provided by writers such as Conti (1993, 1997) and Hillman (1994) but an all-embracing definition is provided by the EFQM (1998).

> Self-assessment is a comprehensive, systematic and regular review of an organisation's activities and results referenced against a model of business excellence.
>
> The self-assessment process allows the organisation to discern clearly its strengths and areas in which improvements can be made and culminates in planned improvement actions which are monitored for progress.

Self-assessment implies the use of a model on which to base the evaluation and diagnostics. There are a number of internationally recognized models, the main ones being the Deming Application Prize in Japan, the MBNQA in the USA and the EFQM model for business excellence in Europe. Although there are some differences between the models, they have a number of common elements and themes. In addition, there are many national quality awards (e.g. the British Quality Award,

Irish National Business Excellence Award and the Australian Quality Award) and regional quality awards (e.g. North West Quality Award). Most of the national and regional awards are more or less duplicates of the international models, with some modifications to suit issues of national or local interest. In the USA alone, there are over 60 state and regional award schemes. Sometimes an organization will adjust the criteria of one of these models to cater for their own specific situation. The models on which these awards are based comprise definitions of TQM in a broad sense; they are comprehensive considering the whole organization and its various activities, practices and processes. Since the establishment of these awards there has been an explosion in published material describing them, e.g. Brown (1996), Cole (1991), Conti (1993, 1997), Hakes (1998), Lascelles and Peacock (1996), Nakhai and Neves (1994) and Steeples (1993).

The models on which the awards are based, and the guidelines for application, are helpful in defining TQM in a way in which management can easily understand. This is one of the reasons behind the distribution of thousands of booklets outlining the guidelines and award criteria. The majority of companies requesting them have no intention, in the short term, of applying for the respective awards. These organizations are simply using the criteria of the chosen model to assist them in diagnosing the state of health of their improvement process and providing indications of how to achieve business excellence. They help organizations to develop and manage their improvement activities in a number of ways:

- They provide a definition and description of TQM which gives a better understanding of the concept, improves awareness and generates ownership for TQM among senior managers.
- They enable measurement of the progress with TQM to be made, along with its benefits and outcomes.
- Year-on-year improvement is encouraged and this provides the basis for assessing the rate of improvement.
- They force management to think about the basic elements of the organization and how it operates.
- The scoring criteria provides an objective fact-based measurement, gains consensus on the strengths and weaknesses of the current approach and helps to pinpoint improvement opportunities.
- Benchmarking and organizational learning is facilitated.
- Training in TQM is encouraged.

A full listing of the benefits which have been found to result from the self-assessment process are given in the EFQM *Self-Assessment Guidelines for Companies* (1998). There is little doubt that the MBNQA and EQA has helped to raise the profile of TQM in the USA and Europe.

To use any self-assessment method effectively as a business tool for continuous improvement, various elements and practices have to be in place, and management needs to have had some TQM experience to understand the questions underpinning the concept. What has not been implemented cannot be assessed. The decision to undertake self-assessment needs to be fully considered from all angles, and management must be fully committed to its use. In the author's view, the use of self-assessment methods based on the quality award models are best suited to those organizations that have had a formal improvement process in place for at least three years, although there is a clear need to assess progress before this time has elapsed. This is supported by Sherer (1995), the MD of Rank Xerox (Germany), who, in explaining how the Corporation won the EQA, says: 'Do not use the Award Programme, your application for the EQA, as an entry point into your quality journey. It is something you should do after you have been on the road for a long time.' He also goes on to comment: 'Do not try to run for the award too early.' A similar point is made in *The Deming Prize Guide for Overseas Companies* (JUSE, 1998): 'It is advisable to apply for the Prize after two to three years of company-wide TQM implementation efforts or after top management has become fully committed and has begun to assume a leadership role.' Having made this point, the models underpinning the quality awards are also helpful in demonstrating to those managers in organizations inexperienced in TQM of what is involved. However, they must understand the potential gap that can exist between where they currently stand in relation to TQM and the model of the award being used to make comparisons.

TQM and Business Performance

A number of reports have been published in recent times which claim that TQM is not working, it is not successful, TQM has been replaced with BPR, the interest in TQM is fading, the number of applicants for the MBNQA is down in comparison to previous years, etc. Senior management are judged on results, and if TQM does not improve business performance then, they simply channel the resources of the organization in other directions. It is little comfort for senior managers to be told that superior performing organizations know that TQM is crucial to achieving significant and lasting improvement to the business; they want to see the evidence of this on their bottom-line results. This evidence is now increasingly surfacing in the form of analysis of the results of organizations who have won quality awards or have been judged worthy of a site visit. Here are some examples:

- Kano et al. (1983) carried out an examination of 26 companies which won the Deming Application Prize between 1961 and 1980, and found that financial performance of these companies – in terms of earning rate, productivity, growth rate, liquidity, and net worth – was above the average for their industrial sector.
- A report published by the US General Accounting Office (1991) focused on the top 20 scorers of the MBNQA in the period 1988–1989. Using a combination of questionnaire and interview methods, the companies were asked to provide information on four broad classes of performance measures – employee-related indicators, operating indicators, customer satisfaction indicators and business performance indicators. Improvements were claimed in all these indicators, e.g. market share, sales per employee, return on assets, and return on sales. Useful information on financial performance was obtained from 15 of the 20 companies, who experienced these annual average increases:

  - Market share, 13.7%
  - Sales per employee, 8.6%
  - Return on assets, 1.3%
  - Return on sales, 0.4%

- Larry (1993) reports on a study carried out on the winners of the MBNQA and found that they 'yielded a cumulative 89% gain, whereas the same investment in the Standard and Poor 500 – Stock Index delivered only 33.1%'.
- Wisner and Eakins (1994) also carried out an operation and financial review of the MBNQA winners, 1988–1993. One of the conclusions reached was that the winners appear to be performing financially as well or better than their competitors.
- The 'Baldrige Index' is made up of publicly-traded US companies that have received the MBNQA during the years 1988–1997. The National Institute of Standards and Technology (NIST) 'invested' a hypothetical $1,000 in each of the six whole company winners of the MBNQA. The investments were tracked from the first business day of the month following the announcement of award recipients (or the date they began public trading) to 1 December 1998. Adjustments were made for stock splits. Another $1,000 was hypothetically invested in the S&P 500 at the same time. NIST found that the group of six outperformed the S&P 500 by more than 2.6 to 1, achieving a 460 per cent return on investment compared to a 175 per cent return for the S&P 500. This is the fifth year in a row that the fictitious 'Baldrige Index' has outperformed the S&P 500 by almost 3 to 1, says the NIST (1999). NIST also tracked a similar investment in a group made up of the six whole company MBNQA winners and the parent companies of 17 subsidiary winners. This group of 23 companies outperformed the S&P 500 by 2.5 to 1, a 426 per cent return on investment compared to a 173 per cent return for the S&P 500.

  In addition, a fact sheet 'Why Apply' by NIST outlines the benefits reported by recipients of the award under topics such as time to market, new product sales, employee involvement, customer satisfaction, return on assets, revenue, etc.

- The Aeroquip Corporation, a Trinova company involved in aerospace, automotive and industrial markets, have 9,000 employees in 12 countries and on 40 manufacturing sites. They have developed their own version of the MBNQA called Aeroquip quality plus (AQ+). Each of their operating sites is required to obtain a score of 700 out of 1,000 points to attain an AQ+ award. These are the details of the 1994 performance of the nine sites who have attained the award compared to those sites who are still working towards it:

  - 64% of Aeroquip operating income is generated from 31% of sales
  - 15.1% return on sales against 3.9% for remainder of the Aeroquip companies
  - 21% sales growth against 5.0% for the remainder of the Aeroquip companies
  - 31% income growth against a 3.2% decrease for the remainder of the Aeroquip companies

- The Bradford Study (Letza et al., 1997), carried out at the University of Bradford Management Centre, identified 29 companies within the UK which display characteristics associated with TQM. The study was first carried out over the period 1987–1991 and has been repeated for the period 1991–1995. Nine measures have been used by the study team to compare company performance with the median for the particular industry. The second study reveals these details:

- 81% of companies are above the industry median for turnover per employee.
- 81% of the companies provide a higher salary to turnover ratio than their peers.
- 74% of the organizations remunerate their employees above the median for the industry.
- 65% of the organizations produce above median profit per employee for their industry.
- 62% of the organizations have a higher net asset turnover than their peer group.

The authors also go on to say that 'four of the nine measures are marginally below the median for their industry but this is to be expected as quality becomes institutionalised and more widespread'.

Award Models

Deming application prize

The Deming Prize was set up in the honour of Dr W. E. Deming, back in 1951. It was in recognition of his friendship and achievements in the cause of industrial quality. Deming, through the royalties received from the text of his 'eight day course on Quality Control', contributed to the initial funding of the Deming Prize. The prize was developed to ensure that good results are achieved through the implementation of company-wide control activities. It is based on the application of a set of principles and statistical techniques.

The author has led four Missions of European manufacturing executives to Japan to study how they manage quality. It is clear from the evidence collected that the Deming Application Prize criteria has produced an almost standard method of managing quality; see Dale (1993). Compared to the West, there is much less company-to-company variation in the level of understanding of TQM and in the degree of attainment. This has helped to promote a deep understanding of TQM among all employees. Rather than argue about the merits of a particular approach, system, method or technique, the Japanese tend to discuss how to apply the TQM approach more vigorously through a common core level of understanding. JUSE (1998) outline these results which have been achieved in applying for the Deming Application Prize:

- Quality stabilization and improvement
- Production improvement/cost reduction
- Expanded sales
- Increased profits
- Thorough implementation of management plans/business results
- Realization of top management's dreams
- Participation and improvement of the organizational constitution
- Heightened motivation to manage and improve as well as to promote standardization
- Converged large power from the bottom of the organization and enhanced morale
- Establishment of various management systems and the total management system

The original intention of the Deming Application Prize was to assess a company's use and application of statistical methods; later, in 1964, it was broadened out to assess how TQM activities were being practised. The award is managed by the Deming Application Prize Committee and administered by JUSE. It recognizes outstanding achievements in quality strategy, management and execution. There are three separate divisions for the award: The Deming Application Prize, the Deming Prize for individuals and the Quality Control Award for Factories. The Deming Application Prize is open to individual sites, a division of a company, small companies and overseas companies. It is awarded each year and there is no limit on the number of winners. On the other hand, the Committee reserves the right not to award the prize in any year. It is made to those 'companies or divisions of companies that have achieved distinct performance improvement through the application of company-wide quality control' (JUSE, 1998). Data collected by Dale (1993) suggest that it has become customary in Japan for organizations wishing to improve their performance to apply for the Deming Application Prize. This arises from the continuous improvements which are necessary to qualify for the award, along with the considerable prestige associated with winning the prize.

The Deming Application Prize is comprised of ten primary categories (table 22.1) which in turn are divided into 66 sub-categories. Each primary category has six sub-categories apart from the QA activities which has twelve categories. There are no predesignated points allocated to the individual sub-categories. It is claimed that the reason for this is to maintain flexibility. However, discussions with JUSE indicate that the maximum score for each subcategory is 10 points. This checklist is prescriptive in that it identifies factors, procedures, techniques and approaches that underpin TQM. The examiners for the Deming Application Prize are selected by JUSE from quality management experts from not-for-profit organizations. The applicants are required to submit a detailed document on each of the prize's criteria. The size of the report is dependent upon the number of employees in each of the applicant company's business units, including the Head Office. The Deming Prize Committee examines the application document and decides if the applicant is eligible for on-site examination. The committee chooses the two or more examiners to conduct this examination. Discussions by the author with JUSE suggest that considerable emphasis is placed on the on-site examination of the applicant organization's practices. It is also evident that the applicant organization rely a great deal on advice from the JUSE consultants. JUSE would also advise an organization when they should apply for the prize.

In 1996, the Japanese Quality Award was established. This is an annual award that recognizes the excellence of the management of quality. The concept of the award is similar to the EFQM model with emphasis placed on the measurement of quality with respect to customer, employees and society. The eight criteria on which the award is based are similar to the MBNQA.

The Malcolm Baldrige National Quality Award (MBNQA)

The MBNQ Improvement Act of 1987, signed by President Reagan on 20 August, 1987, established this annual US quality award, some 37 years after the introduction of the Deming Prize. The award is named after a former American Secretary of Commerce in the Reagan Administration, Malcolm Baldrige. The MBNQA programme is the result of the co-operative efforts of government leaders and US business. The purposes of the award are to promote an understanding of the requirements for

Table 22.1 Quality award criteria

Deming Application Prize
Category
Policies
Organisation
Information
Standardization
HR development and utilization
QA activities
Maintenance/control activities
Improvement
Effects
Future plans
Total

Malcolm Baldrige National Quality Award

Category	*Max.*
Leadership	110
Strategic planning	80
Customer and market focus	80
Information and analysis	80
HR focus	100
Process management	100
Business results	450
Total	1,000

European Quality Award

Category	*Max.*
Leadership	100
People management	90
Policy and strategy	80
Resources	90
Processes	140
People satisfaction	90
Customer satisfaction	200
Impact on society	60
Business results	150
Total	1,000

performance excellence and competitiveness improvements and to promote the sharing of information on successful performance strategies. The MBNQA guidelines contain detailed criteria that describe a world class total quality organization. The US Department of Commerce and the NIST are responsible for administering the Award scheme.

Up to two awards can be given each year, out of the average number of 100 applicants in each of three categories:

- Manufacturing companies or subunits
- Service companies or subunits
- Small business (defined as independently owned, and with not more than 500 employees)

Since its inception, in a single year there has never been less than two and no more than five awards. Any for-profit, domestic or foreign organization located in the US that is incorporated or a partnership can apply. The applicant can be a whole firm or a legitimate business unit. The award is made by the President of the US, with the recipients receiving a specially designed crystal trophy mounted with a gold-plated medallion. They may publicize and advertise their award provided they agree to share information and best practice about their successful quality management and improvement strategies with other US organizations.

Every MBNQA application is evaluated in seven major categories with a maximum total score of 1,000, US Department of Commerce (1998); see table 22.1 and figure 22.1. Each of the seven categories are then subdivided into 20 items and the items are further defined by 29 areas to address. The seven categories embody 11 core values and concepts – customer driven quality, leadership, continuous improvement and learning, valuing employees, fast response, design quality and prevention, long-range view of the future, management by fact, partnership, company responsibility and citizenship and results.

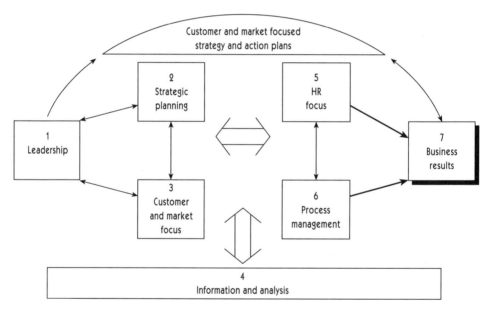

Figure 22.1 Baldridge criteria for performance excellence framework – a systems perspective
Source: US Department of Commerce (1998)

The criteria and processes are reviewed each year to ensure that they remain relevant and reflect current thinking and, based on experience during the intervening period, their wording and relative scores are updated. It should be mentioned that, like the EFQM model, the MBNQA criteria were developed originally by the business fraternity, management consultants and academics.

The framework (as shown in figure 22.1) has three basic elements: strategy and action plans, system, and information and analysis. Strategy and action plans are the set of customer and market focused company-level requirements, derived from short- and long-term strategic planning, that must be done well for the company's strategy to succeed. They guide overall resource decisions and drive the alignment of measures for all work units to ensure customer satisfaction and market success. The system is comprised of the six Baldrige categories in the centre of the figure 22.1 that define the organization, its operations and its results. Information and analysis (Category 4) are critical to the effective management of the company and to a fact-based system for improving company performance and competitiveness.

The evaluation by the Baldrige examiners is based on a written application (this summarizes the organization's practices and results in response to the Criteria for Performance Excellence) of up to 50 pages and looks for three major indications of success:

1 *Approach* – Appropriateness of the methods, effectiveness of the use of the methods with respect to the degree to which the approach is systematic, integrated and consistently applied, embodies evaluation/improvement/learning cycles and is based on reliable information, and evidence of innovation and/ or significant and effective adoptions of approaches used in other types of applications or businesses.
2 *Deployment* – The extent to which the approach is applied to all requirements of the item, including use of the approach in addressing business and item requirements and use of the approach by all appropriate work units.
3 *Results* – The outcomes in achieving the purposes given in the item, including current performance, performance relative to appropriate comparisons and/ or benchmarks, rate, breadth, and importance of performance improvements, demonstration of sustained improvement and/or sustained high level performance and linkage of results to key performance measures.

The assessors will use these three dimensions to score an applicant. Most entrants tend to score within a fairly narrow range on 'approach', and a few fall down on 'deployment', but it is 'results' that separates the real contenders from the rest. High scoring on 'results', which are heavily weighted towards customer satisfaction, requires convincing data that demonstrates steady improvement over time, both internally and externally. Experience has shown that, even with a good internal approach and deployment strategy, it takes time for results to show.

Following a first-stage review of the application by quality management experts (i.e. leading consultants, practitioners and academics), a decision is made as to which organizations should receive a site visit. The site visit takes 2–5 days from a team of 6–8 assessors. The assessors have to be fair, honest and impartial in their approach. A panel of judges reviews all the data both from the written applications and site visits and recommends the award recipients to the NIST. Quantitative results weight heavily in the judging process, so applicants must be able to prove that their quality efforts have resulted in sustained improvements. The thoroughness of the judging process means that applicants not selected as finalists receive valuable written feedback on their strengths and areas for improvement. The detail of the report is related to the scores achieved; see Heathy and Gruska (1995). This is considered by many organizations to be valuable consultancy advice.

The European Quality Award (EQA)

The EQA was launched in October 1991 and first awarded in 1992. According to the EFQM, it was intended to 'focus attention on business excellence, provide a stimulus to companies and individuals to develop business improvement initiatives and demonstrate results achievable in all aspects of organisational activity'. While only one EQA is made each year for company, public sector and SME, several EQAs are awarded to those companies who demonstrate excellence in the management of quality through a process of continuous improvement. The EQA is awarded to the best of the prize winners in the categories of companies and public service organizations – i.e. healthcare, education and local and central government – that is the most successful exponent of TQM in Europe. The winner of each of the three awards retains the EQA trophy for a year and all prizewinners receive a framed holographic image of the trophy. The winners are expected to share their experiences of TQM at conferences and seminars organized by the EFQM.

The EFQM model is intended to help the management of European organizations to better understand best practices and to support them in their leadership role. The model provides a generic framework of criteria that can be applied to any organization or its component parts. The EQA is administered by the EFQM with the support of the European Organisation for Quality (EOQ) and the European Commission. The EFQM in developing the model of business excellence and the EQA drew upon the experience in use and application of the MBNQA. The model is structured on these nine criteria which companies can use to assess and measure their own performance:

1 *Leadership*, 100 points (10%)
   The behaviour of all managers in driving the company towards business excellence
   How the executive team and all other managers inspire and drive excellence as the organization's fundamental process for continuous improvement
2 *People management*, 90 points (9%)
   The management of the organization's people
   How the organization releases the full potential of its people to improve its business continuously
3 *Policy and strategy*, 80 points (8%)
   The organization's values, vision and strategic direction and the manner in which it achieves them
   How the organization incorporates the concept of excellence in the determination, communication, implementation, review and improvement of its policy and strategy
4 *Resources*, 90 points (9%)
   The management, utilization and preservation of resources
   How the organization improves its business continuously by optimization of resources, based on the concept of excellence
5 *Processes*, 140 points (14%)
   The management of all the value-adding activities within the organization
   How key and support processes are identified, reviewed and if necessary revised to ensure continuous improvement of the organization's business
6 *People satisfaction*, 90 points (9%)
   What the people's (employees) feelings are about the organization
   The organization's success in satisfying the needs and expectations of its people
7 *Customer satisfaction*, 200 points (20%)
   What the perception of the external customers, direct and indirect, is of the organization and of its products and services
   The organization's success in satisfying the needs and expectations of customers

8 *Impact on society*, 60 points (6%)
   What the perception of the organization is among the community at large
   This includes views of the organization's approach to quality of life, the environment and to the preservation of global resources. It is about the organization's success in satisfying the needs and expectations of the community at large
9 *Business results*, 115 points (15%)
   What the organization is achieving in relation to its planned business performance
   The organization's continuing success in achieving its financial and other business targets and objectives and in satisfying the needs and expectations of everyone with a financial interest in the organization

The criteria which are shown in table 22.1 are split into two groups: 'Enablers' and 'Results' and illustrated in figure 22.2. The nine elements of the model are further divided into 32 criteria parts. For example, leadership is divided into four parts and people management into six parts. The model is based on the principle that processes are the means by which the organization harnesses and releases the talents of its people to produce results. In other words, the processes and the people are the enablers which provide the results. The results aspects of the award are concerned with what the organization has achieved and is continuing to achieve, and the enablers with how the results are being achieved. The rationale for this is that customer satisfaction, people satisfaction, and impact on society are achieved through the leadership driving policy and strategy, people management and the management of resources and processes leading to excellence in business results. Each of these nine criteria can be used to assess the organization's progress to business excellence.

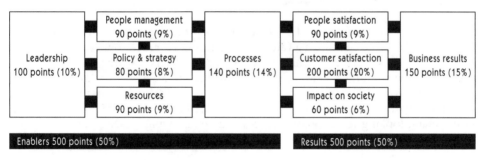

Figure 22.2 The EFQM model for business excellence
Source: EFQM (1998)

The enablers, i.e. the 'hows', are scored in terms of approach and deployment. The approach is concerned with how the requirements of a particular item are approached and met:

● The appropriateness of the methods, tools and techniques used
● The degree to which the approach is systematic and prevention based
● The use of review cycles
● The implementation of improvements
● The degree to which the approach has been integrated into normal operations

The deployment is the extent to which the approach has been deployed and implemented vertically and horizontally in all relevant processes and to all relevant products and services within the organization. The results (i.e. the 'whats') criteria are evaluated in terms of degree of excellence and the scope or breadth (i.e. all relevant areas, full range of results and understanding) of the results presented. They include positive trends, performance against trends, understanding of negative results, comparison of results with competitors, similar organizations and best in class organizations, and the ability to sustain performance. The results criteria do not cover just financial performance. The scoring framework consists of 1,000 points with 500 points each being allocated to enablers and results, i.e. existence of positive trends, comparison with both internal targets and external organizations, and the ability to sustain performance.

The EFQM model does not stipulate any particular techniques, methods or procedures which should be in place. The organizations that put themselves forward for the award are expected to have undertaken at least one self-assessment cycle. Following this, a 75-page report is written and once the application has been submitted to the EFQM headquarters, a team of six fully trained independent assessors examine each application and decide whether to conduct a site visit. The assessors comprise mainly practising managers, but also include academics and quality professionals. Irrespective of whether the company is subject to a site visit, a feedback report is provided to the company that gives a general assessment of the organization, a scoring profile for the different criteria and a comparison with the average scores of other applicants. For each part-criterion, the key strengths and areas for improvement are listed. A jury, comprising of seven members, reviews the findings of the assessors to decide who will win the award.

The Self-assessment Process

Self-assessment was defined in the introduction to this chapter. In short, it uses one of the models underpinning an award to pinpoint improvement opportunities and to identify new ways in which to encourage the organization down the road of business excellence. On the other hand, audits, with which self-assessment is often confused by the less advanced organizations with respect to their development of TQM, are carried out with respect to a quality system standard such as the ISO9000 series are, in the main, looking for non-compliances and are assessing to see if the system and underlying procedures are being followed. In ISO8402, audits are defined as:

> systematic and independent examination to determine whether quality activities and related results comply with planned arrangements and whether these arrangements are implemented effectively and are suitable to achieve objectives.

After gaining the commitment of management to the self-assessment process and carrying out the necessary education and training, these are the main steps which an organization should follow in setting about self-assessment:

- Assess what the organization has done well
- Identify what aspects could be improved upon
- Pinpoint gaps and what elements are missing
- Develop an action plan to pick up the pace of the improvement process

A key aspect of the process is take a good hard and honest look at the organization and to identify its shortcomings, keeping in mind at all times a golfing analogy: 'You will never become a better golfer by cheating.'

There are several methods by which an organization may undertake self-assessment. Each method has advantages and disadvantages and an organization must choose the one(s) most suited to its circumstances. These methods are outlined in detail in EFQM's *Self-Assessment Guidelines for Companies* (1998). These are the broad approaches which can be used separately or in combinations:

- *Award simulation*: This approach, which can create a significant workload for an organization, involves the writing of a full submission document (up to 75 pages) using the criteria of the chosen quality award model and employing the complete assessment methodology including the involvement of a team of trained assessors (internal) and site visits. The scoring of the application, strengths, and areas for improvement are then reported back and used by the management team for developing action plans.

  Some organizations have modified and developed the criteria of the chosen award model to suit their own particular circumstances, provide more emphasis on areas which are critical to them, make the criteria easier to understand and use, and to reduce some of the effort in preparing the application document. In some cases, a Corporation or Holding Company has set a minimum score which each of its facilities has to achieve within a set time frame. Once an internal award has been achieved, its continuation will require the successful completion of a subsequent assessment, usually within two years after the initial award has been granted.

- *Peer involvement*: This is similar but less rigid to the award simulation approach in that there is no formal procedure for data collection. It gives freedom to the organization undertaking the self-assessment to pull together all relevant documents, reports and factual evidence in whatever format they choose against the appropriate model being used.

- *Pro forma*: In this approach the criterion is described and the person(s) carrying out the assessment outlines the organization's strengths, areas for improvement, score and evidence which supports the assessment in the space provided on the form. It is usual to use one or two pages per assessment criterion.

- *Workshop*: This approach is one in which managers are responsible for gathering the data and presenting the evidence to colleagues at a workshop. The workshop aims to reach a consensus score on the criterion and details of strengths and areas for improvement identified and agreed.

- *Matrix chart*: This involves rating a prepared series of statements, based on the appropriate award model on a scoring scale. The statements are usually contained within a workbook which contains the appropriate instructions. The person(s) carrying out the assessment finds the statement which is most suited to the organization and notes the associated score.

- *Questionnaire*: This is usually used to carry out a quick assessment of the organization's standing in relation to the award model being used. It involves answering a series of questions and statements, which are based on the criteria of the award model being used, using a yes/no format or a graduated response scale.

The choice of approach is dependent upon the level of TQM maturity. Organizations with less experience should use the simpler methods; those more advanced should adopt the more searching methods.

In recent times, a number of self-assessment packages, based on software have come onto the market which claim to simplify the self-assessment process and provide a benchmark of progress against other organizations. Typical examples are the British Quality Foundation's Assess *Rapid Score* – which employs a questionnaire completed and compiled by a team, and is useful when starting out on self-assessment since it requires little previous experience – and *Assess Valid Score*, which is similar to Rapid Score but is more sophisticated with the ability to store strength, opportunities for improvement and evidence.

Assessment against a model, whether by internal or external assessors, has three discrete phases:

1 The gathering of data for each criterion
2 The assessment of the data gathered
3 Developing plans and actions arising from the assessment and monitoring the progress and effectiveness of the plan of action

There are a number of flow diagrams which have been produced, which outline the self-assessment process; figure 22.3 shows one reproduced from EFQM's *Self-Assessment Guidelines* (1998). It is not the purpose of this chapter to regurgitate the details of a self-assessment process but simply to list the key issues which need to be considered undertaking by those organizations self-assessment for the first time:

- Ensure that senior management are committed to the self-assessment process and are prepared to use the results to develop improvement plans.
- Arrange for the people involved in the process to be trained.
- Communicate within the business the reasons for and what is involved in self-assessment.
- Decide the self-assessment method(s) to be used.
- Plan the means of collecting the data.

  – Decide the team and allocate roles and responsibilities for each criteria of the model.
  – Develop a data collection methodology and identify data sources.
  – Agree an activity schedule and manage as a project.

- Decide the best way of organizing the data which has been collected.
- Present the data, reach agreement on strengths and areas for improvement and agree the scores for the criteria.
- Prioritize the improvements and develop an action plan.
- Regular review of progress against the plan.
- Repeat the self-assessment.

Self-assessment: What is the State of the Art?

The first European survey on self-assessment was completed by a research team drawn from UMIST, UK, Ecole Supérieure de Commerce de Paris, France, University

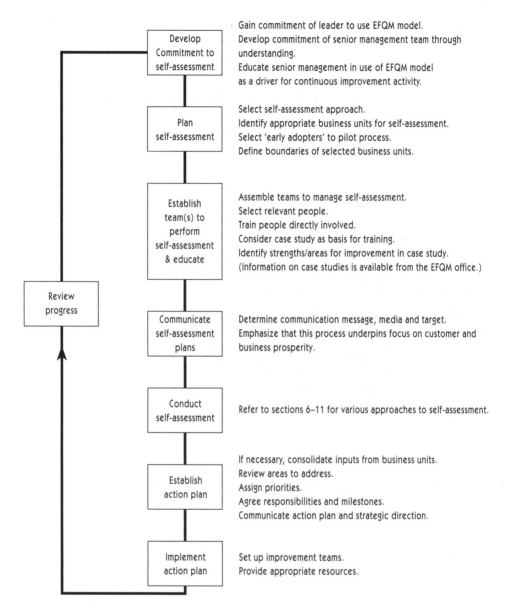

Figure 22.3 Self-assessment: general process
Source: EFQM (1998)

of Valencia, Spain, Universität Kaiserslautern, Germany, University of Limerick, Ireland and Erasmus University Rotterdam, The Netherlands. The research which was carried out by postal questionnaire has obtained data from 519 organizations and is reported by van der Wiele (1996a, b). Some of the main findings of this research are presented in summary form.

Reasons for starting self-assessment

These are the five most important reasons for organizations starting self-assessment:

1 To find opportunities for improvement
2 To create a focus on a TQM based on either the EFQM or MBNQA model criteria
3 To direct the improvement process
4 To provide new motivation for the improvement process
5 To manage the business

This ranking provides a clear indication that internal issues are the most important motivation for organizations starting formal self-assessment. The need for improvement is now recognized in most cases, however well an organization may be doing. This is encapsulated by the comment: 'Even if you are good now, you still have to get better.'

Mechanics of the self-assessment process

A number of steps which could be part of the self-assessment process were defined; here are the top five in the ranking of importance, by the respondents:

1 Business unit develops an improvement plan.
2 Outcomes of the self-assessment are linked to the business planning process.
3 Assessors present their findings in written form to the management team of the business unit.
4 Senior management level monitors improvement targets.
5 The management team of the business unit presents their improvement plan based on the self-assessment to senior management.

The findings of this ranking are consistent with the typical goals set out for self-assessment by writers such as Soin (1992).

These were the lowest ranked steps:

● Business unit employees write a full application report.
● Assessments are carried out with the help of a computer toolkit.
● The management team receive a bonus which is dependent upon the success of the self-assessment, i.e. the score achieved.

It is clear that in this sample of organizations there is a strong understanding that the outcomes from self-assessment have to be linked with improvements identified as important by the business plan. This is important to ensure that the areas for improvement are turned into actions which are implemented. Therefore, only if an organization has a business plan that is known to its various business units, and that business plan has specified within it items for improvement related to whatever model is being used, will self-assessment be considered a success.

The issues of training (training of assessors, training of employees who gather data, and training of employees who are going to be assessed) is not seen as important as it should be, if organizations are serious about self-assessment. For example, some companies have started self-assessment along the lines of the models without making use of case studies in their training or even without assessment and scoring guidelines. In other organizations, the training has been treated as part of the launch of self-assessment.

Feedback is most important for organizational learning. However, not all organizations communicate the results of their self-assessments companywide. It is often only the self-assessment results of their own unit which are available, not the scores of other units or detailed knowledge of other units assessments. However, in most cases, there is the intention to use the results of the self-assessment for internal benchmarking.

In relation to the feedback, there is the issue of the 'power of the written word'. The respondents provided firm indications that a key to the success of self-assessments is that the assessments have to be written down by the assessors. If the assessments are purely verbal, it is claimed that they have far less power. Something written down has a life of its own. It can be referred to again and again, and it can be related to the business plan. It can be related to a subsequent improvement plan and can be part of a PDCA cycle. Written assessments also mean they will be taken much more seriously by both assessors and the assessed.

Is self-assessment worthwhile?

The respondents rated the success of their first self-assessment as an average of 3.39 on a scale from 1 (not very successful) to 5 (very successful). After subsequent self-assessment activities the score increased to 3.79. This provides an indication of the continuous improvement which is evident in the self-assessment process and organizational learning of how to use the technique. Those who have tried self-assessment intend to continue it and they have positive feelings about it. It does not appear to result in management revolution, or complaints about too much bureaucracy, or rivalry, etc.

Respondents were asked to rate the extent to which improvements have been realized in the EFQM and MBNQA categories since the implementation of self-assessment. The highest ranking was given for the award categories 'customer satisfaction', 'management of processes', and 'business results'. In addition to the specific EFQM and MBNQA criteria, the respondents were also asked to rank a list of 21 more specific issues. These five issues were ranked the most important in relation to the improvements realized:

1   Line management have a much better understanding of TQM.
2   Line management have a greater understanding of the importance of TQM.
3   Errors of defects.
4   Costs of (non)-quality.
5   Customer complaints.

The issues related to the more financial aspects (cost savings, return on sales, return on assets, sales per employee, market share, and others) appear in the middle of this ranking.

These were the lowest ranked issues:

- Customer retention
- Inventory turnover

- Attendance of employees
- Safety/health of employees
- Employee turnover

It will always be difficult to clarify the impact of self-assessment on an organization's business results. However, those respondents with considerable experiences of self-assessment do have a very positive perception of the impact of the techniques on their business performance.

Respondents mentioned that four issues have been the key learning points based on the current experiences with self-assessment:

- Start self-assessment with senior management.
- Senior management must review the improvements.
- Involve the CEO.
- Train the people who will do the self-assessment.

A significant positive result is that managers gain a much greater understanding of what TQM means in practical terms and the importance of it for their organization.

In summarizing the findings of this survey, it is clear that self-assessment has a greater chance of success if these conditions exist:

- Senior management are committed to the process and are involved.
- The business unit (BU) management team develop an improvement plan from the outcomes.
- The outcomes from the self-assessment are linked to the business planning process.
- Senior management monitor targets for the improvement plan developed.
- The management team of a BU present their plan to the senior management.
- The people who undertake the self-assessment are given relevant training.

Summary

Self-assessment on a systematic basis, by an organization against one of the models described in this chapter can prove extremely useful in assisting it to improve its business performance. However, if used in an artless manner by organizations just starting out on the quality journey, and without an adequate vision of TQM by the senior management team, it will not provide the necessary results and may even push the organization down blind alleys. It can also lead to the risk of gathering a considerable amount of data which cannot then be put to effective use. When used in such a naïve way, the emphasis tends to be on training staff as assessors, assembling data, preparing long reports and assessment and annual points scoring, without the development of the all-important action plans and the solving of the day-to-day quality problems. The focus tends to be on meeting a minimum set number of points for an internal award and what activities should be concentrated on to increase the score, rather than what are the priorities to increase the velocity of the improvement process. As a consequence the ongoing day-to-day quality problems which beset the organization will not resolved. It is also observed that senior management become obsessive about gaining some form of award (regional or national) within a set time frame.

In using self-assessment, it is important that management attention is focused on the identification and implementation of planned and prioritized improvements and not on the mechanics and techniques of the assessment process and with the obsession of the scoring of points. If this is not done, they will run into the problems of self-deception.

The benefit of using self-assessment against one of the recognized models is not the winning of the award; it is its adoption as a methodology to assess progress, using appropriate diagnostics, and to identify opportunities for improvement, not forgetting the need to satisfy and delight customers. This measurement of progress on a regular basis and comparison of scores from assessments is a confirmation to the management team that real improvement and achievement has taken place. The quantification of performance in terms of numbers is important for senior management. It is also important that the management team of the organization buy in to the self-assessment process and are enthusiastic about its use. This applies, in particular, to developing action plans to address the outcomes from the self-assessment. They must also be clear on their objectives for self-assessment. When used in the correct manner, the challenge, effort and involvement helps to generate an environment in which it is enjoyable to work.

It would appear that the MBNQA and EQA have generated an industry of its own in running training courses and advising how to understand the assessment process and detail requirements of the award criteria. In organizations, this often creates an internal expert who, after intensive external training, applies the knowledge gained in providing advice to the local management team as to how each of the individual criterion can be interpreted and applied to their own particular area of activity. A danger inherent in this is that the 'expert' keen to demonstrate their knowledge ends up in detailed discussion on the details of the mechanics of self-assessment and consequently the purpose of self-assessment is often lost in the ensuing debate. Another worrying trend is that some organizations seem to believe that using one of the models as the standard and almost as a checklist approach will automatically lead them to TQM. In such organizations, people will continually use the term 'business excellence model' in their language almost as a comfort factor that all will be right with their continuous improvement efforts. There is also the danger of treating self-assessment against one of the recognized models as a panacea which is clearly not the case.

An organization has to be fairly advanced in TQM to be able to use self-assessment in an effective manner, what is not in place cannot be assessed. ISO9000 series registration can be a useful first step towards TQM; however, there is a large gap between the requirements of ISO9001 and what is portrayed in the EFQM and MBNQA models. Those organizations which have recently acquired ISO9000 series registration, and are not advanced in their quality management activity, would benefit from studying one of these models to gain an insight into what is necessary to develop a TQM approach to managing the business. Having identified the gap, they need to look at methods of introducing the basics of TQM, such as a consultancy package, the teachings of the quality management gurus, or a simple improvement framework. Once the basics are in place, then the organization should return to self-assessment to assess progress, and identify the next steps, etc.

References

Brown, G. 1996: How to determine your quality quotient: measuring your company against the Baldrige Criteria. *Journal for Quality and Participation*, June, 82–88.

Cole, R. E. 1991: Comparing the Baldrige and Deming awards. *Journal for Quality and Participation*, July–August, 94–104.

Conti, T. 1993: *Building Total Quality: A Guide to Management*. London: Chapman and Hall.

Conti, T. 1997: *Organisational Self-Assessment*. London: Chapman and Hall.

Dale, B. G. 1993: The key features of Japanese total quality control. *Quality and Reliability Engineering International*, 9(3), 169–78.

EFQM (European Foundation for Quality Management) 1998: *Self-Assessment 1998 Guidelines for Companies*. Brussels: EFQM.

Hakes, C. 1998: *Total Quality Management: The Key to Business Improvement*. 3rd edn. London: Chapman and Hall.

Heathy, M. S. and Gruska, G. F. 1995: *The Malcolm Baldrige National Quality Award: a Yardstick for Quality Growth*. Massachusetts: Addison-Wesley.

Hillman, P. G. 1994: Making self-assessment successful. *The TQM Magazine*, 6(3), 29–31.

JUSE, Deming Prize Committee, 1998: *The Deming Prize Guide for Overseas Companies*. Tokyo: Union of Japanese Scientists and Engineers.

Kano, N., Tanaka, H. and Yamaga, Y. 1983: *The TQC Activity of Deming Prize Recipients and its Economic Impact*. Tokyo: Union of Japanese Scientists and Engineers.

Larry, L. 1993: Betting to win on the Baldrige winners. *Business Week*, 18 October, 16–17.

Lascelles, D. M. and Peacock, R. 1996: *Self-Assessment for Business Excellence*. Maidenhead, Berks.: McGraw Hill.

Letza, S. R., Zairi, M. and Whymark, J. 1997: *TQM – Fad or Tool for Sustainable Competitive Advantage: An Empirical Study of the Impact of TQM on Bottom Line Business Results*. Bradford: University of Bradford Management Centre.

Nakhai, B. and Neves, J. 1994: The Deming, Baldrige and European quality awards. *Quality Progress*, April, 33–7.

NIST 1999: Baldrige Index outperforms S and P 500 for fourth year, *National Institute of Standards and Technology*, February, 9. http://www.nist.gov/publicaffairs/stockstudy.htm

Sherer, F. 1995: Winning the European quality award: a Xerox perspective. *Managing Service Quality*, 5(2), 28–32.

Soin, S. 1992: *Total Quality Control, Essentials: Key Elements, Methodologies, and Managing for Success*. New York: McGraw Hill.

Steeples, M. M. 1993: *The Corporate Guide to the Malcolm Baldrige National Quality Award*. Milwaukee: ASQC Quality Press.

US Department of Commerce. 1998: *Malcolm Baldrige National Quality Award 1998 Criteria for Performance Excellence*, United States Department of Commerce, National Institute of Standards and Technology.

US General Accounting Office. 1991: *Management Practices: US Companies Improve Performance Through Quality Efforts*. Washington: United States General Accounting Office.

van der Wiele, T. and Williams, A. R. T., Dale, B. G., Carter, G., Kolb, F., Luzon, D. M., Schmidt, A. and Wallace, M. 1996a: Self-assessment: a study of progress in Europe's leading organisations in quality management practices. *International Journal of Quality and Reliability Management*, 13(1), 84–104.

van der Wiele, T. and Williams, A. R. T., Dale, B. G., Carter, G., Kolb, F., Luzon, D. M., Schmidt, A. and Wallace, M. 1996b: Quality management self-assessment: an examination in European business. *Journal of General Management*, 22(1), 48–67.

Wisner, J. D. and Eakins, S. G. 1994: Competitive assessment of the Baldrige winners. *International Journal of Quality and Reliability Management*, 11(2), 8–25.

part five

TQM Through Continuous Improvement

This final chapter draws together some of the common themes which have emerged in the individual chapters. It covers a number of issues including the importance of quality, TQM as a continuous process and measuring progress towards TQM. The chapter also identifies and describes a number of TQM issues to which organizations need to give attention if they are to achieve world class quality status. These issues also present potential research challenges.

chapter twenty-three

Managing Quality: Epilogue

B. G. Dale

Introduction

This concluding chapter of *Managing Quality* pulls together the main themes and strands running through the book, and identifies issues to which organizations will need to give particular attention in the future. It starts by examining what quality means to different people and its importance in business transactions. The case is made that improvement is a continuous process which is systematic, incremental and cyclic. It is argued that the senior management of an organization are always keen to know where they are positioned in relation to the competition and also their perceived status within the industry and the market-place. The means of carrying out such an assessment are explored. The chapter and the book is concluded by outlining a number of issues to which organizations will need to give more attention if they are to achieve world class quality status.

The Importance of Quality

Most people now accept that quality is an important business issue. But what is quality? What do people mean when they speak of the quality of product, service, communications, or people? It is important for them to have a clear understanding of what they mean when the word is used in whatever context, so they know what to do to attain it and to improve on it continuously. It is unfortunate that there are so many different interpretations of quality, but by being amenable to wide and differing interpretations, it remains appropriate in widely differing situations and circumstances. Thus it has a unifying effect in that all genuine aspirations to improve are known to be going in the same direction, irrespective of the definitions put on it in individual cases. Indeed, it may be that quality has become a common goal rather more readily than other desirable aims (e.g. productivity, profit, market share) simply because everyone understands its importance and can identify with it. It perhaps matters little that the designer, the HR manager, the operations manager, the manufacturing engineer, the salesman, the installer, and the service engineer all have different interpretations of quality to assist them in developing their own contributions to the total quality image. The total quality image is the sum of a set of attributes, each of which has its own quality criteria. However, it is the responsibility of senior management to see to it that every contributor plays his or her part fully in fashioning the image of the organization and its products and services, i.e. that held by the customer.

Common threads running through all the contributions to the book are that customers are increasingly demanding improvements in the quality of products and services they receive, and that the provision, improvement and maintenance of quality has become an important part of business policy in superior performing enterprises. It is rare these days to find a thriving and successful organization where quality is not a basic business principle, integrated with their corporate objectives and strategies. Many businesses are experiencing massive changes in customer's expectations, e.g. rapid changes in technology, pressure for instantaneous delivery, radical changes in distribution methods and an attitude of 'more value for less money'. An organization which does not continually satisfy its customers needs and expectations will almost inevitably suffer a fall in their market share and return on assets and, in certain sectors, could lose their 'licence to operate', to use a term from *Tomorrow's Company* (RSA, 1995). Indeed, it is significant that an increasing number of organizations are talking not just about satisfying the customer but *delighting* them by exceeding and going beyond their expectations, e.g. meeting latent requirements; selling value to the customer being a prime organizational theme. The enlightened executive knows that while price and delivery are negotiable, quality in its widest sense is not.

There are also clear signs that the argument that ensuring products and services conform to customer requirements causes productivity to fall and costs to rise, is now recognized by many executives as being fallacious; quality and productivity improvements and cost reduction should always be joint organizational objectives in striving for good business results.

TQM: A Continuous Process

From the various contributions, the reader should have received the clear message that improvement is a process which, once started, should never end; all employees are involved with changing the organization in a gradual manner. This process of improvement also concentrates on the elimination of waste and non-value added activity through the creative involvement of all employees. The process is based on systematic, incremental and habitual improvement rather than, for example, relying on 'breakthrough' and 'innovative' advances as is the case with BPR. The argument advanced is that small step improvements are cumulative in nature and, ultimately, can lead to greater overall effect that a single large and radical change which can lose its value with time; see Imai (1986) and chapter 1. It should be said that TQM can also deliver 'breakthrough' or 'outrageous' improvements through activities such as benchmarking.

A question commonly encountered is: How will an organization know when they have achieved TQM? The short answer is: they won't. Because TQM is based on a continuous process which is both proactive and reactive to the changing needs, the market-place, the environment, the business and its customers and competitors, an organization will never arrive at TQM; it can only keep going further along the road. Terms commonly used to describe this are 'a race without a finishing line', 'a road without an end' and 'attempting to reach the end of a rainbow'.

There are many ways of incorporating a TQM approach into an organization's day-to-day activities. There is no single route leading to success; different management styles and corporate cultures will need to take different paths. The introduction and subsequent development of TQM must be led by the company's senior managers and accepted from the outset that it will be liable to setbacks, owing mainly to resistance to change; see chapter 12. There will be points in the process at which little headway will appear to be made and only if the senior management team are monitoring the process proactively using a set of key metrics will they be able to act positively and maintain progress. Management's commitment to TQM must be demonstrated to all employees through, for example, the time they devote to the concept, their day-to-day leadership actions, behaviour and decision making, and proving to employees that they genuinely care about improvement.

It is wise also for an organization to understand that their competitors are making continual advances and that, to catch-up or keep ahead, it is necessary to develop the process at a faster rate than that which the competition are achieving; today's state-of-the-art, delight and latent features becomes tomorrow's standard performance. Because the competitors' position can never be known with certainty, there is no prudent alternative other than to pursue perfection in all aspects of organizational activity.

Measuring Progress Towards TQM

The evidence presented by the contributors corroborates the case argued in chapter 1 that there are distinct stages or levels in the evolution of quality management, the stages being broadly characterized as inspection, quality control, QA and TQM. It is evident that in some organizations, because of the type of business they are in, their cultures, systems, and procedures will be heavily biased towards inspection and quality control type of activities. Clearly, these organizations will have greater difficulty in progressing from one stage to the next than companies without such limitations and they will tend to display the characteristics of 'uncommitted', 'drifters' or 'tool pushers' rather than 'improvers', as outlined in chapter 4.

Issues which seem to concern executives are where they stand in relation to their competitors, and their perceived status within the industry and the market-place. There are many widely accepted business performance criteria which can be applied using readily available information. Examples are market share, sales turnover, volume of exports, profit, return on net assets, yield performance, share price, manufacturing output, complexity of the product or service and its prestige, sophistication of technology and systems, etc. However, a company's senior managers should be no less interested in issues such as the organization's progress towards TQM, the effectiveness of its QA and improvement activities, and the efficacy of the organization's expenditure on promoting TQM. This assessment of quality standing is not as straightforward as in other organizational areas. Scrap rates, process yield performances, process capability indices, quality costs, non-conformances found at product audit, customer complaints, warranty claims, service quality index, number of hours of defect-free operations recorded by employees and departments, numbers of quality-related incidents, and the number of product recall programmes are all measures which can provide some indication of a company's progress from an internal baseline, but it is unlikely that similar detailed data will be available from competitors, even though there is an increased sharing of data through the formation of benchmarking clubs and other types of networks. If no such comparative data is available and there are no absolute measures, the question remains how to gauge a company's progress towards TQM.

This kind of assessment can be approached in a number of ways:

- By regular assessment of the progress being made by a company against internal benchmarks, including past performance and a 'perfect' situation – it is usual to quantify these key measurables and plot and monitor their performance over time
- Self-assessment of internal performance using the EFQM (1998) and MBNQA models criteria
- By general comparison of the level of TQM activity against companies of high standing within and outside the particular industrial sector, for example, by benchmarking
- Analysis of internal and external audit results and assessments by people external to the company
- By attempting to understand how an outside independent observer might see the company

These different approaches raise again the question of the definition of quality.

- The first measure, using internal benchmarks will employ scrap costs, level of quality costs, customer complaints, quality levels as measured by the customer, number of line complaints raised at customer plants, defect reports, etc. as its measures i.e. quality can be expressed in numbers.
- The second measure is critical self-assessment of the organization's activities and results against a specific set of criteria and framework. For each of the EFQM model's nine criteria, data is available on the scores achieved by the 'best in class' per criterion for applicants.
- The third measure, comparison with companies of high standing, will use published information, visits to companies and discussions with managers, and will be concerned with advanced quality planning, improvement teams, SPC, mistake-proofing, quality skills and competencies, cycle time reduction, internal recognition, etc. Thus the measures of quality become subjective assessment of tools and techniques in use, systems in place, sophistication of TQM, and achievements and benefits.
- The fourth measure will mainly be concerned with reports and comments on systems, planning carried out, attitudes of management, training undertaken and customer awards based on such criteria.
- In the fifth measure, an outside observer who is not necessarily knowledgeable about TQM, will have other different criteria. This could very well be the end user customer who may not be able to articulate their views and subsequently 'votes with his or her feet'. His or her judgement will probably be subjective, perhaps based on superficial knowledge of the product and/or service, perhaps based on little experience, and influenced by hearsay and propaganda. These measures of quality will include: appearance, utility, cost, value

for money, reported performance, reliability and serviceability. This type of qualitative assessment can extend beyond the product and/or service by making a judgement on the manner in which the producer, seller, service provider conducts their business (i.e. ethical, morale, economic and environment type issues).

Clearly these measures are so different, it is not possible to reconcile them one with another, and managers must make the best judgements they can from them.

However, it is the in-house measures of quality and those based on the customers' direct measures of product and service quality which are of the most immediate and direct use because they are the most visible, meaningful and motivational to the company's workforce. Here are some in-house and active performance indicators which surface when attempting to assess an organization's standing with respect to TQM:

- Scores attained using the EFQM or MBNQA models criteria
- Number of second- and third-party approvals and regional and national quality awards held
- Number of preferred supplier status awards held
- Scores allocated by customers in their formal assessments of the organization's quality management system
- Strengths and weaknesses of the quality management system indicated in a second- or third-party assessment
- Frequency of incidence of quality management system failures
- Internal and external quality levels per product, production line, and service
- Lead time and schedule compliance
- Number of defect-free hours of work registered by employees and departments
- Total quality costs
- Process capability indices
- Number and type of tools and techniques employed, the order in which they were adopted, and how they are integrated one with another
- Proportion of indirect personnel employed in the quality department
- Number of invoice queries
- The time taken to respond to customer problems
- Number of people in the organization who recognize the difference between a quick fix and long-term corrective action, who go to the root cause of a problem rather than merely curing symptoms, and those who react to the signal from a process rather than the noise
- Resources allocated by management to long-term corrective actions, including budget and staff
- Training budget as a percentage of annual sales and extent of staff training in TQM
- Number of improvement teams in operation
- Number of staff and areas involved in teamwork and improvement activities
- Number of improvement projects being pursued and those which are successfully completed
- Proportion of staff who have identified their internal customers and suppliers
- Proportion of employees who practise continuous improvement
- Proportion of employees who are satisfied that the company is customer-focused

- Proportion of employees who are satisfied that the company is a 'quality' organization
- Number of agreed departmental performance measures being used
- Percentage of staff who speak the common language of improvement
- Customer access to staff and attitudes of staff to customer complaints
- Number of product recall programmes
- Number of new products and services introduced and time to market
- Staff turnover and absenteeism rate
- Training days per person each year

While in-house performance indicators are important, it is the customer assessment of the product and/or service which really counts, so it is important to have a set of measures which reflect the customer's viewpoint. There are a variety of means used to assess customer perceptions, obtain customer feedback and understand the market-place including, surveys, interviews, customer focus meetings, clinics, shows, product launches, mystery shoppers, field contacts; see chapter 9. It is helpful to combine the collected data in this way into a customer satisfaction index.

The measurement of progress in continuous improvement and TQM is now being written about in the literature. Burstein and Sedlock (1988), Saraph et al. (1989), Schaffer and Thomson (1992) and Wortham (1988), among others, touch on the subject; Crosby's (1979) quality management maturity grid and the spectrum of Quality Management Implementation Grid of Dale and Smith (1997) details some milestones on the journey of transformation and, of course, the criteria of the MBNQA and EQA provide extremely useful route maps.

Measurement of performance and progress in meaningful terms is a difficult subject and is one to which more research effort needs to be devoted. However, it is vital to review the performance trend of the key measurables to ensure that the improvement initiatives and projects are having the desired impact and that the organization is progressing towards world class.

TQM Issues which need to be Considered in the Future

Chapter 1 was brought to a close by outlining a number of issues which need to be considered by an organization to assist them to develop TQM. Here, I conclude *Managing Quality* by listing a number of issues to which organizations will need to give more attention if they are to achieve world class quality status.

Tools and techniques such as self-assessment (chapter 22), SPC (chapter 18), FMEA (chapter 17), quality costing (chapter 7), DOE (chapter 16), QFD (chapter 15), mistake-proofing (chapter 14), benchmarking (chapter 19), and the seven management tools (chapter 14) will continue to be seen as part of the core quantitative disciplines employed by an increasing number of organizations as important aids in facilitating and measuring continuous improvement. More attention will focus on the lesser used tools and techniques, such as policy deployment (chapter 5), QFD and the seven management tools, in particular the latter for making the best use of qualitative data in relation to the application of QFD. The assessment of BPR (chapter 20) will continue with respect to its role in business improvement and its connection with TQM. The EFQM and MBNQA models will become increasingly recognized by business as general management models useful as a starting point which individual business units then need to develop to fit their own situations. It is expected the misuse of such models will tend to fall as managers become familiar with them, rely less on the use of management consultancies, the hype surrounding them dies away and management consultants switch their attention to the latest money-generating concept.

There is considerable scope for improving the use and exploitation of tools and techniques, and organizations need to give consideration to a number of issues:

- A route map for their use and application
- Identifying which tools and techniques should be used together
- The type of organizational changes which are needed to make the most effective use of tools and techniques
- The role that particular tools and techniques play
- Ensuring that people make the best use of tools and techniques, in particular, remembering the purpose of the tools they are applying
- The use of assessment methods to evaluate the use of tools and techniques; see Dale and McQuater (1998).

In relation to the collection and use of quality costs, *ABC and throughput accounting* will grow in importance. Other issues which need to be evaluated, include the different types of approaches and strategies which can be employed in the identification and collection of quality cost, development of quality cost models, justification of investment in prevention type activities, development of quality cost performance indicators, and the best means of identifying and reporting 'bottom-line' and intangible benefits to demonstrate the effectiveness of TQM.

A considerable number of organizations have based their *quality systems* on the ISO9000 series of quality standards (chapter 13), or that of a major purchaser (e.g. QS-9000). Looking forward, organizations without an ISO9000 series certificate of registration will find it increasingly difficult to do business in the world marketplace; this trend will be reinforced by the exponential interest of US industry in the series, driven by QS9000. However, this series of quality management system standards should be regarded by organizations as the minimum; their objective should be to surpass the specified requirements. In particular, the challenge is to develop effective preventive action disciplines and mechanisms, and to ensure that these drive continuous improvement and broaden the vision from merely a paperwork system audit. It is predicted that the development of environmental management systems to meet the requirements of ISO14001 will help to make quality management systems which are based on the ISO9000 series more improvement orientated.

Many SMEs have ISO9000 series registration and remain stuck on this quality management foundation stone. They require simple, effective and pragmatic advice on what are *the next steps on the improvement journey*, the TQM framework outlined in chapter 8 has proved an effective means of providing this guidance to aid development. The challenge is providing to SMEs practical and pragmatic advice, in appropriate and easily understandable stages, which can move them from ISO9000 series registration to EQA prize winner status. However, the gap between the requirements of the ISO9000 series and the holistic nature of the EFQM model for business excellence cannot be bridged just by taking another list of criteria by which an organization can be measured. More of the basics need to be put in place before the EFQM model can be effectively used for assessing an organization; see van der Wiele et al. (1997).

There will be a development in the direction of *integrating quality* into the normal management procedures and operations of a business. This will be aided by the development of integrated management systems dealing with quality management, environment, occupational health and safety and data protection; see Wilkinson and Dale (1998).

Attention needs to be given to developing, in a continuous manner, the problem-solving skills, competencies and talents of *all* employees in the organization.

The *impact of corporate culture on TQM and vice versa* needs to be fully evaluated. Here are some issues that need to be examined:

- How does an organization develop its culture so that *everyone* is committed to continuous improvement?
- What is the best means of managing the change process?
- Did those companies who are successful with TQM have a culture, prior to its introduction, different from that typified by traditionally managed companies?
- What was the predominant management style?
- What is the best means of facilitating such changes in traditionally managed organizations, in particular those in public ownership and monopoly/regulated supply situations and also in government departments?
- How, when, where and at what pace does culture change take place?
- What are the best means of measuring change?
- How to change the attitudes of middle management
- How to ensure that production/operations personnel think quality as well as numbers and value not just costs
- What are the best means of empowering people to take ownership for their own quality and its improvement?
- What is the effect of national cultures on TQM?
- Are the impediments to progress common across different cultures?
- How can TQM be developed in a downsizing situation?

In this current age of privatization, contracting-out of government services and pressure for value for money services, government departments, public services and service providers are coming under increasingly competitive pressures for *the pursuit of excellence*. In these organizations, the challenge is how to apply the principles and mechanisms of continuous improvement effectively and to change the 'civil service' mentality which typically exists in such environments.

Continuous improvement initiatives must reach *every* part of an organization, and every employee and every function need to be involved if TQM is to become total. Quality needs to be seen and treated as an integral part of each department's activities. However, some functions and staff are more resistant to the concept of TQM than others. How to convert the cynics, 'blockers' and 'resistors' is a major problem in most organizations and the same can be said for ensuring that improvement becomes a daily issue in situations when resources and people are already fully stretched and feel overworked. A related issue which needs attention is how to measure the 'conversion' of cynics – lip service versus commitment.

A set of issues relate to employee relations:

- What is the role of employee representation in TQM and will it have a diminishing or increasing influence?

- What are the effects of the democratizing process in TQM and the increasing values placed on the workforce and their skills on the traditional balance of power in the workplace?
- What, if any, effects will European Labour Laws have on TQM?

Quality will continue to permeate every function of an organization and become more integrated with business activities. More organizations will start to use policy deployment as the means to align all efforts in the organization towards its major goals. The *role of the quality professional* will need to change in response to this trend of increasing integration in both an operational and strategic sense. Bertsch et al. (1999) provides some details of the logic behind this and what will be required of quality managers/directors in the future. They argue that when TQM is considered by an organization to be of strategic importance then fundamental changes will be needed not only in the role of the quality manager but in the type of skills they possess.

There will be a greater focus on *process streams* linked directly to customer groups and suppliers, replacing the traditional functional oriented structure. The challenge will be to integrate these process streams owned by different business organizations, to align them to satisfy the requirements of a common end-user and to exploit specific market opportunities.

The best means of *managing and organizing across a number of sites and locations* is an issue being faced by many businesses with a multi-site operation, in particular, when it embraces a number of countries. They typically seek answers to these questions:

- What is the right type of organization, structure and framework?
- What are the benefits of a controlled and managed development of across sites compared with a 'do as they feel fit' approach?
- How can we cater for site-to-site and country-to-country differences?

Revitalizing TQM after a period of stagnation is currently being faced by a number of organizations. Here are some typical issues with which organizations are wrestling:

- Why has stagnation occurred?
- Is stagnation a natural phenomenon?
- What are the best means of revitalizing it?

Chapters 4 and 12 provides some guidance to identifying these issues and what can be done to overcome them. Most people in an organization will know why TQM has stagnated but, of more immediate concern, is what is the best means of restarting it again and sustaining its momentum. This will continue in the future, with management coping with the effects of redundancy, recession, organizational restructuring, downsizing and changes in senior management, products, services and process and attempting to minimize the effects of these on TQM.

Some organizations are facing a situation which is much more difficult to deal with than TQM stagnation. This is when all the improvement initiatives have collapsed and nothing more than ISO9000 series registration remains. They require guidance on the best means of *rekindling the process.* This needs to take into account the conditions which caused the current conditions and whether they have changed, the views from different levels of the organizational hierarchy on the reasons for the failure, current attitudes, what initiatives to take-up, etc. for which chapters 4, 8 and 12 provides some clues.

A number of companies, who have received considerable publicity because of their perceived success with TQM, have built up myths supported by considerable and readily available documentation of how good they are. The rhetoric surrounding this is perpetuated both inside and outside the organization. At the operating level of these businesses, *the reality often does not live up to the communicated word*, and what senior and some middle management believe the situation to be, in particular, at corporate headquarters.

- There is a detailed and fully documented policy deployment procedure but it is all top-down cascade with little 'catchball', bottom-up feedback and little audit of the agreed plans and targets
- It is a requirement that every business unit carries out a self-assessment which is subject to peer review but the plans to address the chosen areas for improvement are only given serious attention prior to such a review taking place.

A challenge facing the senior managers of these organizations is to have the courage to stop believing their own self-perpetuating story of success, understand why things have not happened at the grass roots of the business as was intended by the corporate headquarters, and to address the deficiencies to ensure that the message reaches the operation; this requires strong and committed leadership.

Organizations should have *measures of performance* based on hard measures of customer satisfaction. The measures should be regularly monitored and fed back to all internal suppliers and customers (chapters 9 and 15) and a system of planning in place to close any gaps between actual performance and expectations. The relevancy and value of these measures will continue to present a challenge to management.

Teamwork, in all its forms, should be encouraged and the different types of team activity need to be integrated to obtain the best influence of synergy (chapter 21). Attention needs to be paid to which teams work best in which situations and why, and the effects which teams have on the day-to-day operation of a section/department.

Winning the 'hearts and minds' of all employees and *cultivating motivation and commitment* among the workforce is, and will remain, a key issue. The senior management team must work harder at sharing the organization's vision, mission and values and ensuring that they become a reality and, also, at fostering and promoting an environment where people feel secure, trusted, and respected. Selfishness and indifference to the problems of others works against continuous improvement.

Timely and accurate data is a prerequisite of effective quality-related decision making, quality information systems and quality databases need to be developed further to facilitate this, feedback of data internally and externally being a key issue.

A high proportion of quality problems are caused by *poor communications*. Organizations need to develop effective methods and channels which encourage open and honest communication in terms everyone can understand between employees at all levels, and between themselves, their suppliers, and their customers; chapter 3 on Japanese experiences of TQC and chapter 10 on the HR issues in TQM provide some good examples. In this way, employees will be encouraged to question what and why things are done in a certain way. Many major purchasers are using electronic data interchange systems to communicate more effectively with their supplier communities (see chapter 11).

A key concern of major organizations is how to develop *effective working relationships with their supplier base* and jointly pursue improvement initiatives; see chapter 11. While there have been a number of attempts at these, doubts still remain among some major purchasers about their ability to convert all their suppliers to TQM and, where it is possible, the most effective means of achieving it and integrating them into the improvement process. One clear principle for success is that the purchaser must be a good role model. There is also evidence that some organizations talk partnership but, in practice, do not act in this way. There are also different kinds of partnerships and that organizations must decide which best suits them and their suppliers. These type of issues are explored in Burnes and Dale (1998) and will continue to dominate the partnership sourcing and supplier development literature throughout the remainder of this decade. In the working in partnership with stakeholders section in *Tomorrow's Company* (RSA, 1995) a very relevant point is made:

> Tomorrow's company views key suppliers as true extensions of the company. It sets target costs and pursues them jointly with suppliers, sharing information and new ideas to reduce waste and improve performance. Yesterday's companies regard suppliers as inter-changeable vendors. They see cost cutting as a zero-sum game by which profits are increased only at the expense of suppliers.

Quality must start with education. Organizations must invest to train employees at all levels in the organization in improvement skills to facilitate changes in behaviour and attitude. Deciding what type of improvement training is required and how this training should be conducted and used. In spite of all the quality propaganda, many production/operations people still view their first priority as meeting the production schedule, quota and cost targets; only after achieving these objectives will they give some consideration to quality performance. Habits of a lifetime are slow in dying. Having said this, there is an increasing realization that while meeting the schedule pays salaries, shipping product which does not conform to the customer's requirements is self-defeating. This change in view is more likely to take place in organizations where the CEO and members of the senior management team act as a role model.

It is vital that members of the *senior management* team continue to develop their understanding of TQM; see chapters 1 and 2. A key issue is how to keep management's attention focused on TQM and ensure that they devote sufficient time to improvement activities and initiatives. A similar issue is how to maintain a strategic focus on a small number of projects. It is not uncommon to find that management believe they need to justify their TQM endeavours along with the requisite improvement resources. Detailed examination of why profitable businesses fail may help to provide the right type of evidence on this matter. More detailed guidance is required on what type of activities senior management should be involved with and what they need to do about TQM. Senior management also need help on the best means of conveying their commitment throughout the organization. The efforts made by both senior and middle management are often not visible to junior members of staff who will often comment on their lack of perceived commitment, when this is not the case.

In the late 1980s and the 1990s, there has been almost a clarion call that the reason why some introductions of *TQM had been unsuccessful* – e.g. Wilkinson (1992) – was a lack of focus on the so-called soft issues of TQM. The EFQM model with the people management and people satisfaction being the second largest element after customer satisfaction, in terms of the number of available points, should have changed this perception. A future challenge is to decide how much influence the model has had on these people and soft quality issues, in particular, management style.

The subject of TQM is now being given more attention in the European higher educational system and courses featuring the subject are on the increase; see van der Wiele and Dale (1996). This trend needs to be encouraged because until TQM is recognized as a subject in its own right, the brightest young people will be deterred from studying TQM and the best graduates will not be attracted into the quality profession. An issue which is currently under debate is whether TQM should be taught as a separate subject in relation to undergraduate and postgraduate degrees awarded in quality management or whether it should be treated as an essential component of all courses, in particular, at postgraduate level. Another debate which is starting to surface is whether universities and business schools should be structuring their MBA courses around the EFQM model.

Organizations, in the main, have some difficulty in seeing the need for TQM research undertaken by the academic fraternity, its relevance to their immediate requirements, how they might use the findings and what is the starting point for collaboration. A challenge facing both business and academics is to develop a closer working relationship with each other.

Two important factors hindering the development of TQM in European business is the shortage of people qualified to take up quality management positions and the lack of exposure to quality management principles and methods of recently recruited graduates. The more advanced organizations now see the function of quality management as crucial to their corporate success and are appointing suitable qualified people. With respect to the lack of quality management in the course curriculum of many undergraduate and postgraduate degree courses, this situation is now changing. An increasing number of universities and business schools are starting to teach TQM as part of the degree courses and graduates, through such exposure, start to recognize the potential of employment prospects in quality management; see van der Wiele and Dale (1996).

Summary

During the course of the UMIST research on TQM carried out over the last 18 or so years, I have observed and been involved in a large number of TQM initiatives. A number of these have been successful, others not so. What are the reasons for this? The lack of success is certainly not related to the concept of TQM. Rather, it is the way that TQM has been introduced. It is surprising how many fundamental mistakes are made by senior managers and their advisors (both internal and external) in relation to issues such as communication, training, infrastructure, teams and projects, involvement and measurement. In addition, there is a fundamental failure to stick to the basics; too many become distracted by vogue concepts, systems and techniques. These mistakes are avoidable by improved knowledge and understanding of the subject and better planning. I hope this book will assist on all three counts.

In drawing to a close this book I quote one of the reviewers of the manuscript, a senior production executive of a major British company:

I have found that reading the manuscript has helped me to reflect on:

  (i) the things that we could have done better
 (ii) areas that have been well managed
(iii) the topics that we need to concentrate on in the immediate future
 (iv) the longer term issues.

With these thoughts in mind, happy reading!

References

Bertsch, B., Williams, A. R. T., Dale, B. G. and van der Wiele, T. 1999: *The Changing Role of the Quality Manager: a Critical Examination*, European Quality (awaiting publication).

Burnes, B. and Dale, B. G. (eds) 1998: *Working in Partnerships: Best Practice in Customer-Supplier Relations*. Aldershot, Berks: McGraw Hill.

Burstein, C. and Sedlock, K. 1988: The federal quality and productivity improvement effort. *Quality Progress*, October, 38–41.

Crosby, P. B. 1979: *Quality is Free*. New York: McGraw Hill.

Dale, B. G. and McQuater, R. E. 1998: *Managing Business Improvement and Quality: Implementing Key Tools and Techniques*. Oxford: Blackwell Business.

Dale, B. G. and Smith, M. 1997: Spectrum of quality management implementation grid: development and use. *Managing Service Quality*, 7(6), 307–11.

EFQM (European Foundation for Quality Management) 1998: *Self-Assessment 1998 Guidelines for companies*. Brussels: EFQM.

Imai, M. 1986: *Kaizen: the Key to Japan's Competitive Success*. New York: Random House.

RSA 1995: *Tomorrow's Company*. London: The Royal Society for the Encouragement of Arts, Manufacturers and Commerce.

Saraph, J. V., Benson, P. G. and Schroeder, R. C. 1989: An instrument for measuring the critical factors of quality management. *Decision Sciences*, 20(6), 810–29.

Schaffer, R. H. and Thomson, H. A. 1992: Successful change programs begin with results. *Harvard Business Review*, January/February, 80–89.

US Department of Commerce, 1998: *Malcolm Baldrige National Quality Award 1998 Criteria for Performance Excellence*. Gaithersberg, USA: National Institute of Standards and Technology.

van der Wiele, T. and Dale, B. G. 1996: *Total Quality Directory 1996: TQM at European Universities and Business Schools*. Rotterdam: Erasmus University.

van der Wiele, T., Dale, B. G., Williams, A. R. T. 1997: ISO9000 series registration to total quality management: the transformation journey. *International Journal of Quality Science*, 2(4), 236–52.

Wilkinson, A. 1992: The other side of quality: soft issues and the human resources dimension. *Total Quality Management* 3(3), 323–29.

Wilkinson, A. and Dale, B. G. 1998: Manufacturing companies' attitudes to system integration: A case study examination. *Quality Engineering*, 11(1), 249–56.

Wortham, A. W. 1988: Rating quality assurance programs. *Quality Progress*, September, 53–54.

Index